Quantitative Psychological Research

Quantitative Psychological Research

A STUDENT'S HANDBOOK

David Clark-Carter
Psychology Department, Staffordshire University

Ψ Psychology Press
Taylor & Francis Group
HOVE AND NEW YORK

First published 2004 by Psychology Press
27 Church Road, Hove, East Sussex BN3 2FA

Simultaneously published in the USA and Canada
by Psychology Press
29 West 35th Street, New York, NY 10001

Psychology Press is a part of the Taylor & Francis Group

Copyright © 2004 David Clark-Carter

Typeset in 10/12pt Palatino by Graphicraft Limited, Hong Kong
Printed and bound in Great Britain by Biddles Ltd, King's Lynn
Cover design by Richard Massing

This publication has been produced with paper manufactured
    to strict environmental standards and with pulp derived from
    sustainable forests.

British Library Cataloguing in Publication Data
A catalogue record for this book is available from the British Library

Library of Congress Cataloging-in-Publication Data

Clark-Carter, David.
    Quantitative psychological research : a student's handbook / David
Clark-Carter.—2nd ed.
        p. cm.
Rev. ed. of: Doing quantitative psychological research. c1997.
Includes bibliographical references and indexes.
        ISBN 1-84169-225-5 (pbk.)—ISBN 1-84169-520-3 (hbk.)
        1. Psychology—Research—Methodology—Textbooks. I. Clark-Carter,
David. Doing quantitative psychological research. II. Title.
        BF76.5.C53 2004
        150'.72—dc22   2003021775

ISBN 1-84169-520-3 (hbk)
ISBN 1-84169-225-5 (pbk)

To Anne, Tim and Rebecca

Contents

Preface to the second edition   ix

Preface to the first edition   x

Part 1
Introduction   1

1 The methods used in psychological research   3

Part 2
Choice of topic, measures and research design   19

2 The preliminary stages of research   21
3 Variables and the validity of research designs   36
4 Research designs and their internal validity   48

Part 3
Methods   67

5 Asking questions I: Interviews and surveys   69
6 Asking questions II: Measuring attitudes and meaning   84
7 Observation and content analysis   96

Part 4
Data and analysis   105

8 Scales of measurement   107
9 Summarising and describing data   114
10 Going beyond description   142
11 Samples and populations   152
12 Analysis of differences between a single sample and a population   163
13 Effect size and power   180
14 Parametric and non-parametric tests   188
15 Analysis of differences between two levels of an independent variable   198
16 Preliminary analysis of designs with one IV with more than two levels   222
17 Analysis of designs with more than one independent variable   244
18 Subsequent analysis after ANOVA or χ^2 261

19 Analysis of relationships I: Correlation   287
20 Analysis of relationships II: Regression   317
21 Multivariate analysis   341
22 Meta-analysis   353

Part 5
Sharing the results   363

23 Reporting research   365

Appendixes

I.   Descriptive statistics   387
      (linked to Chapter 9)
II.   Sampling and confidence intervals for proportions   397
      (linked to Chapter 11)
III. Comparing a sample with a population   402
      (linked to Chapter 12)
IV.   The power of a one-group *z*-test   409
      (linked to Chapter 13)
V.   Data transformations and goodness-of-fit tests   412
      (linked to Chapter 14)
VI.   Seeking differences between two levels of an independent variable   419
      (linked to Chapter 15)
VII. Seeking differences between more than two levels of an independent variable   441
      (linked to Chapter 16)
VIII. Analysis of designs with more than one independent variable   462
      (linked to Chapter 17)
IX.   Subsequent analysis after ANOVA or χ^2 477
      (linked to Chapter 18)
X.   Correlation and reliability   496
      (linked to Chapter 19)
XI.   Regression   517
      (linked to Chapter 20)
XII. Item and discriminative analysis on Likert scales   533
      (linked to Chapter 6)
XIII. Meta-analysis   535
      (linked to Chapter 22)
XIV. Probability tables   547
XV.   Power tables   582
XVI. Miscellaneous tables   618

References   629

Glossary of symbols   633

Author index   635

Subject index   637

PREFACE TO THE SECOND EDITION

All that I said in the preface to the first edition of the book remains true so I refer the reader to that for details of my ideas about the book, including the rationale for the layout and possible approaches people new to the subject could take to reading the book.

Most chapters and appendices have been altered to a certain extent. Given the constraints on space and the main focus of the book, I reluctantly took out the section on specific qualitative methods which had been in the first edition. In its place are details of two books on the topic. I have continued to assume that, where possible, you will conduct analysis using a computer package, but have avoided trying to provide a manual on how to do analyses in any specific package as such things frequently change. Nonetheless, in this edition I have made more reference than last time to what you can expect from SPSS. There are many *how to* books for computer packages and I recommend Kinnear and Gray (2000) for SPSS.

Acknowledgements

In addition to all those who helped with the first edition I want to mention the following. Peter Harris, Darren Van Laar and John Towse all made helpful comments on the proposals I put forward about this edition. Chris Dracup, Astrid Schepman, Mark Shevlin and A. H. Wallymahmed made helpful comments on the first draft of the second edition. A number of people at Psychology Press and Taylor & Francis (some of whom have moved on) have had a hand in the way this edition has developed. In fact, there were so many that I apologise if I've left anyone out of the following list: Alison Dixon, Caroline Osborne, Sue Rudkin and Vivien Ward. I would also like to thank all the students and colleagues at Staffordshire University who commented on the first edition or asked questions which have suggested ways in which the first edition could be amended or added to. Finally, although I have already thanked them in the preface to the first edition, I want again to thank Anne, Tim and Rebecca for their forbearance and for dragging me from the study when I was in danger, rather like Flann O'Brien's cycling policeman, of exchanging atoms with the chair and computer keyboard.

PREFACE TO THE FIRST EDITION

This book is designed to take the reader through all the stages of research: from choosing the method to be employed, through the aspects of design, conduct and analysis, to reporting the results of the research. The book provides an overview of the methods which psychologists employ in their research but concentrates on the practice of quantitative methods.

However, such an emphasis does not mean that the text is brimming with mathematical equations. The aim of the book is to explain how to do research, not how to calculate statistical techniques by hand or by simple calculator. The assumption is that the reader will have access to a computer and appropriate statistical software to perform the necessary calculations. Accordingly, the equations in the body of the text are there to enhance understanding of the technique being described. Nonetheless, the equations and worked examples for given techniques are contained in appendices for more numerate readers who wish to try out the calculations themselves and for those occasions when no computer is available to carry out the analysis. In addition, some more complex ideas are only dealt with in the appendices.

The structure of the book

A book on research methods has to perform a number of functions. Initially, it introduces researchers to basic concepts and techniques. Once they are mastered, it introduces more complex concepts and techniques. Finally, it acts as a reference work. The experienced researcher often is aware that a method exists or that there is a restriction on the use of a statistical technique but needs to be reminded of the exact details.

This book is structured in such a way that the person new to the subject can read selected parts of selected chapters. Thus, first-level undergraduates will need an overview of the methods used in psychology, a rationale for their use and ethical aspects of such research. They will then look at the stages of research, followed by a discussion of variables and an overview of research designs and their internal validity. Then, depending on the methods they are to conduct, they will read selected parts of the chapters on specific research methods. In order to analyse data they will need to be aware of the issues to do with scales of measurement and how to explore and summarise data. Next they will move on to trying to draw inferences from their data—how likely their results are to have occurred by chance. They should be aware of how samples can be chosen to take part in a study and how to compare the results from a sample with those from a population.

It is important that, as well as finding out about how likely their results are to have occurred by chance, they know how to state the size of any effect they have detected and how likely they were to detect a real effect if it exists. They need to know the limitations on the type of data that certain statistical tests can handle and of alternative tests that are available which do not have the same limitations. They may restrict analysis to situations involving looking at differences between two conditions and simple analysis of the relationships between two measures. Finally, they will need to know how to report their research as a laboratory report. Therefore, a first-level course could involve the following chapters and parts of chapters:

1. The methods used in psychological research.
2. The preliminary stages of research.
3. Variables and the validity of research designs.

The sections on types of designs and on terminology in:

4. Research designs and their internal validity.

One or more of:

5. Asking questions I: Interviews and surveys.
6. Asking questions II: Measuring attitudes and meaning.
7. Observation and content analysis.

Then:

8. Scales of measurement.
9. Summarising and describing data.
10. Going beyond description.

The sections on statistics, parameters and choosing a sample from:

11. Samples and populations.

The sections on z-tests and t-tests in:

12. Analysis of differences between a single sample and a population.
13. Effect size and power.
14. Parametric and non-parametric tests.
15. Analysis of differences between two levels of an independent variable.

The first section in:

19. Analysis of relationships I: Correlation.

Possibly the section on simple regression in:

20. Analysis of relationships II: Regression.

The sections on non-sexist language and on the written report in:

23. Reporting research.

Students in their second level should be dealing with more complex designs. Accordingly, they will need to look at more on the methods, the designs and their analysis. They may look at further analysis of relationships and be aware of other forms of reporting research. Therefore they are likely to look at:

The section on specific examples of research designs in:

4. Research designs and their internal validity.

Anything not already read in:

5. Asking questions I: Interviews and surveys.
6. Asking questions II: Measuring attitudes and meaning.
7. Observation and content analysis.

The section on confidence intervals in:

11. Samples and populations.

16. Preliminary analysis of designs with one IV with more than two levels.
17. Analysis of designs with more than one IV.

At least the section on contrasts in:

18. Subsequent analysis after ANOVA.

The remaining material in:

19. Analysis of relationships I: Correlation.

At subsequent levels I would hope that students would learn about other ways of analysing data once they have conducted an analysis of variance, that they would learn about multiple regression and meta-analysis and that they would be aware of the range of multivariate analyses.

As psychologists we have to treat methods as tools that help us carry out our research, not as ends in themselves. However, we must be aware of the correct use of the methods and be aware of their limitations. Above all, the things that I hope readers gain from conducting and analysing research is the excitement of taking an idea, designing a way to test it empirically and seeing whether the evidence is consistent with your original idea.

A note to tutors

Tutors will notice that I have tried to place greater emphasis on statistical power, effect size and confidence intervals than is often the case in statistical texts aimed at psychologists. Without these tools psychologists are in danger of producing findings that lack generalisability because they are overly dependent on what have become conventional inferential statistics.

I have not given specific examples of how to perform particular analyses in any particular computer package because of lack of space, because I do not want the book to be tied to any one package and because the different generations of the packages involve different ways of achieving the same analysis.

Acknowledgements

I would like to thank those people who started me off on my career as a researcher and in particular John Valentine, Ray Meddis and John Wilding, who introduced me to research design and statistics. I have learned a lot from many others in the intervening years, not least from all the colleagues and students who have asked questions that have forced me to clarify my own thoughts. I would also like to thank Marian Pitts who encouraged me when I first contemplated writing this book. Ian Watts and Julie Adams, from Staffordshire University's Information Technology Services, often gave me advice on how to use the numerous generations of my word-processing package to achieve what I wanted. Rachel Windwood, Rohays Perry, Paul Dukes, Kathryn James and Kirsten Buchanan from Psychology Press all gave me help and advice as the book went from original idea to published work.

Paul Kinnear, Sandy Lovie and John Valentine all made very helpful comments on an earlier version of the book. Tess and Steve Moore initiated me into some of the mysteries of colour printing. Anne Clark-Carter acted as my person on the Stoke-on-Trent omnibus and pointed out where I was making the explanation particularly complicated. This effort was especially heroic given her aversion to statistics. In addition, she, Tim and Rebecca all tolerated, with various levels of equanimity, my being frequently superglued to a computer. Despite all the efforts of others, any mistakes which are still contained in the book are my own.

PART 1
Introduction

THE METHODS USED IN PSYCHOLOGICAL RESEARCH

1

Introduction

This chapter deals with the purposes of psychological research. It explains why psychologists employ a method in their research and describes the range of quantitative methods employed by psychologists. It addresses the question of whether psychology is a science. Finally it deals with ethical issues to do with psychological research.

What is the purpose of research?

The purpose of psychological research is to increase our knowledge of humans. Research is generally seen as having one of four aims, which can also be seen as stages: the first is to describe, the second is to under-stand, leading to the third, which is to predict, and then finally to control. In the case of research in psychology the final stage is better seen as trying to intervene to improve human life. As an example, take the case of non-verbal communication (NVC). First, psychologists might describe the various forms of NVC, such as eye contact, body posture and gesture. Next, they will try to understand the functions of the different forms and then predict what will happen when people display abnormal forms of NVC, such as making too little eye contact or standing too close to others. Finally, they might devise a means of training such people in ways of improving their NVC. This last stage will also include some evaluation of the success of the training.

What is a method?

A method is a systematic approach to a piece of research. Psychologists use a wide range of methods. There are a number of ways in which the methods adopted by psychologists are classified. One common distinction which is made is between quantitative and qualitative methods. As their names suggest, quantitative methods involve some form of numerical measurement while qualitative methods involve verbal description.

Why have a method?

The simple answer to this question is that without a method the research of a psychologist is no better than the speculations of a lay person. For, without a method, there is little protection against our hunches overly guiding what information is available to us and how we interpret it. In addition, without method our research is not open to the scrutiny of other psychologists. As an example of the dangers of not employing a method I will explore the idea that the consumption of coffee in the evening causes people to have a poor night's sleep.

I have plenty of evidence to support this idea. Firstly, I have my own experience of the link between coffee consumption and poor sleep. Secondly, when I have discussed it with others they confirm that they have the same experience. Thirdly, I know that caffeine is a stimulant and so it seems a perfectly reasonable assumption that it will keep me awake.

There are a number of flaws in my argument. In the first place I know my prediction. Therefore the effect may actually be a consequence of that knowledge. To control for this possibility I should study people who are unaware of the prediction. Alternatively, I should give some people who are aware of the prediction what is called a placebo—a substance which will be indistinguishable from the substance being tested but which does not have the same physical effect—in this case a drink which they think contains caffeine. Secondly, because of my prediction I normally tend to avoid drinking coffee in the evening; I only drink it on special occasions and it may be that other aspects of these occasions are contributing to my poor sleep.

The occasions when I do drink coffee are when I have gone out for a meal at a restaurant or at a friend's house or when friends come to my house. It is likely that I will eat differently on these occasions: I will have a larger meal or a richer meal and I will eat later than usual. In addition, I may drink alcohol on these occasions and the occasions may be more stimulating in that we will talk about more interesting things than usual and I may disrupt my sleeping pattern by staying up later than usual. Finally, I have not checked on the nature of my sleep when I do not drink coffee; I have no baseline for comparison.

Thus, there are a number of factors that may contribute to my poor sleep, which I need to control for if I am going to study the relationship between coffee consumption and poor sleep properly. Applying a method to my research allows me to test my ideas more systematically and more completely.

Tensions between control and ecological validity

Throughout science there is a tension between two approaches. One is to investigate a phenomenon in isolation, or, at least, with a minimum of other factors, that could affect it, being present. For example, I may isolate the consumption of caffeine as the factor that contributes to poor sleep. The alternative approach is to investigate the phenomenon in its natural setting. For example, I may investigate the effect of coffee consumption on my sleep in its usual context. There are good reasons for adopting each of these approaches.

By minimising the number of factors present, researchers can exercise control over the situation. Thus, by varying one aspect at a time and observing any changes, they can try to identify relationships between factors. Thus, I may be able to show that caffeine alone is not the cause of my poor sleep. In order to minimise the variation that is experienced by the different people whom they are studying, psychologists often conduct research in a laboratory.

However, often when a phenomenon is taken out of its natural setting it changes. It may have been the result of a large number of factors working together or it may be that, by conducting my research in a laboratory, I have made it so artificial that it bears no relation to the real world. The term *ecological validity* is used to refer to research that *does* relate to real-world events. Thus, the researcher has to adopt an approach that maximises control while at the same time being aware of the problem of artificiality.

Distinctions between quantitative and qualitative methods

The distinction between quantitative and qualitative methods can be a false one in that they may be two approaches to studying the same phenomena. Or they may be two stages in the same piece of research, with a qualitative approach yielding ideas which can then be investigated via a quantitative approach. The problem arises when they provide different answers. None-theless, the distinction can be a convenient fiction for classifying methods.

Quantitative methods

One way to classify quantitative methods is under the headings of experimenting, asking questions and observing. The main distinction between the three is that in the experimental method researchers manipulate certain aspects of the situation and measure the presumed effects of those manipulations. Questioning and observational methods generally involve measurement in the absence of manipulation. Questioning involves asking people about details such as their behaviour and their beliefs and attitudes. Observational methods, not surprisingly, involve watching people's behaviour.

Thus, in an experiment to investigate the relationship between coffee drinking and sleep patterns I might give one group of people no coffee, another group one cup of normal coffee and a third group decaffeinated coffee, and then measure how much sleep members of each group had. Alternatively, I might question a group of people about their patterns of sleep and of coffee consumption, while in an observational study I might stay with a group of people for a week, note each person's coffee consumption and then, using a closed-circuit television system, watch how well they sleep each night.

The distinction between the three methods is, once again, artificial, for the measures used in an experiment could involve asking questions or making observations. Before I deal with the three methods referred to above I want to mention a method which is often left out of consideration and gives the most control to the researcher—modelling.

Modelling and artificial intelligence

Modelling

Modelling refers to the development of theory through the construction of models to account for the results of research and to explore more fully the consequences of the theory. The consequences can then be subjected to empirical research to test how well the model represents reality. Models can take many forms. They have often been based on metaphors borrowed from other disciplines. For example, the information-processing model of human cognition can be seen to be based on the computer. As Gregg (1986) points out, Plato viewed human memory as being like a wax tablet, with forgetting being due to the trace being worn away or effaced.

Modelling can be in the form of the equivalent of flow diagrams as in Atkinson and Shiffrin's (1971) model of human memory, where memory is seen as being in three parts: immediate, short-term and long-term. Alternatively, it can be in the form of mathematical formulae, as were Hull's models of animal and human learning (see Estes, 1993).

With the advent of the computer, models can now be explored through computer programs. For example, Newell and Simon (1972) explored human reasoning through the use of computers. This approach to modelling is called computer simulation. Miller (1985) has a good account of the nature of computer simulation.

Artificial intelligence

A distinction needs to be made between computer simulation and artificial intelligence. The goal of computer simulation is to mimic human behaviour on a computer in as close a way as possible to the way humans perform that behaviour. The goal of artificial intelligence is to use computers to perform tasks in the most efficient way that they can and not necessarily in the way that humans perform the tasks. Nonetheless, the results of computer simulation and of artificial intelligence can feed back into each other, so that the results of one may suggest ways to improve the other. See Boden (1987) for an account of artificial intelligence.

The experiment

Experiments can take many forms, as you will see when you read Chapter 4 on designs of research. For the moment I simply want to re-emphasise that the experimenter manipulates an aspect of the situation and measures what are presumed to be the consequences of those manipulations. I use the term *presumed* because an important issue in research is attempting to identify causal relationships between phenomena. As explained earlier, I may have poorer sleep when I drink coffee but it might not be the cause of my poor sleep; rather it might take place when other aspects of the situation, which do impair my sleep, are also present. It is felt that the properly designed experiment is the best way to identify causal relationships.

By a properly designed experiment I mean one in which all those aspects of the situation which may be relevant are being controlled for in some way. Chapter 4 discusses the various means of control which can be exercised by researchers.

The quasi-experiment

The quasi-experiment can be seen as a less rigorous version of the experiment: for example, where the researcher does not manipulate an aspect of the situation, such as coffee consumption, but treats people as being in different groups on the basis of their existing consumption, or lack of it, and then compares the sleep patterns of the groups. Because the quasi-experiment is less well controlled than an experiment, identifying causal relationships can be more problematic. Nonetheless, this method can be used for at least two good reasons. Firstly, it may not be possible to manipulate the situation. Secondly, it can have better ecological validity than the experimental equivalent.

Asking questions

There are at least three formats for asking questions and at least three ways in which questions can be presented and responded to. The formats are unstructured (or free) interviews, semi-structured interviews and structured questionnaires. The presentation modes are face-to-face, by telephone and through written questionnaire. Surveys of people usually employ some method for asking questions.

Unstructured interviews
An unstructured interview is likely to involve a particular topic or topics to be discussed but the interviewer has no fixed wording in mind and is happy to let the conversation deviate from the original topic if potentially interesting material is touched upon. Such a technique could be used when a researcher is initially exploring an area with a view to designing a more structured format for subsequent use. In addition, this technique can be used to produce the data for a content analysis (see below) or even for a qualitative method such as discourse analysis (see Potter & Wetherall, 1995).

Semi-structured interviews
Semi-structured interviews are used when the researcher has a clearer idea about the questions that are to be asked but is not necessarily concerned

about the exact wording, or the order in which they are to be asked. It is likely that the interviewer will have a list of questions to be asked in the course of the interview. The interviewer will allow the conversation to flow comparatively freely but will tend to steer it in such a way that he or she can introduce specific questions when the opportunity arises. An example of the semi-structured interview is the typical job interview.

The structured questionnaire

The structured questionnaire will be used when researchers have a clear idea about the range of possible answers they wish to elicit. It will involve precise wording of questions, which are asked in a fixed order and each one of which is likely to require respondents to answer one of a number of alternatives that are presented to them. For example:

People should not be allowed to keep animals as pets:

| *strongly agree* | *agree* | *no opinion* | *disagree* | *strongly disagree* |

There are a number of advantages of this approach to asking questions. Firstly, respondents could fill in the questionnaire themselves, which means that it could save the researcher's time both in interviewing and in travelling to where the respondent lives. Secondly, a standard format can minimise the effect of the way in which a question is asked of the respondent and on his or her response. Without this check any differences that are found between people's responses could be due to the way the question was asked rather than any inherent differences between the respondents. A third advantage of this technique is that the responses are more immediately quantifiable. In the above example, respondents can be said to have scored 1 if they said that they strongly agreed with the statement and 5 if they strongly disagreed.

Structured questionnaires are mainly used in health and social psychology, by market researchers and by those conducting opinion polls. Focus groups can be used to assess the opinions and attitudes of a group of people. They allow discussion to take place during or prior to the completion of a questionnaire and the discussion itself can be recorded. They can be particularly useful in the early stages of a piece of research when the researchers are trying to get a feel for a new area. Interviews and surveys are discussed further in Chapters 5 and 6.

Observational methods

There is often an assumption that observation is not really a method as a researcher can simply watch a person or group of people and note down what happened. However, if an observation did start with this approach it would soon be evident to the observer that, unless there was little behaviour taking place, it was difficult to note everything down.

There are at least three possible ways to cope with this problem. The first is to rely on memory and write up what was observed subsequently.

This approach has the obvious problem of the selectivity and poor retention of memory. A second approach is to use some permanent recording device, such as an audio or video recorder, which would allow repeated listening or viewing. If this is not possible, the third possibility is to decide beforehand what aspects of the situation to concentrate on. This can be helped by devising a coding system for behaviour and preparing a checklist beforehand.

You may argue that this would prejudge what you were going to observe. However, you must realise that even when you do not prepare for an observation, whatever *is* noted down is at the expense of other things that were not noted. You are being selective and that selectivity is guided by some implicit notion, on your part, as to what is relevant. As a preliminary stage you can observe without a checklist and then devise your checklist as a result of that initial observation but you cannot escape from the selective process, even during the initial stage, unless you are using a means of permanently recording the proceedings. Remember, however, that even a video camera will be pointed in a particular direction and so may miss things.

Methods involving asking questions and observational methods span the qualitative–quantitative divide.

Structured observation
Structured observation involves a set of classifications for behaviour and the use of a checklist to record the behaviour. An early version, which is still used for observing small groups, is the interaction process analysis (IPA) devised by Bales (1950) (see Hewstone, Stroebe & Stephenson, 1996).

Using this technique verbal behaviour can be classified according to certain categories, such as 'Gives suggestion and direction, implying autonomy for others'. Observers have a checklist on which they record the nature of the behaviour and to whom it was addressed. The recording is made simply by making a mark in the appropriate box on the checklist every time an utterance is made. The IPA loses a lot of the original information but that is because it has developed out of a particular theory about group behaviour: in this case, that groups develop leaders, that leaders can be of two types, that these two can coexist in the same group and that interactions with the leaders will be of a particular type. A more complicated system could involve symbols for particular types of behaviour, including non-verbal behaviour.

Structured observation is not only used when one is present at the original event. It is also often used to summarise the information on a video or audio recording. It has the advantage that it prepares the information for quantitative statistical analysis.

A critical point about structured observation, as with any measure that involves a subjective judgement, is that the observer, or preferably observers, should be clear about the classificatory system before implementing it. In Chapter 2 I return to this theme under the heading of *the reliability of measures*. For the moment, it is important to stress that an observer should classify the same piece of behaviour in the same way from one occasion to another. Otherwise, any attempt to quantify the behaviour is subject to error, which in turn will affect the results of the research. Observers should undergo a training phase until they can classify behaviour with a high degree of accuracy. It is preferable to have more than one observer because if they disagree over a classification this will show that the classification is unclear and needs to be defined further. Structured observation is dealt with in Chapter 7.

Content analysis

Content analysis is a technique used to quantify aspects of written or spoken text or of some form of visual representation. The role of the analyst is to decide on the unit of measurement and then apply that measure to the text or other form of representation. For example, Pitts and Jackson (1989) looked at the presence of articles on the subject of AIDS in Zimbabwean newspapers, to see whether there was a change with a government campaign designed to raise awareness and whether any change was sustained. In a separate study, Manstead and McCulloch (1981) looked at the ways in which males and females were represented in television adverts. Content analysis is dealt with in Chapter 7.

Meta-analysis

Meta-analysis is a means of reviewing quantitatively the results of the research in a given area from a number of researchers. It allows the reviewer to capitalise on the fact that while individual researchers may have used small samples in their research, an overview can be based on a number of such small samples. Thus, if different pieces of research come to different conclusions, the overview will show the direction in which the general trend of relevant research points. Techniques have been devised that allow the reviewer to overcome the fact that individual pieces of research may have used different statistical procedures in producing the summary. A fuller discussion can be found in Chapter 22.

Case studies

Case studies are in-depth analyses of one individual or, possibly, one institution or organisation at a time. They are not strictly a distinct method but employ other methods to investigate the individual. Thus, a case study may involve both interviews and experiments. They are generally used when an individual is unusual: for example, when an individual has a particular skill such as a phenomenal memory (see Luria, 1975a). Alternatively, they are used when an individual has a particular deficit such as a form of aphasia—an impairment of memory (see Luria, 1975b). Cognitive neuropsychologists frequently use case studies with impaired people to help understand how normal cognition might work (see Humphreys & Riddoch, 1987).

Qualitative methods

Two misunderstandings that exist about the qualitative approach to research are, firstly, that it does not involve method and, secondly, that it is easier than quantitative research. While this may be true of bad research, good qualitative research will be just as rigorous as good quantitative research. Many forms of qualitative research start from the point of view that measuring people's behaviour and their views fails to get at the essence of what it is to be human. To reduce aspects of human psychology to numbers is, according to this view, to adopt a reductionist and positivist approach to understanding people.

Reductionism refers to reducing the object of study to a simpler form. Critics of reductionism would argue, for example, that you cannot understand human memory by giving participants lists of unrelated words, measuring recall and looking at an average performance. Rather, you have to understand the nature of memories for individuals in the wider context of their experience, including their interaction with other people. Positivism refers to a mechanistic view of humans that seeks understanding in terms of cause and effect relationships rather than the meanings of individuals. The point is made that the same piece of behaviour can mean different things to different people and even to the same person in different contexts. Thus, a handshake can be a greeting, a farewell, the conclusion of a contest or the sealing of a bargain. To understand the significance of a given piece of behaviour, the researcher needs to be aware of the meaning it has for the participants. The most extreme form of positivism that has been applied in psychology is the approach adopted by behaviourism.

In the first edition of this book I briefly described some qualitative methods. In this edition I had a dilemma in that I wanted to expand that section to cover some more methods while at the same time I needed to include other new material elsewhere and yet keep the book to roughly the same size. Given the title of the book I decided to remove that section. Instead I would recommend that interested readers look at Banister, Burman, Parker, Taylor and Tindall (1994) and Hayes (1997). These provide an introduction to a number of such methods and references for those wishing to pursue them further.

Is psychology a science?

The classic view of science is that it is conducted in a number of set stages. Firstly, the researcher identifies a hypothesis that he or she wishes to test. The term *hypothesis* is derived from the Greek prefix *hypo* meaning less than or below or not quite and *thesis* meaning theory. Thus a hypothesis is a tentative statement that does not yet have the status of a theory. For example, I think that when people consume coffee in the evening they have poorer sleep. Usually the hypothesis will have been derived from previous work in the area or from some observations of the researcher. Popper (1972) makes the point that, as far as the process of science is concerned, the source of the hypothesis is, in fact, immaterial. While this is true, anyone assessing your research would not look favourably upon it if it appeared to have originated without any justification.

The next stage is to choose an appropriate method. Once the method is chosen, the researcher designs a particular way of conducting the method and applies the method. The results of the research are then analysed and the hypothesis is supported by the evidence, abandoned in the light of the evidence or modified to take account of any counter-evidence. This approach is described as the hypothetico-deductive approach and has been derived from the way that the natural sciences—such as physics—are considered to conduct research.

The assertion that psychology is a science has been discussed at great length. Interested readers can pursue this more fully by referring to Valentine (1992). The case usually presented for its being a science is that it practises the hypothetico-deductive method and that this renders it a science. Popper (1974) argues that for a subject to be a science the hypotheses it generates should be capable of being falsified by the evidence. In other words, if my hypothesis will remain intact regardless of the outcome of any piece of research designed to evaluate it then I am not practising science. Popper has attacked both psycho-analysis and Marxism on these grounds as not being scientific. Rather than explain the counter-arguments to Popper, I want to question whether use of the hypothetico-deductive approach defines a discipline as a science. I will return to the Popperian approach in Chapter 10 when I explain how we test hypotheses statistically.

Putnam (1979) points out that even in physics there are at least two other ways in which the science is conducted. The first is where the existing theory cannot explain a given phenomenon. Rather than scrap the theory, researchers look for the special conditions that could explain the phenomenon. Putnam uses the example of the orbit of Uranus not conforming to Newton's theory of gravity. The special condition was the existence of another planet—Neptune—which was distorting the orbit of Uranus. Researchers, having arrived at the hypothesis that another planet existed, proceeded to look for it. The second approach that is not hypothetico-deductive is where a theory exists but the predictions that can be derived from it have not been fully explored. At this point mathematics has to be employed to elucidate the predictions, and only once this has been achieved can hypotheses be tested.

The moral that psychologists can draw from Putnam's argument is that there is more than one approach that is accepted as scientific, and that in its attempts to be scientific, psychology need not simply follow one approach. Modelling is an example of how psychology also conducts research in the absence of the hypothetico-deductive approach. Cognitive neuropsychologists build models of human cognition from the results of their experiments with humans and posit areas of the brain that might account for particular phenomena: for example, when an individual is found to have a specific deficit in memory or recognition, such as prosopagnosia—the inability to recognise faces. Computer simulation is the extension of exploring a theory mathematically to generate and test hypotheses.

Ethical issues in psychological research

Whatever the research method you have chosen, there are certain principles that should guide how you treat the people you approach to take part in your research, and in particular the participants who do take part in your research. Also, there are principles that should govern how you behave towards fellow psychologists.

Both the BPS (British Psychological Society, 2000) and the APA (American Psychological Association, 1992) have written guidelines on how to conduct ethical research and both are available via their web sites. Shaughnessy, Zechmeister and Zechmeister (2003) outline the APA's guidelines and include a commentary on them about their implications for researchers.

To emphasise the point that behaving ethically can have benefits as well as obligations, I have summarised the issues under the headings of *obligations* and *benefits*. I have further subdivided the obligations into the stages of planning, conduct and reporting of the research. Many of the topics covered are a matter of judgement so that a given decision about what is and what is not ethical behaviour will depend on the context.

Obligations

Planning

As researchers, we should assess the risk/benefit ratio. In other words, we should look to see whether any psychological risks, to which we are proposing to expose participants, are outweighed by the benefits the research could show. Thus, if we were investigating a possible means of alleviating psychological suffering we might be willing to put our participants at more risk than if we were trying to satisfy intellectual curiosity over a matter that has no obvious benefit to people.

Linked to this is the notion of what constitutes a risk. The term 'minimal risk' is used to describe the level of risk that a given participant might have in his or her normal life. Thus, if the research involved no more than this minimum of risk it would be more likely to be considered ethically acceptable than research that went beyond this minimum.

It is always good practice to be aware of what other researchers have done in an area, before conducting a piece of research. This will prevent research being conducted that is an unnecessary replication of previous research. In addition, it may reveal alternative techniques that would be less ethically questionable. It is also a good idea, particularly as a novice researcher, to seek advice from more experienced researchers. This will be even more important if you are proposing to conduct research with people from a special group, such as those with a sensory impairment. This will alert you to ethical issues that are particular to such a group. In addition, it will prevent you from making basic errors that will give your research a less professional feel and possibly make the participants less co-operative.

What constitutes a risk worth taking will also depend on the researcher. An experienced researcher with a good track record is likely to show a greater benefit than a novice.

If risks are entailed that go beyond the minimum, then the researchers should put safeguards in place, such as having counselling available.

Conduct

Work within your own level of competence. That is, if you are not clinically trained and you are trying to do research in such an area, then have a clinically trained person on your team.

Approach potential participants with the recognition that they have a perfect right to refuse; approach them politely and accept rejection gracefully. Secondly, always treat your participants with respect. They have put themselves out to take part in your research and you owe them the common courtesy of not treating them as research-fodder, to be rushed in when you need them and out when you have finished with them. You may be bored stiff by going through the same procedure many times but think how *you* feel when you are treated as though you are an object on a conveyor belt.

Participants may be anxious about their performance and see themselves as being tested. If it is appropriate, reassure them that you will not be looking at individual performances but at the performance of people in general.

Resist the temptation to comment on their performance while they are taking part in the study; this can be a particular danger when there is more than one researcher. I remember, with horror, working with a colleague who had high investment in a particular outcome from the experiments on which we were working and who would loudly comment on participants who were not performing in line with the hypothesis.

Obtain informed consent. In other words, where possible, obtain the agreement from each participant to taking part, with the full knowledge of the greatest possible risk that the research could entail. In some cases, the consent may need to be obtained from a parent or guardian, or even someone who is acting *in loco parentis*—acting in the role of parent, for example a teacher.

Obviously, there are situations in which it will be difficult, and counterproductive, to obtain such consent. For example, you may be doing an observation in a natural setting. If the behaviour is taking place in a public place then the research would be less ethically questionable than if you were having to utilise specialist equipment to obtain the data.

Although you should ideally obtain informed consent, do not reveal your hypotheses beforehand to your participants: neither explicitly by telling them directly at the beginning nor implicitly by your behaviour during the experiment. This may affect their behaviour in one of two ways. On the one hand, they may try to be kind to you and give you the results you predict. On the other hand, they may be determined not to behave in the way you predict; this can be particularly true if you are investigating an aspect of human behaviour such as conformity.

If you are not using a cover story, it is enough to give a general description of the area of the research, such as that it is an experiment on memory. Be careful that your own behaviour does not inadvertently signal the behaviour you are expecting. Remember the story of the horse Clever Hans who appeared to be able to calculate mathematically, counting out the answer by pawing with his hoof. It was discovered that he was reacting to the unconscious signals that were being sent by his trainer (Pfungst, 1911/1965). One way around such a danger is to have the research conducted by someone who is unaware of the hypotheses or of the particular treatment a given group have received and in this case is unaware of the expected response—a blind condition.

Do not apply undue pressure on people to take part. This could be a particular problem if the people you are studying are in some form of institution, such as a prison or mental hospital. They should not get the impression that they will in some way be penalised if they do not take part in the research. On the other hand, neither should you offer unnecessarily large inducements, such as disproportionate amounts of money. I have seen participants who were clearly only interested in the money on offer, who completed a task in a totally artificial way just to get it over with and to obtain the reward.

Assure participants of confidentiality: that you will not reveal to others what you learn about your individual participants. If you need to follow up people at a later date you may need to identify who provided you with what data. If this is the case then you can use a code to identify people and then, in a separate place from the data, have your own way to translate from the code to find who provided the particular data. In this way, if someone came across, say, a sensitive questionnaire, they would not be able to identify the person whose responses were shown.

If you do not need to follow up your participants then they can remain anonymous. For example, if you are conducting an opinion poll and are collecting your information from participants you gather from outside a supermarket, then they can remain anonymous.

Make clear to participants that they have a right to withdraw at any time during the research. In addition, they have the right to say that you cannot use any information that you have collected up to that point.

If you learn of something about a participant during the research which it could be important for them to know then you are obliged to inform them. For example, if while conducting research you found that a person appeared to suffer from colour blindness then they should be told. Obviously you should break such news gently. In addition, keep within your level of competence. In the previous example, recommend that they see an eye specialist. Do not make diagnoses in an area for which you are not trained.

There can be a particular issue over psychometric tests—such as personality tests. Only a fully trained person should utilise these for diagnostic purposes. However, a researcher can use such tests as long as he or she does not tell others about the results of individual cases.

In research that involves more than one researcher there is collective responsibility to ensure that the research is being conducted within ethical guidelines. Thus, if you suspect that someone on the team may not be behaving ethically it is your responsibility to bring them into line.

You should debrief participants. In other words, after they have taken part you should discuss the research with them. You may not want to do this, in full, immediately, as you may not want others to learn about your full intentions. However, under these circumstances you can offer to talk more fully once the data have been collected from all participants.

Reporting

Be honest about what you found. If you do make alterations to the data, such as removing some participants' scores, then explain what you have done and why.

Maintain confidentiality. If you are reporting only summary statistics, such as averages for a group, rather than individual details, then this will help to prevent individuals being identified. However, if you are working with special groups, such as those in a unique school or those with prodigious memories, or even with individual case studies, then confidentiality may be more difficult. Where feasible, false names or initials can improve confidentiality. However, in some cases participants may need to be aware of the possibility of their being identified and at this point given the opportunity to veto publication.

Many obligations are to fellow psychologists.

If, after reporting the results of the research, you find that you have made important errors, you should make those who have access to the research aware of your mistake. In the case of an article published in a journal you will need to write to the editor.

Do not use other people's work as though it were your own. In other words, avoid plagiarism. Similarly, if you have learned about another researcher's results before they have been published anywhere, report them only if you have received permission from the researcher. Once published, they are in the public domain and can be freely discussed but must be credited accordingly. You should also give due credit to all those who have worked with you on the research. This may entail joint authorship if the contribution has been sufficiently large. Alternatively, an acknowledgement may be more appropriate.

Once you have published your research and are not expecting to analyse the data further, you should be willing to share those data with other psychologists. They may wish to analyse them from another perspective.

Benefits

In addition to all the obligations, acting ethically can produce benefits for the research.

If you treat participants as fellow human beings whose opinions are important then you are likely to receive greater co-operation. In addition, if you are as open as you can be, within the constraints of not divulging your expectations before participants have taken part in the research, then the research may have more meaning to them and this may prevent them from searching for some hidden motive behind it. In this way, their behaviour will be less affected by a suspicion about what the research might be about, and the results will be more valid.

If you have employed a cover story you can use this opportunity to disclose the true intentions behind the research, to find out how convincing the cover story was and to discuss how participants feel. This is particularly important if you have required them to behave in a way that they may feel worried about. For example, in Milgram's experiments where participants thought that they were delivering electric shocks to another person, participants were given a long debriefing (Milgram, 1974).

Another useful aspect of debriefing is that participants may reveal strategies that they employed to perform tasks, such as using a particular mnemonic technique in research into memory. Such information may help to explain variation between participants in their results, as well as giving further insight into human behaviour in the area you are studying.

Summary

The purpose of psychological research is to advance knowledge about humans by describing, predicting and eventually allowing intervention to help people. Psychology can legitimately be seen as a science because it employs rigorous methods in its research in order to avoid mere conjecture and to allow fellow psychologists to evaluate the research. However, in common with the natural sciences, such as physics, psychologists employ a range of methods in their research. These vary in the amount of control the researcher has over the situation and the degree to which the context relates to people's daily lives. Such research is often classified as being either quantitative—involving the collection of numerical data—or qualitative—to do with the qualities of the situation.

Throughout the research process psychologists should bear in mind that they should behave ethically not only to their participants but also to their fellow psychologists.

The next chapter outlines the preliminary stages of research.

PART 2
Choice of topic, measures and research design

THE PRELIMINARY STAGES OF RESEARCH

2

Introduction

This chapter describes the preliminary stages through which researchers have to go before they actually conduct their research with participants. In addition, it highlights the choices researchers have to make at each stage. The need to check, through a trial run—a pilot study—that the research is well designed, is emphasised.

There are a number of stages that have to be undertaken prior to collecting data. You need to choose a topic, read about the topic, focus on a particular aspect of the topic and choose a method. Where appropriate, you need to decide on your hypotheses. You will also need to choose a design, choose your measure(s) and how you are going to analyse the results. In addition, you need to choose the people whom you are going to study.

Choice of topic

The first thing that should guide your choice of a topic to study is your interest. If you are not interested in the subject then you are unlikely to enjoy the experience of research. A second contribution to your choice should be the ethics of conducting the research. Research with humans or animals should follow a careful cost–benefit analysis. That is, you should be clear that if the participants are paying some cost, such as being deceived or undertaking an unpleasant experience, then the benefits derived from the research should outweigh those costs. Using these criteria means that research that is not designed to increase human knowledge, including most student projects, should show the maximum consideration for the participants. See Chapter 1 for a fuller discussion of ethical issues.

A third point should be the practicalities of researching in your chosen area. There are some areas where the difficulties of conducting empirical research, as a student, are evident before you read further. For example, your particular interest may be in the profiling of criminals by forensic psychologists but it is unlikely, unless you have special contacts, that you are going to be able to carry out more than library research in that area.

However, before you can decide how practical it would be to conduct research in a given area you will often need to read other people's research and then focus on a specific aspect of the area that interests you.

Reviewing the literature

Before conducting any research you need to be aware of what other people have done in the area. Even if you are trying to replicate a piece of research in order to check its results, you will need to know how that research has been conducted in the past. In addition, you may have thought of what you consider to be an original approach to an area, in which case it would be wise to check that it *is* original.

There are two quick ways to find out about what research has been conducted in the area. The first is to ask an expert in the field. The second is to use some form of database of previous research.

Asking an expert

Firstly, you have to identify who the experts are in your chosen field. This can be achieved by asking more experienced researchers in your department for advice, by interrogating the databases referred to in a later section or by searching on the Internet. Once you have identified the expert, you have to think what to ask him or her. Too often I have received letters or e-mails that tell me that the writer wants to conduct research in the area of blindness and then go on to ask me to give them any information that might be useful to them. This is far too open-ended a request. I have no idea what aspect of blindness they wish to investigate and so the only thing I can offer is for them to visit or phone me to discuss the matter. Researchers are far more likely to respond if you can give them a clear idea of your research interest. Unless you can be sufficiently specific, I recommend that you explore the literature through a database of research.

Places where research is reported

Psychologists have four main ways of reporting their research—at conferences, in journal articles, in books and on the Internet. A conference is the place where research that has yet to be published in other forms is reported, so it will tend to be the most up-to-date source of research. However, when researchers become more eminent they are invited to present reviews of their work at conferences.

Conferences are of two types. Firstly, there are general conferences, such as the annual conferences of the British Psychological Society or the American Psychological Association, in which psychologists of many types present papers. Secondly, there are specialist conferences, which are devoted to a more specific area of psychology such as cognitive psychology or developmental psychology. However, even in the more general conferences there are usually symposia that contain a number of papers on the same theme.

There are problems with using conferences as your source of information. Firstly, they tend to be annual and so they may not coincide with when you need the information. A bigger problem is that they may not have any papers on the area of your interest. However, abstracts of the proceedings of previous conferences can be useful to identify who the active researchers are in a given area. A third problem can be that research reported at a conference often has not been fully assessed by other psychologists who are expert in the area, and so it should be treated with greater caution.

Accordingly, you are more likely to find out about previous research from academic journal articles or books. Psychologists tend to follow other sciences and publish their research first in journal articles. The articles will generally have been reviewed by other researchers and only those that are considered to be well conducted and of interest will be published.

Once they have become sufficiently well-known, researchers may be invited to contribute a chapter to a book on their topic. When they have conducted sufficient research they may produce a book devoted to their own research—what is sometimes called a research monograph. Alternatively, they may write a general book that reports their research and that of others in their area of interest. The most general source will be a textbook devoted to a wider area of psychology, such as social psychology, or even a general textbook on all areas of psychology.

Most books take a while to get published and so they tend to report slightly older research. Although there is a time lag between an article being submitted to a journal and its publication, journals are the best source for the most up-to-date research.

Journals, like conferences, can be either general, such as the *British Journal of Psychology* or *Psychological Bulletin*, or more specific, such as *Cognition* or *Memory and Language*. Many journal articles are available on the Internet and this is likely to be a growing phenomenon once problems over copyright have been resolved. Publishers have a number of arrangements that will allow you access to an Internet-based version of their journals. In some cases your institution will have subscribed to a particular package that will include access to electronic versions of certain journals. Under other schemes an electronic version will be available if your institution already subscribes to the paper version.

Beyond the electronic versions of journals, and the research databases that are mentioned later, the Internet can be a mixed blessing. On the one hand, it can be a very quick way to find out about research that has been conducted in the area you are interested in. On the other hand, there is no quality control at all and so you could be reading complete drivel that is masquerading as science. Accordingly, you have to treat what you find on the Internet with more caution than any of the other sources. Nonetheless, if you can find the Web pages of a known researcher in a field, they can often tell you what papers that person has published on the topic.

While it is possible to identify relevant research by looking through copies of journals, a more efficient search strategy is to use some form of database of research.

Databases of previous research

The main databases of psychological research are *Psychological Abstracts*, *PsycINFO*, the *Social Science Citation Index* (*SSCI*) and *Current Contents*.

Psychological Abstracts

An abstract is a brief summary of a piece of research; a fuller description of an abstract is given in Chapter 23. *Psychological Abstracts* is a monthly publication that lists all the research that has been published in psychology. In addition, every year a single version is produced of the research that has been reported in that year. Approximately every 10 years a compilation is made of the research that has been published during the preceding decade. You can consult *Psychological Abstracts* in two ways. Firstly, you can use an index of topics to find out what has been published in that area. Secondly, you can use an index of authors to find out what each author has published during that period. Each piece of research is given a unique number and both ways of consulting *Psychological Abstracts* will refer you to those numbers. Armed with those numbers you can then look up a third part of *Psychological Abstracts* which contains the name(s) of the author(s), the journal reference and an abstract of the research. At that point you can decide whether you want to read the full version of any reference.

The disadvantage of *Psychological Abstracts* is that when you do not have a compiled version for the decade or for the year you will have to search through a number of copies. In addition, you can only search for one key word at a time.

PsycINFO

PsycINFO is a Web-based version of a compilation of *Psychological Abstracts*. *PsycINFO* allows you to search for more than one keyword at a time. For example, you may be interested in AIDS in African countries. By simply searching for articles about AIDS you will be presented with thousands of references. If you search for references that are to do both with AIDS and with Africa you will reduce the number of references you are offered. Once you have made your search, you can look up each reference where you will be given the same details as those contained in *Psychological Abstracts*: the author(s), the journal and an abstract of the article. You then have the option of marking each reference you wish to pursue so that when you have finished scanning them you can have a printout of the marked references, complete with their abstracts. Once again, you can then use this information to find the original of any article for more details.

Social Science Citation Index

Social Science Citation Index (*SSCI*) allows you to find references in the same way as for *PsycINFO*. However, it has the additional benefit that you can find out who has cited a particular work in their references. In this way, if you have found a study and are interested in identifying who has also worked in the same area, then you can use the study as a way of finding out other more recent work in that area.

There are Web-based, CD-ROM and paper versions of the SSCI. If you have searched using the Web-based version you can have the results of your search emailed to you. There is also a *Science Citation Index* (*SCI*) which could prove useful.

Current Contents

There are various versions of *Current Contents* for different collections of disciplines. The most relevant for psychologists is the one for *Social and Behavioral Sciences*, which includes, among others, psychology, education, psychiatry, sociology and anthropology. *Current Contents* is published weekly and is simply a list of the contents pages of academic journals and some books published recently.

It is available in a number of formats. At the time of writing these include a Web-based version and a diskette version. Each allows you to search according to keywords. They also provide you with the address of the person from whom the article can be obtained. There is an additional facility—*Request-a-print*—which allows you to print a postcard to the author asking for a reprint of the article.

Inter-library loans

Sometimes you will identify an article or a book that your library does not have. It is possible in some libraries to borrow a copy of such a book or journal article through what is termed an inter-library loan. You will need to talk to your librarians about whether this facility is available and what the restrictions are at your institution with regard to the number you can have, whether you have to pay for them and, if so, how much they will cost you.

Focusing on a specific area of research

It is likely that in the process of finding out about previous research you will have expanded your understanding of an area, not only of the subject matter but also of the types of methods and designs that have been employed. This should help you narrow your focus to a specific aspect of the area that interests you particularly and that you think needs investigating. In addition, you are now in a better position to consider the practicalities of doing research in the area. You will have seen various aspects of the research that may constrain you: the possible need for specialised equipment, such as an eye-movement recorder, and the number of participants considered necessary for a particular piece of research. In addition, you will have an idea of the time it would take to conduct the research.

An additional consideration that should motivate you to narrow your focus is that if you try to include too many aspects of an area into one piece of research you will be making a common mistake of novice researchers. By trying to be too all-encompassing you will make the results of the research difficult to interpret. Generally, a large-scale research project involves a number of smaller-scale pieces of research that, when put together, address a larger area. Accordingly, I advise you not to be too ambitious; better a well-conducted, simple piece of research that is easy to interpret than an over-ambitious one that yields no clear-cut results: scientific knowledge mainly increases in small increments.

Choice of method

See Chapter 1 for a description of the range of quantitative methods that are employed by psychologists.

In choosing a method you have to take account of a number of factors. The first criterion must be the expectations you have of the research. The point has already been made, in Chapter 1, that you need to balance the advantages of greater control against the concomitant loss of ecological validity. Thus, if your aim is to refine understanding in an area that has already been researched quite thoroughly, then you may use a tightly controlled experimental design. However, if you are entering a new area you may use a more exploratory method such as one of the qualitative methods. Similarly, if you are interested in people's behaviour but not in their beliefs and intentions then an experiment may be appropriate. On the other hand, if you want to know the meaning that that behaviour has for the participants then you may use a qualitative method.

It is worth making the point that if a number of methods are used to focus on the same area of research—usually termed 'triangulation'—and they indicate a similar result to each other then the standing of those findings is enhanced. In other words, do not feel totally constrained to employ the same method as those whose research you have read. By taking a fresh method to an area you can add something to our understanding of that area.

Once again, not least to be considered are the practicalities of the situation. You may desire to have the control of an experiment but be forced to use a quasi-experimental method because an experiment would be impractical. For example, you may wish to compare two ways of teaching children to read. However, if your time is limited you may be forced to compare children in different schools where the two techniques are already being used rather than train the children yourself. Nonetheless, you should be aware of the problems that can exist for interpreting such a design (see Chapter 4).

Choice of hypotheses

A sign of a clearly focused piece of research can be that you are making specific predictions as to the outcomes—you are stating a hypothesis. Stating a hypothesis can help to direct your attention to particular aspects of the research and help you to choose the design and measures. The phrasing of hypotheses is inextricably linked with how they are tested and is dealt with in Chapter 10.

Choice of research design

Chapter 4 describes the research designs that are most frequently employed by psychologists.

Once you have chosen a method, you need to consider whether you are seeking a finding that might be generalisable to other settings, in which case you ought to choose an appropriate design that has good external validity (see Chapter 3). Similarly, if you are investigating cause and effect relationships within your research then you need to choose a design that is not just appropriate to the area of research but one that has high internal validity (see Chapters 3 and 4). Once again, there are likely to be certain constraints on the type of design you can employ. For example, if you have less than a year to conduct the research and you want to conduct longitudinal research then you can only do so with some phenomenon that has a cycle of less than a year.

An aspect of your design will be the measure(s) that you take in the research. The next section considers the types of measures that are available to psychologists and factors that you have to take into account when choosing a measure.

Measurement in psychology

The phenomena that psychologists measure can be seen as falling under three main headings: overt non-verbal behaviour, verbal behaviour and covert non-verbal behaviour.

Overt non-verbal behaviour

By this term I mean behaviour that can be observed directly. This can take at least two forms. Firstly, an observer can note down behaviour at a distance, for example, that involved in non-verbal communication, such as gestures and facial expressions. Alternatively, more proximal measures can be taken, such as the speed with which a participant makes an overt judgement about recognising a face (reaction times).

Verbal behaviour

Verbal behaviour can be of a number of forms. Researchers can record naturally occurring language. Alternatively, they can elicit it either in spoken form through an interview or in written form through a questionnaire or a personality test.

Covert behaviour

By covert behaviour I mean behaviour that cannot be observed directly, for example, physiological responses, such as heart rate.

As psychologists we are interested in the range of human experience: behaviour, thought and emotion. However, all the measures I have outlined are at one remove from thought and emotion. We can only *infer* the existence and nature of such things from our measures. For example, we may use heart rate as a measure of how psychologically stressed our participants are. However, we cannot be certain that we have really measured the entities in which we are interested, for there is no perfect one-to-one relationship between such measures and emotions or thoughts. For example, heart rate can also indicate the level of a person's physical exertion.

It might be thought that by measuring verbal behaviour we are getting nearer to thought and emotion. However, verbal behaviour has to be treated with caution. Even if people are trying to be honest, there are at least two types of verbal behaviour that are suspect. Firstly, if we are asking participants to rely on their memories then the information they give us may be misremembered. Secondly, there are forms of knowledge, sometimes called 'procedural knowledge', to which we do not have direct access.

For example, as a cyclist, I could not tell you how to cycle. When I wanted to teach my children how to cycle I did not give them an illustrated talk and then expect them to climb on their bicycles and know how to ride. The only way they learned was through my running alongside them and letting go for a brief moment and allowing them to try to maintain their balance. As the moments grew longer their bodies began to learn how to cycle. Accordingly, to be an acceptable measure verbal behaviour usually has to be about the present and be about knowledge to which participants do have access (see Nisbett & Wilson, 1977; Ericsson & Simon, 1980).

The choice of measures

The measures you choose will obviously be guided by the type of study you are conducting. If you are interested in the speed with which people can recognise a face then you are likely to use reaction times which are measured using a standard piece of apparatus. On the other hand, if you want to measure aspects of people's personalities then you may use an available test of personality. Alternatively, you may wish to measure something that has not been measured before or has not been measured in the way you intend, in which case you will need to devise your own measure.

Whatever the measures you are contemplating using, there are two points you must consider: whether the measures are reliable and whether they are valid. To answer these questions more fully involves a level of statistical detail that I have yet to give. Accordingly, at this stage, I am going to give a brief account of the two concepts and postpone the fuller account until Chapter 19.

Reliability

Reliability refers to the degree to which a measure would produce the same result from one occasion to another: its consistency. There are at least two forms of reliability. Firstly, if a measure is taken from a participant on two occasions, a measure with good reliability will produce a very similar result. Thus, a participant who on two occasions takes an IQ test that has high reliability, should achieve the same score, within certain limits. No psychological measure is 100% reliable and therefore you need to know just how reliable the measure is in order to allow for the degree of error that is inherent in it. If the person achieves a slightly higher IQ on the second occasion he or she takes the test, you want to know if this is a real improvement or one that could have been due to the lack of reliability of the test.

If you are developing a measure then you should check its reliability, using one of the methods described in Chapter 19. If you are using an existing psychometric measure, such as an IQ test or a test of personality, then the manual to the test should report its reliability.

A second form of reliability has to do with measures that involve a certain amount of judgement on the part of the researchers. For example, if you were interested in classifying the non-verbal behaviour of participants, you would want to be sure that you and your fellow researchers are being consistent in applying your classification. This form of reliability can be termed *intra-rater* reliability if you are checking how consistent one person is in classifying the same behaviour on two occasions. It is termed *inter-rater* reliability when the check is that two or more raters are classifying the same behaviour in the same way.

If you are using such a subjective measure then you should check the intra- and inter-rater reliability before employing the measure. It is usual for raters to need to be trained and for the classificatory system to need refining in the light of unresolvable disagreements. This has the advantage of making any classification explicit rather than relying on 'a feeling'.

Obviously, there are measures that are designed to pick up changes and so you do not want a consistent score from occasion to occasion. For example, in the area of anxiety, it is recognised that there are two forms: state-specific anxiety and trait anxiety. The former should change depending on the state the person is in. Thus, the measure should produce a similar score when the person is in the same state but should be sensitive enough to identify changes in anxiety across states. On the other hand, trait anxiety should be relatively constant.

Validity

The validity of a test refers to the degree to which what is being measured is what the researchers intended. There are a number of aspects of the validity of a measure that should be checked.

Face validity

Face validity refers to the perception that the people being measured, or the people administering the measures, have of the measure. If participants in your research misperceive the nature of the measure then they may behave in such a way as to make the measure invalid. For example, if children are given a test of intelligence but perceive the occasion as one for having a chat with an adult then their performance may be poorer than if they had correctly perceived the nature of the test. Similarly, if the person administering the test does not understand what it is designed to test, or does not believe that it is an effective measure, then the way he or she administers it may affect the results.

The problem of face validity has to be weighed against the dangers of the participants being aware of the hypothesis being tested by the researchers. Participants may try to help you get the effect you are predicting. Alternatively, they may deliberately work against your hypothesis. However, it is naive to assume that because you have disguised the true purpose of a measure, participants will not arrive at their own conclusions and behave accordingly. Orne (1962) described the clues that participants pick up about a researcher's expectations as the *demand characteristics* of the research. He pointed out that these will help to determine participants' behaviour. He noted that in some situations it was enough to engineer different demand characteristics for participants for them to alter their behaviour even though there had been no other experimental manipulation. Therefore, if you do not want the people you are studying to know your real intentions you have to present them with a cover story that convinces them. Milgram (1974) would not have obtained the results he did in his studies of obedience if he had told participants that he was studying obedience. Before you do give participants a cover story you must weigh the costs of lying to your participants against the benefits of the knowledge to be gained.

Bear in mind the fact that you can give a vague explanation of what you are researching if this does not give the game away. For example, you can say that you are researching memory rather than the effect of delay on recall.

Construct validity

If a measure has high construct validity, then it is assessing some theoretical construct well. In fact, many measures that psychologists use are assessing theoretical entities, such as intelligence or extroversion. In order to check the construct validity of a measure it is necessary to make the construct explicit. This can often be the point at which a psychological definition starts to differ from a lay definition of the same term, because the usage made by non-psychologists is too imprecise. That is not to say that psychologists will agree about the definition. For example, some psychologists argue that IQ tests test intelligence while others have simply said that IQ tests test what IQ tests test.

Further evidence of construct validity can be provided if the measure shows links with tests of related constructs—it converges with them (convergent construct validity)—and shows a difference from measures of unrelated constructs—it diverges from them (divergent construct validity).

Convergence
For example, if we believe that intelligence is a general ability and if we have devised a measure of numerical intelligence then our measure should produce a similar pattern to that of tests of verbal intelligence.

Divergence

If we had devised a measure of reading ability we would not want it producing too similar a pattern to that produced by an intelligence test. For if the patterns were too similar it would suggest that our new test was merely one of intelligence.

Content validity

Content validity refers to the degree to which a measure covers the full range of behaviour of the ability being measured. For example, if I had devised a measure of mathematical ability, it would have low content validity if it only included measures of the ability to add numbers. One way of checking the content validity of a measure is to ask experts in the field whether it covers the range that they would expect. Nonetheless, it is worth checking whether certain aspects of a measure are redundant and can be omitted because they are measuring the same thing. Staying with the mathematical example, if it could be shown that the ability to perform addition went with the ability to perform higher forms of mathematics successfully then there is no need to include the full content of mathematics in a measure of mathematical ability. Thus, a shorter and quicker measure could be devised.

Criterion-related validity

Criterion-related validity addresses the question of whether a measure fulfils certain criteria. In general this means that it should produce a similar pattern to another existing measure. There are two forms of criteria that can be taken into account: concurrent and predictive.

Concurrent validity

A measure has concurrent validity if it produces a similar result to that of an existing measure that is taken around the same time. Thus, if I devise a test of intelligence I can check its concurrent validity by administering an established test of intelligence at the same time.

This procedure obviously depends on having a pre-existing and valid measure against which to check the validity of the new measure. This raises the question of why one would want another test of the same thing. There are a number of situations in which a different test might be required. A common reason is the desire to produce a measure that takes less time to administer and is less onerous for the participants: people are more likely to allow themselves to be measured if the task is quicker.

Another reason for devising a new measure when one already exists is that it is to be administered in a different way from the original. For example, suppose that the pre-existing measure was for use in a face-to-face interview, such as by a psychiatrist, and it was now meant to be used when the researcher was not present (such as a questionnaire). Alternatively, a common need is for a measure that can be administered to a group at the same time, rather than individually.

Predictive validity

A measure has predictive validity if it correctly predicts some future state of affairs. Thus, if a measure has been devised of academic aptitude it could be used to select students for entry to university. The measure would have good predictive validity if the scores it provided predicted the class of degree achieved by the students.

With both forms of criterion validity one needs to check that *criterion contamination* does not exist. This means that those providing the criteria should be unaware of the results of the measure. If a psychiatrist or a teacher knows the results of the measure it may affect the way they treat the person when they are taking their own measures. Such an effect would suggest that the measure has better criterion validity than it really has.

Floor and ceiling effects

There are two phenomena that you should avoid when choosing a measure, both of which entail restricting the range of possible scores that participants can achieve. A floor effect in a measure means that participants cannot achieve a score below a certain point. An example would be a measure of reading age that did not go below a reading age of 7 years. A ceiling effect in a measure occurs when people cannot score higher than a particular level. An example would be when an IQ test is given to high achievers. Floor and ceiling effects hide differences between individuals and can prevent changes from being detected. Thus a child's reading might have improved but if it is still below the level for a 7-year-old then the test will not detect the change.

Once the area of research, the method, the design, the hypotheses and the measures to be used in a study have been chosen, you need to decide the method of analysis you are going to employ.

Choice of analysis

Chapters 9 to 22 describe various forms of analysis. Particular forms will be appropriate for particular types of measure and for particular designs. It is good practice to decide what form of analysis you are going to employ prior to collecting the data. This may stop you collecting data that cannot be analysed in ways that would address your hypotheses and would stop you collecting data that you will not be analysing. There is a temptation, particularly among students, to take a range of measures, only to drop a number of them when arriving at the analysis stage. An additional advantage of planning the analysis will become clearer in Chapter 18, where it will be shown that your hypotheses can be given a fairer chance of being supported if the analysis is planned than when it is unplanned.

Chapter 13 shows that knowing the form of analysis you will employ can provide you with a means of choosing an appropriate sample size.

Choice of participants—the sample

Next you need to choose whom you are going to study. There are two aspects to the choice of participants: firstly, what characteristics they should have; secondly, the number of participants. The answer to the first question will depend on the aims of your research. If you are investigating a particular population because you want to relate the results of your study to the population from which your sample came then you will need to select a representative sample. For example, you might want to investigate the effect of different types of slot machine on the gambling behaviour of adolescents who are regular gamblers. In this case you would have to define what you meant by a regular gambler (devise an operational definition) and then sample a range of people who conformed to your definition, in such a way that you had a representative sample of the age range and levels of gambling behaviour and any other variables you considered to be relevant. See Chapter 11 for methods of sampling from a population.

Often researchers who are employing an experimental method are interested in the wider population of all people and wish to make generalisations that refer to people in general rather than some particular subpopulation. This can be a naive approach as it can lead to the sample merely comprising those who were most available to the researchers, which generally means undergraduate psychologists. This may in turn mean that the findings do not generalise beyond undergraduate psychologists. However, even within this restricted sample there is generally some attempt to make sure that males and females are equally represented.

The number of participants you use in a study depends on the design you are employing for at least three reasons. The first guide is likely to be the practical one of the nature of your participants. If you are studying a special population, such as people with a particular form of brain damage, then the size of your sample will be restricted by their availability. A second practical point is the willingness of participants to take part in your research—the more onerous the task the fewer participants you will get. A third guide should be the statistics you will be employing to analyse your research. As you will see in Chapter 13, it is possible to work out how many participants you need for a given design, in order to give the research the chance of supporting your hypothesis if it is correct. There is no point in reducing the likelihood of supporting a correct hypothesis by using too few participants. Similarly, it is possible to use an unnecessarily large sample if you do not calculate how many participants your design requires.

The procedure

The procedure is the way that the study is conducted: how the design decisions are carried out. This includes what the participants are told, what they do, in what order they do it and whether they are debriefed (see Chapter 1).

When there is more than one researcher or when the person carrying out the study is not the person who designed it, each person dealing with the participants needs to be clear about the design and needs to run it in the same way. This can be helped by having standardised instructions for the researchers and for the participants.

New researchers are often concerned that having a number of researchers on a project can invalidate the results: firstly, because there were different researchers, and secondly, because each researcher may have tested participants in a different place. As long as such variations do not vary systematically with aspects of the design this will not be a problem—if anything it can be a strength. Examples of systematic variation would be if one researcher only tested people in one condition of the study or only tested one type of person, such as only the males. Under these circumstances, any results could be a consequence of such limitations. However, if such potential problems have been eradicated then the results will be more generalisable to other situations than research conducted by one researcher in one place.

Finally, regardless of the method you are employing in your research, it is important that a pilot study be conducted.

Pilot studies

A pilot study is a trial run of the study which should be conducted on a smaller sample than that to be used in the final version of the study. Regardless of the method you adopt, it is essential that you carry out a pilot study first. The purpose of a pilot study is to check that the basic aspects of the design and procedure work. Accordingly, you want to know whether participants understand the instructions they are given and whether your measures have face validity or, if you are using a cover story, it is seen as plausible. In an experiment you will be checking that any apparatus works as intended and that participants are able to use the apparatus. Finally, you can get an idea of how long the procedure takes with each participant so that you can give people an indication of how long they will be required for, when you ask them to take part, and you can allow enough time between participants. It is particularly useful to debrief the people who take part in your pilot study as their thoughts on the study will help to reveal any flaws, including possible demand characteristics.

Without the information gained from a pilot study you may be presented with a dilemma if you discover flaws during the study: you can either alter the design midway through the study or you can plough on regardless with a poor design. Changing the design during the study obviously means that participants in the same condition are likely not to have been treated similarly. This will mean that you are adding an extra source of variation in the results, which can be a problem for their interpretation. On the other hand, to continue with a design that you know is flawed is simply a waste of both your time and that of your participants. Save yourself from confronting this dilemma by conducting a pilot study.

It is particularly important to conduct a pilot study when you are using measures that you have devised, such as in a questionnaire or in designs where training is needed in taking the measures. In the chapters devoted to asking questions and observations (Chapters 5 to 7) I will describe how to conduct the necessary pilot studies for those methods.

The pilot study should be conducted on a small number of people from your target population. There is not much point in checking whether the design works with people from a population other than the one from which you will be sampling. As, in most cases, you should not use these people again in your main study, the number you use can be dictated by the availability of participants from your population. Thus, if the population is small or you have limited access to members of the population, for example, people born totally blind, then you may choose only to use two or three in the pilot study. Nonetheless, it is preferable if you can try out every condition that is involved in the study.

Chapter 13 also describes a further advantage of using a pilot study, namely that it can help you decide on the appropriate sample size for your main study.

Once you have completed the pilot study you can make any alterations to the design that it reveals as being necessary and then conduct the final version of the study.

Summary

Prior to conducting a piece of research you have to narrow your focus to a specific aspect of your chosen area. This can be helped by reading previous research that has been conducted in the area and possibly through talking to experts in the field. You have to choose a method from those described in Chapter 1. You have to choose a design from those described in Chapter 4. You have to choose the measure(s) you are going to take during your research and you will need to check that they are both reliable and valid. You have to choose whom you are going to study and this will depend partly on the particular method you are employing. Finally, you must conduct a pilot study of your design. Once these decisions have been made and the pilot study has been completed, you are ready to conduct the final version of your research.

The next two chapters consider aspects of the variables that are involved in psychological research and the most common research designs that psychologists employ. In addition, they explain the importance of checking whether any findings from a piece of research that employs a given design can be generalised to people and settings other than those used in the research and whether given designs can be said to identify the cause and effect relationships within that research.

3
VARIABLES AND THE VALIDITY OF RESEARCH DESIGNS

Introduction

This chapter describes the different types of variables that are involved in research. It then explains why psychologists need to consider the factors in their research that determine whether their findings are generalisable to situations beyond the scope of their original research. It goes on to explore the aspects of research that have to be considered if researchers are investigating the causes of human behaviour. Finally, it discusses the ways in which hypotheses are formulated.

Variables

Variables are entities that can have more than one value. The values do not necessarily have to be numerical. For example, the variable gender can have the value *male* or the value *female*.

Independent variables

An independent variable is a variable that it is considered could affect another variable. For example, if I consider that income affects happiness, then I will treat *income* as an independent variable that is affecting the variable *happiness*.

In experiments an independent variable is a variable that the researchers have manipulated to see what effect it has on another variable. For example, in a study comparing three methods of teaching reading, children are taught to recognise words by sight—the whole-word method—or to learn to recognise the sound of parts of words that are common across words—the phonetic method—or by a combination of the whole-word and phonetic methods. In this case the researchers have manipulated the independent variable—*teaching method*—which has three possible values in this study: whole-word, phonetic or combined. The researchers are interested in whether teaching method has an effect on the variable *reading ability*. In other words, whether different teaching methods produce different performances on reading.

The term *level* is used to describe one of the values that an independent variable has in a given study. Thus, in the above study, the independent variable—teaching method—has three levels: whole-word, phonetic and combined.

The term *condition* is also used to describe a level of an independent variable. The above study of teaching methods has a whole-word condition, a phonetic condition and a combined condition.

Independent variables can be of two basic types—fixed and random—depending on how the levels of that variable were selected.

Fixed variables

A fixed variable is one where the researcher has chosen the specific levels to be used in the study. Thus, in the experiment on reading, the variable—*teaching method*—is a fixed variable.

Random variables

A random variable is one where the researcher has randomly selected the levels of that variable from a larger set of possible levels. Thus, if I had a complete list of all the possible methods for teaching reading and had picked three randomly from the list to include in my study, *teaching method* would now be a random variable.

It is unlikely that I would want to pick *teaching method* randomly; the following is a more realistic example. Assume that I am interested in seeing what effect listening to relaxation tapes of different lengths has on stress levels. In this study, *duration of tape* is the independent variable. I could choose the levels of the independent variable in two ways. Firstly, I could decide to have durations of 5, 10, 15 and 30 minutes. *Duration of tape* would then be a fixed independent variable. Alternatively, I could randomly choose four durations from the range 1 to 30 minutes. This would give a random independent variable. Participants are usually treated as a random variable in statistical analysis.

The decision as to whether to use fixed or random variables has two consequences. Firstly, the use of a fixed variable prevents researchers from trying to generalise to other possible levels of the independent variable, while the use of a random variable allows more generalisation. Secondly, the statistical analysis can be affected by whether a fixed or a random variable was used.

Dependent variables

A dependent variable is a variable on which an independent variable could have an effect. In other words, the value the dependent variable has is dependent on the level of the independent variable. Thus, in the study of reading, a measure of reading ability would be the dependent variable, while in the study of relaxation tapes, a measure of stress would be the dependent variable. Notice that in each of these examples of an experiment the dependent variable is the measure provided by the participants in the study: a reading score or a stress score.

Variables in non-experimental research

The description of variables given above is appropriate when the design is experimental and the researcher has manipulated a variable (the independent variable, IV) to find out what effect the manipulation could have on another variable (the dependent variable, DV). However, there are situations when no manipulation has occurred but such terminology is being used as shorthand. In quasi-experimental research the equivalent of the IV could be gender or smoking status or some other pre-existing grouping. In research where relationships between variables are being investigated, for example, age and IQ, using the techniques described in Chapter 19, neither term is necessary. However, when the values of one variable are being used to predict the values of another, using the techniques described in Chapter 20, then the often preferred terms are *predictor variable* and *criterion variable*. This usage emphasises the point that no manipulation has occurred.

Other forms of variable

In any study there are numerous possible variables. Some of these will be part of the study as independent or dependent variables. However, others will exist that the researchers need to consider.

Confounding variables

Some variables could potentially affect the relationship between the independent and dependent variables that are being sought. Such variables are termed *confounding variables*. For example, in the teaching methods study, different teachers may have taken the different groups. If the teachers have different levels of skill in teaching reading, then any differences in reading ability between the children in the three teaching methods may be due to the teachers' abilities and not the teaching methods. Thus, teachers' skill is a confounding variable. Alternatively, in the relaxation study it could be that the people who receive the longest-duration tape are inherently less relaxed than those who receive the shortest tape and this may mask any improvements which might be a consequence of listening to a longer tape. In this case, the participant's initial stress level is a confounding variable.

There are ways of trying to minimise the effects of confounding variables and many of the designs described in the next chapter have been developed for this purpose.

Irrelevant variables

Fortunately, many of the variables that are present in a study are not going to affect the dependent variable and are thus not relevant to the study and do not have to be controlled for. For example, it is unlikely that what the teacher was wearing had an effect on the children's reading ability. However, researchers must consider which variables are and which are not relevant. In another study, say on obedience, what the experimenter wore might well affect obedience.

Researchers have been criticised for assuming that certain variables are irrelevant. As Sears (1986) noted, frequently psychology undergraduates are used as participants in research. There are dangers in generalising findings of such research to people in general, to non-students of the same age or even to students who are not studying psychology.

In addition, it has been suggested that the experimenter should not be treated as an irrelevant variable (Bonge, Schuldt & Harper, 1992). It is highly likely, particularly in social psychology experiments, that aspects of the experimenter are going to affect the results of the study.

The validity of research designs

The ultimate aim of a piece of research may be to establish a connection between one or more independent variables and a dependent variable. In addition, it may be to generalise the results found with the particular participants used in the study to other groups of people. No design will achieve these goals perfectly. Researchers have to be aware of how valid their design is for the particular goals of the research. The threats to validity of designs are of two main types: threats to what are called external validity and internal validity.

External validity

External validity refers to the generalisability of the findings of a piece of research. Similarities can be seen between this form of validity and ecological validity. There are two main areas where the generalisability of the research could be in question. Firstly, there may be a question over the degree to which the particular conditions pertaining in the study can allow the results of the study to be generalised to other conditions—the tasks required of the participants, the setting in which the study took place or the time when the study was conducted. Secondly, we can question whether aspects of the participants can allow the results of a study to be generalised to other people—whether they are representative of the group from which they come, and whether they are representative of a wider range of people.

Threats to external validity

Particular conditions of the study

Task
Researchers will have made choices about aspects of their research and these may limit the generalisability of the findings. For example, in an experiment

on face recognition, the researchers will have presented the pictures for a particular length of time. The findings of their research may only be valid for that particular duration of exposure to the pictures. A further criticism could be that presenting people with two-dimensional pictures, which are static, does not mimic what is involved in recognising a person in the street: is the task ecologically valid?

Setting

Many experiments are conducted in a laboratory and so generalisability to other settings may be in question. However, it is not only laboratory research that may have limited generalisability with respect to the setting in which it is conducted. For example, a clinical psychologist may have devised a way to lessen people's fear of spiders through listening to audio tapes of a soothing voice talking about spiders. The fact that it has been found to be effective in the psychologist's consulting room does not necessarily mean that it will be so elsewhere.

Time

Some phenomena may be affected by the time of day, for example, just after lunch, in which case, if a study were conducted at that time only, the results might not generalise to other times. Alternatively, a study carried out at one historical time might produce results that were valid then but subsequently cease to be generalisable due to subsequent events. For example, early research in which people were subjected to sensory deprivation found that they were extremely distressed. However, with the advent of people exploring mystical experiences, participants started to enjoy the experience and it has even been used for therapeutic purposes (see Suedfeld, 1980).

Aspects of the participants

Researchers may wish to generalise from the particular participants they have used in their study—their sample—to the group from which those participants come—the population. For example, a study of student life may have been conducted with a sample selected from people studying a particular subject, at a particular university. Unless the sample is a fair representation of the group from which they were selected, there are limitations on generalising any findings to the wider group.

Generalising to other groups

As mentioned earlier, even if the research can legitimately be generalised to other students studying that subject at that university, this does not mean that they can be generalised to other students studying the same subject at another institution, never mind to those studying other subjects or even to non-students.

Many aspects of the participants may be relevant to the findings of a particular piece of research: for example, their age, gender, educational level and occupation.

Laboratory experiments are particularly open to criticism about their external validity because they often treat their participants as though they were representative of people in general. However, the aim of the researchers may not be to generalise but simply to establish that a particular phenomenon exists. For example, they may investigate whether people take longer to recognise faces when they are presented upside down than when presented the right way up. Nonetheless, they should be aware of the possible limitations of generalising from the people they have studied to other people.

Improving external validity

The two main ways to improve external validity are replication and the careful selection of participants.

Replication

Replication is the term used to describe repeating a piece of research. Replications can be conducted under as many of the original conditions as possible. While such studies will help to see whether the original findings were unique and merely a result of chance happenings, they do little to improve external validity. This can be helped by replications that vary an aspect of the original study, for example, by including participants of a different age or using a new setting. If similar results are obtained then this can increase their generalisability.

Selection of participants

There are a number of ways of selecting participants and these are dealt with in greater detail in Chapter 11. For the moment, I simply want to note that randomly selecting participants from the wider group that they represent gives researchers the best case for generalising from their participants to that wider group. In this way researchers are less likely to have a biased sample of people because each person from the wider group has an equal likelihood of being chosen. I will define 'random' more thoroughly in Chapter 11 but it is worth saying here what is not random. If I select the first 20 people that I meet in the university refectory, I have not achieved a random sample but an opportunity sample—my sample is only representative of people who go to the refectory, at that particular time and on that particular day.

Internal validity

Internal validity is the degree to which a design successfully demonstrates that changes in a dependent variable are caused by changes in an independent variable. For example, you may find a relationship between television viewing and violent behaviour, such that those who watch more television are more violent, and you may wish to find out whether watching violent

TV programmes causes people to be violent. Internal validity tends to be more of a problem in quasi-experimental research where researchers do not have control over the allocation of participants to different conditions and so cannot assign them on a random basis or in research where the researchers have simply observed how two variables—such as TV watching and violent behaviour—are related.

Threats to internal validity

Selection

The presence of participants in different levels of an independent variable may be confounded with other variables that affect performance on the dependent variable. A study of television and violence may investigate a naturally occurring relationship between television watching and violent behaviour. In other words, people are in the different levels of the independent variable, *television watching*, on the basis of their existing watching habits, rather than because a researcher has randomly assigned them to different levels. There is a danger that additional variables may influence violent behaviour: for example, if those with poorer social skills watched more television. Thus, poor social skills may lead to both increased television watching and more violent behaviour but the researchers may only note the television and violence connection.

Maturation

In studies that look for a change in a dependent variable, over time, in the same participants, there is a danger that some other change has occurred for those participants which also influences the dependent variable. Imagine that researchers have established that there is a link between television watching and violence. They devise a training programme to reduce the violence, implement the training and then assess levels of violence among their participants. They find that violence has reduced over time. However, they have failed to note that other changes have also occurred which have possibly caused the reduction. For example, a number of the participants have found partners and, although they now watch as much television as before, they do not put themselves into as many situations where they might be violent. Thus, the possible continued effects of television have been masked and the training programme is falsely held to have been successful.

History

An event that is out of the researchers' control may have produced a change in the dependent variable. Television executives may have decided, as a consequence of public concern over the link between television and violence, to alter the schedules and censor violent programmes. Once again, any changes in violent behaviour may be a consequence of these alterations rather than any manipulations by researchers. Duncan (2001) found an example of the effects of history when he was called in by an organisation to reduce the number of staff who were leaving. He devised a programme that he then implemented and he found that staff turn-over was reduced. However, during the same time the unemployment rate had increased and this is likely also to have affected people's willingness to leave a job, or their ability to find alternative employment.

Instrumentation

If researchers measure variables on more than one occasion, changes in results between the occasions could be a consequence of changes in the measures rather than in the phenomenon that is being measured. This is a particular danger if a different measure is used, for example, a different measure of violence might be employed because it is considered to be an improvement over an older one.

Testing

Participants' responses to the same measure may change with time. For example, with practice participants may become more expert at performing a task. Alternatively, they may change their attitude to the measure. For example, they may become more honest about the levels of violence in which they participate. Thus, changes that are noted between two occasions when a measure is taken may not be due to any manipulations of researchers but due to the way the participants have reacted to the measure used.

Mortality

This is a rather unfortunate term referring to loss of participants from the study; an alternative that is sometimes used is *attrition*. In a study some of the original participants might not take part in later stages of the research. There may be a characteristic that those who dropped out of the research share and that is relevant to the study. In this case, an impression of the relationship between independent and dependent variables may be falsely created or a real one masked. For example, if the more violent members of a sample dropped out of the research then a false impression would be created of a reduction in violence among the sample. Accordingly, we should always examine aspects of those who drop out of a study to see whether they share any characteristics that are relevant to the study.

Selection by maturation

Two of the above threats to internal validity may work together and affect the results of research. Imagine that you have two groups—high television watchers and low television watchers. You have tried to control for selection by matching participants on the basis of the amount of violence they indulge in. It is possible that changes that affect levels of violence occur to one of the groups and not the other and that this is confounded with the amount of television watched; for example, if those who watch more television also have more siblings and learn violent behaviour from them. Thus, your basis of selection may introduce a confounding variable, whereby the members of one group will change in some relevant way relative to the members of the other group, regardless of the way they are treated in the research.

The next four threats to internal validity refer to designs in which there is more than one condition and where those in one group are affected by the existence of another group—there is contamination across the groups.

Imitation (diffusion of treatments)

Participants who are in one group may learn from those in another group aspects of the study that affect their responses. For example, in a study of the relative effects of different training films to improve awareness of AIDS, those watching one film may tell those in other groups about its content.

Compensation

Research can be undermined by those who are dealing with the participants, particularly if they are not the researchers, in the ways they treat particip- ants in different groups. For example, researchers may be trying to compare a group that is receiving some training with a group that is not. Teachers who are working with the group not receiving the training programme may treat that group, because it is not being given the programme, in a way that improves that group's performance, anyway. This would have the tendency of reducing any differences between the groups that were a consequence of the training.

Compensatory rivalry

This can occur if people in one group make an extra effort in order to be better than those in another group, for example, in a study comparing the effects of different working conditions on productivity.

Demoralisation

The reverse to compensatory rivalry would be if those in one group felt that they were missing out and decided to make less effort than they would normally. This would have the effect of artificially lowering the results for that group.

Regression to the mean

As I explained in Chapter 2, most measures are imperfect in some way and will be subject to a certain amount of error and are thus not 100% reliable. In other words, they are unlikely to produce exactly the same result from one occasion to the next; for example, if a person's IQ is measured on two occasions and the IQ test is not perfectly reliable then the person is likely to produce a slightly different score on the two occasions. There is a statistical phenomenon called 'the regression to the mean'. This refers to the fact that, if people score above the average, for their population, on one occasion, when they are measured the next time their scores are likely to be nearer the average, while those who scored below average on the first occasion will also tend to score nearer the average on a second occasion. Thus, those scoring above the average will tend to show a drop in score between the two occasions, while those scoring below the average will tend to show a rise in score.

If participants are selected to go into different levels of an independent variable on the basis of their score on some measure, then the results of the study may be affected by regression to the mean. For example, imagine a study into the effects of giving extra tuition to people who have a low IQ. In this study participants are selected from a population with a normal range of IQ scores and from a population with a low range of IQ scores. A sample from each population is given an IQ test and, on the basis of the results, two groups are formed with similar IQs, one comprising people with low IQs from the normal-IQ population and one of people with the higher IQs in the low-IQ population. The samples have been matched for IQ so that those in the normal IQ group can act as a control group which receives no treatment, while those from the low IQ population are given extra tuition. The participants in the two groups then have their IQs measured again. Regression to the mean will have the consequence that the average IQ for the sample from the normal-IQ population will appear to have risen towards the mean for that population, while the average IQ for the sample from the low-IQ population will appear to have lowered towards its population mean. Thus, even if the extra tuition had a beneficial effect, the average scores of the two groups may have become closer and may suggest to the unwary researcher that the tuition was not beneficial.

Improving internal validity

Many of the threats to internal validity can be lessened by the use of a control group which does not receive any treatment. In this way, any changes in a dependent variable over time will only occur in a treatment group if the independent variable is affecting the dependent variable. The threats that involve some form of contamination between groups need more careful briefing of participants and those conducting the study such as teachers implementing a training package. Whenever possible, participants should be allocated to different conditions on a random basis. This will lessen the dangers of selection and selection by maturation being a threat to internal validity. In addition, it conforms to one of the underlying assumptions of most statistical techniques.

Efficacy and effectiveness

When looking at therapeutic interventions, for example to reduce anxiety, a distinction is sometimes made between the *efficacy* and the *effectiveness* of the intervention. Efficacy refers to whether the therapy works. Effectiveness, on the other hand, refers to whether the therapy works in the usual therapeutic conditions rather than only as part of a highly controlled experiment. As Chambless and Ollendick (2001) point out, this distinction is similar to the one made between internal and external validity: an efficacious treatment may be shown to work in controlled conditions but may not generalise to a clinical setting.

The choice of hypotheses

An explicit hypothesis or set of hypotheses is usually tested in experiments and often in studies that employ other research methods. When hypotheses are to be evaluated statistically, there is a formal way in which they are expressed and in the way they are tested. The procedure is to form what are termed a *Null Hypothesis* and an *Alternative Hypothesis*. In experiments the Null Hypothesis is generally stated in the form that the manipulation of the independent variable will not have an effect upon the dependent variable. For example, imagine that researchers are comparing the effects of two therapeutic techniques on participants' level of stress—listening to a relaxation tape and doing exercise. The Null Hypothesis, often symbolised as H_0, is likely to be of the form: *There is no difference, after therapy, in the stress levels of participants who listened to a relaxation tape and those who took exercise.* The Alternative Hypothesis (H_A), which is the outcome predicted by the researchers, is also known as the Research Hypothesis or the Experimental Hypothesis (in an experiment) or even H_1, if there is more than one prediction.

Researchers will only propose one Alternative Hypothesis for each Null Hypothesis but that Alternative Hypothesis can be chosen from three possible versions. The basic distinction between Alternative Hypotheses is whether they are non-directional or directional. A non-directional (or bi-directional) hypothesis is one that does not predict the direction of the outcome. In the above example the non-directional Alternative Hypothesis would take the form: *There will be a difference between the stress levels of the participants who experienced the two different therapeutic regimes.* Thus, this hypothesis predicts a difference between the two therapies but it does not predict which will be more beneficial.

A directional (or uni-directional) hypothesis, in this example, can be of two types. On the one hand, it could state that *the participants who received the relaxation therapy will be less stressed than those who took the exercise*. On the other hand, it could state that *participants who took the exercise will be less stressed than those who received the relaxation therapy*. In other words, a directional hypothesis not only states that there will be a difference between the levels of the independent variable but it predicts which direction the difference will take.

It may seem odd that in order to test a prediction researchers have not only to state that prediction but also to state a Null Hypothesis that goes against their prediction. The reason follows from the point that it is logically impossible to *prove* that something is true while it *is* possible to prove that something is false. For example, if my hypothesis is that I like all flavours of whisky then, however many whiskies I might have tried, even if I have liked them all to date, there is always the possibility that the next whisky I try I will dislike; and that one example will be enough to disprove my hypothesis. Accordingly, if the evidence does not support the Null Hypothesis it is taken as support for our Alternative Hypothesis; not as proof of the Alternative Hypothesis, because that can never be obtained, but support for it.

Chapter 10 will show how we use statistics to decide whether the Null Hypothesis or its Alternative Hypothesis is the more likely to be true.

Summary

Researchers often manipulate *independent variables* in their research and observe the consequences of such manipulations on *dependent variables*. In so doing, they have to take account of other aspects of the research which could interfere with the results that they have obtained. In addition, if they wish their findings to be generalisable, they have to consider the *external validity* of their research designs. If researchers want to investigate the causal relationship between the independent and dependent variables in their research they have to consider the *internal validity* of their research designs. Researchers who are testing an explicit hypothesis, statistically, have to formulate it as an *Alternative Hypothesis* and propose a *Null Hypothesis* to match it. The research will then provide evidence that will allow the researchers to choose between the hypotheses.

The next chapter introduces a number of research designs that can be employed and points out the ways in which each design might fail to fulfil the requirements of internal validity. Remember, however, that internal validity is only a problem if you are trying to establish a causal link between independent and dependent variables.

4

RESEARCH DESIGNS AND THEIR INTERNAL VALIDITY

Introduction

This chapter describes a range of designs that are employed in psychological research. It introduces and defines a number of terms that are used to distinguish designs. In addition, it describes particular versions of designs and evaluates the problems that can prevent each design from being used to answer the question of whether a dependent variable can be shown to be affected by independent variables.

The three sections of this chapter need to be treated differently. The initial overview of the types of designs and the terminology that is used to distinguish designs should be read before moving on to other chapters. However, the remainder of the chapter, which gives specific examples of the designs, should be treated more for reference or when you have more experience in research.

Types of designs

Designs can be classified in a number of ways. One consideration that should guide your choice of design and measures should be the statistical analysis you are going to employ on your data. It is better to be clear about this before you conduct your study rather than find afterwards that you are having to do the best you can with a poor design and measures that do not allow you to test your hypotheses.

Accordingly, I am choosing to classify the designs according to the possible aims of the research and the type of analysis that could be conducted on the data derived from them. In this way, there will be a link between the types of designs and the chapters devoted to their analysis. The designs are of seven basic types:

1. Measures of a single variable are taken from an individual or a group. For example, the IQ of an individual or those of members of a group are measured. Such designs could be used for descriptive purposes; descriptive statistics are dealt with in Chapter 9. Alternatively, these designs could be used to compare an individual or a group with

others, such as a population, to see whether the individual or group is unusual. This form of analysis is dealt with in Chapter 12.

2. A single independent variable (IV) is employed with two levels and a single dependent variable (DV). Such designs are used to look for differences in the DV between the levels of the IV. An example would be if researchers compared the reading abilities of children taught using two techniques. The analysis of such designs is dealt with in Chapter 15.

3. A single independent variable is employed with more than two levels and a single dependent variable. This is an extension of the previous type of design, which could include the comparison of the reading abilities of children taught under three different techniques. The analysis of such designs is dealt with in Chapter 16.

4. More than one independent variable is involved but there is a single dependent variable. An example of such a design would be where one IV is type of reasoning problem with three levels—verbal, numerical and spatial—and a second IV is gender, with number of problems solved as the DV. As with Designs 2 and 3, researchers would be looking for differences in the dependent variable between the levels of the independent variables. In addition, they can explore any ways in which the two IVs interact—an example of an interaction in this case would be if females were better than males at verbal tasks but there was no difference between the genders on the other tasks. The analysis of such designs is covered in Chapter 17.

5. An alternative version of the previous design would be where researchers were interested in how well they could use measures (treated as IVs or predictor variables), such as students' school performance and motivation, to predict what level of university degree (treated as a DV or criterion variable) students would achieve. The analysis of this version of such designs is dealt with in the later half of Chapter 20.

The first five types of design are usually described as *univariate* because they contain a single DV.

6.   Designs used to assess a relationship between two variables.

6a. This design is described as *bivariate* because it involves two variables but neither can necessarily be classified as an independent or a dependent variable: for example, where researchers are looking at the relationship between performance at school and performance at university. The analysis of such designs is dealt with in Chapter 19.

6b. This is fundamentally the same design (and a simpler version of Design 5), but one of the variables is treated as an IV (or predictor variable) and is used to predict the other, treated as a DV (or criterion variable): for example, if admissions tutors to a university wanted to be able to predict from school performance what performance at university would be. The analysis is dealt with in the first part of Chapter 20.

7. Finally, there are designs with more than one dependent variable. For example, where children have been trained according to more than one reading method and researchers have measured a range of abilities, such as fluency in reading, spelling ability and ability to complete sentences. Such designs are described as *multivariate* because there is more than one DV. Brief descriptions of such designs and the techniques used to analyse them are contained in Chapter 21.

Further description of designs of types 5, 6 and 7 will be left until the chapters which deal with their analysis.

All the designs that are described in the rest of this chapter are used to see whether an individual differs from a group or whether groups differ. Typically the designs look to see whether a group that is treated in one way differs from a group that is treated in another way. Usually, the members of a group are providing a single summary statistic—often an average for the group—which is used for comparison with other groups. This approach treats variation by individuals within the same group as a form of error.[1] There are a number of factors that contribute to individuals *in the same group* giving different scores:

1. Individual differences, such as differences in ability or motivation.
2. The reliability of the measure being used.
3. Differences in the way individuals have been treated in the research.

The more variation in scores that is present within groups, the less likely it is that any differences between groups will be detected. Therefore, where possible, such sources of variation are minimised in designs. An *efficient* design is one that can detect genuine differences between groups. However, researchers wish to avoid introducing any confounding variables which could produce spurious differences between different treatments or mask genuine difference between treatments. Some attempts to counter confounding variables in designs can increase individual differences within groups and thus can produce less efficient designs.

[1] See Danziger (1990) for an account of how psychologists came to adopt this approach. Designs 5 and 6b take a different approach and are interested in individual differences.

Terminology

As with many areas of research methods, there is a proliferation of terms that are used to describe designs. What makes it more complex for the newcomer is that similar designs are described in different ways in some instances, and the same designs are referred to in different ways by different writers. I will describe the most common terms and then try to stick to one consistent set.

Replication

'Replication' is used in at least two senses in research. In Chapter 3 I mentioned that replication can mean re-running a piece of research. However, the term is also used to describe designs in which more than one participant is treated in the same way. Thus, a study of different approaches to teaching is likely to have more than one child in each teaching group. Otherwise, the results of the research would be overly dependent on the particular characteristics of the very limited sample used.

Most studies involve some form of replication, for this has the advantage that the average score across participants for that condition can be used in an analysis. This will tend to lessen the effect of the variation in scores that is due to differences between people in the same condition. Nonetheless, there may be situations where replication is kept to a minimum because the task for participants is onerous or time-consuming or because there are too few participants available, for example, in a study of patients with a rare form of brain damage.

The allocation of participants

The biggest variation in terminology is over descriptions of the way in which participants have been employed in a piece of research. As a starting point I will use as an example a design that has one IV with two levels.

Between-subjects designs

One of the simplest designs would involve selecting a sample of people and assigning each person to one of the two levels of the IV: for example, when two ways of teaching children to read are being compared.

Such designs have a large number of names: *unrelated, between-subjects, between-groups, unpaired* (in the case of an IV with two levels), *factorial* or even *independent groups*. I will use the term *between-subjects*. These designs are relatively inefficient because the overall variation in scores (both within and between groups) is likely to be relatively large as the people in each group differ and there is more scope for individual differences.

Such designs have the additional disadvantage that the participants in the different levels of the independent variable may differ in some relevant way such that those in one group have an advantage that will enhance their performance on the dependent variable. For example, if the children in one group were predominantly from middle-class families that encourage reading; this could mean that that group will perform better on a reading test regardless of the teaching method employed.

There are a number of ways around the danger of confounding some aspect of the participants with the condition to which they are allocated. One is to use a random basis to allocate them to the conditions. Many statistical techniques are based on the assumption that participants have been randomly assigned to the different conditions. This approach would be preferable if researchers were not aware of the existing abilities of the participants, as it would save testing them before allocating them to groups. An alternative that is frequently used, when more obvious characteristics of the participants are known, is to control for the factor in some way.

A method of control that is not recommended is to select only people with one background—for example, only middle-class children—to take part in the research. Such a study would clearly have limited generalisability to other groups; it would lack external validity.

A more useful approach comes under the heading of 'blocking'.

Blocks

Blocking involves identifying participants who are similar in some relevant way and forming them into a subgroup or block. You then ensure that the members of a block are randomly assigned to each of the levels of the IV being studied. In this way, researchers could guarantee that the same number of children from each socio-economic group experienced each of the reading methods.

One example of blocking is where specific individuals are *matched* within a block for a characteristic. For example, if existing reading age score were being used to form blocks of children. Matching can be of at least two forms. *Precision matching* would involve having blocks of children with the same reading ages, within a block, while *range matching* would entail the children in each block having similar reading ages. Block designs are more efficient than simple between-subjects designs because they attempt to remove the variability that is due to the blocking factor. However, they involve a slightly more complex analysis as they have introduced a second IV: the block.

One problem with matching is that many factors may be relevant to the study so that perfect matching becomes difficult. In addition, matching can introduce an extra stage in the research: we have to assess the participants on the relevant variables, if the information is not already available. A way around these problems is to have the ultimate match, where the same person acts as his or her own match. It is then a *within-subjects* design.

Within-subjects designs

If every participant takes part in both levels of the IV then the design can be described as *related, paired, repeated measures, within-subjects* or even *dependent*. If an IV with more than two levels is used then *within-subjects* or *repeated measures* tend to be the preferred terms. I am going to use *within-subjects* to describe such designs.

This type of design can introduce its own problems. Two such problems are order effects and carry-over effects.

Order effects

If the order in which participants complete the levels of the IV is constant, then it is possible that they may become more practised and so they will perform better with later tasks—a practice effect—or they may suffer from fatigue or boredom as the study progresses and so perform less well with the later tasks—a fatigue effect. In this way, any differences between levels of an IV could be due to an order effect or alternatively a genuine difference between treatments could be masked by an order effect.

One way to counter possible order effects would be to randomise the order for each participant. A second way would be to alternate the order in which the tasks are performed by each participant; to *counterbalance* the order. Some of the participants would do the levels in one order while others would complete them in another order. A negative effect of random orders and counterbalancing is that they are likely to introduce more variation in the scores, because people in the same condition have been treated differently; the design is less efficient. However, this can be dealt with by one of two systematic methods which can be seen as forms of blocking: complete counterbalancing or Latin squares.

Complete counterbalancing

An example would be where researchers wished to compare the number of words recalled from a list after two different durations of delay: 5 seconds and 30 seconds. They could form the participants into two equally sized groups (blocks) and give those in one block a list of words to recall after a 5-second delay followed by another list to recall after a 30-second delay. The second group would receive the delay conditions in the order: 30 seconds then 5 seconds. This design has introduced a second IV—order. Thus we have a within-subjects IV—delay before recall—and a between-subjects IV—order. Designs that contain both within- and between-subjects IVs are called *mixed* or *split-plot*. However, some writers and some computer programs refer to them as *repeated measures* because they have at least one IV that entails repeated measures.

Latin squares

I will deal here, briefly, with Latin squares. Without replication of an order, they require as many participants as there are levels of the independent variable for each Latin square. Thus, for three levels of an independent variable there will need to be three participants: for example, if the effects of three different delay conditions (5, 10 and 20 seconds) on recall are being compared. Notice that each participant has been in each treatment and that each treatment has been in each order once.

There are twelve different possible Latin squares for such a 3 by 3 table; I will let sceptics work them out for themselves. If further replication is required, extra participants can be allocated an order for completing the levels

Table 4.1 A Latin square for a design with three treatments

	Order of treatment		
	first	second	third
Participant 1	Treatment 1	Treatment 2	Treatment 3
Participant 2	Treatment 2	Treatment 3	Treatment 1
Participant 3	Treatment 3	Treatment 1	Treatment 2

of the independent variable by drawing up a fresh Latin square for every three participants. In this way, when there are three treatments, more than 36 participants would be involved before any Latin square need be re-used. Those wishing to read more on Latin squares can refer to Myers and Well (1991), which has an entire chapter devoted to the subject.

Carry-over effects

If taking part in one level of an independent variable leaves a residue of that participation, this is called a *carry-over effect*. One example would be if participants were to be tested on two occasions, using the same version of a test. They are likely to remember, for a while after taking the test for the first time, some of the items in the test and some of the answers. A second example would be where a drug such as alcohol has been taken and its effects will be present for a while after any measurement has been taken.

One way around carry-over effects is to use a longer delay between the different levels of the IV. However, this may not always be possible as the residue may be permanent: for example, once a child has learned to read by one method the ability cannot be erased so that the child can be trained by another method.

Another way around carry-over effects (and another solution for order effects) is to use different participants for the different levels of the independent variable. This brings us full circle, back either to a between-subjects design or some form of blocking (matching) with more than one participant in each block.

In quasi-experiments, researchers may have limited control over the allocation of participants to treatments, in which case there are potential threats to the internal validity of the design.

A further aspect of designs is whether every level of one independent variable is combined with every level of all other IVs. If they are then the design is described as *crossed*, if they are not the design is called *nested*.

Crossed designs

Crossed designs are those in which every level of one independent variable is combined with every level of another independent variable. For example, in an experiment on speed of face recognition the design would be crossed if it included all possible combinations of the levels of the independent variables, orientation and familiarity: upside-down familiar faces, upside-down unfamiliar faces, correctly oriented familiar faces and correctly oriented unfamiliar faces.[2] Such designs allow researchers to investigate *interactions* between the independent variables: that is, how the two variables combine to affect the dependent variable. (Interactions are discussed in Chapter 17.)

One example of a crossed design is the standard within-subjects design—participants are crossed with the IV(s), every participant takes part in every condition.

[2] By 'unfamiliar' I mean faces that were not familiar to the participants before the study but have been shown during the study prior to the testing phase.

Nested designs

A disadvantage of crossed designs can be that they necessitate exhaustively testing each possible combination of the levels of the independent variables, which means that the task will take longer for participants in a within-subjects design or the study will require more participants in a between-subjects design. An alternative approach is to nest one variable within another: in other words, to refrain from crossing every level of one independent variable with every level of another. In fact, between-subjects designs have participants nested within the levels of the independent variable(s).

Some quasi-experiments may force the use of nested designs. For example, if researchers wished to compare two approaches to teaching mathematics—formal and 'new' mathematics—they might have to test children in schools that have already adopted one of these approaches. Thus, the schools would be nested in the approaches. Designs that involve the nesting of one variable within another in this way are termed *hierarchical* designs. A disadvantage of this design is that it is not possible to assess the interaction between IVs: in this case, school and teaching approach. Hence, hierarchical nesting should only be adopted when the researcher is forced to or where no interaction is suspected.

Balanced designs

Whenever using between-subjects or mixed designs it is advisable to have equal numbers of participants in each level of each IV. This produces what is termed a 'well-balanced design' and is much more easily analysed and interpreted than a poorly balanced design.

The remainder of the chapter describes specific versions of the first four designs that were identified at the beginning of the chapter. As mentioned in the Introduction, I recommend treating this part of the chapter more for reference purposes than for reading at one sitting.

Specific examples of research designs

Designs that have one variable with one level

Design 1: The one-shot case study
This type of design can take a number of forms; each involves deriving one measure on one occasion either from an individual or from a group. It allows researchers to compare the measure taken from the individual or group with that of a wider group. In this way, I could compare the performance of an individual who has brain damage with the performance of people who do not have brain damage to see whether he or she has impaired abilities on specific tasks.

Design 1.1: A single score from an individual
An example of this design would be measuring the IQ (intelligence quotient) of a stroke patient.

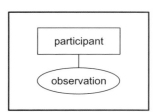

FIGURE 4.1 A one-shot case study involving a single measure from one person

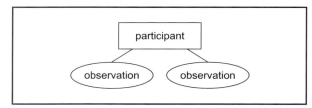

FIGURE 4.2 A one-shot case study with a summary statistic from one person

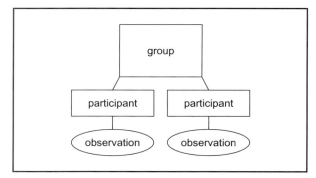

FIGURE 4.3 A one-shot case study with a summary statistic from a group

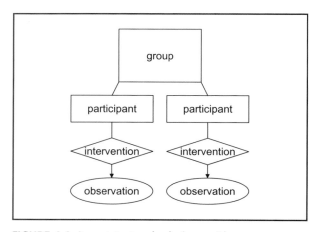

FIGURE 4.4 A post-test-only design, with one group

Design 1.2a: An average score from an individual

An example would be setting an individual a number of similar logic puzzles, timing how long he or she took to solve them, then noting the average time taken.

Design 1.2b: A one-shot case study with a summary statistic from a group

This can be a replicated version either of design 1.1, where the average IQ of a group is noted, or of design 1.2a where the average time taken to solve the logic puzzles is noted for a group.

Such designs are mainly useful for describing an individual or a group. For example, in a survey of students, participants are asked whether they smoke and the percentages who do and do not smoke are noted. Alternatively, such designs can be used to see whether an individual or a particular group differs from the general population. For example, researchers could compare the IQs of a group of mature students with the scores that other researchers have found for the general population to see whether the mature students have unusually high or low IQs.

Design 1.2c: Post-test only, with one group

This type of design could involve an intervention or manipulation by researchers: for example, if a group of criminals were given a programme that is designed to prevent them from re-offending.

There are no problems of internal validity with this type of design because it is pointless to use it to try to establish causal relationships. For, even in the example of the programme for criminals, as a study on its own, there is no basis for assessing the efficacy of the programme. Even if we find that the group offends less than criminals in general, we do not know whether the group would have re-offended less without the intervention. To answer such questions, researchers would have to compare the results of the programme with other programmes and with a control group. In so doing they would be employing another type of design.

Designs that have one independent variable with two levels

Between-subjects designs

Design 2.1a: Cross-sectional design, two groups

Two groups are treated as levels of an IV and the members of each are measured on a single vari-. able. It is likely that the two groups will differ in some inherent way—such as gender—in which case the design can be described as a *static* group or *non-equivalent* group comparison. Examples of such a design would be if researchers asked a sample of males and a sample of females whether they smoked or tested their mathematical abilities.

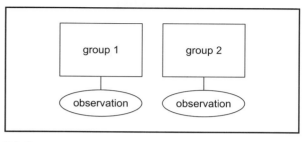

FIGURE 4.5 A cross-sectional design with two groups

This design may include time as an assumed variable by taking different participants at different stages in a process, but measured at the same time. For example, if researchers wanted to study differences in IQ with age, they might test the IQs of two different age groups—at 20 years and at 50 years. This design suffers from the problems of history: if educational standards had changed with time, differences in IQ between the age groups could be a consequence of this rather than a change for the individuals. A way around this problem is to use a longitudinal design in which the same people are measured at the different ages, which would be an example of the panel design given later in the chapter.

Design 2.1b: Two-group, post-test only

Two groups are formed, each is treated in a different way and then a measure is taken. An example of a study that utilised this design would be one in which two training methods for radiographers to recognise tumours on X-rays were being compared. However, preferably, one of the groups would be a control group. The advantage of a control group is that it helps to set a base-line against which to compare the training method(s). For, if we found no difference between groups who had been trained, without a control group we could not say whether either training was beneficial; it may be that both are equally benefi-cial or that neither is. However, if those in training groups were no better than the controls we have failed to show any benefit of training. Thus, if we wish to compare two interventions we are better using a different design.

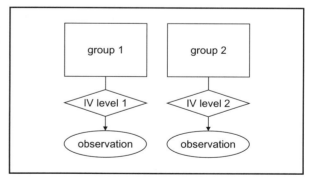

FIGURE 4.6 A two-group, post-test-only design

When naturally occurring groups are used, rather than randomly assigned participants, designs 2.1b can also be described as *static* or

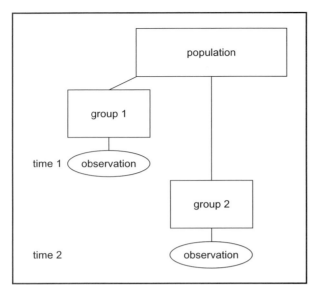

FIGURE 4.7 The quasi-panel design

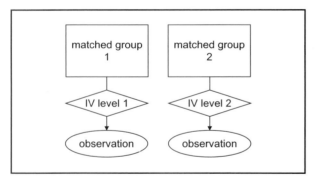

FIGURE 4.8 A post-test-only design with two matched groups

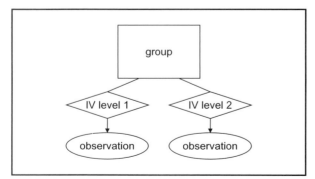

FIGURE 4.9 A within-subjects post-test-only design

non-equivalent group comparison designs. They can be subject to selection as a threat to internal validity.

Design 2.1c: Quasi-panel

One purpose of this design can be to measure participants prior to an event and then attempt to assess the effect of the event. For example, we could take a sample of drama students prior to their attendance on a drama course and measure how extrovert they are. After the first year of the course, we could take another sample from the same population of students, which may or may not include some of those we originally tested, and measure their extroversion. In addition to selection, maturation and selection by maturation are potential threats to internal validity, as could be instrumentation.

Matched participants

Design 2.2a: Two matched groups, post-test only

This design could compare two levels of an IV or one treatment with a control group.

Within-subjects designs

Design 2.3a: Within-subjects, post-test only, two conditions

For example, participants are given two types of logic puzzle to solve and the time taken to solve each type is noted. Here *type of logic puzzle* is the independent variable with two levels and *time taken* is the dependent variable.

In this design it would be better to have one condition as a control condition, if an intervention is being tested. Where possible the order of conditions should be varied between participants so that order effects can be controlled for.

Design 2.3b: One-group, pre-test post-test
The measures could be taken before and after training in some skill. There are a number of variants of this design; for example, a single treatment could occur—such as being required to learn a list—after which participants are tested following an initial duration and again following a longer duration.

This design could be subject to a number of criticisms. Firstly, because no control group is included, we have no protection against maturation and history, particularly if there is an appreciable delay between the times when the two measures are taken; we do not know whether any differences between the two occasions could have come about even without any training. Secondly, we have to be careful that any differences that are detected are not due to instrumentation, mortality, order or carry-over effects.

In the context of surveys, where the intervention could be some event that has not been under the control of the researchers then the design is described as a *simple panel* design. An example would be of a sample of the electorate whose voting intentions are sought before and after a speech made by a prominent politician.

Another variant of this design would be where time is introduced as a variable, retrospectively, by measuring participants after an event and then having them recall how they were prior to the event—a *retrospective panel* design. For example, we might ask students to rate their attitude to computers after they had attended a computing course and then ask them to rate what they thought their attitudes had been prior to the course. An additional problem with retrospective designs is that they rely on people's memories, which can be fallible.

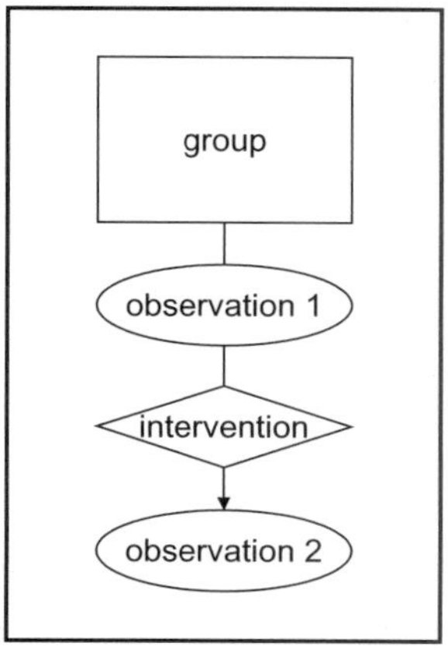

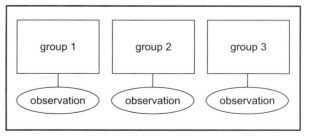

FIGURE 4.10 A one-group, pre-test, post-test design

Designs that have one independent variable with more than two levels

The following designs are simple extensions of the designs described in the previous section. However, they are worth describing separately as the way they are analysed is different. I am mainly going to give examples with three levels of the independent variable but the principle is the same regardless of the number of levels. Needless to say, each design suffers from the same problems as its equivalent with only two levels of an IV, except that two treatments can be compared and a control condition can be included.

Between-subjects designs

Design 3.1a: Multi-group cross-sectional (static or non-equivalent)
This is a quasi-experimental design in which participants are in three groups (as three levels of an IV) and are measured on a DV. For example, children in three age groups have their understanding of the parts of the body assessed.

FIGURE 4.11 A multi-group cross-sectional design

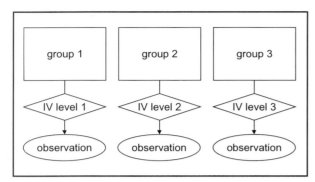

FIGURE 4.12 A multi-group, post-test-only design

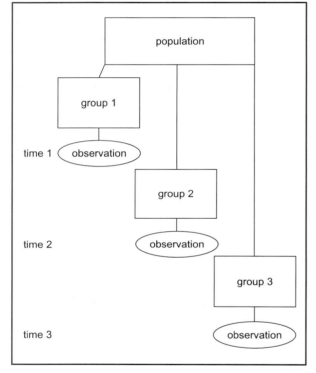

FIGURE 4.13 The multi-group, quasi-panel design

Design 3.1b: Multi-group, post-test only

Each group is given a different treatment and then a measure is taken. For example, children are placed in three groups. Their task is to select a piece of clay that is as large as a chocolate bar that they have been shown. Prior to making the judgement, one group is prevented from eating for six hours. A second group is prevented from eating for three hours; the final group is given food just prior to being tested. Here *time without food* is the independent variable, with three levels, and *the weight of the clay* is the dependent variable. The advantage of this design over the equivalent with only two levels of an IV is that one of the levels of the independent variable could be a control group. In this way, two treatments can be compared with each other and with a control group.

Design 3.1c: The multi-group quasi-panel

This is an extension of the two-group quasi-panel (2.1c) in which three samples are taken from a population at different times to measure if changes have occurred. Imagine that a third sample of drama students had their extroversion levels measured after the second year of their course.

Matched participants designs

Design 3.2: Multiple-group, matched, post-test only

This design is the equivalent of design 3.1b but three matched groups are each treated in a different way and then a measure is taken. Once again, one group could be a control group.

FIGURE 4.14 A multi-group, matched, post-test-only design

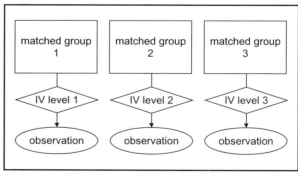

Within-subjects designs

Design 3.3a: Within-subjects, post-test only, more than two conditions

Participants each provide a measure for three different conditions. For example, each participant in a group is asked to rate physics, sociology and psychology on a scale that ranges from 'very scientific' to 'not very scientific'. As with other within-subjects designs, the order in which the observations from the different levels of the IV are taken should be varied between participants to control for order effects.

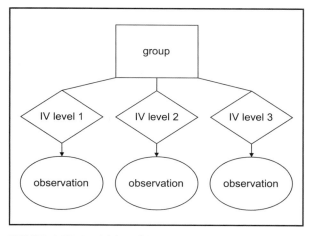

FIGURE 4.15 A within-subjects, post-test-only design with more than two conditions

Design 3.3b: Interrupted time series

This is an extension of the one-group, pre-test, post-test design which can help to protect against instrumentation and, to a certain extent, maturation and history. An interrupted time series is a design in which measures are taken at a number of points. For example, a study could be made of training designed to help sufferers from Alzheimer's disease to be better at doing basic tasks. Once again, in the context of a survey this can be called a *panel* design.

Gradual effects of history and maturation should show up as a trend, while any effects of the intervention should show up as a change in the trend. An additional advantage of taking measures on a number of occasions after the intervention is that it will help to monitor the longer-term effects of the intervention. This design can be carried out retrospectively when appropriate records are kept. However, when the intervention is not under the control of the researchers and where records are not normally kept, the researchers obviously have to know about the impending change, well in advance, in order to start taking the measures.

A problem with this design is that sometimes it can be difficult to identify the effects of an intervention when there is a general trend. For example, if I had devised a method for improving the language ability of stroke patients I would obviously need to demonstrate that any change in language ability after the intervention of my training technique was not simply part of a general trend to improve. The analysis of such designs can involve time series analysis to ascertain whether there is a trend that needs to be allowed for. Such analysis is beyond the scope of this book. For details on time series analysis see McCain and McCleary (1979) or Tabachnick and Fidell (2001).

This design can be used for single-case designs such as with an individual sufferer of Alzheimer's disease. There is an additional complication with such designs in that we clearly cannot randomly assign a participant to a condition. However, we can circumvent this problem to a certain extent by starting the intervention at a random point in the sequence of observations we take. This will allow analysis to be conducted that can try to distinguish the results from chance effects. See Todman and Dugard (2001) for details

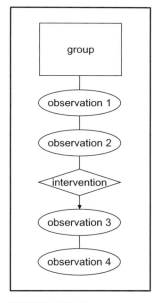

FIGURE 4.16 An interrupted time series design

on the randomisation process and analysis of such designs when single cases or small samples are being used.

Designs that have more than one independent variable and only one dependent variable

The following examples will be of designs that have a maximum of two independent variables. Designs with more than two IVs are simple extensions of these examples. In addition, most of the examples given here show only two or three levels of an IV. This is for simplicity in the diagrams and not because there is such a limit on the designs.

Between-subjects designs

Design 4.1a: Fully factorial
In this design each participant is placed in only one condition; that is, one combination of the levels of the two IVs. For example, one IV is photographs of faces with the levels *familiar* and *unfamiliar* and the other IV is the orientation in which the photographs are presented, with the levels *upside down* and *normal way up*. Speed of naming the person would be the DV. The number of IVs in a design is usually indicated: a one-way design has one IV, a two-way design has two IVs, and so on.

FIGURE 4.17 A two-way, fully factorial design

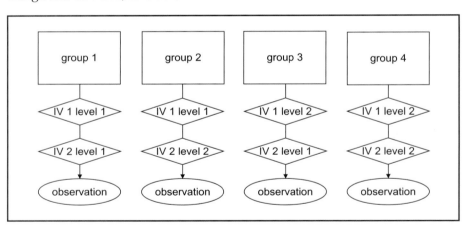

Design 4.1b: Two-way with blocking on one IV
For example, in a study of the effects of memory techniques, age might be considered to be a factor that needs to be controlled. Participants are placed in three blocks depending on their age. Participants in each age group are formed into two subgroups, with one subgroup being told simply to repeat a list of pairs of numbers while the other subgroup is told to form an image of a date that is related to each pair of numbers, e.g. 45 produces an image of the end of the Second World War. Thus, the independent variables are age (with three levels) and memory technique (with two levels). The dependent variable is *number of pairs correctly recalled*.

Quasi-experiments and surveys or experiments that entail a number of levels of the independent variables but have a limited number of participants may force the researchers to use a less exhaustive design. A hierarchical design with one variable nested within another is one form of such designs.

Design 4.2: Nesting

In the example given earlier in which mathematics teaching method was nested within school, imagine there are two methods being compared: formal and topic-based. Imagine also that four schools are involved: two adopting one approach and two adopting the other. This design involves two independent variables: the school and the teaching method, with schools (and children) nested within teaching methods.

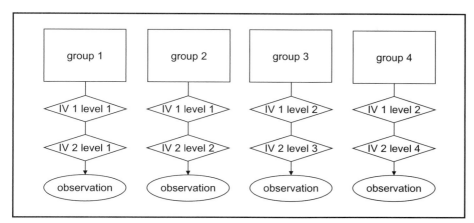

FIGURE 4.18 A design with one IV nested within another

Mixed (split-plot) designs

Design 4.3a: The classic experiment or two-group, pre-test, post-test

In this design two groups are formed, and, as the name suggests, each is tested prior to an intervention. Each is then treated differently and then tested again. One group could be a control group. For example, participants are randomly assigned to two groups. Their stress levels are measured. Members of one group are given relaxation training at a clinic and in a group. Members of a second group are given no treatment. After two months each participant's stress level is measured again. Here the first IV, which is between-subjects, is type of treatment (control or relaxation), while the second IV, which is within-subjects, is stage (pre- or post-test).

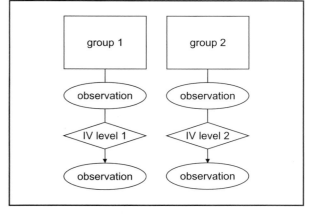

FIGURE 4.19 The two-group, pre-test, post-test design

Design 4.3b: Two-way mixed

A variant of this design could entail two different IVs but with one of them being a within-subjects variable and the other a between-subjects variable. For example, if in the face recognition study, some participants are measured on photographs (both familiar and unfamiliar) in an upside-down orientation while others are measured only on faces that are presented the normal way up.

FIGURE 4.20 A mixed design involving two IVs

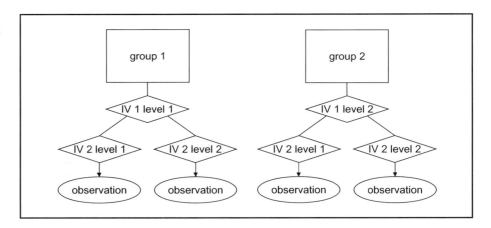

Another example of the above would be where one IV is block, where the blocks have been formed in order to counter order effects. For example, if in a memory experiment, one IV were length of delay before recall, with two levels—after 5 seconds and after 20 seconds—then one block of participants would do the levels in the order 5 seconds then 20 seconds, while another block would do them in the order 20 seconds then 5 seconds.

Yet another variant would be a Latin squares design with the order of treatments varying between participants.

Time can be built into the design in the same way as for designs with a single independent variable, retrospectively or as part of a time series; again the inclusion of a control group should improve internal validity. However, once again, if participants are not randomly assigned to the groups—non-equivalent groups—there could be problems of selection.

Design 4.4: Solomon four-group

One design that attempts to control for various threats to internal validity is the Solomon four-group. It combines two previously mentioned designs. As with design 2.1b, it is used in situations where two levels of an independent variable are being compared or where a control group and an experimental group are being employed. However, as with design 4.3a, some of the groups are given pre- and post-tests. This allows researchers to identify effects of testing.

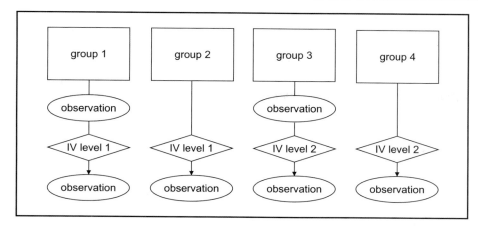

FIGURE 4.21 A Solomon four-group design comparing two treatments

An example of this design would be if researchers wished to test the effect of conditioning on young children's liking for a given food. One experimental and one control group would be tested for their liking for the food, then the experimental groups would go through an intervention whereby the researchers tried to condition the children to associate eating the food with pleasant experiences; during this phase the control groups would eat the food under neutral conditions. Subsequently, all groups would be given a post-test to measure their liking for the food.

This design is particularly expensive, as far as the number of participants used is concerned, because it involves double the number of participants as in design 2.1b or design 4.3a, for the same comparisons.

Design 4.5: A replicated, interrupted time series

This design is a modification of the interrupted time series given above. The modification involves an additional, comparison group, which can either be a control group or a group in which the intervention occurs at a different point from where it does in the original group. Once again, the study could be of training designed to help sufferers from Alzheimer's disease.

This design should be even better than the interrupted time series at detecting changes due to maturation or history as these should show up in both groups, whereas the effects of an intervention should appear as a discontinuity at the relevant point only.

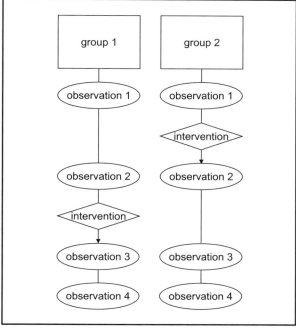

FIGURE 4.22 A replicated, interrupted time series

Within-subjects designs

Design 4.6: Multi-way within-subjects design
If the example of speed of recognition required every participant to be presented with familiar and unfamiliar faces, which were either presented upside down or the normal way up, this would be a two-way within-subjects design.

FIGURE 4.23 A two-way, within-subjects design

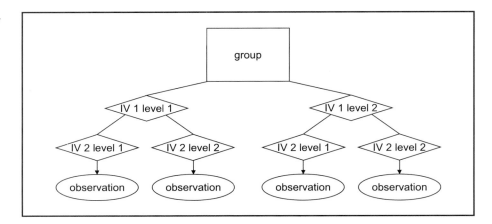

For more details on designs see Cochran and Cox (1957), Cook and Campbell (1979), Myers and Well (1991), or Winer, Brown and Michels (1991).

Summary

Designs can be classified according to the number of independent and dependent variables that they contain and the aims of the research. They can involve the same participants in more than one condition or they can employ different participants in different conditions. Designs also differ in the degree to which they measure participants at different stages in a process. Although it is possible to maximise the internal validity of a design in laboratory experiments, much research is conducted outside the laboratory. In this case, researchers have to choose the most internally valid design that is available to them in the circumstances. No design is perfect but some are more appropriate than others to answer a particular research question. Where possible it is best to allocate participants to the different conditions on a random basis.

The details for using an experimental method are contained in the first four chapters of this book. Other quantitative methods need further explanation. The next three chapters describe the conduct of research using different methods: those involving asking questions and observational methods.

PART 3
Methods

Asking questions 1: Interviews and Surveys

Introduction

This chapter describes the topics that can be covered in questions and the formats for the questions, ranging from informal to formal. It then concentrates on more formal questioning formats and discusses the different settings in which interviews and surveys can take place. It considers the wording and order of questions and the layout of a questionnaire. Finally, it emphasises the particular importance of conducting a pilot study when designing a questionnaire.

Topics for questions

The sorts of questions that can be asked fall under three general headings: demographic, behaviour and what can variously be termed opinions or beliefs or attitudes. In addition, questions can be asked about a person's state of health.

Demographic questions

These are to elicit descriptions of people: such as their age, gender, income and where they live.

Behaviour questions

Questions about behaviour could include whether, and how much, people smoke or drink.

Questions about opinions, beliefs and attitudes

These could include questions about what respondents think is the case, such as whether all politicians are corrupt. Alternatively, they could ask about what respondents think should be the case, such as whether politicians should be allowed to have a second job. The next chapter concentrates on how to devise measures of opinions, beliefs and attitudes.

Health status questions

These might include how much pain a person with a given condition was feeling or how nauseous a person felt after a given treatment.

The formats for asking questions

There are at least three formats for asking questions, ranging from the formal to the informal. When the person asking the questions is to be present then it is possible to work with just one participant at a time or with a group such as a focus group.

Structured interviews/questionnaires

The most formal format is that of a questionnaire. The exact wording of each question is selected beforehand and each participant is asked the same question in the same order. For this particular format the participant and researcher do not have to be involved in an interview.

Semi-structured interviews

Less formal than the questionnaire is the semi-structured interview. Here the questioner has an agenda: a specific topic to ask about and a set of questions he or she wants answered. However, the exact wording of the questions is not considered critical and the order in which the questions are asked is not fixed. This allows the interview to flow more like a conversation. Nonetheless, the interviewer will have to steer the conversation back to the given topic and check that the questions have been answered.

Free or unstructured interviews

Free interviews, as their name implies, need have no agenda and no pre-arranged questions. The conversation can be allowed to take whatever path the participants find most interesting. In the context of research, however, the researcher is likely to have some preliminary ideas which will guide at least the initial questions. Nonetheless, he or she is not going to constrain the conversation.

Choosing between the formats

The choice of format will depend on three factors. Firstly, the aims of the particular stage in the research will guide your choice. If the area you are studying is already well researched or you have a clear idea of the questions you wish to ask then you are likely to want to use either a structured or a semi-structured interview. However, if you are exploring a relatively unresearched area and you do not want to predetermine the direction of the interview then you are more likely to use a free interview.

Secondly, the choice between the structured and semi-structured formats will depend on how worried you are about interviewer effects. If you use a structured format then you will minimise the dangers of different participants responding differently because questions were phrased differently and asked in a different order. A third factor that will determine your choice of format will be the setting in which the questioning will take place: you cannot conduct a free interview when respondents are not present, talking on the phone or responding via computer.

The settings for asking questions

Face-to-face interviews

Face-to-face interviews involve the interviewer and participant being present together. The interviewer asks the questions and notes down the responses. Such interviews can occur in a number of places. They can be conducted on the interviewer's territory, when participants visit the researcher's place of work, or on the participant's territory, when the interviewer visits the participant's home or place of work. Finally, they can be conducted on neutral territory such as outside a shop. When conducted on the participant's territory you obviously need to take the usual precautions you would when entering a strange area and more particularly a stranger's home. It would be worth letting someone know where you are going and when to expect you back.

Self-completed surveys

Self-completed questionnaires are read by the participant who then records his or her own responses. They can take a number of forms and occur in a number of places.

Interviewer present

Like the face-to-face interview, the researcher can be present. This has the advantage that if a participant wants to ask a question it can be answered quickly. As with face-to-face interviews, these can be conducted on the researcher's territory, the participant's territory or in a neutral place. The arrangement could entail each participant being dealt with individually. Alternatively, the interviewer could introduce the questionnaire to a group of participants and then each participant could complete his or her copy of the questionnaire.

Postal surveys

Participants are given the questionnaire to complete on their own. They then have to return it to the researchers.

Internet and e-mail surveys

In the former a questionnaire can be posted on a web site and responses sent to the researcher. In the latter particular user groups can be sent a questionnaire again for returning to the researcher (see Hewson, 2003).

Telephone surveys

The questioner asks the questions and notes down the participant's responses.

The relative merits of the different settings

The nature of the sample

If it is important that the sample in a survey be representative of a particular population, then how the participants are chosen is important. See Chapter 11 for details of how to select a sample.

Response rate

An additional problem for attempts to obtain a representative sample is the proportion of people for whom questionnaires are not successfully completed. The people who have not taken part may share some characteristic that undermines the original basis for sampling. For example, the sample may lack many people from a particular socio-economic group because they have chosen not to take part.

The response rate for a postal survey is generally the poorest of the methods, although it is possible to remind the sample, for example, by post or even telephone, which can improve the response rate. In a survey about student accommodation at Staffordshire University the initial response rate was 50% but with a poster campaign reminding people to return their questionnaires this was improved to 70%.

Telephone surveys can produce a better response rate as the survey can be completed, there and then, rather than left and forgotten. The response rate can be improved if you send a letter beforehand introducing yourself and possibly including a copy of the questionnaire. In this way, the respondents have some warning, as some people react badly to 'cold-calling'. However, we found (McGowan, Pitts & Clark-Carter, 1999), when trying to survey general practitioners, a heavily surveyed group may be quite resistant, even to telephone surveys and even when they have received a copy of the questionnaire. Although many may not refuse outright, they may put the researcher off to a future occasion.

Face-to-face surveys produce the best response rate but you can still meet resistance. I found when trying to survey visually impaired people in their own homes that one person was suspicious, despite my assurances, that I might pass the information to the Inland Revenue. If you are going to other people's houses you also have the obvious problem that the person may not be in when you call. In the case of both telephone and face-to-face interviews, it is worth setting yourself a target that you will not make more than a certain number of attempts to survey a given person.

You should send an introductory letter beforehand, possibly mentioning a time when you would like to call. Also include a stamped addressed postcard which allows respondents to say that the time you suggest is inconvenient and to suggest an alternative. This serves the dual purpose of being polite and lessening the likelihood that the person will be out. Always carry some official means of identification as people are often encouraged not to let strangers into their houses. Do not assume that because you have sent a letter beforehand that respondents will remember any of the details, so be prepared to explain once again.

Motivation of respondents

If you want people to be honest and, more particularly, if you want them to disclose more sensitive details about themselves, then there can be an advantage in being able to establish a rapport with them. This is obviously not easily achieved in a postal survey, or even in other situations where participants complete a questionnaire themselves, though a carefully worded letter can help. It is more possible to establish rapport over the phone and more so still with face-to-face interviews.

The anonymity of respondents

You may be more likely to get honest responses to sensitive questions if the respondents remain anonymous but, because you have not managed to establish any relationship with them, they have less personal investment in the survey.

Interviewer effects

While establishing rapport has certain advantages, as with any research, there can be a danger that the researcher has an unintended effect upon participants' behaviour. In the case of interviewers, many aspects of the researcher may affect responses, and affect them differently for different respondents. In face-to-face interviews, the way researchers dress, their accents, their gender, the particular intonation they use when asking a question and other aspects of non-verbal communication can all have an effect on respondents. This can lead to answers that are felt by the respondent to be acceptable to the researcher. You can try to minimise the effects by dressing as neutrally as possible. However, what you consider neutral may be very formal to one person or overly casual to someone else.

If your sample is of a particular subgroup then it would be reasonable to modify your dress to a certain extent. I do not mean by this that when interviewing punks you should wear their type of clothes unless you yourself are a punk; the attempt to dress appropriately may jar with other aspects of your behaviour and make your attempts seem comic or condescending. For this group simply dress more casually than you might have for visiting a sample of elderly people. Some of these factors, such as accent, intonation and gender, are present during a telephone conversation and none, bar possibly the gender of the researcher, is present in a postal survey.

As an interviewer you want to create a professional impression, so make sure that you are thoroughly familiar with the questionnaire. In this way, you should avoid stumbling over the wording and be aware of the particular routes through the questionnaire. That is, you will know what questions are appropriate for each respondent.

To avoid affecting a respondent's answers it is important that the interviewer use the exact wording that has been chosen for each question. Changing the wording can produce a different meaning and therefore a different response. Sometimes it may be necessary to use what are described as 'probes' to elicit an appropriate response: for example, when the answer that is required to a given question is either yes or no, but the interviewee says 'I'm not sure'. The important thing to remember about probes is that they should not lead in a particular direction; they should be neutral. Silence and a quizzical look may be enough to produce an appropriate response. If this does not work then you could draw the interviewee's attention to the nature of the permissible responses, or with other questions you could say 'is there anything else?'

Beware of rephrasing what respondents say, particularly when they are answering open-ended questions. During the analysis stage of the research you will be looking for patterns of responses and common themes. These may be hidden if the answers have not been recorded exactly.

Maximum length of interview

Another advantage of being able to establish rapport can be that respondents will be more motivated to continue with a longer interview. If your questionnaire takes a long time to complete then a postal survey is ill-advised. The length of telephone interviews and face-to-face interviews will depend on how busy the person is, how useful they perceive your survey as being and, possibly, how lonely they are. With face-to-face interviews in the person's own house an interview can extend across a number of visits.

Cost

The question of cost will depend on the aims of the survey and who is conducting it. If the sample is to be representative and the population from which it is drawn is geographically widespread then face-to-face interviewing will be the most expensive. Telephoning will be expensive if researchers cannot take advantage of cheap-rate calls. Postal surveys will be the cheapest, though a follow-up, designed to improve response rate, will add to the costs. If the quality of the sample is less important then a face-to-face interview can be relatively cheap. Interviewers can stand in particularly popular places and attempt to interview passers-by—an opportunity sample. However, if the interviewers have to be employed by the researchers then this can add to the cost.

Whether interviewers can be supervised

When employing others to administer a questionnaire it is important to supervise them in some way. Firstly, you should give them some training. You may be sampling from a special population and using terminology that you and your potential respondents may know but which you could not assume that your questioners would know. For example, you may be surveying blind people and be using technical terms related to the causes of their visual impairment. You may also want to give the questioners an idea of how to interact with a particular group. This could involve role play. You also want to reassure yourself that their manner will be appropriate for someone interviewing other people.

The second point is that there may be advantages in your being available to deal with questions from interviewers during the interview. If the interviews are being conducted in a central place, either face-to-face or over the phone, then it is possible to be available to answer questions. When the interviewers phone from their own homes or visit respondents' territory you do not have this facility.

A third point is that you may wish to check the honesty of your interviewers. One way to do this is to contact a random subsample of the people they claim to have interviewed to see that the interview did take place and that it took the predicted length of time.

The ability to check responses

A badly completed questionnaire can render that participant's data unusable. Obviously, clear instructions and simple questions can help but with a paper version of a self-completed questionnaire you have no check that the person has filled in all the relevant questions; sometimes they may even have turned over two pages and left a whole page of questions uncompleted. A well-laid-out questionnaire will allow interviewers, either face-to-face or over the telephone, to guide the person through the questionnaire.

The questionnaire can be computerised and this could guide the interviewer or respondent through the questions and record the responses at the same time. Computers can be used for self-administered questionnaires but this is only likely to be the case when the respondent comes to a central point or is using the Internet and has his or her own computer and link. A portable computer could be used by a questioner in the respondent's home.

The speed with which the survey can be conducted

If the responses for the whole sample are needed quickly then the telephone can be the quickest method. For example, political opinion pollsters often use telephone surveys when they want to gauge the response to a given pronouncement from a politician. However, if the nature of the sample is not critical then other quick methods can be to stand in a public place and ask passers-by, or use the Internet or e-mail.

Aspects of the respondents that may affect the sample

If you go to people's homes during the day you will miss those who go out to work; you also will not sample the homeless. You can go in the evening but if you need to be accompanied by a translator or sign language user, their availability may be a problem.

If you use the telephone you will have difficulty with those who are deaf or do not speak your language, and you will miss those who do not have a phone. In addition, if you sample using the phone book you will miss those who are ex-directory and those who have just moved into the area and not been put in the phone book. You could get around these latter problems by dialling random numbers that are plausible for the area you wish to sample. You may get some business numbers but if they were not required in your sample you could stop the interview once you were aware that they were businesses.

If you use a postal survey you will miss those who cannot read print—people who are visually impaired, dyslexic, illiterate or unable to read the language in which you have printed the questionnaire. At greater expense you could send a cassette version or even a video version but this also depends on people having the correct equipment. You could also translate the questionnaire into another language or into Braille. However, in the latter case, only a small proportion of visually impaired people would be able to read it. You obviously need to do preliminary research to familiarise yourself with the problems that your sample may present.

Degree of control over the order in which questions are answered

For some questionnaires, the order in which the questions are asked can have an effect on the responses that are given. For example, it is generally advisable to put more sensitive questions later in the questionnaire so that respondents are not put off straight away, but meet such questions once they have invested some time and have become more motivated to complete the questionnaire. A self-administered paper-and-pencil questionnaire allows respondents to look ahead and realise the overall context of the questions. In addition, they can check that they have not contradicted them-selves by looking back at their previous responses and in this way they can create a false impression of consistency.

Group size

When you want a discussion to take place among a group of participants, for example in a focus group, then there can be an optimal number of people. If you include too few people this may not provide a sufficient range of ideas to generate a useful discussion, while having too many people is likely to inhibit discussion. Morgan (1998) says that a group size of between six and ten people is usual. However, he notes that when you are dealing with a complex topic, you are sampling experts or want more detail from each person you may be better choosing even fewer than six, while when the members of your sample have low personal involvement in the topic or you want a wide range of opinion then you might go for more than ten.

The choice of setting

If speed is important, the questionnaire is not too long, cost is a consideration and a relatively good response rate is required then use a telephone survey or the Internet or e-mail.

If none of cost, time and the danger of interviewer bias are problems, if the questionnaire is long, a very high response rate is required, and if the sample may be so varied or is of a special group where language may be a problem, then use a face-to-face technique.

If cost or anonymity are over-riding considerations, if the response rate is not critical and the questionnaire is short then use a postal survey.

The choice of participants

The population

The population will be defined by the aims of the research, which in turn will be guided partly by the aspect of the topic that you are interested in and partly by whether you wish to generalise to a clearly defined population. Your research topic may define your population. For example, you may be interested in female students who smoke. Alternatively, your population might be less well specified, such as all potential voters in a given election.

The sample

How you select your sample will depend on three considerations. Firstly, it will depend on whether you wish to make estimates about the nature of your population from what you have found within your sample; for example, if you wanted to be able to estimate how many females in the student population smoked. A second consideration will be the setting you are adopting for the research. This in turn will interact with the third set of considerations, which will be practicalities such as the distance apart of participants and the costs of sampling.

See Chapter 11 for a description of the methods of sampling and for details of the statistical methods that can be used in sampling, including decisions about how many participants to include in the sample.

A census

A census is a survey that has attempted to include all the members of the population. In the UK, every 10 years there is a national census: a questionnaire is sent to every household. Householders are legally obliged to fill in the questionnaire.

What questions to include

Before any question is included ask yourself why you want to include that particular one. It is often tempting to include a question because it seemed interesting at the time but when you come to analyse the data you fail to do anything with it; think about what you are going to do with the information. You may have an idea of how people are going to respond to a given question, but also consider what additional information you would want if they responded in a way that was possible but unexpected. Not to include such a follow-up question may lose useful information and even force the need for a follow-up questionnaire to find the answer.

Types of questions

Open-ended questions

Open-ended questions are those where respondents are not constrained to a pre-specified set of responses; for example, 'What brand of cigarettes do you smoke?' or 'How old are you?'

Closed questions

Closed questions constrain the way the respondent can answer to a fixed set of alternatives. Thus they could be of the form 'Do you smoke?' or 'Mark which age group you are in: 20–29, 30–39, 40–49 or 50–59'. A closed version of the question about the brands of cigarettes smoked would list the alternatives. One way to allow a certain flexibility in a closed question is to include the alternative *other* which allows unexpected alternatives to be given by the respondent, but remember to ask them to specify what that other is. Another form of closed question would be to give alternatives and ask respondents to rate them on some dimension. For example, you could give respondents a set of pictures of people and ask for a rating of how attractive the people portrayed are, on a scale from 'very attractive' to 'very unattractive'. Alternatively, the photos could be ranked on attractiveness; that is, placed in an order based on their perceived attractiveness. In addition to the above, there are standard forms of closed questions that are used for attitude questions; see Chapter 6 for a description of these.

Closed questions have certain advantages in that they give respondents a context for their replies and they can help jog their memories. In addition, they can increase the likelihood that a questionnaire will be completed because they are easier for self-administration and quicker to complete. Finally, they are easier to score for the analysis phase. However, they can overly constrain the possible answers. It is a good idea to include more open-ended questions in the original version of a questionnaire. During the pilot study respondents will provide a number of alternative responses which can be used to produce a closed version of the question.

A popular format for questions about health status, such as the amount of pain being experienced, is the visual analogue scale (VAS). Typically this involves a horizontal line, frequently 10 centimetres long, with a word or phrase at each end of the scale. The participant is asked to mark a point on the line which they feel reflects their experience.

No pain _____ The worst pain I have ever experienced

The score would then be the number of millimetres, from the left end of the line, where the person has marked.

There are various alternative visual analogue scales including having a line of cartoon faces that represent degrees of pain from ☺ through ☺ to ☹ or in the form of a thermometer like the ones sometimes used outside churches to show how the appeal fund is progressing.

Filter questions

Your sample may include people who will respond in some fundamentally different ways and you may wish to explore those differences further. In this case, rather than ask inappropriate questions of some people you can include filter questions which guide people to the section that is appropriate for them. For example, 'If you smoke go to question 7, otherwise go to question 31'.

Badly worded questions

There are many ways in which you can create bad questions. They should be avoided as they can create an impression that the questionnaire has been created sloppily and can confuse participants as to what the question means. Alternatively, they can suggest what response is expected or desired. The outcome can be that the answers will be less valid and the participants may be less motivated to fill in the questionnaire. Why should they invest time if you do not appear to have done so? In addition, you may not know the meaning of the responses. Many of the points below pertain to bad writing in general.

Questions that contain technical language or jargon
There is not much point in asking a question if your respondents do not know the terms you are using. It is generally possible to express yourself in simpler words but this can be at the cost of a longer question which in itself can be difficult to understand. The advantage of a phone or face-to-face interview is that you can find out whether respondents understand the terms and explain them, if necessary. Nonetheless, keep technical terminology to a minimum and do not use unnecessary abbreviations for the same reason.

Ambiguous questions
An example of an ambiguous question would be 'Do you remember where you were when Kennedy was assassinated?' Even if the person was aware that you were talking about members of the famous American family, both John and Robert Kennedy were assassinated so it is unclear which one you mean.

Vague questions

Vague questions are those that, like ambiguous questions, could be interpreted by different people in different ways because you have failed to give sufficient guidance. For example, the answer to 'Do you drink much alcohol?' depends on what you mean by *much*. I might drink a glass of wine every day and consider that to be moderate, while another person might see me as a near-alcoholic and a third person see me as a near-teetotaller, depending on their own habits, and each would see themselves as moderate drinkers. It is better to give a range of possible amounts of alcohol from which they can indicate their consumption.

Leading questions

A leading question is one that indicates to the participant the response that is expected. For example, 'Do you believe in the myth that big boys don't cry?' suggests that the participant should not agree with the statement.

Questions with poor range indicators

If you give alternatives and you only want respondents to choose one, then they must be mutually exclusive; in other words, it should not to be possible to fulfil more than one alternative. Imagine the difficulty for a 30-year-old when asked to 'Indicate which age group you are in: 20–30, 30–40, 40–50, 50–60'.

Questions with built-in assumptions

Some questions are inappropriate for some respondents and yet imply that everyone can answer them. An example would be 'What word processor do you use?' without giving the option *none*. A more common occurrence can be a question of the form: 'Does your mother smoke?' There are a number of reasons why this might not be appropriate—the person never knew his or her mother, or the mother is now dead.

Double-barrelled questions

Some questions involve two or more elements but only allow the respondent to answer one of them. Often they can be an extension of the question with a built-in assumption. For example, 'When you have a shower do you use a shower gel?' If you only have baths you have difficulty answering this question, for if you reply *no* then this might suggest that you do have showers but only use a bar of soap with which to wash.

The use of double negatives

Double negatives are difficult to understand. For example, 'Do you agree with the statement: Lawyers are paid a not inconsiderable amount?' If the questioner wants to know whether people think that lawyers are paid a large amount then it would be better to say so directly.

Sensitive questions

Sensitive questions can range from demographic ones about age and income to questions about illegal behaviour or behaviour that transgresses social norms. Sensitive questions about demographic details can be made more acceptable by giving ranges rather than requiring exact information. Some-times the sensitivity may simply apply to saying a person's age out loud, in which case you could ask for dates of birth and work out ages afterwards.

Behaviour questions can be more problematic. Assurances of anonymity can help but it may be necessary to word the question in a way that defuses the sensitivity of the question to a certain extent. For example, if asking about drug taking you may lead up to the question in a roundabout way, by having preliminary comments that suggest that you are aware that many people take drugs and possibly asking if the participant's friends take drugs, then asking the participant if he or she does.

The layout of the questionnaire

The layout of a questionnaire can make it more readable and help to create a more professional air for the research, which in turn will make particip-ants more motivated to complete it. This is not only true for self-completed questionnaires but can help the interview run more smoothly when it is administered face-to-face or over the telephone.

Break the questionnaire down into sections. For example, in a question-naire on smoking you might have a section for demographic questions, a section on smoking behaviour, a section on attitudes to smoking, a section on knowledge about health and a section on the influence of others. This gives the questionnaire a coherence and a context for the questions in a given section. Include filter questions where necessary. This may increase the complexity of administering the questionnaire but it will mean that participants are not asked inappropriate questions.

Provide instructions and explanatory notes for the entire questionnaire and for each section.

The use of space

Use only one side of the paper as this will lessen the likelihood that a page of questions will be missed. Follow the usual guidance for the layout of text by giving a good ratio of 'white space' to text (Wright, 1983). This will not only make it more readable but will also allow the person scoring the sheets reasonable space to make comments and make coding easier. Use reason-ably sized margins, particularly side margins. When giving alternatives in a closed question list them vertically rather than horizontally. For example:

How do you travel to work?

> *on foot*
> *by bicycle*
> *by bus*
> *by train*
> *by another person's car*
> *by own car*
> *other (please specify)*

Leave enough space for people to respond as much as they want to to open-ended questions but not so much space that they feel daunted by it.

Order of questions

You want to motivate respondents, not put them off. Accordingly, put interesting but simple questions first, closed rather than open-ended first for ease of completion, and put the more sensitive questions last. Vary the question format, if possible, to maintain interest and to prevent participants from responding automatically without considering the question properly. You may wish to control the order of the sections so that when participants answer one section, they are not fully aware of other questions you are going to ask. For example, you may ask behaviour questions before asking attitude questions.

If you are concerned that the specific order of questions or the wording of given questions can affect the responses then you can adopt a split-ballot approach. This simply means that you create two versions of the questionnaire with the different orders/wording and give half your sample one version and half the other. You can then compare responses to see whether the participants who received the different versions responded differently. If you do have such concerns then try them out at the pilot stage.

The pilot study

The pilot study is critical for a questionnaire for which you have created the questions or when you are trying an existing questionnaire on a new population. As usual it should be conducted on people who are from your target population. It is worth using a larger number of people in a pilot study where you are devising the measure than you would when using an existing measure such as in an experiment.

The pilot study can perform two roles. Firstly, it can help you refine your questionnaire. It can provide you with a range of responses to your open-ended questions and so you can turn them into closed ones by including the alternatives that you have been given. Secondly, it can tell you the usefulness of a question. If everyone answers the question in the same way then it can be dropped as it is redundant. If a question is badly worded then this should become clear during the pilot study and you can rephrase the question.

Summary

Researchers who wish to ask questions of their participants have to choose the topics of the questions—demographic, behavioural and attitude/opinion/belief or, where required, aspects of health status. They have to choose the format of the questioning—structured, semi-structured or free. In addition, they have to choose the settings for the questioning—face-to-face, self-completed by participants or over the telephone. Once these choices have been made it is necessary to refine the wording of the questions, choose the order in which they are asked and the layout of the questionnaire. Before the final study is carried out it is essential that a pilot study be conducted. This is particularly important when the researchers have devised the questionnaire.

The next chapter deals with the design and conduct of attitude questionnaires.

6 ASKING QUESTIONS II: MEASURING ATTITUDES AND MEANING

Introduction

There are many situations in which researchers want to measure people's attitudes. They may wish to explore a particular area to find out the variety of attitudes that exist—for example, people's views on animal welfare. Alternatively, they may want to find out how people feel about a specific thing—for example, whether the government is doing a good job. Yet again, they may wish to relate attitudes to aspects of behaviour—for example, to find out how people's attitudes to various forms of contraception relate to their use of such methods.

One way to find out people's attitudes is to ask them. A number of techniques have been devised to do this. This chapter describes three attitude scales you are likely to meet when reading research into attitudes: the Thurstone, Guttman and Likert scales. It explains why the Likert scale has become the most frequently employed measure of attitudes. In addition, it describes four other methods that have been used to explore what certain entities mean to people: the semantic differential, Q-methodology, repertory grids and facet theory.

Reliability of measures

If we wanted to find out a person's attitude towards something, such as his or her political attitude, we might be tempted to ask a single question, for example:

Do you like the policies of Conservative politicians? (Yes/No)

If you are trying to predict voting behaviour this may be a reasonable question. However, the question would fail to identify the subtleties of political attitude, as it assumes that there is a simple dichotomy between those who do and those who do not like such policies. Frequently, when confronted with such a question people, will say that it depends on which policy is being considered. Thus, if a particular policy with which they disagreed was being given prominence in the media they might answer

No, whereas if a policy with which they agreed was more prominent, they are likely to answer *Yes*. Yet, if attitudes are relatively constant we would want a measure that reflected this constancy. In other words, we want a reliable measure. A single question is generally an unreliable measure of attitudes.

To avoid the unreliability of single questions, researchers have devised multi-item scales. The answer to a single question may change from occasion to occasion but the responses to a set of questions will provide a score that should remain relatively constant. A multi-item scale has the additional advantage that a given person's attitude can be placed on a dimension from having a positive attitude towards something to having a negative attitude towards it. In this way, the relative attitudes of different people can be compared in a more precise way.

Dimensions

The use of multi-item scales also allows researchers to explore the subtleties of attitudes to see whether a single dimension exists or whether there is more than one dimension. For example, in political attitudes it might be felt that there exists a single dimension from left-wing to right-wing. However, other dimensions also exist, for example libertarian–authoritarian. Thus, there are right-wing libertarians and left-wing libertarians, just as there are right-wing authoritarians and left-wing authoritarians. Therefore, if researchers wished to explore the domain of political attitude they would want some questions that identified where a person was on the left–right dimension and some questions that identified where he or she was on the libertarian–authoritarian dimension.

The three scales described below deal with the issue of dimensions in different ways. The Thurstone scale ignores the problem and treats attitudes as though they were on a single dimension. The Guttman scale recognises the problem and tries to produce a scale that is uni-dimensional (having one dimension) by removing questions that refer to other dimensions. The Likert scale explores the range of attitudes and can contain subscales that address different dimensions. The creation of any of these three scales involves producing a set of questions or statements and then selecting the most appropriate among them on the basis of how a sample of people have responded to them. As you will see, the criteria for what constitutes an appropriate statement depends on the particular scale.

However, the criteria of all three types of scale share certain features. As with all questionnaires, try to avoid badly worded questions or statements; refer to the previous chapter for a description of the common mistakes. Once you have produced an initial set of statements, as with any research, carry out a small pilot study to check that the wording of the statements, despite your best efforts, is not faulty. Then, once you have satisfied yourself on this point, you are ready to carry out the fuller study to explore your attitude scale.

Attitude scales

Thurstone scale

A Thurstone scale (Thurstone, 1931; Thurstone and Chave, 1929) is designed to have a set of questions that have different values from each other on a dimension. Respondents identify the statements with which they agree. For example, in a scale designed to measure attitudes about animal welfare, the statements might range from:

Humans have a perfect right to hunt animals for pleasure

to

No animal should be killed for the benefit of humans

The designer of the scale gets judges to rate each statement as to where it lies on the dimension—for example, from totally unconcerned about animal welfare to highly concerned about animal welfare. On the basis of the ratings, a set of statements is chosen, such that the statements have ratings that are as equally spaced as possible across the range of possible values. Once the final set of statements has been chosen, it can be used in research and a participant's score on the scale is the mean value of the statements with which he or she has agreed.

Choosing the statements

Compile a set of approximately 60 statements that are relevant to the attitude you wish to measure. Word the statements in such a way that they represent the complete range of possible attitudes. Place the statements in a random order rather than one based on their assumed position on the dimension.

Exploring the scale

Ask at least 100 judges to rate each statement on an 11-point scale. For example, a judge might be asked to rate the statements given above as to where they lie on the dimension ranging from totally unconcerned about animal welfare (which would get a rating of 1) to highly concerned about animal welfare (which would get a rating of 11). They are not being asked to give their own attitudes to animals but their opinions about where each statement lies on the dimension.

Item analysis

The average (mean) rating for each statement is calculated, as is a measure of how well judges agreed about each statement's rating (the standard deviation). The calculation of these two statistics is dealt with in Chapter 9.

Put the statements in order, based on the size of the mean rating for each statement and identify statements that are given, approximately, mean ratings for each half-point on the scale. Thus, there should be statements with a rating of 1, others with a rating of 1.5 and so on up to a rating of 11. It is likely that you will have statements with similar ratings. Choose, for each interval on the scale, the question over which there was the most agreement: that is, with the smallest standard deviation. Discard the other statements. Place the selected statements in random order and add the possible response (agree/disagree) to each statement.

Criticisms of the Thurstone scale

The first criticism was mentioned earlier. Thurstone scales assume that the attitude being measured is on a single dimension but do not check whether this is the case. Secondly, two people achieving the same score on the scale, particularly in the mid-range of scores, could have achieved their scores from different patterns of responses. Thus, a given score does not denote a single attitude and so is not distinguishing clearly between people. A third criticism is that a large number of statements have to be created, to begin with, in order to stand a chance of ending with a set of equally spaced questions across the assumed dimension. Finally, a lot of people have to act as judges.

A Guttman scale deals with all but the last of these problems.

Guttman scale

The creation of a Guttman scale (Guttman, 1944) also involves statements with which respondents agree or disagree. Once again, a set of statements is designed to sample the range of possible attitudes. They are given to a sample of people and the pattern of responses is examined. The structure of a Guttman scale is such that the statements are forced to be on a single dimension. The statements are phrased in such a way that a person with an attitude at one end of the scale would agree with none of the items while a person with an attitude at the other end of the dimension would agree with all of the statements. Thus, a measure of attitudes to animal welfare might have statements ranging from

It is acceptable to experiment on animals for medical purposes

through

It is acceptable to experiment on animals for cosmetic purposes

to

It is acceptable to experiment on animals for any reason

If these items formed a Guttman scale then a person agreeing with the final item should also agree with the previous ones and a person disagreeing with the first item should disagree with all the other items. Statements that do not fit into this pattern would be discarded. In this way, a person's score is based on how far along the dimension he or she is willing to agree with statements. Thus, if these statements formed a 3-point scale, agreeing with the first one would score one, agreeing with the second one would score two and agreeing with the last one would score three. Accordingly, two people with the same score can be said to lie at the same point on the dimension.

Bogardus social distance scales

The Bogardus social distance scale (Bogardus, 1925) can be seen as a version of the Guttman scale, in that it produces a scale that is uni-dimensional. In this case, the dimension is to do with how much contact a person would be willing to have with people who have certain characteristics, such as race or a disability. The items on the scale could range from asking about the respondent's willingness to allow people of a given race to visit his or her country to willingness to let them marry a member of the respondent's family.

Criticism of the Guttman scale

The very strength of dealing strictly with a single dimension means that, unless subscales are created to look at different, related dimensions, a Guttman scale misses the subtleties of attitudes about a given topic. For example, a Guttman scale looking at attitudes to race issues would probably require different scales for different races.

A Likert scale explores the dimensions within attitudes to a given topic and can contain subscales. It has become the most popular scaling technique.

Likert scale

Each item in a Likert scale (Likert, 1932) is a statement with which respondents can indicate their level of agreement on a dimension of possible responses. An example of the type of statement could again be:

No animal should be killed for the benefit of humans

Typically the range of possible responses will be of the following form:

| Strongly agree | Agree | Undecided | Disagree | Strongly disagree |

I recommend that a five- or a seven-point scale be used. Fewer points on the scale will miss the range of attitudes, while more points will require an artificial level of precision, as people will often not be able to provide such a subtle response. In addition, an odd number of possible responses can include a neutral position; not having such a possible response forces people to make a decision in a particular direction, when they may be undecided, and this can produce an unreliable measure.

Choosing the statements

I think you need at least 20 statements that are designed to evaluate a person's attitude to the topic you have chosen, because some are likely to be found not to be useful when you analyse people's responses. Remember that you want to distinguish between people's attitudes, so don't include items that everyone will agree with or that everyone will disagree with, for they will be redundant.

Wording of statements

In accordance with the previous point, don't make the statements too extreme; let the respondent indicate his or her level of agreement by the response chosen.

Phrase roughly half of the statements in the opposite direction to the rest. For example, if your scale was to do with attitudes to smoking, then half the statements should require people who were positively disposed towards smoking to reply *Agree* or *Strongly agree*, while the other half of the statements should require them to reply *Disagree* or *Strongly disagree*. In this way, you force respondents to read the statements and you may avoid what is termed a response bias—that is, a tendency by a given person to use one side of the range of responses. This does not mean that you simply take an existing, positively worded statement and produce a negative version of the same statement to add to the scale.

Part of the reason for the last point is that you are trying to explore the range of attitudes that exist and so you do not want redundant statements which add nothing to what is already covered by other questions. However, it may not always be possible to identify what will be a redundant question in advance of conducting the study.

Sample size

Chapter 13 contains an explanation for the choice of sample size for a given study. For the moment I will give the rule of thumb that sampling at least 68 people will mean that you are giving your questions a reasonable chance of showing themselves as useful in the analysis that you will conduct. To use fewer people would increase the likelihood that you would reject a question as not useful when it is measuring an aspect of the attitude under consideration.

Analysing the scale

There are two analyses that can be conducted of the responses you have been given by those in your sample. The first—an item analysis—looks to see whether the attitude scale is measuring one or more dimensions; this will also identify statements that do not appear to be sufficiently related to the other statements in the scale. The second analysis checks whether a given statement is receiving a sufficient range of responses—the discriminative power of the statement; remember that if everyone gives the same or very similar responses to a statement, even though their attitudes differ, then there is no point in including it as it does not tell you how people differ.

Chapters 9 and 19 cover the material on the statistical techniques used in the two analyses. Below is given a description of what these analyses entail. For a fuller description of the process see Appendix XII.

Scoring the responses

Using a 5-point scale as an example, choose to score the negative side of the scale as 1 and the positive end as 5. For example, if your scale was about attitudes to animals, then a response that implied an extremely unfavourable attitude to animals would be scored 1, while a response that implied an extremely favourable attitude to animals would be scored 5. Thus, you will need to reverse the scoring of those statements that are worded so that agreement suggested a negative attitude to animals. For example, if the statement was of the form *Fox hunting is a good thing* then extreme agreement would be scored 1, while extreme disagreement would be scored 5. This can be done in a straightforward manner and you can get the computer to do the reversing for you. Entering the data into the computer in their original form is less prone to error than trying to reverse the scores before putting them into the computer. Appendix XII describes how to reverse scores once they are entered into the computer.

Once the responses have been scored, and those items that need it have been reversed, find the total score for each respondent by simply adding together all that person's responses for each statement.

Conducting an item analysis

Statements that are part of a single dimension should correlate well with each other and with the total score; for two statements to correlate, people who give a high score to one statement will tend to give a high score to the other and those who give a low score to one will tend to give a low score to the other. Those statements that form a separate dimension will not correlate well with the total score but will correlate with each other. For example, in a study on attitudes to the British royal family, a group of students found that, in addition to the main dimension, there was a dimension that related to the way the royal family was portrayed in the newspapers.

If a statement does not correlate reasonably well with the total score nor with other statements then it should be discarded. It would be worth examining such statements to see what you could identify about them that might have produced this result. They may still be badly worded, despite having been tested in the pilot study. It could be that people differed little in the way they responded to a given item; for if there was not a range of scores for that statement then it would not correlate with the total. Alternatively, although you included the statement because you thought that it was relevant to the attitude, this result may demonstrate that it is not relevant, after all.

Analysing discriminatory power

Discard the items that failed the item analysis and conduct a separate analysis of discriminatory power for each dimension (or subscale) that you have identified. For each dimension find a new total score for each respondent. Find out which respondents were giving the top 25% of total scores and which were giving the bottom 25% of total scores.[1] You can then take each statement that is relevant to that dimension and see whether these two groups differ in the way they responded to it. If a statement fails to distinguish between those who give high scores and those who give low scores on the total scale, then that statement has poor discriminative power and can be dropped.

[1] Other proportions can be used, such as the top and bottom third.

Criticism of Likert scales

Like Thurstone scales, two people with the same score on a Likert scale may have different patterns of responding. Accordingly, we cannot treat a given score as having a unique meaning about a person's attitude.

Techniques to measure meaning

Q-methodology

Q-methodology is an approach to research that was devised by Stephenson (1953). It requires participants or judges to rate statements or other elements on a given dimension or on a given basis. One technique that Q-methodology employs is getting participants to perform Q-sorts. Typically a Q-sort involves participants being presented with a set of statements, each on an individual card, and being asked to place those statements on a dimension, such as *very important to me* to *not important to me*. (Kerlinger, 1973, recommends that, for a Q-sort to be reliable, the number of statements should normally be no fewer than 60 but no more than 90.) The ratings can then be used in at least three ways. Firstly, similarities between people in the way they rate the elements can be sought. For example, researchers could ask potential voters to rank a set of statements in order of importance. The statements might include *inflation should be kept low, pensions should be increased, the current funding of health care should be maintained* and *we should maintain our present expenditure on defence*. The rankings could then be explored to see whether there is a consensus among voters as to what issues are seen to be the most important.

A second, and more interesting, use of Q-methodology can be to explore different subgroups of people who would produce similar rankings but would differ from other subgroups. Thus, in the previous example you might find that some people ranked pensions and the funding of health care as the most important while others put higher priorities on defence and inflation and a third group might see environmental issues as paramount.

A third use of Q-methodology can be to examine the degree of agreement an individual has when rating different objects on the same scale. I could explore the degree to which a person views his or her parents as being similar by getting him or her to rank a set of statements on the basis of how well they describe one parent and then to repeat the ranking of the statements for the second parent. Once again, I could get a number of people to do these rankings for each of their parents and then look to see whether there is a group of people who rank both their parents in a similar fashion and another group who rank each parent differently.

Rogers (1951, 1961) has used Q-sorts in the context of counselling. For example, a person attending counselling could be asked to rate statements on an 11-point scale on the basis of how typical the statements are of him- or herself. This Q-sort could be compared with another done on the basis of how typical the statements are of how the person would like to be (his or her ideal self). At various points during the period when the person is receiving counselling, the Q-sorts would be repeated. The aim of counselling would be to bring these two Q-sorts into greater agreement, either by improving a person's self-image or by making his or her ideal self more realistic. In addition, Rogers has used Q-methodology to investigate how closely counsellors and their clients agree over certain issues. In this case, the counsellor and his or her client are given statements and asked to rank them in order of importance. According to Rogers, the degree of agreement between the two orderings can be a good predictor of the outcome of counselling.

Q-methodology can be used to explore theories. For example, rankings or sortings could be used to explore the different meanings a concept has. Stenner and Marshall (1995) used this technique to investigate the different meanings people have for *rebelliousness*. It is this latest use of the method that has produced a resurgence of interest, with other areas being investigated including *maturity* (Stenner & Marshall, 1999) and *jealousy* (Stenner & Stainton Rogers, 1988).

Criticisms of Q-methodology

Sometimes the people doing the sorting are forced to sort the statements according to a certain pattern. For example, they may be told how many statements can be given the score 1, how many 2 and so on throughout the scale. A typical pattern would be so that the piles of statements formed a normal distribution (see Chapter 9 for an explanation of this term). A second criticism is over the statistical techniques that are applied to Q-methodology. As you will see in the relevant chapters on data analysis, certain techniques, such as analysis of variance (see Chapter 16) or factor analysis (see Chapter 21), are looking at the pattern of data across a number of people. However, some users of Q-methodology use such statistical techniques on data derived from a single person or to find clusters of people with similar sortings rather than clusters of statements that are similar.

Taking these criticisms into consideration, it would be best to use Q-methodology for exploratory purposes rather than to place too much faith in the statistical techniques that have been applied to it; in fact, that is how Stainton Rogers and his co-workers have been using it (see Stainton Rogers, 1995).

The semantic differential

Osgood, Suci and Tannenbaum (1957) devised the semantic differential as a way of exploring a person's way of thinking about some entity or, as they put it, of measuring meaning quantitatively. An example they give is investigating how people view politicians. They suggested that there is a semantic space with many dimensions, in which a person's meaning for a given entity (e.g. a politician) will lie. They contrasted their method with other contemporary ones in that theirs was explicitly multi-dimensional, while others involved only one dimension.

Participants are given a list of bipolar adjective pairs such as *good–bad, fast–slow, active--passive, dry–wet, sharp–dull* and *hard–soft* and are asked to rate the entities (the politicians), one at a time, on a 7-point scale—1 for *good* and 7 for *bad*—for each of the adjective pairs. They recommend the following layout:

Margaret Thatcher

fair								X	unfair
fast	X								slow
active	X								passive

The person making the ratings puts a cross in the open-topped box that seems most appropriate for that entity for each adjective pair.

Semantic differentiation is the process of placing a concept within the semantic space by rating it on each of the bipolar adjective pairs. The difference in meaning between two concepts can be seen by where they are placed in the semantic space. The responses for a given person or a group of people are analysed to see whether they form any patterns (factors). A common pattern is for the ratings to form three dimensions: *evaluation*, e.g. *clean–dirty*; *potency*, e.g. *strong–weak*; and *activity*, e.g. *fast–slow*.

The particular set of bipolar adjective pairs that are useful will depend on the particular study. Osgood et al. (1957) note that *beautiful–ugly* may be irrelevant when rating a presidential candidate but *fair–unfair* may be relevant, while for rating paintings the reverse is likely to be true. They provide a list of 50 adjective pairs.

The semantic differential can be used for a number of purposes: to explore an individual's attitudes, say to a political party; to compare individuals to see what differences existed between people in the meanings that entities had for them; or to evaluate change after a therapy or after an experimental manipulation.

The results of the ratings gleaned from using the semantic differential can be analysed via multi-dimensional scaling (MDS, see Chapter 21). Osgood and Luria (1954) applied the method to a famous case of a patient who had been diagnosed with multiple personality. They looked at sortings from the three 'personalities' taken at two times separated by a period of two months to see how they differed and how they changed over time.

Repertory grids

Kelly (1955) developed a number of techniques that allow investigators or therapists to explore an individual's meanings and associations. For example, they could be used to explore how a smoker views smoking, by looking at how he or she views smokers and non-smokers and people who are not identified as either. The techniques stem from Kelly's personal construct theory, in which he views individuals as thinking in similar ways to scientists in that they build up a mental model of the world in which *elements* (for example, people) are categorised according to the presence or absence of certain *constructs* (for example, likeableness).

A repertory grid typically involves asking an individual to think of two people (for example, the person's parents) and to think of one way in which they are similar. That similarity then forms the first construct in the grid. The nature of the constructs that people provide says something about them, as this shows what is salient to them, what bases they use to classify aspects of their world, in this case, people. They could use psychological constructs such as *nice*, or purely physical ones such as *old*. After providing the first construct, the person will be asked to consider a third person (say, a sibling) and think of a way in which this third person differs from the previous two. If this entails a new construct then this is added to the grid. This process is continued until a set of elements is created and each is evaluated on each construct. The way the elements are perceived in terms of the constructs is analysed to look for patterns using techniques such as cluster analysis (see Chapter 21). Repertory grids can be used in a therapeutic setting to see how a patient views the world and how that view changes during therapy. Alternatively, it could be used for research purposes to see how a particular group is viewed, for example, how blind people are thought of by those who do not have a visual impairment. For an account of the use of repertory grids and other aspects of personal construct theory, as used in clinical psychology, see Winter (1992).

Facet theory

Another approach that had early origins but has shown a relatively recent resurgence of interest is facet theory. It was developed by Guttman in the 1950s but has been taken up by others wishing to explore the meanings and ways of structuring the elements in such diverse domains as intelligence, fairness, colour or even criminal behaviour. The Guttman scale, described earlier, can be seen as the simplest way in which people conceptualise a domain, i.e. on a single dimension. More complex conceptions take into account the multi-dimensional nature of much of what we think about. Thus, intelligence could be thought of as ranging from low intelligence to high intelligence, while more complex conceptions would include the type of task—numerical, spatial, verbal or social. Greater complexity still would be taken into account if types of tasks were separated into those where a rule is being identified, those where one is being recalled and those where a rule is being applied. A final layer of complexity would come if we allowed for the 'mode of expression' such as whether the task were performed by the manipulation of objects or by pencil and paper tests. Although the two-dimensional structures can be analysed using standard statistical software, for example Multiple Dimensional Scaling in SPSS (see Chapter 21), more complex structures involve specialist software (see Shye, Elizur & Hoffman, 1994).

Summary

Multi-item scales are preferred for assessing people's attitudes because they are more reliable than single questions that are designed to assess the same attitude. Such scales require the creation of a large number of items that have to be evaluated on a reasonable sample of people before they are used in research. You should never devise a set of questions to measure an attitude and use it without having conducted an analysis of the items to see whether they do form a scale. The most popular scale at present is the Likert scale. Psychologists also use a number of other means to assess what people think of aspects of their lives; in particular, what such things mean to people.

The next chapter deals with observing people's behaviour.

7 OBSERVATION AND CONTENT ANALYSIS

Introduction

The present chapter describes two methods that, on the surface, may not appear the same but in fact entail similar problems and similar solutions. Observation tends to be thought of in the context of noting the behaviour of people, while content analysis is usually associated with analysing text. However, given that one can observe behaviour that has been videoed and that content analysis has been applied to television adverts, the distinctions between the two methods can become blurred. In fact, as was pointed out in Chapter 2, all psychological research can be seen as being based on the observation and measurement of behaviour—whether it involves overt movement, language or physiological states—for we cannot directly observe thought. Nonetheless, I will restrict the meaning of observation, in this chapter, to the observation of some form of movement or speech.

Both observation and content analysis can be conducted qualitatively or quantitatively. I am going to concentrate on the quantitative approach but many of the methodological points made in this chapter should guide someone conducting qualitative research. Because of the overlap between the two methods I will start by describing observation, then look at aspects of research that are common to the two methods. I will describe a form of structured observation and, finally, look at content analysis, including the use of diaries and logs as sources of data.

Observation

When applicable

There are a number of situations in which we might want to conduct an observation. Usually, it will be when there is no accurate verbal report available. One such occasion would be when the people being studied had little or no language, such as young children. Alternatively, we might wish to observe behaviour that occurs without the person producing it being aware of what he or she is doing, as in much non-verbal communication, such as making eye-contact. Another area worth exploring is where researchers are interested in problem solving. Experts, such as doctors who, when attempting to diagnose diseases, often do not follow the path of reasoning that they were taught but when asked to describe the procedure they use will report the method they were originally taught. Observation would help to clarify the stages such diagnosis takes.

A fourth situation in which it would be appropriate to use observation would be when participants may wish to present themselves in a favourable light, such as people who are prejudiced against an ethnic minority and might not admit how they would behave towards members of that minority group. However, even if accurate verbal reports are available it would be worth conducting observation to complement such reports.

Types of observation

There are numerous ways in which observations can be classified. One way is based on the degree to which the observer is part of the behaviour being observed. This can range from the *complete participant*, whose role as an observer might be hidden from the other participants, to the *complete observer*, who does not participate at all and whose role is also kept from the people who are being observed. An example of the first could be a researcher who covertly joins an organisation to observe it from within. The second could involve watching people in a shopping centre to see how they utilise the space. Between these two extremes are a number of gradations. One is the *participant-as-observer*, which, as the name suggests, involves researchers taking part in the activity to be observed but revealing that they are researchers. The complete participant and the participant-as-observer are sometimes described as doing ethnographic research.

Next in distance from direct participation is the *marginal participant*. Researchers might have taken steps, such as wearing particular clothing, in order to be unobtrusive. Next comes the *observer-as-participant*. Researchers would reveal the fact that they were observing but not participate directly in the action being observed. Such a classification makes the important point that the presence of researchers can have an effect on others' behaviour and so, at some level, most observers are participating.

Another way in which types of observation are classified relates to the level at which the behaviour is being observed and recorded. *Molar* behaviour refers to larger-scale behaviour such as greeting a person who enters the room; this level of observation can involve interpretation by the observer as to the nature of the behaviour. On the other hand, *molecular* behaviour refers to the components that make up molar behaviour, and is less likely to involve interpretation. For example, a molecular description of the behaviour described earlier as greeting a person who enters the room might be described thus: 'extends hand to newcomer; grips newcomer's hand and shakes it; turns corners of mouth up and makes eye-contact, briefly; lets go of newcomer's hand'.

A further way of classifying observation depends on the degree to which the nature of the observation is predetermined. This can range from what is termed *informal* or *casual* observation to *formal* or *systematic* observation. In informal observation the researchers might note what strikes them as being of interest at the time; this approach may often be a precursor to systematic observation and will be used to get a feel for the range of possible behaviours. In systematic observation, researchers may be looking for specific aspects of behaviour with the view to testing hypotheses.

A final way to view types of observation is according to the theoretical perspectives of the researchers. *Ethology*—the study of animals and humans in their natural setting—is likely to entail observation of more molecular behaviour and use little interpretation. *Structured* observation may use more interpretation and observe more molar behaviour. *Ethnography* may entail more casual observation and interpretation, as well as introspection on the part of the observer. Those employing *ecological* observation will be interested in the context and setting in which the behaviour occurred and will be interested in inferring the meanings and intentions of the participants.

The use of words such as *may* and *likely* in the previous paragraph comes from my belief that none of these ways of classifying observation is describing mutually exclusive ways of conducting observation. Different ways are complementary and may be used by the same researchers, in a form of triangulation. Alternatively, different approaches may form different stages in a single piece of research, as suggested earlier.

Gaining access

If you are going to observe a situation that does not have public access—for example, a school, a prison, a mental institution or a company—you have an initial hurdle to overcome: gaining access to the people carrying out their daily tasks. If you are going to be totally covert then you will probably have to join the institution by the same means that the other members joined it. Before choosing to be totally covert you should consider the ethical issues involved (see Chapter 1). On the other hand, you can gain access without revealing to everyone what your intentions are if you take someone in the organisation into your confidence. However, even if you are going to be completely open about your role as a researcher you are going to need someone who will help introduce you and give your task some legitimacy.

Beware of becoming too identified with that person; people may not like that person or may worry about what you might reveal to that person and this may colour their behaviour towards you.

You will need to reassure people about your aims. This may involve modifying what you say so that they are not put unnecessarily on their guard or even made hostile. Think whether you need to tell school teachers that, as a psychologist, you are trying to compare teachers' approaches to teaching mathematics with the recommendations of theorists. It might be better to say that you are interested in the way teachers teach this particular subject and in their opinions. I am not advocating deceit; what you are saying is true, but if you present your full brief the teachers may behave and talk to you in a way that conforms to what they think you ought to hear rather than reflecting what they really do. It is worth stressing the value, to them, of any research you are doing; guarantee confidentiality so that individuals will not be identified and show your willingness to share your findings with them; do keep such promises.

Methods of recording

The ideal method of recording what is observed is one that is both unobtrusive and preserves as much of the original behaviour as possible. An unobtrusive measure will minimise the effect of the observer on the participants, for there is little point in having a perfect record of behaviour that lacks ecological validity because the participants have altered their behaviour as a consequence of being observed. Equally, there is little point in observing behaviour that is thoroughly ecologically valid if you cannot record what you want. In the right circumstances, video cameras linked to a good sound recording system can provide the best of these two worlds.

It is possible to have a purpose-built room with cameras and microphones that can be controlled from a separate room. Movements of the camera such as changes in focus and angle need to be as silent as possible, and with modern cameras this can be achieved. Video provides a visual record which can be useful, even if the research is concentrating on language, because it can put the language in context. Having the cameras as near the ceiling as possible minimises their salience but means that a good-sized room is required so that more is recorded than just a view of people's heads.

A single camera can mean that, unless the people being observed have been highly constrained as to where they can place themselves, what is observed may be only part of the action. A combination of two or three cameras can minimise the number of blind spots in a room. It is possible to record the images from more than one camera directly onto a single video tape. This allows researchers to see the faces of two people conversing face-to-face, or to observe a single individual both in close-up and from a distance.

Apart from the advantages just given, video allows researchers to view the same piece of behaviour many times. In this way, the same behaviour can be observed at a number of different levels and it allows researchers to concentrate, on different occasions, on different aspects of the behaviour. It also allows a measure of elapsed time to be recorded on the tape, which helps in sampling and in noting the duration of certain behaviours. A further advantage is that the tape can be played at different speeds so that behaviours that occur for a very short duration can be detected. Video also allows the reliability of measures to be checked more easily.

There are many reasons why you may not be able to use the purpose-built laboratory. However, even with field research you can use a hand-held camera or a camera on a tripod. Fortunately, people tend to habituate to the presence of a camera or an audio tape-recorder if it is not too obtrusive. If people are hesitant about allowing themselves to be recorded, allow them to say when they want the recording device switched off and reassure them about the use to which the recordings will be put. Nonetheless, there will be situations in which you cannot take recordings in the field, such as when you are observing covertly or when you have been denied permission to record. Under these circumstances you have a problem of selectivity and of when to note down what has happened.

If you are trying to achieve a more impressionistic observation then you may need to take comparatively frequent breaks during which to write down your observations; you obviously have problems over relying on your memory and over being able to check on reliability. Even if you have taken notes, you need time to expand on them as soon as possible after the event. If you want a more formal observation, it would be advisable to create a checklist of behaviour in the most convenient form for noting down the occurrence and, if required, the duration of relevant behaviour. Under the latter circumstances you may be able to check the reliability of that particular set of observations by having a second observer using the checklist at the same time. Alternatively, you should at least check the general reliability of the checklist by having two or more observers use it while they are observing some relevant behaviour. More information can be noted by using multiple observers so that each concentrates on different aspects of behaviour or monitors different people.

Issues shared between observation and content analysis

As has been emphasised in earlier chapters, we need to be confident that our measures are both reliable and valid. In observation and content analysis these issues can be particularly problematic as we may start to employ more subjective measures. For example, in both methods we may wish to classify speech or text as being humorous or sarcastic. In order that others can use our classificatory system we will need to operationalise how we define these concepts. However, in so doing we have to be careful that we do not produce a reliable measure that lacks validity.

The categories in the classificatory system need to be mutually exclusive— that is, a piece of behaviour cannot be placed in more than one category.

Once you have devised a classificatory system, it should be written down, with examples, and another researcher should be trained in its use. Then, using a new episode of behaviour or piece of text, you will need to check the inter-rater reliability—that is, the degree to which raters, working separately, agree on their classification of behaviour or text. If the agreement is poor then the classificatory system will need to be refined and differences between raters negotiated. See Chapter 19 for ways to quantify reliability and for what constitutes an acceptable level of agreement.

There is always a problem of observer or rater bias, where the rater allows his or her knowledge to affect the judgements. This can be lessened if they are blind to any hypotheses the researchers may have, and also to the particular condition being observed. For example, if researchers were comparing participants given alcohol with those given a placebo they should not tell the raters which condition a given participant was in, or even what the possible conditions were. In addition, raters need to be blind to the judgements of other raters.

Another problem can be observer drift where, possibly through boredom, reliability worsens over time. Raters are likely to remain more vigilant and reliable if they think that a random sample of their ratings will be checked.

Transcribing

A disadvantage of video, and to a lesser extent of audio tape, is the vast amount of information to be sifted through. This can be very time-consuming. It can be tempting to hand the tapes over to someone else to transcribe into descriptions or more particularly the words spoken. While this may save time for the researchers and can help to provide a record that may be more convenient to peruse, it is a good idea to view and listen to the original tapes. Having the context in which behaviour and speech occurred and the intonation of the original speech is very useful. A compromise would be to have a transcription that you then annotate from your observations of the original recording.

Types of data

Firstly, you will probably draw up a list of categories and sub-categories of relevant behaviour. Then you need to decide whether you are going to record the frequency with which a particular behaviour occurs, its duration, or a combination of the two. In addition, you might be interested in particular sequences of events in order to look for patterns in the ways certain behaviours follow others. Even if you are simply interested in the frequency with which certain behaviour occurs, it can be worth putting this into different time frames to see whether there is a change over time. Also, with more subjective judgements you may want to get ratings of aspects such as degree of emotion.

Sampling

Sampling can be done on the basis of time or place as well as people. *Continuous real-time sampling* would be observing an entire duration. This can be very time-consuming and so there exist ways to select shorter durations from the complete duration. *Time point sampling* involves deciding on specific times and noting whether target behaviours are occurring then. This could be done on a regular basis or on a random basis. Alternatively, *time interval sampling* would be choosing periods of a fixed duration at selected stages in the overall duration and noting the frequency of target behaviours during the fixed durations.

You need to think about the different periods and settings you might want to sample. Thus, if studying student behaviour at university, researchers would probably want to observe lectures, tutorials, seminars, libraries, refectories and living accommodation. In addition, they would want to observe during freshers' week, at various times during each of the years, including during examination periods, and at graduation.

An example of systematic sampling for a content analysis of television adverts could be to get adverts that represented the output from the different periods during the day, such as breakfast television, daytime television, late afternoon and early evening programmes when mainly children will be watching, peak-time viewing and late at night. The random approach could involve picking a certain number of issues from the previous year of a magazine, randomly, on the basis of their issue number. See Chapter 11 for a discussion of random selection.

Structured observation

A widely used form of structured observation is interaction process analysis (IPA) which was devised by Bales (1950).

Bales's interaction process analysis

This can be used to look at the dynamics in a small group in order to identify the different styles of interaction that are adopted by the members of the group. For example, different types of leader may emerge—those who are predominantly focused on the task and those who are concentrating on group cohesiveness. In addition, the period of the interaction can be sub-divided so that changes in behaviour over time can be sought. A checklist of behaviours is used for noting down particular classes of behaviour, who made them and to whom they were addressed, including whether they were to the whole group. The behaviours fall into four general categories: positive, negative, asking questions and providing answers. If the study is being conducted live, ideally there would be as many observers as participants, while more observers still would allow some check on inter-rater reliability.

Content analysis

Content analysis can be seen as a non-intrusive form of observation, in that the observer is not present when the actions are being performed but is analysing the traces left by the actions. It usually involves analysing text such as newspaper articles or the transcript of a speech or conversation. However, it can be conducted on some other medium such as television adverts or even the amount of wear suffered by particular books in a library or areas of carpet in an art gallery. It can be conducted on recent material or on more historical material such as early text books on a subject or personal diaries.

A typical content analysis might involve looking at the ways people represent themselves and the people they are seeking through adverts in lonely hearts columns of a magazine. The analyst could be investigating whether males and females differ in the approaches they adopt and the words they use. For example, do males concentrate on their own wealth and possessions but refer to the physical attributes of the hoped-for partner? Do males and females make different uses of humour? The categories being sought could be derived from a theory of how males and females are likely to behave or from a preliminary look at a sample of adverts to see what the salient dimensions are. Once the categories had been defined, such an analysis could involve counting the numbers of males and females who deploy particular styles in their adverts.

Another example of a content analysis was conducted by Manstead and McCulloch (1981). They analysed advertisements that had been shown on British television to see whether males and females were being represented differently. To begin with they identified, where possible, the key male and female characters. Then they classified the adverts according to the nature of the product being sold and the roles in the adverts played by males and females—whether as imparters or receivers of information.

Diaries and logs

An important source of material for a content analysis can be diaries or logs. These can range from diaries written spontaneously, either for the writer's own interest or for publication, to a log kept according to a researcher's specification. In the latter case they are sometimes indistinguishable from a questionnaire that is completed on more than one occasion. The frequency with which entries are made can also range widely, from more than once a day at regular intervals, through being triggered by a particular event such as a conversation, to being sampled randomly, possibly on receipt of a signal generated by a researcher. The duration of the period studied can range from one week to many years.

Diaries and logs can be used in many contexts. They can be used to generate theory such as by Reason and Lucas (1984, cited in Baddeley, 1990) who looked at slips of memory, such as getting out the keys for a door at work when approaching a door at home, while Young, Hay and Ellis (1985) looked at errors in recognising people. The technique can be used to investigate people's dreams, to find the baseline of a type of behaviour, such as obsessional hand-washing or amount of exercise taken by people, it can look at social behaviour in couples or groups, and can look at consumer behaviour such as types of purchases made or television viewing.

It has certain advantages over laboratory-based methods in that it can be more ecologically valid and can allow researchers to study behaviour across a range of settings and under circumstances that it would be either difficult or ethically questionable to create such as subjecting participants to stress. It doesn't have to rely on a person's memory as much as would a method where a person was interviewed at intervals. In this way, less salient events will be recorded rather than being masked by more salient ones and the order of events will be more accurately noted. It is particularly useful for plotting change over time, for example in degrees of pain suffered by a client, and there won't be a tendency for the average to be reported across a range of experiences.

Disadvantages include, among others, the fact that participants are likely to be highly self-selected, that because it may be onerous people may drop out, that they may forget to complete it on occasions, that the person may be more sensitised to the entity being recorded such as their experience of pain. Finally there is the cost.

Ways have been found to lessen a number of the drawbacks and what is appropriate will depend on the nature of the task and the duration of the study. These include: interviewing potential participants to establish a rapport and so reduce self-selection; explaining the nature of the task thoroughly; giving small, regular rewards, such as a lottery ticket; keeping in touch by sending a birthday card, counteracting forgetting by phoning to remind, supplying a pager and paging the person, or even having a pre-programmed device that sends out a signal, such as a sound or vibration when the data is due to be recorded; making the task as easy as possible by supplying a printed booklet and even a pen; making contact with the researchers as easy as possible by supplying contact numbers and e-mail addresses; making submission of the data as straightforward as possible such as by supplying stamped addressed envelopes, collecting the material or telephoning for it. It is important not to try to counter the cost by trying to squeeze too much out of the research; by making the task more onerous the likelihood of self-selection and dropout are increased.

Summary

Observation and content analysis are two non-experimental methods that look at behaviour. In the case of observation the observer is usually present when the action occurs and the degree to which participants are aware of the observer's presence and intentions can vary. On the other hand, content analysis is conducted on the product of the action, including data from diaries or logs, with the analyst not being present when the action is performed. Both can involve the analyst in devising a system for classifying the material being analysed. Therefore, both need to have the validity and reliability of such classificatory systems examined.

The next part, Chapters 8 to 22, deals with the data collected in research and how they can be analysed.

PART 4
Data and analysis

Scales of Measurement

Introduction

Chapter 2 discussed the different forms of measurement that are used by psychologists. In addition, it emphasised the need to check that the measures are valid and reliable. The present chapter shows how all the measures psychologists make can be classified under four different scales. It contrasts this with the way that statisticians refer to scales. The consequences of using a particular scale of measurement are discussed.

Examples of measures

The following questions produce answers that differ in the type of measurement they involve. Before moving on to the next section look at the questions and see whether you can find differences in the type and precision of information that each answer provides.

1. Gender: Female or Male?
2. What is your mother's occupation?
3. How tall are you? (in centimetres)
4. How old are you? (in years)

   10–19   20–29   30–39   40–49   50–59

5. What is your favourite colour?
6. What daily newspaper do you read?
7. How many brothers have you?
8. What is your favourite non-alcoholic drink?
9. Do you eat meat?
10. How many hours do you like to sleep per night?
11. What colour are your eyes?
12. How many units of alcohol do you drink per week?
    (1 unit = half a pint of beer, a measure of spirit or a glass of wine)
13. Is your memory:

well above average	above average	average	below average	well below average

14. How old is your father?
15. At what room temperature (in degrees Celsius) do you feel comfortable?
16. What is your current yearly income?

Scales of measurement

There are four scales that are used to describe the measures we can take. Read the descriptions of the four scales below and then try to classify the 16 questions above into the four scales. The answers are given at the end of the next section.

Nominal

The nominal scale of measurement is used to describe data that comprise simply names or categories (hence another name for this level of measurement: *categorical*). Thus, the answer to the question: *Do you live in university accommodation?* is a form of nominal data; there are two categories: those who do live in university accommodation and those who don't. Nominal data are not only binary (or dichotomous) data, that is, data where there are only two possible answers. The answer to the question *How do you travel to the university?* is also nominal data.

Ordinal

The ordinal scale, as its name implies, refers to data that can be placed in an order. For example, the classifications of university degrees into 1st, 2(i), 2(ii) and 3rd forms an ordinal scale.

Interval

The interval scale includes data that tell you more than simply an order; it tells you the degree of difference between two scores. For example, if you are told the temperature, in degrees Fahrenheit, of two different rooms, you know not only that one is warmer than the other but by how much.

Ratio

The ratio scale, like the interval scale, gives you information about the magnitude of differences between the things you are measuring. However, it has the additional property that the data should have a true zero; in other words, zero means the property being measured has no quantity. For example, weight in kilograms is on a ratio scale. This can be confusing as, when asking for a person's weight, he or she cannot sensibly reply that it is zero kilograms. Zero kilograms would mean that there was no weight. The reason why temperature in Fahrenheit is on an interval and not a ratio scale is because zero degrees Fahrenheit is a measurable temperature. Hence, with a ratio scale, because there is a fixed starting point for the measure, we can talk about the ratio of two entities measured on that scale. For example, if we are comparing two people's height—one of 100 centimetres and another of 200 centimetres—we can say that the first person is half the height of the second. With temperature, as there is no fixed starting point for the scale, it is not true to say that 40 degrees Celsius is half 80 degrees Celsius.

The point can be made by converting the scale into a different form of units to see whether the ratio between two points remains the same. If the height example is changed to inches, where every inch is the equivalent of 2.54 centimetres and zero centimetres is the same as zero inches, the shorter person is 39.37 inches tall and the taller person is 78.74 inches tall. The conversion has not changed the ratio between the two people: the first person is half the height of the second person. However, if we convert the temperatures from Celsius to Fahrenheit, we get 104 degrees and 176 degrees respectively. Notice that the first temperature is now clearly not half the second one. Fortunately, for any reader who may still not understand the distinction between interval and ratio scales, the statistics covered in this book treat ratio and interval data in the same way.

The relevance of the four scales

As you move from nominal towards ratio data you gain more information about what is being measured. For example, if you ask:

Do you smoke? (Yes/No)

you will get nominal data. If you ask:

Do you smoke:

>   *not at all?*
>   *between one and 10 cigarettes a day?*
>   *more than 10 cigarettes a day?*

you will get ordinal data that help you to distinguish, among those who do smoke, between heavier and lighter smokers. Finally, if you ask:

How many cigarettes do you smoke per day?

You will receive ratio data that tell you more precisely about how much people smoke. The important difference between these three versions of the question is that you can apply different statistical techniques depending on whether you have interval/ratio data, ordinal data or nominal data. The more information you can provide the more informative will be the statistics you can derive from it.

Accordingly, if you are provided with a measure that is on a ratio scale you will be throwing information away if you treat it as ordinal or nominal.

The following questions provide you with nominal data:

1. Gender: Female or Male?
2. What is your mother's occupation?
5. What is your favourite colour?
6. What daily newspaper do you read?
8. What is your favourite non-alcoholic drink?
9. Do you eat meat?
11. What colour are your eyes?

The following questions yield ordinal data:

4. How old are you?

10–19   20–29   30–39   40–49   50–59

13. Is your memory:

| well above average | above average | average | below average | well below average |

This last example can confuse people as they point out that the possible alternatives are simply names or categories, but you have to note that they form an order; a person who claims to have an above-average memory is claiming that his or her memory is better than someone with an average memory, someone with a below-average memory or someone with a well-below-average memory.

The following question is one of the few physical measures that gives interval but not ratio data:

15. At what room temperature (in degrees Celsius) do you feel comfortable?

The following questions would give you ratio data:

3. How tall are you? (in centimetres)
7. How many brothers have you?
10. How many hours do you like to sleep per night?
12. How many units of alcohol do you drink per week?
(1 unit = half a pint of beer, a measure of spirit or a glass of wine)
14. How old is your father?
16. What is your current yearly income?

Indicators

An additional consideration over the level of a particular measurement is how it is to be used—what it is indicating. It has already been pointed out that psychologists rarely have direct measures of that which they wish to observe. This can be particularly so if they are dealing with something, such as socio-economic status, which they may be attempting to define. Measures such as years in education or income are at the ratio level but when used to indicate socio-economic status, they may be merely ordinal because the same-sized difference in income will mean different things at different points on the scale. Thus, a person earning £20,000 per year is much better off than someone who is earning £10,000, whereas a person earning £260,000 a year is not that much better paid than a person earning £250,000. The previous example showed that an absolute increase will have different meaning at different points on the scale. However, even the same ratio increase can have different meanings at different points on the scale. A 10% increase for people on £10,000 is likely to be more important to them, and may lead them to be classified in a different socio-economic group, than a 10% increase will be for a person on £250,000. Another example of how a scale's level of measurement depends on what it is being used to indicate is mother's occupation. If you wanted to put the occupations in an order on the basis, say, of status, then you would have converted the data into an ordinal scale. However, if you did not have an order then they remain on a nominal scale.

Pedhazur and Schmelkin (1991) point out that few measures that psychologists use are truly on a ratio scale even though they appear to have a true zero. As an example of this, if we create a test of mathematical ability and a person scores zero on it we cannot conclude that they have no knowledge of mathematics. Therefore, we cannot talk meaningfully about the ratio of maths ability of two people on the basis of this test.

Statisticians and scales

Statisticians tend to classify numerical scales into three types: continuous, discrete and dichotomous. The distinction between continuous and discrete can be illustrated by two types of clock. An analogue clock—one with hands that go round to indicate the time—gives time on a continuous scale because it is capable of indicating every possible time. The digital clock, however, chops time up into equal units and when one unit has passed, it indicates the next unit but does not indicate the time in between the units—it gives time on a discrete scale. The distinction between a continuous and a discrete scale can become blurred. The clock examples can be used to illustrate this point. Unless the analogue clock is particularly large, it will be difficult to make very fine measurements; it may only be usable to give time in multiples of seconds, whereas a digital clock may give very precise measurement so that it can be used to record time in milliseconds.

Dichotomous refers to a variable that can have only two values, such as yes or no. Another term for dichotomous is 'binary'.

Return to the 16 questions given at the beginning of the chapter and try to identify those that could be classified as continuous, discrete or dichotomous.

The following questions yield answers that are measured on a continuous scale (as long as they are interpreted as allowing that level of precision):

 3. How tall are you? (in centimetres)
10. How many hours do you like to sleep per night?
12. How many units of alcohol do you drink per week?
    (1 unit = half a pint of beer, a measure of spirit or a glass of wine)
14. How old is your father?
15. At what room temperature (in degrees Celsius) do you feel comfortable?
16. What is your current yearly income?

The following questions yield answers which are on a discrete scale:

 2. What is your mother's occupation?
 4. How old are you? (in years)

         10–19   20–29   30–39   40–49   50–59

 5. What is your favourite colour?
 6. What daily newspaper do you read?
 7. How many brothers have you?
 8. What is your favourite non-alcoholic drink?
11. What colour are your eyes?
13. Is your memory:

well above average	above average	average	below average	well below average

The following questions yield answers that are on a dichotomous scale:

 1. Gender: Female or Male?
 9. Do you eat meat?

Psychologists fall into at least two camps—those who apply the nominal, ordinal or interval/ratio classification of measures to decide what statistics to employ, and those who prefer to follow the statisticians' classificatory system. However, both systems need to be taken into account. As you will see in Chapter 14, there are other important criteria that indicate which version of a statistical procedure to employ. My feeling is that both ways of classifying the scales are valid and we can follow the statisticians' advice as far as choice of statistical test is concerned, but we must be aware of what the measures mean—what they indicate—and therefore what we can meaningfully conclude from the results of statistical analysis. In addition, as will be seen in the next chapter, when we wish to summarise the data we have collected, the scale that they are on determines what are sensible ways of presenting the information.

Summary

There are two approaches to the classification of scales of measurement. Psychologists tend to describe four scales: nominal, ordinal, interval and ratio. Each provides a certain level of information, with nominal providing the least and ratio the most. For the purposes of the statistical techniques described in this book, interval and ratio scales of measurement can be treated as the same. Statisticians prefer to talk of continuous, discrete and dichotomous scales. Both classificatory systems need to be considered. A further consideration that determines how a measure should be classified is what it is being used to indicate. The scale of a measure has an effect on the type of statistics that can be employed on that measure.

The next chapter introduces the ways in which data can be described, both numerically and graphically.

9 SUMMARISING AND DESCRIBING DATA

Introduction

The first phase of data analysis is the production of a summary of the data. This way of describing the data can be done numerically or graphically. It is particularly useful because it can show whether the results of research are in line with the researcher's hypotheses. Statisticians see an increasing importance for this stage and have described it as exploratory data analysis (EDA) (see Tukey, 1977). Psychologists have tended to under-use EDA as a stage in their analysis.

Numerical methods

Ratio, interval or ordinal data

Measures of central tendency

When you have collected data about participants you will want to produce a summary that will give an impression of the results for the participants you have studied. Imagine that you have given a group of 15 adults a list of 100 words and you have asked each person to recall as many of the words as he or she can. The recall scores are as follows:

3, 7, 5, 9, 4, 6, 5, 7, 8, 11, 10, 7, 4, 6, 8

This is a list of what are termed the *raw data*. As it stands it provides little information about the phenomenon being studied. The reader could scan the raw data and try to get a feel for what they are like but it is more useful to use some form of summary statistic or graphical display to present the data. This is even truer when there are even more data points.

The most common type of summary statistic is one that tries to present some sort of central value for the data. This is often termed an *average*. However, there is more than one average; the three most common are given below.

Mean

The mean is what people often think of when they use the term 'average'. It is found by adding the scores together and dividing the answer by the number of scores. To find the mean recall of the group of 15 participants, you would add the 15 recall scores, giving a total of 100, and then divide the result by 15, which gives a mean of 6.667. Statisticians use lower-case letters from the English alphabet to symbolise statistics that have been calculated from a sample. The most common symbol for the mean of a sample is $\bar{x}$. However, the APA (American Psychological Association, 2001) recommend using M to symbolise the mean in the reports of research.

Median

The median is the value that is in the middle of all the values. Thus, to find the median recall of the group of 15 participants, put the recall scores in order.

Now count up to the person with the eighth best recall (the person who has as many people with recall that is poorer than or as good as his or hers as there are people with recall that is as good or better). That person's recall is the median recall for the group. In this case, the median recall is 7. If there

Table 9.1 The number of words recalled by participants, in rank order

order	recall	
1	3	
2	4	
3	4	
4	5	
5	5	
6	6	
7	6	
8	7	← Median
9	7	
10	7	
11	8	
12	8	
13	9	
14	10	
15	11	

is an even number of people then there will be no one person in the middle of the group. In such a case, the median will lie between the half with the lowest recall and the half with the highest recall. Take the mean of the person with the best recall of the lower half of the group and the person who has the poorest recall of the upper half of the group. That value is the median for the group. If a person with a score of below 7 was added to the 15 scores shown in Table 9.1 then the median would be between the current 7th and 8th ranks at 6.5. However, if a person with a score of 7 or more was added to the 15 then the median would be between the current 8th and 9th ranks at 7.

Mode

The mode is the most frequently occurring value among your participants. In Table 9.1 the most frequently occurring recall score was 7. As with the median, the mode can best be identified by putting the scores in order of magnitude.

The relative merits of the measures of central tendency

The mean is the most common measure of central tendency used by psychologists. This is probably for three reasons. Its calculation takes into account all the values of the data. It is used in many statistical tests, as you will see in future chapters. It can be used in conjunction with other measures to give an impression of what range of scores most people will have obtained.

Nonetheless, the mean has at least two disadvantages. Firstly, far from representing the whole group it may represent no one in the group. The point can be made most clearly when the mean produces a value that is not possible: for example, when you are told that the average family has 2.4 children. Thus, we have to accept that the central point as represented by a mean is *mathematically* central. A value has been produced that is on a continuous scale whereas the original measure—number of children—was on a discrete scale.

A second, more serious, problem with the mean is that it can be affected by one score that is very different from the rest. For example, if the mean recall for a group of 15 people is 6.667 words and another person, whose recall is 100 words, is also sampled, then the mean for the new group will now be 12.5. This is higher than all but one of the group and therefore does not provide a useful summary statistic.

Ways have been devised to deal with such an effect. Firstly, the trimmed mean can be calculated whereby the more extreme scores have been left out of the calculation. Different versions of the trimmed mean exist. The simplest involves removing the highest and lowest scores. However, often the top and bottom 10% of scores are removed. This version can be symbolised as $\bar{x}_{10}$. Alternatively, such an unusual person may be identified as an *outlier* or an extreme score, and removed. Identifying possible outliers can be done by using a box plot (see below) or by other techniques given in Chapter 12.

The median, like the mean, may be a value that represents no one when there are an even number of participants involved. If the median recall for the group had been 7.5 words this would be a score that no member of the group had achieved. However, the median is not affected by extreme values. If the person who has recalled 100 words joins the group, the median will stay at 7, whereas the mean rises by over 5.5 words. Another way to deal with the effect of outliers on central tendency is to report the median rather than, or as well as, the mean.

The mode is rarely used by psychologists. It has at least three disadvantages, the first two of which refer to the fact that a single mode may not even exist. Firstly, if no two values are the same then there is no mode; for example, if all 15 people had different recall scores. Secondly, if there are two values that tie for having the most number of people, then again there is no single mode; for example, if in the sample of people, two had recalled 5 words and two 7 words. You may come across the terms *bi-modal*, which means having two modes, or *multi-modal*, which means having more than one mode. The third problem with the mode is that it can be severely unrepresentative when all but a very few values are different. For example, if in a sample of 100 people, with scores ranging from 1 to 100, all but two had different recall scores, but those two both recalled 99 words, then the mode would be 99, which could hardly be seen as a central value. If there is no mode then one strategy is to place the scores in ranges, e.g. 1 to 10 etc., and then find the range that has the highest number of scores: the modal range.

A measure of central tendency alone gives insufficient detail about the sample you are describing because the same value can be produced from very different sets of figures. For example, you can have two samples, each of which has a mean recall of 7, yet one could comprise people all of whose recall was 7, while the other sample may include a person with a recall of 3 and another with a recall of 11. Accordingly, it is useful to report some measure of this spread or dispersion of scores, to put the measure of central tendency in context.

Measures of spread or dispersion

Maxima and minima

If you report the largest value (the maximum) and the smallest value (the minimum) in the sample this can give an impression of the spread of that sample. Thus, if everyone in the sample recalled 7 words then the maximum and minimum would both be 7, while the wider-spread sample would have a maximum of 11 and a minimum of 3.

Range

An alternative way of expressing the maxima and minima is to subtract the minimum from the maximum to give the range of values. This figure allows for the fact that different samples can have similar ranges even though their maxima and minima differ. For example, one sample may have a maximum recall of 9 and a minimum recall of 1, whereas a second sample may have a maximum recall of 11 and a minimum recall of 3. By reporting their range you can make clear that they both have the same spread of 8 words.

Both range and maxima and minima still fail to summarise the group sufficiently, because they only deal with the extreme values. They fail to take account of how common those extremes are. Thus, one sample of 15 people could have one person with a recall of 3, one person with a recall of 11 and the remaining people all with the same recall of 7. This group would have the same maximum and minimum (and therefore, range) as another group in which the recall scores were more evenly distributed between 3 and 11.

The interquartile range

This is calculated by finding the score that is at the 25th percentile (in other words, the value of the score that is the largest of the bottom 25% of scores) and the score that is at the 75th percentile (the value of the score that is the largest of the bottom 75% of scores) and noting their difference. Referring to Table 9.1 we see that the 25th percentile is 5 and the 75th percentile is 8. Therefore the interquartile range is $8 - 5 = 3$. The interquartile range has the advantage that it is less affected by extreme scores than the range, which is calculated from the maximum and minimum.

Variance

The variance takes into account the degree to which the value for each person differs from the mean for the group. It is calculated by noting how much each score differs (or deviates) from the mean. I am going to use, as an example, the recall scores of a sample of five people.

Words recalled

1
2
3
4
5

The mean has to be calculated: $\bar{x} = 3$ words. Next we find the deviation of each score from the mean, by subtracting the mean from each score.

Words recalled	Deviation from the mean
1	−2
2	−1
3	0
4	1
5	2

Now we want to summarise the deviations. However, if we were to add the deviations we would get zero, and this will always be true for any set of numbers. A way to get around this is to square the deviations before adding them, because this gets rid of the negative signs:

Words recalled	Deviation from the mean	Squared deviation
1	−2	4
2	−1	1
3	0	0
4	1	1
5	2	4

Now when we add the squared deviations we get 10. To get the variance we now divide the sum of the squared deviations by the number of scores (5) and get a variance of 2.

A more evenly spread group will have a higher variance, because there will be more people whose recall differs from the mean. If two out of fifteen participants have recall scores of 3 and 11 words while the rest all recall 7 words then the variance is 2.134. On the other hand, the more evenly distributed sample shown in Table 9.1 has a variance of 4.889. The variance, like the mean, is used in many statistical techniques.

To confuse the issue, statisticians have noted that if they are trying to estimate, from the data they have collected, the variance for the population from which the participants came, then a more accurate estimate is given by dividing the sum of squared deviations by one fewer than the number in the sample. This version of the variance is the one usually given by computer programs and the one that is used in statistical tests. This version of the variance for the more evenly spread set of scores is thus 5.238.

Standard deviation

The standard deviation (s or SD) is directly linked to the variance because it is the square root of the variance; for this reason the variance of a sample is often represented as s^2. The usual standard deviation that is given by computer programs is derived from the variance that entailed dividing the sum of the squared deviations by one fewer than the number of scores, as it is also the best estimate of the population's standard deviation.

There are three reasons why the standard deviation is preferred over all the other measures of spread when summarising data. Firstly, like the variance, it is a measure of spread that relates to the mean. Thus, when reporting the mean it is appropriate to report the standard deviation. Secondly, the units in which the standard deviation are expressed are the same as the original measure. In other words, one can talk about the standard deviation of recall being 2.289 words for the more evenly spread set of scores. Thirdly, in certain circumstances, the standard deviation can be used to give an indication of the proportion of people in a population who fall within a given range of values. See Chapter 12 for a fuller explanation of this point.

Semi-interquartile range

When quoting a median the appropriate measure of spread is the semi-interquartile range (sometimes referred to as the 'quartile deviation'). This is the interquartile range divided by 2. In the example of the fifteen recall scores the semi-interquartile range is $\frac{3}{2} = 1.5$.

Nominal data

When dealing with variables that have levels in the form of categories, the numbers are frequencies: that is, the number of people who are in a particular category. For example, when we have found out how many people in a group are smokers, it makes little sense to use the techniques shown above to summarise the data. We can use a number of presentation methods that are based on the number of people who were in a given category. For example, we can simply report the number of smokers—say 10—and the number of non-smokers—say 15. Alternatively, we can express these figures as fractions, proportions or percentages.

Fractions

To find a fraction we find the total number of people—25—and express the number of smokers as a fraction of this total. Thus, 10 out of 25, or $\frac{10}{25}$, of the sample were smokers, and 15 out of 25, or $\frac{15}{25}$, were non-smokers. We can further simplify this, because 10, 15 and 25 are all divisible by 5. Accordingly, we can say that $\frac{2}{5}$ were smokers and $\frac{3}{5}$ were non-smokers.

Proportions

We can find proportions from fractions by converting the fractions to decimals. Thus, dividing 10 by 25 (or 2 by 5) tells us that 0.4 of the sample were smokers, while 15 divided by 25 (or 3 divided by 5) tells us that 0.6 of the sample were non-smokers. Notice that the proportions for all the subgroups should add up to 1: 0.4 + 0.6 = 1; this can be a check that the calculations are correct.

Percentages

To find a percentage multiply a proportion by 100. Thus, 40% of the sample were smokers and 60% were non-smokers. The percentages for all the subgroups should add up to 100.

Frequency distributions

If we have asked a sample of 120 people what their age group is we can represent it as a simple table:

Table 9.2 The frequency distribution of participants' ages

age (in years)	20–29	30–39	40–49	50–59	60–69
number of people	15	45	30	20	10

From this table the reader can see what the distribution of ages is within our sample.

Note that if we were presented with the data in this form and we wanted to calculate the mean or median we could not do so exactly as we only know the range of possible ages in which a person lies. The people in the 20–29 age group might all be 20 years old, 29 years old or evenly distributed within that age range. Techniques for calculating means and medians in such a situation are given in Appendix I.

Contingency tables

When the levels of the variables are nominal (or ordinal as in the last example) but two variables are being considered, the data can be presented as a contingency table. Imagine that we have asked 80 people—50 males and 30 females—whether they smoke.

Table 9.3 The distribution of smokers and non-smokers among males and females

	smokers	non-smokers
males	20	30
females	12	18

However, sometimes it is more appropriate, particularly for comparison across groups with unequal samples, to report proportions or percentages. Reporting the raw data that 20 males and 12 females were smokers makes comparison between the genders difficult. However, 20 out of 50 becomes $\frac{20}{50} = 0.4$ or 4 in 10, while 12 out of 30 becomes $\frac{12}{30} = 0.4$ or 4 in 10, as well. When it is expressed this way the reader can see that, despite the different sample sizes, there are equivalent proportions of smokers among the male and female samples.

Table 9.4 The percentage of smokers and non-smokers among males and females

	smokers	non-smokers	total
males	40%	60%	100%
females	40%	60%	100%

An additional advantage of reporting proportions or percentages is that the reader can quickly calculate the proportions or percentages who do not fall into a category. Thus 0.6 or 60% of males and 60% females in the sample did not smoke. When reporting percentages or proportions it is a good idea to report the original numbers, from which they were derived, as well.

There is a danger when using computers to analyse nominal data. It is usually necessary to code the data numerically, for example, smokers may be coded as 1 and non-smokers as 2. I have seen a number of people learning to analyse data who get the computer to provide means and SDs of these numbers. Thus, in the above example, they would find that the mean score of males was 1.6. Remember that these numbers are totally arbitrary ways to tell the computer which category a person was in—smokers could have been coded as 25 and non-smokers as 7—so it doesn't make sense to treat them as you would ordinal, interval or ratio data.

Graphical methods

There are many ways in which data can be summarised graphically. The advantage of a graphical summary is that it can convey aspects of the data, such as relative size, more immediately to the reader than the equivalent table. There are at least two disadvantages. Firstly, it is sometimes difficult to obtain the exact values from a graph. Secondly, the person who produces them often is unaware that some readers may not be used to the conventions that are involved in graphs. This can be less of a problem when they are in an article because the reader can spend time working out what is being represented. The main danger arises when they are used to illustrate a talk and listeners are given insufficient time to view them and insufficient explanation of the particular conventions being used. The first problem can be solved by providing both tables and graphs but some journals discourage this practice.

The majority of graphical displays of data use two dimensions, or axes, one for the values of the independent variable and one for the dependent variable. There is a convention that the vertical axis represents the dependent variable, while the horizontal axis represents the independent variable. Often there may be no obvious independent or dependent variable, in which case, place the variables on the axes in the way that makes most sense in the light of the convention. Thus, if I were creating a graph with age and IQ, although I might not think of age as affecting IQ, putting age on the horizontal axis would be more consistent with the convention than placing it on the vertical axis and by so doing possibly implying that age could be affected by IQ.

Plots of totals and subtotals

Bar charts

A bar chart can be used when the levels of the variable are categorical, as in the example of male and female smokers.

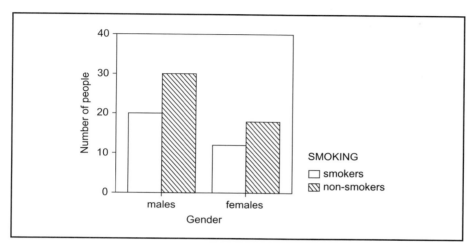

FIGURE 9.1 The number of smokers and non-smokers among males and females

Alternatively, with unequal sample sizes, a preferable method is to show the numbers of smokers and non-smokers in the same bar.

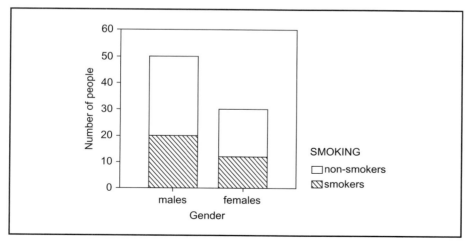

FIGURE 9.2 The number of smokers and non-smokers among males and females

Histograms

Histograms are similar to bar charts but the latter are for more discrete measures such as gender, while the former are for more continuous measures such as age. Nonetheless, histograms can be used when the variable is discrete, as in the example shown in Table 9.2 where age groups have been formed.

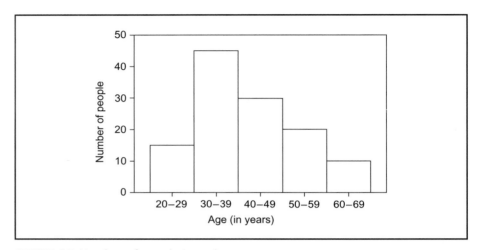

FIGURE 9.3 Number of people in each age group

Pie charts

The pie chart differs from most of the graphs in that it does not use axes but represents the subtotals as slices of a pie. See Appendix I for a description of how to calculate the amount of the pie for each category.

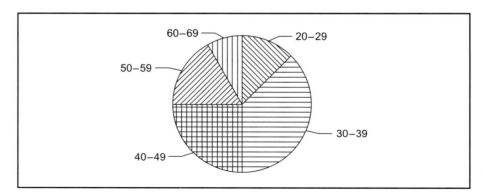

FIGURE 9.4 Number of people in each age group

Alternatively the areas could be expressed as percentages.

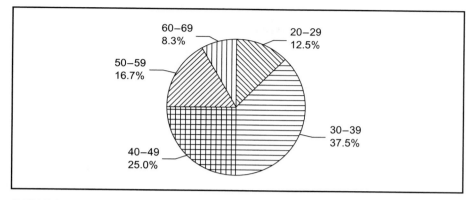

FIGURE 9.5 Percentage of people in each age group

It is possible to emphasise one or more subtotals by lifting them out of the pie.

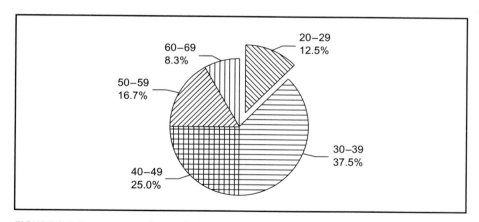

FIGURE 9.6 Percentage of people in each age group

It is also possible to show more than one set of data in separate pie charts so that readers can compare them.

FIGURE 9.7 Percentage of smokers and non-smokers among males and females

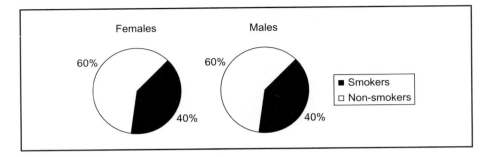

An added visual aid can come from representing the different numbers of participants in each pie by having a larger pie for a larger sample. One way to do this is to have the areas of the two pie charts in the same ratio as the two sample sizes (Appendix I shows how to calculate the appropriate relative area for a second pie chart).

FIGURE 9.8 Percentage of smokers and non-smokers among males and females

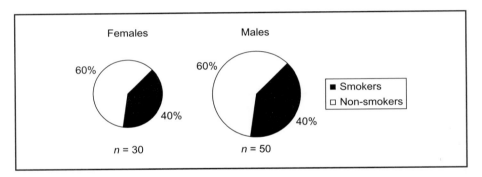

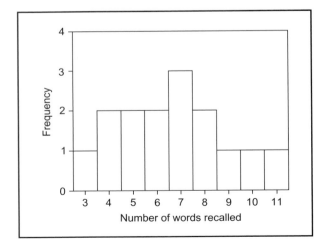

FIGURE 9.9 Frequency distribution of number of words recalled

Frequency distributions

A frequency distribution can be shown as a histogram that presents a picture of the number of participants who gave a particular score or a range of scores. The width of the bars can be chosen to give the level of precision required. Figure 9.9 shows the recall scores from Table 9.1, with the width of bar being such that each bar represents those who recalled a particular number of words. From Figure 9.9 we can see at a glance that 7 is the mode, that the mode is roughly in the middle of the spread of scores, that the minimum was 3 and the maximum 11. Figure 9.3 is a frequency distribution of age but the bars have widths of 10 years.

Stem-and-leaf plots

Stem-and-leaf plots are a variant of the histogram. Normally they are presented with the values of the variable (the stem) on the vertical axis and the frequencies (the leaves) on the horizontal axis. The recall scores for the 15 participants are plotted in Figure 9.10.

2	0
4	0000
6	00000
8	000
10	00

FIGURE 9.10 Stem-and-leaf plot of number of words recalled

The values on the stem give the first number in the range of scores contained in the leaf. In this version of a stem-and-leaf plot the 0s in the leaves simply denote the number of scores that fell in a particular range. Thus the 2 denotes that scores in the range 2 to 3 are contained on that leaf and the single 0 on the leaf shows that there was only one score in that range.

The nature of the stem can change depending on the distribution of scores. The plot when a 16th score of 25 and a 17th score of 15 are added is given in Figure 9.11.

0	344
0	5566777889
1	01
1	7
2	
2	5

FIGURE 9.11 Stem-and-leaf plot of number of words recalled (with two additional scores)

In this example, the distribution has been split into ranges of five figures: 0 to 4, 5 to 9 and so on. The plot assumes that all the numbers have two digits in them and so treats 3 as 03. The stem shows the first digit for each number. Accordingly, we can see that there are three scores in the range 0 to 4 and ten in the range 5 to 9. Also we can see that there were no scores in the range 20 to 24. The advantage of this version of the stem-and-leaf plot over the histogram is that we can read the actual scores from the stem-and-leaf plot, even when each stem is based on a broad range of scores, as in the last example. Note that, even when a part of the stem has no corresponding leaf, that part of the stem should still be shown (see Figure 9.11). SPSS adopts a slightly different convention, whereby it treats scores that are more than one-and-a-half times the interquartile range above and below the interquartile range as *extreme* scores and doesn't display them as was done in Figure 9.11. See Figure 9.12.

```
 Frequency      Stem &   Leaf

     3.00         0  .   344
    10.00         0  .   5566777889
     2.00         1  .   01
     2.00  Extremes     (>=15)

Stem width:        10.00
Each leaf:          1 case(s)
```

FIGURE 9.12 Stem-and-leaf plot from SPSS of the data displayed in Figure 9.11

From this we can see that two data points are equal to or greater than 15 and are classified as extreme.

Plots of bivariate scores

Scattergrams

A scattergram (or scatterplot) is a useful way to present the data for two variables that have been provided by each participant. This would be the case if, in the memory example, we had also tested the time it took for each participant to say the original list out aloud (the articulation speed).

Table 9.5 Number of words recalled and articulation
speed, ranked according to number of words recalled

recall	articulation speed
3	30
4	25
4	28
5	30
5	25
6	23
6	24
7	23
7	21
7	23
8	23
8	18
9	19
10	20
11	19

FIGURE 9.13 Scattergram of articulation time and number of words recalled

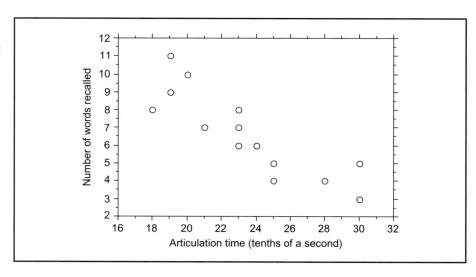

The position of each score on the graph is given by finding its value on the articulation speed axis and drawing an imaginary vertical line through that point, then finding its value on the recall axis and drawing an imaginary horizontal line through this point. The circle is drawn where the two imaginary lines cross. Try this with the first pair of data points: 30 and 3.

The advantage of the scattergram is that the reader can see any trends at a glance. In this case it suggests that faster articulation is accompanied by better recall.

In the example, two participants recalled the same number of words and had the same articulation rate. The scattergram in Figure 9.13 has not shown this. However, there are ways of representing situations where scores coincide.

Ways of representing scores that are the same (ties)
There are a number of ways of showing that more than one data point is the same. One method is to use numbers as the symbols and to represent the number of data points that coincide by the value of the number.

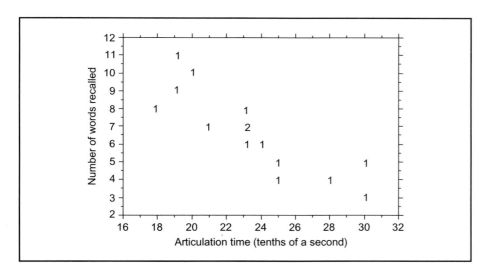

FIGURE 9.14 Scattergram of articulation time and number of words recalled (with ties shown by numbers)

Another method is to make the size of the symbol denote the number of coinciding data points.

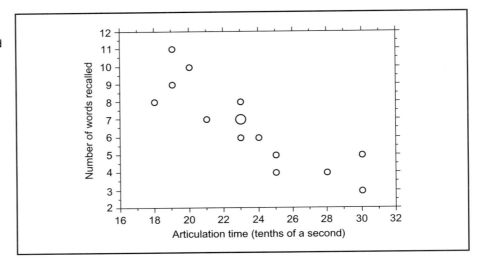

FIGURE 9.15 Scattergram of articulation time and number of words recalled (showing ties as larger points)

A further technique is to use what is called a *sunflower*. Here the number of data points that coincide is represented by the number of petals on the flower.

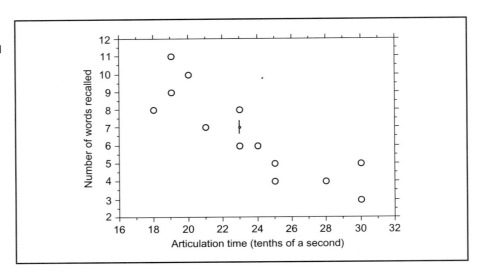

FIGURE 9.16 Scattergram of articulation time and number of words recalled (showing ties as sunflower petals)

Plots of means

One independent variable

Line charts

Imagine for this example that researchers wish to explore the effectiveness of two different mnemonic techniques. The first technique involves participants in relating the items in a list of words to a set of pre-learned items which form a rhyme: *one–bun, two–shoe* and so on. For example, the list to be learned might begin with the words *horse* and *duck*. Participants are encouraged to form an image of a horse eating a bun and a duck wearing a shoe. This mnemonic technique is called *pegwords*. The second technique involves participants imagining that they are walking a route with which they are familiar and that they are placing each item from a list of words on the route, so that when they wish to recall the items they imagine themselves walking the route again (known as the *method of loci*). The researchers also include a control condition in which participants are not given any training.

The means and standard deviations for the three conditions are shown in Table 9.6 and in Figure 9.17. This suggests that using mnemonics improved recall and that the method of loci was the better of the two mnemonic

Table 9.6 The mean and standard deviations of words recalled under three memory conditions

	control	pegword	method of loci
M	7.2	8.9	9.6
SD	1.62	1.91	1.58

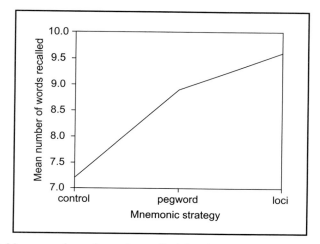

FIGURE 9.17 Mean number of words recalled for three mnemonic strategies

techniques. However, it is important to be wary of how the information is displayed. Note that the range of possible memory scores shown on the vertical axis only runs between 7 and 10. Such truncation of the range of values can suggest a greater difference between groups than actually exists. Figure 9.18 shows the same means but with the vertical axis not truncated.

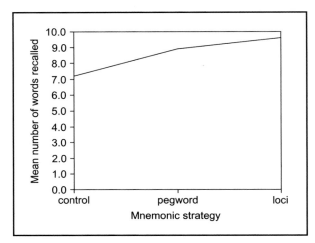

FIGURE 9.18 The mean word recall for three different memory groups (vertical axis not truncated)

Notice that the difference between the means does not seem so marked in this graph.

Bar charts

Means can also be shown using bar charts. In fact, given that the measure on the horizontal axis is discrete (and nominal in this case), then bar charts

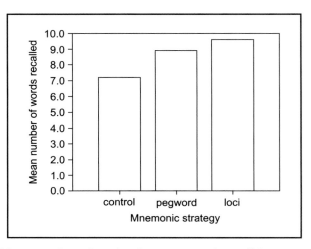

FIGURE 9.19 Mean word recall under three mnemonic conditions

could be considered more appropriate as they do not have lines connecting the means which might imply a continuity between the levels of the IV that were used in the research.

Two independent variables

Line charts

When you have more than one independent variable it is usual to place the levels of one of them on the horizontal axis and the other as separate lines within the graph. An example of this would be if the previous design were enlarged to incorporate a second independent variable—the degree to which the words in the list were conceptually linked—with two levels, linked and unlinked; the linked list includes items that are found in a kitchen. The means are shown in Table 9.7 and Figure 9.20.

From this the reader can see that recall was generally better from linked lists but this produced the greatest improvement, over unlinked lists, when participants were in the control condition where they were not using any mnemonics.

Table 9.7 The mean word recall of groups given linked and unlinked lists of words to remember using different mnemonic techniques

	control	pegword	loci
linked	11.0	10.6	10.6
unlinked	6.4	8.4	8.8

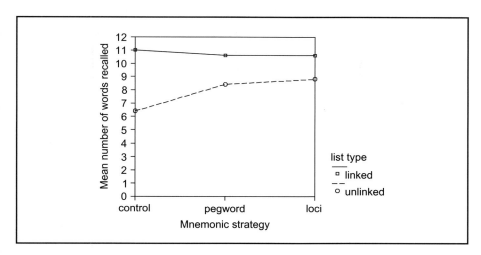

FIGURE 9.20 Mean number of words recalled for three mnemonic strategies when words in lists are linked or unlinked

Bar charts

It is also possible to present the means of two independent variables using a bar chart.

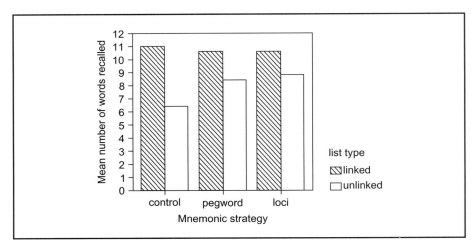

FIGURE 9.21 Mean number of words recalled for three mnemonic strategies when words in lists are linked or unlinked

Plots of means and spread

As was pointed out under the discussion of numerical methods of describing data, means on their own do not tell the full story about the data. It can be useful to show the spread as well in a graph because it gives an idea about how much overlap there is between the scores for the different levels of the independent variable. This can be done using a line chart, a bar chart or a box plot.

Error bar graphs

If we plot means and standard deviations for the three recall conditions we get the following graph:

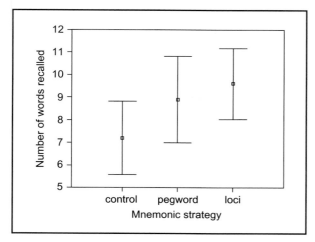

FIGURE 9.22 The means and standard deviations of words recalled for the three mnemonic strategies

The vertical lines show one standard deviation above and below the mean. This shows that the difference between the three conditions is not as clear as was suggested by the graph that just included the means. Here we can see that the three methods had a large degree of overlap. Chapter 12 shows other measures of spread that can be put on a line chart.

When more than one independent variable is involved in the study it is best not to show the standard deviation as well on a line chart, because it will make reading the graph more difficult, as the standard deviation bars may lie on top of each other. However, if the lines are sufficiently well separated so that error bars do not overlap then do include them.

Bar charts

With a bar chart, particularly if the bars are to be shaded, it is best to show just one standard deviation *above* the mean.

It would be possible to represent the standard deviations for the levels of two IVs on a bar chart.

Box plots

A box plot provides the reader with a large amount of useful information. In this example I have illustrated the data for 17 people who were given a list to recall as represented in Figure 9.12.

The box represents the middle 50% of scores and the horizontal line in the box is the median.

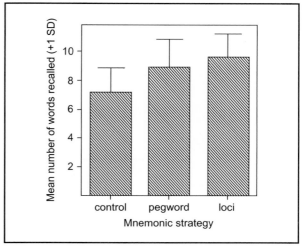

FIGURE 9.23 The means and standard deviations of words recalled for the three mnemonic strategies

FIGURE 9.24 A box plot of number of words recalled

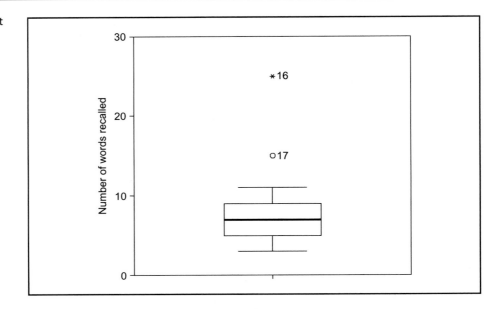

FIGURE 9.25 A box plot of words recalled, with elements of the box plot labelled

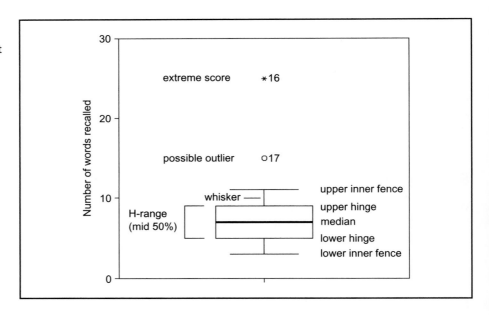

The upper and lower edges of the box are known as the *upper* and *lower hinges* and the range of scores within the box is known as the *H-range*, which is the same as the interquartile range given earlier in this chapter. The vertical lines above and below the box are known as *whiskers*—hence the box plot is sometimes called the *box-and-whisker plot*. The whiskers extend across what are known as the *upper* and *lower inner fences*. Figures 9.24 and 9.25 are created using SPSS which has represented the upper and lower fences as extending as far as the highest and lowest data points that aren't considered to be outliers. It treats as outliers data points that are more than one-and-a-half times the box length above or below the box, and they are symbolised by a circle and the 'case number' of the participant who provided that score. It treats as an extreme score one that is more than three times the box length above and below the box, and this is denoted by an asterisk. An alternative version of the box plot is given by Cleveland (1985). Appendix I contains details of a more common convention for the position of the whiskers and how to calculate their length.

Looking at Figures 9.24 and 9.25, we have good grounds for treating participant 16 who has a score of 25, and possibly participant 17 who scored 15, as outliers whom we may wish to drop from further analysis. Nonetheless, we should be interested in how someone achieves such scores. I would recommend exploring why these data points are so discrepant from the rest, by checking that they have not been entered incorrectly into the computer or, possibly, by interviewing the people involved. Debriefing participants can help with identifying reasons for outlying scores. Chapter 12 gives another version of the box plot and another way of identifying what could be outlying scores.

The distribution of data

One reason for producing a histogram or stem-and-leaf plot is to see how the data are distributed. This can be important as a number of statistical tests should only be applied to a set of data if the population from which the sample came conforms to a particular distribution—the *normal distribution*. In the remainder of this chapter histograms are going to be used to examine the distribution of data. However, in Chapter 12 I will introduce the normal quantile–quantile plot which can be another useful way to examine distributions.

The normal distribution

When a variable is normally distributed, the mean, the median and the mode are all the same. In addition, the histogram shows that it has a symmetrical distribution either side of the mean (median and mode). For example, if an IQ test has a mean of 100 and a standard deviation of 15 then, if enough people are given the test, the distribution of their scores will be normally distributed as shown in Figure 9.26, where 16,000 people were in the sample.

Notice that as the IQ being plotted on the graph moves further from the mean, fewer people have that IQ. Thus, fewer people have an IQ of 90 than

FIGURE 9.26 The distribution of IQ scores in a sample of 16,000 people

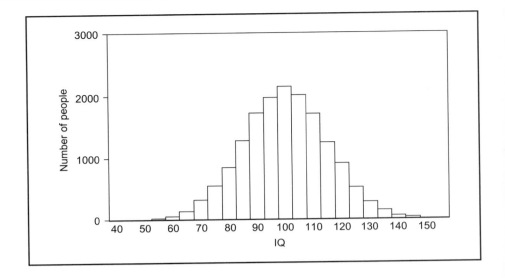

have an IQ of 100. Because of its shape it is sometimes referred to as the 'bell-shaped curve'. Yet another name is the 'Gaussian curve' after one of the mathematicians—Gauss—who identified it.

In fact, the normal distribution is a *theoretical* distribution; that is, one that does not ever truly exist. Data are considered to be normally distributed when they closely resemble the theoretical distribution. The normal distribution is continuous and, therefore, it forms a smooth curve, as shown in Figure 9.27.

FIGURE 9.27 The normal distribution curve

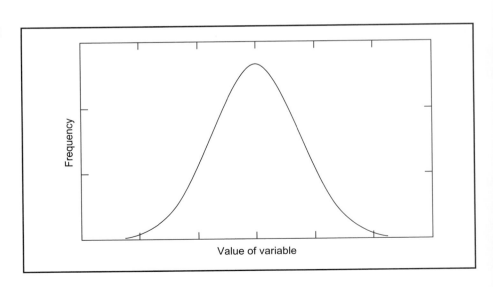

Skew

A distribution is said to be *skewed* when it is not symmetrical around the mean (median and mode). Skew can be positive or negative.

Positive skew

For example, we might test the recall of a sample of people and find that some people had particularly good memories. Note that the *tail* of the distribution is longer on the side where the recall scores are larger.

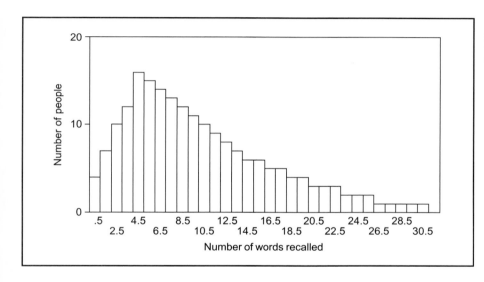

FIGURE 9.28 A positively skewed frequency distribution of word recall

The mean of the distribution in Figure 9.28 is 9.69 words, the median is 8 words and the mode is 4 words. Notice that the measures of central tendency, when placed in alphabetical order, are decreasing.

Negative skew

Our sample of people might include a large proportion who have been practising mnemonic techniques. Now the tail of the distribution is longer where the recall scores are smallest.

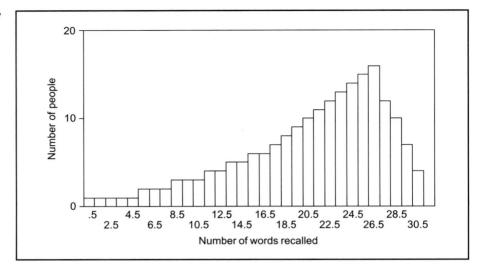

The mean of this distribution is 20.31 words, the median 22 words and the mode 26 words. Notice that this time the measures of central tendency, when placed in alphabetical order, are increasing.

Kurtosis

Kurtosis is a term used to describe how thin or broad the distribution is. When the distribution is relatively flat it is described as *platykurtic*, when it is relatively tall and thin it is described as *leptokurtic*, and the normal distribution is *mesokurtic*.

A platykurtic distribution

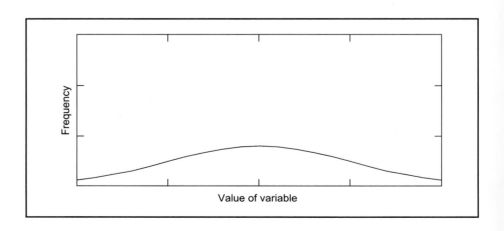

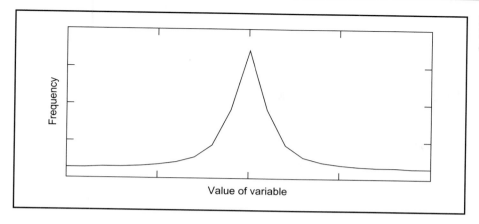

FIGURE 9.31 A leptokurtic frequency distribution

A leptokurtic distribution

Skew and kurtosis can affect how data should be analysed and interpreted. Statistics packages give indices of skew and kurtosis. However, as you will see when we look at statistical tests, the presence of skew in data is often more problematic than the presence of kurtosis. The effects of non-normal distributions are discussed in the appropriate chapters on analysis. Interpretation of the indices is discussed in Appendix I.

Summary

The first stage of data analysis should always involve some form of summary of the data. This can be done numerically and/or graphically. This process can give a preliminary idea of whether the results of the research are in line with the researcher's hypotheses. In addition, they will be useful for helping to identify unusual scores and, when reporting the results, as a way of describing the data.

A frequent use of graphs is to identify the distribution of data. The normal distribution is a particularly important pattern for data to possess as, if it is present, certain statistical techniques can be applied to the data. The distribution of data can vary from normal by being skewed—non-symmetrical—or having kurtosis—forming a flat or a tall and thin shape.

The next chapter describes the process that researchers use to help them decide whether the results of their research have supported their hypotheses.

10 GOING BEYOND DESCRIPTION

Introduction

This chapter explains how the results of research are used to test hypotheses. It introduces the notion of probability and shows how the decision as to whether to reject or accept a hypothesis is dependent on how likely the results were to have occurred if the Null Hypothesis were true.

Hypothesis testing

The formal expression of a research hypothesis is always in terms of two related hypotheses. One hypothesis is the experimental, alternative or research hypothesis (often shown as H_A or H_1). It is a statement of what the researchers predict will be the outcome of the research. For example, in Chapter 9 we looked at a study that investigated the relationship between the speed with which people could speak a list of words (articulation speed) and memory for those words. In this case, the research hypothesis could have been: *there is a positive relationship between articulation speed and short-term memory*. The second hypothesis is the Null Hypothesis (H_0). It is, generally, a statement that there is no effect of an independent variable on a dependent variable or that there is no relationship between variables. For example, *there is no relationship between articulation speed and short-term memory*.

Only one H_A is ever set up for each H_0, even if more than one hypothesis is being tested in the research. In other words, each H_A should have a matching H_0. You will find that psychologists, when reporting their research, rarely mention their research hypotheses explicitly and even more rarely do they mention their Null Hypotheses. I recommend that during the stage when you are learning about research and hypothesis testing, you do make both research and Null Hypotheses explicit. In this way you will understand better the results of your hypothesis testing.

Probability

As was discussed in Chapter 1, it is never possible to prove that a hypothesis is true. The best we can do is evaluate the evidence to see whether H_0

is unlikely to be true. We can only do this on the basis of the probability of the result we have obtained having occurred, if H_0 were true. If it is unlikely that our result occurred if H_0 were true then we can reject H_0 and accept H_A. On the other hand, if it *is* likely that our result occurred if H_0 were true then we cannot reject H_0.

To discuss the meaning of probability I am going to use a simple example where the likelihood of a given chance outcome can be calculated straight-forwardly. This is designed to demonstrate the point that different outcomes from the same chance event can have different likelihoods of occurring.

If we take a single coin that is not in any way biased and we toss it in the air and let it fall, then there are only two, equally possible, outcomes: it could fall as a head or it could fall as a tail. In other words, the probability that it will fall as a head is one out of two or 1/2. Similarly, the probability that it will fall as a tail is 1/2. Note that when we add the two probabilities the result is one. This last point is true of any situation: however many possible outcomes there are in a given situation, if we calculate the prob-ability of each of them and add those probabilities they will sum to one. This simply means that the probability that at least one of the outcomes will occur is one. Probabilities are usually expressed as proportions out of one. For example, the probability of a head is 0.5 and the probability of a tail is also 0.5. Probabilities are also sometimes expressed as percentages. For example, there is a fifty per cent chance that a single coin will fall as a head and there is a one hundred per cent chance that the coin will fall as a head or a tail.

Imagine that a friend says that she can affect the outcome of the fall of coins by making them fall as heads. Let us turn this into a study to test her claim. We would set up our hypotheses:

H_A: Our friend can make coins fall as heads.
H_0: Our friend cannot affect the fall of coins.

We know that the likelihood of a coin falling as a head by chance is 0.5. Thus, if we tossed a single coin and it fell as a head we would know that it was highly likely to have been a chance event and we would not have sufficient evidence for rejecting the Null Hypothesis. In fact this is not a fair test of our hypothesis, for no outcome, in this particular study, is sufficiently unlikely by chance to act as evidence against the Null Hypothesis.

To give our hypothesis a fair chance we would need to have a situation where some possible outcomes were unlikely to happen by chance. If we make the situation slightly more complicated we can see that different out-comes can have different probabilities.

If we toss five coins at a time and note how they fall we have increased the number of possible outcomes. The possibilities range from all being heads through some being heads and some tails to all being tails. There are in fact six possible outcomes: five heads, four heads, three heads, two heads, one head and no heads.

However, some of the outcomes could have happened in more than one way, while others could only have been achieved in one way. For example,

Table 10.1 The possible ways in which five coins could land

outcome	coin 1	coin 2	coin 3	coin 4	coin 5	number of heads
1	T	T	T	T	T	0
2	H	T	T	T	T	1
3	T	H	T	T	T	1
4	T	T	H	T	T	1
5	T	T	T	H	T	1
6	T	T	T	T	H	1
7	H	H	T	T	T	2
8	H	T	H	T	T	2
9	H	T	T	H	T	2
10	H	T	T	T	H	2
11	T	H	H	T	T	2
12	T	H	T	H	T	2
13	T	H	T	T	H	2
14	T	T	H	H	T	2
15	T	T	H	T	H	2
16	T	T	T	H	H	2
17	H	H	H	T	T	3
18	H	H	T	H	T	3
19	H	H	T	T	H	3
20	H	T	H	H	T	3
21	H	T	H	T	H	3
22	H	T	T	H	H	3
23	T	H	H	H	T	3
24	T	H	H	T	H	3
25	T	H	T	H	H	3
26	T	T	H	H	H	3
27	H	H	H	H	T	4
28	H	H	H	T	H	4
29	H	H	T	H	H	4
30	H	T	H	H	H	4
31	T	H	H	H	H	4
32	H	H	H	H	H	5

there are five ways in which we could have got four heads. Coin one could have been a tail while all the others were heads, coin two could have been a tail while all the others were heads, coin three could have been a tail while all the others were heads, coin four could have been a tail while all the others were heads, and finally coin five could have been a tail while all the others were heads. On the other hand, there is only one way in which we would have got five heads: all five coins fell as heads. Table 10.1 shows all the possible ways in which the five coins could have landed.

Note that there are 32 different ways in which the coins could have landed. We can produce a frequency distribution from these possible results, see Figure 10.1.

From Table 10.1 we can calculate the probability of each outcome by taking the number of ways in which a particular outcome could have been achieved and dividing that by 32—the total number of different ways in which the coins could have fallen.

Thus, the least likely outcomes are all heads and all tails, each with a probability of 1/32, or 0.031, of having occurred by chance. Remember that

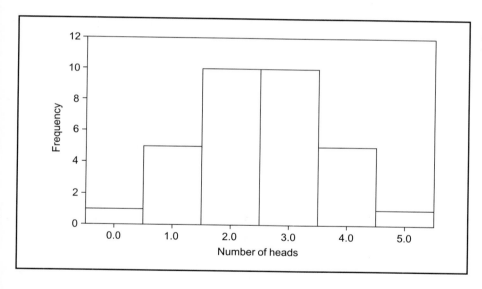

FIGURE 10.1 The distribution of heads from tosses of five coins

Table 10.2 The probabilities of different outcomes when five coins are tossed

Number of heads	Number of ways achieved	Probability
5	1	0.031
4	5	0.156
3	10	0.313
2	10	0.313
1	5	0.156
0	1	0.031

this can also be expressed as a 3.1% chance of getting five heads. Put another way, if we tossed the five coins and noted the number of heads and the number of tails, and continued to do this until we had tossed the five coins 100 times, we would expect by chance to have got five heads on only approximately three occasions.

The most likely outcomes are that there will be three heads and two tails or that there will be two heads and three tails, each with the probability of $10/32$, or 0.313, of occurring by chance. In other words, if we tossed the five coins 100 times we would expect to get exactly three heads approximately 31 times.

Now imagine that we have conducted the study to test whether our friend can affect the fall of coins such that they land as heads. We toss the five coins and they all land as heads. We know that this result *could* have occurred by chance but the question is, is it sufficiently unlikely to have been by chance for us to risk saying that we think that the Null Hypothesis can be rejected and our research hypothesis supported?

Before testing a hypothesis researchers set a critical probability level, such that the outcome of their research must have a probability that is equal to or less than the critical level before they will reject the Null Hypothesis that the outcome occurred by chance. They say that the range of outcomes that are as likely or less likely than the critical probability are in the *rejection region*; in other words, such outcomes are sufficiently unlikely to occur when the Null Hypothesis is true that we can reject the Null Hypothesis.

Statistical significance

If the outcome of the research is in the rejection region the outcome is said to be *statistically significant*. If its probability is outside the rejection region then the outcome is not statistically significant. By convention, generally attributed to Fisher (1925), in research the critical probability is frequently set at 0.05. The symbol α (the Greek letter alpha) is usually used to denote the critical probability. Thus, $\alpha = 0.05$ in much research. This level may seem rather high as it is another way of saying a one-in-twenty chance, but it has been chosen as a compromise between two types of error that researchers could commit when deciding whether they can reject the Null Hypothesis. If the probability of our outcome having occurred if the Null Hypothesis is true is the same as or less than α it is *statistically significant* and we can reject H_0. However, if the probability is greater than α it is not statistically significant and we cannot reject H_0.

As the probability of getting five heads by chance is 0.031 (usually expressed as $p = 0.031$) and as p is less than 0.05 (our critical level of probability, α) then we would reject the Null Hypothesis and accept our research hypothesis. Thus, we conclude that our friend can affect the fall of coins to produce heads.

A further convention covers the writing about statistical significance. Often the word *statistical* is dropped and a result is simply described as being *significant*. In some ways this is unfortunate because it makes less explicit the fact that the significance is according to certain statistical criteria. However, it becomes cumbersome to describe a result as *statistically significantly different* and so I will follow the convention and avoid such expressions.

Error types

Any result *could* have been a chance event, even if it is very unlikely, but we have to decide whether we are willing to risk rejecting the Null Hypothesis despite this possibility. Given that we cannot know for sure that our hypothesis is correct, there are four possible outcomes of our decision process and these are based on which decision we make and the nature of reality (which we cannot know):

Table 10.3 The possible errors that can be made in hypothesis testing

		Reality	
		H_0 false	H_0 true
Our decision	Reject H_0	Correct	Type I error
	Do not reject H_0	Type II error	Correct

Thus, there are two ways in which we can be correct and two types of error we could commit. When we make a decision we cannot know whether it is correct so we always risk making one type of error. A Type I error occurs when we choose to reject the Null Hypothesis even though it is true. A Type II error occurs when we reject our research hypothesis (H_A) even though *it* is true. The probability we are willing to risk of committing a Type I error is α. If we set α very small, although we lessen the danger of making a Type I error, we increase the likelihood that we will make a Type II error. Hence the convention that α is set at 0.05.

However, the actual level of α we set for a given piece of research will depend on the relative importance of making a Type I or a Type II error. If it is more important to avoid a Type I error than to avoid a Type II error then we can set α as smaller than 0.05. For example, if we were testing a drug that had unpleasant side-effects to see whether it cured an illness that was not life-threatening then it would be important not to commit a Type I error. However, if we were testing a drug that had few side-effects but might save lives then we would be more concerned about committing a Type II error, and we could set the α level to be larger than 0.05.

You may feel that this seems like making the statistics say whatever you want them to. While that is not true, unless there is good reason for setting α at a different level, psychologists often play safe and use an α level of 0.05.

Thus, if you are uncomfortable with varying α, you could stick to 0.05 and not be seen as unusual by most other psychologists.

Calculating the probability of the outcome of research

Often in psychological research we do not make an exact prediction in our research hypotheses. Rather than say that our friend can make exactly five coins fall as heads, we say that she can affect the fall of coins so that they land as heads. Imagine that we re-ran the experiment but that now, instead of getting five heads, we get four heads. Remember that our friend did not say that she could make four out of five coins land as heads. If she had, the probability of this outcome would be 5/32 or 0.156 (see Table 10.2). Now, it may be the case that she *can* affect the coins but was having a slight off-day. We have to say that the probability of this result having occurred by chance is the probability of the actual outcome plus the probabilities of all the other possible outcomes that are more extreme than the one achieved but are in line with the research hypothesis; the reason is that if we only take account of the exact probability of the outcome, even though this was not the prediction made, we are unfairly advantaging the research hypothesis. The probability we are now using is that of getting four heads or more than four heads, that is, $0.156 + 0.031 = 0.187$. Thus, if we only got four heads we would not be justified in rejecting the Null Hypothesis, as the probability is greater than 0.05. We therefore conclude that there is insufficient evidence to support the hypothesis that our friend can affect the fall of coins to make them land as heads.

In the case of five coins we could only reject the Null Hypothesis if all the coins fell as heads. However, there are situations in which our prediction may not be totally fulfilled and yet we can still reject the Null Hypothesis.

To demonstrate this point, let us look at the situation where we throw ten coins. Table 10.4 shows that in this case there are eleven possible results ranging from no heads to ten heads, but now there are 1024 ways in which they could be achieved.

Imagine that to test our research hypothesis we toss the ten coins but only nine fall as heads. The probability of this result (or ones more extreme and in the direction of our research hypothesis) would be the probability of getting nine heads plus the probability of getting ten heads: $0.00976 + 0.00098 = 0.01074$. In this case, we would be justified in rejecting the Null Hypothesis. Thus, the outcome does not have to be totally in line with our research hypothesis before we can treat it as supported.

Fortunately, it is very unlikely that you will ever find it necessary to calculate the probability for the outcome of your research yourself. The next chapter will demonstrate that you can use standard statistical tests to evaluate your research and that statisticians have already calculated the probabilities for you.

Table 10.4 The possible outcomes and their probabilities when ten coins are tossed

Number of heads	Number of possible ways achieved	Probability
0	1	0.00098
1	10	0.00976
2	45	0.04395
3	120	0.11719
4	210	0.20508
5	252	0.24609
6	210	0.20508
7	120	0.11719
8	45	0.04395
9	10	0.00976
10	1	0.00098

One- and two-tailed tests

So far we have considered the situation in which our friend tells us that she can cause coins to fall as *heads*. She has predicted the direction in which the outcome will occur. Imagine now instead that she has kept us guessing and has simply said that she can affect the fall of the coins such that there will be a majority of one type of side but she has not said whether we will get a majority of heads or a majority of tails.

We will again toss five coins and the hypotheses will be:

H_A: Our friend can cause the coins to fall such that a majority of them fall on the same side.

H_0 (as before): Our friend cannot affect the fall of coins.

When we made our original hypothesis, that the coins will fall as heads, we were saying that the result will be in the right-hand side of the distribution of Figure 10.1 (or the right-hand *tail* of the distribution). That is described as a *directional* or *uni-directional* hypothesis.

However, the new research hypothesis is *non-directional* or *bi-directional*, as we are not predicting the direction of the outcome; we are not saying in which tail of the distribution we expect the result to be. We can calculate the probability for this situation but now we have to take into account both tails of the distribution. If the coins now fall as five heads, the probability that the coins will all fall on the same side is the probability that they are all heads plus the probability that they are all tails. In other words, $0.031 + 0.031 = 0.062$. Thus, in this new version of the experiment we would not reject the Null Hypothesis, because this outcome, or more extreme ones, in the direction of our hypothesis, is too likely to have occurred when the Null Hypothesis is true (i.e. p is greater than 0.05, usually written as $p > 0.05$).

When the hypothesis states the direction of the outcome, we apply what is described as a *one-tailed test* of the hypothesis because the probability is only calculated in one 'tail' (or end) of the distribution. However, when the hypothesis is not directional the test is described as a *two-tailed test* because the probability is calculated for both tails (or ends) of the distribution.

With a one-tailed test the rejection region is in one tail of the distribution and so we are willing to accept a result as statistically significant as long as its probability is 0.05 or less, on the predicted side of the distribution.

FIGURE 10.2 The rejection region for a one-tailed test with $\alpha = 0.05$

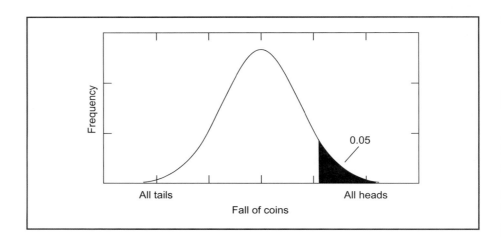

FIGURE 10.3 The rejection regions for a two-tailed test with $\alpha = 0.05$

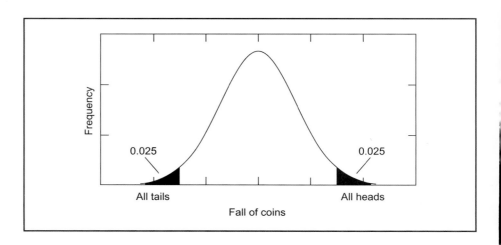

In other words, 5% of possible occurrences are within the rejection region (see Figure 10.2).

With a two-tailed test we usually split the probability of 0.05 into 0.025 on one side of the distribution and 0.025 in the other tail. In other words, 2.5% of possible occurrences are in one rejection region and 2.5% of them are in the other rejection region (see Figure 10.3).

If you compare Figures 10.2 and 10.3 you will see that for an outcome to be in the rejection region when we apply a one-tailed test, it can have fewer heads and still be statistically significant, than it would have needed in order to be statistically significant had we applied a two-tailed test.

Summary

Researchers can never accept their hypotheses unequivocally. They have to evaluate how likely the results they achieved were to have occurred if the Null Hypothesis were true. On this basis they can choose whether or not to reject the Null Hypothesis. There is a convention that if the result has a probability of occurring if the Null Hypothesis were true of 0.05 or less then the result is described as statistically significant and the Null Hypothesis can be rejected. This probability level has been chosen as the best value for avoiding both a Type I error—rejecting the Null Hypothesis when it is true— and a Type II error—failing to reject the Null Hypothesis when it is false.

This chapter has only dealt with the way in which researchers take into account the danger of making a Type I error. Chapter 13 will show how they can also try to minimise the probability of committing a Type II error. In addition, it will show other ways to present our results that are less reliant on significance testing.

The next chapter explains how researchers can use summary statistics to draw conclusions about the population from which their sample came. It also discusses issues of how to select a sample from a population.

11 SAMPLES AND POPULATIONS

Introduction

This chapter introduces the notion of population parameters and describes two basic approaches to choosing a sample from a population: random and non-random sampling. It explains the notion of a confidence interval and shows how proportions in a population may be estimated from the proportions found in a sample.

Statistics

The summary statistics, such as mean ($\bar{x}$ or M), variance (s^2) and standard deviation (s or SD), which were referred to in Chapter 9, describe the sample that was measured. Each statistic has an equivalent that describes the population from which the sample came: these are known as *parameters*.

Parameters

Each parameter is symbolised by a lower-case letter from the Greek alphabet. The equivalent of the sample mean is the population mean and is denoted by μ (the Greek letter mu, pronounced 'mew'). The equivalent of the variance for the sample is the variance for the population which is shown as σ^2 (the square of the Greek letter sigma). The equivalent of the standard deviation for the sample is the standard deviation for the population, denoted by σ. There is a rationale for the choice of Greek letter in each case: μ is the equivalent of m in our alphabet, while σ is the equivalent of our s.

When a research hypothesis is proposed, the researcher is usually not only interested in the particular sample of participants that is involved in the research. Rather, the hypothesis will make a more general statement about the population from which the sample came. For example, the hypothesis *males do fewer domestic chores than their female partners* may be tested on a particular sample but the assumption is being made that the finding is generalisable to the wider population of males and females.

Parameters are often estimated from surveys that have been conducted to identify voting patterns or particular characteristics in a population, such as the proportion of people who take recommended amounts of daily exercise.

In addition, many statistical tests involve estimations of the parameters for the population, in order to assess the probability that the results of the particular study were likely to occur if the Null Hypothesis were true.

Choosing a sample

Often when experiments are conducted there is an implicit assumption, unless particular groups are being studied, such as young children, that any sample of people will be representative of their population: people in general. This can lead to mistaken conclusions when the sample is limited to a group whose members come from a subpopulation, such as students. What may be true of students' performance on a task may not be true of non-students.

However, when researchers conduct a survey they frequently wish to be able to generalise explicitly from what they have found in their sample to the population from which the sample came. To do this they try to ensure that they have a sample that is representative of the wider population.

Before a sample can be chosen researchers have to be clear about what constitutes their population. In doing this they must decide what their unit of analysis is: that is, what constitutes a *population element*. Often the units of analysis will be people. However, many of the principles of sampling also apply when the population elements are places, times, pieces of behaviour or even television programmes. For simplicity, the discussion will be based on the assumption that people are the population elements that are to be sampled.

The next decision about the population is what are the limiting factors: that is, what constraints are to be put on what constitutes a population element, for example, people who are eligible to vote or people in full-time education. Sudman (1976) recommends that you operationalise the definition of a population element more precisely, at the risk of excluding some people. He gives the example of defining a precise age range rather than using the term 'of child-bearing age'. He does, however, note that it is possible to make the definition too rigid and in so doing increase the costs of the survey by forcing the researchers to have to screen many people before the sample is identified.

The aims of the research will help to define the population and, to a large extent, the constitution of the sample. For example, if a comparison is desired between members of subpopulations, such as across the genders or across age groups, then researchers may try to achieve equal representation of the subgroups in the sample.

There are two general methods of sampling that are employed for surveys: random (or probability) sampling and non-random (or non-probability) sampling. Which you choose will depend on the aims of your study and such considerations as accuracy, time and money.

Random samples

Random samples are those in which each population element has an equal probability, or a quantifiable probability of being selected. The principle of random sampling can be most readily understood from a description of the process of simple random sampling.

Simple random sampling

Once the population has been chosen, the first stage is to choose the sample size. This will depend on the degree of accuracy the researchers wish to have over their generalisations to the population. Clearly, the larger the sample, the more accurate the generalisations that can be made about the population from which the sample came. (Details are given in Appendix II on how to calculate the appropriate sample size.) Secondly, each population element is identified. Thirdly, if it does not already possess one, each element is given a unique identifying code, for example a number. Fourthly, codes are selected randomly until all the elements in the potential sample are identified.

Random selection can be done using a computer program, a table of random numbers or putting all the numbers on separate pieces of paper and drawing them out of a hat. (Appendix XVI contains tables of random numbers.)

Problems in identifying the population elements

There can be a difficulty in using published lists of people because there may be systematic reasons why certain people are missing. For example, in the United Kingdom there was a tax imposed in the 1990s that necessitated that the tax collectors knew where each person lived. Accordingly, many people tried to keep their names off lists that could be used to identify them, particularly lists of voters. If such a list had been used to identify people for a survey, some people who were either too poor or who were politically opposed to the tax would have been excluded, thus producing a biased sample.

Another example comes from the field of visual impairment. Local authorities in England and Wales keep a register of visually impaired people. However, for a person to have been registered they must have been recommended by an ophthalmologist. It is likely that many elderly people have simply accepted their visual impairment and have not visited an ophthalmologist, in which case elderly people will be under-represented in the register.

It may be that in order to identify population elements a wider survey has to be conducted. In the case of the visually impaired, it may be necessary to sample people in general to estimate what proportion of the population have a visual impairment and to estimate their characteristics.

Telephone surveys

When conducting a telephone survey it can be tempting to use a telephone directory. However, at least four groups will be excluded by this method: those who do not have a telephone, those who only have a mobile phone, those who have moved so recently to the area that they are not in the book, and those who have chosen to be ex-directory. In each case missing such people may produce a biased sample.

One way around the last two problems is to select telephone numbers randomly from all possible permissible combinations for the given area(s) being sampled.

Alternative methods of random sampling

Simple random sampling is only one of many techniques. There are at least three other forms of random sampling that can be simpler to administer but can make parameter estimation more complicated: systematic, stratified and cluster sampling.

Systematic sampling

Systematic sampling involves deciding on a sample size and then dividing the population size by the sample size. This will give a figure (rounded to the nearest whole number) that can be used as the basis for sampling. As an example, if a sample of 100 people was required from a population of 2500, then the figure is $2500/100 = 25$. Randomly choose a starting number among the population; let us say 70. The first person in the sample is the 70th person, the next is the $70 + 25 = 95$th person and the next is the $95 + 25 = 120$th person and so on until we have a sample of 100. Note, however, that the 97th person we select for the sample will be the 2495th person in the population, and if we carry on adding 25 we will get 2520, which is 20 larger than the size of the population. To get around this, we can subtract 2500 from 2520 and say that we will continue by picking the 20th person followed by the $20 + 25 = 45$th person.

One danger of systematic sampling could be if the cycle fits in with some naturally occurring cycle in the population. For example, if a sample was taken from people who lived on a particular road and the sampling basis used an even number then only people who lived on one side of the road might be included. This could be particularly important if one side of the road was in one local authority area and the other side in another.

Stratified sampling

A stratified sample involves breaking the population into mutually exclusive subgroups or strata. A typical example might be to break the sample down, on the basis of gender, into male and female strata. Once the strata have been chosen, simple random sampling or systematic sampling can then be carried out within each stratum to choose the sample. An advantage of stratified sampling can be that there is a guarantee that the sample will contain sufficient representatives from each of the strata. A danger of both simple random and systematic sampling is that you cannot guarantee how well represented members of particular subgroups will be. There are two ways in which stratified sampling can be conducted: proportionately and disproportionately.

Proportionate sampling

Proportionate sampling would be involved if sampling from the strata reflected the proportions in the population. For example, a colleague wanted to interview people who were visiting a clinic for sexually transmitted diseases. She was aware that approximately one-seventh of the visitors to the clinic were female. Accordingly, if she wanted a proportionate stratified sample she would have sampled in such a way as to obtain six-sevenths males and one-seventh females.

Disproportionate sampling

If the researchers do not require their sample to have the proportions of the population they can choose to have the sampling being disproportionate. My colleague may have wanted her sample to have 50% males and 50% females. Clearly, it would not be reasonable simply to combine the subsamples from a disproportionate sample and try to extrapolate any results to the population. Such extrapolation would involve more sophisticated analysis (see Sudman, 1976).

Cluster sampling

Cluster sampling involves initially sampling on the basis of a larger unit than the population element. This can be done in one of two ways: in a single stage or in more stages (multi-stage).

Single-stage cluster sampling

An example would be if researchers wished to survey students studying psychology in Great Britain but instead of identifying all the psychology students in Great Britain they identified all the places where psychology courses were being run. They could randomly select a number of courses and then survey all the students on those courses.

Multi-stage cluster sampling

A multi-stage cluster sample could be used if researchers wished to survey children at secondary school. They could start by identifying all the education authorities in the country and selecting randomly from them. Then, within the selected authorities they would identify all the schools and randomly select from those schools. They could then survey all the children in the selected schools or take random samples from each school that had been selected.

Cluster sampling has the advantage that if the population elements are widely spread geographically then the sample is clustered in a limited number of locations. Thus, if the research necessitates the researchers meeting the participants then fewer places would need to be visited. Similarly, if the research was to be conducted by trained interviewers, then these interviewers could be concentrated in a limited number of places.

Dealing with non-responders

Whatever random sampling technique you use, how you deal with non-responders can have an important effect on the random nature of your sampling. There will be occasions when a person selected is not available. You should make more than one attempt to include this person. If you still cannot sample this person then do not go to the next population element, from the original list of the whole population, in order to complete your sample. By so doing you will have undermined the randomness of the sample because that population element will already have been rejected by the sampling procedure. When identifying the initial potential sample, it is better to include more people than are required. Then if someone cannot be sampled move to the next person in the potential sample.

Non-random samples

Accidental/opportunity/convenience sampling

As the names imply this involves sampling those people one happens to meet. For example, researchers could stand outside a supermarket and approach as many people as are required. It is advisable, unless you are only interested in people who shop at a particular branch of a particular supermarket chain, to vary your location. I would recommend noting the refusal rate and some indication of who is refusing. In this way you can get an indication of any biases in your sample.

Quota sampling

A quota sample is an opportunity sample but with quotas set for the numbers of people from subsamples to be included. For example, researchers might want an equal number of males and females. Once they have achieved their quota for one gender they will only approach members of the other gender until they have sufficient people.

Sometimes the quota might be based on something, such as age group or socio-economic status, where it may be necessary to approach everyone and ask them a filter question to see if they are in one of the subgroups to be sampled.

If quotas are being set on a number of dimensions then the term *dimensional sampling* is sometimes used, for example, if researchers wanted to sample people with different levels of visual impairment, from different age groups and from different ages of onset for the visual condition. Such research could involve trying to find people who fulfilled quite precise specifications.

Purposive sampling

Purposive sampling is used when researchers wish to study a clearly defined sample. One example that is often given is where the researchers have a notion of what constitutes a typical example of what they are interested in. This could be a region where the voting pattern in elections has usually reflected the national pattern. The danger of this approach is that the region may no longer be typical.

Another use of purposive sampling is where participants with particular characteristics are being sought, such as people from each echelon in an organisation.

Snowball sampling

Snowball sampling involves using initial contacts to identify other potential participants. For example, in research into the way blind writers compose, a colleague and I used our existing contacts to identify blind writers and then asked those writers of others whom they knew.

The advantages of a random sample

If a random sample has been employed, then it is possible to generalise the results obtained from the sample to the population with a certain degree of accuracy. If a non-random sample has been used it is not possible to generalise to the population with any accuracy. The generalisation from a random sample can be achieved by calculating a *confidence interval* for any statistic obtained from the sample.

Confidence intervals

As with any estimate we can never be totally certain that our estimate of a parameter is exact. However, what we can do is find a range of values within which we can have a certain level of confidence that the parameter may lie. This range is called a *confidence interval*. The level of confidence we can have that the parameter will be within the range is generally expressed in terms of a percentage. A common level of confidence chosen is 95%. Not surprisingly, the higher the percentage of confidence we require, the larger the size of the interval in which the parameter may lie, in order that we can be more confident that we have included the parameter in the interval.

Appendix II contains an explanation of how confidence intervals are obtained and details of the calculations that would be necessary for each of the examples given below. It also describes how you can decide on a sample size if you require a given amount of accuracy in your estimates.

For example, in the run-up to an election, a market research company runs an opinion poll to predict which party will win the election. It uses a random sample of 2500 voters and finds that 36% of the sample say that they will vote for a right-wing party—The Right Way—while 42% say that they will vote for a left-wing party—The Workers' Party. The pollsters calculate the appropriate confidence intervals. They find that they can be 95% confident that the percentage in the population who would vote for The Right Way is between 34.1% and 37.9%, and that the percentage who would vote for The Workers' Party is between 40.1% and 43.9%. Because the two confidence intervals do not overlap we can predict that if an election were held more people would vote for The Workers' Party than for The Right Way.

You may have noticed that polling organisations sometimes report what they call the *margin of error* for their results. In this case, the margin of error would be approximately 2%, for the predicted voting for either party is in a range that is between approximately 2% below and 2% above the figures found in the sample. The margin of error is half the confidence interval.

At least three factors affect the size of the confidence interval for the same degree of confidence: the proportion of the sample for which the confidence interval is being computed, the size of the sample, and the relative sizes of the sample and the population.

The effect of the proportion on the confidence interval

The further the proportion, for which the confidence interval is being estimated, is from 0.5 (or 50%), the smaller the size of the confidence interval. For example, imagine that the pollsters also found that 0.05 (or 5%) of their sample would vote for the far-left party—The Very Very Left-Wing Party. When the confidence interval is calculated, it is estimated that the percentage in the population who would vote for The Very Very Left-Wing Party would be between 4.15% and 5.85%. Notice that the range for this confidence interval is only 1.7%, whereas with the same sample size the range of the confidence interval for those voting for The Workers' Party is just under 4%.

Table 11.1 gives examples of how the confidence interval of a subsample is affected by the size of the proportion that a subsample forms.

Table 11.1 The 95% confidence interval for a subsample depending on the proportion that the subsample forms of the sample of 2500

	Subsample as a proportion of entire sample					
	0.05 or 0.95	0.10 or 0.90	0.20 or 0.80	0.30 or 0.70	0.40 or 0.60	0.50
Confidence interval	1.7%	2.4%	3.1%	3.6%	3.8%	3.9%

The effect of sample size on the confidence interval

The degree of accuracy that can be obtained depends less on the relative size of the sample to the population, than on the absolute size of the sample. This is true as long as the sample is less than approximately five per cent (one-twentieth) the size of the population. The larger the sample size the smaller the range of the confidence interval for the same level of confidence; that is, the more accurately we can pinpoint the population parameter.

To demonstrate that sample size affects the confidence interval imagine that a second polling company only samples 100 people to find out how they will vote. Coincidentally, they get the same results as the first company. However, when they calculate the confidence interval, with 95% confidence for the percentage in the population who would vote for The Workers' Party, they find that it is between 32.33% and 51.67%, a range of 19.34%, or a margin of error of nearly 10%.

The larger the sample size, the greater the increase in sample size that would be required to reduce the confidence interval by an equivalent amount. Note that the confidence interval shrank from 19.34% to 3.86%, a reduction of 15.48%, when an extra 2400 participants were sampled. If a further 2400 participants were added to make the sample 4900, the confidence interval would become 2.76%, which is only a reduction of a further 1.1%. In fact, you would need a sample of nearly 10,000 before you would get the confidence interval down to 2%. Table 11.2 shows the effect sample size has on the width of the confidence interval for a subsample. You obviously have to

Table 11.2 The 95% confidence interval for a subsample, depending on the sample size, when the subsample forms half of the sample

Size of sample	Confidence interval
50	27.7%
100	19.6%
200	13.9%
300	11.3%
400	9.8%
500	8.8%
1000	6.2%
2000	4.4%
2500	3.9%
5000	2.8%
10,000	2.0%

think carefully before you invest the extra time and effort to sample 10,000 people as opposed to 2500 when you are only going to gain 1% in the margin of error.

The effect of sample size as a proportion of the population

The larger the sample is as a proportion of the population the more accurate the confidence interval (see Table 11.3). Obviously, if you have taken a census of your population—that is, everyone in the population—then there is no confidence interval, for the statistics you calculate *are* the population parameters.

Table 11.3 The effect on the 95% confidence interval of varying the sample as a proportion of the population (for a subsample of 500 from a sample of 1000)

| | Sample as percentage of population | | | | | | | | |
	10	20	30	40	50	60	70	80	90
Confidence interval	5.9%	5.5%	5.2%	4.8%	4.4%	3.9%	3.4%	2.8%	2.0%

The final factor that affects the size of the confidence interval is the degree of confidence that you require about the size of the confidence interval.

The effect of degree of confidence on the size of a confidence interval

The figures that have been quoted above have been for a 95% confidence interval, that is a confidence interval when we wish to have 95% confidence that it contains the parameter we are estimating, which is the one usually calculated. However, it is possible to have other levels of confidence. The more confident you wish to be about where the parameter lies, the larger the margin of error and therefore the larger the confidence interval. If we wished to be 99% confident about the proportion of supporters of The Right Way in the population, the margin of error would rise to 2.5% and the confidence interval would be between 0.335 and 0.385, or 33.5% and 38.5%. Table 11.4 shows the effects of varying confidence level on the width of the confidence interval when the subsample is 0.5 (50%) of the sample.

Table 11.4 The effect of varying confidence level on confidence interval (for a subsample of 500 from a sample of 1000)

| | Confidence level | | | | |
	80%	85%	90%	95%	99%
Confidence interval	4.0%	4.6%	5.2%	6.2%	8.1%

The figures given above are only true for a simple random sample. The reader wishing to calculate confidence intervals or the sample size for other forms of random sample should consult a more advanced text, such as Sudman (1976). It must be borne in mind that this degree of accuracy is based on the assumption that the sample is in no way biased.

Summary

Researchers can choose the sample they wish to study either by random sampling or by non-random sampling. If they employ a random sample they can estimate from the figures they have obtained with their sample, with a certain degree of accuracy, the equivalent parameters for the population. The degree of accuracy of such estimates will depend on the sample size and the proportion of the population that they have sampled.

The next chapter describes how researchers can decide how likely it is that a sample comes from a particular population.

ANALYSIS OF DIFFERENCES BETWEEN A SINGLE SAMPLE AND A POPULATION

12

Introduction

Sometimes researchers, having obtained a score for a person or a sample, wish to know how common such a score is within a population. In addition, researchers want to know whether a measure they have taken from a person, or a sample of people, is statistically different from the equivalent measure from a population. This chapter introduces a family of statistical tests—z-tests—which allow both these sorts of questions to be answered. In addition, it introduces a related family of tests—t-tests—which can be applied in some circumstances when there is insufficient information to use a z-test.

The chapter also includes additional versions of graphs and another way to identify outliers.

Z-tests

Z-tests allow researchers to compare a given statistic with the population mean for that statistic to see how common that statistic is within the population. In addition, they allow us to find out how likely the person, or sample of people, is to have come from a population that has a particular mean and standard deviation. A z-test can be used to test the statistical significance of a wide range of summary statistics, including the size of a single score, the size of a mean or the size of the difference between two means. In this chapter I will keep the examples to looking at a total for an individual participant or a mean that has come from one sample.

All z-tests are based on the same principle. They assess the distance that the particular statistic being evaluated is from the population's mean in terms of population standard deviations. For example, the statistic could be an individual's score on an IQ test, the population mean would be the mean IQ score for a given population and the standard deviation would be the standard deviation for the IQs of those in the population. The population parameters (or *norms*) will have been ascertained by the people who devised the test and will be reported in the manual that explains the appropriate use of the test.

The equation for a z-test that compares a single participant's score with that for the population is of the form:

$$z = \frac{\text{single score} - \text{population mean for the measure}}{\text{population standard deviation for the measure}}$$

At an intuitive level we can say that the z-test is looking at how large the difference is between the sample statistic and the population mean (the parameter) for the statistic. Therefore, the bigger the difference the bigger z will be. However, z also takes into account the amount of spread that that statistic has in the population, expressed in terms of the standard deviation. Thus, the bigger the spread, the smaller z will be. Therefore for z to be large, the difference between the statistic and the population mean for the statistic must be sufficiently large to counteract the effect of the size of the spread.

This stage in the explanation is critical because I am now introducing the general principle for most inferential statistics. So far when talking about a normal distribution (see Chapter 9) I have referred to a concrete entity such as an IQ score. Figure 12.1 shows the distribution of IQ scores for 16,000 people, on a test that has a population mean of 100 IQ points and a standard deviation of 15 IQ points. Remember that in a normal distribution the mean value is also the most frequent value—the mode.

Imagine, now, that we select a person from the above sample. We put the IQ for that person into the equation for z and calculate z, then we plot that z-value on a frequency graph. We repeat this for the entire sample; we select each person, one at a time, test their IQ, calculate the new z-value and then plot it on the graph. Under these conditions, the most likely value of z would be zero because the most frequent IQ score will be the mean for the population:

FIGURE 12.1 The distribution of IQ scores in a sample of 16,000 people, for a test with mean = 100 and SD = 15

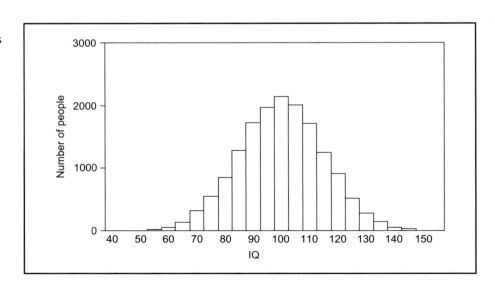

$$z = \frac{100 - 100}{15}$$

$$= 0$$

The larger the difference between the IQ score we are testing and the mean IQ for the population the less frequently it will occur. Thus the distribution of the z-scores from the sample looks like this:

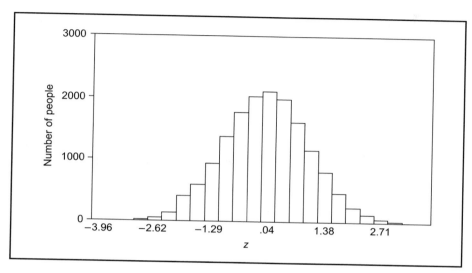

FIGURE 12.2 The distribution for 16,000 z-scores calculated from the data in Figure 12.1

The theoretical distribution of z (the *standardised normal distribution*) is shown in Figure 12.3. We can see that, as with all normal distributions, the distribution is symmetrical around the mean (and mode and median). However, the mean for z is 0. The standard deviation for z has the value 1.

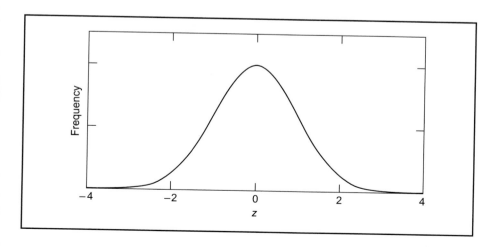

FIGURE 12.3 The standardised normal distribution

Using the z-distribution, statisticians have calculated the proportion of a population that will have a particular score on a normally distributed measure.

Thus, if we have any measure that we know to be normally distributed in the population, we can work out how likely a given value for that measure is by applying a z-test. For example, if we know that a given IQ test has a mean of 100 and a standard deviation of 15, we can test a particular person's IQ and see how many people have an IQ that is as high (or low) as this person's. Imagine that the person scores 120 on the IQ test. Using the equation for z we can see how many standard deviations this is above the mean:

$$z = \frac{120 - 100}{15}$$

$$= 1.333$$

We can now find out what proportion of people have a z-score that is at least this large by referring to z-tables.

Reading *z*-tables

Appendix XIV contains the table of z-values that can be used to find their significance. Table 12.1 shows a portion of Table A14.1 from Appendix XIV. To find the proportion for a z of 1.333, look in the first column until you find the row that indicates the first decimal place: 1.3. Now, because the figure (1.333) has more than one decimal place, look along the columns until you find the value of the second decimal place (3). Now look at the entry in the table where the row 1.3 meets the column 3 and this will give us the

Table 12.1 An extract of the z-tables from Appendix XIV

z	0	1	2	3	4	5	6	7	8	9
				2nd decimal place						
1	0.1587	0.1562	0.1539	0.1515	0.1492	0.1469	0.1446	0.1423	0.1401	0.1379
1.1	0.1357	0.1335	0.1314	0.1292	0.1271	0.1251	0.1230	0.1210	0.1190	0.1170
1.2	0.1151	0.1131	0.1112	0.1093	0.1075	0.1056	0.1038	0.1020	0.1003	0.0985
1.3	0.0968	0.0951	0.0934	0.0918	0.0901	0.0885	0.0869	0.0853	0.0838	0.0823
1.4	0.0808	0.0793	0.0778	0.0764	0.0749	0.0735	0.0721	0.0708	0.0694	0.0681
1.5	0.0668	0.0655	0.0643	0.0630	0.0618	0.0606	0.0594	0.0582	0.0571	0.0559
1.6	0.0548	0.0537	0.0526	0.0516	0.0505	0.0495	0.0485	0.0475	0.0465	0.0455
1.7	0.0446	0.0436	0.0427	0.0418	0.0409	0.0401	0.0392	0.0384	0.0375	0.0367
1.8	0.0359	0.0351	0.0344	0.0336	0.0329	0.0322	0.0314	0.0307	0.0301	0.0294
1.9	0.0287	0.0281	0.0274	0.0268	0.0262	0.0256	0.0250	0.0244	0.0239	0.0233
2	0.0228	0.0222	0.0217	0.0212	0.0207	0.0202	0.0197	0.0192	0.0188	0.0183

proportion of the population that would produce a z-score of 1.33 (or larger); we cannot look up a more precise z-score than one that has two decimal places in this table. The cell gives the figure 0.0918. This is the proportion of people who will have a score that is high enough to yield a z of *at least* 1.33: in other words, in this example, the proportion of people who have an IQ of 120 or more.

Converting the proportion to a percentage (by multiplying it by 100) tells us that the person whose IQ we have measured has an IQ that is in the top 9.18%. By subtracting this figure from 100% we can say that 90.82% of the population have a lower IQ than this person.

If a z-score is negative, then, because the z-distribution is symmetrical, we can still use Table 12.1 but now the proportions should be read as those below the z-score. Thus, if $z = -1.333$ (for a person with an IQ of 80), then 9.18% of people in the population have a score as low or lower than this.

Using z-scores in this way it can be shown that a standard deviation can be a particularly useful summary statistic. If we know the mean and the standard deviation for a population (which is normally distributed), then if someone has a score that is one standard deviation higher than the mean, the z for that person will be 1.

For example, we know that the standard deviation for the IQ test is 15. If a person has an IQ one standard deviation higher than the mean his or her IQ will be 115. Therefore,

$$z = \frac{115 - 100}{15}$$

$$= 1$$

If we look up, in Table 12.1, the proportion for $z = 1$ we use the column of Table 12.1 that is headed by 0 as a z of 1 is the same as a z of 1.00—to two decimal places. The table shows the value 0.1587. In other words, 15.87% of the population have an IQ as large as or larger than one standard deviation above the mean. Similarly, if a person has an IQ that is one standard deviation below the mean (i.e. $100 - 15 = 85$) then the z of their score will equal −1, in other words, 15.87% of the population have an IQ that is one or more standard deviations below the population mean.

Using these two bits of information we can see that 15.87% + 15.87% = 31.74% of the population have an IQ that is either one, or more, standard deviations above, or one, or more, standard deviations below the population mean. Therefore, the remainder of the population, approximately 68%, have an IQ that is within one standard deviation of the mean. That is, approximately 68% of the population will have an IQ in the range 85 to 115. Hence, if we assume that a given statistic is normally distributed we know that 68% of the population will lie within one standard deviation of the mean for that population.

Testing the significance of a single score when the population mean and standard deviation are known

Another way of looking at the z-test is to treat the z-distribution as telling us how likely a given score, or a more extreme score, is to occur in a given population. Thus, in the earlier example we can say that there is a probability of 0.0918 of someone who is picked randomly from the population achieving an IQ score as high as 120, or higher. In this way, we can test hypotheses about whether a given score is likely to have come from a population of scores with a particular mean and standard deviation.

For example, if an educational psychologist tests the IQ of a person, he or she can perform a z-test on that person's IQ to see whether it is significantly different from what would be expected if the client came from the given population.

Let us say, again, that the mean for the IQ test is 100 and its standard deviation is 15. The educational psychologist could test the hypothesis:

H_A: The client has an IQ that is too low to be from the given population.

for which the Null Hypothesis would be:

H_0: The client has an IQ that is from the given population.

The educational psychologist tests the client's IQ and it is 70. In order to evaluate the alternative hypothesis the psychologist applies a z-test to the data.

$$z = \frac{70 - 100}{15}$$
$$= -2.$$

In other words, the client's IQ is 2 standard deviations below the population mean.

Finding out the statistical significance of a z-score

Computer programs will usually report the statistical significance of a z-score that they have calculated. However, sometimes you will need to refer to statistical tables to find out its significance.

To find out the probability that this person came from the population with a mean IQ of 100 and an SD of 15 we again read the z-tables. We take the negative sign as indicating a score below the population mean but for the purposes of reading the z-tables we ignore the sign, as the distribution is symmetrical.

The body of Table 12.1 (and Table A14.1) gives one-tailed probabilities for zs. In other words, it is testing a directional hypothesis. As the psychologist is assessing whether the person's IQ is lower than the mean IQ for the population he or she has a directional hypothesis.

Looking at Table 12.1, we can see that with $z = 2$, $p = 0.0228$. This is the probability that a person with an IQ as low as (or lower than) 70 has come from the population on which the IQ test was standardised. As 0.0228 is smaller than 0.05, the educational psychologist can say that the client's IQ is significantly lower than the population mean and can reject the Null Hypothesis that this client comes from the given population.

Testing a non-directional hypothesis

If the educational psychologist had not had a directional hypothesis he or she would conduct a two-tailed test. To find a two-tailed probability, find the one-tailed probability (in this case 0.0228) and multiply it by two ($0.0228 \times 2 = 0.0456$). The reason we can do this is that we need to look in both tails of the distribution: for a positive z-value *and* a negative z-value. In addition, as the distribution is symmetrical, the negative z will have the same probability as the positive z.

Examining the difference between a sample mean and a population mean

For the following discussion, imagine that researchers believe that children who have been brought up in a particular institution have been deprived of intellectual stimulation and that this will have detrimentally affected the children's IQs. They wish to test their hypothesis:

H_A: Children brought up in the institution have lower IQs than the general population.

The Null Hypothesis will be:

H_0: Children brought up in the institution have normal IQs.

Under these conditions we can employ a new version of the z-test: one to test a sample mean. However, in order to be able to apply a z-test to a given statistic we need to know how that statistic is distributed. Thus, in this case, we need to know what the distribution of means is.

The distribution of means

Instead of taking all the single scores from a population and looking at their distribution, we would need to take a random sample of a given size from the population and calculate the mean for the sample, and then repeat the exercise for another sample of the same size from the same population. If we did this often enough we would produce a distribution for the means, which would have its own mean and its own standard deviation.

Statisticians have calculated how means are distributed. They have found that the mean of such a distribution is the same as the population mean.

However, the standard deviation of means depends on the sample size, such that the population of such means has a standard deviation that is $\frac{\sigma}{\sqrt{n}}$, that is, the standard deviation for the original scores divided by the square root of the sample size. The standard deviation of means is sometimes called the *standard error of the mean*.

Thus, if we know the mean and the standard deviation for the original population of scores, we can use a z-test to calculate the significance of the difference between a mean of a sample and the mean of the population, using the following equation:

$$z = \frac{\text{mean of sample} - \text{population mean}}{\left(\dfrac{\text{population standard deviation}}{\sqrt{\text{sample size}}} \right)}$$

In this way we can calculate how likely a mean from a given sample is to have come from a particular population.

Let us assume that 20 children from the institution are tested and that their mean IQ is 90, using a test that has a mean of 100 and a standard deviation of 15. We can calculate a z-score using the appropriate equation and this shows that $z = -2.98$. Referring to the table of probabilities for z-scores in Appendix XIV tells us that the one-tailed probability of such a z-score is 0.0014. As this is below 0.05, we can reject the Null Hypothesis and conclude that the institutionalised children have a significantly lower IQ compared with the normal population.

A z-test can be used when we know the necessary parameters for the population. However, when not all the parameters are known, alternative tests will be necessary. One such test is the *t*-test.

One-group *t*-tests

Evaluating a single sample mean when the population mean is known but the population standard deviation is not known

When we know, or are assuming that we know, the mean of a population but do not know the standard deviation for the population, the best we can do is to use an approximation of that standard deviation from the standard deviation for the sample. Statisticians have worked out that it is not possible to produce such an approximation that is sufficiently close to the standard deviation of the population to be usable in a z-test. Instead they have devised a different type of distribution, which can be used to test the significance of the difference between the sample mean and the population mean, the *t*-distribution. You will sometimes see it described as Student's *t*. This is because William Gossett, who first published work describing it, worked for the brewers Guinness and chose this name as a pseudonym.

Using t-tests to test the significance of a single mean

The equation to calculate this version of t is similar to the equation for the z when we are comparing a sample mean with a population mean: in this case the sample standard deviation is used instead of the population standard deviation:

$$t = \frac{\text{mean of sample} - \text{population mean}}{\left(\dfrac{\text{sample standard deviation}}{\sqrt{\text{sample size}}}\right)}$$

The distribution of t is also similar to the distribution of z. It is bell-shaped with the mean at zero. However, it has the added complication that its distribution is partly dependent on the size of the sample, or rather, the degrees of freedom (df). Degrees of freedom are explained in the next section; for the present version of the t-test the degrees of freedom are one fewer than the sample size. Figure 12.4 shows the t-distribution when df is 1 and when df is 50.

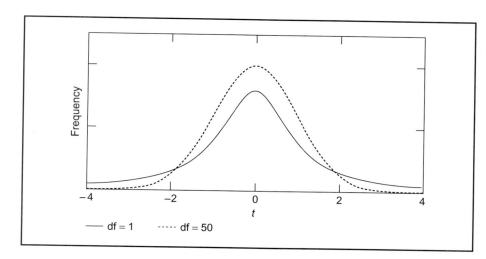

FIGURE 12.4
t-distributions with 1 and 50 degrees of freedom

As the degrees of freedom increase so the distribution begins to look more like a normal distribution. Because the shape of the distribution depends on the degrees of freedom, instead of being able to produce a single distribution for t there is a different distribution of t for each sized sample.

The significance of a number of different statistics, not just single means, can be tested using t-tests. Unlike z-tables, the probabilities shown in t-tables are dependent on the sample size and on the version of the t-test that is used. Statisticians have worked out that the distribution of t is dependent on a factor other than just the simple sample size: the degrees of freedom involved in the particular version of t. Instead of creating a different set of probability tables for each version of the t-test, the same table can be used if we know the degrees of freedom involved in the particular version of the *t*-test that we are using.

Degrees of freedom

The degrees of freedom for many statistical tests are partly dependent on the sample size and partly on the number of entities that are fixed in the equation for that test, in order that parameters can be estimated. In the case of a *t*-test, based on a single mean, only one entity is fixed—the mean—as it is being used to estimate the standard deviation for the population.

To demonstrate the meaning of degrees of freedom, imagine that we have given five people a maths exam. Their scores out of 10 were as follows:

Participant	Maths score
1	7
2	8
3	6
4	5
5	9

The mean score is 7. I can alter one number and, as long as I alter one or more of the other numbers to compensate, they will still have a mean of 7. In fact, I have the freedom to alter four of the numbers to whatever values I like but this will mean that the value of the fifth number will be fixed. For example, if I add one to each of the first four numbers then the last number will have to be 5 for the mean to remain at 7. Hence, I have four degrees of freedom. Therefore, to obtain the degrees of freedom for this equation, we have to subtract one from the sample size.

The method of calculating the degrees of freedom for each version of the *t*-test will be given as each version is introduced. However, most computer programs will report the degrees of freedom for the *t*-test.

(Incidentally, as the sample gets larger, the sample standard deviation produces a better approximation of the population standard deviation. Hence, when the degrees of freedom for the *t*-test are over about 200 the probability for a given *t*-value is almost the same as for the same *z*-value.)

As an example of the use of this version of the *t*-test, known as the *one-group t*-test, let us stay with the scores on the maths exam. Imagine that researchers had devised a training method for improving maths performance in children. Ten 6-year-olds are given the training and then they are tested on the maths test which produces an AA (arithmetic age) score.

The research hypothesis was directional:

H_A: The maths score of those given the training will be better than that of the general population of 6-year-olds.

The Null Hypothesis was:

H_0: The maths score of those given training will not be different from that of the population of 6-year-olds.

The mean for the sample was 7 and the SD was 1.247. The mean is consistent with the research hypothesis, in that the performance is better than for the population (which would be 6, their chronological age), but we want to know whether it is significantly so. Therefore the results were entered into the equation for a one-group t-test, with the result:

$$t_{(9)} = \frac{7 - 6}{\left(\dfrac{1.247}{\sqrt{10}}\right)}$$

$$= 2.536$$

where the 9 in brackets shows the degrees of freedom.

Finding the significance of t

To find out the likelihood of achieving this size of t-value if the Null Hypothesis were true we need to look up the t-tables. A full version is given in Appendix XIV. Table 12.2 gives an extract of that table. Note that the t-tables are laid out differently from the z-tables. Here, probability levels are given at the top of the table, the degrees of freedom are given in the first column and the t-values are given in the body of the table. Note also that the one- and two-tailed probabilities are given.

To read the table find the degrees of freedom, in this case 9. Read along that row until you come to a t-value that is just smaller than the result from your research ($t = 2.536$). Note that 2.262 is smaller than 2.536, while 2.821 is larger than it. Therefore, look to the top of the column that contains 2.262. As the research hypothesis is directional we want the one-tailed probability. We are told that had the t-value been 2.262 then the probability would have been 0.025. Our t-value is larger still and so we know that the probability is less than 0.025. This can be written $p < 0.025$, where the symbol $<$ means *is less than*. As 0.025 is smaller than the critical value of 0.05, the researchers can reject the Null Hypothesis and accept their hypothesis that the group who received maths training had better performance than the general population.

Table 12.2 An extract of the t-table (from Appendix XIV)

Critical values for the t-test

One-tailed probabilities

0.4	0.3	0.2	0.1	0.05	0.025	0.01	0.005	0.001	0.0005

Two-tailed probabilities

df	0.8	0.6	0.4	0.2	0.1	0.05	0.02	0.01	0.002	0.001
8	0.262	0.546	0.889	1.397	1.860	2.306	2.896	3.355	4.501	5.041
9	0.261	0.543	0.883	1.383	1.833	2.262	2.821	3.250	4.297	4.781
10	0.260	0.542	0.879	1.372	1.812	2.228	2.764	3.169	4.144	4.587

Reporting the results of a t-*test*

The column for the one-tailed $p = 0.01$ level in Table 12.2 shows that the t-value would have to be 2.821 to be significant at this level. As the t-value obtained in the research was larger than 2.262 but smaller than 2.821, we know that the probability level lies between 0.025 and 0.01. This can be represented as:

$$0.01 < p < 0.025.$$

There are many suggestions as to how to report probability levels. If you have been given the exact probability level by a computer program then report the exact level; in this case it is $p = 0.016$. However, if you have to obtain the level from t-tables, I recommend the format that shows the range in which the p-level lies, as this is the most informative way of presenting the information. If you simply write $p < 0.025$, the reader does not know whether p is less than or more than 0.001. The APA states that you shouldn't use a zero before the decimal point if the value of the number couldn't be greater than 1, for example when reporting a probability. Personally, I don't like this convention but I will stick to it when showing how to report results formally. Another recommendation is that, unless you need greater precision, you should round decimals to two decimal places. Accordingly, if the third decimal place is 5 or greater then you round up the second decimal place; in other words, increase it by 1. Therefore, 2.536 becomes 2.54. If the third decimal place is 4 or smaller then leave the second decimal place as it is.

To report the results of the t-test use the following format:

$$t_{(9)} = 2.54, .01 < p < .025, \text{one-tailed test}$$

Dealing with unexpected results

Sometimes researchers make a directional hypothesis but the result goes in the opposite way to that predicted. Clearly the result is outside the original rejection region (within which the Null Hypothesis could be rejected), because it is in the wrong tail of the distribution. However, it is possible, rather than simply rejecting the research hypothesis, to ask whether the result would have been statistically significant had the hypothesis been non-directional. Abelson (1995) suggests that, if this happens, you look to see whether the result is statistically significant in the other tail of the distribution, but set the new α-level at 0.005 for a one-tailed test. In this way the overall α-level for the two assessments is the equivalent of a two-tailed probability of $0.05 + 0.005 = 0.055$, which is only just over the conventional α-level. Abelson calls this the *lopsided test*, because the regions in the two tails of the distribution are not the same, as they are in a conventional two-tailed test. As this is an unusual procedure, I recommend that if you use it, you explain thoroughly what you have done.

Another approach is to set up three hypotheses: a Null Hypothesis (H_0)—for example that the means of two groups do not differ—and two directional hypotheses, one suggesting that group A has larger mean than group B (H_1) and one suggesting that group B has a larger mean than group A (H_2) (in other words, two directional hypotheses). The results of our statistical test can lead to one of three decisions: fail to reject H_0, reject H_0 and favour H_1 or reject H_0 and favour H_2. See Dracup (2000), Harris (1997), Jones and Tukey (2000) and Leventhal and Huynh (1996) for more on this approach.

Confidence intervals for means

Confidence intervals (CIs) were introduced in Chapter 11 where the example used concerned proportions. Remember that a confidence interval is a range of possible values within which a population parameter is likely to lie and that it is estimated from the statistic that has been found for a sample. You now have the necessary information to allow the confidence intervals of a mean to be described. There are two ways in which the CI for the population mean can be calculated. The first is based on the z-test and would be used when the sample is as large as 30. The second is based on the t-test and is used when the sample is smaller than 30.

Appendix III gives worked examples of both methods of calculating the CI for a mean. The CI for the mean performance on the maths exam tells us where the mean is likely to lie if we gave the population of children the enhanced maths training. The 95% confidence interval is 0.892 above and below the sample mean. The sample mean was 7 so the CI is between $7 - 0.892 = 6.108$ and $7 + 0.892 = 7.892$. Note that the interval does not include 6, which was the mean on the maths exam for the general population. This gives more evidence for the conclusion that the enhanced maths training does produce better performance than would be expected from the general population.

Further graphical displays

We can now introduce three new versions of graphs that were originally discussed in Chapter 9: line charts of means with standard error of the mean, line charts with means and confidence intervals, and notched box-plots. In addition, we can introduce another graph which explores whether a set of data is normally distributed: the normal quantile–quantile plot.

Line charts with means and standard error of the mean

Some researchers, including those working in psychophysics, prefer to present the standard error of the mean as the measure of spread on a line chart. A line chart of means with standard deviations as the measure of spread (as shown in Figure 9.22) presents the range of scores that approximately 68% of the population would have if the measure were normally distributed.

A line chart with the standard error of the mean as the measure of spread is presenting the range of scores that approximately 68% of *means* would have if the study were repeated with the same sample size.

Figure 12.5 presents the mean recall for the three mnemonic strategies referred to in Chapter 9, but with the standard error of the mean as the measure of spread.

FIGURE 12.5 The mean recall and standard error of the mean for the three mnemonic strategies

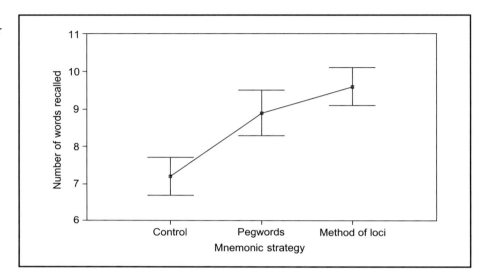

Line charts with means and confidence intervals

An alternative measure that can be presented on a line chart is the confidence interval. This allows comparison across groups to see whether the confidence intervals overlap. If they do, as in Figure 12.6, this suggests that even if the result from the sample showed a significant difference between the means, the means for the three populations may not in fact differ.

Notched box-plots

Figure 12.7 shows the notched version of the box plot for the data given in Table 9.1 of participants' recall of words. This variant of the box plot allows the confidence interval for the median to be presented in the notch. The way to calculate this confidence interval is shown in Appendix III.

Normal quantile–quantile plots

Another form of graph, the normal quantile–quantile (normal Q–Q) plot, can help evaluate whether a distribution is normal. Quantiles are points on

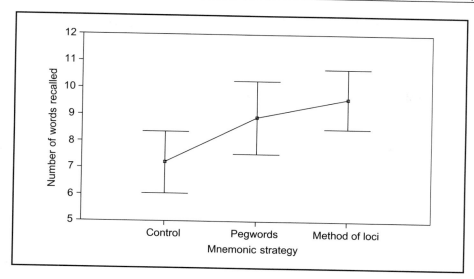

FIGURE 12.6 The mean word recall and 95% confidence interval for the three mnemonic strategies

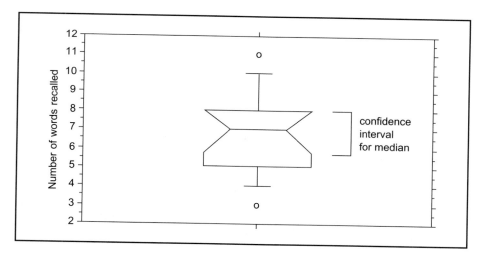

FIGURE 12.7 A notched box-plot of number of words recalled

a distribution that split it into equal-sized proportions; for example, the median would be Q(.5), the lower quartile would be Q(.25) and the upper quartile Q(.75); together these quartiles split distribution into four equal parts. This graph is like a scattergram but it plots, on the horizontal axis, the quantiles against, on the vertical axis, what the quantiles would have been had the data been normally distributed. To find the *normal expected value* for an observed value, initially the quantile for the observed data point is calculated. The z-score that would have such a quantile in a normal distribution is then found. This is then converted back, based on the mean and SD of the original distribution, into the value the data point would have had had the

FIGURE 12.8 A normal
Q–Q plot of data that
are positively skewed

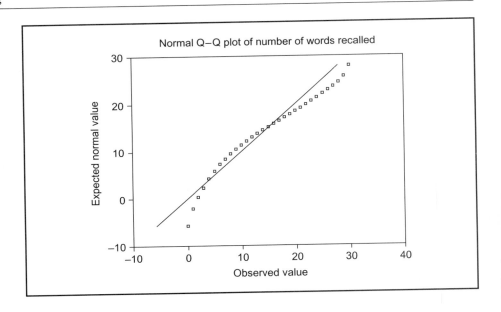

distribution been normal. (An example of how this is calculated is given in Appendix III.) If the original data were normally distributed then the points should form a straight line on the normal Q–Q plot. However, if the data were non-normal then the points will not lie on a straight line. Figure 12.8 shows the Normal Q–Q plot of the positively skewed data shown in Figure 9.28.

Identifying outliers with standardised scores

In addition to using box plots or stem-and-leaf plots to identify outliers, it is possible to standardise a set of numbers using a variant of the z-score and see how extreme any of the numbers are. To standardise the scores the following equation is used:

$$\text{standardised score} = \frac{\text{score} - \text{sample mean}}{\text{sample SD}}$$

Chapter 9 gave an example of the recall scores for a sixteenth person being added to the original group of fifteen people. The sixteenth person had a score of 25 which was much higher than the rest. The mean for the enlarged sample is 7.8125 and the sample SD is 5.088. Table 12.3 shows the original and the standardised recall scores. A standardised score of greater than 3 or less than –3 should be investigated further as a potential outlier. Note that the score of 25 produced a standardised score of 3.378.

Table 12.3 The original and standardised scores
for the word recall of sixteen participants

original score	standardised score
3	−.946
4	−.749
4	−.749
5	−.553
5	−.553
6	−.356
6	−.356
7	−.160
7	−.160
7	−.160
8	.037
8	.037
9	.233
10	.430
11	.626
25	3.378

Summary

When researchers know the population mean and standard deviation for a given summary statistic they can compare a value for the statistic that has been obtained from one person or a sample of people with the population mean for that statistic, using a z-test. In this way, they can see how common the value they have obtained is among the population and thus how likely the person or group is to have come from a population with that mean and standard deviation. When only the population mean is known for the statistic a t-test has to be employed rather than a z-test.

The present chapter has largely concentrated on statistical significance as a way of deciding between a research hypothesis and a Null Hypothesis. In other words, it has only addressed the probability of making a Type I error (rejecting the Null Hypothesis when it is true). The next chapter explains how researchers can attempt to avoid a Type II error and introduces additional summary statistics that can help researchers in their decisions.

13 EFFECT SIZE AND POWER

Introduction

There has been a tendency for psychologists and other behavioural scientists to concentrate on whether a result is statistically significant, to the exclusion of any other statistical consideration (Cohen, 1962; Sedlmeier & Gigerenzer, 1989; Clark-Carter, 1997). Early descriptions of the method of hypothesis testing (e.g. Fisher, 1935) only involved the Null Hypothesis. This chapter deals with the consequences of this approach and describes additional techniques, which come from the ideas of Neyman and Pearson (1933), which can enable researchers to make more informed decisions.

Limitations of statistical significance testing

Concentration on statistical significance misses an important aspect of inferential statistics—statistical significance is affected by sample size. This has two consequences. Firstly, statistical probability cannot be used as a measure of the magnitude of a result; two studies may produce very different results, in terms of statistical significance, simply because they have employed different sample sizes. Therefore, if only statistical significance is employed then results cannot be sensibly compared. Secondly, two studies conducted in the same way in every respect except sample size may lead to different conclusions. The one with the larger sample size may achieve a statistically significant result while the other one does not. Thus, the researchers in the first study will reject the Null Hypothesis of no effect while the researchers in the smaller study will reject their research hypothesis. Accordingly, the smaller the sample size the more likely we are to commit a Type II error—rejecting the research hypothesis when in fact it is correct.

Two new concepts will provide solutions to the two problems. *Effect size* gives a measure of magnitude of a result that is independent of sample size. Calculating the *power* of a statistical test helps researchers decide on the likelihood that a Type II error will be avoided.

Effect size

To allow the results of studies to be compared we need a measure that is independent of sample size. Effect sizes provide such a measure. In future chapters appropriate measures of effect size will be introduced for each research design. In this chapter I will deal with the designs described in the previous chapter, where a mean of a set of scores is being compared with a population mean. A number of different versions exist for some effect size measures. In general I am going to use the measures suggested by Cohen (1988).

In the case of the difference between two means we can use Cohen's d as the measure of effect size:

$$d = \frac{\mu_2 - \mu_1}{\sigma}$$

where μ_1 is the mean for one population, μ_2 is the mean for the other population, σ is the standard deviation for the population (explained below). To make this less abstract, recall the example, used in the last chapter, in which the IQs of children brought up in an institution are compared with the IQs of children not reared in an institution. Then, μ_1 is the mean IQ of the population of children reared in institutions, μ_2 is the mean for the population of children not reared in institutions and σ is the standard deviation of IQ scores, which is assumed to be the same for both groups. This assumption will be explained in the next chapter but need not concern us here. Usually, we do not know the values of all the parameters that are needed to calculate an effect size and so we use the equivalent sample statistics.

Accordingly, d is a measure of how many standard deviations apart the two means are. Note that although this is similar to the equations for calculating z, given in the last chapter, d fulfils our requirement for a measure that is independent of the sample size.[1]

In the previous chapter we were told that, as usual, the mean for the 'normal' population's IQ is 100; the standard deviation for the particular test was 15 and the mean IQ for the institutionalised children was 90. Therefore:

$$d = \frac{90 - 100}{15}$$

$$= -0.67$$

[1] The equation used to calculate effect size is independent of sample size. However, as with any statistic calculated from a sample, the larger the sample the more accurate the statistic will be as an estimate of the value in the population (the parameter).

After surveying published research, Cohen has defined, for each effect size measure, what constitutes a small effect, a medium effect and a large effect. In the case of d, a d of 0.2 (meaning that the mean IQs of the groups are just under $\frac{1}{4}$ of an SD apart) represents a small effect size, a d of 0.5 ($\frac{1}{2}$ an SD) constitutes a medium effect size and a d of 0.8 (just over $\frac{3}{4}$ of an SD) would be a large effect size (when evaluating the magnitude of an effect size ignore the negative sign). Thus, in this study we can say that being reared in an institution has between a medium and a large effect on the IQs of children.

An additional use of effect size is that it allows the results of a number of related studies to be combined to see whether they produce a consistent effect. This technique—meta-analysis—will be dealt with in Chapter 22.

The importance of an effect size

As Rosnow and Rosenthal (1989) have pointed out, the importance of an effect size will depend on the nature of the research being conducted. If a study into the effectiveness of a drug at saving lives found only a small effect size, even though the lives of only a small proportion of participants were being saved, this would be an important effect. However, if the study was into something trivial like a technique for enhancing performance on a computer game, then even a large effect might not be considered to be important.

Statistical power

Statistical power is defined as the probability of *avoiding* a Type II error. The probability of making a Type II error is usually symbolised by β (the Greek letter beta). Therefore, the power of a test is $1 - \beta$.

Figure 13.1 represents the situation where two means are being compared; for example, the mean IQ for the population on which a test has been standardised (μ_1) and the mean for the population of people given special training to enhance their IQs (μ_2). Formally stated H_0 is: $\mu_2 = \mu_1$, while the research hypothesis (H_A) is $\mu_2 > \mu_1$. As usual an α-level is set (say $\alpha = 0.05$). This determines the critical mean, that is the mean IQ, for a given sample size, that would be just large enough to allow us to reject H_0. It determines β which will be the area (in the distribution that is centred on μ_2) to the

FIGURE 13.1 A graphical representation of the links between statistical power, β and α

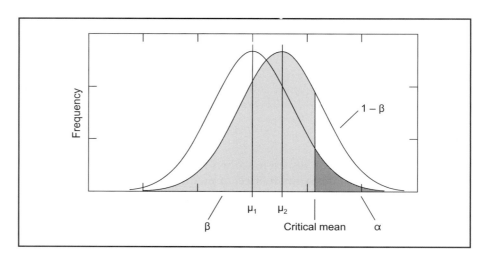

left of the critical mean. It also then determines the power $(1 - \beta)$ which is the area (in the distribution that is centred on μ_2) that lies to the right of the critical mean.

   The power we require for a given piece of research will depend on the aims of the research. Thus, if it is particularly important that we avoid making a Type II error we will aim for a level of power that is as near 1 as possible. For example, if we were testing the effectiveness of a drug that could save lives we would not want wrongly to reject the research hypothesis that the drug was effective. However, as you will see, achieving such a level of power may involve an impractically large sample size. Therefore, Cohen and others recommend, as a rule of thumb, that a reasonable minimum level of power to aim for, under normal circumstances, is 0.8. In other words, the probability of making a Type II error (β) is $1 -$ power $= 0.2$. With an α-level set at 0.05 this will give us a ratio of the probabilities of committing a Type I and a Type II error of 1:4. However, as was stated in Chapter 10, it is possible to set a different level of α.

   Statistical power depends on many factors, including the type of test being employed, the effect size, the design—whether it is a between-subjects or a within-subjects design—the α-level set, whether the test is one- or two-tailed and, in the case of between-subjects designs, the relative size of the samples.

   Power analysis can be used in two ways. It can be used prospectively during the design stage to decide on the sample size required to achieve a given level of power. It can also be used retrospectively once the data have been collected, to ascertain what power the test had. The more useful approach is prospective power analysis. Once the design, α-level, and tail of test have been decided, researchers can calculate the sample size they require. However, they still have the problem of arriving at an indication of the effect size before they can do the power calculations. But as the study has yet to be conducted this is unknown.

Choosing the effect size prior to conducting a study

There are at least three ways in which effect size can be chosen before a study is conducted. Firstly, researchers can look at previous research in the area to get an impression of the size of effects that have been found. This would be helped if researchers routinely reported the effect sizes they have found. The latest version of the APA's *Publication Manual* (American Psychological Association, 2001) recommends the inclusion of effect sizes in the report of research. Nonetheless, if the appropriate descriptive statistics have been reported (such as means and SDs) then an effect size can be calculated. Secondly, in the absence of such information, researchers can calculate an effect size from the results of their pilot studies. A final way around the problem is to decide beforehand what size of effect they wish to detect. This is where Cohen's classification of effects into small, medium and large can be useful. Researchers can decide that even a small effect is important in the context of their particular study. Alternatively, they can aim for the necessary power for detecting a medium or even a large effect if this is appropriate for their research. It should be emphasised that they are not saying that they know what effect size *will* be found—only that this is the effect size that they would be willing to put the effort in to detect as statistically significant.

I would only recommend this last approach if there is no other indication of what effect size your research is likely to entail. Nonetheless, this approach does at least allow you to do power calculations in the absence of any other information on the likely effect size.

To aid the reader with this approach I have provided power tables in the appendices for each statistical test and as each test is introduced I will explain the use of the appropriate table.

The power of a one-group *z*-test

Power analysis for this test is probably the simplest, and for the interested reader I have provided, in Appendix IV, a description of how to calculate the exact power for the test and how to calculate the sample size needed for a given level of power. Here I will describe how to use power tables to decide sample size.

Table 13.1 shows part of the power table for a one-group *z*-test, from Appendix XV. The top row of the table shows effect sizes (*d*). The first column shows the sample size. Each Figure in the body of the table is the statistical power that will be achieved for a given effect size if a given sample size is used.

The table shows that for a one-group *z*-test with a medium effect size (*d* = 0.5), a one-tailed test and an α-level of 0.05, to achieve power of 0.80, 25 participants are required.

The following examples show the effect that altering one of these variables at a time has on power. Although these examples are for the one-group *z*-test, the power of all statistical tests will be similarly affected by changes in sample size, effect size, the α-level and, where a one-tailed test is possible for the given statistical test, the nature of the research hypothesis.

Table 13.1 An extract of the power tables for a one-group *z*-test, one-tailed probability, α = 0.05 (* denotes that the power is over 0.995)

n	0.1	0.2	0.3	0.4	0.5	0.6	0.7	0.8	0.9	1.0	1.1	1.2	1.3	1.4
15	0.10	0.19	0.31	0.46	0.61	0.75	0.86	0.93	0.97	0.99	*	*	*	*
16	0.11	0.20	0.33	0.48	0.64	0.77	0.88	0.94	0.97	0.99	*	*	*	*
17	0.11	0.21	0.34	0.50	0.66	0.80	0.89	0.95	0.98	0.99	*	*	*	*
18	0.11	0.21	0.35	0.52	0.68	0.82	0.91	0.96	0.99	*	*	*	*	*
19	0.11	0.22	0.37	0.54	0.70	0.83	0.92	0.97	0.99	*	*	*	*	*
20	0.12	0.23	0.38	0.56	0.72	0.85	0.93	0.97	0.99	*	*	*	*	*
25	0.13	0.26	0.44	0.64	0.80	0.91	0.97	0.99	*	*	*	*	*	*
30	0.14	0.29	0.50	0.71	0.86	0.95	0.99	*	*	*	*	*	*	*
35	0.15	0.32	0.55	0.76	0.91	0.97	0.99	*	*	*	*	*	*	*
40	0.16	0.35	0.60	0.81	0.94	0.98	*	*	*	*	*	*	*	*

Effect size (d)

Sample size and power

Increased sample size produces greater power. If everything else is held constant but we use 40 participants then power rises to 0.94.

Effect size and power

The larger the effect size the greater the power. With an effect size of 0.7, power rises to 0.97 for 25 participants with a one-tailed α-level of 0.05.

Research hypothesis and power

A one-tailed test is more powerful than a two-tailed test. A two-tailed test using 25 people for an effect size of $d = 0.5$ would have given power of 0.71 (see Appendix XV), whereas the one-tailed version gave power of 0.8.

α-level and power

The smaller the α-level the lower the power. In other words, if everything else is held constant then reducing the likelihood of making a Type I error increases the likelihood of making a Type II error. Setting α at 0.01 reduces power from 0.8 to 0.57. On the other hand, setting α at 0.1 increases power to nearly 0.99. These effects can be seen in Figure 13.1; as α gets smaller (the critical mean moves to the right) so $1 - \beta$ gets smaller, and as α gets larger (the critical mean moves to the left) so $1 - \beta$ gets larger.

The power of a one-group *t*-test

To assess the power of a one-group *t*-test or to decide on the sample size necessary to achieve a desired level of power use the table provided in Appendix XV, part of which is reproduced in Table 13.2. The tables for a

Table 13.2 An extract of a power table for one-group *t*-tests, one-tailed probability, $\alpha = 0.05$ (* denotes that the power is over 0.995)

n	0.1	0.2	0.3	0.4	0.5	0.6	0.7	0.8	0.9	1	1.1	1.2	1.3	1.4
140	0.32	0.76	0.97	*	*	*	*	*	*	*	*	*	*	*
150	0.33	0.79	0.98	*	*	*	*	*	*	*	*	*	*	*
160	0.35	0.81	0.98	*	*	*	*	*	*	*	*	*	*	*
170	0.36	0.83	0.99	*	*	*	*	*	*	*	*	*	*	*
180	0.38	0.85	0.99	*	*	*	*	*	*	*	*	*	*	*
190	0.39	0.86	0.99	*	*	*	*	*	*	*	*	*	*	*
200	0.41	0.88	0.99	*	*	*	*	*	*	*	*	*	*	*
300	0.53	0.96	*	*	*	*	*	*	*	*	*	*	*	*
400	0.64	0.99	*	*	*	*	*	*	*	*	*	*	*	*
500	0.72	*	*	*	*	*	*	*	*	*	*	*	*	*
600	0.79	*	*	*	*	*	*	*	*	*	*	*	*	*
700	0.84	*	*	*	*	*	*	*	*	*	*	*	*	*
800	0.88	*	*	*	*	*	*	*	*	*	*	*	*	*

Effect size (d)

one-group t-test can be read in the same way as those for the one-group z-test. As an example, imagine that researchers wished to detect a small effect size ($d = 0.2$) and have power of 0.8. They would need to have between 150 and 160 participants in their study. Therefore, as 0.80 lies midway between 0.79 and 0.81, we can say that the sample would need to be 155 (midway between 150 and 160).

Retrospective power analysis

If a study fails to support the research hypothesis, there are two possible explanations. The one that is usually assumed is that the hypothesis was in some way incorrect. However, an alternative explanation is that the test had insufficient power to achieve statistical significance. If statistical significance is not achieved I recommend that the power of the test be calculated. This will allow the researchers, and anyone reading a report of the research, to see how likely it was that a Type II error would be committed. I then recommend that researchers calculate the sample size that would be necessary, for the given effect size, to achieve power of 0.8.

Sometimes researchers, particularly students, state that had they used more participants they might have achieved a statistically significant result. This is not a very useful statement, as it will almost always be true if a big enough sample is employed, however small the effect size. For example, if a one-group t-test were being used, with $\alpha = 0.05$ and the effect size was as small as $d = 0.03$, a sample size of approximately 10,000 would give power of 0.8 for a one-tailed test. This effect size is achieved if the sample mean is only one-thirtieth of a standard deviation from the population mean—a difference of half an IQ point if the SD for the test is 15 IQ points.

It is far more useful to specify the number of participants that would be required to achieve power of 0.8. This would put the results in perspective. If the effect size is particularly small and the sample size required is vast then it questions the value of trying to replicate the study as it stands, whereas if the sample size were reasonable then it could be worth replicating the study.

As a demonstration of retrospective power analysis, imagine that researchers conducted a study with 50 participants. They analysed their data using a one-group t-test, with a one-tailed probability and α-level of 0.05. The probability of their result having occurred if the Null Hypothesis were true was greater than 0.05 and so they had insufficient information to reject the Null Hypothesis. When they calculated the effect size, it was found to be $d = 0.1$. They then went on to calculate the power of the test and found that it was 0.17. In other words, the probability of committing a Type II error was $1 - 0.17 = 0.83$. Therefore, there was an 83% chance that they would reject their research hypothesis when it was true. They were hardly giving it a fair chance. Referring to Table 13.2 again, we can see that over 600 participants would be needed to give the test power of 0.8. The need for such a large sample should make researchers think twice before attempting a replication of the study. If they wished to test the same hypothesis, they might examine the efficiency of their design to see whether they could reduce the overall variability of the data.

As a second example, imagine that researchers used 25 participants in a study but found after analysis of the data that the one-tailed, one-group t-test was not statistically significant at the 0.05 level. Effect size was found to be $d = 0.4$. The test, therefore, only had power of 0.61. In order to achieve the desired power of 0.8, 40 participants would have to be used. In this example the effect size is between a small and a medium one and as a sample size of 40 is not unreasonable, it would be worth replicating the study with the enlarged sample.

Summary

Effect size is a measure of the degree to which an independent variable is seen to affect a dependent variable or the degree to which two or more variables are related. As it is independent of the sample size it is useful for comparisons between studies.

The more powerful a statistical test the more likely a Type II error will be avoided. A major contributor to a test's power is the sample size. During the design stage researchers should conduct some form of power analysis to decide on the optimum sample size for the study. If they fail to achieve statistical significance then they should calculate the level of power their test had and work out what sample size would be required to achieve a reasonable level of statistical power for the same effect size. This chapter has shown how to find statistical power using tables. However, computer programs exist for power analysis. These include Gpower which is available via the Internet (see Erdfelder, Faul & Buchner, 1996) and SamplePower (Borenstein, Rothstein & Cohen, 1997).

The next chapter discusses the distinction between two types of statistical test: parametric and non-parametric tests.

14 PARAMETRIC AND NON-PARAMETRIC TESTS

Introduction

One way in which statistical tests are classified is into two types: parametric tests, such as the *t*-test, and non-parametric tests (sometimes known as distribution-free tests), such as the Kolmogorov–Smirnov referred to below. The distinction is based on certain assumptions about the population parameters that exist and the type of data that can be analysed.

The χ^2 (*chi-squared*, pronounced *kie-squared*) goodness-of-fit test is introduced for analysing data from one group when the level of measurement is nominal.

Parametric tests

Parametric tests have two characteristics which can be seen as giving them their name. Firstly, they make assumptions about the nature of certain parameters for the measures that have been taken. Secondly, their calculation usually involves the estimation, from the sampled data, of population parameters.

The assumptions of parametric tests

Parametric tests require that the population of scores, from which the sample came, is normally distributed. Additional criteria exist for certain parametric tests, and these will be outlined as each test is introduced. In the case of the one-group *t*-test the assumption is made that the data are independent of each other. This means that no person should contribute more than one score. In addition, there should be no influence from one person to another. In Chapter 12 an example was given where a group of people received enhanced maths training. The participants were then given a maths test. For the scores to be independent there should be no opportunity for the participants to confer over the answers to the questions in the test.

A common instance where data are unlikely to be independent is in social psychology research where data are provided by people who were tested in groups. An example would be if participants were in groups to discuss their opinions about a painting, with the dependent variable being each person's rating of his or her liking of the picture. Clearly people in a group may be affected by the opinions of others in the group. One way to achieve independence of scores in this situation is to take *group mean* as the dependent variable rather than individual scores. To do this, and maintain a reasonable level of statistical power, would mean having a larger number of participants than would be required if the individuals' ratings could be used.

An additional criterion that psychologists often set for a parametric test is that the data must be interval or ratio. As has already been pointed out in Chapter 8, statisticians are less concerned with this criterion. Adhering to it can set constraints on what analyses are possible with the data. The following guidelines allow a less strict adherence to the rule. In the case of nominal data with more than two levels it makes no sense to apply parametric tests because there is no inherent order in the levels; for example, if the variable is *political party*, with the levels conservative, liberal and radical. However, if the variable is ordinal but has sufficient levels—say 7 or more as in a Likert scale—then, as long as the other parametric requirements are fulfilled, it is considered legitimate to conduct parametric tests on the data (e.g. Tabachnick & Fidell, 2001). Zimmerman and Zumbo (1993) point out that many non-parametric tests produce the same probability as converting the original data into ranks (and therefore ordinal level of measurement) and performing the equivalent parametric test on the ranked data. Accordingly, the restriction of parametric tests to interval or ratio data ignores the derivation of some non-parametric tests.

If the criteria for a given parametric test are not fulfilled then it is inappropriate to use that parametric test. However, another misunderstanding among researchers is the belief that non-parametric statistics are free of any assumptions about the distribution of the data. Therefore, even when the assumptions of a parametric test are not fulfilled, the use of a non-parametric equivalent may not be recommended. Some variants of parametric tests have been developed for use even when some of the assumptions have been violated.

A further disadvantage of a non-parametric test is that it may have less power than its parametric equivalent. In other words, we may be more likely to commit a Type II error when using a non-parametric test. However, this is only usually true when the data fulfil the requirements of a parametric test and yet we still use a non-parametric test. *When those requirements are not fulfilled a non-parametric test can be the more powerful.*

Robustness

Despite the criteria that have been stated, statisticians have found that parametric tests are quite accurate even when some of their assumptions are violated: they are robust. However, this notion has to be treated with care. If more than one assumption underlying a particular parametric test is not fulfilled by the data, it would be better to use a parametric test that relaxes some of the assumptions or a non-parametric equivalent, as the probability levels given by standard tables or by computer may not reflect the true probabilities. The advent of computers has meant that researchers have been able to evaluate the effects of violations of assumptions on both parametric and non-parametric statistics. These studies have shown that, under certain conditions, both types of tests can be badly affected by such violations, in such a way that the probabilities that they report can be misleading; we may have very low power under some circumstances and under others the probability of making a Type I error may be markedly higher than the tables or computer programs tell us.

Tests have been devised to tell whether an assumption of a parametric test has been violated. The trouble with these is that they rely on the same hypothesis testing procedure as the inferential test. Therefore they are going to suffer the same problems over statistical power. Accordingly, if the sample is small the assumptions of the test could be violated quite badly but they would suggest that there is not a problem. Alternatively, if a large sample is used then a small and unimportant degree of violation could be shown to be significant. Therefore I do not recommend using such tests. Fortunately, there are rules of thumb as to how far away from the ideal conditions our data can be before we should do something to counteract the problem, and these will be given as each test is introduced.

One factor that can help to solve problems over assumptions of tests is that in psychology we are often interested in a summary statistic rather than the original scores that provided the statistic. Thus, we are usually interested in how the mean for a sample differs from the population or from another sample, rather than how the score for an individual differs from the population.

There is a rather convenient phenomenon—described by the *central limit theorem*—which is that if we take a summary statistic such as the mean, it has a normal distribution, even if the original population of scores from which it came does not. To understand the distribution of the mean, imagine that we take a sample of a given size from a population and work out the mean for that sample. We then take another sample of the same size from the same population and work out its mean. We continue to do this until we have found the means of a large number of samples from the population. If we produce a frequency distribution of those means it will be normally distributed. However, there is a caveat, that the sample size must be sufficiently large. Most authors seem to agree that a sample of 40 or more is sufficiently large, even if the original distribution of individual scores is quite skewed.

Often we do not know the distribution of scores in the population. I have said that the population has to be normally distributed. We may only have the data for our sample. Nonetheless, we can get an impression of the population's distribution from our sample. For example, I sampled 20 people's IQs from a normally distributed population, and it resulted in the distribution shown in Figure 14.1.

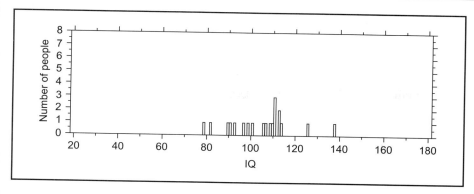

FIGURE 14.1 The distribution of IQs of 20 people selected from a normally distributed population

By creating a frequency distribution of the data from our sample we can see whether it is markedly skewed. If it is not then we could continue with a parametric test. If it is skewed and the sample is smaller than about 40, then we could *transform* the data.

Data transformation

It is possible to apply a mathematical formula to each item of data and produce a data set that is more normally distributed. For example, if the data form a negatively skewed distribution then squaring each score could reduce the skew and then it would be permissible to employ a parametric test on the data. If you are using a statistical test that looks for differences between the means of different levels of an independent variable then you must use the same transformation on all the data. Data transformation is a perfectly legitimate procedure as long as you do not try out a number of transformations in order to find one that produces a statistically significant result. Nonetheless, many students are suspicious of this procedure. For those wishing to pursue the topic further, possible transformations for different distributions are given in Appendix V, along with illustrations of the effects of some transformations.

Finding statistical significance for non-parametric tests

There are two routes to finding the statistical significance of a test: one is to work out the exact probability; the other is to work out, from the non-parametric statistic, a value for a statistic that does have a known distribution, for example a z-score, often called a *z-approximation*. The latter approach produces a probability that is reasonably close to the exact probability but only if the sample size is large enough. However, what constitutes a large enough sample depends on the non-parametric statistic being used.

Exact probabilities involve what are sometimes called *permutation tests*. These entail finding a value for a statistic from the data that have been collected. Every possible alternative permutation of the data is then produced and the value of the statistic is calculated for each permutation. The proportion of the permutations that are as extreme as the value that came from the way the data did fall, or more extreme and in line with the research hypothesis, is then calculated and that proportion is the probability of the test. The example of tossing coins, given in Chapter 10, is a version of this form of test. Here the number of heads is the statistic. We then worked out every possible fall of the coins and noted what proportion would have as many, or more heads, compared with those we actually got when the coins were tossed.

Clearly, where possible, we want to know the exact probability. Unfortunately, the number of permutations will sometimes be very large, particularly when a large sample is involved. However, powerful desktop computer programs can now handle samples up to a certain size and statistical packages, such as SPSS, include an option, which may have to be bought as an addition to the basic package, that will calculate some exact probabilities. When even these programs cannot cope with the number of permutations they can use what is sometimes called a *Monte Carlo method* which takes a pre-specified number of samples of the data and calculates the statistic for each sample. Again the proportion of statistics that are as big, or bigger and in line with the research hypothesis, is the probability for the test.

I recommend the following procedure for finding the probability of non-parametric tests. If you are analysing the data using a program that can calculate exact statistics *and* can cope with the sample size you have employed then find the exact statistic. Otherwise, you have to find out, for the test you are using, whether the sample you are using is small enough that tables of exact probabilities exist. Finally, if the sample is bigger than the appropriate table allows for then you will have to use the approximation test that has been found for that statistic. Be careful when using statistical packages where you don't have access to exact probabilities as they sometimes provide the approximation and its probability regardless of how small the sample is.

Non-parametric tests for one-group designs

At least ordinal data

When the data are on an ordinal scale it is possible to use the Kolmogorov–Smirnov one-sample test. However, this is an infrequently used test and the test used for nominal data—the one-sample χ^2 test—is often used in its place. Accordingly, the Kolmogorov–Smirnov one-sample test is only described in Appendix V.

Nominal data

One-sample χ^2 test

Sometimes we may wish to see whether a pattern of results from a sample differs from what could have been expected according to some assumption about what that pattern might have been. An example would be where we are studying children's initial preferences for particular paintings in an art gallery. We observe 25 children as they enter a room that has five paintings in it and we note, in each child's case, which painting he or she approaches first. Our research hypothesis could be that the children will approach one painting first more than the other paintings. The Null Hypothesis would be that the number of children approaching each painting first will be the same for all the paintings. Thus, according to the Null Hypothesis we would expect each painting to be approached by $\frac{25}{5} = 5$ children first.

The data can be seen in Table 14.1. The χ^2 test compares the actual, or observed, numbers with the expected numbers (according to the Null Hypothesis) to see whether they differ significantly. This example produces $\chi^2 = 10$. The way in which a one-group χ^2 is calculated is shown in Appendix V.

Table 14.1 The number of children approaching a particular painting first and the expected number according to the Null Hypothesis

Painter	Approached first	Expected by H_0
Klee	11	5
Picasso	5	5
Modigliani	3	5
Cézanne	4	5
Rubens	2	5

Finding the statistical significance of χ^2

If you conducted the χ^2 using a computer it would tell you that the result was $p = 0.0404$ (SPSS provides, as an option, an exact probability for this test, which is $p = 0.042$). Both the exact and the probabilities from chi-squared tables would be considered statistically significant and we could reject the Null Hypothesis. The probability for a χ^2 test given by computers, and in statistical tables, is always for a non-directional hypothesis. The notion of a one- or two-tailed test is not applicable here as there are many ways in which the data could have fallen: any one of the paintings could have been preferred.

If we do not know the exact probability of a χ^2, we can use a table that gives the probabilities for what is called the *chi-squared distribution*. As this table can be used for finding out the probabilities of statistical tests other than just the χ^2 tests, I am going to follow the practice of some authors and refer to *chi-squared* when I am talking about the table and χ^2 for the test.

In order to look up the probability of the results of a χ^2 test, you need to know the degrees of freedom. In the one-group version of the χ^2 test, they are based on the number of categories, which in this case was five (i.e. the number of paintings). The df is calculated by subtracting one from the number of categories. This is because the total number of participants is the fixed element in this test. In this case, as the total number of participants was 25, the number of participants who were in four of the categories could be changed but the number in the fifth category would have to be such that the total was 25. Therefore there are four degrees of freedom.

The probability table for the chi-squared distribution is given in Appendix XIV. Table 14.2 shows an extract of that table.

Table 14.2 An extract of the probability table for the chi-squared distribution

	Probability												
df	0.99	0.95	0.90	0.80	0.70	0.50	0.30	0.20	0.10	0.05	0.02	0.01	0.001
1	0.00	0.00	0.02	0.06	0.15	0.45	1.07	1.64	2.71	3.84	5.41	6.63	10.83
2	0.02	0.10	0.21	0.45	0.71	1.39	2.41	3.22	4.61	5.99	7.82	9.21	13.82
3	0.11	0.35	0.58	1.01	1.42	2.37	3.66	4.64	6.25	7.81	9.84	11.34	16.27
4	0.30	0.71	1.06	1.65	2.19	3.36	4.88	5.99	7.78	9.49	11.67	13.28	18.47
5	0.55	1.15	1.61	2.34	3.00	4.35	6.06	7.29	9.24	11.07	13.39	15.09	20.51

When there are four degrees of freedom, the critical level for χ^2 at $p = 0.05$ is 9.49 and for $p = 0.02$ it is 11.67. Therefore, as our χ^2 was 10 and this is larger than 9.49, the probability that this result occurred by chance is less than 0.05. However, as 10 is smaller than 11.67, the probability is greater than 0.02. In this case, we would report the probability as $0.02 < p < 0.05$. The complete way to report the result of a χ^2 test, when you do not know the more exact probability, is: $\chi^2_{(4)} = 10$, $.02 < p < .05$, $N = 25$.

Notice that you should report N (the sample size) as, with this test, the df are not based on the sample size.

The effect size of χ^2

Cohen (1988) uses w as his effect size measure for χ^2, where:

$$w = \sqrt{\frac{\chi^2}{N}}$$

and N is the sample size. Therefore, in the present case:

$$w = \sqrt{\frac{10}{25}}$$

$$= \sqrt{0.4}$$

$$= 0.632$$

Cohen defines a w of 0.1 as a small effect size, a w of 0.3 as a medium effect size and a w of 0.5 as a large effect size. Therefore, in this example, we can say that the effect size was large.

The power of the χ^2 test

The tables in Appendix XV give the power of the χ^2 test. Table 14.3 gives an extract of the power tables when df = 4. From the table we can see that, with $\alpha = 0.05$, df = 4, the power of the test lies between 0.64 and 0.69 (for $w = 0.6$) and 0.80 and 0.83 (for $w = 0.7$). In fact, the power, when $w = 0.632$ and $N = 25$, is 0.71. That is, there is approximately a 71% probability of avoiding a Type II error. Appendix XV explains how to find power levels for samples or effect sizes that are not presented inthe tables.

Table 14.3 An extract of the power tables for w when df = 4 and $\alpha = 0.05$ (* denotes that the power is over 0.995)

				df = 4 effect size (w)					
n	0.1	0.2	0.3	0.4	0.5	0.6	0.7	0.8	0.9
22	<0.20	<0.20	<0.20	0.29	0.43	0.60	0.75	0.87	0.94
24	<0.20	<0.20	<0.20	0.31	0.47	0.64	0.80	0.90	0.96
26	<0.20	<0.20	0.20	0.33	0.50	0.69	0.83	0.92	0.97
28	<0.20	<0.20	0.21	0.36	0.54	0.72	0.86	0.94	0.99
30	<0.20	<0.20	0.23	0.38	0.57	0.76	0.88	0.96	0.99
35	<0.20	<0.20	0.26	0.44	0.65	0.82	0.93	0.98	*

The assumptions of the χ^2 test

The first assumption is that all the observations are independent. In other words, in this case, each child should only be counted once—for 25 scores there should be 25 children. The second assumption is that the *expected* frequencies (if the Null Hypothesis is correct) will be at least a certain size. In the case where there is only one degree of freedom—for example, only two paintings—all expected frequencies should be at least 5. When the degrees of freedom are more than one, then no more than 20% of the expected frequencies may be under 5. In the case of five categories, it would mean that only one of the expected frequencies could be less than 5. As the expected frequencies are partly governed by the sample size, in order to try to avoid the problem of small expected frequencies, it is advisable to have at least five participants per category. Therefore, the minimum sample size for this research would have been 25.

If too many categories have expected frequencies below 5, then it is possible to combine categories. For example, if the sample had had only 20 participants in it, as shown in Table 14.4, then we could combine the numbers for different paintings.

Table 14.4 The number of children approaching a particular painting first and the expected number according to the Null Hypothesis

Painter	Approached first	Expected by H_0
Klee	9	4
Picasso	4	4
Modigliani	2	4
Cézanne	3	4
Rubens	2	4

Table 14.5 The number of children approaching a particular painting first and the expected number according to the Null Hypothesis

Painting	Approached first	Expected by H_0
Klee or Picasso	13	8
Other paintings	7	12

We could compare the numbers approaching the Klee or the Picasso with those approaching the other paintings, as in Table 14.5. We can only do this if it makes sense in terms of our research hypothesis. Thus we could only do this if our hypothesis was that different paintings would be approached by more children than would other paintings.

Note that the expected frequencies for the paintings in a given row in Table 14.5 is the sum (or total) of the expected frequencies for each of the paintings in that row. The result of a χ^2 carried out on these data is $\chi^2_{(1)} = 7.81$, $p = .022$, $N = 20$, which is also statistically significant.

This last example demonstrates that the expected frequencies do not have to be the same as each other. The original example was testing whether the pictures had an equal likelihood of being approached first. However, another use for the one-group χ^2 test is as a *goodness-of-fit* test. There may be situations in which we think that a set of data is distributed in a particular way and we wish to test whether this assumption is correct. For example, imagine that we are told that the population contains 20% smokers and 80% non-smokers. We have a sample of 100 participants whose smoking status we have noted and we wish to check that the sample is representative of the population. The data are shown in Table 14.6. Unlike the usual inferential statistic where we are seeking a statistically significant result, in this case we are looking for a result that suggests that the difference between the expected and observed frequencies is not statistically significant. The analysis produces the following result: $\chi^2_{(1)} = 1.56$, $p = .21$, $N = 100$. We would conclude that the sample was not significantly unrepresentative with respect to smoking status.

Table 14.6 The number of smokers and non-smokers in a sample and the expected numbers as predicted from the population

Smoking Status	Observed	Expected
smoker	25	20
non-smoker	75	80

However, this use of inferential tests is problematic because it is reversing the usual process, as our prediction is that there will be no difference. Therefore we are attempting to confirm an H_0 that assumes that the distribution does not differ from what would be expected if the sample had been selected randomly from the population. We have the problem that the lower the power of the test, the more likely this assumption is to be supported.

To take an extreme example, imagine that we were unwise enough to have a sample of only 25 people in this survey. If we found that 8 of those were smokers (that is 32% rather than the 20% we are told is in the population) then the analysis produces the following result: $\chi^2_{(1)} = 2.25$, $p = .13$, $N = 25$, despite the fact that the effect size would be $w = 0.3$, which is a medium effect size. The power of the test would be 0.32. In other words, β—the probability of making a Type II error (that is, missing an effect when it was present)—would be 0.68 or 68%.

Cohen (1988) has suggested that one way round the problem is to select a sample size that would set the power of the test at 0.95. This would mean that β would be 0.05 and therefore the same as α. We would have to set the effect size we were seeking as particularly small, say a w of less than 0.1. The consequence of this would be that with df = 1 we would need around 800 participants to have the required power for the test.

Summary

Parametric tests such as the *t*-test make certain assumptions about the measure being analysed. Most require that the data being analysed are independent of each other and have a normal distribution in the population. If the assumptions are not met then modified versions of the parametric tests or non-parametric tests should be employed.

The next chapter describes statistical tests that allow us to compare the data from two levels of an independent variable to see whether they are significantly different.

15

ANALYSIS OF DIFFERENCES BETWEEN TWO LEVELS OF AN INDEPENDENT VARIABLE

Introduction

The present chapter deals with designs that involve one independent variable with only two levels. Parametric and non-parametric tests are introduced that analyse between- and within-subjects designs. The use of z-tests to evaluate larger samples in non-parametric tests is explained. The power and effect size of the two-sample t-test and its non-parametric equivalents are discussed. An additional measure of effect size for certain designs with nominal data—the odds ratio—is presented.

Parametric tests

The distribution of the difference between two means

Because we are now looking at the difference between two sample means rather than a sample mean and a population mean, statisticians have had to identify how this new statistic is distributed—what its mean and standard error are—so that an inferential statistic can be used to evaluate it. In fact, there are different versions of the test, depending on whether the design is between- or within-subjects. The complete equations for the tests are shown in Appendix VI, where worked examples are given. All the versions of the test use the t-distribution and so the same probability table can be used as for the one-group t-test.

t-tests to evaluate the difference between two sample means

Between-subjects designs

An additional assumption of the between-subjects t-*test*
In Chapter 14 it was pointed out that certain criteria have to be met before it is appropriate to use a parametric test such as the t-test. The level of measurement should be at least interval or, if ordinal, should potentially

have 7 or more values. The scores contributing to a given mean should be independent. The population of scores should be normally distributed, or at least the summary statistic being evaluated should be normally distributed, which in the case of the t-test of means is likely to be true if the sample has at least 40 participants in it.

In addition to the above, the t-test for comparison between two independent sample means requires what is called *homogeneity of variance*. This term means that the variances of the populations of the two sets of scores are the same. Usually researchers will be dealing with data from samples rather than from populations, and so it is unlikely that the two samples will have exactly the same variance, even if the populations from which they come do.

Fortunately, the t-test has been shown to be sufficiently robust that the variances can be different to a certain degree and yet the test will not be badly affected. As a rule of thumb, if the larger variance of the two samples is no more than four times the smaller variance then it is still legitimate to use the t-test. However, if the population of scores is markedly non-normal *and* the variances differ, even by less than four times, the test becomes less robust. In addition, this rule of thumb should only be used when the sample sizes, in the two groups, are equal.

For this example researchers wish to evaluate the effectiveness of a therapeutic technique designed to rid people of arachnophobia (extreme aversion to spiders). They intend to have two groups of arachnophobes. One group is to act as the experimental group and receive therapy, the other is the control group which does not receive therapy. The researchers measure anxiety using a self-report checklist that yields a score between 20 and 100 and is known to be normally distributed among the population; a high score means that the person is more anxious. The independent variable is therefore experience of therapy, with two levels: *experience* and *no experience*. The dependent variable is *anxiety level*. The research hypothesis is:

H_A: Those receiving therapy have lower anxiety levels than those not receiving it.

with the Null Hypothesis:

H_0: There is no difference in mean anxiety level between those receiving therapy and those not receiving therapy.

Put formally, the Null Hypothesis is that the mean anxiety level for the population of people who receive the therapy (μ_t) is the same as that for the population of those who do not receive the therapy (μ_c); that is: $\mu_t = \mu_c$ or $(\mu_t - \mu_c) = 0$. The research hypothesis is $\mu_t < \mu_c$ or $(\mu_t - \mu_c) < 0$.

In order to decide on a sample size the researchers conduct a power analysis.

Power analysis

The hypothesis is directional and so a one-tailed test will be appropriate. Alpha will be set to 0.05. The researchers are expecting that the therapy will produce a large effect size ($d = 0.8$). They are seeking power of 0.8. They look in the appropriate power tables (see Appendix XV) which show that they need 20 people in each group. They find 40 arachnophobes and randomly assign them to the two groups.

The results of the study are shown in Table 15.1 and Figure 15.1.

Table 15.1 The means and SDs of anxiety level in the therapy and control groups

	Therapy	Control
Mean	71.5	79.5
sd	6.56	7.64

FIGURE 15.1 Means and SDs of anxiety levels of therapy and control groups

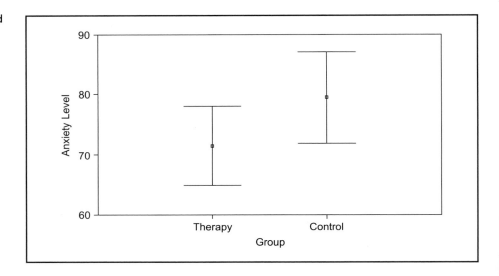

Effect size

In a case like the present study, where the effect we are looking at is the change between a control condition and an experimental condition, it makes sense to calculate d using the following equation, where the SD used is that for the control group:

$$d = \frac{\text{mean}_{\text{(for experimental group)}} - \text{mean}_{\text{(for control group)}}}{\text{SD}_{\text{(for control group)}}}$$

In this example:

$$d = \frac{71.5 - 79.5}{7.64}$$

$$= -1.047$$

This tells us that the therapy reduced anxiety by over 1 SD, which in Cohen's terms can be considered to be a large effect size.

If the research had involved comparing the means of two experimental groups, it would be more legitimate to use an SD that combines the information from both groups (the pooled SD) in the above equation rather than the SD of one group. (See Appendix VI for the equation for a pooled SD.)

We have seen that the result has gone in the hypothesised direction; now we wish to find out whether the result is statistically significant. But first it is necessary to check whether the data fulfil the requirements of a t-test. An additional requirement of the between-subjects t-test is that the data for the two conditions should be independent. This has been guaranteed by the researchers. However, they need to check whether there is homogeneity of variance between the two sets of data. Squaring the standard deviations gives the variances. The variance for the therapy group is 43.03 and for the control group it is 58.37. As the variance for the control group (the larger variance) is not more than four times that of the therapy group, and the anxiety scale is a ratio measure that is normally distributed in the population, the researchers decide that it is legitimate to use a t-test.

This version of the t-test is formed by:

$$\frac{\text{difference between the means} - \text{difference between the means if } H_0 \text{ is correct}}{\text{standard error of the difference between means}}$$

The difference between the means, if H_0 is true, is 0, in which case the equation can be rewritten:

$$\text{between-subjects } t = \frac{\text{difference between the means}}{\text{standard error of the difference between means}}$$

In the present case, this becomes:

$$t = \frac{71.5 - 79.5}{2.25131}$$

$$= -3.553$$

Finding the statistical significance of a between-subjects *t*-test

The same table can be used for this version of the *t*-test as for all other versions (see Appendix XIV). However, before the probability of this value can be evaluated we need to know the appropriate degrees of freedom for this version of the *t*-test.

Degrees of freedom for a between-subjects t-test

This version of the *t*-test is based on the means of two groups and so has two degrees of freedom fewer than the sample size. Therefore, in this case, the degrees of freedom are $40 - 2 = 38$.

Table 15.2 shows part of the *t*-tables from Appendix XIV. Looking along the row for df = 38, we see that the *t*-value of 3.553 (remember to ignore the negative sign if the calculated *t*-value is negative) is between 3.319 and 3.566. Therefore, the one-tailed probability of the *t*-value is less than 0.001 but greater than 0.0005; we can say that $0.0005 < p < 0.001$. In fact, the computer gives the *p*-value as 0.00052. It is clear that the *p*-value is less than the α-level and so the researchers can reject the Null Hypothesis and conclude that their therapeutic technique reduces the anxiety of arachnophobes. We would report the result as follows: *Participants in the therapeutic group had significantly lower anxiety levels than those in the control group ($t_{(38)} = 3.55$, $p < .001$, one-tailed test, d = −1.05).*

If the exact df is not shown on tables it is often not a problem. The *t*-value will usually either be clearly statistically significant when the df are smaller than the exact value (for example when df = 45 and $t = 1.69$), in which case the result will also be significant with the exact level, or alternatively, the result will not be significant even with the next higher df for which the table has an entry (for example when df = 45 and $t = 1.67$), in which case it would not be statistically significant with the exact df. A problem arises, if you are dependent on tables, when the *t*-value is not

Table 15.2 An extract of the *t*-tables (from Appendix XIV)

	One-tailed probabilities									
	0.4	0.3	0.2	0.1	0.05	0.025	0.01	0.005	0.001	0.0005
	Two-tailed probabilities									
df	0.8	0.6	0.4	0.2	0.1	0.05	0.02	0.01	0.002	0.001
35	0.255	0.529	0.852	1.306	1.690	2.030	2.438	2.724	3.340	3.591
36	0.255	0.529	0.852	1.306	1.688	2.028	2.434	2.719	3.333	3.582
37	0.255	0.529	0.851	1.305	1.687	2.026	2.431	2.715	3.326	3.574
38	0.255	0.529	0.851	1.304	1.686	2.024	2.429	2.712	3.319	3.566
39	0.255	0.529	0.851	1.304	1.685	2.023	2.426	2.708	3.313	3.558
40	0.255	0.529	0.851	1.303	1.684	2.021	2.423	2.704	3.307	3.551
50	0.255	0.528	0.849	1.299	1.676	2.009	2.403	2.678	3.261	3.496

clearly in one of these two positions; for example, if it had been 1.682 with df = 43. (Appendix XIV shows how a more exact critical t-value can be found using *interpolation*.)

The effect on power of unequal sample sizes

In a between-subjects t-test the power of the test is reduced by having unequal sample sizes. For example, if in the above example the researchers had used a control group of 10 and an experimental group of 30, although the overall sample size would be the same, the power for a large effect size of $d = 0.8$ would be reduced to 0.69, a drop of 0.11. Thus, when designing the research try to have equally sized samples. Appendix XV shows how to calculate the sample size that is appropriate for reading power tables for a between-subjects t-test, when the sample sizes for the two groups are different.

Heterogeneity of variance

If the variances for the two samples differ by more than four times (and the samples have equal numbers of participants) then you are advised to use a modified version of the t-test. When the samples' sizes are unequal, then use the modified t-test if the variances differ by more than twice. In the version of the t-test given above, the variances for the two conditions have been pooled, or summarised in a single measure. When the two variances are different it is more appropriate to estimate the standard error for the difference between the means without pooling the two variances.

This new version of the t-test, sometimes known as 'Welch's t-test', is not distributed in exactly the same way as the other versions. However, the standard tables can be used if an adjustment is made to the degrees of freedom. The calculation of this version of the t-test and of the degrees of freedom is shown in Appendix VI. Some computer programs report this version, along with the more usual t-value. In SPSS it is shown as the version of the t-test for which *equal variances are not assumed*. If the variances pass the rule of thumb for being considered sufficiently homogeneous, then quote the more usual t-value, with its df and p. However, if the variances are heterogeneous then quote the modified version. If you are reporting the latter version, explain that you are doing so.

Within-subjects or matched designs

In this example sports psychologists have devised a technique that they hope will enhance the performance of racing cyclists. They decide to compare performance, in terms of time taken to complete a route, before training with performance after training. Therefore the independent variable is *training stage*, with two levels: *pre-training* and *post-training*. The dependent variable is *time to complete the route*. Their research hypothesis is:

H$_A$: Cyclists take less time to complete the route after training than before training.

the Null Hypothesis is:

> H_0: Cyclists take the same time after training as before training to complete a route.

Formally stated, the Null Hypothesis is that the mean of the differences (μ_d), for each cyclist, between the times taken on the two occasions, is zero; that is: $\mu_d = 0$. The research hypothesis is $\mu_d > 0$.

In order to choose an appropriate sample size the researchers conduct a power analysis.

Power analysis

The nature of the hypothesis means that a one-tailed test is appropriate. Alpha is set at 0.05. As the training takes a long time, the psychologists are only interested in detecting a large effect ($d = 0.8$) and they want power of 0.8. They look in the power tables for the within-subjects t-test (see Appendix XV) and decide that 11 cyclists are needed to take part in the study. As each participant in a within-subjects design provides a score for each level of the independent variable, fewer participants will be required than in a between-subjects design, for the same level of power. In addition, within-subjects designs are more powerful than between-subjects designs, as there should be less variability in the overall set of scores, because the same person is providing two scores, and so they will need even fewer participants to achieve the same level of power. As will be seen later, this way of assessing power is very approximate and should only be used when no other guidelines about the effect size are available.

Degrees of freedom for a within-subjects or matched-pairs t-test

In this case the t-value is calculated on the basis of the differences between each pair of scores, from each participant, and so the degrees of freedom are one fewer than the number of pairs of scores (or one fewer than the number of participants). Therefore, in this example df = 11 − 1 = 10.

The results of the experiment are shown in Table 15.3 and Figure 15.2.

Table 15.3 The means and SDs of time taken (in minutes) to complete a route by cyclists pre- and post-training

	Stage of training	
	Pre	Post
Mean	184.0909	182.5455
sd	21.66	20.68

(I have given the means to four decimal places in order that the calculations shown below produce consistent results. I do not recommend that you report results with such levels of accuracy.)

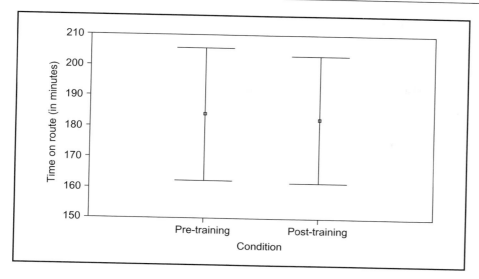

FIGURE 15.2 The means and SDs of time taken to complete a route by cyclists pre- and post-training

From the summary statistics we can see that there is a slight improvement in the mean time in the post-training condition but that there is a large overlap between the spreads of the two conditions.

Effect size

The calculation of d and the guidelines that Cohen (1988) has proposed for what constitute small, medium and large effects sizes are all based on between-subjects designs. This means that when we have a within-subjects design there are two ways in which d can be calculated: one for the purposes of judging the magnitude of the effect relative to a between-subjects design and one for the purposes of reading the power tables. In order to be consistent with the way that effect size is calculated for a between-subjects design, and because the pre-training condition can be treated as a control condition, we can use the following equation:

$$d = \frac{\text{mean for pre-training} - \text{mean for post-training}}{\text{SD for pre-training}}$$

If neither condition could be treated as a control we would have found the pooled SD as in the between-subjects design.

In the present case:

$$d = \frac{184.0909 - 182.5455}{21.66}$$

$$= 0.07$$

Which, according to Cohen (1988), is below a small effect size.

This version of the t-test is formed by:

$$\text{within-subjects } t = \frac{\text{mean difference} - \text{mean difference if } H_0 \text{ correct}}{\text{standard error of differences}}$$

The mean difference if H_0 is correct is 0. Therefore the equation can be rewritten as:

$$\text{within-subjects } t = \frac{\text{mean difference}}{\text{standard error of differences}}$$

In the present case:

$$t = \frac{184.091 - 182.546}{1.021}$$

$$= 1.513$$

Referring to the appropriate part of the t-tables from Appendix XV, the researchers find that with df = 10, p lies between 0.1 and 0.05, for a one-tailed test; the computer shows the probability as 0.08. Accordingly, the psychologists cannot reject the Null Hypothesis and are forced to conclude that their training technique does not improve performance. The result would be reported as: *Cyclists showed no significant improvement in time taken to complete the route after training ($t_{(10)} = 1.51$, $p = .08$, one-tailed test, $d = 0.07$).*

Retrospective power analysis

Because the result was not statistically significant, in order to guide future research, the psychologists wish to know the power the test had. There is a slight complication with within-subjects designs. The effect size measure allows comparison with between-subjects designs but will underestimate the power of the test because the t-value for a within-subjects design utilises the standard deviation of the differences between the scores for each participant (s_{diff}) and therefore, if we have this information, the effect size (d'), which we can use to calculate the power, is found from:

$$d' = \frac{\bar{x}_1 - \bar{x}_2}{s_{\text{diff}}}$$

As $s_{\text{diff}} = 3.387$,

$$d' = \frac{184.0909 - 182.5455}{3.387}$$

$$= 0.456$$

When the within-subjects t-value is known d' can be calculated from:

$$d' = \frac{t}{\sqrt{n}}$$

Thus,

$$d' = \frac{1.513}{\sqrt{11}} = 0.456$$

The researchers note that, with such an effect size ($d = 0.456$) and a sample of 11 participants, the power of their test was between 0.32 (for $d = 0.4$) and 0.44 (for $d = 0.5$). Therefore, as the effect lies approximately midway between the two tabled values, the power will be approximately the mean of the two levels, that is $(0.32 + 0.44)/2 = 0.38$. In order to achieve power of 0.8 they would have needed to use between 30 and 40 participants, or approximately 35 cyclists. Thus they can conclude that this study may be worth repeating with the larger sample size.

(The discrepancy between the two values—for d and d'—that have been calculated for this study is explained in Appendix XV.)

Non-parametric tests

Tests to evaluate the difference between two levels of an independent variable: at least ordinal scale

Between-subjects designs: the Mann–Whitney U-test

The Mann–Whitney U-test assumes that the distributions, in the population, of the two groups to be compared are the same. Thus, it is not as restrictive as the t-test and so can be used when the distributions are not normal. However, it does assume homogeneity of variance. This latter restriction may be less of a problem because the test entails placing the data in order rather than noting the size of any differences between scores, and therefore the effect of extreme scores will be reduced. Nonetheless, if the original scores have heterogeneous variances, then it would be worth converting the data into ranks, with both samples being ranked together, and then checking that the variance of the ranks of one group is no greater than four times the variance of the other group. If the variances still remain heterogeneous then Zimmerman and Zumbo (1993) recommend conducting a t-test for separate variances, Welch's t-test, mentioned earlier in the chapter, on the ranked data. As with the between-subjects t-test, the Mann–Whitney U-test assumes that the scores are independent of each other.

Researchers wished to compare the attitudes of two groups of students—those studying physics and those studying sociology—about the hunting of animals. Each student was asked to rate his or her agreement with the statement 'hunting wild animals is cruel'. The ratings were made on a five-point scale, ranging from *disagree strongly* to *agree strongly*, with a high score denoting an anti-hunting attitude.

The research hypothesis is:

H_A: Sociology students will be more anti-hunting than physics students.

with the Null Hypothesis:

H_0: There is no difference between sociology and physics students in their attitude to hunting.

Expressed formally, the Null Hypothesis is that the medians of the two groups do not differ.

Deciding on sample size

Effect size

There is no straightforward way to present effect sizes for non-parametric tests that involve small samples. However, as we will see, we can make certain assumptions based on the equivalent parametric test when we wish to do prospective power analysis. In addition, when we have a sufficiently large sample size (for many non-parametric tests this is around 20 to 25 participants, for within-subjects designs, or pairs of participants in a between-subjects design) then it is possible to calculate an effect size. This method will be shown later in the chapter.

Power

The power of non-parametric tests tends to be reported in terms of how they compare with their parametric equivalents, when the assumptions of the parametric test are fulfilled. The term *power efficiency* is used, meaning the relative number of participants that would be needed to achieve the same power as for the parametric test. As was noted in Chapter 14, when the assumptions of the parametric test are not fulfilled then the non-parametric test may have more power than its parametric equivalent. However, calculating the power under these circumstances is not straightforward, as it depends on the way in which the parametric assumptions have been violated. Accordingly, the procedure I will adopt is, where possible, to utilise the tables that are given for the equivalent parametric test, but suggest adjustments that can be made to the sample size to compensate for the relative power efficiency of the non-parametric test.

In the case of the Mann–Whitney U-test, if we multiply the sample size suggested for the t-test by 1.05, then we will have, at least, the power suggested for the t-test. Thus, if the researchers wanted to detect a large effect size of $d = 0.8$, they would be told that they needed 20 participants per group to get power of 0.8 for a one-tailed between-subjects t-test, with $\alpha = 0.05$. Accordingly, they needed $20 \times 1.05 = 21$ participants per group for the Mann–Whitney U-test.

The researchers collect the data and create the following table:

Table 15.4 The mean, median and SDs of attitudes of sociology and physics students towards a question about hunting wild animals

	Sociology	Physics
Mean	4.14	2.67
Median	4	3
SD	0.91	1.24

Statistical significance of the Mann–Whitney U-test

The Mann–Whitney U-Test involves placing all the data in numerical order and then calculating how many data points are not in the hypothesised order. In the present case a data point that was out of order would be a physics student who was more anti-hunting than any sociology student.

The original data and calculations for the test are shown in Appendix VI. The analysis was performed and it gave a U of 79.5. As was explained in Chapter 14, there are three possible ways of finding the probability for this result. The most appropriate one depends on whether you are using a statistical package that provides exact probabilities and, if you are not, then it depends on the sample size. SPSS reports the exact probability as $p = 0.00009$. If we hadn't had this information, as the sample size in both groups is greater than 20, then it would have been necessary to use a version of a z-test to calculate the probability (see Appendix VI). In the present example, with 21 participants in each group, $z = -3.5469$, $p = 0.0002$, one-tailed test. Had both samples been 20 or smaller then we could have found the probability from tables in Appendix XIV.

Correction for ties

It is likely that your computer program will also offer you an alternative value of z that has taken into account the number of scores that had the same value (tied scores). The calculation for this is also shown in Appendix VI. The version allowing for ties gives $z = -3.6389$, $p = 0.00015$, one-tailed test. The correction for the ties is the more accurate version so only report that result, when it is given, and the sample size is large enough to make the z-test appropriate. SPSS only provides the version corrected for ties. The two versions produce the same result when there are no ties.

Reporting the results of a Mann–Whitney U-test

Here I would say *sociology students were significantly more opposed to hunting than were physics students ($U = 79.5$, $p < .001$, $N = 42$, one-tailed test)*. If the probability was an exact one found from a statistical package then add something along the lines of: *the probability is exact and was found using* SPSS *version 11*. Report the value for *U* even if you had to use a *z*-test to find the probability, but in that case also report the *z*-score.

Effect size revisited

Now that we have a *z*-score for the result we can convert this into an effect size (*r*) using the equation shown in Appendix VI. Putting the *z*-score corrected for ties (−3.64) into the equation gives an effect size of $r = −0.56$, which in Cohen's (1988) terms would be considered a large effect size. (This effect size measure is discussed more fully in Chapter 19.)

Within-subjects designs: the Wilcoxon signed rank test for matched pairs

When comparing two levels of an independent variable, in a within-subjects design with at least ordinal data that do not conform to the assumptions of a within-subjects *t*-test, it may be appropriate to use the Wilcoxon signed-rank test for matched pairs. The test assumes that the distribution of the difference scores between the two conditions forms a symmetrical distribution in the population. Thus, it is less restrictive than the *t*-test. As with the within-subjects *t*-test it assumes that the scores in a given condition are independent of each other.

This test could be appropriate if researchers were comparing people's views of psychology as a science before and after hearing a talk on the nature of psychology. Their views were found from their responses to the statement: *Psychology is a science*. They used a 5-point rating scale ranging from *agree strongly* to *disagree strongly*, with a higher score denoting a belief that psychology is a science.

Power

The researchers assumed a large effect size, set α to 0.05 and because they were making the directional hypothesis—*People will rate psychology more clearly as a science after they have heard a talk on it*—they would use a one-tailed probability. They wanted to have power of 0.8. The Wilcoxon test has the same power efficiency as the Mann–Whitney *U*-test. Accordingly, we can look for the sample size for a within-subjects *t*-test with an effect size of

Table 15.5 The mean, median and SDs of ratings given by participants of psychology before and after a talk on the subject

	Before	After
Mean	2.667	3.883
Median	2.5	4.0
SD	1.23	0.94

$d = 0.8$ and power of 0.8 and multiply the sample size by 1.05. Using the tables in Appendix XV we find that the sample size for the equivalent t-test would need to be 11. Therefore the sample size required for a Wilcoxon test is $11 \times 1.05 = 11.55$. We round this up to the nearest whole number, giving a sample size of 12 participants.

The Wilcoxon test looks at the size of differences between the two levels of the IV. It ranks the differences according to their size and gives each difference either a positive or a negative sign, depending on whether the second level is bigger or smaller than the first level. The ranks of the sign that occurs least frequently are then added together and the result forms the statistic T. In this case, a Wilcoxon test was conducted with the result that $T = 0$ (because there were no people for whom the second result was smaller than the first); the original data and workings are shown in Appendix VI.

Tied scores

The Wilcoxon test has two types of tied score—those where a participant gave the same score for each condition and those where the difference scores for different participants were the same.

This test discards those cases where there is no difference between the two levels of the IV and the sample size includes only those who did show a difference. Thus, in the present example, as 4 people did not change their ratings between the two occasions, the sample size is considered to be $12 - 4 = 8$. If the range of possible scores is limited, there could be a high proportion of such ties and this could reduce the power of the test dramatically by reducing the effective sample size.

Statistical significance

SPSS reported the exact probability as $p = 0.004$. When you are not using a computer that calculates exact probabilities and the sample size is 25, or smaller, then use the table in Appendix XIV. With the revised sample size of 8 we learn that $p < 0.005$, for a one-tailed test. Alternatively, when the sample size is greater than 25 then you would need to use a z-test to calculate the probability that T could have occurred by chance. If more than one person had the same size difference between the two levels of the IV then a z-value that allows for such tied values is usually calculated by computer programs. As with the Mann–Whitney U-test, the z corrected for ties is the more accurate. Workings for the z-test are given in Appendix VI.

Reporting the result of a Wilcoxon signed rank test for matched pairs

As with the Mann–Whitney U-test always report the original statistic from the test, in this case the T-value, and then, if appropriate, the z-value. If you are reporting the exact statistics say so and give the statistical program you have used and the version: e.g. SPSS version 11. In this case I would say *The ratings given after the talk on psychology gave psychology a significantly higher rating as a science than before the talk (T = 0, p = .004, one-tailed test, N = 8). You could also mention that 4 participants showed no change and were removed from the analysis.*

Tests to evaluate the difference between two levels of an independent variable: nominal scale

Between-subjects designs: the χ^2 test of contingencies

The χ^2 test of contingencies is appropriate if you have two variables meas-ured at the nominal (or categorical) level and you wish to see whether different levels of one variable differ over the pattern that they form on the other variable. However, it is important that no person be counted more than once; the entries in the table must be independent.

As an example, researchers had heard that there appeared to be a large number of female students who smoked. They wanted to see whether there were different proportions of males and females who smoked.

Effect size
The effect size for this version of the χ^2 test is the same as for the one-group χ^2 goodness-of-fit test. The measure of effect size given by Cohen (1988) is *w*, with 0.1, 0.3 and 0.5 being the values of *w* that he suggests constitute small, medium and large effect sizes.

Power
The researchers wish to detect, at least, a medium effect size (*w* = 0.3) and so they look in the tables in Appendix XV for a medium effect size, with $\alpha = 0.05$ and df = 1 (to be explained later). They find that, for power of 0.8, the recommended sample size is 88. They decide that they would like an equal number of males and females, to make comparison of proportions simpler and so they sample 44 males and 44 females.

The researchers asked the participants in their study whether they smoked and put the results into a table:

Table 15.6 The numbers of male and female smokers and non-smokers in a sample

Observed Frequency Table

	male	female	Totals:
smoker	17	21	38
non-smoker	27	23	50
Totals:	44	44	88

This version of the χ^2 test tests the Null Hypothesis that smoking status and gender are not related (are independent). It does this by noting the proportions of males and females in the sample (44 out of 88 or 0.5 for each) and the proportions of smokers and non-smokers (38 out of 88, or approximately 0.43 for smokers, and 50 out of 88 or 0.57 for non-smokers). If the two variables *gender* and *smoking* are not related then there should be the same proportion of smokers among the males as among the females (that is, 0.43 or 43%). Thus, under the Null Hypothesis that the proportion of males and females who smoke is the same, the expected frequencies would produce the following table:

Table 15.7 The expected frequencies of male and female smokers and non-smokers if smoking and gender are not linked

Expected Values

	male	female	Totals:
smoker	19	19	38
non-smoker	25	25	50
Totals:	44	44	88

However, 17 of the males, or 38.64%, were smokers, while 21, or 47.73%, of the females were smokers.

Table 15.8 The percentages of male and female smokers and non-smokers

Percents of Column Totals

	male	female	Totals:
smoker	38.64%	47.73%	43.18%
non-smoker	61.36%	52.27%	56.82%
Totals:	100%	100%	100%

The χ^2 test compares the expected frequencies with those that actually occurred (the observed frequencies). Workings for this example are given in Appendix VI. The result is that $\chi^2 = 0.741$. SPSS gives an exact probability of $p = 0.519$, while the probability based on the chi-squared distribution as calculated by the computer is $p = 0.3893$. Looking in the table for the chi-squared distribution in Appendix XIV shows that the probability that this result, with df = 1, would occur if the Null Hypothesis were true is $0.3 < p < 0.5$.

Degrees of freedom and χ^2

The fixed elements in the calculation of a χ^2 test on contingency tables are what are termed the *marginal totals*—the number of smokers and non-smokers and the numbers of males and females—because the expected frequencies are calculated from these totals. Thus, in a 2×2 table, as above, as soon as one frequency is placed in the table, all the others are fixed. For example, given that the sample size was 88, if we are told that 17 males smoked, then we know how many females smoked ($38 - 17 = 21$) and how many males did not smoke ($44 - 17 = 27$), and we also then know how many females did not smoke ($44 - 21 = 23$). Thus, we only had the freedom to alter one of the four frequencies, and so df = 1. This particular version of the χ^2 test is not only usable on a 2×2 table: we can have more levels of either variable, for example, *smoking status* could have had the levels *never smoked*, *ex-smoker* and *currently a smoker*. The rule for working out the degrees of freedom is to take one from the number of columns in the table and one from the number of rows in the table and multiply the results:

$$\text{df} = (\text{columns} - 1) \times (\text{rows} - 1).$$

Thus, in a 2×2 table we had $(2 - 1) \times (2 - 1) = 1 \times 1 = 1$.

One- and two-tailed tests and χ^2

As was mentioned in Chapter 14, the probability given in chi-squared tables and by computer programs is for a non-directional hypothesis. With a contingency table that is larger than 2×2 the possible directions in which a significant result could have gone are more than two. For example, if we looked at a study of smoking that included three possible smoking statuses, then we would reject the Null Hypothesis of no difference between the genders if smokers, non-smokers, or ex-smokers were particularly high (or low) in either gender. However, in the case of a 2×2 table there are only two directions that the result could have gone when there was a difference between the groups: either a higher proportion of males were smokers or a higher proportion of females were smokers. In such a situation, if the result did go in the direction predicted then we can find the probability by dividing the usual probability for a non-directional hypothesis by two. Imagine that the researcher had predicted that there would be a higher proportion of smokers among the females than among the males. The result, summarised in Table 15.6, did go in the predicted direction and so we can divide the originally reported probability by two; as a result $p = 0.259$. In fact, SPSS will report what it describes as an *Exact Sig. (1-sided)* when you ask it to calculate exact probabilities. If you do calculate such a probability, it would be advisable to explain this process, as, although legitimate, it is not a common practice. To avoid the need for explanation, as the result remained non-significant even after being converted to a directional probability, I would simply report the non-directional probability.

Reporting the results of a χ^2 test

As usual, report what test was used, what conclusion you draw from the result and your evidence for the conclusion. Thus, I would say: *A 2 × 2 χ^2 test was conducted to compare the proportions of smokers and non-smokers among* the males and females. *There was no significant difference in the proportions of smokers between females and males ($\chi^2_{(1)} = 0.741$, df = 1, p = .52, N = 88).* If you leave the probability as the one given by a computer or from a table then there is no need to report that it is a two-tailed probability. Alternatively, if you had a directional hypothesis and the result went in the direction you predicted, then you could halve the probability and report that, as long as you explained what you had done.

Effect size revisited

The effect size w can be calculated from the following equation:

$$w = \sqrt{\frac{\chi^2}{N}}$$

where N is the total sample size. Thus, in the present example:

$$w = \sqrt{\frac{0.741}{88}}$$

$$= 0.0918$$

which, in Cohen's terms, is a small effect size. Given this effect size, power was less than 0.2. To achieve power of 0.8 for this effect size it would be necessary to have a sample size of over 700 participants. Thus, it is unlikely that you would recommend replicating the study without, at least, some modification of the design to increase the effect size and so reduce the necessary sample size.

Correction for continuity

The probability that the result of the χ^2 test would have occurred if the Null Hypothesis were true is calculated with reference to a particular distribution—the chi-squared distribution. The chi-squared distribution is what is termed a *continuous distribution*. This means that every possible value for chi-squared could exist. However, the majority of tests that produce a χ^2 value cannot produce a truly continuous range of possible values and this will be particularly true with small sample sizes and a small number of categories. Thus, below a certain sample size and number of categories it was suggested that the χ^2 statistic did not have a distribution that was accurately represented by the chi-squared distribution.

Yates (1934) devised a way of correcting for continuity for a 2 × 2 contingency table that will often be quoted by computer packages. In the *gender* by *smoking status* example, the corrected version gives $\chi^2 = 0.417$, $p = 0.5185$. Twenty-five years ago Yates's corrected version of χ^2 was still considered to be the appropriate one to report. However, since then there has been a dispute over its appropriateness. My advice would be that, if the corrected and non-corrected versions of the test agree over whether the result was statistically significant, as in the smoking example, then there is no problem—report the uncorrected version. However, if the two versions disagree report them both and draw attention to the discrepancy. The reader can then make his or her own judgement. If you are using exact probabilities then the problem is solved and you can just accept that probability.

Small expected frequencies

Another way to try to avoid the problem of χ^2 not being reflected in the chi-squared distribution, under certain circumstances, is to have reasonably sized expected frequencies. The usual rule of thumb is that all the expected frequencies in a 2×2 table should be at least five. In the case of tables that are larger than 2×2, at least 80% of expected frequencies should be at least five. These restrictions mean that even if we were not using statistical power to guide sample size we would want a minimum of five participants per cell of the contingency table, which means that a study that will be analysed by a 2×2 table should have at least 20 participants in it. Chapter 16 shows ways of solving the problem of small expected frequencies in contingency tables that are larger than 2×2.

Fisher's exact probability test

Fisher devised a test to cope with 2×2 contingency tables with small samples. Unfortunately, it is only applicable when all the marginal totals are fixed (Neave & Worthington, 1988). A fixed marginal total is where the numbers in that total have been specified before the study is conducted. In the smoking example the totals for males and females were fixed at 44 each, whereas the totals for smokers and non-smokers were free; that is, they were not known until the data were collected. In fact, it would be unusual to have all the marginal totals fixed and would have made no sense in the smoking example as it would have meant specifying how many smokers and non-smokers to sample, as well as how many males and females. Nonetheless, the method for calculating Fisher's exact probability test are provided in Appendix VI and probability tables for it are in Appendix XIV.

2×2 frequency table quick test

A preferable way to deal with small expected frequencies is a modified version of the χ^2 test using the following equation (provided here as it is not generally available on computers):

$$\text{modified } \chi^2 = \frac{(N - 1) \times [(A \times D) - (B \times C)]^2}{(A + B) \times (C + D) \times (A + C) \times (B + D)}$$

As an example, imagine that researchers explore whether having a pet improves the life expectancy of elderly people. They choose ten people who are aged over 75 years, who have no pets and who are living on their own. They randomly choose half of the people to look after a pet dog. After two years they note how many of the people with and without pets are still alive.

Table 15.9 The numbers of elderly people alive and dead by whether they were previously given a dog to look after

	Given a dog	Not given a dog	
Still alive	4 (A)	1 (B)	5
Died	1 (C)	4 (D)	5
	5	5	

$$\text{modified } \chi^2 = \frac{(10-1) \times [(4 \times 4) - (1 \times 1)]^2}{(4+1) \times (1+4) \times (4+1) \times (1+4)}$$

$$= \frac{9 \times (16-1)^2}{5 \times 5 \times 5 \times 5}$$

$$= 3.24$$

As with the previous example of a χ^2 test on a 2×2 contingency table, df = 1. The probability, for a non-directional hypothesis of this result, is $0.05 < p < 0.1$.

Odds ratios

An alternative way to describe the size of an effect in contingency tables is the odds ratio. This is a popular measure in medical research and is becoming increasingly used by psychologists, such as health psychologists and clinical psychologists, who do research alongside medical researchers. In order to explain what an odds ratio is it is necessary to define some other measures first.

Probability

We can take the data for male smokers in Table 15.6 and express the number of male smokers as a proportion of all the males in the sample: 17 out of 44 or $\frac{17}{44}$. Converting this into a proportion, we have 0.38636. We can say that the probability, in this sample, of a male being a smoker is 0.38636.

Odds

The odds is the probability that an event will occur divided by the probability that it will not occur. Therefore, we need to know the probability that a male will not be a smoker. Because we only have two possibilities, we can find this probability by subtracting the probability that a male *is* a smoker from 1:

probability that a male is not a smoker $= 1 - 0.38636 = 0.61364$

Now we can find the odds that a male is a smoker:

$$\text{odds that a male is a smoker} = \frac{\text{probability that a male is a smoker}}{\text{probability that a male is not a smoker}}$$

$$= \frac{0.38636}{0.61364} = 0.6296$$

This is just under 2/3 and so we can interpret these odds as telling us that, among males, for every two smokers there will be approximately three non-smokers, or that non-smokers are one-and-a-half times more likely than smokers.

Odds ratios
An odds ratio, as its name suggests, is the ratio between two odds. There-fore, if we wanted to know the odds ratio of male to female smokers we need the odds for female smokers, which is 0.9130 and shows a higher likelihood of females being smokers. It is still more likely that a female will be a non-smoker than a smoker, but only just. Now we can calculate the odds ratio of males and females being smokers:

$$\text{odds ratio of males and females being smokers}$$

$$= \frac{\text{odds of males being smokers}}{\text{odds of females being smokers}}$$

$$= \frac{0.6296}{0.9130} = 0.6896$$

We can conclude from this that males are only just over two-thirds as likely to be smokers as females. An odds ratio can range from 0 upwards, with an odds ratio of 1 meaning that there was no difference in the two odds. A ratio below 1 means that the first odds is less likely, as it is here, while a ratio that is above 1 shows that the first odds is more likely. The odds ratio can be converted so that it is couched in terms of the other group by dividing it into 1. Thus, the odds ratio can be expressed in terms of female smokers:

$$\text{odds ratio of female to male smokers} = \frac{1}{\text{odds ratio for male smokers}}$$

$$= \frac{1}{0.6896} = 1.4501$$

This confirms that females are more likely to be smokers; in fact nearly one-and-a-half times as likely. This can also be expressed as a percentage: the odds of being smokers for the females is 45% higher than the odds of being smokers for the males.

Confidence intervals for odds ratios

As with other statistics, it is useful to be able to put an odds ratio in context. It is possible to calculate a confidence interval for an odds ratio. If the interval contains 1 then it could be that there is no real difference between the groups. The 95% confidence interval for the odds ratio of male to female smokers is 0.295 to 1.609. (The calculations are contained in Appendix VI.) This tells us that although the odds ratio suggests that males are less likely to be smokers than females in this sample, if we were to repeat the study with another sample we might very well find no difference, as there may be no difference in the population.

Within-subjects designs: McNemar's test of change

If we have within-subjects data for two levels of an IV with nominal levels of measurement then the data breach the requirements of the χ^2 test because the data points are not independent. McNemar's test of change allows us to analyse such data when they can be formed into a 2×2 contingency table for example, if we were again studying people's attitudes to psychology as a science before and after a talk on the subject but this time we simply asked on each occasion whether or not they thought psychology was a science.

Effect size and power

Although McNemar's test produces a χ^2 value I know of no evidence that the effect size (w) that is used for the conventional χ^2 test, is applicable in this instance. To calculate power is also problematic unless we go via the power efficiency of the test relative to a within-subjects t-test. To be on the safe side, we should take the worst case, which is that the power efficiency can be as low as 0.63. Accordingly, we should find the sample size for the within-subjects t-test, with the required effect size and level of power, and multiply that by 1.6. For a one-tailed test, with $\alpha = 0.05$, and a large effect size ($d = 0.8$), we would need a sample of 11 to have power of 0.8 with a within-subjects t-test. Thus, we should have a sample of $11 \times 1.6 = 17.6$ or 18 people with McNemar's test of change.

The data can be put into the following form:

Table 15.10 The numbers of people who agreed or disagreed that psychology is a science before and after hearing a talk

		After agree	After disagree
Before	disagree	9	3
	agree	6	0

This test is only interested in those people who have changed opinion. Accordingly, the Null Hypothesis that it tests is that the number of people changing in one direction will be the same as the number changing in the other direction. If we label the four cells

		After	
		agree	disagree
Before	disagree	A	B
	agree	C	D

we can calculate McNemar's test by

$$\chi^2 = \frac{(A - D)^2}{(A + D)}$$

$$= \frac{(9 - 0)^2}{(9 + 0)}$$

$$= \frac{81}{9}$$

$$= 9$$

The test has df = 1.

The statistical significance of McNemar's test of change

SPSS reports the exact probability as $p = 0.004$. It reports this as having come from the binomial distribution. Appendix VI explains this distribution and how it was used to find this probability. If we were dependent on the tables for the chi-squared distribution in Appendix XIV then we would find that the likelihood of this result occurring by chance is $0.001 < p < 0.01$. As with other tests that use the chi-squared distribution, this probability is for a non-directional hypothesis. If we had made a directional hypothesis that more people would change to agree that psychology was a science than would change to disagree that it was a science, then we could halve the probability. In this case, $0.0005 < p < 0.005$, or $p = 0.002$ for the exact probability.

Summary

When two levels of an independent variable are being compared, the following chart can be used to decide which is the appropriate statistical test. However, remember that if homogeneity of variance is not present but the other requirements of a between-subjects t-test are fulfilled then we should use Welch's t-test.

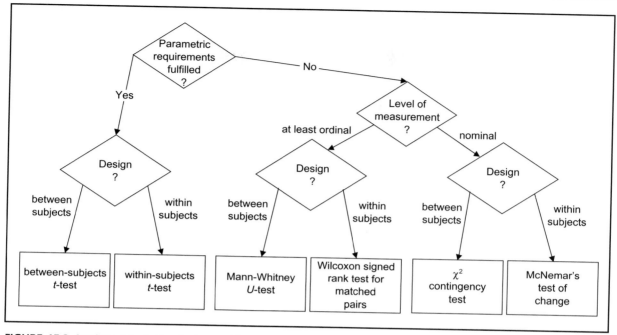

FIGURE 15.3 Statistical tests for designs with one independent variable with two levels

16 PRELIMINARY ANALYSIS OF DESIGNS WITH ONE IV WITH MORE THAN TWO LEVELS

Introduction

So far you have been introduced to the analysis of designs that include a single independent variable that has a maximum of two levels. The present chapter describes how to carry out preliminary analysis of designs that have a single independent variable with more than two levels.

Parametric tests

For an example I will return to one originally introduced in Chapter 9. Researchers wished to compare the recall of participants in three conditions: using the mnemonic system of pegwords, using the method of loci and not using any mnemonics (the control condition). In order not to have practice effects and introduce problems of having to match lists for difficulty, a between-subjects design is chosen.

The researchers now have a design that includes one independent variable—type of mnemonic—which has three levels: pegword, method of loci and the control condition. They also have a single dependent variable—number of words recalled. When they come to analysing the results of their research, they could employ t-tests to compare pairs of levels. However, they will have to perform three t-tests: one between pegwords and method of loci, one between pegwords and the control group and one between method of loci and the control group. This approach would be possible but there is a statistical problem that renders it inadvisable.

The rationale behind statistical significance testing is that when we decide to accept our hypothesis and reject the Null Hypothesis we are taking a risk—the risk of making a Type I error. Imagine that we have set $\alpha = 0.05$. We are saying that if the result we found were really to be by chance, and we were to repeat the research a large number of times and analyse the data each time, we would expect that on about 5% of occasions the result would be as extreme or more extreme than this and therefore statistically significant. Therefore, if we perform the test more than once we are increasing the likelihood that we will find a significant result even when the Null Hypothesis is true.

It is possible to try to allow for the fact that a number of tests are being performed by making the α-level smaller and thus reducing the danger of making a Type I error. However, such techniques are rather inexact. It is considered better, at least initially, to perform a single test that takes into account all the data that have been collected in a piece of research. If this initial test demonstrates that there is a significant difference between the levels of the independent variable we are justified in exploring the data further to try to identify the specific contributions to that significant effect.

The test that is the most appropriate for analysing the memory experiment described above is the analysis of variance (usually abbreviated to ANOVA). ANOVA can be seen as an extension of the *t*-test in that it compares the means for the different levels of the independent variable and, as with the *t*-test, the Null Hypothesis is that the means do not differ. In formal terms, the Null Hypothesis is that the three sets of data for the groups actually come from the same population and thus have the same mean. Also, as with the *t*-test, even if there is a difference between the means, if the variation in scores *within the groups* is large then a significant difference will not be obtained. However, because we are now dealing with three rather than two means the way to evaluate the difference between them is to see how much they vary.

To look at the nature of ANOVA entails re-introducing certain concepts and then expanding on your existing knowledge. This will help to read the summary table which comes from performing an ANOVA.

As was shown in Chapter 9, one way to ask how typical or atypical a particular score is, is to calculate how far away it is from the mean for its group: that is, its deviation from the group mean. If we want a measure of the spread within a group of scores we can square the deviation for each score and add them together; this is known as *the Sum of Squared Deviations* which is often shortened to *the Sum of Squares*. If we divide the Sum of Squares by the appropriate degrees of freedom we arrive at the variance for the group of scores, usually described as a *Mean Square* (MS) in ANOVA. This is an estimate of the variance in the population. If the Null Hypothesis is correct then all the scores come from the same population; the different levels of the IV do not produce differences in the DV. ANOVA relies on the fact that there is more than one way to estimate the population variance; in particular, it involves one estimate that is derived from the variance between the levels of the IV and another derived from the variance within the levels.

The estimate of the population variance which comes from within the levels of the IV is only going to be due to individual differences,[1] sometimes referred to as 'error'. This is true regardless of whether the Null Hypothesis is true or false. The estimate of the population variance that comes from between the levels of the IV will contain only variance due to individual differences if the Null Hypothesis is correct. However, if the Null Hypothesis is false, it will also contain variance due to the differences between the treatments.

[1] Individuals treated in the same way will have different scores on most measures for at least two reasons: firstly, the participants have an inherent difference in ability; secondly, the measure that is being used is not 100% reliable and so is going to vary in the degree to which it manages to assess a person's 'true' score.

ANOVA has its own statistic—the F-test or F-ratio. It is called a ratio because it calculates the ratio between the variance that can be explained as being due to the differences between the groups and the error or unexplained variance. Thus,

$$F\text{-ratio} = \frac{\text{between-group estimate of population variance}}{\text{within-group estimate of population variance}}$$

In our example this would mean:

$$F\text{-ratio} = \frac{\text{variation between the recall conditions}}{\text{variation within the recall conditions}}$$

If the Null Hypothesis is true then both estimates of the population variance should be roughly the same. In which case, the F-ratio should equal approximately one.

However, if the Null Hypothesis is false the estimate of the population variance that comes from looking at the between-group variation should be larger. In this case, the F-ratio should be larger than one.

In the process of making the estimates of variance due to different sources, the overall sum of squares for all the data, that is the total variation in all the data, is split (or partitioned) into the different sources that are producing it. This has the consequence of identifying a specific amount of the overall variation as being linked to a particular IV and its related error variation. Hence, another way to view the F-ratio is to see it as:

$$F = \frac{\text{variation between the means}}{\text{unexplained (error) variation}}$$

How the partitioning occurs depends on the research design and will be explained as each design is introduced.

Between-subjects designs

The simplest form of ANOVA to interpret (and to calculate) is a between-subjects design, as with the memory example. Figure 16.1 shows that the overall variation is split into two sources. There will only be one F-ratio which will be of the following form:

$$F = \frac{\text{between-groups variance}}{\text{within-groups variance}}$$

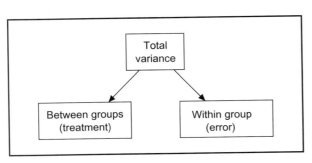

FIGURE 16.1 Partitioning of variance in a between-subjects ANOVA

Imagine that the researchers randomly allocated 10 people to each group for the experiment. (I will leave power analysis until later in the chapter.) They gave the appropriate instructions to the members of each group and then presented them with 20 words. Twenty-four hours later the researchers asked them to recall as many words as they could, in any order. The research hypothesis is that the method of loci produces the best recall. Note, however, that ANOVA cannot test that hypothesis directly. At this stage the researchers can only ask whether the recall for the three groups differs significantly. Therefore their research hypothesis has another, preliminary, hypothesis, which is tested first:

H_A: The mean recall of the three conditions is different.

which has the Null Hypothesis:

H_0: The mean recall of the three conditions does not differ.

Formally, the Null Hypothesis is that the means for the populations for the different conditions are the same. In the case of three means H_0 would be: $\mu_1 = \mu_2 = \mu_3$.

If the preliminary hypothesis is not supported then the research hypothesis will not be supported and it is not worth trying to test it. If, however, the preliminary hypothesis *is* supported then it is worth conducting further analysis to see whether the research hypothesis is also supported.[2]

Table 16.1 and Figure 16.2 summarise the results of the experiment. We can see that the means are different. However, Figure 16.2 shows that there

2 This account is true for most follow-up analysis that researchers currently conduct. However, situations are described in Chapter 18 that are exceptions to this rule.

Table 16.1 Means and SDs of word recall for the three memory conditions

	Control	Pegword	Loci
Mean	7.2	8.9	9.6
SD	1.62	1.91	1.58

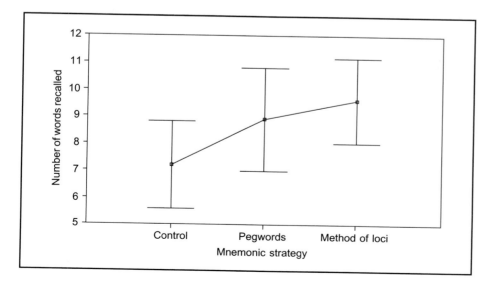

FIGURE 16.2 Means and SDs of word recall for the three memory conditions

is some overlap between the three sets of scores. To test whether the differences between the means are statistically significant we need to carry out an ANOVA on the data. See Appendix VII for a worked example. Table 16.2 shows the results of the analysis; the term *one-way* is used to describe an ANOVA conducted on a design with a single IV.

Table 16.2 A summary table for a one-way between-subjects ANOVA comparing recall under the three mnemonic conditions

Source	Sum of Squares	df	Mean Square	F-test	p
Between Groups	30.467	2	15.233	5.213	0.0122
Within Groups	78.9	27	2.922		
Total	109.367	29			

Interpreting a one-way between-subjects ANOVA

I will explain what the different elements of Table 16.2 mean. The first column (source) indicates what the figures in the other columns refer to and in particular to what the amounts of the variation in the data are attributable. In this case, you will see that some of the variation in scores is due to the difference between the groups; this is the variation we are interested in because it tells us about the differences between the mean recall for the three groups. Next we have the variation within the groups, that is the error variation, which will be due to differences between people within the groups. Finally, we have the total variation for the experiment.

The next column gives the Sum of Squares for each of the sources of variation in the data. Recall that a Sum of Squares is a descriptive statistic that describes amount of spread in data. The next column tells us about the degrees of freedom (df). Note that the df for groups is 2. This is simply one fewer than the number of groups because we are looking at the variation between the means for the groups. The df for the total is 29 which is one fewer than the number of participants used in the experiment. The df for within groups is 27, which is the difference between the total df and the df for between groups. The within-group df can also be calculated by saying that there are three groups each with nine degrees of freedom, that is, one fewer than the number in each group.

The next column gives the Mean Square for each source of variation in the study. If you take the Sum of Squares for a given source of variation and divide it by its df you arrive at the appropriate Mean Square; the Mean Squares are the estimates of variance. The next column provides the F-ratio, which in this case is found by dividing the Mean Square for between groups by the Mean Square for within groups (or error MS).

Tails of test

With the majority of the statistical tests that have been introduced thus far, we have wanted to know what tail of test we should employ. However, when there are more than two levels of an independent variable being tested in an ANOVA there is no choice—the test will be the equivalent of a two-tailed test. To find the reason for this we have to return to the nature of the Null Hypothesis for research designs that are analysed by ANOVA. The Null Hypothesis states that the means for the different conditions do not differ (because they come from the same population). The Alternative Hypothesis states that they do differ (because they come from different populations). The ANOVA as described so far is incapable of testing more precise hypotheses, such *as recall from the control group will be poorer than for the other two conditions.*

If you think about it, you will see that when there are three levels of an independent variable, such a precise hypothesis is only one of many possible directional alternative hypotheses that could have been stated, rather than the two that are possible when there are only two levels of an independent variable. If we wish to test a more precise, directional hypothesis, the convention is that we first check whether the non-directional hypothesis is supported. If it is, we can explore further, using the techniques shown in Chapter 18. If it is not, then we have little evidence for a directional hypothesis.

Evaluating the statistical significance of an F-ratio

Usually, when you calculate an ANOVA by computer you will be told the significance of any resulting *F*-ratio. However, it is worth being able to read the significance tables for *F*-ratios. An *F*-ratio is evaluated in a slightly different way from other tests described so far. As it is the ratio between two variance estimates (Mean Squares), each with its own df, we need both dfs to evaluate the significance of an *F*-ratio. Table 16.3 is an extract from a table of the probabilities of *F*-ratios in Appendix XIV.

It is usual for significance tables for *F*-ratios to come in a set, with one table for each significance level. Frequently the tables are limited to $\alpha = 0.05$, $\alpha = 0.025$, $\alpha = 0.01$ and $\alpha = 0.001$, or an even smaller range, as in the present book which only contains tables for $\alpha = 0.05$ and $\alpha = 0.01$. In this way, we can only tell that an *F*-ratio did or did not reach statistical significance and cannot be much more precise than that.

When reading Table 16.3 note that the degrees of freedom for the treatment are shown in the first row of the table (df_1), such that there is a column devoted to each different treatment df. The df for the error term are shown in the first column so that each row has a different df for the error term—in this case the *within-groups* source of variance—(df_2). Therefore, to find the critical value of *F* to be significant at $p = 0.05$ we look in the column for

Table 16.3 An extract from the $\alpha = 0.05$ probability tables for an *F*-ratio

df_2 \ df_1	1	2	3	4	5	6	7	8	9	10	12	14
26	4.23	3.37	2.98	2.74	2.59	2.47	2.39	2.32	2.27	2.22	2.15	2.09
27	4.21	3.35	2.96	2.73	2.57	2.46	2.37	2.31	2.25	2.20	2.13	2.08
28	4.20	3.34	2.95	2.71	2.56	2.45	2.36	2.29	2.24	2.19	2.12	2.06

df = 2 and the row for df = 27. This shows us that the critical value is F = 3.35. As the *F*-value that we found from our analysis is larger than this we can say that our result is statistically significant at the *p* < 0.05 level. We could look further in the tables for lower significance levels, in which case we would learn that *p* lies between 0.01 and 0.05, i.e. 0.01 < *p* < 0.05.

The researchers can therefore reject the Null Hypothesis and accept the preliminary research hypothesis that recall is different in the different recall conditions. Remember that they had a more specific hypothesis. Given that the preliminary research hypothesis has been supported, they are justified in conducting further analysis to evaluate their more specific hypothesis. I want to leave description of that analysis until the next but one chapter, by which time I will have introduced the various forms of ANOVA.

Reporting the results of an ANOVA

The minimum details that are needed are the following. *There was a significant effect of mnemonic strategy on recall (F$_{(2,27)}$ = 5.213, p = .012).* This entails reporting the source of the *F*-ratio, the appropriate degrees of freedom, the *F*-ratio and the probability level. In addition to this you should report the effect size which is described later.

Within-subjects designs

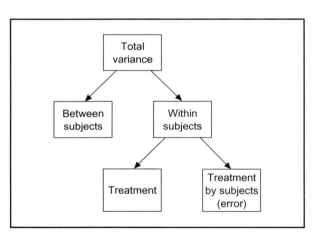

FIGURE 16.3 Partitioning of variance in a within-subjects ANOVA

These designs are also known as *repeated-measures* designs. In a within-subjects design, with a single independent variable, the total variation in the data can be seen as being due to two main sources: differences between the participants (between-subjects variance) and differences within the participants (within-subjects variance), that is, how individuals varied across the different conditions. Within-subjects variance can be further divided into variance between the levels of the independent variable—the conditions—(treatments variance) and variance due to the way the different participants showed a different pattern of responses across the conditions (treatment by subjects, also known as 'error variance' or 'residual variance'). An example of the latter would be if the previous study had been a within-subjects design and the first participant had recalled most words in the pegword condition, while the second participant had recalled most in the loci condition.

The *F*-ratio that addresses the hypothesis we are interested in is:

$$F = \frac{\text{treatment variation}}{\text{error variation}}$$

It will tell us whether the treatment conditions differed significantly. Although we are not usually interested in knowing whether the participants differed, the advantage of this design is that the variation in scores that can be seen as being due to the difference between participants can be removed from the analysis and so a smaller amount of variance which is not attributable to the differences between the treatments will remain. Hence this is a more efficient design which has more statistical power than a between-subjects design.

Note that there cannot be variance that is attributable to variation within participants in a between-subjects design because each participant only provides one data point and so we cannot ascertain how the same person varies across the levels of an independent variable.

For this example, imagine that a team of researchers is looking at the effects of the presence of others on judgements about the treatment of offenders. Participants are given a description of a crime and have to decide how much time the criminal should spend in prison. The experiment involves three conditions: in one each participant is alone and is unaware of anyone else's judgement; in a second condition each participant is alone but can see on a computer screen what others have 'decided'; in the third condition each participant is in a group and is aware of what the others have 'decided'. The decisions that the participants learn that others have made are, in fact, pre-set by the experimenters but the participants are unaware of this. There are three different crimes, considered by a panel of judges to be of similar severity, so that the participants do not have to make their three judgements about the same crime. The confederates of the experimenters have been told to suggest a long sentence, even though the crimes are comparatively mild.

The experimental hypothesis is that participants will recommend longer sentences when they are aware of what others have recommended, and even longer sentences when they are in the presence of the confederates. However, remember that the initial ANOVA cannot test a directional hypothesis; it can only test the preliminary research hypothesis:

H_A: The mean length of sentence recommended by participants will differ between the three conditions.

The Null Hypothesis will be:

H_0: The mean length of sentence will not differ between the three conditions.

If the preliminary research hypothesis is supported then analysis to evaluate the more specific research hypothesis is justified.

The experiment is run with ten participants with the order in which each participant takes part in each condition being randomised. The dependent variable, length of sentence in months, is noted for each decision. Again, power will be dealt with later. The results of the experiment are shown in Table 16.4 and Figure 16.4.

The results suggest that the sentences recommended do differ between the three different conditions. However, note that there is also quite a spread

Table 16.4 The means and SDs of sentence length (in months) recommended by participants

	Alone	Computer	Group
Mean	14.7	18.2	20.0
SD	6.55	4.52	5.48

FIGURE 16.4 The means and SDs of sentence length (in months) recommended by participants

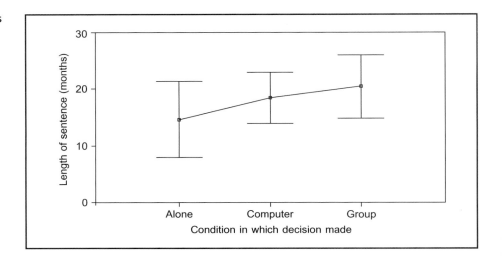

around the means and quite an overlap between the three different conditions. As usual, the descriptive statistics can only indicate in which direction the results are going; they cannot tell us how likely the results are to have occurred if the Null Hypothesis were true. Therefore, we cannot decide between the Null and Experimental Hypotheses until we have carried out an ANOVA on the data.

Table 16.5 shows the summary table for the analysis of variance for this experiment. Note that the summary table for the ANOVA of a

Table 16.5 A summary table for a one-way within-subjects ANOVA comparing the sentences given to criminals when the decisions were made under three different conditions

Source	Sum of Squares	df	Mean Square	F-ratio	p
Between subjects	776.3	9			
Within subjects	208.667	20			
Treatments	145.267	2	72.633	20.621	0.0001
Residual*	63.399	18	3.522		
Total	984.967	29			

*shown as treatment by subjects in Figure 16.3

within-subjects design looks more complicated than that for a between-subjects design. This is because we can identify more sources for the variation between all the scores.

The first column splits the sources of variance initially into two parts. There is the variance between subjects and the variance within subjects. The variance within subjects is then further divided into that which is due to the treatments (i.e. differences between the conditions) and the residual (i.e. the error or the variance that cannot be explained by the differences between subjects or by the differences between the conditions).

The second column tells us the size of the sum of squared deviations (Sum of Squares) for each of the sources of variance; see Appendix VII for a description of how these are obtained. The total Sum of Squares has been split into that which is attributable to between-subjects variation and that which can be attributed to within-subjects variation. The latter is then further subdivided into the variation due to the treatments and the variation due to error (the residual).

The third column informs us that the total degrees of freedom are 29; this is produced by noting how many scores we have—three for each of the ten participants—and subtracting one from the result. The 29 degrees of freedom are initially split into 9 for the between-subjects variance—one fewer than the ten participants—and 20 for the within-subjects variance—the difference between the total df and the between-subjects df. The within-subjects df can be further divided into 2 for the treatments—the number of treatments less one—and 18 for the residual—one subtracted from the number of conditions multiplied by one subtracted from the number of participants $(3 - 1) \times (10 - 1)$.

We are now in a position to calculate the estimates of the variance from the different sources (the Mean Square or MS) by dividing the Sum of Squares by the appropriate degrees of freedom. These estimates are shown in the fourth column. Remember that under the Null Hypothesis each is an estimate of the same variance—that of the single population of scores from which the present sample of scores is considered to have come.

The summary table (Table 16.5) shows that we have two estimates for the population variance and from these an F-ratio is calculated for the difference between the conditions. The MS for the residual contains the variation that is unexplained by either the overall variation between subjects or the overall variation between conditions.

If the conditions overall do not produce a difference in the length of recommended sentence then the MS for treatments will only be an estimate of the general variance among scores (error). Therefore, the F-ratio for treatments is found by dividing the MS for treatments by the MS for residuals:

$$F(\text{treatments}) = \frac{\text{MS treatments}}{\text{MS residual}}$$

If the Null Hypothesis is correct then F(treatments) will equal approximately 1, whereas, if the Null Hypothesis is false then F(treatments) will tend be greater than 1. Note, however, that it does not automatically follow that because an *F*-ratio is greater than 1 it is statistically significant; the critical level for *F* to be statistically significant depends on factors such as the sample size and the number of levels of the IV.

Interpreting a one-way within-subjects ANOVA

We are provided with the probability value for the difference between the conditions. If the computer does not provide probabilities then the same *F*-tables described in the section on ANOVA for between-subjects designs (see Appendix XIV) can be used.

The experimental hypothesis is dealt with by the *F*-ratio for treatments. In this case the preliminary version of the experimental hypothesis is supported. Recommendations about the length of sentence for a crime *are* affected by knowledge of others' judgements. To test the directional hypothesis that length of sentence will be greater the greater the proximity to other judges we will have to wait until we know how to compare the individual conditions; this is shown in Chapter 18. What we do know is that it is worth conducting further analysis.

Reporting the results of a one-way within-subjects ANOVA

Report the relevant details for the *F*-ratio, including an explanation of the conclusions you draw from it. The results would be reported in the following way:

> *There was a significant difference in the length of sentence recommended between the different conditions under which sentences were made ($F_{(2,18)} = 20.621$, p = .0001).*

Also include the effect size which is described later in the chapter.

The assumptions of ANOVA

You will recall that the use of a *t*-test requires certain assumptions to be fulfilled about the nature of the data. The use of ANOVA is also restricted to certain situations.

The form of ANOVA I have described thus far is a parametric test. The restrictions on its use are related to the level of measurement, the nature of the distribution, the nature of the variance and the independence of the scores. However, as I will demonstrate, ANOVA can cope to a certain extent with cases in which some of these assumptions are contravened. In other words, ANOVA is a robust test.

Level of measurement

As with other parametric tests, psychologists agree that this version of ANOVA is appropriate when the dependent variable is an interval or ratio measure. However, statisticians are less restrictive in their advice over its use for ordinal data. Nonetheless, one suggestion is that if you are using ordinal data then it should have at least seven possible values on the scale, for example on a 7-point Likert scale (Tabachnick & Fidell, 2001).

Homogeneity of variance

As with the between-subjects t-test, the between-subjects ANOVA assumes that the variance for the population of scores for each of the conditions is the same.

Normal distribution

As with the between-subjects t-test, the between-subjects ANOVA assumes that the scores for each of the conditions comes from a population that has a normal distribution.

Independence

ANOVA assumes that the scores for a given condition are independent of each other. In other words, that the scores of one person have not been affected by the scores of another participant. This would not be a problem for the experiment on recommendations of sentence length because we have not included in our analysis the recommendations of the confederates. However, if we had been looking at the judgements of participants after they had discussed the topic in groups and included all those judgements in our analysis, then each judgement in a given condition would not be independent of the others in a group.

The robustness of ANOVA

ANOVA can cope, to a certain extent, with contraventions of some of its assumptions and still be a valid test. However, if the assumptions are poorly met and if more than one is not met then we increase the likelihood that we will make a Type I or a Type II error.

As long as the samples in a between-subjects design are roughly the same size, the recommendation is that ANOVA can cope with differences in variance between the groups, such that the largest variance can be as much as four times the smallest variance. Note that in the example given above the variances of the different conditions do not differ by more than four times. If the variances do differ by more than four times then it may be possible to transform the data in some way to reduce the variance (see Appendix V for ways to transform data). Alternatively, as with the t-test, there is a version of ANOVA (the Welch formula, F') that is designed for use with data that do not have homogeneity of variance. SPSS has introduced the use of this statistic as an option you can choose in version 11 of the program. Appendix VII gives the Welch formula and an example of its use. If sample sizes are unequal, then treat the data as having *heterogeneous* variances if the largest variance is more than *two* times the smallest variance.

The assumption about normal distribution for the population of scores can also be contravened to a certain extent. Unfortunately, we often do not know what the distribution of the population of scores is as we only have the scores from our sample. I recommend that you produce a graph of the frequencies and if the distribution for any of the conditions differs markedly from normal then again the data can be transformed to make it more normal.

Following the reasoning of Zimmerman and Zumbo (1993), if you have both heterogeneity of variance and non-normal distributions then you convert the data into ranks and analyse the ranks using the Welch formula.

Dealing with lack of independence

If the data in a given condition are not independent then we can render the scores independent. If the scores were taken after participants had discussed the recommendations about sentence length then we could take the mean score for each discussion group and use the means as the dependent variable. The problem with this move is that we will reduce the number of scores that we are analysing and so we will make our test less powerful. In other words, we will increase the likelihood of making a Type II error. However, if we did not use the means we could be seriously violating the assumptions of the ANOVA and would thus be increasing the likelihood of making a Type I error.

Within-subjects designs

Sphericity (or circularity)

Within-subjects ANOVA has another assumption that the data should fulfil—*sphericity*. If we were to find, for each participant, the difference between his or her score on two of the levels of an IV, for example, that between the sentence given when alone and the sentence given when in a group, then we would have a set of difference scores. We could then calculate the variance of those difference scores. If we found the difference scores for each pair of levels of the IV and calculated the variance for each set of difference scores we would be in a position to check whether sphericity were present in the data. It would be present if the variances of the difference scores were homogeneous. When an IV only has two levels, and therefore df = 1, there is only one set of difference scores and so sphericity is not an issue.

When sphericity is not present, there are at least two possible ways around the problem. One is to use a different form of ANOVA: multivariate ANOVA or MANOVA. This technique is briefly described in Chapter 21 but its method of calculation is beyond the scope of this book. An alternative approach comes from the finding that even when sphericity is not present, the *F*-ratio calculated from a within-subjects ANOVA still conforms to the *F*-distribution. However, it is necessary to adjust the degrees of freedom to allow for the lack of sphericity. Computer programs such as SPSS and *SuperANOVA* report two such adjustments, so it is worth your while knowing about them; both are given the symbol ε (the Greek letter *epsilon*). The first is the Greenhouse–Geisser epsilon (G–G) and the second is the Huynh–Feldt epsilon (H–F). The first is conservative, in other words it is more likely to avoid a Type I error but increases the likelihood of a Type II error, and the second is more liberal.

Reworking the analysis for within-subjects ANOVA, the computer reported that the G–G epsilon was 0.913 and the H–F epsilon was 1.134. If H–F epsilon is greater than 1 then it is treated as though it were 1, in which case the original degrees of freedom remain unaltered. To find the new dfs use the following equations:

$$\text{adjusted treatment df} = \text{treatment df} \times \varepsilon$$

$$\text{adjusted error df} = \text{error df} \times \varepsilon$$

Therefore in the present example, for G–G epsilon:

$$\text{adjusted treatment df} = 2 \times 0.913 = 1.826$$

$$\text{adjusted error df} = 18 \times 0.913 = 16.434$$

In fact, the probability of the result, reported by the computer as $p = 0.0001$, is little affected by the adjustment. If we had to rely on tables then we would round the dfs to the nearest whole numbers, which in this case would be 2 and 16. Reading such tables would show that the results were statistically significant at the $p < 0.01$ level.

If you are using a computer program that reports the epsilon values then check whether the three probability values that are given for each *F*-ratio agree over whether the result is statistically significant. As usual, if they agree then there is no problem. If they disagree then you have to report the different values and discuss the differences.

If the program does not compute the epsilon values, then the following can show whether they need to be calculated:

1. If the *F*-ratio is not statistically significant with unadjusted dfs then it certainly will not be after adjustment, so there is no need to calculate either epsilon.
2. If the *F*-ratio is statistically significant with the unadjusted dfs and is still statistically significant even with df of 1 for the treatment and $n - 1$ (1 fewer than the number of participants) for the error term, then there is no need to calculate epsilon as the result is clearly statistically significant.
3. If the *F*-ratio is statistically significant with the unadjusted dfs but is not so with dfs of 1 and $n - 1$, then you need to calculate the epsilons.

In the current example, as the result was statistically significant with the unadjusted df, we should check the probability of the *F*-ratio with df of 1 and 9 (as there were 10 participants). As the critical level of *F* for $p \leq 0.01$ is 10.56, the calculated level of *F* (20.621) is clearly statistically significant and so we would not have needed to calculate the epsilons, had the computer not provided them.

The equations for the two forms of epsilon are given in Appendix VII.

Unequal sample sizes in between-subjects ANOVA

As was noted earlier, to minimise the effects of not having homogeneity of variance, in a between-subjects design it is best to try to have equal numbers of participants in each level of the independent variable (a balanced design). However, sometimes this will not be possible. When the samples are unequal, the computation of ANOVA is different from when the samples are equal. However, there are two possible ways in which the analysis can be conducted and these should depend on why the samples are unequal.

In some circumstances there may be good reason to have unequal samples; for example, if we were comparing people with normal memories with those with unusually good memories. In this case, there would be fewer of the latter group in the population. Under such circumstances, it makes sense to use what are described as *weighted means*. In other words, means that come from a larger sample are given more weight in the analysis. This is the analysis used by most computer programs when the samples are unequal.

However, there are situations in which the reason for the unequal samples is arbitrary. An example would be if some participants in a study, who were due to be included, were not available when required. As long as the reasons for their absence are not systematic, it makes more sense to use unweighted means. An example of systematic absence would be if we had originally selected our sample so that we could compare people from different socio-economic backgrounds but found that a disproportionate number of people from one type of background were subsequently unavailable to take part in the research.

The two methods for calculating ANOVAs when sample sizes are unequal are given in Appendix VII.

Effect size and ANOVA

There are a number of measures for the effect size of a treatment in ANOVA. The simplest to find is η^2 (eta-squared), which is the proportion of the overall Sum of Squares which can be attributed to the treatment and can be used to see the proportion (or percentage) of overall variance that is attributable to a given treatment. Thus,

$$\eta^2 = \frac{\text{Sum of Squares for treatments}}{\text{total Sum of Squares}}$$

Therefore, in the memory example:

$$\eta^2 = \frac{30.467}{109.367} = 0.279$$

In this case, 0.279×100 or 27.9% of the overall variance in scores can be explained as being due to the differences between the mnemonic strategies. In the sentencing example:

$$\eta^2 = \frac{145.267}{984.967}$$

$$= 0.147$$

Cohen (1988) uses a different measure of effect size which can be derived from η^2. However, for consistency I have converted his recommendations into values for η^2. Accordingly, he states that an η^2 of 0.01 is a small effect size, η^2 of 0.059 is a medium effect size and η^2 of 0.138 is a large effect size. In this case, both studies produced large effect sizes.

Some computer packages, including SPSS, report what is described as *partial* eta-squared, the equation for which is shown in Appendix VII. I prefer the version of eta-squared described above as it relates more clearly to the notion of proportion of variance accounted for than does partial eta-squared. For one thing, when there is more than one IV in the analysis the amount of variance accounted for by the different elements in the design may add up to more than 100%. In addition, it is simpler to calculate and, as explained in Chapter 20, eta-squared is more straightforwardly analogous to the information provided by other ways of analysing the same data than is partial eta-squared. However, with a one-way between-subjects ANOVA eta-squared and partial eta-squared produce the same result.

Calculating the power of a parametric one-way ANOVA

Appendix XV gives tables of the relationship between effect size, power and sample size for ANOVA. This shows that with 10 participants in each group and $\eta^2 = 0.279$, the power of the test for treatment df of 2 is between 0.77 and 0.87 (the exact figure is 0.83).

The power of within-subjects ANOVAs

The calculation of the power of within-subjects ANOVA is complicated by the fact that under certain circumstances, for the same number of data points, it will be more powerful than its equivalent between-subjects design, whereas under other circumstances the power will be reduced. To keep the process as simple as possible, I have followed other authors in only providing power tables for between-subjects ANOVA, where the values can be specified more precisely. These tables can be used for within-subjects designs to give approximate guidelines for sample size and power.

The relationship between *t* and *F*

If we are analysing an experimental design with one independent variable that only has two levels we can obviously use a *t*-test. However, we can also use an ANOVA on the same data. In fact, under these conditions, and only these conditions, they will give us the same answer as far as the probability is concerned. However, this is only true when we are using a two-tailed test for the *t*-test, because ANOVA only tests non-directional hypotheses. Under these circumstances the value for the *F*-ratio is the square of the value for *t*. In mathematical terms:

$$F = t^2$$

That is:

$$t = \sqrt{F}$$

Thus, if $F = 4$ with 1 and 15 degrees of freedom, then $t = 2$ with 15 degrees of freedom. To confirm this look at the critical values for *F* and *t* in their respective tables. You will see that when $\alpha = 0.05$ the critical value for *F* with 1 and 15 degrees of freedom is $F = 4.54$. The equivalent critical value for a two-tailed *t*-test with 15 degrees of freedom is 2.131 or $\sqrt{4.54}$.

Non-parametric equivalents of ANOVA

At least ordinal data

Between-subjects designs: Kruskal–Wallis one-way ANOVA by ranks

When the research design is between-subjects with more than two levels of the independent variable and the requirements of a parametric ANOVA are not fulfilled then the analysis can be conducted using the Kruskal–Wallis one-way Analysis of Variance, which is based on its parametric equivalent. This test does not assume that the distribution in the population is normal but that the distributions of the different conditions are the same. Therefore it is not as restrictive as the parametric one-way between-subjects ANOVA. Nonetheless, it does assume that the individual scores are independent of each other.

In a study researchers wished to compare the grades given by lecturers to essays that were shown either to be by a male or a female, or the gender was not specified. The research hypothesis was that the grades given to the three different categories of author would be different. Formally, the Null Hypothesis would be that the medians for the three conditions do not differ.

Twenty-four college lecturers were each given an essay to mark and they were told that the writer of the essay was either a male student or a female student, or they were not given any indication of the student's

Table 16.6 The mean, median and SDs of grades given for the essay and the supposed gender of the author

	Gender of author		
	female	neutral	male
mean	3.25	4	4.25
median	3	4	4
SD	1.04	1.07	1.67

gender. In fact, the same essay was given to all the lecturers. Each essay was given a grade between C− and A+, which was converted to a numerical grade ranging from 1 to 9. The summary statistics for the ratings of the essays of the three different 'authors' are shown in Table 16.6.

A Kruskal–Wallis ANOVA was performed on the data; the workings are shown in Appendix VII. As with the Wilcoxon signed-rank test for matched pairs, a rank is given to each grade and a statistic, H in this case, is calculated from these grades. In this example, $H = 2.086$. When some scores are the same, there is a version of the test that adjusts for ties. This is the more accurate version and the one that SPSS reports. In the present example, there were five places where the grades tied and the H corrected for ties was 2.231. SPSS gave the exact probability as 0.340. If you don't have access to programs that produce exact probabilities then for an independent variable with three levels and sample size no greater than 8 in any of the groups, the critical values for H to produce significance at $p = 0.05$ and $p = 0.01$ are given in Appendix XIV (the critical values are also given for an IV with 4 levels with up to 4 participants in each and for an IV with 5 levels with up to 3 participants in each). Otherwise, H is distributed like χ^2, with degrees of freedom of one fewer than the number of levels of the IV. The probability based on the chi-squared distribution is $p = 0.328$ and if we look in the table of the chi-squared distribution in Appendix XIV for df = 2 we will find that p lies between 0.5 and 0.3 (i.e. $0.3 < p < 0.5$). This means that there is insufficient evidence to reject the Null Hypothesis.

Reporting the results of a Kruskal–Wallis ANOVA
The above result would be reported in the following way: *There was no significant difference in the median grades given to the three authors* ($H = 2.231$, *df = 2, p = .34, N = 24*). From this we could conclude that the lecturers did not differ in the grades they gave to essays on the basis of their knowledge of the author's gender.

Power and the Kruskal–Wallis ANOVA
As with previous non-parametric tests, the power of the Kruskal–Wallis ANOVA is given in terms of power efficiency: that is, how statistically powerful it is relative to the parametric equivalent, when the assumptions of the parametric test are fulfilled. Accordingly, I advise finding the sample size that would be required for the one-way between-subjects parametric ANOVA and then adjusting the sample size according to the rule given below. If the

researchers had been expecting a medium effect size then they would have found, for $\alpha = 0.05$, they needed a sample of 52 in each group in order to have power of 0.8 when running a parametric ANOVA. As they were using the Kruskal–Wallis test, they needed $52 \times 1.05 = 54.6$, in other words, 55 people in each group for the same level of power. As with other non-parametric tests, if the assumptions of the parametric ANOVA are not met, the Kruskal–Wallis may well have greater power than its parametric equivalent.

Within-subjects designs: Friedman two-way ANOVA

When the design is within-subjects and the independent variable has more than two levels but the assumptions of the parametric ANOVA are not met, if the level of measurement is at least ordinal, then the Friedman two-way ANOVA is the appropriate test. The name of the test is somewhat confusing as it is used for one-way within-subjects designs. As usual, the data in a given condition are assumed to be independent.

Researchers wished to see whether a group of seven students rated a particular course differently as they spent more time on the course. Each student was asked to rate the course on a 7-point scale ranging from *not enjoyable at all* to *very enjoyable*, on three occasions: after one week, after five weeks and after ten weeks.

Friedman's ANOVA tests whether the medians of the levels of the IV are the same. The median ratings for weeks 1, 5 and 10 were 4, 4 and 5, respectively, suggesting a slight improvement in rating over time. However, to see whether this was likely by chance, the Friedman ANOVA was used to analyse the data; workings are given in Appendix VII. The test produces a statistic called χ_F^2 (sometimes given as χ_r^2). It also has a version corrected for ties which is the more accurate statistic and the one reported by SPSS. In this example, $\chi_F^2 = 4.071$ and χ_F^2 corrected for ties = 5.429. SPSS reported the exact probability as $p = 0.063$. When you do not have access to a program that provides the exact probability, for IVs with levels of 3, 4, 5 or 6, Table A14.10 in Appendix XIV gives critical values for χ_F^2 that are based on sample sizes of up to 20 per group and for IVs with 3 levels additional critical values are given for sample sizes of up to 50. When the number of levels and the sample size are both sufficiently large, the distribution of χ_F^2 is like chi-squared, with degrees of freedom that are one fewer than the number of levels of the IV. The probability based on the chi-squared distribution is $p = 0.066$.

Reporting the results of Friedman's test
Report the result in the following way: *There was not a significantly different rating given to the three different weeks ($\chi_F^2 = 5.429$, df = 2, p = .06, N = 7).* However, if the probability is given in Table A14.10 then report the result without the degrees of freedom: ($\chi_F^2 = 5.429$, p > 0.05, N = 7).

Power and Friedman's test
The power efficiency of the Friedman test depends on the number of levels of the IV: the smaller the number of levels the poorer the power efficiency.

Appendix VII gives guidelines on how to adjust the sample size that is necessary for the within-subjects parametric ANOVA in order to get power of a particular size for Friedman's test; for example, when the IV has only three levels the sample size for a Friedman's test would have to be nearly one-and-a-half times that of a parametric ANOVA.

Further analysis after an initial non-parametric ANOVA

If the results of a non-parametric ANOVA show a significant difference between the levels of the IV then further analysis can be conducted that will help to pinpoint the source of the significance. Chapter 18 deals with such analysis.

Nominal data

Between-subjects designs: χ^2 contingency test

When a contingency table has variables with more than two levels, the analysis is basically the same as for one with variables that have only two levels. Thus, the appropriate test is the χ^2 contingency test (sometimes known as the 'test of independence'), described in Chapter 15. For example, if one variable was type of smoker—with smoker, ex-smoker and non-smoker—and the other variable was gender we would have a 3 by 2 contingency table. In this case, the terms 'independent' and 'dependent' variable are often misnomers in the χ^2 test, as neither has been manipulated; the test is looking to see whether the pattern of one variable is different for different levels of another variable—for example, whether the proportions in each of the different smoking statuses differ between the males and the females.

Remember that the frequencies should be independent—each person should only appear under one category—and that not more than 20% of the *expected* frequencies should be smaller than 5; see Chapter 15 for a fuller explanation. If too many expected frequencies are below 5 then it is possible to combine categories for variables that have more than two levels. Thus, if the ex-smoker categories had expected frequencies that were too small then a new category could be formed that combined ex-smokers and non-smokers. This would only make sense if the researchers were particularly interested in comparing those who smoke now with those who do not. If they were interested in comparing those who had smoked at some time with those who never had then it would make more sense to combine ex-smokers with smokers.

Within-subjects designs: Cochran's Q

If the measure taken is dichotomous, for example, yes or no, or can be converted into one or more dichotomies, then Cochran's Q can be used. An example would be if researchers wanted to compare students' choices of modules on *social psychology*, *research methods* and *historical issues* to see whether some modules were more popular than others. It is recommended that the test be conducted with at least 16 participants, and so the researchers asked this number of students what their module choices were. Twelve had chosen social psychology, eight research methods and six historical issues. Appendix VII shows the workings for Cochran's Q. In the example $Q = 4.668$ and df $= 3 - 1 = 2$. SPSS reports the exact probability as $p = 0.125$. However, if you do not have access to exact probabilities, then, with at least this sample size, Q is considered to be distributed like chi-squared with df = one fewer than the number of levels of the IV. The probability based on the chi-squared distribution is $p = 0.097$. Accordingly, it was concluded that there was insufficient evidence to reject the Null Hypothesis that the numbers choosing the different modules are the same.

Converting nominal data with more than two levels into dichotomous data

In order to use Cochran's Q, it may be necessary to create dichotomous variables from non-dichotomous nominal (categorical) data. In this example, each student could choose more than one of the modules but for the analysis the response to each module was treated as a separate level of the IV with *yes* (coded as *1*) being the score if a student did take that module and *no* (coded as *0*) if he or she did not.

Power analysis and Cochran's Q
I do not know of a means to do power analysis on Cochran's Q as there is no parametric equivalent for such data.

Summary

When there are more than two levels of an independent variable it is not considered appropriate to use a series of tests of the difference between pairs of those conditions. Instead, as a preliminary stage, it is advisable to see whether there is an overall difference between the conditions. Such analysis can be conducted using the appropriate form of the Analysis of Variance, or equivalent for nominal data; see Figure 16.5. However, remember that if homogeneity of variance is not present but the other requirements of a parametric between-subjects ANOVA are fulfilled then we use Welch's F-test. If there is an overall difference between the conditions then its precise source can be sought using techniques given in Chapter 18.

The next chapter looks at the analysis of designs with more than one independent variable.

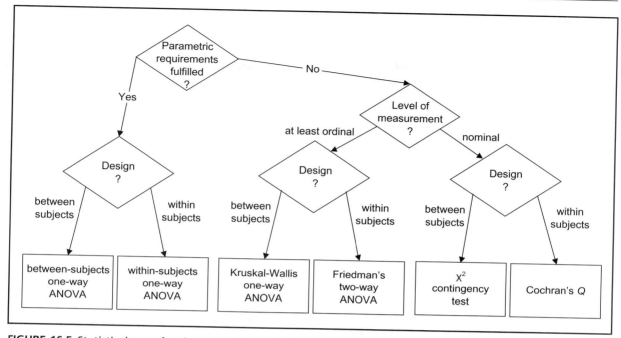

FIGURE 16.5 Statistical tests for designs with one independent variable with more than two levels

17 ANALYSIS OF DESIGNS WITH MORE THAN ONE INDEPENDENT VARIABLE

Introduction

In many psychological experiments we are not only interested in the effects of a single independent variable on the dependent variable. Rather, we can be interested in the effects of two or more independent variables. The main reason for this is because we may hypothesise that the independent variables work together in their effects; that is, that the independent variables interact with each other. The present chapter gives full examples in which two independent variables are involved and then describes how this can be extended to situations that entail more than two independent variables.

How to evaluate effect size and conduct power analysis in such designs are also discussed. Worked examples of each of the stages are given in Appendix VIII.

Interactions between independent variables

An interaction is where a pattern that is found across the levels of one independent variable differs according to the levels of another independent variable. Imagine that, in a study of face recognition, researchers have two independent variables: familiarity, with two levels—familiar and unfamiliar (that is familiar and unfamiliar prior to the experiment); and orientation of face, with two levels—correct and upside down. The dependent variable is *time taken to recognise a face shown in a photograph*. An interaction between the two variables would exist if familiar faces were more quickly recognised than unfamiliar faces when they were presented in the correct orientation, while there was no difference in speed of recognition

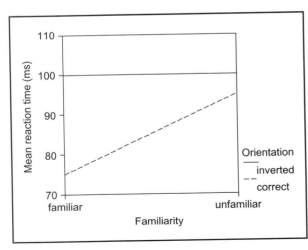

FIGURE 17.1 An example of an interaction between two independent variables

between the two levels of familiarity when faces were presented upside down. Orientation could be described as a *moderator* variable because it moderates the relationship between degree of familiarity and reaction time. Similarly, familiarity could be seen as a moderator of the relationship between orientation and reaction time.

An interaction would also be present if familiar faces were recognised more slowly than unfamiliar ones when presented upside down but the pattern was reversed for correctly oriented faces.

It is important to note that if the trend for familiar faces to be more quickly recognised were true to the same degree regardless of orientation, an interaction would not be present, even if correctly oriented faces were recognised more quickly than upside-down ones. In this last case orientation is not moderating the relationship between degree of familiarity and reaction time. When the lines representing the two levels of one of the IVs are roughly parallel, there is unlikely to be an interaction between the IVs.

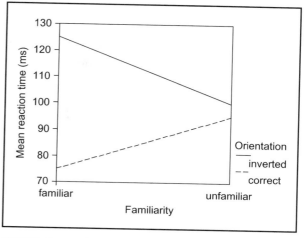

FIGURE 17.2 A further example of an interaction between two independent variables

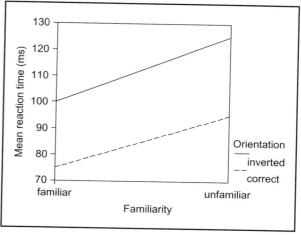

FIGURE 17.3 An example of a lack of interaction between two independent variables

Parametric tests

Two between-subjects independent variables

The simplest version of ANOVA, with two IVs, to calculate and to interpret is where both IVs are between-subjects.

For the first example I am going to expand the between-subjects example from the previous chapter. This time imagine that the researchers not only want to look at the effect of mnemonic strategy on recall but they also want to investigate the effect of the nature of the list of words to be recalled. As before, one independent variable is *mnemonic strategy*, with groups either receiving no training (the control group), being trained to use pegwords or the method of loci. A second independent variable is introduced, *the nature of the list*, with two levels: a list of words that are conceptually linked—all are things found in the kitchen—and words that are not conceptually linked. This design means that we have six different conditions; see Table 17.1. The design of this experiment is totally between-subjects. In other words, each participant is only in one condition. Therefore, there are six groups altogether. A totally between-subjects design is sometimes described as a *factorial* design.

Table 17.1 The conditions involved in a design for testing memory strategy and type of word list

List type	Control	Pegword	Loci
Linked	x	x	x
Unlinked	x	x	x

It is possible to analyse the data from this type of design using a version of Analysis of Variance (ANOVA). In this case, it is a two-way ANOVA: two-way because there are two independent variables: *nature of list* and *mnemonic strategy*.

A two-way ANOVA will test three hypotheses; the use of numbers helps to distinguish the hypotheses from each other. The first is

H_1: The means for the levels of the first IV are different.

with the Null Hypothesis:

H_{01}: The means for the levels of the first IV are not different.

The second is

H_2: The means for the levels of the second IV are different.

with the Null Hypothesis:

H_{02}: The means for the levels of the second IV are not different.

The third is

H_3: The pattern of the means for one IV differs between the levels of the other IV.

with the Null Hypothesis:

H_{03}: The pattern of means for one IV does not differ between the levels of the other IV.

The third hypothesis deals with an interaction between IVs.

The researchers conduct the experiment with five participants in each condition. They calculate the means (see Table 17.2) and plot them on a graph (see Figure 17.4). If we look at the column means in Table 17.2 we see

Table 17.2 The mean recall for participants showing effects of list type and mnemonic strategy

List	Control	Mnemonic strategy Pegword	Loci	Row mean
Linked	11.00	10.60	10.60	10.73
Unlinked	6.40	8.40	8.80	7.87
Column mean	8.70	9.50	9.70	9.30

the means for each mnemonic strategy, regardless of which list was presented. This suggests that there is a difference between the strategies, with the best recall produced by those using the method of loci (9.70 words), the next best by those using pegwords (9.50 words) and the worst by those using no strategy, the control group (8.70 words).

If we look at the row means for Table 17.2 we see the means for the two types of list, regardless of the mnemonic strategy employed. This suggests that those who were shown the list of linked words recalled more (10.73 words) than those who were shown the unlinked list (7.87 words).

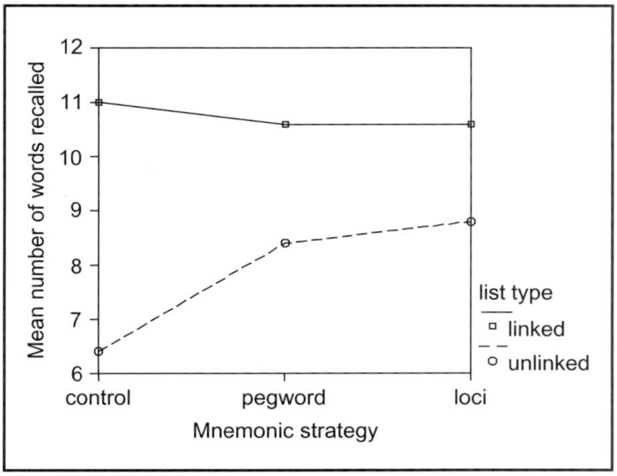

Finally, if we look at the means for each of the six groups (sometimes called the 'cell means') in Table 17.2 and look at their relative position in Figure 17.4, this suggests that there is a different pattern between the two lists for the mnemonic strategies. It would appear that those in the control group have particularly poor recall compared with the other two mnemonic strategies when the list contained unlinked words. However, when the list contained linked words, the control group was no worse than those who used the two mnemonic strategies. This difference in the two patterns suggests that there is an interaction between the independent variables: the relative performance of the participants in the three mnemonic conditions depends on the type of list used.

FIGURE 17.4 Mean recall of participants by list type and mnemonic strategy

Partitioning the variance in a two-way between-subjects ANOVA

When there are two between-subjects variables, there are only between-subjects sources of variance. As with the one-way between-subjects ANOVA, the total variance can be split into between-groups and within-groups variance. Between-groups variance can be further divided into variance due to one independent variable, variance due to the other independent variable and variance due to the interaction between the two independent variables. Within-groups variance is the residual (or error) term that will be needed to form F-ratios with each of the between-group sources of variance.

Returning to the example, as usual we want to know whether the impressions that are given by the summary statistics are supported by the inferential statistics. Therefore we will need to conduct a two-way between-subjects ANOVA, the results of which are given in Table 17.3. Sometimes when

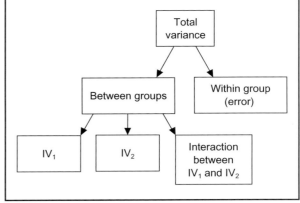

FIGURE 17.5 Partitioning of variance in two-way between-subjects ANOVA

Table 17.3 The summary table for a 2 × 3, two-way between-subjects ANOVA

Source	Sum of Squares	df	Mean Square	F	p
List	61.633	1	61.633	37.354	0.0001
Mnemonic	5.600	2	2.800	1.697	0.2045
List * Mnemonic	11.467	2	5.733	3.475	0.0473
Error	39.600	24	1.650		
Total	118.300	29			

describing multi-way ANOVAs (that is, having more than one IV) the numbers of levels of each IV are included in the description. Accordingly, the current analysis is a 2 × 3, two-way ANOVA.

Interpreting the output from a two-way between-subjects ANOVA

Once again the first column shows the sources of variation in the data (the recall scores). We are shown that the total amount of variation can be split into four sources:

(i)   the variation that can be attributed to the differences between the two list types;

(ii)   the variation that can be attributed to the difference between mnemonic strategies;

(iii) the variation that can be attributed to the interaction between list type and mnemonic strategy. In other words, the way in which the pattern of recall across the mnemonic strategies differs between the two lists; and

(iv)   the residual or variation that cannot be attributed to the actions of the IVs—the within-groups variation.

The second column shows the sum of squared deviations for each source of variance. The variation for the interaction needs further explanation. It measures the variation between the groups that remains once the variation due to differences between the list types and the variation due to differences between the mnemonic strategies have been subtracted from the overall variation between the groups.

The third column shows the degrees of freedom for each source of variation. The total degrees of freedom are one fewer than the number of scores, that is $30 - 1 = 29$. The df for each of the IVs is simply one fewer than the number of levels in that IV: list df $= 2 - 1 = 1$; mnemonic-strategy df $= 3 - 1 = 2$. The df for interaction is calculated by multiplying the df for each of the IVs: interaction df $= 1 \times 2 = 2$. The df for within-groups (error) is the number of degrees of freedom that is left once all the dfs for the IVs have been removed from the total: error df $= 29 - 1 - 2 - 2 = 29 - 5 = 24$. Another way to look at the error df is that there are six groups, each of which has five participants in it. There is one fewer degree of freedom in each group than the number of participants in that group: $5 - 1 = 4$. Therefore, error df $= 6 \times 4 = 24$.

The fourth column shows the Mean Squares for each of the sources of variation. The Mean Square is the estimate of the population variance. As usual, each Mean Square is calculated by dividing the sum of squares by its df.

The fifth column shows the F-ratios for the analysis.

In this experiment we are interested in evaluating all three between-groups sources of variation. The last source, within-groups, is unwanted variation, as far as we are concerned. Therefore, there are three F-ratios that will need to be calculated to test our hypotheses: one for each of the IVs—list type and mnemonic strategy—and one for the interaction between them. In this particular design the within-groups source of variation is the appropriate error term for each of the three F-ratios. Thus:

$$F_{(list)} = \frac{\text{variance estimate from list type}}{\text{variance estimate from within groups}}$$

$$F_{(mnemonic)} = \frac{\text{variance estimate from mnemonic strategy}}{\text{variance estimate from within groups}}$$

$$F_{(interaction)} = \frac{\text{variance estimate from interaction between list type and mnemonic strategy}}{\text{variance estimate from within groups}}$$

As with one-way ANOVA, if a Null Hypothesis is correct then the F-ratio for that hypothesis is the ratio between two estimates of the same variance. That is, the variance within a single population of scores which have not been affected by the experimental manipulations. Therefore the F-ratio will be close to 1. However, if the Null Hypothesis is incorrect then the appropriate between-groups variance estimate will contain an additional amount of variance due to the effect of the given treatment or treatments. In this case, the F-ratio will tend to be greater than 1.

Note that the F-ratio for list type is well above 1, while the F-ratios for mnemonic strategy and for the interaction are closer to 1. As usual, we still need to know how likely each of these outcomes is to have occurred if the Null Hypothesis is true.

The sixth column shows the probability for each F-ratio. From this we can see that, overall, the lists produced significantly different recall; that, overall, the mnemonic types did not produce significantly different recall; and that the lists and mnemonic strategies interacted with each other to produce a significant effect.

Interpreting a two-way between-subjects ANOVA

A two-way design introduces the need to test the interaction between the two independent variables, regardless of whether we had any hypothesis about an interaction. This introduces a complication because the effects of the IVs alone have to be evaluated in the context of an interaction.

When talking about a single IV in an ANOVA that has more than one IV, we talk about the *main effect* of that IV. This is because there is more than one way to look at the effect of that IV. The main effect of the IV is when we ignore how it varies as a consequence of the other IV. Thus, in the present case, the overall pattern of the means for mnemonic strategy (the main effect) is not echoed in each case when only one type of word list is used. When linked words were presented, the control condition produced the best recall, whereas when unlinked words were presented, the control condition produced the worst recall.

We can say that there is a significant main effect of list type ($F_{(1,24)} = 37.354$, $p = .0001$, $\eta^2 = .521$). We can also say that there is no significant main effect of mnemonic strategy ($F_{(2,24)} = 1.697$, $p = .205$, $\eta^2 = .047$). However, these results are complicated by the presence of a significant interaction between list type and mnemonic strategy ($F_{(2,24)} = 3.475$, $p = .047$, $\eta^2 = .097$). Without further analysis we can only say that the interaction *appears* to be produced by the marked improvement in recall for the control group when they are given a list of linked words as opposed to one that contains unlinked words. The type of further analysis that is appropriate depends on our hypotheses and on the nature of these preliminary results. See the sections on *contrasts* and *simple effects* in the next chapter for details of how to analyse the results further.

Unequal sample size

In the previous chapter it was stated that there are two basic ways to analyse a design that does not have the same sample size in each condition (an unbalanced design): by weighted means and by unweighted means. There is also the method of least squares. Whereas most computer programs use weighted means as the standard for one-way ANOVA, they do not for multi-way ANOVA.

There are at least three situations in which you might have an unbalanced design. One is if the samples are proportional and reflect an imbalance in the population from which the sample came. Thus, if we knew that two-thirds of psychology students were female and one-third male, we might have a sample of psychology students with a 2:1 ratio of females to males. For example, we might look at the way male and female psychology students differ in their exam performance after receiving two teaching techniques—seminars or lectures. The samples might be the following:

Table 17.4 The numbers of male and female psychology students used in a study of gender and teaching technique

Gender	Teaching technique seminar	lecture
male	10	10
female	20	20

With such proportional data it is legitimate to use the weighted means analysis.

A second possible reason for an unbalanced design is that participants were not available for particular treatments but there was no systematic reason for their unavailability, that is, there is no connection between the treatment to which they were assigned and the lack of data for them. Under these circumstances it is legitimate to use the unweighted means method or the least squares method of analysis.

A third possible reason for an unbalanced design would be if there were a systematic link between the treatment group and the failure to have data for such participants; this is more likely in a quasi-experiment. For example, if research involved criminals who were allocated to different groups on the basis of the severity of their crimes. If the design lacked more of one type of criminal, even though the imbalance was not a reflection of the population, then, in such a case of self-selection by the participants, none of the three options can solve the problem.

Given the difficulties with unbalanced designs, unless you are dealing with proportional samples, some people recommend randomly removing data points from the treatments that have more than the others. Alternatively, it is possible to replace missing data with the mean for the group, or even the overall mean. If you put in the group mean you may artificially enhance any differences between conditions, and if you use the overall mean to replace missing data you may obscure any genuine differences between groups. If either of these methods is used then the total degrees of freedom (and, as a consequence, the error df) should be reduced by one for each data point estimated.

My own preference would be to remove data but I would only recommend this if you have a reasonable sample size, given the effect that removing data will have on the statistical power of the test.

Two within-subjects independent variables

For the example of a two-way, within-subjects design I will expand the one-way design used in the previous chapter to evaluate how participants will differ in the length of sentence they recommend for a criminal, depending on the conditions under which they are making the decision. As before, the first independent variable—the condition under which sentencing was decided—has three levels: alone, communicating with others via computer and in the presence of others. A second independent variable is now introduced—the nature of the defendant. In this case, the defendants will be of two types: those with no previous record (novices) and habitual criminals (experienced).

We now have six possible conditions in this experiment (see Table 17.5) and because both independent variables are within-subjects every participant provides a score for each of the six conditions. As with the between-subjects design, the ANOVA will test for three hypotheses: two main effects and an interaction.

Table 17.5 The conditions involved in a two-way within-subjects design

Defendant	Context Alone	Context Computer	Context Face-to-face
Novice	x	x	x
Experienced	x	x	x

Table 17.6 The mean sentence length, in months, recommended for defendants under different contexts

	Context Alone	Context Computer	Context Face-to-face	Row mean
Novice	13.2	13.6	16.2	14.33
Experienced	16.0	17.6	20.6	18.07
Column mean	14.6	15.6	18.4	

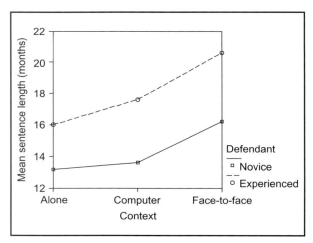

FIGURE 17.6 The mean sentence length recommended for defendants under different contexts

The experimenters collect the data from five participants and produce a table (see Table 17.6) and graph of the results (see Figure 17.6). It would appear that a novice defendant receives a shorter sentence than an experienced criminal but that both criminals will receive a heavier sentence if the judge is aware of the recommendations that have been made by others. The fact that the lines for the two defendant types are roughly parallel suggests that there is no interaction between defendant type and the context in which the sentencing occurred.

Partitioning the variance in a two-way within-subjects ANOVA

In designs with two within-subjects independent variables, as with the one-way within-subjects design, there are two main sources of variance: between-subjects and within-subjects.

Within-subjects variance can be further divided into:

(i)   variance due to the first independent variable;
(ii)   variance due to the interaction between the subjects and the first independent variable;
(iii) variance due to the second independent variable;
(iv)   variance due to the interaction between the subjects and the second independent variable;

(v)   variance due to the interaction between the two independent variables;

(vi)   variance due to the interaction between the two independent variables and subjects.

Each of the interactions that involves subjects constitutes an error term for use in calculating an *F*-ratio.

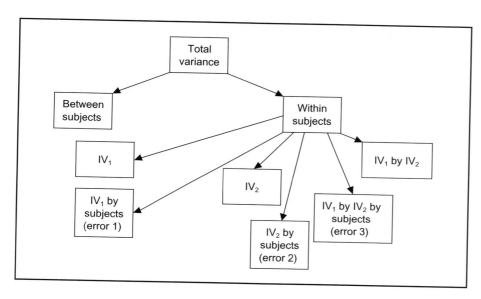

FIGURE 17.7 Partitioning of variance in two-way within-subjects ANOVA

Before the researchers can evaluate their hypotheses properly they need to conduct a two-way within-subjects ANOVA on their data, the results of which are shown in Table 17.7.

Table 17.7 The summary table for a 2 × 3, two-way within-subjects ANOVA

Source	S of S	df	MS	F	p	G–G	H–F
subject	2.467	4	.617				
defendant	104.533	1	104.533	93.612	.0006	.0006	.0006
defendant by subject	4.467	4	1.117				
context	77.600	2	38.800	46.099	.0001	.0007	.0001
context by subject	6.733	8	.842				
defendant by context	3.467	2	1.733	1.455	.2892	.2946	.2948
defendant by context by subject	9.533	8	1.192				
Total	208.8	29					

Interpreting a two-way within-subjects ANOVA

The first column shows the sources of the variation in the experiment. The between-subjects variance is simply the main effect of subjects—the variation in sentencing between participants, regardless of conditions. In all there are seven identifiable sources of variation in the sentences: one between-subjects and six within-subjects.

The second column shows the sum of squared deviations for each of the sources of variation in the experiment, while the third column shows the degrees of freedom. The total degrees of freedom are one fewer than the number of scores: total df = 30 − 1 = 29. These can be split into the df for each of the other sources of variance. The df for between-subjects variance is one fewer than the number of participants, df = 5 − 1 = 4.

The df for within-subjects sources of variance can be split into:

defendant df = 2 − 1 = 1;

context df = 3 − 1 = 2;

interaction between defendant and context df = 1 × 2 = 2;

defendant by subject interaction df = 1 × 4 = 4;

context by subject interaction df = 2 × 4 = 8;

defendant by context by subject interaction df = 1 × 2 × 4 = 8.

The fourth column shows the Mean Squares for each of the sources of variation, created by dividing each sum of squares by its df.

The fifth column shows the *F*-ratios for each of the within-subjects sources of variation. The appropriate error term for each within-subjects source of variation is the interaction between subject and that source of variation. Thus:

$$F_{(\text{defendant})} = \frac{MS_{\text{defendant}}}{MS_{\text{defendant by subject}}}$$

$$F_{(\text{context})} = \frac{MS_{\text{context}}}{MS_{\text{context by subject}}}$$

$$F_{(\text{defendant by context})} = \frac{MS_{\text{defendant by context}}}{MS_{\text{defendant by context by subject}}}$$

As usual, in each case the Null Hypothesis assumes that the variation is due solely to random differences within subjects, while, if the Null Hypothesis is incorrect, the treatment MS will have variation due to the treatment.

The sixth column tells us the probability of each treatment effect having occurred if the Null Hypothesis were true. From this we can see that there was a significant main effect of defendant type ($F_{(1,4)} = 93.612$, $p = .0006$, $\eta^2 = .501$); there was a significant main effect of context ($F_{(2,8)} = 46.099$, $p = .0001$, $\eta^2 = .372$); but there was no significant interaction between defendant type and context ($F_{(2,8)} = 1.455$, $p = .29$, $\eta^2 = .017$). I have added the effect sizes which have been calculated in the usual way of dividing the sum of squares for a given effect by the total sum of squares.

Those using SPSS to analyse the data will find that the results are laid out differently from how they are shown in Table 17.7. In the first place the between-subjects element will be in a separate table. Secondly, each error term, instead of being described as *by Subject*, as in *defendant by Subject*, is shown as *Error(defendant)*.

Sphericity

The term *sphericity* was introduced in the previous chapter. It refers to the need for within-subjects designs to have homogeneity of variance among difference scores. The columns headed G–G (for Greenhouse–Geisser) and H–F (for Huynh–Feldt) in Table 17.7 show where adjustments have been made, to compensate for possible lack of sphericity, to the degrees of freedom and the effects the adjustments have on the probability of a given *F*-ratio. As the probabilities shown for the adjustments are in line with the unadjusted probabilities, in that they agree over whether a result is significant or not, there is not a problem over sphericity. When df = 1 sphericity is not an issue and so no adjustment is made. In SPSS each method of adjusting for possible lack of sphericity is shown in a separate row, which includes the adjusted df. For Context, G–G epsilon = 0.658, df = 1.317, 5.266; H–F epsilon = 0.854, df = 1.708, 6.831. For Defendant by Context, G–G epsilon = .524, df = 1.049, 4.195; H–F epsilon = .550, df = 1.099, 4.397.

The results from the experiment could be further analysed by comparing the means to identify the source of the significant main effect of context. Remember that a significant result in an ANOVA does not specify the precise contributions to that significance if there are more than two levels of the independent variable. In the case of defendant type, because there are only two means involved, we know that the significant difference is due to higher sentences being passed on habitual criminals. The next chapter deals with ways to conduct the necessary further analysis.

Mixed (split-plot) designs

So far the designs that have been described have been straightforward in that they have either entailed independent variables which are both between-subjects, in which case the design is between-subjects or factorial, or both have been within-subjects, in which case the design is within-subjects or repeated-measures. However, we now move to a design that contains both a between-subjects and a within-subjects independent variable. Such a design is described as *mixed*, *split-plot* or *repeated measures with one between-subjects factor*.

Imagine that experimenters want to compare the way that males and females rate their parents' IQs. In this design the independent variable *gender* which has two levels—male and female—is a between-subjects variable. The independent variable *parent* which has two levels—mother and father—is a within-subjects variable because each participant supplies data for each level of that variable.

Table 17.8 The mean estimates of parental IQ by males and females

	Parent Father	Parent Mother	Row mean
Male	115	103	109.0
Female	109	108	108.5
Column mean	112.0	105.5	

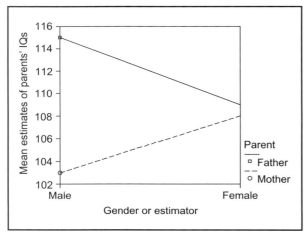

FIGURE 17.8 The mean IQ estimates by males and females of parental IQ

The researchers hypothesise that males and females will differ in the way that they rate their parents' IQs, such that both may rate their fathers' IQs higher than they rate their mothers' IQs, but that males will show a larger difference between the ratings. Thus they are predicting an effect of parents' IQ estimate and an interaction between gender and parental IQ. They collect the estimates from five males and five females and the results are shown in Table 17.8 and Figure 17.8.

The results suggest that the males do estimate their fathers' IQs to be much higher than their mothers' IQs but females estimate their fathers' IQs to be only slightly higher than their mothers' IQs. Thus, there would appear to be a main effect of parental IQ, even though it is not totally in line with the hypothesis, while there would appear to be an interaction between gender and parental IQ that *is* in line with the hypothesis.

Partitioning of variance in a two-way mixed ANOVA

When a design combines between- and within-subjects independent variables, it follows the rules described above for the other types of design. Thus, the overall variance can be split into between-subjects and within-subjects sources of variance. The between-subjects variance pertains to the between-subjects variable and is split into variance due to the differences between the levels of the between-subjects variable (IV_1 or between-groups variance) and differences between subjects within the groups (subjects-within-groups variance). This latter forms the error term for the between-group variance.

The within-subjects variance is split into:

(i)   the variance due to differences between levels of the second (within-subjects) independent variable (IV_2);

(ii) the variance due to the interaction between the two independent variables (IV_1 by IV_2); and

(iii) the variance due to the interaction between the second independent variable and the subjects within the groups for the first independent variable.

This last source of variance forms the error term for the other two within-subjects sources of variance.

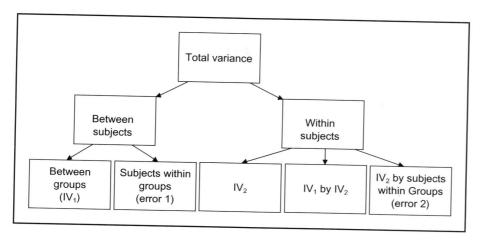

FIGURE 17.9 Partitioning of variance in a two-way mixed ANOVA

The next stage is to conduct a two-way mixed ANOVA on the data to see if the effects are statistically significant (see Table 17.9).

Table 17.9 The summary table of a 2 × 2, two-way mixed ANOVA

	Source	S of S	df	MS	F	p	G–G	H–F
(a)	gender	1.250	1	1.250	.007	.9376		
(b)	subject (group)	1530.000	8	191.250				
(c)	parent	211.250	1	211.250	5.633	.0450	.0450	.0450
(d)	parent by gender	151.250	1	151.250	4.033	.0795	.0795	.0795
(e)	parent by subject (group)	300.000	8	37.500				
	Total	2193.75	19					

Reading the summary table of a two-way mixed ANOVA

The first column of Table 17.9 shows the sources for the variation in the study. Total variation can be split into between-subjects variation and within-subjects variation. These can be further divided. The between-subjects variation can be split into:

(a) variation between the genders, regardless of which parent they were making the estimate about;

(b) the variation between subjects within the two genders (subject within groups).

The within-subjects variation can be split into:

(c)   the differences in estimates for the two parents;
(d)   the interaction between parent and gender;
(e)   the interaction between parent and subject within group.

The second column shows the Sum of Squares, while the third column shows the degrees of freedom. The total df is number of scores less 1: $20 - 1 = 19$. This can be split into between-subjects sources and within-subjects sources:

*   Between-subjects
    gender df = $2 - 1 = 1$
    subjects within group df, each group has df = $5 - 1 = 4$, therefore the
        subjects within groups df = $2 \times 4 = 8$
*   Within-subjects
    parent df = $2 - 1 = 1$
    interaction between parent and gender df = $1 \times 1 = 1$
    parent by subject within group df = $1 \times 8 = 8$

The fourth column shows the Mean Squares for each of the sources of variance, while the fifth column shows the F-ratios, which are formed from the following equations:

$$F_{(gender)} = \frac{MS_{gender}}{MS_{subjects\ within\ gender}}$$

$$F_{(parent)} = \frac{MS_{parent}}{MS_{parent\ by\ subjects\ within\ groups}}$$

$$F_{(interaction)} = \frac{MS_{gender\ by\ parent}}{MS_{parent\ by\ subjects\ within\ groups}}$$

Interpreting a two-way mixed ANOVA

The summary table shows that there is no significant main effect of gender on ratings of IQ ($F_{(1,8)} = 0.007$, $p = .938$, $\eta^2 = .0006$). There is a significant main effect of parent on ratings of IQ ($F_{(1,8)} = 5.663$, $p = .045$, $\eta^2 = .096$). There is no significant interaction between gender and parent on ratings of IQ ($F_{(1,8)} = 4.033$, $p = .0795$, $\eta^2 = .069$).

Note that the table only reports adjusted probabilities for the F-ratios that entail a within-subjects element. As in each case df = 1, there is no adjustment as sphericity isn't an issue and so the probability remains the same.

Missing data
In designs with at least one within-subjects independent variable computers usually delete all the data for participants for whom there are missing values, although other options are sometimes available. Two possibilities

mentioned earlier under unequal samples for between-subjects designs are also available here: to estimate the missing data by using the mean for the condition or by using the overall mean. Once again the appropriate degrees of freedom will have to be reduced to take account of each data point that is estimated.

Designs with more than two independent variables

The principles that have been outlined for the previous designs can be extended to designs that have three or more independent variables. The problem with such designs is that they will have more sources of variance which are due to interactions and they will have what are called 'higher-order interactions'. Imagine that we extended the design in which we had participants recommend a sentence for a defendant so that we had gender of participant as one IV, nature of defendant as a second and context in which the judgement was made as a third. In addition to the three main effects, we would have the following interactions: defendant by context, defendant by gender, context by gender and defendant by context by gender. This makes interpretation of the results more difficult. In addition, it makes presentation of the results in graphical form more difficult, for we will need to represent the new dimension somehow. It is possible (though it is difficult to read), to represent a three-way design on a single graph, or you can produce a separate two-way graph for each level of a third IV. For example, you could have a context by defendant graph for each level of gender. However, once you adopt a four-way design either approach ceases to be possible.

The account I have given of ANOVA has been simplified over such issues as whether the levels of the independent variable(s) can be viewed as fixed (selected arbitrarily) or random (randomly chosen); see Chapter 3. The analyses I have described have treated the levels of the IV(s) as fixed. This limits the conclusions that can be drawn from the results; we cannot safely generalise from the effects of the levels we have used to what effects other levels might have produced. If you have randomly selected the levels and wish to generalise I recommend that you read the accounts given in Myers and Well (1991), Howell (2002) or Winer, Brown and Michels (1991).

Effect size and ANOVA

For each effect I have reported the η^2. I have calculated them in the same way that I did for the one-way ANOVA as shown in the previous chapter: the sum of squares for the effect is divided by the total sum of squares. SPSS reports partial-η^2 but I think that this can be confusing and is different from η^2 even in the completely between-subjects design. Accordingly, I would calculate them myself for the reasons explained in the previous chapter.

Power and ANOVA

The power tables that were used for one-way ANOVAs (see Appendix XV) can be used to estimate the power and sample size required for a multi-way ANOVA. However, the power of each F-ratio can be estimated separately. If you are trying to work out the necessary sample size to achieve a given level of power, you will need to include the largest sample size that your power analyses suggest.

Non-parametric tests

Standard tests for multi-way ANOVA with data that do not conform to the assumptions of parametric ANOVA are not generally available on computer. However, Meddis (1984) describes two-way ANOVAs for data that are at least ordinal and for nominal data. In addition, Neave and Worthington (1988) describe tests that can evaluate the interactions between two such variables. It is also possible to use more advanced techniques on such data. These techniques—log-linear modelling, and logistic regression—are described briefly in Chapter 21 but their full use is beyond the scope of this book.

Summary

Multi-way ANOVA (for designs with more than one independent variable) allows the interaction between IVs to be evaluated, as well as the main effects of each IV. Beyond two-way ANOVA interpretation begins to be complicated and the results can be difficult to display graphically.

You have now been introduced to the preliminary analysis for one-way and two-way ANOVAs. The next chapter explains the types of analysis that can be conducted to follow up the findings from an ANOVA in order to test the more specific hypotheses that researchers often have.

SUBSEQUENT ANALYSIS AFTER ANOVA OR χ^2 18

Introduction

The previous two chapters have introduced the first stage of analysis when a design has a single independent variable with more than two levels or more than one IV. As was pointed out, the preliminary analysis asks the limited question: do the means for the different levels of one or more IVs appear to differ? If they do appear to differ then the source of that difference may not be obvious. Therefore, in order to identify the source it is necessary to conduct further analysis. However, despite the title of this chapter, the methods described here can be used without having ascertained whether the F-ratios in an ANOVA are statistically significant.

This chapter describes three types of subsequent analysis—contrasts, trend tests and simple effects.

Contrasts

Parametric tests

Contrasts are comparisons between means in the case of parametric tests. To discuss them I am going to return to the word-recall experiment, described in Chapter 16, which involves a group using pegwords, a group using the method of loci and a control group. The mean recall of participants in the three conditions were found to be significantly different. The types of contrast you can perform are almost infinite in number. The main distinction is between pairwise contrasts, where you compare two means at a time, and other forms of contrast, such as a comparison of the control condition with the mean of the two other conditions. There are numerous tests of contrasts. Rather than describe all of them I will give a set of tests that cover most situations and an explanation of when each is appropriate.

The rationale behind all the tests of contrasts is an attempt to get round the problem I described when introducing ANOVA. If you have more than two means then identifying which ones are significantly different involves more than one test; in the case of three means you would need to do three pairwise comparisons and in the case of four means you would need to do six pairwise comparisons. The probability given by the inferential statistics described in this book is the likelihood that an outcome would have occurred even if the Null Hypothesis were correct. That probability is based on the observation that if the same test is conducted repeatedly on sets of data for which the Null Hypothesis is correct then a result will be shown to be significant at the $p = 0.05$ level on approximately 5% of occasions. In other words, a Type I error will be committed on 5% of occasions. Therefore, whenever the same statistical test is repeated the likelihood of making a Type I error is increased.

The family of contrasts

A group of contrasts is sometimes described as a *family of contrasts*. Tests of contrasts adjust the probability level so that the probability is for the family of contrasts (the *error rate per family*, EF) rather than the individual contrast (*error rate per contrast*, EC). Thus, the probability for the family of contrasts is set at $\alpha = 0.05$. How the adjustment is made depends on the nature and size of the family of contrasts. As a rule of thumb, treat the family of contrasts as those contrasts that are relevant to a single *F*-ratio from the original ANOVA. Thus, in a two-way ANOVA there will be three families of contrasts—one for each of the main effects and one for the interaction.

A test that makes too great an adjustment and thus overly decreases the likelihood of making a Type I error is described as being *conservative*. Remember that a conservative test will increase the likelihood of making a Type II error. It is important that you choose the correct contrast test, and therefore the correct adjustment, to avoid reducing the power of your test unnecessarily.

Planned and unplanned comparisons

An important distinction between comparisons is whether you decided which ones to do before looking at the data or afterwards. If you choose what comparisons you are going to conduct before looking at the data they are described as *planned* or *a priori* comparisons. If you choose them after looking at the data then they are described as *unplanned*, *post hoc* or *a posteriori* comparisons.

The distinction is not a trivial one because the test employed on unplanned comparisons will be more conservative than the one applied to planned comparisons. An example should make the reason clear. If I look at the means for the memory experiment and then decide to do a pairwise comparison of the mean for the control group and the mean for the method of loci group because these two means are the furthest apart, then it is as if I had conducted all three possible comparisons. Therefore, the family of contrasts, in this case, is all three contrasts and so the adjustment to the α-level will be made accordingly conservative. However, if, before looking at the data, I had planned to conduct a contrast between the means for controls and method of loci then the family of contrasts contains only one and there will be no adjustment to the α-level.

Another distinction between planned and unplanned contrasts is that, if the contrasts are planned, then it is perfectly legitimate to conduct them, even when the original *F*-ratio from the ANOVA was not statistically significant. Unplanned contrasts should only be conducted when the *F*-ratio is statistically significant because they are exploratory rather than testing a specific hypothesis.

Before introducing the specific contrast tests I will deal with one last concept—orthogonality.

Orthogonality

You will recall that ANOVA takes the overall variation in scores in a study and attempts to identify the sources of that variation; in other words, it partitions the variance of the scores. Contrasts similarly partition the variance. The amount of variance that can be identified as being due to the treatments can be split into specific sources of variance, each based on a different contrast.

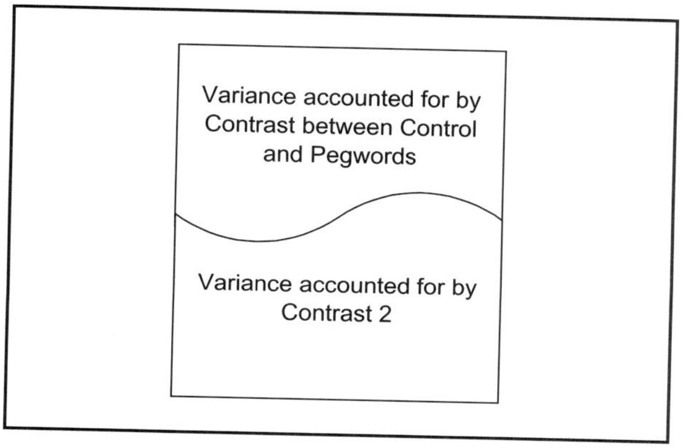

If you are going to split the overall variance into parts, such that each accounts for a different part of the variance, then the contrasts are described as *orthogonal*. Figure 18.1 is a schematic representation of the variance explained by a given IV, for example, the mnemonic strategy: the rectangle denotes the overall variance for the treatments, while each segment represents the variance that has been accounted for by a particular contrast. The two contrasts are orthogonal because they are accounting for different parts of the overall variation in scores.

On the other hand, if the variance accounted for by one contrast includes some of the variance accounted for by another contrast, then the contrasts are non-orthogonal. Figure 18.2 shows the case where two contrasts are not orthogonal because they are trying to account for some of the same variance.

A consequence of limiting your contrasts to being orthogonal is that you can only conduct as many contrasts as there are degrees of freedom in the treatment. Thus, in the case of the memory experiment, as the treatment (memory condition) has two degrees of freedom, only two contrasts could be conducted and remain orthogonal.

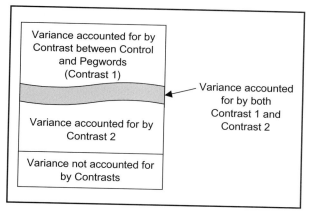

FIGURE 18.1 The variance accounted for by two orthogonal contrasts

FIGURE 18.2 The variance accounted for by two non-orthogonal contrasts

How one checks that a set of contrasts is orthogonal is difficult to understand without sufficient mathematical description. The check is given in Appendix IX. However, while statisticians used to see keeping contrasts orthogonal as important, this is no longer the case, and all the tests of contrasts mentioned in this chapter can be legitimately conducted on non-orthogonal contrasts. Therefore, it should be possible to understand the rest of the chapter without having referred to Appendix IX. Nonetheless, it is important to be aware of the notion of orthogonality because some tests of contrasts are more conservative when the contrasts are not orthogonal.

The simplest, and most frequently used, contrast is the pairwise contrast where two means are compared. The description in this chapter will therefore be restricted to pairwise contrasts. How to conduct more complex contrasts is described in Appendix IX.

All the pairwise contrasts described in this chapter are based on a t-value which is then compared with a critical value of t to see whether it is statistically significant. The method of calculation of t depends on whether the data are from a between- or a within-subjects design.

Contrasts on data from between-subjects designs

For between-subjects designs, use the following equation:

$$t = \frac{\text{mean}_1 - \text{mean}_2}{\sqrt{\left(\frac{1}{n_1} + \frac{1}{n_2}\right) \times \text{MS}_{\text{error}}}} \tag{18.1}$$

where mean_1 is the mean for one of the conditions (condition 1); mean_2 is the mean for the other condition (condition 2); n_1 is the sample size of the group producing mean_1; n_2 is the sample size of the group producing mean_2; MS_{error} is the mean square for the appropriate error term in the original F-ratio.

When there are equal numbers in the groups this equation simplifies to:

$$t = \frac{\text{mean}_1 - \text{mean}_2}{\sqrt{\left(\frac{2}{n}\right) \times \text{MS}_{\text{error}}}} \tag{18.2}$$

where n is the sample size of the group producing one of the means.

Heterogeneous variances

If the groups for the ANOVA do not have similar variances, then the above equations are not appropriate. Following the rule of thumb given in Chapter 16 we can say that as long as the largest variance is no more than four times the smallest variance we have sufficient homogeneity of variance to use the above equations, *as long as the sample sizes are equal*. If we have a lack of homogeneity then it would be advisable, for pairwise contrasts, to use the t-test for separate variances (Welch's t-test) which is discussed in Chapter 15 and Appendix VI. If the sample sizes are unequal, the largest variance should be no more than twice the smallest to be treated as homogeneous.

Contrasts on data from within-subjects designs

If the design is within-subjects and the data lack sphericity (see Chapter 16 for an explanation of this term), then once again neither of the above equations will be the correct one. To be on the safe side, therefore, for pairwise contrasts, the t for each contrast should be computed using the standard equation for a within-subjects design with two levels, given in Appendix VI and referred to in Chapter 15. Myers and Well (1991) note that most, if not all, computer programs use this version of t for contrasts on within-subjects designs. This option is not available for one of the tests—the Scheffé test; the Scheffé test is not recommended for pairwise contrasts as it is considered too conservative to be used for such contrasts.

Conducting only one contrast

For data from either design, if you are only conducting one contrast, as you might with a planned contrast, then the probability of the t-value for that contrast can be checked using the standard t-tables. However, when more than one contrast is involved, you will need to use one of the procedures described below.

Table 18.1 gives the means and standard deviations for the memory experiment and Table 18.2 provides the summary of the ANOVA conducted on those data. Thus, if we wished to compare the method of loci condition with the control condition, we would have the following figures:

$$\text{mean}_1 = 9.6$$

$$\text{mean}_2 = 7.2$$

$$n = 10$$

$$\text{MS}_{\text{error}} = 2.922$$

$$\text{df}_{\text{error}} = 27$$

Table 18.1 Means and SDs of word recall for the three memory conditions

	Control	Pegword	Loci
Mean	7.2	8.9	9.6
SD	1.62	1.91	1.58

Table 18.2 The summary table for the one-way between-subjects ANOVA on the recall data

Source	Sum of Squares	df	Mean Square	F-test	p
Between Groups	30.467	2	15.233	5.213	0.0122
Within Groups	78.9	27	2.922		
Total	109.367	29			

and we can use Equation 18.2 because the design is between-subjects and the groups have the same sample size:

$$t_{(27)} = \frac{9.6 - 7.2}{\sqrt{\left(\frac{2}{10}\right) \times 2.922}}$$

$$= 3.139$$

Bonferroni's t

Bonferroni's t (sometimes known as the Dunn multiple comparison test) takes into consideration the actual number of contrasts that you are going to conduct. It is most appropriate when you have planned your comparisons and are keeping them to a minimum. It is conservative when the contrasts are not orthogonal. The adjustment it makes is based on an equation that, when the original α is set at 0.05 or lower, simplifies approximately to dividing α by the number of contrasts to be conducted. The α-level from the adjustment is for each contrast. However, it is more usual to express the α-level of the family. Appendix XIV gives the α-levels for the family of contrasts.

Choose the number of contrasts you are going to make. Look up the critical t-value in the tables of Bonferroni corrections for contrasts in Appendix XIV for that number of contrasts, using the df from the appropriate MS_{error} for the treatment you are investigating, in the case of a between-subjects design with homogeneity of variance, the df appropriate for a t-test with independent variances when there is heterogeneity of variance, or the df for the standard within-subjects t-test in the case of a within-subjects design. For the contrast to be statistically significant, the t computed for the contrast has to be as large as or larger than the critical t.

Table 18.3 gives a part of Table A14.11 in Appendix XIV. In the present example, if we planned to conduct all three contrasts in the memory experiment then, with df of 27, the critical t would be 2.552. The t computed for the contrast (3.139) shows us that the means for the control and the method of loci are significantly different at the $p < 0.05$ level.

The contrast t-value for control versus pegwords is 2.224, and for pegwords versus method of loci is 0.916. Therefore, neither of them is statistically

Table 18.3 An extract from the Bonferroni tables for an error rate per family of $\alpha = 0.05$

df error	2	3	4	5	6	7	8	9	10	12	15
25	2.385	2.566	2.692	2.787	2.865	2.930	2.986	3.035	3.078	3.153	3.244
26	2.379	2.559	2.684	2.779	2.856	2.920	2.975	3.024	3.067	3.141	3.231
27	2.373	2.552	2.676	2.771	2.847	2.911	2.966	3.014	3.057	3.130	3.219
28	2.368	2.546	2.669	2.763	2.839	2.902	2.957	3.004	3.047	3.120	3.208
29	2.364	2.541	2.663	2.756	2.832	2.894	2.949	2.996	3.038	3.110	3.198
30	2.360	2.536	2.657	2.750	2.825	2.887	2.941	2.988	3.030	3.102	3.189

(column group header spanning columns 2–15: Number of contrasts)

significant at $\alpha = 0.05$. Using Bonferroni's t we can conclude that the method of loci produces recall significantly better than the control condition but not than the pegword method. In addition, the pegword condition does not produce significantly better recall than the control condition.

Dunnett's t

Dunnett's t (sometimes also known as d) is normally used when a particular mean (say for a control group) is being contrasted with other means, one at a time. It is less conservative than Bonferroni's t because it does not assume that the contrasts are orthogonal.

Firstly, look up the critical value for t, with the error df (or df for Welch's t-test for between-subjects designs with heterogeneous variances, or df for the within-subjects t-test in within-subjects designs), in the table for Dunnett's t in Appendix XIV, and compare the computed t for the contrast with that critical value. If the computed t is as large as, or larger than, the critical value it is statistically significant.

Table 18.4 gives an extract of Table A14.12 in Appendix XIV. Assuming two contrasts are being conducted, each with 27 degrees of freedom, we have a critical value of d between 2.32 and 2.35, because the Table 18.4 does not give values for df = 27. This agrees with the pattern of results suggested by Bonferroni's t: the contrast between loci and control conditions was statistically significant, while that between pegwords and control conditions was not.

Table 18.4 An extract from the Dunnett's t tables for an error rate per family of $\alpha = 0.05$

df error	Number of means (including the control)												
	3	4	5	6	7	8	9	10	11	12	13	16	21
24	2.35	2.51	2.61	2.70	2.76	2.81	2.86	2.90	2.94	2.97	3.00	3.07	3.16
30	2.32	2.47	2.58	2.66	2.72	2.77	2.82	2.86	2.89	2.92	2.95	3.02	3.11

Scheffé's t

Scheffé's test is very conservative as it allows you to conduct any type of *post hoc* contrast. It is sufficiently conservative that there is no point in conducting it if the original F-ratio was not statistically significant. There are a confusing number of ways of calculating and expressing Scheffé's test—sometimes as a t-value and sometimes as an F-ratio. However, they will all give the same protection against making a Type I error. Here I give one version. Appendix IX gives three others because computer programs produce such versions.

Treated as a t-test we can take the calculated t-value and check it using standard F-tables (see Appendix XIV; yes, I do mean F-tables). To find the critical t-value, use the following equation:

$$\text{critical } t = \sqrt{df_{\text{treatment}} \times F(df_{\text{treatment}}, df_{\text{error}})}$$

In words, take the critical F-value that the F-tables give for the treatment df and error df (i.e. the original degrees of freedom for the F-ratio we are now trying to explain) and multiply it by the degrees of freedom for the treatment. The square root of the result is the critical value against which the calculated t-value has to be evaluated.

Table 18.5 shows the relevant part of the F-tables in Appendix XIV.

Table 18.5 An extract from the $\alpha = 0.05$ probability tables for an F-ratio

df_2	1	2	3	4	5	6	7	8	9	10	12	14
26	4.23	3.37	2.98	2.74	2.59	2.47	2.39	2.32	2.27	2.22	2.15	2.09
27	4.21	3.35	2.96	2.73	2.57	2.46	2.37	2.31	2.25	2.20	2.13	2.08
28	4.20	3.34	2.95	2.71	2.56	2.45	2.36	2.29	2.24	2.19	2.12	2.06

(column group header: df_1)

The treatment and error dfs for the original F-ratio were 2 and 27, respectively. Looking in Table 18.5 we see that the critical F-ratio for these degrees of freedom is 3.35 for $p = 0.05$. Therefore:

$$\text{critical } t = \sqrt{(2 \times 3.35)}$$
$$= 2.588$$

This means that the only contrast that is statistically significant at $p < 0.05$ is the control group versus the method of loci group.

Scheffé's test is so conservative that it is not recommended for pairwise comparisons. Appendix IX shows its use with more complex comparisons.

Within-subjects designs

As was mentioned earlier, if the data in a within-subjects design lack sphericity, then it is not appropriate to use Equation 18.1 or 18.2 to make contrasts. Given that Scheffé's test should not be used for pairwise contrasts, we do not have the option of computing a standard t-test (that is, one for comparing two means) for the more complex contrasts for which Scheffé's test is appropriate. Instead, if we wish to use Scheffé's test we have to check the sphericity of the data first. If the original ANOVA did not show the need to make an adjustment to the degrees of freedom then the data have sphericity. If your computer program does not give such information, Appendix VII shows how the need for such an adjustment can be checked. If the data do have sphericity then we can continue to conduct the Scheffé test as described above.

Tukey's honestly significant difference (HSD)

This test is for use when the group sizes are the same. A variant—the Tukey–Kramer test—is for use when the groups are not the same size.

This method is less conservative than Scheffé's, as it assumes that not all possible types of comparison between the means are going to be made. However, it is more conservative than Dunnett's t.

To calculate Tukey's HSD, look up the critical q-value from the tables of the Studentised range statistic (given in Appendix XIV) for the number of means involved in the contrasts and the error df (or df for Welch's t-test for between-subjects designs with heterogeneous variances, or df for the standard within-subjects t-test, in within-subjects designs). Place the value found for q in the following equation:

$$\text{critical } t = \frac{q}{\sqrt{2}}$$

Then compare the computed t-value for the contrast with the critical t. A comparison will only be significant when the value for computed t is as large as or greater than the critical t.

Table 18.6 is part of the Studentised range statistic (q) from Table A14.13 in Appendix XIV.

Table 18.6 An extract from the studentised range statistic (q), $\alpha = 0.05$

df error	Number of means to be contrasted										
	3	4	5	6	7	8	9	10	11	12	15
24	3.53	3.90	4.17	4.37	4.54	4.68	4.81	4.92	6.01	5.10	5.32
30	3.49	3.85	4.10	4.30	4.46	4.60	4.72	4.82	4.92	5.00	5.21

With three means and error df of 27, the critical q is between 3.49 and 3.53 for $p = 0.05$. Therefore:

$$\text{critical } t \text{ is between } \frac{3.49}{\sqrt{2}} \text{ and } \frac{3.53}{\sqrt{2}}$$

$$= \text{between } 2.468 \text{ and } 2.496$$

In this case, only the contrast between method of loci and control conditions is statistically significant at $p < 0.05$.

Tukey–Kramer

This test is for between-subjects pairwise contrasts when the sample sizes for the two groups are not the same. It uses a variant of Equation 18.1 for contrasts:

$$t = \frac{\text{mean}_1 - \text{mean}_2}{\sqrt{\dfrac{\left(\dfrac{MS_{error}}{n_2}\right) + \left(\dfrac{MS_{error}}{n_1}\right)}{2}}} \tag{18.3}$$

where n_1 and n_2 are the sizes of the two subsamples involved in the contrast. The critical t is found in exactly the same way as for the Tukey HSD method.

Other contrast tests

The tests of contrasts described thus far are sufficient for most situations. However, for completeness, further tests are described briefly in Appendix IX. You may find them in computer programs. In addition, as experienced researchers often have their favourite contrast tests, they may require you to use them.

One- and two-tailed tests and contrasts

The probabilities quoted in the extracts in this chapter from tables for the contrast tests are all two-tailed. Clearly, when using unplanned comparisons, the hypothesis that underlies the test, is non-directional. However, when using a planned comparison, if it is testing a directional hypothesis, then it is legitimate to use a one-tailed probability. Accordingly, tables of one-tailed probabilities have been provided in Appendix XIV for Bonferroni's t and Dunnett's t for $\alpha = 0.05$.

Table 18.7 Summary of equations to be used to calculate t-values and df for critical t-values for pairwise contrasts

Design	Equation for t	df for critical t
Between-subjects		
homogeneous variance	Equation 18.1 or 18.2 if sample sizes are equal	df for MS_{error} of original ANOVA
heterogeneous variance	Welch's t-test (Chapter 15 and Appendix VI)	Adjusted df for Welch's t-test (Appendix VI)
Within-subjects	Standard t-test for within-subjects designs (Chapter 15 and Appendix VI)	$n - 1$ where n is the number of participants

Summary of contrast tests for parametric tests

You should be reassured by the fact that, of the recommended tests, all agreed over which contrasts were and were not statistically significant. However, Dunnett's t, the least conservative, would have made the contrast between method of loci and the control condition statistically significant at $p < 0.01$ (even if all three contrasts had been conducted), while the others set the probability at $0.01 < p < 0.05$. (Incidentally, for reasons of space, for Dunnett's t I have only included probability tables for $\alpha = 0.05$ in this book.)

Using a computer to conduct contrasts

Post hoc *contrasts*
For between-subjects designs, most of the procedures I have described can be made simpler if you have access to a computer program that will run

Table 18.8 A summary of the tests of contrasts and when each is appropriate

Test	When to use
Bonferroni	A small number of planned or unplanned contrasts
Dunnett	Comparing one particular mean against others
Scheffé	Any post hoc contrast
Tukey's HSD	A set of post hoc pairwise contrasts, equal sample sizes
Tukey–Kramer	A set of post hoc pairwise contrasts, unequal sample sizes

them. However, you have to be careful about what probability it is reporting. Thus far I have described how you look in a table of critical values to find out what the t-value would have to be to achieve significance when the error rate per family of contrasts is being maintained at 0.05. In SPSS when a named *post hoc* contrast is conducted the probability that is reported is an adjusted version for the *individual* contrast that allows for the contrast test being employed and the size of the family of contrasts. To decide whether a contrast is statistically significant we compare the probability reported by the computer against an unadjusted alpha level (usually 0.05). In SPSS you can run *Dunnett's t* and *Tukey's HSD* (which will also do *Tukey–Kramer* when the sample sizes are unequal). It is described as *Tukey* in SPSS (also included is a different test, called *Tukey-b*, which is *Tukey's WSD* and is described in Appendix IX). In addition, when the variances aren't homogeneous, by running *Games–Howell* you will be doing the equivalent of Tukey (or Tukey–Kramer) via a Welch's t-test as described above. Although *Bonferroni* is included among the *post hoc* tests, the probabilities will be adjusted by too much as it will assume that you are conducting all the possible pairwise contrasts.

Planned contrasts

SPSS will do the appropriate analysis under its *Contrasts* option when you tell it which particular pairs you are contrasting. In addition, you can set up more complex contrasts. However, it will make no adjustment to the probability, and so, if you are conducting more than one contrast, you will need to adjust alpha (using Bonferroni's adjustment) and compare the probability that SPSS reports against the adjusted alpha.

Non-parametric tests

At least ordinal data

One way to contrast two levels of an independent variable at a time, following a Kruskal–Wallis one-way ANOVA or Friedman's two-way ANOVA, would be to conduct for each contrast the appropriate test for an IV with two levels. Thus, a Mann–Whitney U-test would be used for contrasts on between-subjects designs and a Wilcoxon signed-rank test for matched pairs would be used for contrasts on within-subjects designs. However, it would be necessary to adjust the α-level, using a Bonferroni adjustment by dividing the α-level by the number of contrasts being made. Therefore, for four contrasts, the error rate per contrast becomes:

$$EC = \frac{0.05}{4} = 0.0125$$

There are also specific tests of contrasts for such data, as long as all the levels of the IV have five or more participants and the original statistical test was statistically significant. There are two types of such tests. One type is for use when any pair of levels of the IV are being contrasted and the other is analogous to Dunnett's t in that it is for contrasting a control condition with another level of the IV. I include the former technique in Appendix IX. Those wishing to learn about the second technique can refer to Siegel and Castellan (1988).

Categorical data

When analysing a contingency table that is more than a 2×2 table there are a number of ways in which the result could be statistically significant: for example, if researchers are looking at the proportions of males and females who are smokers, non-smokers and ex-smokers. It is possible to conduct further analysis by *partitioning* the contingency table into a number of 2×2 subtables. Thus, the researchers could focus on smokers versus non-smokers and other more specific comparisons than are provided by the original analysis.

The analysis is also rather specialised and so is given in Appendix IX rather than here.

Trend tests

Trend tests are an extension of contrasts between means and use a very similar procedure. They are designed to test whether a group of means form a single pattern, or *trend*. The most appropriate use for trend analysis is when the levels of the independent variable being tested are quantities rather than categories. For example, researchers hypothesise that reaction times will be slower as a result of the amount of alcohol consumed. They predict that the effect of the alcohol will be to increase reaction time by a regular amount: that is, that there is a *linear trend* for reaction time to increase with alcohol consumed.

In the example, 24 participants are placed into three equal-sized groups. Each group is given a different amount of alcohol: one, two or three units. Each participant is then given a task in which he or she has to detect the presence of an object on a computer screen.

There are a variety of possible trends that can be tested for but the number is dependent on the number of means involved and is the same as the df of the treatment being analysed. Thus, in the case of three means there are two types of possible trend—linear and quadratic. Figures 18.3 and 18.4 show the patterns that would constitute linear and quadratic trends.

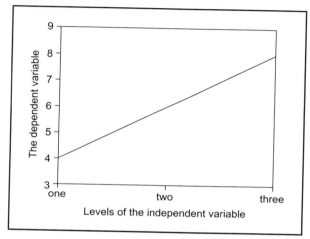

FIGURE 18.3 An illustration of a linear trend

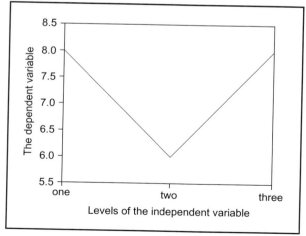

FIGURE 18.4 An illustration of a quadratic trend

In the case of four means an additional possible trend is a cubic one.

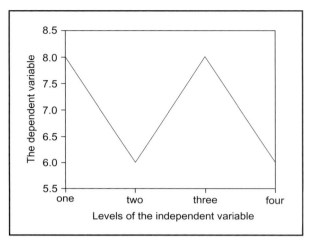

FIGURE 18.5 An illustration of a cubic trend

Table 18.9 and Figure 18.6 show the results of the experiment.

Table 18.9 The means and SDs of reaction times
(in tenths of seconds) by number of units of alcohol consumed

	Units of alcohol consumed		
	one	two	three
Mean	151.25	163.38	168.75
SD	14.12	10.53	12.94

FIGURE 18.6 Mean reaction times with SDs, by number of units of alcohol consumed

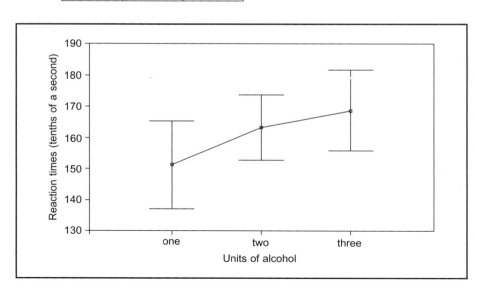

Notice that the means are going in the direction suggested but that they do not form a completely straight line. Before looking for any trend the convention is to conduct an initial ANOVA to find whether the treatment effect is statistically significant. In fact this is not essential as the trend test could still be statistically significant even when the initial ANOVA is not. Table 18.10 shows the results of a between-subjects one-way ANOVA on the data.

Table 18.10 Summary table of the between-subjects ANOVA on the effects of alcohol on reaction times

Source	Sum of Squares	df	Mean Square	F	p
Between Groups	1285.750	2	642.875	4.039	.0328
Within Groups	3342.875	21	159.185		
Total	4628.625	23			

The fact that the means do not form a perfectly straight line suggests that the trend could be of a type other than linear.

For a trend analysis with three means with equal sample sizes you create a Sum of Squares (SS) for the trend you are testing according to the following equation:

$$SS_{trend} = \frac{n \times [(coef_1 \times \bar{x}_1) + (coef_2 \times \bar{x}_2) + (coef_3 \times \bar{x}_3)]^2}{coef_1^2 + coef_2^2 + coef_3^2}$$

where n is the number of participants in each group; $coef_1$, $coef_2$ and $coef_3$ are coefficients that are designed to test for a particular trend; $\bar{x}_1$, $\bar{x}_2$ and $\bar{x}_3$ are the means for the three groups. Appendix IX gives the general equation for trend tests from which this has been derived. A table of the coefficients can be found in Appendix XVI. Table 18.11 shows the coefficients for trends involving three means.

$$SS_{lin} = \frac{8 \times [(-1 \times 151.25) + (0 \times 163.38) + (1 \times 168.75)]^2}{(-1)^2 + (0)^2 + (1)^2}$$

$$= \frac{2450}{2}$$

$$= 1225$$

Table 18.11 Coefficients for analysing trends with three means

Number of levels of IV	Type of trend	Level of IV									
		1	2	3	4	5	6	7	8	9	10
3	linear	−1	0	1							
	quadratic	1	−2	1							

Each trend test always has 1 degree of freedom. Therefore the MS_{trend} is also 1225.

The F-ratio for the MS_{trend} is found by dividing the MS_{trend} by the MS_{error}, which in this case is 159.185 (from Table 18.10). Thus,

$$F_{(1,21)} = 7.695$$

We can use standard F-tables to assess the statistical significance of this result. The critical F for this trend test is 4.32, in which case there is a significant linear trend in this study between quantity of alcohol consumed and reaction time.

The coefficients for trend tests have been chosen so that the trend tests partition the treatment sum of squares into separate sources of variation; they are orthogonal. In other words, if you add the sum of squares for all the permissible trend tests, the result will be the same as the treatment sum of squares.

We can therefore work out whether it is worth looking for other trends. Given that the overall sum of squares for alcohol consumption was 1285.75 (see Table 18.9) and the sum of squares for the linear trend was 1225, then the sum of squares for any remaining trend (in this case quadratic) is:

$$1285.75 - 1225 = 60.75$$

As the df for any trend is 1, the MS for a quadratic trend will also be 60.75 and so the F-ratio for such a trend would be:

$$\frac{60.75}{159.185} = 0.382$$

which is not statistically significant. Accordingly, we can conclude that there is solely a significant linear trend.

Simple effects

When there is an interaction between two independent variables it is worth attempting to explore the nature of that interaction further. Let us return to the example, from Chapter 17, in which participants were shown a list of words and asked to recall as many words as they could. The two independent variables were *type of list* (with words which were either linked or unlinked) and *mnemonic strategy* (method of loci, pegwords or a control condition). One method of analysing the interaction of the two IVs is to separate out the treatment effects of one independent variable for each of the levels of the other independent variable. In the example this would mean looking at the effects of mnemonic strategy on the recall of linked words and the effect of mnemonic strategy on recall of unlinked words. It could also mean looking at the effect of type of list on recall of those using method of loci, the effect of type of list on recall of those using pegwords and the effect of type of list on recall of the control group. Each of these analyses is described as a *simple effect* (sometimes referred to as a 'simple main effect').

Some books advise only looking for simple effects when there is a significant interaction. I disagree, because useful information can sometimes be found when the interaction is not significant, such as finding the pattern of a significant main effect only reproduced in some levels of the second IV. It is particularly worth testing simple effects when you have predicted that there will be an interaction. Remember that the interaction that has been tested deals with the variance remaining once the main effects have been tested and so a non-significant interaction can be followed by one or more significant simple effects. Nonetheless, if the interaction is far from being statistically significant then the simple effects are not worth conducting. The method that is used to find the simple effects depends on whether the variable being considered is a within-subjects variable or a between-subjects variable. I am going to be more specific and say that you should use one technique when the design is totally between-subjects and one when it is either totally within-subject or mixed (i.e. has some IVs that are within-subjects).

Between-subjects designs

The two-way ANOVA produced the following summary table:

Table 18.12 The summary table from the ANOVA of a 2 × 3, two-way, between-subjects ANOVA

Source	Sum of Squares	df	Mean Square	F	p
List	61.633	1	61.633	37.354	0.0001
Mnemonic	5.600	2	2.800	1.697	0.2045
List * Mnemonic	11.467	2	5.733	3.475	0.0473
Error	39.600	24	1.650		
Total	118.300	29			

This tells us that there was a significant interaction between list type and mnemonic strategy.

A warning about heterogeneity of variance

The following procedure is only appropriate if the variances for all the conditions in the interaction are similar. Therefore, before you conduct a simple effects analysis on a between-subjects design examine the variances. If they are different then you should follow the procedure suggested for within-subjects and mixed designs shown below. In the example the following table shows the variances for the six conditions:

Table 18.13 The variances for the six memory conditions

List	Mnemonic strategy control	pegword	loci
linked	1.50	1.86	1.30
unlinked	2.30	1.30	1.70

If the largest variance is no more than twice the smallest variance then we can continue with the procedure. In this case, 2.3, the largest variance, is less than twice 1.3, the smallest variance. Notice that the variances have to be closer together in this situation than they have to be to perform the initial ANOVA. See Myers and Well (1991) for a discussion of the problems of heterogeneity of variance when performing simple effects.

To analyse simple effects we need to form an F-ratio for each simple effect. When the design is completely between-subjects, and there is homogeneity of variance, the F-ratio for each level of one of the independent variables is formed from the following equation:

$$F = \frac{MS_{\text{level of IV}}}{MS_{\text{error for interaction}}}$$

Thus, in the case of the above example, if we were looking at the simple effect of mnemonic strategy on unlinked words we would find the MS for unlinked words and divide it by the MS error for the original interaction (i.e. MS_{residual}). The appropriate degrees of freedom for the F-ratio, as usual, would be the df from the MS for the level, in this case the df for the mnemonic strategies with unlinked words (2), and the df for the original interaction error term (24).

To simplify the process you can find the MS for each level by running a one-way ANOVA on just the data for the level in which you are interested. In this case, you would just include the data for participants who were shown unlinked words. The following summary table is of a one-way between-subjects ANOVA comparing the recall for the three mnemonic strategies on the unlinked lists.

Table 18.14 The one-way between-subjects ANOVA on mnemonic strategy for unlinked lists

Source	Sum of Squares	df	Mean Square	F-value	p
Mnemonic	16.533	2	8.267	4.679	0.0315
Residual	21.200	12	1.767		

From this analysis we can see that the $MS_{\text{mnemonic for unlinked}}$ is 8.267 with df = 2. The error term for the simple effect is the same as the one used for the two-way ANOVA, that is 1.650 with df = 24 (see Table 18.12).

Therefore the simple effect for unlinked words is:

$$F_{(2,24)} = \frac{8.267}{1.650}$$

$$= 5.010$$

Referring to F-tables tells us that the critical F-ratio for $p = 0.05$ with df of 2 and 24 is 3.4. In this case, we can report that, for unlinked words, recall differed significantly between the three mnemonic strategies. ($F_{(2,24)} = 5.010$, $p < 0.05$, $\eta^2 = .14$ as a proportion of the recall of the original data, $\eta^2 = .438$ as a proportion of the recall of unlinked words.) I am reporting both effect sizes as they inform the future researcher about the effects for different aspects of the design.

The analysis could be repeated for linked words:

Table 18.15 The one-way between-subjects ANOVA on mnemonic strategy for linked lists

Source	Sum of Squares	df	Mean Square	F-value	p
Mnemonic	0.533	2	0.267	0.174	0.8425
Residual	18.400	12	1.533		

Here,

$$F_{\text{linked}} = \frac{MS_{\text{linked}}}{MS_{\text{error}}}$$

$$F_{(2,24)} = \frac{0.267}{1.650}$$

$$= 0.162.$$

As this F-value is less than 1, it is definitely not statistically significant. We now have a clearer picture of what produced the significant interaction in the two-way ANOVA. Mnemonic strategy significantly affects recall when lists are unlinked but not when lists are linked.

To complete the analysis we would now perform comparisons on the means of the unlinked conditions to identify even more specifically the source of the significant effect. I leave that as an exercise for you to do.

Partitioning the Sums of Squares in simple effects

In analysing the simple effects you are taking the Sum of Squares for the interaction and for the IV, which will be tested in the simple effect, from the original two-way ANOVA and splitting this into separate parts for each simple effect. Looking at the original two-way ANOVA, the Sum of Squares for the interaction is 11.467 and for mnemonic is 5.600. Adding these together gives a Sum of Squares of 17.067. Notice that the Sum of Squares for the unlinked words is 16.533 and for linked words is 0.533. Adding these together gives 17.066 (which is only different from 17.067 because the figures have been rounded).

Designs with within-subjects variables

Totally within-subjects designs

To conduct simple effects on one independent variable, simply ignore the data for the other levels of that IV and conduct a one-way within-subjects ANOVA on the remaining data. The F-ratio from that analysis is the appropriate F-ratio for the simple effect, with the dfs from that analysis.

Recall the study, described in Chapter 17, in which participants had to decide on a sentence for a crime. There were two IVs: the context in which the decision was made (alone, at a computer or face-to-face with other judges) and the nature of the defendant (experienced criminal or novice). The results did not show a significant interaction. However, for the purposes of illustration, I will analyse the simple effects for each level of the context.[1]

Tables 18.16 to 18.18 show the simple effects comparing defendant type for each of the three contexts. From these simple effects we can see that, whatever the context, the experienced defendant will be given a significantly more severe sentence than a novice defendant. As there were only two levels in each simple effect, we could have conducted the analysis using within-subjects t-tests.

[1] The more appropriate analysis, when the interaction is not significant but a main effect with more than two levels is significant, is contrasts on the main effect, which is described later in the chapter.

Table 18.16 The one-way, within-subjects ANOVA of the effects of defendant type on suggested sentence length (for participants who made the decision alone)

Source	Sum of Squares	df	Mean Square	F-value	P-value
Subject	2.4	4	0.6		
Experience	19.6	1	19.6	12.25	0.0249
Experience by Subject	6.4	4	1.6		
Total	28.4	9			

Table 18.17 The one-way, within-subjects ANOVA of the effects of defendant type on suggested sentence length (for participants who made the decision while seeing other judges' decisions on computer)

Source	Sum of Squares	df	Mean Square	F-value	P-value
Subject	5.4	4	1.35		
Experience	40.0	1	40.00	160	0.0002
Experience by Subject	1.0	4	0.25		
Total	46.4	9			

Table 18.18 The one-way, within-subjects ANOVA of the effects of defendant type on suggested sentence length (for participants who made the decision in the presence of other judges)

Source	Sum of Squares	df	Mean Square	F-value	P-value
Subject	1.4	4	0.35		
Experience	48.4	1	48.40	29.333	0.0056
Experience by Subject	6.6	4	1.65		
Total	56.4	9			

Mixed designs

The example given in Chapter 17 of this design was of males and females giving ratings of their mother's and father's IQ. When you are looking at the simple effects of the within-subjects variable (parent), conduct a one-way, between-subjects ANOVA on the between-subjects variable for each level of the within-subjects variable. Thus, you would conduct a one-way, between-subjects ANOVA on each level of parent. When looking at the simple effects of the between-subjects variable (gender), conduct a one-way, within-subjects ANOVA on each of the levels of the between-subjects variable. Thus, you would conduct a one-way, within-subjects ANOVA on each level of gender. These recommendations are designed to simplify the analysis. Those of you who wish to pursue this further should read Howell's (2002) account for a more thorough way of conducting simple effects under these circumstances.

The original prediction of the researchers was that males and females would rate their parents differently. The graph of the means suggested that an interaction was present between gender and parent's IQ; see Figure 18.7. However, the F-ratio for interaction did not reach statistical significance ($p = 0.0795$, see Table 17.9).

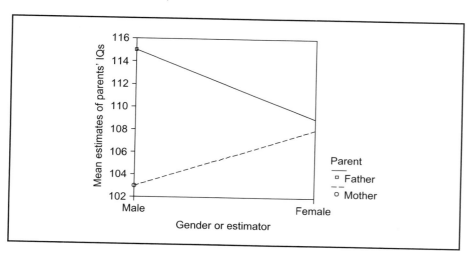

FIGURE 18.7 The mean rating of parental IQ by males and females

The simple effect of the IQ ratings made by females produced the following result:

Table 18.19 A one-way, within-subjects ANOVA of females' judgements of their parents' IQs

Source	Sum of Squares	df	Mean Square	F-value	P-value
Subject	315.00	4	78.75		
Parent	2.50	1	2.50	0.286	.6213
Parent by Subject	35.00	4	8.75		

The simple effect of the IQ ratings made by males produced the following result:

Table 18.20 A one-way, within-subjects ANOVA of males' judgements of their parents' IQs

Source	Sum of Squares	df	Mean Square	F-value	P-value
Subject	1215.00	4	303.75		
Parent	360.00	1	360.00	5.434	.0802
Parent by Subject	265.00	4	66.25		

The researchers are forced to conclude that the simple effects for males and for females do not show a significant difference in their ratings of their mothers' and fathers' IQs. Nonetheless, it looks as though there is a possible effect that is worth further research.

My advice would be to repeat the research with a larger sample size in order to give the test more power. Note that by analysing the simple effects we have based each ANOVA on five raters. The effect size (η^2) of parent being rated for the male raters is 0.196, which is a large effect size, according to Cohen's criteria. However, with the small sample size the test only had power of about 0.29. In order to achieve power of 0.8, with such an effect size, we need about 16 male raters. The effect size for female raters is 0.007, which is small.

A warning about Type I errors

We could be conducting a number of analyses for simple effects. If we continue to use an alpha level of $p = 0.05$ we are increasing the danger of making a Type I error. Accordingly, we could use a Bonferroni adjustment. In the case of the three simple effects on sentencing patterns, the adjusted α-level for each simple effect would be:

$$\frac{0.05}{3} = 0.0167$$

in order to leave the overall α-level at 0.05. It is best to keep the number of simple effects analyses to a minimum as the power of each test will be reduced by the adjustment to alpha.

Notice that, with this more stringent α-level, the simple effect for decisions made when the participants were on their own would not be statistically significant. When the probability for a given analysis reaches $p < 0.05$ but does not reach the adjusted level, I would suggest that it should not automatically be dismissed as not statistically significant but that it should be treated with more caution and the reader's attention should be drawn to the need to do more research on this particular aspect of the study.

Interpreting main effects

When a two-way ANOVA does not reveal an interaction between the IVs then it is possible to interpret the main effects more straightforwardly as they are not being complicated by the presence of an interaction. How we interpret the main effects depends on the number of levels that a significant main effect has. If there are only two levels then we can refer directly to the means to see which group has the higher score. The means we will need to examine will be ones that are found by ignoring the presence of the other IV (the marginal means). In the two-way within-subjects design described earlier there was a significant main effect of the type of defendant (novice or experienced) on the length of sentence recommended and a significant main effect of the context in which the recommendation was made (alone, via computer or in a face-to-face group). As type of defendant had only two levels we can find the mean length of sentence that was made for the novice and for the experienced defendant. These were 43 and 54.2 respectively. Therefore we can conclude that a significantly longer sentence was recommended for an experienced defendant than for a novice.

To interpret the significant main effect of context we have to conduct further analysis as there are more than two levels. As with any such ANOVA, all the significant result has told us is that the conditions differ from each other but not how they differ.

For the follow-up analysis I am going to cover only paired contrasts as these are the most likely ones that people are going to want to conduct. Nonetheless, other tests could be applied, including trend tests, where appropriate. As with contrasts following a one-way ANOVA, we need to know two things: how to calculate the appropriate statistic and how to decide its significance. The reasoning is the same as for paired contrasts described earlier. The method of calculating the t-value for a contrast is dependent on whether the design was completely between-subjects, completely within-subjects or mixed and, if it was between-subjects, whether the groups had homogeneity of variance or not and whether the groups had equal-sized samples. To decide the significance of the t-value if we planned a set of contrasts before the analysis then we would use Bonferroni's test or Dunnett's test if other groups were being compared with a control group. If the contrasts were unplanned then we would use Tukey's test.

Between-subjects design

Throughout this explanation I am going to use the mnemonic by list example. However, remember that in that example the IV that has three levels (mnemonic) did not have a significant main effect and there was a significant interaction so we would not normally conduct such analysis on the data.

Homogeneity of variance present

We can use Equation 18.1 or 18.2 as appropriate or, if we are using the Tukey–Kramer test, then Equation 18.3. In each case the MS_{error} would be the MS_{error} from the original ANOVA (in the mnemonic by list example the MS_{error} was 1.650). To find the means for the contrast ignore the presence of the IV that you are not analysing in the contrast. In the mnemonic by list example if we are conducting contrasts comparing two mnemonic conditions then we would calculate the means as though there had not been separate lists in the design. Table 17.2 shows that the means for the control, pegword and loci methods were 8.7, 9.5 and 9.7 respectively. The sample sizes to go in the equations come from the number of participants who contributed to the means involved in the contrast. In the mnemonic by list example $n = 10$ for each of the mnemonic conditions. To find the critical value for t we would need to read the appropriate table using the df from the MS_{error}, which in the mnemonic by list example was 24.

Homogeneity of variance not present across the conditions of the two-way ANOVA

Although the full set of conditions in the two-way ANOVA may not have been homogeneous, if we ignore the presence of one variable we could find that we have sufficient homogeneity to conduct a standard one-way ANOVA that ignores the IV that will not be involved in the contrasts. In the mnemonic by list example the variances for the control, pegword and loci conditions are 7.57, 2.72 and 2.23 respectively. As the sample sizes are the same for the three groups these variances are sufficiently homogeneous to allow a standard one-way between-subjects ANOVA to be conducted, followed by contrasts based on Equation 18.1, 18.2 or 18.3 as appropriate, but with the MS_{error} and df from the one-way ANOVA rather than from the original two-way ANOVA.

If variances for the levels of the IV that is to involve the contrast are not homogeneous even when the presence of the other IV has been ignored then conduct the between-subjects t-tests for each contrast, just including the data for the two conditions being contrasted; when the pair of conditions have homogeneity of variance use the standard t-test, otherwise use Welch's t. The df used to find the critical value of t will then come from each t-test.

Within-subjects designs

For each level of the IV that will be involved in the contrasts find the mean across the levels of the IV that won't be in the contrasts. In the defendant by context example, we would find the mean for each participant for each context across the two defendant types. Run within-subjects t-tests for each contrast on the means. Table 18.21 shows the t-values and unadjusted p-values for each contrast; each has df = 4.

Table 18.21 The t- and unadjusted p-values of the paired contrasts from the main effect of context on sentence recommended

Contrast	t	p
Alone—Computer	−1.907	0.129
Alone—Face to face	−14.905	0.000
Computer—Face to face	−6.893	0.002

If we had planned to do certain of the above contrasts then we could divide 0.05 by the number of contrasts we planned (to form our adjusted alpha level) and compare the probabilities for each contrast against them. Alternatively, if we are using Tukey's test to conduct unplanned contrasts then we would find the critical t for the contrasts, with df = 4, using the method described earlier in the chapter. This produces a critical t of 3.56. We would therefore judge that the alone and computer conditions did not produce significantly different lengths of recommended sentence, while sentences given when face-to-face with other members of a group were significantly higher than when the person recommending the sentence was alone and when the person thought he or she knew what the other members of the groups had recommended.

Mixed designs

The method of analysis depends on whether you are looking at a main effect for a between-subjects or for a within-subjects IV. If for a between-subjects IV then find the mean for each participant across the levels of the within-subjects IV. If the variances of the levels of the between-subject IV are homogeneous then run a one-way between-subjects ANOVA and the contrasts using Equation 18.1, 18.2 or 18.3 as appropriate. If the variances are not homogeneous use the appropriate between-subjects t-test for each contrast. For the within-subjects IV, ignore the presence of the between-subjects IV and run within-subjects t-tests for each contrast.

Beyond two-way ANOVA

Earlier in the chapter I described a hypothetical two-way within-subjects ANOVA that requires participants to sentence defendants who are either experienced or novices (IV$_1$) under the conditions of being alone, or seeing what sentences others suggest via a computer or being in the same room as other participants (IV$_2$). In Chapter 17 I described an extension of this design whereby the gender of the participant was a third IV. If the three-way inter-action from this design was significant then we could explore it further by analysing *simple interaction effects*. For example, we could take just the females and run a two-way ANOVA on the other IVs. Then we could do the same just for the males. If either of these interactions were significant (allowing for having adjusted alpha) then we would need to investigate that further via ordinary simple effects.

If the three-way interaction was not significant but one or more two-way interactions were significant then we could investigate these interactions by choosing to ignore the existence of one of the variables. The choice of variable to ignore would be most straightforward if one variable was not involved in any of the two-way interactions. Thus, if the only two-way interaction to be significant was type of defendant by condition under which sentence was given then we could ignore gender and conduct two separate one-way ANOVAs comparing the three conditions under which the sentence was given: one for the sentence given to experienced defend-ants and one for inexperienced defendants.

Summary

After conducting an ANOVA, researchers often wish to explore the data further. Contrasts allow means to be compared to investigate more specific hypotheses than are tested by an ANOVA. Contrasts can be planned before the data have been examined, or be unplanned and conducted once the means have been calculated. A variant on contrasts—trend analysis—can be applied when levels of an independent variable are quantitative rather than qualitative. Trend analysis allows patterns across means to be explored to see whether there is a trend across the levels of the independent variable.

Simple effects analysis allows the nature of an interaction between two IVs to be explored further. It isolates one level of one IV at a time to see how the levels of the other IV vary. Simple effects can be statistically significant even when the original interaction F-ratio is not.

If there is a significant main effect and no interaction, then, if the main effect has only two levels the direction in which the result went can be found by inspecting the marginal means for that IV. However, if the main effect has more than two levels then contrasts need to be conducted to explore the source of the significant result further.

The analysis introduced in this and previous chapters has addressed the question of whether the mean for the dependent variable differs between levels of an independent variable. The next two chapters introduce techniques for analysing relationships between two or more variables.

ANALYSIS OF RELATIONSHIPS I: CORRELATION

Introduction

Researchers are often interested in the relationship between two, or more, variables. For example, they may want to know how the variable *IQ* is related to the variable *earnings*.

The chapter starts by explaining the measures, including correlation, that are used to quantify the relationship between variables and how to interpret those measures. It discusses the basic forms of correlation for different types of data. It then introduces extensions of these techniques and the use of correlation for investigating the reliability and validity of measures.

Correlation

Two variables are said to be correlated when there is some predictability about the relationship between them. If people with low IQs had low incomes, people with medium IQs had medium incomes and people with high IQs had high incomes then, if we knew an individual's IQ, we could predict, with a certain degree of accuracy, what his or her income was. This would be an example of a positive correlation: as one variable gets larger so does the other. If, on the other hand, we investigated the relationship between family size and income we might find that those with large families have low incomes, those with medium-sized families have medium incomes and those with small families have high incomes. We could now predict a person's income from his or her family size with a certain degree of accuracy. However, this example would be of a negative (or inverse) correlation: as one variable gets larger the other gets smaller.

One measure of the relationship between two variables is the covariance between them.

Covariance

Imagine that in the IQ and income example the information presented in Table 19.1 was found for a sample of five people. Covariance, as its name suggests, is a measure of how the two variables vary together. To find the

Table 19.1 The IQ and income of five people

Participant	IQ	Income
1	85	12000
2	90	11000
3	95	15000
4	100	16000
5	110	20000
Mean	96	14800
SD	9.618	3563.706

covariance we calculate how much each person's score on one variable deviates from the mean for that variable and multiply that by how much their score on the other variable deviates from its mean.

Thus for the first person this would be:

$$(85 - 96) \times (12000 - 14800) = 30800$$

Repeat for each person and add the results together; this equals 131000. In order to take account of the sample size, divide by one fewer than the number of people who have provided measures. In this case the covariance is:

$$\frac{131000}{5 - 1} = 32750$$

If the covariance is large and positive then this is because people who were low on one variable tended to be low on the other and people who were high on one tended to be high on the other, and suggests a positive relationship between the two variables. Similarly, a large negative covariance suggests a negative relationship. Covariance of zero shows no relationship between the two variables.

However, there is a problem with covariance being used as the measure of the relationship: it does not take the size of the variance of the variables into account. Hence, if in a study one or both of the variables had a large variance then the covariance would be larger than in another study where the two variances were small, even if the degree of relationship in the two studies were similar. Therefore, using covariance we would not be able to compare relationships to see whether one relationship was closer than another. For example, we might wish to see whether IQ and income were as closely related in one country as they were in another.

Accordingly, we need a measure that takes the variances into account. The correlation coefficient is such a measure.

Correlation coefficients

The correlation coefficient (r), known as *Pearson's Product Moment Correlation Coefficient*, can be found using the following equation:

$$r = \frac{\text{covariance between two variables}}{\text{SD}_1 \times \text{SD}_2}$$

where SD_1 and SD_2 are the standard deviations of the two variables. For the IQ and income example:

$$r = \frac{32750}{9.618 \times 3563.706}$$

$$= 0.9555$$

The effect of dividing by the standard deviations is to limit, mathematically, the range of r, such that the largest positive correlation that can be achieved is +1 and the largest negative correlation that can be achieved is −1. If r is 0 this means there is no relationship between the variables.

The statistical significance of a correlation coefficient

The Null Hypothesis against which r is usually tested is that there is no relationship between the two variables. More particularly, the Null Hypothesis is about the equivalent parameter to r—the correlation in the population, usually shown as ρ (the Greek letter *rho*). Formally stated, the Null Hypothesis is that the sample comes from a population in which the correlation between two variables is $\rho = 0$. Therefore, with a sufficiently large sample size, the frequency distribution of r, under this Null Hypothesis, has roughly the following shape, with 0 as the most frequently occurring value and with +1 and −1 as the least likely values to occur when there is no relationship:

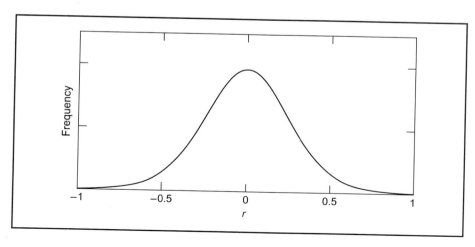

FIGURE 19.1 The frequency distribution of *r*, when the samples are taken from a population in which there is no correlation

Table 19.2 An extract of the probability tables for r (when the Null Hypothesis is that ρ = 0)

One-tailed probabilities

	0.4	0.3	0.2	0.1	0.05	0.025	0.01	0.005	0.001	0.0005

Two-tailed probabilities

df = n−2	0.8	0.6	0.4	0.2	0.1	0.05	0.02	0.01	0.002	0.001
1	0.3090	0.5878	0.8090	0.9511	0.9877	0.9969	0.9995	0.9999	1.0000	1.0000
2	0.2000	0.4000	0.6000	0.8000	0.9000	0.9500	0.9800	0.9900	0.9980	0.9990
3	0.1577	0.3197	0.4919	0.6870	0.8054	0.8783	0.9343	0.9587	0.9859	0.9911
4	0.1341	0.2735	0.4257	0.6084	0.7293	0.8114	0.8822	0.9172	0.9633	0.9741

The exact shape of the distribution is dependent on the sample size, or more particularly, on the degrees of freedom of r, which are two fewer than the sample size because the significance of r is based on the significance of regression (which, as we will see in the next chapter, has to estimate two parameters when two variables are involved). The larger the sample size, the closer the distribution is to being normally distributed. Appendix XIV gives the probabilities for r (when the Null Hypothesis is that ρ = 0) and Table 19.2 is an extract from that table. (The way to find the probability of r, when the Null Hypothesis is not ρ = 0, is explained later in this chapter.) Note that Table 19.2 gives probabilities for both one- and two-tailed tests.

One-tailed probabilities for r

If the research hypothesis is directional then a one-tailed probability is appropriate. An example would be if the research hypothesis was:

H_A: IQ and income are positively correlated.

with the Null Hypothesis:

H_0: There is no relationship between IQ and income.

The Null Hypothesis is that there is no *linear* relationship between the two variables in the population. A *linear relationship* would exist if a scattergram were created between the two variables and the points on the scattergram formed a straight line.

As there were five participants, df = 3. In this case, the one-tailed probability provided by the computer is $p = 0.0056$. This result would be reported as: *There was a significant positive correlation between IQ and income* (r = .956, df = 3, p = .0056, one-tailed test). As with the reporting of other tests, the df can also be shown in the following way: $r_{(3)}$ = .956.

The prediction of a negative correlation between two variables would also be a directional hypothesis. An example would be if the research hypothesis was:

H_A: There is a negative correlation between family size and income.

with the Null Hypothesis:

H_0: There is no relationship between family size and income.

To find the probability of a negative correlation ignore the negative sign and read the table as though the result had been a positive correlation; a correlation of $r = -0.9555$ has the same probability as a correlation of $r = 0.9555$.

Two-tailed probabilities for r

If the research hypothesis is non-directional then you would use a two-tailed probability. An example of a non-directional hypothesis would be if the research hypothesis was:

H_A: There is a relationship between IQ and income.

with the Null Hypothesis as before:

H_0: There is no relationship between IQ and income.

Here we would use a two-tailed probability; with $r = 0.9555$, and df = 3, $p = 0.0112$.

The interpretation of *r*

Causality and correlation

A snare that people should avoid with correlation, but often fall into, is assuming that because two variables are correlated one is affecting or causing the other to vary. An example shows the dangers of this reasoning. Over the year the consumption of ice-cream and the incidence of drownings are correlated. This does not suggest that consuming ice-cream leads to drowning. Here the relationship is produced by the fact that each variable is linked to the weather: the hotter the weather the more likely people are to consume ice-cream and the more likely people are to go swimming and so put themselves in danger.

There are other situations in which two variables may correlate but there is no causal link between them. They may be part of a chain of causality. For example, amount of knowledge about healthy behaviour may be correlated with physical health. However, there may be one or more variables that are acting as *mediators* between them. Amount of knowledge about healthy behaviour may be related to the degree to which people feel in control of their own health, which in turn may be related to the type of behaviour that people display and this may be linked to their health.

Even when there is a causal link between two variables we may not know which is the cause and which the effect. If socio-economic status (SES) and incidence of mental illness were positively related we would not know whether people's SES affects the likelihood of their developing a mental illness or the development of mental illness affects their SES. As has been said in previous chapters, cause and effect are best identified through experiments, where the researchers manipulate the independent variable(s) and look for the effects of the manipulations on the dependent variable(s).

The nature of the correlation

Whenever correlations are being investigated it is important that a scattergram be produced of the relationship between the two variables and that aspects of the variables be considered. This is because in some situations a significant correlation may be produced when there is little or no relationship (a spurious correlation) while in other situations a relationship may exist that is not detected by r.

Figure 19.2 shows the pattern that can be expected when there is a high positive correlation between two variables:

FIGURE 19.2 A scattergram for a high positive correlation (r = 0.9555)

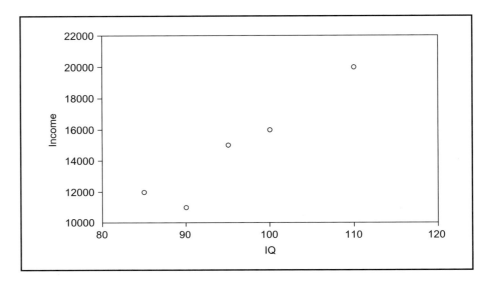

[1] This is a simplification because the measure that is being kept to a minimum is the *square* of the distance between the data points and the line.

A line can be drawn on the diagram, which is sometimes called the *best-fit* line, to depict the relationship between the two variables. The best-fit line is the line that passes through the data points with the minimum distance between itself and all the points.[1]

FIGURE 19.3 The best-fit line on a scattergram of a high positive correlation (r = 0.9555)

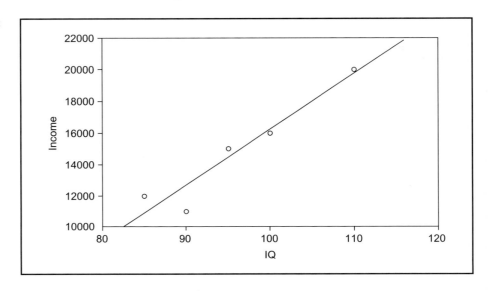

Note that in the case of a positive correlation the line runs from the bottom left-hand corner to the upper right-hand corner of the graph

Figure 19.4 shows the scattergram that can be expected from a high negative correlation. Note that in the case of a negative correlation the line runs from the top left-hand corner to the bottom right-hand corner of the graph.

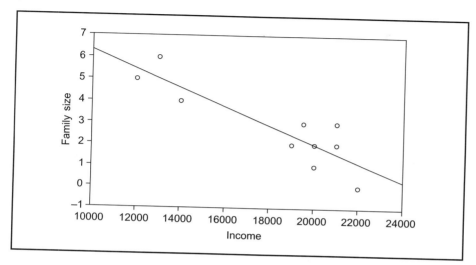

FIGURE 19.4 The scattergram for a high negative correlation ($r = -0.877$)

For a case where there is no relationship between two variables, imagine that we have looked at shoe size and income. In this example the correlation coefficient is $r = -0.041$ (df = 8, $p = 0.9104$, two-tailed test). Note that although the computer has produced a best-fit line it does not represent the data satisfactorily.

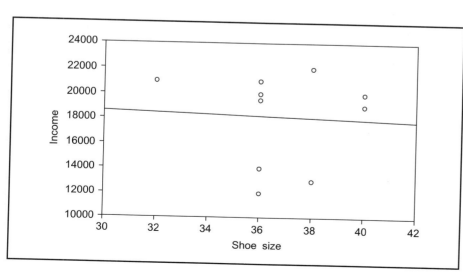

FIGURE 19.5 The scattergram for a low correlation between two variables

Situations in which a statistically significant r is spurious

Like the mean, *r* is highly affected by outliers. Thus, if a single person with a large shoe size and a large income were added to the previous sample we could get the following result:

FIGURE 19.6 A scattergram that includes one outlier

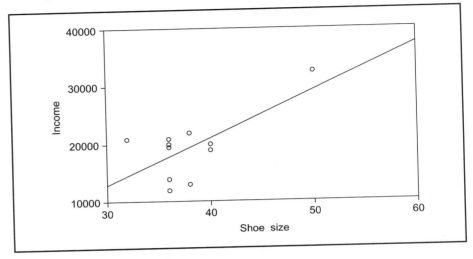

Here the addition of one person has changed the correlation from a very low negative one to a large, statistically significant positive one ($r = 0.666$, df = 9, $p = 0.0252$, two-tailed test).

Another situation that could produce a significant correlation would be if the sample included an unreasonably large range on one or both dimensions. For example, if we included children in the income by shoe size study. Here the correlation has become large, positive and significant ($r = 0.912$,

FIGURE 19.7 A scattergram produced when samples from two populations are combined

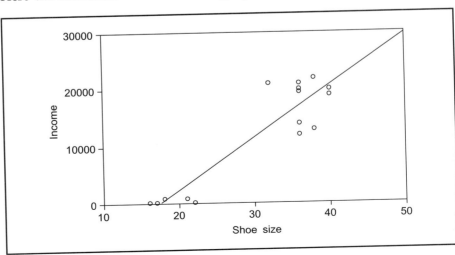

df = 13, p < 0.0001, two-tailed test). The scattergram shows that we have really included samples from two populations, neither of which, on its own, would show the correlation.

Situations in which r fails to detect a relationship

A non-linear relationship
In the example of family size and income we might have found the following pattern:

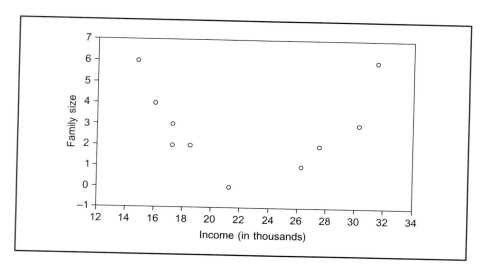

FIGURE 19.8 The scattergram of a non-linear relationship

Here the correlation is given as $r = -0.0243$ (df = 8, $p = 0.947$, two-tailed test). Note that the scattergram forms a U-shaped curve. Below an income of around 22,000 there is a negative relationship between family size and income. Above around 26,000 there is a positive relationship. There clearly is a relationship but it cannot be represented by a straight line. Pearson's Product Moment Correlation Coefficient (r) is a measure of linear, or straight-line relationships. The analysis of non-linear relationships is beyond the scope of this book. This non-linear form of relationship is described as *polynomial*. Under certain circumstances it is possible to transform one or both of the variables in a non-linear relationship so that the relationship becomes linear and then Pearson's r can be applied to the data. This is discussed in Appendix V.

Too restricted a range
The range of scores of one or both variables can be restricted in at least two ways. The first is a consequence of the very nature of correlation: both variables have to have some variability otherwise it is not possible to have a correlation.

If, in the IQ and income example, everyone in the sample had had an IQ of 100 then the correlation would be $r = 0$, because it makes no sense to ask whether income varies with IQ if IQ does not vary. (Recall the equation for r: as the covariance of IQ and income will be 0, so r must be 0.)

A second problem can be where only part of the range has been sampled. For example, if the incomes of only those with IQs in the 120 to 150 range were sampled there might be no relationship between income and IQ, whereas across the range 85 to 115 there might very well be a relationship.

To reiterate, when calculating the correlation between two variables always create and view a scattergram of the variables to see whether the relationship is linear and not affected by outliers or separate clusters of scores. Also always think about the range you have sampled of each variable to check whether you have artificially restricted them and so hidden a possible relationship or extended the ranges too widely so that a relationship is artificially created.

Effect size and correlation

There is a useful measure of effect size in correlation that can be derived simply from the correlation coefficient.

$$\text{effect size (ES)} = r^2 \times 100$$

Thus, in the case of IQ and income:

$$\text{ES} = (0.9555)^2 \times 100$$

$$= 91.298$$

The effect size is a measure of the amount of the variance in one variable that can be explained by the variance in the other. In the example, we can therefore say that 91.298% of the variance in income can be explained by the variance in IQ. In other words, less than 9% of the variance in income is not explicable in terms of the variance in IQ.

Cohen (1988) prefers to use r itself as a measure of effect size and I will keep to his convention for the power tables for r. Cohen judges that $r = 0.1$ constitutes a small effect size, $r = 0.3$ is a medium effect size and $r = 0.5$ is a large effect size in psychological research. Converting these to percentage variance accounted for we have 1% is a small ES, 9% is a medium ES and 25% is a large ES.

Power and correlation

Appendix XV gives the power tables for r. Table 19.3 reproduces part of those tables. The extract shows the power that is achieved for a given effect and sample size. Thus, if we wished to achieve power of 0.8 at $\alpha = 0.05$ with a directional hypothesis, we would need between 600 and 700 participants to detect a small ES, between 60 and 70 participants to detect a medium ES and between 20 and 25 to detect a large ES.

Table 19.3 An extract from the power tables for r, when α = 0.05 for a
one-tailed test (* denotes that power is greater than 0.995)

n	\multicolumn{11}{c}{effect size (r)}										
	0.1	0.2	0.3	0.4	0.5	0.6	0.7	0.8	0.9	0.95	0.99
20	0.10	0.20	0.35	0.54	0.74	0.89	0.98	*	*	*	*
25	0.12	0.24	0.42	0.64	0.83	0.95	0.99	*	*	*	*
60	0.19	0.45	0.76	0.94	0.99	*	*	*	*	*	*
70	0.20	0.51	0.81	0.97	*	*	*	*	*	*	*
600	0.79	*	*	*	*	*	*	*	*	*	*
700	0.84	*	*	*	*	*	*	*	*	*	*

The assumptions of Pearson's Product Moment Correlation

The statistic that has been introduced thus far in this chapter is parametric
and so, when used for inferential statistics, it makes certain assumptions
about the level of measurement obtained and the nature of the populations
from which the sample has come. The first assumption is that the scores
in one variable will be independent; that is, they will not be influenced by
other scores in that variable. The next assumption is that both variables
are of interval or ratio level of measurement, or ordinal with at least 7
different values in the scale. The third assumption is that the variables will
be bivariately normal in the population. This means that not only will each
variable be normally distributed in the population but also, for each value of
one of the variables, the other variable will be normally distributed in the
population. Figure 19.9 shows a bivariate normal distribution. In this graph
the height tells us the proportion of people who had a particular combination of scores on two variables. If were able to look down on the graph it
would look like a scattergram with a net superimposed on it and we would
see an oval shape characteristic of a correlation of r = 0.5. If we were able to
take a vertical slice through the graph we would see a normal distribution.

Once again we have the problem that we are usually dealing with
samples and not populations and so we are unlikely to know what the

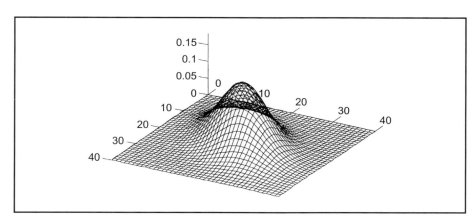

FIGURE 19.9 A 3D
frequency plot showing
a bivariate normal
distribution when the
correlation between the
two variables is r = 0.5

population distributions are like. In fact, few researchers check for bivariate normal distribution for simple correlation, although it becomes important when using the multivariate statistics described in Chapter 21. Nonetheless, it is worth checking the distribution of each variable on its own. If one of the distributions is skewed or if the two distributions are skewed in opposite directions, this can limit the size of the correlation coefficient.

When the assumptions of Pearson's Product Moment Correlation are not fulfilled there are a number of alternative correlation coefficients that can be calculated.

Point-biserial correlation

Sometimes one variable will be measured on a dichotomous scale; for example, male and female. There is a variant of the Pearson's Product Moment Correlation, called the *point-biserial correlation*, that can be used in this situation. For example, researchers might be interested in the relationship, among smokers, between gender and number of cigarettes smoked. However, instead of comparing average number of cigarettes smoked by male and female smokers to see whether there is a difference (using a between-subjects *t*-test or a Mann–Whitney *U*-test), they could look at the correlation between gender and smoking. The usual way to code the dichotomous variable is to call one level 0 and the other level 1. Which way round does not matter, except that it will affect whether the correlation is positive or negative. In Table 19.4 I have recoded the males as 0 and the females as 1.

Table 19.4 The number of cigarettes smoked daily by males and females

Gender	Coding	Smoking
male	0	15
male	0	15
male	0	20
male	0	30
male	0	35
male	0	10
male	0	25
male	0	20
male	0	15
male	0	20
female	1	5
female	1	7
female	1	3
female	1	20
female	1	15
female	1	20
female	1	7
female	1	10
female	1	20
female	1	25

Figure 19.10 shows the scattergram for the recoded data.

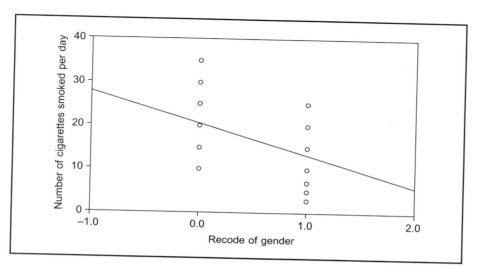

FIGURE 19.10 The best-fit line for the relationship between gender and cigarette smoking (among smokers)

The best-fit line crosses the levels of the IV at their means. Accordingly, it meets the males at 20.5 and the females at 13.2.

The correlation coefficient is $r = -0.4478$, showing a medium-to-large relationship between gender and smoking. Had females been coded as 0 and males as 1 then the correlation would have been positive.

To find the probability of the point-biserial correlation you use the same method as for testing the probability of r. If the hypothesis had been that there would be a negative relationship between gender and smoking (which means, given the coding of males as 0, that males smoke more than females), then we can perform a one-tailed test. Thus with $r = -0.4478$, df = 18, the probability is $p = 0.0239$, one-tailed test.

The discussion of the point-biserial correlation shows that the distinction between tests that are designed to look for differences between groups and those that look for relationships between variables is a little artificial. I will return to this theme in the next chapter.

Biserial correlation

In the previous example, gender is genuinely dichotomous. However, sometimes the dichotomy has been imposed on a variable that really is not dichotomous, for example, if we put people into two groups—old and young. In such cases there is a variant of the point-biserial correlation called the *biserial correlation*. This method is rarely used, partly because it has certain problems entailed in its calculation and in its use when the distributions are not normal, and so interested readers are referred to Howell (1997); in his later edition, Howell (2002) decided not to include it. As an alternative, in such a situation it would be permissible to use phi or Cramér's phi, which are described later in this chapter, under *correlation and nominal data*.

Non-parametric correlation

At least ordinal data

When the data are at least at the ordinal level of measurement we can use one of two measures of correlation: Spearman's rho (ρ)—sometimes known as the 'Spearman rank-order correlation coefficient'—and Kendall's tau (τ)—sometimes known as the 'Kendall rank-order correlation coefficient'. Spearman's rho has become more popular in statistical packages. I think this is partly due to the fact that pre-computers it was the easier to calculate. However, it has the drawback that it cannot be used simply for calculating *partial correlations*, whereas Kendall's tau can. Partial correlation, which is explained more fully later in the chapter, allows the possible effects of a third variable to be removed from the relationship between two variables.

As an example of non-parametric correlation, imagine that researchers wished to investigate the relationship between the length of time students have studied psychology and the degree to which they believe that psychology is a science. Eleven psychology students were asked how long they had studied psychology and were asked to rate, on a 5-point scale, ranging from 1 = *not at all* to 5 = *definitely a science*, their beliefs about whether psychology is a science. Table 19.5 shows the data from the study.

Table 19.5 The length of time students have studied psychology and their opinion of whether it is a science

Participant	Years studied psychology	Rating of psychology as a science
1	1	1
2	2	1
3	3	2
4	4	3
5	5	4
6	1	3
7	2	3
8	3	2
9	4	5
10	5	5
11	6	5

Both Spearman's rho and Kendall's tau can be calculated by converting the scores within a variable to ranks, though this conversion does not need to be used with Kendall's tau. As usual in such tests, scores that have the same value (ties) are given the mean rank. Thus, as two participants had been studying psychology for one year, they occupy the first two ranks and are each given the mean of those ranks: $\frac{1+2}{2} = 1.5$. See the description of the Wilcoxon signed-ranks test for matched pairs in Appendix VI for a fuller explanation of ranking data.

Table 19.6 The years spent studying psychology and the opinion of whether psychology is a science plus rankings

Participant	Years spent studying psychology	Rating of psychology	Rank of years	Rank of rating
1	1	1	1.5	1.5
2	2	1	3.5	1.5
3	3	2	5.5	3.5
4	4	3	7.5	6
5	5	4	9.5	8
6	1	3	1.5	6
7	2	3	3.5	6
8	3	2	5.5	3.5
9	4	5	7.5	10
10	5	5	9.5	10
11	6	5	11	10

Spearman's rho

The calculation of Spearman's rho produces the same result as would be found if the scores in each variable were converted to ranks for that variable, and Pearson's Product Moment Correlation was calculated. However, there is a version of rho that assumes that no scores are the same in a given variable and this is a value commonly given by computers. A worked example is given in Appendix X.

Using the simplified equation, rho = 0.77.

Tied observations
When there are no ties in the data, the two versions of Spearman's rho produce the same result. However, when two or more scores are the same in a given variable, the simplified equation is incorrect and then there is a version of rho that corrects for these 'ties', and produces the same result as would be obtained by applying the Pearson's Product Moment Correlation procedure to the ranks. In the present example there is more than one student in each of the first five years and more than one person gave ratings of 1, 2, 3 or 5. Rho corrected for ties produces rho = 0.762; this is the version that SPSS calculates. The version of rho that corrects for ties is the one you should report.

The probability of Spearman's rho
Unlike for other non-parametric tests, SPSS does not offer the ability to find exact probabilities (at least this is true up to version 11). With a sample of

100 or fewer participants use the table of probabilities given in Appendix XIV. When the sample is over 100 there is an equation that converts rho to a t-value and allows you to use t-tables to check the probability.

Alternatively, when the sample size is greater than 100, there is a z-approximation that can be used to calculate the probability of rho, which, although less accurate than the conversion of rho to t, could be used if you have access to more finely detailed z-tables. Appendix X gives the equations to convert rho to t and z. The probability of this result, as a one-tailed test, is $0.0025 < p < 0.005$. The result should be reported as: *There was a significant positive correlation between the length of time students had spent studying psychology and their opinion that it is a science (rho = .762, .0025 < p < .005, one tailed test, N = 11)*. If the sample size had been sufficiently large to justify using a t-test or a z-test to find the probability, then report the t- or z-value.

Kendall's tau

Kendall's tau differs from Spearman's rho. It places the original scores (or ranks) for one variable in numerical order and examines the order that has been created for the other variable.

Table 19.7 The time spent studying psychology and the ratings of psychology, sorted in the numerical order of time spent studying psychology

Participant	Years spent studying psychology	Rating of psychology
6	1	3
1	1	1
2	2	1
7	2	3
3	3	2
8	3	2
9	4	5
4	4	3
10	5	5
5	5	4
11	6	5

Thus, if the two variables were perfectly positively related then the order of the scores in the second variable should be from the lowest to the highest rating, and none would be out of order. In the above example, if we take the rating of psychology as a science we see that participant 6 had only been studying psychology for a year and yet gave it a rating of 3, while participants 2, 3 and 8 had been studying for longer but gave it a lower rating. Kendall's tau involves calculating how many scores are out of order relative to each person. If there are no scores out of order tau = 1. If all the possible ranks are out of order then tau = −1 which is the same pattern as given by other correlation coefficients; a perfect positive correlation is +1 and a perfect inverse correlation is −1.

If we re-analyse the data from the previous example using Kendall's tau, we get the result that tau = 0.564.

Tied observations

As with Spearman's rho there is an adjustment for ties, which in this case gives tau = 0.639, the one provided by SPSS, which shows it as *Kendall's tau-b*. See Appendix X for a worked example.

The probability of tau

Again SPSS does not offer exact probabilities for this test. As with Spearman's rho there exists an approximation to the normal distribution for Kendall's tau. However, Kendall's tau has the advantage that this approximation is accurate for smaller sample sizes. Thus, if the sample is ten or fewer then you use the appropriate table in Appendix XIV. Above this sample size use the z-approximation shown in Appendix X. The probability in the present example can be calculated via the z-test, as the sample size is over 10. This gives a z-value (adjusted for ties) of $z = 2.738$ with a one-tailed probability of $p = 0.0031$. The result should be reported using the same format as for Spearman's rho.

The relative merits of rho and tau

As has been explained, the two coefficients are based on different calculations, and will often yield different values. Therefore it makes no sense to compare the values derived from the two tests to see whether two relationships differ. With the advent of computers, the fact that Spearman's rho is easier to calculate, particularly for larger samples, is no longer a reason for preferring it. I prefer Kendall's tau because it has a straightforward means for finding a partial correlation. An additional reason for preferring Kendall's tau is, as Howell (1997) points out, that it provides a better estimation of the value that would have been obtained for the population from which the sample came than does Spearman's rho.

Power and ordinal measures of correlation

The power levels of tau and rho are given in terms of their power efficiency relative to their parametric equivalent, Pearson's Product Moment Correlation. In order to achieve the same level of power when using Spearman's rho or Kendall's tau find the sample size necessary for the required effect size and power for Pearson's r and multiply the sample size by 1.1. For example, if we were seeking a medium effect size ($r = 0.3$), with a one-tailed test, an alpha level of 0.05 and we wished to have power of 0.8 then we would need 68 participants. Therefore, if we were using Spearman's rho or Kendall's tau, then we would need $68 \times 1.1 = 74.8$ or 75 participants to achieve the same level of power.

Correlation and nominal data

In Chapter 15 the proportion of males and females in a sample who were smokers was compared with the proportion who were non-smokers, using a χ^2 test for contingency tables. We can re-analyse the data to ask whether there is a relationship between gender and smoking status.

Table 19.8 The number of smokers and non-smokers in a sample of males and females

Observed Frequency Table

	male	female	Totals:
smoker	17	21	38
non-smoker	27	23	50
Totals:	44	44	88

The χ^2 value for this contingency table was 0.741.

There are a number of measures of correlation that can be used with categorical data, all of which are based on χ^2: the contingency coefficient (C), phi (ϕ) and Cramér's phi (ϕ_c).

$$\text{contingency coefficient} = \sqrt{\frac{\chi^2}{\chi^2 + N}}$$

Howell (2002) points out that the contingency coefficient is limited in two ways. Firstly, it can never have the value 1 because of the way it is calculated. Secondly, the maximum value it can have is limited by the number of cells in the contingency table, such that it can only reach a maximum possible value of 0.707 with a 2×2 table.

$$\text{phi} = \sqrt{\frac{\chi^2}{N}}$$

Phi is limited to analysing 2×2 tables but there is an alternative version that is not—Cramér's phi (shown as Cramér's V in SPSS).

$$\text{Cramér's phi} = \sqrt{\frac{\chi^2}{N \times (k-1)}}$$

where k is the number of rows or the number of columns in the contingency table, whichever is smaller. With a 2×2 table Cramér's phi becomes the same as phi. In addition, with a 2×2 table, both give the same result as would a Pearson's Product Moment Correlation, with each dichotomy being recoded into zeros and ones.

In the present case:

$$\text{contingency coefficient} = \sqrt{\frac{0.741}{0.741 + 88}}$$

$$= \sqrt{0.00835}$$

$$= 0.091$$

$$\text{phi} = \sqrt{\frac{0.741}{88}}$$

$$= \sqrt{0.00842}$$

$$= 0.092$$

Finding the probability of correlations based on categorical data

As each of the measures described utilises χ^2 there is no need to find a separate source for the probability; we can use the probability for the χ^2 value.

Effect size and χ^2 revisited

In Chapter 15 the effect size (w) for χ^2 was introduced. If you compare the equation for w and that for phi you will see that they are the same. Thus, for a 2×2 χ^2 the effect size measure is the same as the recommended correlation measure for the same data. In addition, note that phi gives the same result as a Product Moment Correlation (r) conducted on the same data and that the recommended values for small, medium and large effect sizes for w are the same (0.1, 0.3 and 0.5, respectively) as those recommended for r.

Summary of correlation methods

This is shown in Table 19.9.

Table 19.9 A summary of the different forms of correlation introduced in this chapter

Coefficient	Symbol	When appropriate
Pearson's Product Moment	r	both variables at least ordinal
Point-biserial	r_{pb}	one variable at least ordinal, the other a true dichotomy
Biserial	r_b	one variable at least ordinal, the other an artificial dichotomy
Spearman's rho	ρ	both variables at least ordinal but not fulfilling criteria for Pearson's r (cannot be used, simply, for partial correlation)
Kendall's tau	τ	both variables at least ordinal but not fulfilling criteria for Pearson's r (can be used for partial correlation)
Contingency coefficient	C	both variables nominal (provides restricted range of values)
phi	ϕ	both variables nominal but with only 2 levels each
Cramér's phi	ϕ_c	both variables nominal

Other uses of correlation

This section shows how the possible influences of a third variable can be removed from the relationship between two variables, how two correlation coefficients can be compared, how a sample's correlation coefficient can be compared with a population's actual or hypothesised correlation coefficient and how confidence intervals can be obtained from r.

Partial and semi-partial correlation

Sometimes, as in the ice-cream and drownings example, two variables may correlate although this is due to some third variable that correlates with both of the original variables. In such cases, if we know how each pair of variables correlate we can remove the effect of the third variable; we can *partial out* that effect using partial or semi-partial correlation.

Partial correlation with Pearson's r

In a study researchers wished to see whether mathematical ability and ability at English correlate among children but they were aware that age is likely to correlate with each of them and may explain any relationship they have. They gave a sample of 10 children, with ages ranging between 12 and 14 years, tests of maths and English and they noted each child's age.

When a correlation coefficient has been calculated for every possible combination of pairs from a set of variables, the results are usually represented

Table 19.10 The correlation matrix of mathematical ability, English ability and age

	Maths	English	Age
Maths	1		
English	.888	1	
Age	.748	.862	1

in what is called a *correlation matrix*. Table 19.10 gives the correlation matrix for the correlations between maths ability, English ability and age. The figures in the correlation matrix are the correlation coefficients between pairs of variables. The correlation for a given pair of variables is given at the point where the column labelled with one variable's name meets the row that is labelled with the other variable's name. The first column shows correlations with maths and the second row shows correlations with English. This tells us that the correlation between maths and English abilities is $r = 0.888$, which with df = 8 is statistically significant at $p < 0.0005$ (one-tailed test).

Notice that the diagonal from the top left-hand to the bottom right-hand of the matrix contains the figure 1 in each cell. This is because this is the correlation of each variable with itself. Notice also that the top right-hand part of the matrix is empty. This is because all the cells in this part of the matrix would represent correlations that are already shown in the matrix. Some computer programs give the full matrix but the present format makes it easier to read.

The matrix tells us that there is a large correlation between ability at maths and English but there is also a large correlation between each of the abilities and age. The equation for calculating the correlation coefficient of maths and English ability with the effect of age partialled out is:

$$r_{me.a} = \frac{r_{me} - r_{ma} \times r_{ea}}{\sqrt{[1 - (r_{ma})^2] \times [1 - (r_{ea})^2]}}$$

where $r_{me.a}$ is the correlation between maths and English ability, with age partialled out; r_{me} is the correlation between maths and English ability; r_{ma} is the correlation between maths ability and age; r_{ea} is the correlation between English ability and age. Therefore

$$r_{me.a} = \frac{0.888 - 0.748 \times 0.862}{\sqrt{[1 - (0.748)^2] \times [1 - (0.862)^2]}}$$

$$= 0.723$$

To assess the statistical significance of a partial correlation read the standard r-tables but with df of three fewer than the sample size (when, as in this case, one variable has been partialled out). From the r-tables we learn that the correlation between mathematical and English abilities with age partialled out is still statistically significant ($0.01 < p < 0.025$, df = 7, one-tailed test).

One way to view the original and the partial correlations between mathematical and English abilities is to note that the former suggests that the variance in English ability accounts for $(0.888)^2 \times 100 = 78.85\%$ of the variance in mathematical ability. However, the variance in age accounts for $(0.748)^2 \times 100 = 55.95\%$ of the variance in mathematics and $(0.862)^2 \times 100 = 74.30\%$ of the variance in English ability. Partial correlation takes out the part of the variance in English ability that is accountable for in terms of the variance in age and the part of the variance in maths ability that can be accounted for by age, and looks at the amount of shared variance that is left, namely $(0.723)^2 \times 100 = 52.27\%$.

It is possible to partial out the effects of more than one variable on a relationship. For example, we could partial out the effect of socio-economic status as well as age. This is dealt with in Appendix X.

Semi-partial correlation with Pearson's r

Sometimes, rather than look at the relationship between two variables with the effect of a third variable on each partialled out, researchers wish only to partial the effect of the third variable on one of them; this is termed *semi-partial correlation*. I have never used semi-partial correlation in this context but it becomes useful as part of multiple regression, as will be shown in the next chapter.

If researchers were particularly interested in finding how well English ability predicts mathematics ability when the degree to which age predicts English ability has been removed, then they can use semi-partial correlation (also known as 'part correlation'), via the following equation:

$$r_{m(e.a.)} = \frac{r_{me} - r_{ma} \times r_{ea}}{\sqrt{(1 - r_{ea}^2)}}$$

where $r_{m(e.a)}$ is the semi-partial correlation between maths and English ability with the relationship between English ability and age removed; r_{me} is the correlation between maths and English ability; r_{ma} is the correlation between maths ability and age; r_{ea} is the correlation between English ability and age.

In the example:

$$r_{m(e.a.)} = \frac{0.888 - 0.748 \times 0.862}{\sqrt{(1 - (0.862)^2)}}$$

$$= 0.4798$$

Expressed as percentage of variance, $(0.4798)^2 \times 100 = 23.02\%$, we can interpret this semi-partial correlation as showing that English ability explains an additional 23.02% of the variance in mathematical ability over and above the variance in mathematical ability that is explained by age.

Partial correlation using Kendall's tau

The equation for partial correlation using Kendall's tau is basically the same as that for partial correlation with Pearson's Product Moment Correlation. If the data for age, ability at mathematics and ability at English are re-analysed using Kendall's tau, we find that maths and English ability correlate, tau = 0.786. However, age correlates with maths (tau = 0.593) and English (tau = 0.723). Using the following equation, the effect of age can be partialled out of the relationship between maths and English:

$$\tau_{me.a} = \frac{\tau_{me} - \tau_{ma} \times \tau_{ea}}{\sqrt{[1 - (\tau_{ma})^2] \times [1 - (\tau_{ea})^2]}}$$

where $\tau_{me.a}$ is the correlation between maths and English with age partialled out; τ_{me} is the correlation between maths and English; τ_{ea} is the correlation between English and age; τ_{ma} is the correlation between maths and age. Thus,

$$\tau_{me.a} = \frac{0.786 - 0.593 \times 0.723}{\sqrt{[1 - (0.593)^2] \times [1 - (0.723)^2]}}$$

$$= \frac{0.357}{\sqrt{0.309}}$$

$$= 0.6422$$

The probability of the partial correlation using Kendall's tau
To find the probability of Kendall's tau as a partial correlation use Table A14.17 in Appendix XIV. This shows that, with a sample size of 10, a tau of 0.6422 has a one-tailed probability of $0.001 < p < 0.005$.

The difference between two correlations

Sometimes researchers want to compare two correlation coefficients to see whether they are significantly different. It is not sufficient to compare the significance levels of the two correlations and note that one is more statistically significant than the other. It is necessary to conduct a statistical test that compares the two correlations. As with other forms of analysis, different tests are used when the two correlations are from different groups of participants (independent groups) or from the same or related groups of participants (non-independent groups).

Independent groups

Researchers predicted that adults would have a more accurate idea of their memory ability (their metamemory) than children have. They devised a measure of metamemory which they gave to a group of 30 adults and a group of 30 children. They also tested the actual memories of both groups.

They obtained the following results: the correlation for children's metamemory and actual memory was $r = 0.5$, the correlation for adult's metamemory and actual memory was $r = 0.8$. Before the equation for the test can be introduced it is necessary to deal with a complication.

As we are testing the difference between two correlation coefficients, rather than a correlation coefficient against the Null Hypothesis that the correlation is zero, the distribution can be skewed. Fisher devised a way of transforming r into r' that is more symmetrically distributed and allows the use of a z-test to compare the correlations. (Confusingly, this transformation is sometimes described as Fisher's Z_r. However, r' is preferable to prevent confusion with z-tests.)

Appendix XVI provides the equivalent r' for a range of r-values and the equation devised by Fisher for those wanting a more exact transformation when the r-value is not tabled.

The equation for comparing two independent correlation coefficients is:

$$z = \frac{r'_1 - r'_2}{\sqrt{\dfrac{1}{n_1 - 3} + \dfrac{1}{n_2 - 3}}}$$

where r'_1 is the Fisher's transformation of one correlation coefficient; r'_2 is the Fisher's transformation of the other correlation coefficient; n_1 is the sample size of one group; n_2 is the sample size of the other group. Looking up the r to r' conversion tables shows that $r = 0.8$ becomes $r' = 1.099$ and $r = 0.5$ becomes $r' = 0.549$. Therefore, the z-test for comparison between the two correlation coefficients is:

$$z = \frac{1.099 - 0.549}{\sqrt{\dfrac{1}{30 - 3} + \dfrac{1}{30 - 3}}}$$

$$= 2.02$$

Looking up the one-tailed probability of this value in the z-tables (Appendix XIV), we find that $p = 0.0217$. The researchers therefore conclude that adults have more accurate metamemories than children.

Non-independent groups

The equations for the difference between non-independent correlation coefficients are different from the one for independent groups and are of such complexity that I have included their explanation in Appendix X.

The difference between a sample correlation and a population correlation (when H_0 is not $\rho = 0$)

As was noted earlier, r has an equivalent parameter for the population: ρ (not to be confused with Spearman's rho). Researchers sometimes wish to compare the correlation coefficient from a given study with that known, or assumed, to exist for a population. For example, researchers may know, from previous research, that the correlation between extroversion scores of monozygotic (identical) twins reared together is $r = 0.7$. They have a sample of 20 monozygotic twins reared apart whose extroversion scores correlate with $r = 0.4$ and they want to see whether those reared apart have a significantly lower correlation than those reared together.

This form of comparison is similar to the one for two independent correlations and uses the equation:

$$z = \frac{r' - \rho'}{\sqrt{\dfrac{1}{n-3}}}$$

where r' is the Fisher's transformation of the sample's correlation coefficient; ρ' is the Fisher's transformation of the population's correlation coefficient; n is the size of the sample (in this case, the number of pairs of twins). A ρ of 0.7 converts to $\rho' = 0.867$ and an r of 0.4 converts to $r' = 0.424$. Therefore,

$$z = \frac{0.424 - 0.867}{\sqrt{\dfrac{1}{17}}}$$

$$= -1.83$$

The researchers hypothesised that the twins reared separately had a lower correlation (prior, of course, to collecting the data) and so they were justified in using the one-tailed probabilities in the z-tables; remember to ignore the negative sign when reading the tables. The likelihood of this result (or one more extreme) having occurred if the monozygotic twins came from a population in which ρ had equalled 0.7 is given as $p = 0.0336$. Therefore, the researchers were justified in rejecting the Null Hypothesis that the correlations did not differ and in concluding that monozygotic twins reared apart show less similarity in extroversion score than do monozygotic twins who are reared together.

Confidence intervals and correlation

Correlation coefficients have a dual function. On the one hand they are used as inferential statistics: researchers can test the likelihood of a correlation coefficient having arisen by chance. On the other hand, they are descriptive statistics describing the relationship between two variables. As with other sample descriptive statistics it is possible to use them to estimate the confidence interval for the equivalent parameter: the correlation within the population (ρ).

Appendix X gives a worked example of the calculation of the confidence interval for the population. Recall that the correlation between metamemory and actual memory was found to be 0.8 with a sample of 30 adults. At the 95% level of confidence, ρ was found to lie within the interval 0.62 to 0.90.

Measures of agreement between more than two people

Sometimes researchers wish to get independent judges to rate objects in order to provide a scale that is not biased by their own views. For example, if researchers wished to look at the link between the physical attractiveness of a person and whether others would show altruistic behaviour towards that person, then they would need a measure of physical attractiveness. To avoid using their own judgements they could present the materials they wished to use in their study (e.g. photographs) to judges and ask them to rank the people in the photographs according to their physical attractiveness. Before they could use the judgements as the basis of their scale, it would be important to know how well the judges agreed. For, if there were lack of agreement, this would suggest that the measure was unreliable. Using *Kendall's coefficient of concordance* they can assess the degree of agreement among their judges.

Kendall's coefficient of concordance

This test yields a statistic W which is a measure of how much a set of judges agree when asked to put a set of objects in rank order. The data are shown in Table 19.11. The equation for calculating W is given in Appendix X along with the workings for this example.

Table 19.11 The attractiveness rankings given by judges for five photographs

| | Photograph | | | | |
Judge	A	B	C	D	E
one	1	2	3	4	5
two	2	1	4	3	5
three	3	2	1	5	4
four	1	3	2	4	5

W was found to be 0.6875. SPSS shows the exact probability for this result as $p = 0.01$ and thus we can conclude that there is a significant degree of agreement among the judges about the attractiveness of the people represented in the photographs. The mean ratings for each photograph could then be used to provide the order of attractiveness of the five photographs. If you don't have access to exact probabilities then Table A14.18 in Appendix XIV provides significance levels for W when the number of items to be rated is between three and seven. If the number of items is greater than seven then Table A14.18 shows a chi-squared approximation which can be used to find the probability.

W cannot have negative values. It ranges between 0 which would be no agreement between the judges to +1 which would denote perfect agreement between them.

Kendall's coefficient of concordance also allows for a judge to give two objects the same rank. In such a case, there is a modified equation for calculating *W* which adjusts for such ties. Appendix X provides the equation and a worked example. SPSS uses the version that corrects for ties; when there are no ties the two versions give the same answer.

The use of correlation to evaluate reliability and validity of measures

Reliability

A reliable measure was defined in Chapter 2 as a measure that will produce a consistent score from one occasion to another. It can be measured using a reliability coefficient.

Two forms of reliability will be dealt with. The first is what I will call *test* reliability, the reliability of a measure when taken from a number of people, for example, a measure of depression or a test of ability. The second, *inter-rater* reliability, is the degree of agreement between two or more judges who are using a measure, for example, two researchers rating the type of interaction that is occurring between a mother and her child.

Test reliability

If a measure is not 100% reliable then the score a person achieves on a given occasion can be seen as being made up of the true score (which they would have achieved if the test had been 100% reliable) and the error (the difference between the true score and the observed score). Formally, the reliability coefficient is the variance in true scores divided by the variance in measured scores. In other words, it tells us what proportion the variance of the true scores is of the variance in the measured scores. Therefore, the closer the proportion is to 1 the more reliable the measure is. We cannot know what a person's true score is. However, we can produce an estimate of the reliability coefficient from the data we have collected (see McDonald, 1999 or Pedhazur & Schmelkin, 1991 for more details).

There are three forms of test reliability that researchers might want to assess, depending on the use to be made of a measure: test–retest, alternative (or parallel or equivalent) form and internal consistency.

Test–retest reliability
If a test is designed to measure something that is considered to be relatively fixed, as some people believe IQ to be, then they will want a measure that will produce the same results from one occasion to the next. To check this,

the designers of a test will give the test to a group of people on two occasions; Kline (2000) recommends that at least 100 people be tested and that the gap should be at least three months between occasions. Pearson's Product Moment Correlation can be used to correlate the results for the two occasions. Kline (2000) sees $r = 0.8$ as a minimum below which we would not want to go.

Alternative-form reliability

There will be occasions when to give the same test on two occasions will not be practical, as taking the test once will affect how an individual performs on the test a second time. Under such circumstances, researchers prepare two versions of the test. Researchers may wish to measure a change over time, for example, in an ability before and after training. They will want to be sure that any differences in performance between the two occasions are not due to inherent differences in the two forms of the test, which could introduce the threat to internal validity known as *instrumentation*. Accordingly, when trying to establish the reliability of the two versions of the test, they will correlate the performance of their participants on the two versions of the test, which can be taken in the same session; once again Pearson's r can be used. (Kline, 2000, says that ideally r would be at least 0.9 but that this is achieved by few tests.)

Internal-consistency reliability

In the absence of two forms of the test, it is possible to check that the test has items that are consistent with each other. There are a number of measures of internal consistency; the simplest is to correlate performance on two halves of the test: split-half reliability.

Split-half reliability

The test can be split into two parts in a number of ways. One would be to correlate the first and second halves. However, as many tests of performance increase the difficulty of items as the test progresses, this would not be ideal. An alternative is to treat all the even-numbered items as one half of the test and the odd-numbered items as the other. Once again Pearson's r could be used for this purpose. One criticism of this is that this measure of reliability is partly affected by the number of items in a test: the more items the more reliable the test will appear. Spearman and Brown produced an adjustment that allowed for this (see Appendix X for the Spearman–Brown equation).

A further criticism of the simple split-half approach is that the allocation of items into the two halves is somewhat arbitrary. To avoid this a reliability coefficient has been devised which is the equivalent of having conducted all the possible split halves—Cronbach's alpha. Kline (2000) notes that alpha should ideally be around 0.9 and never be below 0.7. On the other hand, Pedhazur and Schmelkin (1991) point out that the user of the measure has to determine how reliable the test should be depending on the circumstances of the study. Nonetheless, it is worth pointing out that the 0.7 level is quoted so frequently that you would have to argue quite strongly to go below this level, particularly if you were hoping to get work based on the measure published. (Appendix X provides the equation for Cronbach's alpha.)

An alternative to Cronbach's alpha—the Kuder–Richardson 20 (KR 20)—is available when the test involves questions that only have two possible responses—known as binary or dichotomous items—such as yes/no, correct/incorrect or true/false. (Appendix X provides the equation for the KR 20.) When the data are dichotomous analysing the data in SPSS as though for a Cronbach's alpha produces the appropriate answer.

Standard error of measurement

When a measure is not 100% reliable, the score a person attains on one occasion will not necessarily be the same as that on another occasion. *The standard error of measurement*, which is a statistic based on the reliability of the measure, can be used to find a confidence interval around the person's score, such that the range of scores in the interval is likely to contain the person's 'true' score. (Appendix X shows how the confidence interval can be found for a single score.)

Inter-rater reliability

Often researchers wish to check that a measure can be used consistently by different observers. The simplest checks could be to use the percentage of agreement between the two observers or a correlation coefficient. Percentage agreement fails to take into account the amount of agreement that could have been expected by chance. A large positive correlation coefficient does not necessarily show that two observers are agreeing. Two lecturers could mark a set of essays and not give the same mark to any of them and yet the correlation between their marks could be perfect. This would occur if one lecturer gave each essay ten marks more than the other lecturer; remember that correlation merely tells you about the direction in which the two measures move relative to each other. A measure that solves both these problems is Cohen's kappa (k). (Appendix X gives the equation and a worked example for Cohen's kappa.) It is worth pointing out that Pedhazur and Schmelkin (1991) would say that what I have been describing is more correctly called inter-rater *agreement*. See their account of what *they* term inter-rater reliability.

Indicators and reliability

Bollen and Lennox (1991) make the point that we should not slavishly follow guidelines about reliability, and in particular internal consistency in our measures, without first thinking about the nature of the elements that make up our measure. They draw attention to a distinction between *effect* indicators and *causal* indicators. Effect indicators can be seen as being affected by the phenomenon we are trying to measure. Thus, if we believed that personality is a relatively fixed thing we would expect an individual's personality to affect their responses to items in a personality test and we would want internal consistency in a test of personality. On the other hand, causal indicators are seen as ones that affect the phenomenon we are assessing. We may be trying to measure socio-economic status by asking about education level and salary. In this case, changes in these elements will affect SES. Accordingly, internal consistency between the elements of this measure is not necessarily something we would expect.

Validity

Correlation can also be used to check aspects of the validity of a measure by assessing the degree of similarity between one measure of a concept and the measure being devised. An example would be if researchers correlated their measure of depression with the clinical judgements of psychiatrists. Alternatively, in the case of divergent construct validity, we could find the degree of correlation between our measure (e.g. reading ability) and one that is not designed to measure the same concept (e.g. IQ). If this correlation were to be too high then we might suspect that our test was measuring aspects of IQ rather than being purely a measure of reading.

Standard error of estimate

Just as the standard error of measurement can be used to find a confidence interval around a person's score on a measure when the measure is not totally reliable, so the *standard error of estimate* is a statistic that can be used to find a confidence interval for a person's score when the validity of the measure is expressed as a correlation coefficient. (Appendix X shows how such a confidence interval can be found.)

Summary

A correlation coefficient describes the relationship between two variables. In addition, it can be used to find the statistical significance of a given relationship. It is necessary to produce a scattergram of the data for the two variables and to think about the nature of the sample being tested, otherwise there is a danger of missing a relationship because it is non-linear or suggesting a relationship that is actually an artefact of the sample.

The degree to which a test will produce the same score from one occasion to another—its reliability—and the degree to which judges agree in the way they use a scoring system—inter-rater reliability—can be ascertained, using tests that are based on correlation. In addition, certain forms of validity of a measure can be checked using correlation.

The next chapter introduces an alternative, but related, way of investigating relationships—regression.

ANALYSIS OF RELATIONSHIPS II: REGRESSION

20

Introduction

Regression analysis is another way of describing and evaluating relationships between variables. However, unlike correlation there is an assumption that one variable is a variable to be predicted (a DV) and one or more variables (IVs) are used to predict the outcome of the DV. Strictly speaking, the terms DV and IV are more appropriate in experimental research: their equivalents in non-experimental research are *criterion variable* and *predictor variable* respectively. However, at the risk of annoying those who prefer the latter terms I am going to use DV and IV throughout this chapter. It allows me to use abbreviations without adding new ones in the form of CV and PV which may introduce their own confusion. Although not one of the factors that affected my decision, it is also consistent with the descriptions used by SPSS. As we will see at the end of the chapter, techniques that analyse designs that look for differences between groups, such as ANOVA, and techniques that analyse designs that are looking for relationships among variables, such as regression, are in fact based on the same principles.

Regression analysis can be described as a form of modelling, for a mathematical model of the relationship between variables is created. Regression allows specific predictions to be made from the independent variable(s) about the dependent variable for individual participants. Simple regression involves a single independent variable. Multiple regression allows more than one independent variable to be used to predict the dependent variable and so improve the accuracy of the prediction. The chapter will only deal with linear regression, in other words, where the relationship between variables when represented on a scattergram is best shown as a straight line. Non-linear regression is beyond the scope of this book.

I am assuming that you will do the necessary calculations on a computer. This chapter is written to help you understand what regression is and how to interpret the results. Some of the simpler aspects of the mathematics are given in Appendix XI.

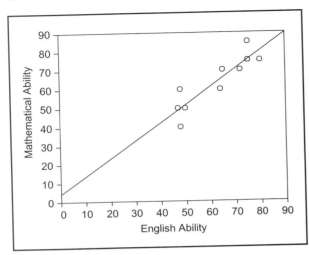

FIGURE 20.1 The relationship between mathematical and English ability

¹ Once again this is a simplification. The best-fit line minimises the square of the distance between itself and the data points. Hence, you will sometimes see the term *least squares* used to describe the method of finding it.

Simple regression

Let us return to the example of mathematical ability, English ability and age, introduced in the previous chapter. Assume that researchers want, initially, to predict mathematical ability from English ability. In other words, they are treating English ability as an independent variable and mathematical ability as a dependent variable. This does not mean that English ability is assumed to be affecting mathematical ability, it simply allows researchers to see how accurately they can make their predictions of a person's mathematical ability if his or her English ability is known. To do this they find the straight line that best summarises the relationship between the two variables (the best-fit line). Figure 20.1 shows the scattergram of mathematical and English ability with the best-fit line superimposed on it. I have intentionally widened the range on both axes of the graph beyond those necessary to show the data, for reasons that will be made clear later. The best-fit line is the line that minimises the distance between itself and the data points on the graph.¹

If we wished to find out what value would be predicted for mathematical ability for a child with a score of 30 on a test of English ability, first read along the horizontal axis (English ability) until you reach the value 30. Then draw a vertical line from that point to the best-fit line. Now draw a horizontal line from where you have met the best-fit line until you reach the vertical axis (mathematical ability). The point on the vertical axis will be the predicted value for mathematical ability.

This suggests that someone with a score of 30 for English would get a score of about 32 for maths.

Those of you who have done sufficient mathematics will know that any straight line on a graph can be described using a standard equation, which will allow any point on the line to be specified. In this way we can get a more exact prediction than by trying to read the graph.

Often a convention is used of calling a value on the vertical axis Y and a value on the horizontal axis X. The equation for a straight line on a graph is always of the form:

$$\text{predicted } Y = a + (b \times X)$$

FIGURE 20.2 Predicting mathematical ability from English ability using the best-fit line

where *a* is the value of *Y* where the best-fit line cuts the *Y*-axis (the intercept) and *b* is a measure of the steepness of the best-fit line (the slope). *a* and *b* are sometimes referred to as *regression coefficients*. (Some versions of this equation will use different letters to represent the different elements in the equation and may even change the order. However, they are, in fact, the same equation.[2])

The larger the measure of the slope the steeper the slope. This makes intuitive sense because the larger the number you multiply the horizontal value by in order to get the vertical value the quicker the vertical value will grow relative to the horizontal value.

Another way to view the equation for regression is:

$$\text{predicted DV} = a + (b \times \text{IV})$$

In this case:

$$\text{mathematical ability} = 4.28832 + (0.94891 \times \text{English ability})$$

The coefficient shown as *b* above can be interpreted as showing that the model predicts that for every increase of 1 in the IV (English ability) there will be an increase by the value of *b* (0.94891) in the DV (mathematical ability). The coefficient shown as *a* above is the value that the DV would have for someone whose score on the IV was 0. Thus, Figures 20.1 and 20.2 show that the best-fit line cuts the vertical axis where the mathematical ability is 4.28832.

The regression equation predicts that if a child scored 65 on the English test then:

mathematical ability

$= 4.28832 + 0.94891 \times 65$

$= 65.967$

Figure 20.3 is an enlargement of the scattergram in the region where English ability is 65. In fact, the person who scored 65 on the English test scored 70 on the maths test. Therefore, the prediction is not perfect. This is no more than we should expect from the correlation coefficient between English and maths abilities of $r = 0.888$, as shown in Chapter 19, which meant that 78.85% of the variance in mathematical ability could be accounted for by the variance in English ability, thus leaving $100 - 78.85 = 21.15\%$ of the variance unexplained.

[2] Those of you who have done some algebra may remember seeing the equation for a straight line written as $y = mx + c$. In that form *m* is the slope and *c* is the intercept.

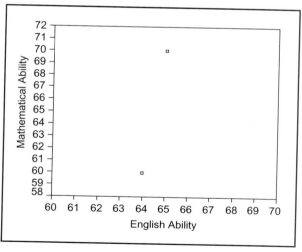

FIGURE 20.3 Enlargement of area around scores of 65 for English ability

Testing the statistical significance of regression analysis

Regression analysis, like correlation, can be presented in terms of percentage of variance accounted for. This means that it could be subjected to an Analysis of Variance, by splitting the variance in the dependent variable into that which can be accounted for by the independent variable and that which remains unaccounted for (residual). The F-ratio is formed by:

$$F = \frac{\text{variance in DV explained by IV}}{\text{variance in DV not explained by IV}}$$

The summary table for the analysis is laid out in the same way as that given when a one-way between-subjects ANOVA is computed (see Table 20.1).

Table 20.1 Summary table of the analysis of variance in a simple regression with ability at English as the predictor and mathematical ability as the dependent variable

ANOVA[b]

Model		Sum of Squares	df	Mean Square	F	Sig.
1	Regression	1381.606	1	1381.606	29.801	.001[a]
	Residual	370.894	8	46.362		
	Total	1752.500	9			

a. Predictors: (Constant), ENGLISH
b. Dependent Variable: MATHS

Reading the summary table for a simple regression

The sources of variance are clearly given as: the regression, the residual and their sum—the total. Sums of squares are the sums of squared deviations from the mean. The total Sum of Squares is the Sum of Squares for the DV. The regression Sum of Squares is calculated by subtracting the mean for the DV from the predicted value of the DV for each person, squaring the result and adding these squared values together (see Appendix XI for a worked example). The residual Sum of Squares is the sum of the squared differences between the predicted value of the DV and the actual value for each person; it can also be found by subtracting the sum of squares for the regression from the total Sum of Squares.

The degrees of freedom for the total are one fewer than the number of participants: $10 - 1 = 9$. The df for the regression is the number of IVs in the analysis, which in this case is 1. The residual df is found by subtracting the regression df from the total df: $9 - 1 = 8$.

Mean Squares (MS) are formed, as usual, by dividing the Sum of Squares by its appropriate df. The *F*-ratio is calculated by dividing the regression MS by the residual MS. The *p*-value can be found from standard *F*-tables using the appropriate two values for the degrees of freedom; in this case 1 and 8. As usual with ANOVA, the *p*-value will be for the equivalent of a two-tailed test. Therefore, we can conclude that English ability predicts a significant proportion of the variance in mathematical ability.

Links between correlation and simple regression

If we divide the Sum of Squares due to the regression by the total sum of squares this tells us the proportion of the overall variance in the DV that is accounted for by the IV in the regression. Multiplying the result by 100 gives the percentage variance accounted for by the regression.

$$\frac{1381.606}{1752.5} \times 100 = 78.84\%$$

This is the same figure (allowing for errors introduced by rounding up) as that found by squaring the correlation coefficient and multiplying the result by 100.

Other similarities between regression and correlation are explored in Appendix XI.

Given the close links between correlation and simple regression, much of the information that one of these analyses provides can be derived from the other. Therefore, unless you are interested in predicting the actual value of the DV from the IV, in psychology it is more usual to analyse the data solely by correlation when there is only one IV.

Multiple regression

Multiple regression can be seen as an extension of simple regression to situations where there is one dependent variable and more than one independent (or predictor) variable. (Incidentally, statisticians refer to regressing the DV onto the IVs.) In the mathematical ability example, we might measure a number of factors, such as IQ and socio-economic status as well as English ability and age. We could then see what combination of these variables best predicts mathematical ability. In this way we might be able to account for more of the variance in mathematical ability and thus have a better model which would allow us to predict it more accurately. A multiple regression is expressed both in terms of an equation that relates the dependent and independent variables and as a multiple correlation coefficient *R*.

Why is multiple regression necessary?

You might feel that it is enough simply to correlate a number of variables with mathematical ability and see which ones produce the highest correlation and retain them as measures you would wish to use to predict mathematical ability in the future. However, as the discussion of partial and semi-partial correlation in Chapter 19 demonstrated, there may be overlap among the IVs in the variance they explain in the DV. This means that without multiple regression we will not have a single mathematical model to predict mathematical ability. In addition, because of the possible overlap between IVs some may not add much, if anything, to our model: the variance they explain may already be explained by other variables. Knowing this would save taking an unnecessarily large number of measures from an individual when we want to predict his or her mathematical ability.

The equation for a multiple regression is an expansion of that for simple regression. If there were two IVs:

$$DV = a + b_1 \times IV_1 + b_2 \times IV_2$$

Thus if we were going to look at the relationship between mathematical ability and English ability and age, the equation would be:

$$\text{mathematical ability} = a + b_1 \times \text{English ability} + b_2 \times \text{age}$$

The regression analysis (with age in months) gives the following values:

$$\text{mathematical ability}$$

$$= 16.979 + 1.012 \times \text{English ability} - 0.107 \times \text{age}$$

Now, if we knew that a child scored 65 on the English test and was 162 months old (13.5 years), the model would predict:

$$\text{mathematical ability} = 16.979 + 1.012 \times 65 - 0.107 \times 162$$

$$= 65.425$$

This is a little farther from the actual figure of 70 than was predicted by English ability alone. It may seem odd that we now have a model that accounts for slightly more of the variance in the DV (79%) than previous models and yet makes a poorer prediction for a given individual. The point is that, although in this individual's case it is making a poorer prediction, over all the participants it is making a smaller error in prediction than the previous models. Let us look at the multiple correlation coefficient (R) and the Analysis of Variance:

Table 20.2 The summary table from a multiple regression with mathematical ability as the dependent variable and English ability and age as the independent variables

Model Summary[b]

Model	R	R Square	Adjusted R Square
1	.889[a]	.790	.729

a. Predictors: (Constant), AGE, ENGLISH
b. Dependent Variable: MATHS

ANOVA[b]

Model		Sum of Squares	df	Mean Square	F	Sig.
1	Regression	1383.705	2	691.852	13.132	.004[a]
	Residual	368.795	7	52.685		
	Total	1752.500	9			

a. Predictors: (Constant), AGE, ENGLISH
b. Dependent Variable: MATHS

R is given as 0.889, which is only slightly larger than the correlation coefficient for English and maths ($r = 0.888$). R^2 is shown as 0.790; to four decimal places it is 0.7896. We can use R^2 to find the proportion of variance accounted for in the same way that we used r^2. Thus, the proportion of variance in mathematical ability that is accounted for by English ability and age together is $0.7896 \times 100 = 78.96\%$. (As with simple regression, the percentage of variance accounted for can also be found by dividing the regression Sum of Squares by the total Sum of Squares: $(1383.705/1752.5) \times 100 = 78.96\%$.) This means that adding age into the equation has accounted for an additional $78.96 - 78.84 = 0.12\%$ of the variance in mathematical ability. This value of 0.12% or 0.0012 (as a proportion of variance) is the square of the semi-partial correlation of mathematical ability and age with English ability partialled out of age. From this we can view regression as giving us:

$$R^2_{\text{m.ea}} = r^2_{\text{me}} + r^2_{\text{m(a.e)}}$$

where $R_{\text{m.ea}}$ is the multiple correlation coefficient of the IVs English ability and age with the DV mathematical ability; r_{me} is the simple correlation of mathematical ability and English ability; $r_{\text{m(a.e)}}$ is the semi-partial correlation of mathematical ability and age with English ability partialled out of age (defined in Chapter 19).

If we added another IV—say socio-economic status (SES)—to the model then the additional variance would be the square of the semi-partial correlation of SES with mathematical ability when English ability and age have been partialled out of SES.

Adjusted R^2

The adjusted R^2 is an estimate of R^2 in the population and takes into account the sample size and the number of IVs; the smaller the sample and the larger the number of IVs the larger the adjustment. In my experience psychologists may show adjusted R^2 in the table of results but they rarely go on to refer to it. The equation for adjusted R^2 is given in Appendix XI.

Types of multiple regression

There are a number of ways of conducting a multiple regression. They differ in the way the IVs are selected to be put into the model.

Standard multiple regression

This involves simply putting all the independent variables into the model in one stage. It is most useful when you are trying to explain as much of the variance in the DV as possible and are not concerned about wasting effort on measures that add only a small amount of information.

Sequential (or hierarchical) multiple regression

This involves the researcher placing the IVs into the model in a prearranged order, which will be determined by the model which the researcher has. In this way an explicit model can be tested and it is possible to see how much variance in the DV is accounted for by certain IVs when one or more other variables are already in the model. In fact, I have already demonstrated a sequential regression. I put English ability into the model first and then age in a second stage. However, it would be more usual to conduct the analysis the other way around. Thus, you are more likely to put demographic details into the model first – e.g. age and gender – and then ask how much extra variance English ability can explain. In this way you find out how much additional variance is explained by a variable that could be subject to being manipulated once variables that can't be manipulated have been accounted for. In addition, it tells us whether variables that involve people taking a test or answering a range of questions (such as an attitude scale) add much information above that already gained from simply knowing their age and gender.

All sub-set multiple regression

This explores all possible combinations of IVs to see which combination is best. There are a number of criteria for assessing what constitutes the best combination. The technique is available on various computer packages but it is not generally recommended as a way of trying to produce a model. If we are using significance as our criterion for evaluating models then we have the problem of multiple testing and the increased danger of making a Type I error.

Statistical multiple regression

Sometimes these are also referred to as 'sequential techniques'. However, they involve the computer choosing the IVs to include in the model, according to some statistical criterion. They will attempt to find the solution that produces the combination of IVs that account for the maximum amount of variance in the dependent variable and will leave out of the equation those IVs that do not contribute significantly to the model. Like any procedure that hands the responsibility for decisions over to a computer, they are controversial and their use is only really appropriate when the researcher is exploring the data rather than testing a specific model.

There are three forms of statistical multiple regression: forward selection, backward deletion and stepwise.

Forward selection
Forward selection involves placing the variables one at a time into the model on the basis of which IV explains the most of the variance in the DV. Once the first IV has been placed into the model the remaining variables are assessed to see which explains the most of the remaining variance. This process continues until none of the remaining variables adds significantly to the model.

Backward deletion
Backward deletion puts all the variables into the model and then extracts the variable that contributes the least to the model to see whether there is a significant reduction in the variance explained. If removing that variable would not detract significantly from the model then it is removed.

Stepwise regression
Stepwise regression is like forward selection in that the variables are placed in the model, one at a time. However, after each new one is added to the model the contribution of each variable already in the model is reassessed and if an earlier one does not contribute significantly, it is removed.

Stepwise regression is considered the safest procedure of the three. Thus, I would recommend that if you are exploring the data for the solution that accounts for the maximum variance for a minimum of IVs then you should use stepwise regression. On the other hand, if you are testing an explicit model use what I am calling *sequential MR*.

The following is an example of stepwise regression with mathematical ability as the DV and English ability, age, SES and IQ as possible IVs. As will be shown later, the sample size at 10 should have been much larger. Table 20.3 shows the correlations between each of the pairs of variables.

Table 20.3 The correlation matrix for mathematical ability, English ability, age, SES and IQ

Correlations

	MATHS	ENGLISH	AGE	SES	IQ
MATHS	1.000				
ENGLISH	.888	1.000			
AGE	.748	.862	1.000		
SES	.056	−.328	−.394	1.000	
IQ	.564	.700	.626	−.390	1.000

The first step of the regression analysis identified English ability as the IV that explains the most variance. This stage in the analysis is the same as the simple regression reported earlier in the chapter.

The remaining three variables were assessed and SES was found to have the largest partial correlation with mathematical ability and so it was added to the model.

Table 20.4 The partial correlations between mathematical ability and the remaining IVs after the first step in the multiple regression analysis

Excluded Variables[c]

Model		Beta In	t	Sig.	Partial Correlation
1	AGE	−.068[a]	−.200	.847	−.075
	SES	.390[a]	3.527	.010	.800
	IQ	−.114[a]	−.475	.649	−.177

a. Predictors in the Model: (Constant), ENGLISH
c. Dependent Variable: MATHS

The remaining two variables were found to explain little of the remaining variance and so were rejected. English ability and SES account for 92.4% of the variance in mathematical ability; adding age and IQ would only have explained a further 0.3%.

TABLE 20.5 The second (and last) step of the stepwise multiple regression analysis with SES entered into the model

Model Summary

Model	R	R Square	Adjusted R Square	Std. Error of the Estimate
2	.961[b]	.924	.902	4.3680

b. Predictors: (Constant), ENGLISH, SES

Coefficients[a]

Model		Unstandardised Coefficients		Standardised Coefficients	t	Sig.
		B	Std. Error	Beta		
2	(Constant)	−14.7767	8.919		−1.657	.142
	ENGLISH	1.0856	.118	1.016	9.196	.000
	SES	4.7887	1.358	.390	3.527	.010

a. Dependent Variable: MATHS

Excluded Variables[c]

Model		Beta In	t	Sig.	Partial Correlation
2	AGE	.106[b]	.470	.655	.189
	IQ	.009[b]	.053	.959	.022

b. Predictors in the Model: (Constant), ENGLISH, SES
c. Dependent Variable: MATHS

Std Error is the standard error of the regression coefficient. The poorer the IV is as a predictor of the DV, the larger the standard error. In addition, the more correlated one IV is with the others in the model, the larger the standard error. The standard error of the regression coefficient can be used to find the statistical significance of the regression coefficient and a confidence interval for it (see Appendix XI for their calculation). The intercorrelation between IVs is discussed under multi-collinearity later in the chapter.

The *Standardised Coefficient* is explained later in the chapter.

From Table 20.5 we learn that the equation for mathematical ability is:

mathematical ability

$$= -14.7767 + 1.0856 \times \text{English ability} + 4.7887 \times \text{SES}$$

Accordingly, a person scoring 65 in the English test and having an SES of 4 will be predicted to have a score of 74.942 on the maths test. The person actually scored 70 on the maths test.

Interpreting a multiple regression

If you want to go beyond simply noting whether the regression accounts for a significant amount of the variance in the DV you can look at the size of the regression coefficients. Looking at the example of mathematical ability, what they mean is that the predicted value of mathematical ability would be raised by 1.086 units for every increase by one unit of English ability, if all other variables in the model were held constant. This is a rather odd idea because we know that the other variable—SES—correlates with English ability and thus would be unlikely to remain constant with changes in English ability.

There is danger in simply comparing the magnitude of the regression coefficients to see which independent variable is the best predictor of the dependent variable. The regression coefficient for SES is larger than that for English ability, yet we already know that English ability explains more of the variance in mathematical ability. The reason for this anomaly is that the magnitude of the regression coefficient is a function of the SD of that variable. A measure which solves this problem is the *standardised regression coefficient* (often denoted as β and called a *beta* coefficient).

A standardised regression coefficient is calculated by the following equation:

$$\beta = \frac{b \times SD_x}{SD_y}$$

where b is the regression coefficient for an IV; SD_x is the standard deviation of the same IV; SD_y is the standard deviation of the DV. When we look again at the summary table we see that the standardised coefficients tell a different story from the regression coefficients and now English ability is seen to contribute the most to the model, as we would expect.

In the case of stepwise regression it makes little sense to utilise the order in which an IV is entered into the model as a criterion for importance. As the description of the method should have made clear, the IV that is entered first could later be eliminated when other variables have been taken into consideration.

Each t-value is calculated from the b value and its standard error. They test the Null Hypothesis that the b is 0 in the population, that is that the IV predicts no variance in the DV. However, the probability tells us whether the particular IV would add significantly to the model if it were added to the model after all the other IVs that have been included in the model have already been entered. Thus we are told that SES adds significantly to the model ($p = 0.01$) even when English ability is already in the model.

The probability from the ANOVA table and the probabilities from the individual IVs tell us different things. The ANOVA tells us whether the overall model predicts a significant proportion of the variance in the DV. The individual probabilities tell us whether a particular IV adds significantly to the model, if it were added last. Thus, you can have an IV that is not considered significant but is part of a model that *is* significant. Also, because the individual probabilities tell us about what would happen if a given IV were added last, in a sequential or statistical model the b and probability will change from stage to stage in the analysis.

Multi-collinearity

Some authors prefer to use the term 'collinearity'. If some IVs intercorrelate too highly—say at 0.8 or higher—then this can make the predicted values more unstable. This is because of the way in which the regression coefficients are calculated. An additional problem is that the analysis can give the wrong impression that a given variable is not a good predictor of the DV simply because most of the variance that it could explain has already been accounted for by other variables in the model. Identifying multi-collinearity can be a problem as, even if no two variables correlate highly multi-collinearity can still be present because a combination of IVs might account for the variance in one of the IVs. In order to detect multi-collinearity, a number of statistics are available. Two common ones, which are directly related, are tolerance and VIF (variance inflation factor).

Tolerance
This is the proportion of variance in an IV that is not predicted by the other IVs. To find tolerance a multiple regression is conducted with the IV of interest treated as the DV which is then regressed on the other IVs. The R^2 from that regression is put into the following equation:

$$tolerance = 1 - R^2$$

High multi-collinearity would be shown by a large R^2 and so a small tolerance value would suggest multi-collinearity. A tolerance value of less than 0.1 is often given as the point when multi-collinearity is likely to be a problem as this would mean that 90% [0.9×100] of the variance in one IV can be explained by the other IVs.

VIF
This is found from the following equation:

$$variance\ inflation\ factor = \frac{1}{tolerance}$$

Therefore a large VIF suggests multi-collinearity. In keeping with the guidance for tolerance, a VIF that is larger than 10 is usually seen as problematic.

Table 20.6 shows the tolerance and VIF values for the regression when mathematical ability was regressed against English ability, age, SES and IQ. From Table 20.6 we can see that, according to the statistics provided there, there is not a problem of multi-collinearity.

Further checks on multi-collinearity can be found in Chatterjee and Hadi (1988), Belsley (1991) or Chatterjee, Hadi and Price (2000).

Table 20.6 Multi-collinearity statistics for the regression of mathematical ability on English ability, age, SES and IQ

Coefficients[a]

Model		Collinearity Statistics	
		Tolerance	VIF
1	ENGLISH	.212	4.720
	AGE	.243	4.112
	SES	.800	1.250
	IQ	.481	2.078

a. Dependent Variable: MATHS

Dealing with multi-collinearity

There are a number of ways in which multi-collinearity can be dealt with. The simplest is to remove one or more of the offending variables and re-run the multiple regression. It is also possible to create composite IVs by combining the problematic IVs either by adding them or by using principal components analysis, a technique that is similar to factor analysis but which, apart from a description in Chapter 21, is beyond the scope of this book. Interested readers should look at Stevens (2002) or Tabachnick & Fidell (2001).

Recommended sample size

In multiple regression there is a requirement to use a reasonable sample size in order to maximise the reliability of the result. However, various figures are proposed. Some writers suggest 15 per independent variable, others 10, others still 5 (though more for stepwise regression), while others argue that the number of participants should be 50 greater than the number of independent variables.

Another way to look at the necessary sample size is in terms of power (the likelihood of avoiding a Type II error). Cohen (1988) recommends power of at least 0.8. However, he also takes into account the effect size that you wish to detect.

Effect size and regression

A convenient measure of effect size is R^2, which tells us the proportion of variance accounted for in the DV and is the same measure as η^2, used as the effect size for ANOVA. Cohen (1988) uses a different effect size from the one I have employed. However, following his guidelines produces R^2 of approximately 0.02 as a small effect size, 0.13 as a medium effect size and 0.26 as a large effect size. You may notice that these are different from the sizes recommended for ANOVA, where the effect size is also a measure of the proportion of variance that is explained. Remember that Cohen has identified these sizes from reviewing the research that utilises each technique. Also remember that these are only guidelines, and that if, for the purposes of choosing a sample size for a study, you have a better estimate of the effect, always use that estimate in preference to these guidelines.

Power and regression

The power of regression is dependent not only on the alpha level set, the sample size and effect size, but also on the number of IVs in the model. Power tables for multiple regression are provided in Appendix XV.

Power analysis shows that if we were holding alpha at 0.05, had one IV in the model and wanted power of 0.8, then for a medium effect size you would need approximately 55 participants. However, when you have 10 independent variables, using power as the basis for choosing sample size, you would need around 120 participants in order to have the same power for a medium effect size. In addition, if a smaller effect size is involved then the sample size would need to be increased further. One way to improve the situation if you have a relatively small sample is again to use principal components analysis to reduce the number of IVs.

I would suggest that if you are exploring the statistical significance of the regression then you should choose the sample size on the basis of power calculations. However, if you are simply interested in the proportion of variance in the DV that is accounted for by the IV(s) then you should use the rule of at least 50 participants more than the number of IVs.

Diagnostic checks

There are certain checks that it is advisable to do to see whether the assumptions of the regression are tenable. A number involve examining the residuals.

Residuals

A residual is the difference between the predicted value for the DV and the actual value. Earlier it was shown that the predicted mathematical ability of an individual was 74.942 yet the actual score was 70. In this case, the residual would be $70 - 74.942 = -4.942$. Statistical packages offer versions of residuals that have been calculated and transformed in a number of ways; a number are described in Appendix XI. The one I recommend using is where they have been standardised by a transformation that gives them a mean of 0 and an SD of 1. This means that we can treat each residual in the same way that we use a z-value: namely to tell us how extreme such a value is. Accordingly, we can look at the standardised residuals to see whether any could be considered as outliers, which would need further investigation. Table 20.7 shows that none of the residuals, taken from the example analysis, are outside the range ±2.01 and are therefore within the normal range as they are not bigger than 3 SDs from the mean.

Although the residuals can be examined from this perspective, I wouldn't simply remove cases that have high standardised residuals. These are people that the model doesn't fit very well. Therefore, to remove them is to

Table 20.7 Maths ability, predicted maths ability, residuals and standardised residuals from the regression of mathematical ability on English ability and SES

Maths ability	Predicted MA	Residual	Std residual
50	49.081	.919	.210
40	42.121	−2.121	−.486
60	56.487	3.513	.804
50	50.613	−.613	−.140
70	74.942	−4.942	−1.131
60	59.490	.510	.117
75	76.221	−1.221	−.279
70	72.964	−2.964	−.679
85	76.221	8.779	2.010
75	76.860	−1.860	−.426

fit the people to the model. An additional problem, if using a standardised value of 3 as the criteria for an outlier, is that with a large sample you may easily have many people whose residuals are that high. One simple way to solve this would be to adjust the alpha level for samples greater than 50 (by dividing 0.05 by the sample size) and then only treating as an outlier those standardised residuals that were equal to or greater than the z-score that would achieve that level of significance. Thus, if the sample size were 100, then the two-tailed, adjusted alpha level would be 0.0005. Looking in Table A14.1 tells us that a z of 3.48 would be necessary to achieve that level of significance (for a two-tailed test) and thus we would only treat standardised residuals that were as big as or bigger than +3.48 or −3.48 as outliers.

A preferable check for outliers and possible influential data points is given later in the chapter. Nonetheless, residuals should be examined, via graphs, to check that they don't form a pattern.

Residual plots

There are two plots of residuals that we require. The first is to check that they are normally distributed (i.e. randomly distributed). We can do this either via a frequency histogram or via a normal quantile–quantile plot. The second type of check can be conducted by producing a scattergram between the predicted values of the dependent variable and the standardised residuals. This should show no obvious pattern and would thus demonstrate that the residuals are randomly distributed relative to the predicted values of the DV.

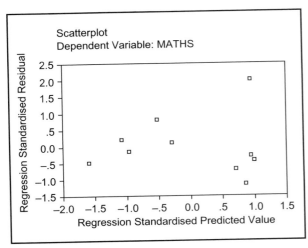

FIGURE 20.4 The plot of standardised predicted values and standardised residuals from the regression of mathematical ability on English ability and SES

To produce Figure 20.4 I have also standardised the predicted values. This plot shows no obvious relationship between the two measures. We will now examine the ways in which the plot could have suggested that the assumptions of regression have been violated.

Heterogeneous variance

Figure 20.5 is an example where there is greater variance of errors for the higher predicted values, which suggests that the model will be better at prediction for the lower values of the DV. *Homoscedasticity* is the term used to denote that a set of residuals have homogeneous variance and *heteroscedasticity* denotes that the residuals have heterogeneous variance – i.e. that they are not randomly distributed.

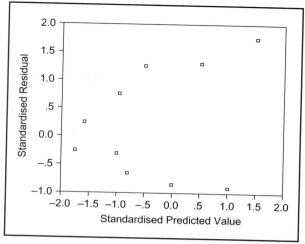

FIGURE 20.5 An example of heterogeneous variance in the residuals from a regression analysis

Curvilinearity

Figure 20.6 suggests that the model will under-estimate the middle values of the DV and over-estimate the more extreme values. Both forms of violation can be countered by adopting an appropriate transformation of the original data.

Leverage and influence

The outcome of a regression analysis can be influenced by outliers among the IVs. One measure of whether an individual person's data contain outliers is *leverage* (also known as *the hat element*). It assesses whether a person's set of scores across the IVs is a *multivariate* outlier. Thus, a person might not be an outlier on any single IV but the pattern of his or her scores across the IVs may be an outlier.

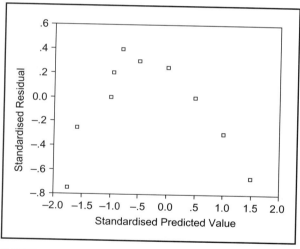

FIGURE 20.6 An example of curvilinear relationship between the residuals and the predicted values of the IV from a regression analysis

An additional measure that looks at how influential a given person's data are on the regression is Cook's distance. This is a measure of the degree to which outliers affect the regression and it takes into account a person's score on the DV as well as the IVs. Table 20.8 shows the Cook's distances and leverage scores for the regression.

Many authors provide rules of thumb for Cook's distance and leverage as to what constitute problematic cases; some of these are given in Appendix XI. A preferable method which other authors suggest is that

Table 20.8 The leverage and Cook's distance statistics for the regression with maths as the DV and ability at English and SES as the IVs

Participant	Cook's Distance	Leverage
1	.00572	.22986
2	.14449	.48592
3	.27161	.42154
4	.00326	.26711
5	.61223	.44381
6	.00176	.23041
7	.00850	.20593
8	.03498	.16059
9	.43977	.20593
10	.04975	.34890

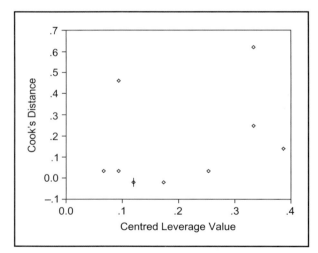

FIGURE 20.7 A scattergram of leverage and Cook's distance for the regression of mathematical ability on English ability and SES

problematic cases are better identified by plotting the leverage and Cook's distance scores against each other, as shown in Figure 20.7.

The scattergram shows that one person has a Cook's distance value that is markedly higher than the others. That person's leverage score is also on the high side relative to the others. In such a situation it is worth re-running the analysis but with such high scorers removed to see whether their removal makes any difference. Table 20.9 shows some of the output from the regression with maths as the variable to be predicted and English ability and SES as the predictors but with the person with high Cook's distance and leverage removed.

Comparing the two models, we see that removing that person's scores has made little difference to the results. The amount of variance accounted for has risen slightly, the model remains significant and the beta coefficients for English and SES do not change much and both remain significant. If removing such potentially influential scores does have a more marked effect on the results then it is important to report the results with and without those scores. This can demonstrate how the model is relatively unstable and how it can be affected by the removal of only a few participants. Other measures of leverage and influence exist and a number are offered by SPSS. These are described in Appendix XI.

Table 20.9 Regression of mathematical ability on English ability and SES with participant with high Cook's distance and leverage scores removed

Model Summary[b]

Model	R	R Square	Adjusted R Square	Std. Error of the Estimate
1	.973[a]	.947	.930	3.8652

a. Predictors: (Constant), SES, ENGLISH
b. Dependent Variable: MATHS

ANOVA[b]

Model		Sum of Squares	df	Mean Square	F	Sig.
1	Regression	1615.918	2	807.959	54.081	.000[a]
	Residual	89.638	6	14.940		
	Total	1705.556	8			

a. Predictors: (Constant), SES, ENGLISH
b. Dependent Variable: MATHS

Coefficients[a]

Model		Unstandardised Coefficients		Standardised Coefficients	t	Sig.
		B	Std. Error	Beta		
1	(Constant)	−21.234	8.745		−2.428	.051
	ENGLISH	1.147	.110	1.085	10.390	.000
	SES	6.398	1.525	.438	4.196	.006

a. Dependent Variable: MATHS

The order of checks on the data and model

Some of the checks can be done before the analysis is conducted, while others are provided as part of the output from the multiple regression. The preliminary checks to conduct are the usual univariate and bivariate ones. Look at the distribution of the variables, in particular the DV. Next plot scattergrams between the DV and individual IVs and between pairs of IVs to check that they are not curvilinear. You could also look at the bivariate correlations to check for collinearity; remembering that this is not the only check for this problem. Then, as part of the regression save the leverage and Cook's distance values and create a scattergram between them. Identifying any problematic cases may solve later problems. Check for multi-collinearity using tolerance or VIF. Finally, check the pattern of the residuals.

Where possible it is a good idea to check the validity of the model you have found. Otherwise there is always a possibility that what you have found is only true for the data you have collected.

Model validation

We obviously want to know how good the predictions are from the model; that is, can they be generalised to other data? I will mention two ways.

Data splitting

If you have a large enough sample you can perform the regression analysis on half the data and then see how well the predictions for that model account for the remaining data. Statistical programs, including SPSS, can be used to select a random subsample of your data for this purpose.

The PRESS statistic

Often you will not have enough data to carry out data splitting and so you can use another technique—PRESS—which repeats the regression by deleting one item and recalculating the predicted value for that item from the remaining data. From this it is possible to calculate a version of R^2 that is based on the PRESS statistic which, if markedly different from the original R^2, would question the latter's reliability. This facility is no longer available in newer versions of SPSS.

Reporting a multiple regression

Start by reporting the correlation matrix of the DV and all the IVs, as shown in Table 20.3. Next give precise details of the type of multiple regression you have conducted and, if you are using sequential analysis, the order in which you entered the variables into the model and the rationale for that order. Thus if I were describing my sequential analysis I would say: *A sequential multiple regression was conducted in two stages with mathematical ability as the variable to be predicted. In the first stage English ability was entered. In the second age was entered.* Describe any problems that there were with the data, such as outliers or influential data points, non-linear relationships, multi-collinearity and heterogeneity in the residuals, and explain what action you took to circumvent the problems. Sometimes it is useful to conduct the analysis with and without the data from particular potentially problematic cases to see whether their inclusion affects the results.

The format for the rest of the results depends largely on the type of analysis you have conducted. Nonetheless, you should include details about the overall model and the individual IVs. For the overall model the necessary details are the R^2, F-ratio with degrees of freedom (for regression and residual) and probability. Thus I would write for the first stage: *With English ability in the model a significant proportion of variance in mathematical ability was accounted for, $R^2 = .7885$, $F_{(1,8)} = 29.80$, $p = .001$.* With a sequential analysis I would report how much variance was added and how much overall variance was accounted for, at each stage. The details for individual IVs should include the *b*, beta, *t* and probability. In addition, a confidence interval for *b* would be useful but if you don't include that then you should report the standard error. If you are using a statistical method (forward, backward or stepwise) then I don't think it is useful to report all these details for each step. However, if you are using sequential analysis then you may want to include that amount of detail, possibly in a table.

The similarity between ANOVA and multiple regression

Except for the discussions of χ^2 and point-biserial correlation, I have maintained the distinction between techniques that are designed to test for differences and techniques that test for relationships. This is a useful distinction to have when you are trying to learn the techniques; as we know, classification helps memory. However, psychologists are often criticised by statisticians for their ignorance of the fact that one technique underlies both approaches. I want to close this chapter with a demonstration that makes this point, by showing that ANOVA is a special case of multiple regression.

You will recall that regression looks at the *relationship* between one dependent variable and one or more independent variables. On the other hand, ANOVA looks at the *difference* between levels of one or more independent variables. The levels are categories, for example *male* or *female*. However, statisticians have pointed out that these are no more than what they term *dummy variables* entered into a regression analysis.

In Chapter 16 an experiment was described in which three groups of participants were asked to recall a list of words. Each group was in a different mnemonic condition—pegwords, method of loci and a control group in which no strategy was used. The data were analysed using a one-way between-subjects ANOVA, the summary table for which is reproduced in Table 20.10.

Table 20.10 A summary table for a one-way between-subjects ANOVA comparing recall under the three mnemonic techniques

Source	Sum of Squares	df	Mean Square	F-test	p
Between Groups	30.467	2	15.233	5.213	0.0122
Within Groups	78.9	27	2.922		
Total	109.367	29			

However, dummy variables can be used to distinguish the three groups (see Table 20.11).

Table 20.11 The data for the recall by mnemonic strategy with dummy variables used to identify the groups

Participant	Group	Recall	Dummy variable 1	Dummy variable 2
1	loci	10	1	0
2	loci	8	1	0
3	loci	11	1	0
4	loci	9	1	0
5	loci	12	1	0
6	loci	10	1	0
7	loci	7	1	0
8	loci	11	1	0
9	loci	8	1	0
10	loci	10	1	0
11	pegword	11	0	1
12	pegword	7	0	1
13	pegword	9	0	1
14	pegword	10	0	1
15	pegword	8	0	1
16	pegword	6	0	1
17	pegword	12	0	1
18	pegword	9	0	1
19	pegword	10	0	1
20	pegword	7	0	1
21	control	10	0	0
22	control	7	0	0
23	control	7	0	0
24	control	9	0	0
25	control	5	0	0
26	control	6	0	0
27	control	8	0	0
28	control	5	0	0
29	control	7	0	0
30	control	8	0	0

Dummy coding is achieved by coding the fact that someone had a given characteristic by a 1 and coding the lack of that characteristic by a 0. Thus, we can use dummy variable 1 to tell us who was in the method of loci condition, and so those in that group are coded as 1 while the others are coded as 0. Then dummy variable 2 tells us who was in the pegword condition. Notice that there is one fewer dummy variable than the number of levels of the IV. This is because with dummy variable 1 and dummy variable 2 we know who was in the final group—the control group. They are the people who were not in either of the other two groups. Thus, people in the method of loci condition are coded as 1 on the first variable and 0 on the other, people in the pegword group as 0 1 and the control group as 0 0.

By treating the dummy variables as independent variables, the same design can be analysed as a multiple regression (see Table 20.12).

Table 20.12 Summary of the regression analysis of recall of words by three groups

Model Summary

Model	R	R Square	Adjusted R Square	Std. Error of the Estimate
1	.528	.279	.225	1.71

ANOVA[b]

Model		Sum of Squares	df	Mean Square	F	Sig.
1	Regression	30.467	2	15.233	5.213	.012[a]
	Residual	78.900	27	2.922		
	Total	109.367	29			

a. Predictors: (Constant), dummy variable 2, dummy variable 1
b. Dependent Variable: RECALL

Note that the regression Sum of Squares is the same as the between-groups Sum of Squares from the one-way ANOVA and that the residual Sum of Squares is the same as the within-groups Sum of Squares. In addition, the value for η^2 in the ANOVA (0.279) is the same as R^2 from the regression. Finally I can explain why I prefer η^2 to partial η^2 as a measure of effect size in ANOVA. The former is the same as the increase in R^2 which would be achieved by putting an additional IV into a multiple regression.

Thus we can see that ANOVA can be treated as an example of regression analysis. Both are models that are described by what is termed *the General Linear Model*, as are three techniques described in the next chapter: Analysis of Covariance (ANCOVA), Multivariate ANOVA (MANOVA) and Multivariate ANCOVA (MANCOVA). Those wishing to read further will find good accounts in Howell (2002) and Tabachnick and Fidell (2001). The moral to be drawn from this point is that looking for differences, as per ANOVA, and looking for relationships, as per regression, are two ways of viewing the same thing. We can ask whether there is a difference in recall between the three mnemonic groups or we can ask whether there is a relationship between the type of mnemonic strategy employed and recall.

Given the similarities between ANOVA and multiple regression, it is important to point out that, as with ANOVA, interactions can be tested in multiple regression. Thus, with the example where mathematical ability is being predicted by age and English ability we can ask whether the interaction between age and English ability adds to the amount of variance of mathematical ability that can be explained. However, unlike with ANOVA, testing an interaction in multiple regression can be a relatively complex process and so I discuss it in Appendix XI.

Summary

Relationships between variables can be explored using regression analysis. Simple regression is used when only one independent variable is involved and multiple regression when more than one IV is included. Such analysis performs two functions. One function is to identify how much of the variance in the DV can be explained by variation in the IV(s). A second function is to build a model of how the DV is related to the IV(s) and so allow the DV to be predicted for specific values of the IV(s).

Multiple regression is sometimes considered to be an example of a multivariate statistic. The next chapter briefly introduces and explains the use of other forms of multivariate statistics.

MULTIVARIATE ANALYSIS

Introduction

The strict definition of multivariate analysis is that more than one dependent variable is involved in the analysis. However, I have included four techniques that do not fulfil this definition—analysis of covariance, log-linear modelling, logit analysis and logistic regression; in order to conduct them you will need to read more about them than there is space to devote to them here.

The techniques described in this chapter are less well understood by most psychologists than many of those covered in earlier chapters. This is partly because they are often not covered in an undergraduate research methods course, except possibly as an advanced option in the final year. To understand how they are calculated involves a level of mathematics that many undergraduates do not possess and the majority of the techniques are not covered in many undergraduate texts. In addition, the results of these techniques are sometimes more difficult to interpret. These factors may contribute to the fact that such techniques are much less frequently used than the univariate and bivariate techniques described in earlier chapters.

However, another contributing factor is that a large number of participants should be used for the results of multivariate techniques to have any validity. For example, for every predictor variable included in a discriminant analysis there should be at least 20 participants.

The role of this chapter is to make the reader aware of the function of each of the techniques described and to warn about the constraints on their use. In this way you can judge when they will be useful to you. In addition, it will enable you to interpret and criticise others' research that has used these techniques. This chapter is not designed to enable you to conduct the techniques. Those who wish to employ the techniques should read Stevens (2002), Tabachnick and Fidell (2001) or the more specific references given in this chapter.

Why use multivariate techniques?

Many multivariate techniques have univariate or bivariate counterparts. When we have more than one dependent variable there are at least two advantages of using a multivariate technique rather than repeating a univariate equivalent for each DV. These advantages are the same as for preferring multi-way ANOVA over a series of one-way ANOVAs or even *t*-tests. Firstly, we do not conduct numerous analyses which would increase the likelihood that we will achieve statistically significant results, even when the data we are analysing are not subject to any real effect. Secondly, we can see how different variables behave in combination, instead of looking at them in isolation.

I have classified the techniques according to whether they are used to seek differences between levels of independent variables or to seek relationships between variables. As I demonstrated in the last chapter, this separation is artificial. Nonetheless, it is a convenient fiction, as it does reflect the type of question we are likely to be asking when we choose a particular statistical technique to analyse our data.

Seeking a difference

Log-linear modelling for categorical data

Log-linear modelling can be seen as an extension of χ^2 analysis of contingency tables. Recall that χ^2 is used when you have categorical data in one or two dimensions.

There are occasions when a simple two-way classification is not enough and we may wish to look at a three-way or more-than-three-way analysis. For example, we may wish to see whether any differences in proportions of smokers have to do with gender, whether parents smoked or both. Hence, log-linear modelling is sometimes referred to as *multi-way frequency analysis*.

Log-linear analysis allows us to compare a number of models to see which best fits the data. Given three variables there are a number of possible models from which we have to choose. In the smoking example there can be any combination of the single variables, interactions between pairs of the variables and the three-way interaction. Take my word for the fact that there are over 15 possible models. I am going to describe just one of many ways of performing a log-linear analysis. The design is called *hierarchical*, in that it assumes that if there are interactions in the model then the main effects will also be present. Thus, if there were an interaction between gender and parental smoking, the effects of gender and of smoking, singly, would also be in the model. Remember, however, from ANOVA, that it is possible to have a statistically significant interaction without having a statistically significant main effect. The method the analysis employs is described as a *backward solution* where it starts with the full model, entailing all possible factors, then selectively removes elements until the optimal solution is found. This can be seen as analogous to the backward solution to multiple regression.

The data to be analysed by log-linear modelling are given in Table 21.1. The log-linear model that was found to fit the data best was one that included the interactions *gender by parents' smoking* and *participant's smoking by parents' smoking*. Left out were the three-way interaction and the interaction between *participant's smoking and gender*. The model was tested statistically,

Table 21.1 The numbers of males and females who smoke and whether their parents smoke

| | Gender of Participant | | | |
| | Male | | Female | |
Parental Smoking	Smoker	Non-smoker	Smoker	Non-smoker
Yes	30	6	40	6
No	12	68	6	32

with the result that $\chi^2 = 0.225$, df = 2, $p = 0.894$. Note that in this case we are testing the fit of a model and not a Null Hypothesis. Thus, if it had been significant we would have had to reject the model. This result can be interpreted as showing that any link between gender and smoking is explicable in terms of the links between parental smoking and participant smoking and between parental smoking and participant's gender. See Agresti (1996, 2002) or Wickens (1989) for details of how to conduct log-linear modelling.

Hotelling's T²

Hotelling's T^2 can be viewed as an extension of the t-test to situations where there are two levels of an independent variable but more than one dependent variable. For example, I might be comparing the effects of two therapeutic techniques. However, instead of looking at only one outcome measure, I might look at how satisfied clients were with the treatment, how much they felt in control of their lives and how anxious they were.

Multivariate Analysis of Variance (MANOVA)

MANOVA is the extension of ANOVA to situations where there is more than one dependent variable and either (a) one independent variable with more than two levels or (b) more than one independent variable. Thus, I might compare three or more therapeutic techniques on a number of outcomes. It can also be used to conduct within-subjects ANOVA as it avoids problems over lack of sphericity.

Controlling for covariates

When a difference is being sought between levels of independent variables but it is suspected that another variable may be affecting the situation, it is possible to control for that variable and so minimise the influence that it is contributing to the variance in the data.

Analysis of Covariance (ANCOVA)

Analysis of Covariance is similar to ANOVA except that it takes into account variables that may be affecting the results but are not the main ones under consideration. There are at least two occasions when ANCOVA can be used. Firstly, it is used in situations where a variable may be confounded with the independent variable and might affect the dependent variable. Secondly, it is used when a test–retest design is used to allow for initial differences between groups that may mask differences in improvements.

As an example of the first type of ANCOVA, imagine I wish to compare the reading age of children in three schools: all-girls, all-boys and co-educational. Thus, I have one independent variable: *school type*, with three levels, and I have one dependent variable: *reading age*. Typically I would analyse this as a one-way ANOVA:

Table 21.2 A one-way between-subjects ANOVA comparing the reading ages of pupils from an all-girls, an all-boys and a co-educational school

Source	Sum of Squares	df	Mean Square	F	p
Between Groups	49.717	2	24.858	3.887	0.0328
Within Groups	172.65	27	6.394		
Total	222.367	29			

The ANOVA suggests a difference in the reading ages between the schools. However, supposing I knew that reading age was correlated with IQ in my sample ($r = 0.641$). It would be sensible to re-examine the reading ages while controlling for IQ to see whether differences between the schools remained; ANCOVA will do this.

Table 21.3 Analysis of covariance comparing the reading ages of pupils from an all-girls, an all-boys and a co-educational school, controlling for IQ

Source of Variation	Sum of Squares	df	Mean Square	F	p
Covariates IQ	91.289	1	91.289	19.866	0.000
Main Effects SCHOOL	11.600	2	5.800	1.262	0.300
Residual	119.478	26	4.595		
Total	222.367	29	7.668		

The ANCOVA shows that there is no longer a statistically significant difference between schools and that the covariate, IQ, accounted for the difference shown in the original one-way ANOVA. ANCOVA is the same as sequential multiple regression, with the covariate added at one stage and the IV added next. It tells us whether our IV adds significantly to the model when the covariate is already in the model.

Multivariate Analysis of Covariance (MANCOVA)

MANCOVA is the multivariate extension of ANCOVA. For example, I might look at the reading ability and the mathematical ability of children in the three school types, while controlling for IQ.

Identifying the basis of difference

Discriminant analysis

Discriminant analysis can be seen as the obverse of Hotelling's T^2, and MANOVA. It is used in two situations: (a) when a difference is presumed in a categorical (or classificatory) variable and more than one predictor variable is used to identify the nature of that difference or (b) when a set of predictor variables is being explored to see whether participants can be classified into categories on the basis of differences on the predictor variables. Huberty (1994) uses the term *descriptive discriminative analysis* (DDA) to describe the former, an example of which would be where two cultures are asked to rate a number of descriptions of people on the dimension of intelligence. Imagine that you were comparing British and Japanese people on the way they rated the intelligence of five hypothetical people whose descriptions you provided. Each hypothetical person had to be rated on the dimension, which ranged from *Intelligent* to *Unintelligent*. Thus, the classificatory variable was culture and the predictor variables were the ratings supplied for each of the hypothetical people.

Discriminant analysis would allow you to see whether the profiles of ratings that the two cultures gave you differed significantly. If they did then you can explore further to find out what was contributing to the difference.

Huberty (1994) describes the second approach as *predictive discriminative analysis* (PDA). An example of its use would be if an organisation wanted to distinguish those who would be successful in training from those who would be unsuccessful on the basis of their profiles on a personality test. If the analysis achieved its aim, successful trainees would have similar profiles and would differ from the unsuccessful trainees. The ways in which the profiles of the two groups differed could then be used to screen applicants for training to decide who is likely to be successful.

Exploring relationships

When we look for relationships between variables there are two basic ways in which we can do this. Firstly, as with correlation and regression, we can seek any relationships between the measures we have taken—our *observed* variables. This assumes that we have measured our variables directly, and implicitly that the measures used were not subject to any error. Alternatively, we can see our measures as indicators of some higher-order variables—*latent* variables. Thus, more than one of our observed variables might be measuring the same latent variable.

Relationships among observed variables

Logit analysis

Logit analysis is the equivalent of multiple regression but with categorical data. For example, you may want to find out how well the dependent variable smoking is predicted by gender and whether parents and/or friends smoked.

Logistic regression

Logistic regression can be seen as a more versatile version of logit analysis in which the restrictions on the levels of measurement are not as severe. Thus, the predictor variables do not have to be categorical and although there is an assumption that the dependent variable is discrete, it is possible to recode other variables so that they form a discrete scale. In addition, prior to analysis, the independent variables are recoded as dichotomous, dummy variables, as shown in the last chapter. The parallels that logistic regression has with multiple regression are many. It is possible to put all the IVs into the model—using direct entry—to specify the order—in sequential analysis—or to hand over the responsibility to the computer using backward, forward or stepwise regression.

Logistic regression can also be used in a similar way to discriminant analysis in that it can attempt to classify participants into their original categories to see how accurate it is at predicting group membership. Probably because of its versatility and the inclusion of more of its features in computer packages it is increasing in popularity and may even replace discriminant analysis. See Agresti (1996, 2002) or Hosmer and Lemeshow (2000) for details of how to conduct logit analysis and logistic regression.

Cluster analysis

Cluster analysis assumes that the elements, say participants, can be classified into some form of hierarchy. It starts by forming groups of participants that are the closest on some dimension (or combination of dimensions) and then forms combinations (or clusters) of those groups and continues to form higher-order combinations until all the elements are in one cluster. For example, I might be interested in classifying patients who had given me scores on a number of tests. The technique is sometimes employed by those using repertory grids derived from Kelly's personal construct theory (see Chapter 6). It allows the researcher to see whether the elements (for example people) that are being evaluated by a person form clusters based on the constructs attributed to them. In this way an analyst might find out the sort of people who are considered by the person to be similar to one of his or her parents. Whereas discriminant analysis starts with knowledge of group membership and looks for the combination of measures that distinguish the groups, cluster analysis looks for possible groups on the basis of the measures. In fact, discriminant analysis is sometimes used to explore further the nature of the groupings that have been identified by cluster analysis.

Canonical correlation

Canonical correlation is an extension of multiple regression to situations where there is more than one dependent variable and more than one independent variable. For example, I might look at the correlation between A-Level, locus of control, achievement motivation and various measures of intelligence as IVs and the results for different courses that each student took at university as the DVs. Unlike multiple regression, because there is more than one DV, there is more than one possible relationship between the IVs and DVs that might be identified.

Path analysis

Path analysis is sometimes referred to as 'hierarchical multiple regression'. It allows researchers to look at the relationships between variables both directly and indirectly. Whereas multiple regression looks at how well a set of IVs can be used to predict a single DV, path analysis can have the same variable acting as a DV at one stage in the model and as an IV in another part of the model. In the simple model shown in Figure 21.1, personality and IQ are seen as predicting a person's previous employment record. In addition they predict a person's present employment performance both directly and via a person's previous employment. Thus, one regression analysis has previous employment as a DV and personality and IQ as IVs, while a second regression has present employment as a DV with personality, IQ and previous employment as the IVs. It is usual to put what are termed *path coefficients* on each of the paths. These are usually standardised regression coefficients and so give an idea of the relative importance of given paths in the prediction process.

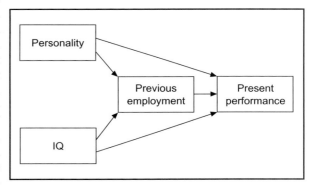

FIGURE 21.1 A path analysis of a model of the relationships between personality, IQ, previous employment and present employment

A danger of path analysis is that researchers will forget what they have been told about correlational techniques, namely, that we cannot identify cause-and-effect relationships. There is a temptation to see the arrow in a path diagram as suggesting a direction of cause. As with regression, it is only telling you about the degree to which one variable can be used to predict another.

Seeking latent variables

There are two basic ways in which we can seek latent (unobserved) variables. Firstly, and at present more commonly, we hand the responsibility over to the computer and ask it to explore the variables to see whether it can identify any latent variables that could explain the relationships among our observed variables. Alternatively we can test a theoretical model by asking the computer whether the latent variables that we assume exist do a good job of explaining the relationships between our observed variables. The problem with the first—*exploratory* techniques—is that they can capitalise on chance and produce models that may only reflect relationships in the particular set of data. The second—*confirmatory* techniques—are preferable because they explicitly test a theory rather than rely on the computer to generate it. Nonetheless, as long as exploratory techniques are treated purely as exploratory and further data collection will follow to confirm the results of the exploration they are perfectly legitimate.

Multidimensional scaling

Multidimensional scaling (MDS) is designed to investigate similarities between entities to try to see whether a set of entities can best be described as lying on two or more dimensions. For example, if I had 20 wines and I asked participants to compare them in pairs and rate how similar they were I would have 190 judgements for each participant. I could then run an MDS program on the data. The result might be that I had two dimensions, one of dryness/sweetness and the other ranging from white to red.

As an example with some real data I have taken the mileage between 10 different cities in England and run an MDS program on the data. The result is the following:

FIGURE 21.2 The results of a multi-dimensional scaling of the distances between a number of English cities

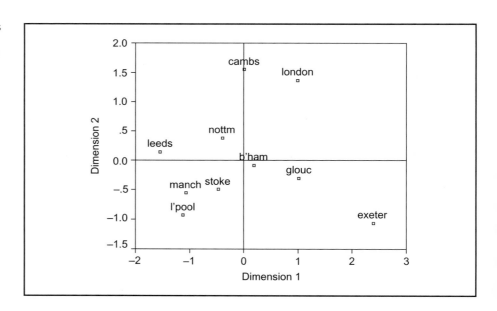

At first this seems to be wrong, in that Cambridge is shown as being north of Manchester. However, this is because the computer was asked to find the dimensions; it was not told about the concepts North and South. Turn

the page through 90 degrees clockwise. Now you can see that Liverpool, Manchester and Stoke have been placed in the North West, Gloucester and Exeter in the South West, Leeds and Nottingham in the North East, Cambridge and London in the South East, and Birmingham in the Midlands. The relationship between this model and the map of England is not perfect but then the original data were based on the road network, not on straight distances. This analysis may not seem very earth-shattering but it does demonstrate that although I did not give the dimensions to the program, it discovered them.

Principal components analysis

Principal components analysis allows you to explore the interrelationships between a number of variables to see whether there are a smaller number of higher-order factors (or components) that account for the pattern of intercorrelations between a set of observed variables. In other words, to see whether the pattern of responses of participants suggests that certain variables are measuring a similar factor or latent variable, while other variables are measuring other factors.

For example, if you were interested in the nature of mathematical ability, you might give a group of participants a battery of tests in mathematics ranging from tests of ability to perform simple calculations, through the ability to interpret graphs, to tests of algebra and calculus. Principal components analysis allows you to test whether participants have a similar profile of ability on all the tests, which would suggest a unitary mathematical ability, or whether there is a pattern that suggests that there exists more than one type of mathematical ability: for example, those that entail calculation, those that involve more abstract concepts and those that involve spatial reasoning.

Figure 21.3 shows the idealised results of a principal components analysis conducted on a test that contained six mathematical questions. It has identified three components or latent variables (notice that the variables that were measured—the questions—are shown in rectangular boxes while the latent variables are in circles; this is a standard convention).

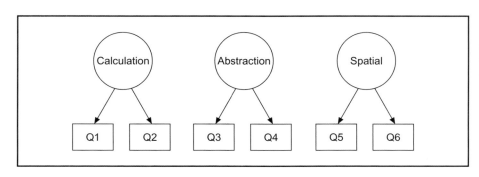

FIGURE 21.3 The results of a principal components analysis on six mathematical questions

Factor analysis

Factor analysis can be seen as an extension of principal components analysis (PCA) that makes different assumptions about the possible patterns between variables. It is quite a controversial technique the use of which has contributed to disagreements among researchers, for example, in research over the nature of intelligence. One anecdote should give a flavour of the controversial nature of the technique. The author asked a mathematician, who was teaching a statistics course, whether he was going to cover factor analysis. He said that he would not cover it as he did not believe in it. It is difficult to imagine a similar response when asking about any other mathematical procedure, for example, algebra.

Both factor analysis and principal components analysis require the researcher to make certain decisions about how the analysis should be conducted and these will affect the results of the analysis. Thus, anyone reporting such analyses should report the options they chose for *their* analysis. Without such information the reader does not know how the results were arrived at. This is important because it could affect as fundamental an issue as how many factors or components were chosen.

PCA, unlike factor analysis, maintains the information such that the correlations between the original variables can be completely reconstructed from the interrelationships among the factors. It includes all the variance in the scores, including that which is unique to a variable and error variance. As such, PCA is summarising the variance in the variables into a (possibly smaller) set of components. Factor analysis, on the other hand, only attempts to account for variance that is shared between variables, under the assumption that such variables are indicators of latent variables or factors. For more on factor analysis see Comrey and Lee (1992).

Structural equation modelling (SEM)

Structural equation modelling allows researchers to perform confirmatory analysis—that is, explicitly to test a theoretical model. It allows them to do this for a number of the techniques described above, individually or in combination. In addition, it allows you to assume that your observed measures could contain an element of error. It can also be used to combine a number of the other techniques in one model.

Figure 21.4 shows how the previous path analysis can be extended so that instead of involving only measured variables it now contains the latent variables that are believed to be being measured by the observed variables. This model combines path analysis (which, if you remember, can be the result of a series of regression analyses) and factor analysis.

Specialist statistical packages are available for analysing structural equation modelling, such as AMOS, LISREL and EQS. They can also be used for path analysis. For more information on structural equation modelling see Schumaker and Lomax (1996), the chapter on the subject in Tabachnick and Fidell (2001), Kline (1998) or, if using AMOS, Byrne (2001).

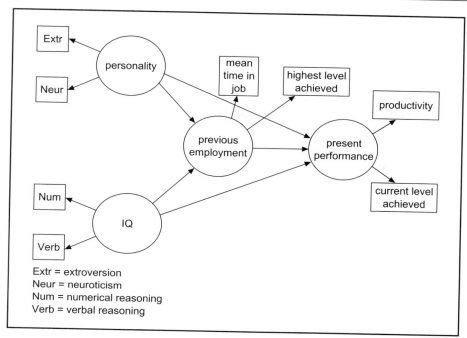

FIGURE 21.4 A structural equation model relating personality, IQ previous and present employment

Extr = extroversion
Neur = neuroticism
Num = numerical reasoning
Verb = verbal reasoning

Summary

There are a number of multivariate techniques that extend the analytic techniques given in the rest of the book to cover situations in which more than one dependent variable is included or to other more complex data sets. They are more complicated to conduct and to interpret than the other techniques and they involve more decisions about how the data will be treated. Such decisions can either be made by the researcher or by a computer program. They can be subject to inappropriate use or they may capitalise on chance

Table 21.4 Summary of multivariate techniques used for exploring differences

DV	Predictor variables	Covariates	Test
1	1+	yes	ANCOVA
>1	1 (2 levels)	–	Hotelling's T^2
>1	1+	–	MANOVA
>1	1+	yes	MANCOVA
1 (nominal)	>1 (nominal)	–	Log-linear modelling
1	1+	–	Discriminant analysis

Table 21.5 Summary of multivariate techniques used to explore relationships between variables

DV	Predictor variables	Latent variables?	Test
1 (nominal)	>1 (nominal)	–	Logit analysis
1	>1	–	Logistic regression
>1	–	–	Cluster analysis
>1	>1	–	Canonical correlation Path analysis
>1	–	yes confirmatory	Principal component analysis Exploratory and factor analysis MDS
>1	>1	yes	Structural equation modelling

and give a solution that is only applicable to the given data and does not provide a reliable model. The particular decisions made, either by researcher or computer, should be fully reported, in order that a reader may put the results in the context of those decisions. They generally require a much larger sample size, both for power and to produce a reliable analysis, than their equivalent univariate technique.

The next chapter describes how to conduct a meta-analysis, which is a quantitative method for combining the results from related studies to produce a general measure of effect size and of probability.

Meta-analysis

Introduction

A meta-analysis is a quantitative equivalent of a narrative literature review. It has three major advantages over a narrative review. Firstly, it allows the reviewer to quantify the trends that are contained in the literature by combining the effect sizes and combining the probabilities that have been found in a number of studies. Secondly, by combining the results of a number of studies the power of the statistical test is increased. In this case, a number of non-significant findings that all show the same trend, may, when combined, prove to be significant. Thirdly, the process of preparing the results of previous research for a meta-analysis forces the reviewer to read the studies more thoroughly than would be the case for a narrative review.

This chapter describes the various stages through which a meta-analysis is conducted. The necessary equations to conduct a meta-analysis are given in Appendix XIII where a worked example of each stage is given. The example is based on a meta-analysis of chronic pelvic pain (McGowan, Clark-Carter & Pitts, 1998).

Choosing the topic of the meta-analysis

As with any research you need to decide on the particular area on which you are going to concentrate. In addition, you will need a specific hypothesis that you are going to test with the meta-analysis. However, initially the exact nature of the hypothesis may be unspecified, only to be refined once you have seen the range of research.

Identifying the research

The next phase of a meta-analysis, as with a narrative review, is to identify the relevant research. This can be done by using the standard abstracting systems such as *PsychINFO*, *Psychological Abstracts* or the *Social Science Citation Index*. The papers that are collected by these means can yield further papers from their reference lists. Another source of material and of people with interests in the research field can be the Internet. In addition, the meta-analyst can write to authors who are known to work in the area to see whether they have any studies, as yet unpublished, the results of which they would be willing to share.

This process will help to show the complexity of the area. It will show the range of designs that have been employed, such as which groups have been used as control groups and what age ranges have been considered: whether children or adults have been employed. For example, in studies of the nature of pelvic pain, a variety of comparison groups have been employed. Comparisons have been made between women who have pelvic pain but no discernible cause and those with some identifiable physical cause. In addition, those with pelvic pain have been compared with those with other forms of chronic pain and with those who have no chronic pain.

The collection of papers will also show what measures have been taken: that is, what dependent variables have been used. For example, in the pelvic pain research measures have ranged from anxiety and depression to experience of childhood sexual abuse.

Choosing the hypotheses to be tested

Once the range of designs and measures has been ascertained it is possible to identify the relevant hypothesis or hypotheses that will be tested in the meta-analysis. Frequently, more than one dependent variable is employed in a single piece of research. The meta-analyst has the choice of conducting meta-analyses on each of the dependent variables or choosing some more global definition of the dependent variable that will allow more studies to be included in each meta-analysis. For example, the experience of childhood sexual abuse and of adult sexual abuse could be combined under the heading of experience of sexual abuse at any age. Such decisions are legitimate as long as the analyst makes them explicit in the report of the analysis.

In each meta-analysis, there has to be a directional hypothesis that is being tested. For, if the direction of effect were ignored in each study then results that pointed in one direction would be combined with results that pointed in the opposite direction and so suggest a more significant finding than is warranted. In fact, positive and negative effects should tend to cancel each other out. By 'direction of the finding' I do not mean whether the results support the overall hypothesis being tested, by being statistically significant, but whether the results have gone in the direction of the hypothesis or in the opposite direction. Whether the original researchers had a directional hypothesis is irrelevant; it is the meta-analyst's hypothesis that determines the direction.

You should draw up criteria that will be used to decide whether a given study will be included in the meta-analysis. For example, in the case of chronic pelvic pain, the generally accepted definition requires that the sufferer has had the condition for at least six months. Therefore, papers that did not apply this way of classifying their participants were excluded from the meta-analysis.

Extracting the necessary information

For each measure the analyst wants to be able to identify the number of participants in each group, a significance level for the results, an effect size and a direction of the finding. Unfortunately, it will not always be possible, directly, to find all this information. In this case, further work will be entailed.

It is good practice to create a coding sheet on which you record, for each paper, the information you have extracted from it. This should include details of design, sample size and summary and inferential statistics.

Dealing with inadequately reported studies

There are a number of factors that render the report of a study inadequate for inclusion in a meta-analysis. Some can be got around by simple re-analysis of the results. Others will involve writing to the author(s) of the research for more details.

Often it is possible to calculate the required information from the detail that has been supplied in the original paper. Sometimes a specific hypothesis will not have been tested because the independent variable has more than two levels and the results are in the form of an Analysis of Variance with more than one degree of freedom for the treatment effect. If means and standard deviations have been reported for the comparison groups then both significance levels and effect sizes can be computed via a t-test. Similarly, if frequencies have been reported then significance levels and effect sizes can be computed via χ^2.

However, sometimes even these details will not be available, particularly if the aspect of the study in which you are interested is only a part of the study and only passing reference has been made to it. In this case, you should write to the author(s) for the necessary information. This can have a useful side-effect in that authors sometimes send you the results of their unpublished research or give you details of other researchers in the field. Another occasion for writing to authors is when you have more than one paper from the same source and are unsure whether they are reports of different aspects of the same study; you do not want to include the same participants, more than once, in the same part of the meta-analysis because to do so would give that particular research undue influence over the outcome of the meta-analysis.

If the researchers do not reply then you may be forced to quantify such vague reporting as 'the results were significant'. Ways of dealing with this are given in Appendix XIII.

The file-drawer problem

There is a bias on the part of both authors and journals towards reporting statistically significant results. This means that other research may have been conducted that did not yield significance and has not been published. This is termed 'the file-drawer problem' on the understanding that researchers' filing cabinets will contain their unpublished studies. This would mean that your meta-analysis is failing to take into account non-significant findings and in so doing gives a false impression of significance. There are standard ways of checking whether there is a file-drawer problem; these are given below.

Classifying previous studies

Once you have collected the studies you can decide on the meta-analyses you are going to conduct. This can be done on the basis of the comparison groups and dependent variables that have been employed. The larger the number of studies included in a given analysis the better. Therefore, I would recommend using a broad categorisation process initially and then identifying relevant subcategories. For example, in the case of pelvic pain you could classify papers that have compared sufferers of pelvic pain with any other group, initially. You could then separate the papers into those that had sufferers from other forms of pain as a comparison group and those that had non-pain-sufferers as a comparison group.

Each meta-analysis can involve two analyses: one of the combined probability for all the studies involved and one of their combined effect size. For each study you will need to convert each measure of probability to a standard measure and each effect size to a standard measure.

Some research papers will report the results from a number of subgroups. For example, in studies of gender differences in mathematical ability, papers may report the results from more than one school or even from more than one country. The meta-analyst has a choice over how to treat the results from such papers. On the one hand, the results for each subsample could be included as a separate element in the meta-analysis. However, it could be argued that this is giving undue weight to a given paper and its method. In this case, it would be better to create a single effect size and probability for all the subsamples in the paper. To be on the safe side, it would be best to conduct two meta-analyses: one with each sub-study treated as a study, in its own right, and one where each paper only contributed once to the meta-analysis. If the two meta-analyses conflict then this clearly questions the reliability of the findings.

Checking the reliability of coding

It is advisable to give a second person blank versions of your coding sheets, details of your inclusion criteria and the papers you have collected (or a sample of them if there are a large number of them). That person should code the studies and then you should check whether you agree over your decisions and the details you have extracted.

Weighting studies

Some texts on meta-analysis recommend that different studies should be given an appropriate weighting. In other words, rather than treat all studies as being of equivalent value, the quality of each, in terms of sample size or methodological soundness, should be taken into account. However, opinions differ over what constitutes an appropriate basis for weighting and even as to whether it is legitimate to apply any weighting. My own preference is simply to weight each study by the number of participants who were employed in that study. In this way, studies that used more participants would have greater influence on the results of the meta-analysis than studies that used smaller samples.

Combining the results of studies

Effect size

Producing a standard measure of effect size

A useful standard measure of effect size is the correlation coefficient r. It is preferred over other measures because it is unaffected by differences in subsample size in between-subjects designs. This is only a problem when the meta-analyst does not have the necessary information about sample sizes to calculate effect sizes that do take account of unequal subsamples. Equations for converting various descriptive and comparative statistics into an r are given in Appendix XIII. However, there is an unfortunate consequence of using r as the measure of effect size: it has itself to be converted into a Fisher's Z-transformation. As there is a danger that this may be confused with the standard z used in the equation for combining probability, I will use the symbol r' to denote a Fisher's Z. The equation for converting r to r' is given in Appendix XVI along with tables for converting r to r'.

Calculating a combined effect size

Once an r' has been calculated for each study they can be used to produce a combined r', which can be converted back to an r to give the combined effect size, either by using the appropriate equation given in Appendix XVI or by using the tables given there.

Probability

Producing a standard measure of probability

The standard measure for finding probability that I recommend is a z-score. Equations are given in Appendix XIII to convert various inferential statistics into a z-score.

Calculating a combined probability

Once you have a z-score for each study a combined z-score can be calculated which can then be treated as a conventional z-score would be and its probability can be found by consulting the standard z-table (see Appendix XIV).

Homogeneity

An important part of the process of meta-analysis is assessing whether the studies in a given meta-analysis are heterogeneous. In other words, do they differ significantly from each other? This is a similar process to the one you would employ when finding a measure of spread for scores from a sample. If they do differ significantly then you need to find which study or studies are contributing to the heterogeneity. You should then examine all the studies to try to ascertain what it is about the aberrant studies that might be contributing to the heterogeneity.

I recommend that you test the heterogeneity of studies on the basis of their effect size and take out the aberrant studies until you have a set of studies that are not significantly heterogeneous, leaving a homogeneous set. You can then report the results of the meta-analyses, with and without the aberrant studies. In the case of probability, remember that it is strongly dependent on sample size and therefore a study might produce a very different probability from others simply because its sample size was different, even when all the studies had similar effect sizes.

Testing the heterogeneity of effect sizes

The heterogeneity of the effect sizes can be found by using an equation which looks at the variation in the Fisher's transformed r-scores (r') of the studies to see whether they are significantly different (see Appendix XIII). If they are significantly different then the probabilities are heterogeneous. In that case, you should remove the study with the r' that contributes most to the variability. If the reduced set of studies is also heterogeneous then continue to remove the study with the r' that contributes most to the heterogeneity until the resultant set is not significantly heterogeneous. You can now report the combined r for these remaining studies as being homogeneous.

Testing the heterogeneity of probabilities

Following the reasoning given above, it may not be felt worth testing whether the probabilities of the studies are heterogeneous. For completeness the method is described (see Appendix XIII) but there is no need to continue testing until you have a non-heterogeneous set of studies, with respect to their probabilities.

Confidence intervals

It is useful to calculate and report the confidence interval for the combined effect size. This takes into account the total number of participants who took part in all the studies in the particular meta-analysis. Remember that a confidence interval is an estimate, based on data from a sample, of where the population parameter is likely to lie. If the confidence interval for the effect size does not contain zero then we can be more confident that there is a real effect being detected. For example, if a confidence interval showed that the effect size for the relationship between gender and smoking, for a number of studies, ranged between −0.1 and +0.4 (where a negative value denoted that a higher proportion of females smoked, while a positive value denoted that a higher proportion of males smoked), then, as this included the possibility that the effect size was zero, it would question whether there was a real difference between the genders in their smoking behaviours.

Checking the file-drawer problem

The fail-safe N

One method of assessing whether there is a file-drawer problem is to compute the number of non-significant studies that would have to be added to the meta-analysis to render it non-significant. This is known as the *fail-safe N* and its calculation is dealt with in Appendix XIII. Rosenthal (1991) suggests that it is reasonable to assume that the number of unreported non-significant studies that exist is around $(5 \times k) + 10$, where k is the number of studies in the meta-analysis. For example, if the meta-analyst has found 6 studies then we can reasonably assume that $(5 \times 6) + 10 = 40$ non-significant studies exist. If the fail-safe N is larger than this critical number of studies then the meta-analysis can be considered to have yielded a result that is robust. In other words, it does not appear to suffer from the file-drawer problem.

Funnel graph

Although effect sizes are less affected by sample size than are tests of significance, it is still the case that the larger the sample the more closely the effect size calculated for that sample will be to the population effect size. Therefore, as sample sizes increase there should be less variability in the effect sizes. Accordingly, if we plot effect size against sample size (in this case using hypothetical data) we should get the pattern seen in Figure 22.1. This plot suggests that the true effect size is just over $r = 0.3$.

However, if there has been publication bias then you are likely to get the pattern shown in Figure 22.2. Here the symmetrical funnel shape shown in Figure 22.1 is not present. The impression we can get from Figure 22.2 is that the true effect size is $r = 0$ but that some studies that employed smaller samples have not been published.

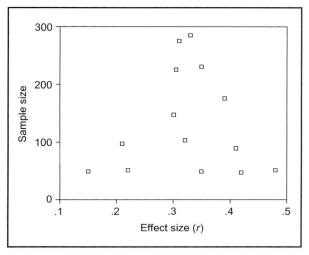

FIGURE 22.1 A funnel graph showing the pattern that can be expected when there is no publication bias

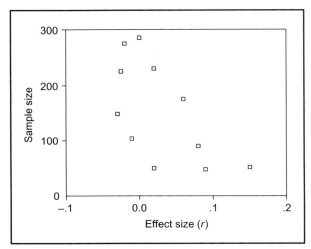

FIGURE 22.2 A funnel graph showing the pattern that can be expected when publication bias is present

Funnel graphs are only really useful when there are a large number of studies in the meta-analysis —otherwise patterns are difficult to discern.

Focused comparison

One way to deal with a non-homogeneous set of studies is to look for a consistent basis for the lack of homogeneity and to test this statistically. For example, in a meta-analysis on the relationship between gender and mathematical ability it might be found that studies give heterogeneous results. The meta-analyst might hypothesise that this is due to the type of mathematics being measured in each study. It would then be possible to classify the studies according to the type of mathematics tested to see whether they produced significantly different results. This technique is beyond the scope of this book; those wishing to conduct a focused comparison should read Rosenthal (1991).

Reporting the results of a meta-analysis

The abstracting systems that were searched to identify the studies, including the key words used, the years covered and when they were last searched, should be reported. All decisions that have been made about how studies were classified and the bases for inclusion and exclusion of studies in a given meta-analysis should be made explicit in the report. Details of how reliability of coding was checked should be given, including how disagreements were resolved. All papers that have been consulted in the meta-analysis should be reported in an appendix to the paper, with an indication of which were included and which excluded.

Probably the best way to present the results of the meta-analyses is in a summary table that includes the following details:

the dependent variable
the nature of the experimental and control groups
the number of studies
the total number of participants in the meta-analysis
the combined effect size (r) and its confidence interval
the combined probability, as a z and as a probability

and, in the case of a significant result:

the number of non-significant studies that would have been needed to render the meta-analysis as not robust to the file-drawer problem (the

Table 22.1 The summary of a meta-analysis of studies that looked at depression in patients with chronic pelvic pain and controls

Groups compared Pelvic pain vs controls	Number of studies	Total number of participants	Combined effect size (r)	Confidence interval	Combined z	Combined p	Fail-safe N	Critical number for drawer
All studies	6	620	0.3418	0.2695 to 0.4104	8.789	<0.0001	166	40
Homogeneous studies	5	510	0.3819	0.3042 to 0.4545	8.966	<0.0001	144	35

fail-safe N) and the number of non-significant studies that are likely to exist. If the result was not statistically significant then it cannot be subject to the file-drawer problem.

Table 22.1 shows the summary table for one meta-analysis based on the depression scores of sufferers of chronic pelvic pain and controls who do not have pelvic pain (the calculations for this meta-analysis are shown in Appendix XIII). Table 22.1 can be interpreted as showing that a meta-analysis was conducted into the relative depression experienced by those suffering chronic pelvic pain and controls who do not suffer pelvic pain. Initially, 6 studies were used in the meta-analysis, with a total of 620 participants. These studies produced a combined effect size of $r = 0.3418$, which Cohen (1988) considers to be above a medium effect size. However, the studies had significantly heterogeneous effect sizes. A non-heterogeneous set of 5 studies was identified. The combined effect size for the homogeneous set was $r = 0.3819$ (also above a medium effect size). The results are highly unlikely to have occurred if the Null Hypothesis of no difference between the groups had been true. It would have needed an additional 166 non-significant studies to render the full meta-analysis non-significant, and 144 for the homogeneous set, which means that the file-drawer problem does not affect this study as only 40, or 35, additional non-significant studies, respectively, are likely to exist. Notice also that the lowest value in the confidence interval for the effect size of all the studies combined is just under 0.3 and for the homogeneous set it is over 0.3. This suggests that the effect in the population is at least a medium effect in Cohen's terms.

Summary

A meta-analysis involves identifying all the available studies that are relevant to the area being explored. These have to be classified according to their design and the dependent variables they have employed. The decision has to be made as to how many meta-analyses will be necessary to describe the area fully. Each meta-analysis can have a combined effect size and a combined probability calculated for it. In addition, the heterogeneity of the effect sizes should be calculated. When heterogeneity of effect size is identified, studies should be removed from the meta-analysis until a homogeneous set of studies has been identified. The combined probabilities for all the studies and for the homogeneous set should be reported, as should the combined effect size for both the complete set of studies and the homogeneous set. All decisions about the inclusion and exclusion of studies should be made explicit in the report of the meta-analysis.

The next chapter explains how to report research.

PART 5
Sharing the results

REPORTING RESEARCH

23

Introduction

There are four points you should communicate to a person reading or hearing an account of your research: what you did, how you did it, why you did it and what you found. A guiding principle is that you should express yourself in the clearest fashion possible for the medium you have chosen and for the audience you can reasonably expect to be reading or hearing your account.

Accordingly, a report written for an academic journal will differ from a verbal presentation to the same audience. In the same way, a written report for an academic audience will differ from that written for a non-academic audience. In addition, you have to be aware of the conventions that exist, because your audience will have certain expectations about what level of detail they will be given and where in the account they will receive it.

Four different audiences can be identified, each of which needs a different approach. Firstly, there is the general public, for whom you have to make the most concessions; explaining and modifying terminology and even simplifying the sentence structure. Secondly, there is the educated lay person, who will still need terminology explained. Thirdly, there is the person from the same discipline as you who may only need aspects of your particular area explained. Finally, there is the researcher in your area, for whom you need make the fewest concessions.

Non-sexist language

Many people no longer find it acceptable to treat pronouns such as *he* and *him* as though they were neutral and do not refer only to males. One way to avoid the necessity to give a person's gender explicitly is to use a plural. For example: *Researchers studied the effects of mnemonic strategy on recall. They selected three groups. . . .* In this way *they* is used rather than *he* or *she*. However, sometimes you do wish to refer to one person. Although some people use *they* as though it were a neutral, singular pronoun, this is not generally accepted and will jar with some readers. It is preferable, in this case, I think, to use the form *he or she*, rather than *s/he* or *he/she*. For example: *Each participant was trained to use one mnemonic strategy; he or she was then asked to remember as many words as possible.*

A written report

A written report can be of many types: for example, it can be for an academic journal, for a professional magazine, such as *The Psychologist*, for a newspaper or popular magazine, for a funding body, or for a client. Students are generally required to adopt a style similar to that of an academic journal article when presenting their research. I am going to concentrate on reports written for an academic audience. Throughout this chapter I will be recommending the conventions of the APA (American Psychological Association). Other publishers have their own house styles, which differ in detail from that of the APA, for example in the treatment of multiple authors. I will start by describing the report of an experiment or quasi-experiment and then explain some variations on the theme.

Academic written reports of experiments or quasi-experiments

Such a report has a clearly defined set of sections. However, students often worry that they are repeating themselves throughout the report because they are having to say the same things in different sections. Each part of the academic report has a specific function and knowing that function should guide what you include in that part.

An academic written report of research differs from an essay in two crucial ways. Firstly, readers may choose not to read it in a linear fashion from the beginning to the end; they may jump about from section to section. Thus, each section needs to be as self-contained as possible. Secondly, you should assume your readers are trained in research practice. Accordingly, there is much that you do not need to explain. For example, if you are using a standard statistical technique you do not need to go into the principles that underlie that technique.

There are two aspects of a report of research, written for fellow academics, that should guide the level of detail you include. Firstly, you need to provide enough detail for someone to replicate your study, such that every essential element is reproduced. Secondly, readers should know precisely what the research entailed so that they can judge its merit.

A convention that is adopted for most academic written reports is that the third person passive voice is preferred over the first person active voice. In other words, write *a study was conducted* rather than *I conducted a study.*

The Title

The wording of the Title is critical, for this will often be all the reader sees, initially, of your report; it may be among a list of the contents of a journal or an entry in a list of publications. Thus, in the Title you have to convey what your research was about to allow readers to decide whether they want to read on. It should be as short as possible, while clearly showing not only the area of research but giving more specific detail about the sub-area. A title of the form *A report of an experiment in social psychology* is an extreme example of what not to do. This has informed the reader about the global area of the research but little else. Most of that title is redundant: the reader knows that it is a report, they can find out that it involves an experiment by reading the abstract and social psychology is a vast area. Generally readers have more specific interests and so will choose whether to read on the basis of the topic of the research. Thus, a better title would have the form: *The effects of the presence of others on altruistic behaviour.*

Another principle is that the title should accurately reflect the content of the report. This may seem obvious, but a sloppy use of terminology can mislead the reader. An ex-colleague was inundated with requests for copies of a paper that had the term *biofeedback* in its Title when the paper was simply about *feedback*.

The Abstract

The Abstract is a very brief summary of the piece of research you are reporting; a typical recommendation is that it should be between 100 and 200 words. However, don't feel that you need to add extra, unnecessary words just to get it to 100 words. As the Abstract is a summary it shouldn't contain details that are not presented elsewhere in the report. If a record of your research is held on a database, such as *PsycINFO*, the Abstract may be the only information that readers have, apart from the Title, about your research. Readers whose interest has been caught by the Title will read the Abstract and, on the basis of what you tell them there, they will choose whether they want to read more. The need for brevity in the Abstract means that it should only include the essential details. It should tell readers what you did in your research, how you did it and what you found; why you did it is less important, here. I do not think that the reader needs to know your hypotheses at this stage. The Abstract needs to be self-contained so don't refer to elements that cannot be understood without access to the rest of the report. For this reason, I also suggest avoiding citations in the Abstract, as the details of the reference will not be available to someone who only has the Abstract and Title. However, if the work referred to is sufficiently well known, then it seems reasonable to refer to it. For example, 'The experiment investigated Baddeley and Hitch's model of working memory'. The following is an example of how to write an Abstract.

Participants were left by an experimenter in a room in one of three situations: alone, with a stranger who was a stooge, or with a friend. The experimenter went into an adjoining room and, after a period, the impression was created that she had had an accident. The stooge implied by his or her behaviour that nothing was wrong. Significantly fewer of the participants who were with the stooge went to the experimenter's aid than in the other two situations; the other two conditions did not differ significantly.

Common mistakes made by students are that they give too much detail about the design, the number and nature of the participants (on occasions when such detail is not necessary), the procedure and the specific statistical tests used. On the other hand, they give too little detail, or even no detail at all, about the results; often the reader is simply told *the results were significant* or even that *the results are discussed*. Tell the reader in which direction the results went.

The Introduction

The function of the Introduction is to put your research in the context of previous relevant research and explain why it was worth conducting your research. The level of detail needs to lie between two extremes: the first is to launch straight into the hypotheses without any explanation; the second is to be so all-encompassing as to explain what social psychology is. Summarise previous research and do not recount every minute detail.

When referring to an author, simply give his or her surname and the date of the publication, as you should in an essay. Do not inform the reader that: *Jean Piaget, a Swiss psychologist from Geneva, stated in 1963 that . . . ,* unless these details are critical to the argument you are presenting. Rather, write: *Piaget (1963) stated that. . . .* When you refer to a work that you have already mentioned in the same paragraph then do not include the date with the name. However, the first time the work is referred to in a new paragraph give the date again. If there are more than two authors (but fewer than seven) the convention is that the first time you refer to them, give the full list of authors. Subsequently, refer to them in the form *Piaget et al. (1977)* rather than list all the authors (et al. simply means *and others*). However, if there are more than six authors then even on the first reference to the work give the first author followed by et al. If you have more than one reference with the same list of authors and the same date then use a lower-case letter as a suffix, starting with a. For example, *Kennedy and Day (1998a)* and *Kennedy and Day (1998b)*. If the list of authors contains some of the same people and the same date then, after the first time the work is referred to, give as many names as necessary to distinguish the two works. For example, if you were citing Page, Plant, Bonham, Jones and Harper (1972) and Page, Plant, Jones, Bonham and Harris (1972) then you would refer to the first as Page, Plant, Bonham et al. (1972) and the second as Page, Plant, Jones et al. (1972). If the first authors of two works have the same surname then give the initials of the first author for each work. For example, *D. Goldberg and Huxley (1985)* and *L. R. Goldberg (1971)*.

There are cases where two dates are given: firstly, when a work has been reprinted after a lapse of time and you have not read the original printing, e.g. Darwin (1859/1960); secondly, when you have read a work in translation, e.g.

Ebbinghaus (1885/1913). In both cases, in the list of references at the end of the report you give the date of the version you read, e.g. Ebbinghaus (1913), with a note at the end of the reference: '(Original work published 1885)'.

Sometimes you will want to cite a personal communication, such as from a conversation or an e-mail, but because no one else can get access to it the APA recommend that you only mention it in the text and not in the list of references. You should give the author's initials, name and as accurate a date as possible. For example, *G. D. Richards (personal communication, July 16, 2002)*.

When you know of a work that has been accepted by a journal or publisher for publication but hasn't yet been printed then use the following form: *Burke, Hallas, Clark-Carter and White (in press)*.

If one or more studies that you have read do not add to the argument but support previous relevant research that you have outlined then it is enough to list the authors after a summary sentence of the form: *These results are supported by Piaget (1963), Hartley (1977) and Cruikshank (1983)*. If you are referring to works in brackets then there are conventions for this as well. Separate the author(s) and the date by a comma. When there is more than one author, use *&* instead of *and*. When there is more than one work separate them by a semi-colon. List them in alphabetical order of the first author's surname. To illustrate all these points: *A number of works have replicated this finding (Hughes & Jarvis, 1985; Milligna, 1956; Wynn, 1990)*.

When you haven't read the original work (the primary source) but are referring to work that you found in a secondary source, then my own preference would be to give the name(s) and date of the original, in the place where you are referring to it. In the references you would then indicate where you read the reference to the work. However, many journals, including those of the British Psychological Society require the use of the APA's conventions (American Psychological Association, 2001). In this method, when you refer to the work you also say where it was cited, e.g. *Miller's study (as cited in Hebb, 1970)*. The disadvantage of this method is that if I want to follow up Miller's work I will have to find Hebb first and look in the reference list of that work to find where to look for Miller's work.

If you are giving a direct quotation then you need to give the page number of the reference, e.g. "The value for which $P = .05$, or 1 in 20, is 1.96 or nearly 2; it is convenient to take this point as a limit in judging whether a deviation is to be considered significant or not" (Fisher, 1925, p. 47). If the quotation is relatively short (fewer than 40 words) then you can include it in the paragraph which introduced it, as I just did, but enclose it in double inverted commas. This allows you to use single inverted commas when the quotation itself contains a quotation or uses quotation marks. (Note that in the usual British convention single inverted commas are used, with double ones for quotations within quotations.) However, if it is longer then it is better to separate it from the rest of the text as in the following example, complete with an indent on the left margin.

> When a graph is constructed, quantitative and categorical information is *encoded*, chiefly through position, size, symbols and color. When a

person looks at a graph, the information is visually *decoded* by the person's visual system. A graphical method is successful only if the decoding process is effective. (Cleveland, 1985, p. 7, italics in the original).

Notice that I have indicated that the emphasis was not added by me. If I had changed any of the formatting then I should indicate this, e.g. *italics added*. If you are quoting selectively then use three full-stops to denote that text has been omitted. However, if you are quoting selectively then do not misrepresent the original. Thus, *this is not the best account I have ever read on the subject* should not become *this is . . . the best account I have ever read on the subject*.

The end of the Introduction should pave the way for the next section: the Method. This can be done by a lead-in sentence along the lines: *It was decided to conduct an experiment to see whether the presence of another person would have an effect on the altruistic behaviour of a participant.* Alternatively, you could formally state your research hypothesis. In a laboratory report it is probably wise to use the latter format—complete with the Null Hypothesis. However, few psychologists report their research in quite such terms when they have graduated, preferring to leave the hypotheses implied. The advantages of the formal approach are two-fold. Firstly, as a student you can demonstrate to the person marking that you know what you are doing. Secondly, you are making clear what criteria will be applied when you carry out the statistics, for example, whether it is appropriate to use a one- or a two-tailed test.

The Method

The function of the Method section is to enable readers to replicate your study, if they want to. Accordingly, you need to decide whether or not you have given enough detail. However, at the same time you should not include irrelevant information, such as the make of word-processing package on which a questionnaire was prepared. The method generally has the subheadings *Design, Participants, Apparatus/Materials* and *Procedure*.

Design

The Design section should, not surprisingly, contain the details about the design that was used in the research. The reader should be told what the independent and dependent variables were, and whether a between-, matched-, within- or mixed-subjects design was used. However, in the case of correlational designs it is not necessary to talk of independent and dependent variables, unless you have manipulated one of the variables, or to talk of between- or within-subjects variables. This section of the report should also include some justification for certain aspects of the design. For example, if, in an experiment on memory, you introduced a task between presentation and recall phases to prevent rehearsal then you should explain why. In short, the Design section is used to explain why participants were required to do what they did, while the Procedure section explains what they were told and what they did.

If you have conducted pilot research, and I strongly recommend that you do, then I think it is clearer if you refer to this in the Design section and then create a subsection entitled *Pilot Study*. In such a section you need to include the usual details about the participants (see below) and some brief reference to modifications that you made in the light of the pilot study. This is particularly important if your study has entailed the creation of a new measure, such as a questionnaire. You need to convince the reader that you have attempted to address the face validity of the measure, at the least.

Although the formal advice might be to state the alpha-level that you will apply to your statistical tests, this is very rarely done in practice.

Participants

In the past, participants have been referred to as *subjects*. There is a feeling that this term implies that people are the objects of research, while *participants* suggests that they are more equal to the researchers. The APA recommends the use of *participants* or more specific terms, such as *university students*, in preference to *subjects* except when discussing statistics or when the people who took part in the study were not able to give consent.

Readers want to know about the representativeness of your sample, to have an idea about how far your findings can be safely generalised. You need to report the number of participants you used, including the numbers of males and females, the age range (preferably with means and standard deviations), and an indication of their occupations. Where you have participants in different groups, for example a control group and a treatment group, it is important to give details for each subgroup in order to reassure the reader that any differences that you find between the groups on some measure are not likely to be due to differences such as age or gender ratio. In addition, you should report the basis on which they were selected: if it was genuinely random, then say how this was done. If some people whom you selected to take part refused, then report how many refused and the basis of the refusal. It is important to know whether you have a sample that could be described as *self-selected* because they are the ones who did not refuse; you may have a biased sample which leads to your results being confounded by the nature of the sample.

Materials/Apparatus

Once again, only include details that are relevant for a person trying to replicate your research. Thus, if the materials or apparatus you used had some distinct characteristics that were critical to the conduct of your study, then give full details of what you used. For example, if you were showing pictures of faces to your participants for a very precise duration then it is worth reporting the make of the device used to present the faces. This is important information because the reader may wish to question the accuracy of the device you have used. Similarly, if you video-recorded behaviour in a room that was designed for the purpose then you should describe the arrangement and the equipment. It is a good idea to include, here, an example of a stimulus or test item to help the reader understand. Thus, if you showed participants drawings of animals put an example here and put the remainder of the items in an Appendix, and remember to refer the reader to the Appendix. If you are including an illustration, it is good practice to put it immediately after the reference to it. Placing it elsewhere means that the reader is less likely to look at it. If you are using a standard statistical technique to analyse your data avoid reporting the statistical package you used. However, if the technique is not generally well-known or if packages differ in the way they handle the data then it is advisable to report the package and even the particular version of the package.

If there was no apparatus or materials used in the research, then do not include this section.

Procedure

The Procedure should simply include what the participants were told, how they were told it and what they were required to do. Any explanation as to *why* participants were required to do things should have been given in the Design section. The reader wants to know what story participants were given; how much they were informed about the purpose of the study; whether they were informed in spoken or written form; whether they had practice trials, if this was appropriate; and whether, after they had completed their task, they were de-briefed. Report the stages of the Procedure in chronological order.

Results

The Results section is only for summary statistics, supported graphically, and related inferential statistics, in that order. However, if you have more than one set of results, report them one set at a time. See Chapter 9 for the best way to present summary statistics and the appropriate chapter for presenting the particular inferential statistics you have used. If you want to include the raw data (that is, unanalysed or summarised for each participant), then put it in an appendix and refer the reader to it.

How you present the statistics depends on how much there is. If there are only a few then they can be contained within the text (usually in brackets). However, this can be tedious to read when there is more information. In this case, place the detail in a table and refer the reader to it. Thus in the case of descriptive statistics you could write: *Recall was better in the method of loci group (M = 9.6, SD = 1.58) than in the pegword group (M = 8.9, SD = 1.91) and both recalled more than the control group (M = 7.2, SD = 1.62).* Where you are including detail in a table introduce it rather than just start the Results section with a table. You could write something of the form: *Table 1 shows the means and standard deviations of the words recalled by participants in each mnemonic group.*

I prefer summary statistics, such as means and standard deviations, to be presented in numerical as well as graphical representation, though some journals forbid the inclusion of both tables and graphs of the same information. The reason for my preference is that tables provide the exact figures, while graphs give a more immediate impression of the results.

Do report the effect size, where one exists, and give the particular version, for example Cohen's *d*, as more than one effect size measure may exist for the same type of data. The APA sees their omission as one of the 'defects in the . . . reporting of research' (American Psychological Association, 2001, p. 5). Do not show equations directly in the text. Put them in either an appendix or in a footnote.

Give every table and figure a number and a title. There is a convention that everything that is not a table is referred to as a figure. Remember to show what units were used in your measures. For example, show that the table provides means and standard deviations of the number of words recalled. Try to make tables and graphs as self-contained as possible rather than force the reader to refer to the text to understand what the illustrations mean. Accordingly, generally avoid using descriptions such as *group 1* when you could put *immediate recall*. Nonetheless, if the description of the group is too complicated then have a key, or, as a last resort, explicitly refer the reader to the text for an explanation.

There is no need to discuss the results in this section. In the case of descriptive statistics, all you need is a sentence that says something of the form: *the mean and standard deviations of words recalled for the immediate and delayed groups are shown in Table 1 and Figure 1.*

When you report inferential statistics I suggest you provide the information in three stages. Firstly, say what test was used and what was being analysed. For example: *a between-subjects t-test was used to compare the recall of those asked to recall immediately after presentation with the recall of those asked to recall after ten minutes.* Secondly, say what the results showed, in words. For example: *those given immediate recall remembered significantly more words than those recalling after ten minutes.* Finally, give the evidence for your statement; for example: $(t_{(15)} = 2.48, p = .013,$ one-tailed test, $d = 0.6)$. Do report the version of the test that you conducted and, where appropriate, explain what the independent and dependent variables were. It is not enough simply to say *a t-test was performed on the data.*

If the result was significant then say so and where appropriate give the direction in which the result went. For example, if two conditions were being compared don't just say that the groups differed but say which one recalled more.

If you have used a statistical package which has provided the exact probability for your result then report that probability. If, on the other hand, you have had to rely on statistical tables then report the probability as accurately as you can. Thus, if the probability lies between two tabled levels, then give the range of possible values, e.g.: $.01 < p < .05$. This tells readers more than $p < .05$, because it shows that p is bigger than 0.01.

The APA recommends that when reporting decimals only give a leading zero if the number could be larger than 1. Thus, for probabilities and correlation coefficients you would start with the decimal place—e.g. $p = .03$— whereas for d you would report $d = 0.6$. When your computer package tells you that the p-value is 0.000, replace the last zero with a 1 and report it as $p < .001$ as no probability is truly 0. Sometimes, for small or large numbers, computers and calculators report a figure in what is often called 'scientific notation', e.g. 2.15E-3. This example can be translated as 2.15×10^{-3}, which means 2.15 divided by $(10 \times 10 \times 10)$, or 2.15 divided by 1000 = 0.00215. The negative sign shows that you are dividing (or multiplying by a fraction, in this case $\frac{1}{1000}$) and the 3 that you are taking the cube of 10. Do not report results using scientific notation. Translate it into normal decimal format. In SPSS such numbers can be reformatted by asking for more decimal places in the output. Avoid reporting a result as *ns* (for *not significant*) as this doesn't tell the reader where between 1 and just greater than 0.05 the probability was.

If you conduct supplementary analyses, such as planned or *post hoc* comparisons after an Analysis of Variance, then report these after the main analysis to which they relate.

Once again the formal advice may be that you should state whether you have chosen to accept or reject your research hypothesis, or some other form of words; this is rarely done in practice but may be advisable when you are learning the statistical techniques.

Unless the statistical techniques you have used are unusual do not explain them. However, if you have to perform preliminary analyses to decide whether or not a given test is appropriate, report the results of such an analysis, for example, if you checked for the homogeneity of variances before conducting a *t*-test. Similarly, if you transform the data, for example, using an arcsine transformation, then report this procedure; see Chapter 14 for a discussion of data transformation. When you have transformed data it is still better to report the descriptive statistics in the original units; the mean of arcsine of number of words doesn't tell people much. Also, if you are using a statistical procedure in which a number of decisions are available then you should report the particular decisions you made. For example, in factor analysis you can choose how the factors are to be identified.

One of the conventions of report writing is that you are trying to present the impression of being an impartial scientist who is letting the figures decide whether your hypothesis is supported. Accordingly, do not undermine this impression with phrases such as *unfortunately, the result was not significant*. Apart from anything else, lack of significance can still be informative.

If you did find a non-significant result then I recommend carrying out a power analysis. From this you would find out the statistical power that your test had, given the effect size you obtained and the sample size you employed. In this way, the reader can see how likely you were to have committed a Type II error. If the power was below 0.8 then I recommend working out the sample size that would be necessary to give power of 0.8 with the same effect size. This puts your result in context. If the effect size was below what Cohen (1988) would call 'small' and you would need a very large sample to have power of 0.8 then ask yourself whether the study is worth attempting to replicate in an unmodified form. On the other hand, if the effect size was small, medium or even large and power was low then it would seem reasonable to recommend replicating the study with the appropriate sample size. Don't conduct power analysis if the result was statistically significant as you won't have committed a Type II error.

Discussion and Conclusion

Here you attempt to set your results in the context of the research you referred to in the Introduction. In addition, you might mention for the first time other research that helps to explain your results. You can also suggest modifications or improvements to your research that would take the investigation further. Do not overdo the criticisms of your own research; some students seem to regard this as an opportunity for public self-humiliation and find fault where it does not exist.

I recommend the following order for a Discussion. Start with a very brief summary of the results. Do not go into the figures for the descriptive or inferential statistics, probability or effect size, just give the direction of the results and whether or not they were statistically significant. Follow this by placing the results in the context of previous research. If your results are in line with previous research then point out that the results confirm the work of whoever you have referred to in the Introduction. There must be some reason why your research was worth conducting and so some new information is likely to be available and need explaining. If your results conflict with previous research then try to explain this. At this point you may wish to criticise your research, particularly if you found a non-significant result but had a low level of statistical power. Avoid lame statements such as *if a larger sample had been used statistical significance might have been achieved*. As I demonstrated in Chapter 13, this is almost always going to be true, and so is pretty meaningless. Be more specific; recommend a particular sample size based on power calculations. This could show whether it is worth pursuing the same effect or whether the design needs modifying to increase effect size. If you are confident that your results reflect a well-designed and conducted piece of research then say what the theoretical implications of those results are. Finally, recommend future, related research but do not go into the realms of fantasy here. Yes, you could look at all sorts of aspects of memory, if that is what your research was about, but try to stick to suggestions that would build on your findings.

If you are reporting more than one study—for example, a series of experiments—in the one report, it is usual to follow a single Introduction with a separate Method, Results and Discussion section devoted to each study. These are then followed by a general Discussion.

References

Your own institution may have a preferred style of reporting references. However, the most popular style among psychology journals and books is that recommended by the APA (American Psychological Association, 2001). It differs slightly when referring to books, chapters in books and journal articles. There is also advice on how to report information you found on the Internet. I am including only the most common types of entry; for more details look at the APA *Publication Manual* where you will find examples of 95 types of reference. For books, chapters in books and journal articles, you start by reporting the author(s), in the order: surname, then initials, starting with the first author and listing all the authors. Where there is more than one author use & in place of *and*. For example, *Smith, M., & Jones G. R.* However, if there are more than six authors give the details of the first six and then follow this with et al. (meaning *and others*). Next, report the year, in brackets, in which the reference was published, making sure, in the case of books, that you report the date of the edition you read.

For journals, give the title of the article next, followed by the journal title (underlined or in italics), the volume number and finally the page numbers of the article. For example:

> Smith, E. (1974) The effect of hunger upon the perception of the size of food. *British Journal of Nutritional Psychology*, 17, 27–35.

For books, report the title (underlined or in italics) with only the first letter of the title in capitals, except where there is a subtitle, in which case the first word of the subtitle also should start with a capital letter. Continue with the edition, if it is later than the first edition, then the place of publication and the publisher's name. For example:

> Brown, A. (1975). *Choice reaction times made simple* (2nd ed.). London: University of Neasden Press.

If you are citing a whole book but one that is edited, in the sense that a number of authors have contributed identified chapters, then follow the name(s) of the editor(s) by (Ed. or Eds.). For example:

> Jones, B. (Ed.). (1990). *Children's understanding of linear algebra*. Manchester: University of Stretford Press.

For chapters within an edited book, report the title of the chapter (not in italics or underlined) followed by the editor name(s), (Ed(s).), the title of the book (underlined or in italics), the page numbers of the chapter, then place of publication and publisher's name. For example:

> Kropotkin, P. (1990). Who needs linear algebra, anyway? In B. Jones (Ed.), *Children's understanding of linear algebra* (pp. 51–73). Manchester: University of Stretford Press.

The use of *pp.* is as an abbreviation for *pages*. Notice that the editor's initials are placed before the surname.

If you are citing a work that is not in English then give the original title but provide an English translation of the title; for example:

> Carpintero, H. (1994) *Historia de la psicología en España* [The history of psychology in Spain]. Madrid: Eudema.

When you are giving the details of a work that is *in press*, as described in the section on writing the Introduction to a report, then provide as much information as you can. In the case of a journal article you are unlikely to know the page numbers.

When you are referring to an Internet site give the web address (the URL) and the last date accessed. For example,

The Code of Conduct for Psychologists. (January 2000). Retrieved August 17, 2002 from http://www.bps.org.uk/about/rules5.cfm

Check the details as close to the point when you last have a chance to update them, for example when you check the proofs when the report is going to be published or just before a verbal presentation is given. At one point someone changed my own Web address and didn't tell me. If the address has changed then update it, and if the pages can't be accessed any more say so. Make sure that you get the details correct. One way to do this is to copy them directly from the Web address line and paste them into your document, as I have done for the address above.

Place the references in alphabetical order, based on the first author's surname. Notice that I have indented the second and subsequent lines of each reference. When the references are put together this makes finding a particular reference easier (see the Reference section of this book).

Appendices

The function of an appendix is to contain supporting evidence from your research that is of such a level of detail that it would affect the reader's flow if included in the main text. Therefore, if you have devised and used a measure that contains a number of items, put only a sufficient number of examples in the main text for the reader to understand the essential elements and refer the reader to an appendix. Similarly, if you wish to list a computer program that has been written or a description of a piece of apparatus, specially designed and used in the study, then place these in appendices. In addition, as mentioned above, if you want to report unanalysed data or calculations or a worked example then put it in an appendix.

It is useful, if you have more than one type of information to go into an appendix, to create an appendix for each rather than lump them together. Thus you could place a listing of a computer program in one appendix and raw data in another. This helps the reader, particularly if the report has a Contents page, to locate the material more quickly.

An academic journal article

Each journal has its own style for layout, reporting of references and other conventions. Some journals contain details of these conventions in each copy of the journal; others, such as those for the American Psychological Association (APA) are contained in a book. Once you have chosen a journal to which you are going to submit your report, read the appropriate details on its conventions and read examples, in a copy of that journal, of studies that are similar to your own before preparing your article. In this way, you will learn such points as whether the first-person active voice is preferred over the third-person passive voice in that particular journal.

Some journals require you to supply a short list of key words that describe the content of your report. This information can be used in databases such as *PsycINFO* and *Current Contents* to help users search for articles on your area of research.

It is usual to submit an article to a journal in single-sided, double-spaced format. Illustrations and tables have to be of high definition and they are generally submitted on separate sheets, with the place you want them put, indicated in the text. Often you are required to submit multiple copies of the manuscript. However, in some cases you can submit the manuscript as an attachment to an e-mail. The majority of journals will pass your article on to one or more referees, who will generally remain anonymous to you. In order that they don't know who you are you should make the manuscript as anonymous as possible yourself. This usually requires you to have a Title page that doesn't give your name and address; these details would be supplied on a separate sheet. Do follow the journal's advice to contributors carefully as you are quite likely to have the manuscript returned by the journal's editor without its having been sent to referees if you haven't. The referees will comment on the quality of the article, recommending whether it should be published and, if so, suggest any alterations or additions they think would improve it; they may make publication dependent on your carrying out some or all of their suggestions. You are obviously free to ignore their advice but if you wanted that journal to publish your article you would need a very good case prepared, particularly if the same suggestions were made by different referees.

Variations in presenting other research methods

A survey or questionnaire study

I will use as an example a survey of smoking behaviour. A survey is more complicated to report than an experiment for a number of reasons. Firstly, unless you are using a pre-existing questionnaire, you are creating a measure. Therefore, you have to check its validity via a pilot study and report this stage. Secondly, as you have not really manipulated any variables, the terms *independent* and *dependent* variable are less clearly defined. Remember that when you are looking at the relationship between two variables, making one an independent and one a dependent variable implies that the former is affecting the latter—in other words a causal relationship is suggested. Thirdly, a survey may not involve testing any specific hypotheses, but simply descriptions of the data and explorations of relationships within the data. The report can seem less obviously focused, as a result. Fourthly, it may feel even less focused because it involves a number of different comparisons between questions.

As a consequence of the above points, the Method, Results and Discussion sections of a report of a survey are going to be different from reports of other research. The Method will be longer because a questionnaire frequently is altered in the light of the pilot study. The best way to maintain the flow in the report is to put the initial and the final versions of the questionnaire in separate appendices to which the reader is referred.

The Results section is likely to be longer as the data may be reported at a number of levels. Firstly, summary statistics will be reported, accompanied by graphs, for example, a bar chart of the ages in the sample. Secondly, two-way contingency tables may be formed, such as gender by smoking status, and inferential statistics may be performed on these. These in turn may be re-analysed on the basis of a third variable, such as the smoking status of parents. There is a danger of putting quite a strain on the reader's memory and of making the finding of subparts of the section difficult.

The best way to deal with the extra content in the Results section is to divide it into subsections into which you place analyses that share some theme. For example, you might have *Health* and *Social Influences* as two separate subsections. The Discussion section is likely to be longer, simply because you have reported more results.

A meta-analysis

Chapter 22 deals with the reporting of the results of a meta-analysis. In a meta-analysis your data are derived from other people's research. The population, in one sense, contains all the papers on the topic of your analysis, while the sample contains all the papers included in the final version of the analysis. You need to explain how you identified your population, such as the databases you used. Then you have to make explicit the criteria you used to select your sample: what constituted satisfactory and unsatisfactory studies. In addition, you have to explain the attempts you made to bring unsatisfactory studies into the sample: for example, by deriving inferential statistics from summary data; by using rules of thumb to quantify terms like *significant*; or by writing to authors for further information.

Given that the aim of an academic report is to allow replication, it is accepted practice that you report all the studies that you considered, in a summary table, placed in an appendix, and identify all those you used in the analysis. You also have to present tables of the statistics that you derived from the studies included in the analysis, complete with sample size and direction of results—i.e. whether or not they support a given hypothesis.

Meta-analysis is still in its comparative infancy and so it is expected that you will report your statistical decisions more explicitly, such as whether you weighted studies on the basis of sample size and the technique you used to convert results to a standard statistic. In addition, it is common for authors to cite specific works on meta-analysis as justification of their decisions.

A verbal presentation

As with all other forms of presentation the style you adopt will depend on your audience. If it is an academic audience then many of the guiding principles for a journal article apply. For non-academics a more journalistic style is appropriate. Nonetheless, remember that speech is a temporal medium; in other words, once you have said something, unless readers have made complete enough notes they have to rely on memory to gain access to it. Therefore, give a pace of delivery that allows listeners to process what you are saying and do not overburden their memories. In addition, listeners cannot consult a dictionary. Accordingly, you should be more willing to explain the terms you use, including abbreviations.

An obvious constraint is the length of time you have. When asking about this, find out if time for questions has to be included and, if so, how much time.

Preparing your talk

Some people speak without notes; this is a rare skill. Others only prepare and use notes. Others still prepare a full version of their talk, which they read. I recommend that, unless you know you can do the first, you do none of these things. I suggest that you start by writing a complete version of the talk. This allows speakers to hone their arguments and to present a coherent story. In addition, it will give experienced speakers a good impression of whether it fits the time allowed and inexperienced speakers the chance to time their presentation.

I then suggest taking notes from the full version of the talk, which act as memory aids when giving the presentation. Keep the notes to a minimum but check that they are sufficient by reading them through again after a period. By putting the talk in note form the speaker is forced to compose the sentences afresh when speaking; and a greater air of naturalness is created. Space the notes well, indenting sub-points, and placing lists in such a way that each item is on a new line. In this way, speakers can find their place more easily and not be too reliant on the notes for what they say. I also mark on my notes where an illustration, such as an overhead projection slide, should go.

Some people use index cards for their notes, others use A4 paper. All this may seem like a lot of preparation. Nonetheless, the better prepared you are the more natural your talk will appear. An additional advantage of preparing a complete version of your talk beforehand is that it is available if someone requests a copy of it.

If you are giving a paper at a conference you are often required to provide an Abstract for your talk. A pamphlet of Titles and Abstracts may be handed out at the conference to help those attending the conference choose which presentations to attend and to act as a fuller record of the conference. In addition, in order to get a paper accepted for a conference you are likely to be required to provide an expanded version of an Abstract which will then be vetted by a committee or by referees, in the same way that a journal article is.

Delivering your talk

You want your audience to understand what you are saying, despite the constraints of the situation. One way to do this is to give the same material more than once at different levels of detail—a bit like a news broadcast: the head-lines, followed by greater depth and concluding with a summary of the main points. Another approach is sometimes characterised as *tell them what you are going to tell them, tell them, then tell them what you told them.*

One way to maximise the chance that the audience will understand is to maintain their interest. I have recommended using notes for your talk in order to create a more natural delivery which will help you establish a rapport with the audience. However, some people read the complete versions of their papers to the audience. The disadvantages of this form of delivery are many. Firstly, often the voice people use for reading aloud differs from the one they use in conversation; it is less animated. Secondly, readers spend more time looking down at their paper. This means that their voices are less well projected and that eye contact with the audience will be reduced.

If you are thinking of reading your paper in this way, ask yourself why. The only justification I can see for it is that every sentence you have written has to be delivered verbatim and any paraphrasing would ruin the meaning. This is very rarely the case. If your fear is that you will forget something critical then go through all the preparation I have described above, having the complete version available as a last resort. If, however, you do have to read the complete version, use print that is large enough, bold enough and sufficiently well spaced to enhance your ability to look up at the audience more frequently and not lose your place. Using a lectern can help. However short the talk, do not try to memorise it and reproduce it verbatim because this also usually lacks naturalness.

Part of maintaining the interest of your audience involves keeping their attention on what you are saying. Thus you have to be aware of your non-verbal behaviour. Give the audience eye-contact but do not concentrate on just one person as it will make them uncomfortable and exclude others. However, do not be surprised when even people you know in the audience have more passive faces than they would have in a conversation; theirs is a passive role. Do not stand like a statue as you will appear uncomfortable and discomfort the audience. Instead, use a reasonable amount of gesture but not so much that it becomes distracting, and try not to fiddle with pens, keys or items of clothing. If you are nervous then remember that a sheet of thin paper ampli-fies any shaking; this can be one advantage of using small index cards for your notes. Try to stay in a constrained area rather than stride around.

Illustrating your talk

Bear in mind the fact that you are talking and that therefore if you present your audience with anything else it may distract them and detract from what you are saying.

Handouts

If you give people a handout that contains prose, before or during your talk, they will read it. Similarly, if you give them pictures they will look at them. In both cases you have no control over the point at which they look at the handout. Think of the function of your handout. If it is to save people taking any notes, then tell them, before you start your talk, that a complete handout will be available at the end. If you want to give a structure to the talk to help note-taking, then give them a handout that merely has headings and sub-headings on it. Make the handout well-spaced so that they have room to make notes and do not have to spend time searching through it. You can include a list of references at the end of the handout.

If you have access to an overhead projector (OHP), a computer package such as *PowerPoint* or a slide projector and the facilities to copy into these formats, do not hand out pictures. Do not give copies of pictures for people to pass round; you will just add further chances for distraction. Offer to pass them round at the end and leave sufficient time to do this.

Audio-visual aids

There used to be a rule for actors: avoid working with animals and children —they are unpredictable and may detract from your performance. The same could be said of supplementing a talk with some form of technology, be it an OHP, a 35 mm slide projector, a video player or a computer. There are two general rules for all such devices. Firstly, do not assume that they will be available for you; ask beforehand. Secondly, even if they can be supplied, do not make your talk so dependent on them that if something goes wrong your performance will be ruined; have contingency plans and do not get flustered by a failure.

Despite the danger of their failing, if used wisely and if they work audio-visual aids can be an asset. This is not only because a picture, particularly a moving one, is often more convincing and more easily understood than the equivalent time spent speaking, but also because in a longer talk they can introduce variety and thus maintain the attention of your audience. In addition, by giving information in more than one medium you can help the retention of details.

Overhead projectors
These are very useful. They allow you to give an outline of your talk, display lists of points, present longer quotations and show graphical displays and pictures. However, do not overuse them. It is pointless to display all your talk on an OHP.

Preparing OHP transparencies
Leave wide margins on both sides and top and bottom of your acetates: not all projectors have the same sized platen (the surface onto which you place the slide). Do not include too much detail and do not make the size of the image too small or feint. If you are using pens to create the image, then I recommend you make a draft of each slide on a piece of paper, beforehand, and use permanent markers on the acetate as the water-soluble ones can smudge, particularly in nervous hands. It is possible to photocopy directly onto them, even in colour. In addition, you can print from a laser printer

directly onto them. However, if you are going to photocopy or print onto them, you must use the correct type of acetate; others melt in the machine. Prepare an introductory transparency which will allow you to check the nature of the display.

Showing OHP transparencies

If you can, allow time to put on your introductory transparency and check various aspects of the display: that it is lined up with the screen; that it is in focus; and by how much, if at all, the mirror obscures your display. You can only check the latter from the perspective of the audience. If the mirror does get in the way, make sure that you move the part of the image that you want the audience to see, out of the way of the mirror, if possible. One technique that can be effective if you have a number of points on the same transparency is to cover the part that is not yet needed, otherwise people will read on. Another technique is to overlay related transparencies on each other, for example, if you are trying to build up a picture to make a point. If you are going to do this give each transparency a common reference mark that will allow you to align them.

Do not stand in front of the screen and do not turn your back on the audience to point to parts of the display projected on the screen—point to the slide. Do not put up a transparency and then talk about something else; talk the audience through the contents of the transparency, for otherwise it will have the same effect as a handout and the audience will have to choose between concentrating on what you are saying or on the content of the transparency. If you are putting up a graphical display or a table, particularly if it is complex or you are using unusual conventions, explain the content, pointing to particular parts of the display as you do. Graphs and tables are forms of abstraction that, like any other means of presenting figures, impose the need for translation on the part of the reader.

Try to keep your transparencies in order after you have used them. During the question time, often questioners want to refer back to a transparency and this will make it easier to find; you and the questioner may remember the contents of the transparency but you may lose the rest of the audience, while the pair of you discuss it, if it has not been projected again.

If there are aspects of the research that are relatively central to your argument but which you have had to summarise to such an extent that you might get questioned about the detail, then it can make sense to have an extra OHP transparency ready, which can simplify your explanation of the details during questions. Speakers sometimes signal points during presentations by saying that they have not got time to deal with them during the talk but could return to them during questions.

35 mm slides

My advice is, if possible, avoid using 35 mm slides, particularly if you are going to have to communicate with someone in a cubicle at the opposite end of the room who has control over the projector. I have lost count of the number of talks I have been to where this set-up fails, leaving the speaker illustration-less, or with the wrong illustration or one that is so badly out of focus that it is worse than useless. You can now do perfectly effective colour OHP transparencies and OHPs are far more commonly available than 35 mm slide projectors. In addition, you can put the content of slides onto computer slide packages such as PowerPoint. Another hazard with slides is that they can be put in the projector in a variety of orientations, including upside down and in mirror-image.

All these hazards take time from the talk while, often in vain, attempts are made to solve the problem. One solution to the orientation problem is to have a mark in the same corner of every slide as a reference point. However, unless you remember in which position the mark should be, you could end up with them all in the same but wrong orientation. As with overhead projector slides, if possible have an introductory slide that you can use to check the display before you start your talk. If you are lucky, the projector used for your talk may be compatible with one for which your institution has a spare carousel. In this case, you can check the orientation of the slides and bring them in the carousel with you. Unfortunately, there is no solution to the problems brought about by having someone else control the display of your slides.

OHP tablets and computer projectors
It is possible to project the image from a computer screen via an OHP or a computer projector onto a large screen. You will obviously need to check that the software, in which you have created your material, is compatible with the machine you will be using during your presentation. Check also that the generation of the software is compatible. If you are using colour and an OHP tablet, then you need to know that the tablet will be capable of reproducing it. At their best such visual aids can be very useful. However, if the wrong projector is used, with insufficient power or if the room lets in too much light in the wrong places, then the image can be so faint as to be virtually useless. As with all OHPs if the image is too small then this too can make this visual aid worthless. Therefore, allow time to load the file onto the host computer or set up your own laptop and check such details when you arrive at the venue. It is possible to send a presentation in advance, either on a floppy disc, if there is space, on a CD-ROM or even as an attachment to an e-mail. This can have the advantage that it can be checked for compatibility and loaded onto the host computer before your talk is due. Too often a sizeable proportion of the time for a talk is spent fiddling with the hardware and software. Even if the program appears to run on the host computer you can find that if you have used unusual symbols they can be presented differently on the host computer from what you intended, e.g. a box shape instead of a letter of the Greek alphabet. One final point is to make sure that you know how to work the software. This may seem obvious but I sat through one PowerPoint presentation where throughout the talk the speaker wasn't able to stop the program moving to the next slide—fascinating but distracting.

A poster presentation

A poster presentation is a way of reporting research at a venue such as a conference. Like a verbal presentation it can be a way of presenting preliminary findings. It has a number of advantages over a verbal presentation and some disadvantages. Firstly, it does not have to compete with other presentations in those conferences where they have parallel sessions; if two presentations are on at the same time you can only attend one of them. Secondly, it cannot be placed at an inconvenient time in the program which would limit its potential audience. Thirdly, it is not as transitory as a talk; readers can refer back to earlier parts of it and, as it may be in place for the duration of the conference, they can return to read it.

However, it will be competing for attention with other poster presentations and other aspects of the conference, such as the book displays that publishers put on. In addition, it will be allocated limited space. Thus, you will have to attract people's attention for them to look at your presentation in the first place and then maintain their attention for them to stay reading it.

The format you need to use for a poster presentation is more akin to that for an OHP slide than that for a written report. Thus, you should summarise as much as possible, only using large areas of print as a last resort. Give clear section headings, use a variety of font sizes to signal different levels of information and space material well; this will help readers find their way round the display. Similarly, you can use different fonts, in underlining, italic and bold, to attract the eye. However, as with all displays, avoid too much variety. Do not use a font just because your word processor can create it. Be selective and look at the overall effect. In the absence of a variety of font sizes mark the levels clearly by using roman or arabic numbers, and upper- or lower-case letters. Use tables and graphs in preference to prose but try to stick to common patterns of visual representation rather than devise your own. For, whereas in a talk you can explain such idiosyncrasies, a poster presentation has to stand alone. However, there are likely to be occasions when you can stand near your presentation and answer questions.

If you know the size allocated to the whole display then it is possible to create a more durable version of the display—rather than a set of individual sheets. One way is to have the individual sheets or even the full display sealed in a plastic film. Another is to have the whole display reproduced on a colour printer. These two techniques should be available through art shops or firms that do work for surveyors or architects. You should also be able to buy tubes in which you can transport the full poster. If neither of these facilities is available to you, I would recommend having a second version of the poster available, in case you damage the first one when putting it up. It would be worth also taking along your own supply of drawing pins, or some other means of fastening your poster, just in case you are not provided with enough to do your display justice; try to find out what sort of fixing the organisers recommend, beforehand.

It is a good idea to provide copies of a complete version of the report for interested people to take away. A better idea still is to offer to send those who are interested a copy; there is a tendency at conferences for people to pick up any handouts that are available and not necessarily to read them. Have a sheet of paper handy for people to write down their addresses and if you do make the offer then do send the paper.

Trying the presentation out

Regardless of the medium in which a report of research is to be presented, it is difficult for an author to stand back and take a detached view of the content of a presentation. After you have finished your preparation on the content, ask someone less closely associated with the work to read it. Apart from telling him or her about the nature of the audience give no other information. This is another advantage of preparing complete versions of a talk. In the case of a poster presentation, let your reader see the poster before he or she looks at a fuller version. In the case of a verbal presentation, particularly if you are inexperienced, give the presentation to a small audience. In all cases, your listener's or reader's comments are likely to be invaluable in improving the quality of your presentation.

Summary

There are a number of different ways in which a piece of research can be reported. Be aware of the conventions and limitations of the particular one you have chosen and of the likely audience of the report. A report of research written for an academic journal needs to have sufficient detail for the reader to be able to evaluate the worth of what you are reporting and to replicate the research in every relevant detail. On the other hand, a spoken presentation, particularly when time is available for questions, needs to have less detail in order to enhance understanding.

APPENDIX I:
DESCRIPTIVE STATISTICS

This appendix illustrates the techniques introduced in Chapter 9.

Calculating the mean ($\bar{x}$)	387
Calculating the variance (s^2)	388
Calculating the standard deviation (s)	389
Calculating the mean and median from frequency distributions	389
Means	389
Medians	390
Winsorised mean	391
Creating a pie chart	392
Representing relative sample size in a second pie chart	393
Creating a box plot	393
The median	394
Hinge location	394
The H-range	394
The inner fences	394
The outer fences	395
Indexes of skew and kurtosis	395
Skew	395
Kurtosis	396

Calculating the mean ($\bar{x}$)

The equation for the mean is:

$$\bar{x} = \frac{\sum x}{n}$$

where $\sum x$ means 'add all the scores'
          n is the number of scores

In words, add all the scores and divide by the number of scores.
   Given the following data

$$3, 7, 5, 9, 4, 6, 5, 7, 8, 11, 10, 7, 4, 6, 8$$

$$\bar{x} = \frac{100}{15}$$

$$= 6.667$$

Calculating the variance (s^2)

The equation for the variance is:

$$s^2 = \frac{\Sigma(x - \bar{x})^2}{n - 1}$$

In words: Find the deviation of each score from the mean and square it. Sum the squared deviations and divide the result by one fewer than the number of scores.

Table A1.1 Obtaining the total sum of the squared deviations from the mean

recall	deviation	squared deviation
3	−3.667	13.447
7	0.333	0.111
5	−1.667	2.779
9	2.333	5.443
4	−2.667	7.113
6	−0.667	0.445
5	−1.667	2.779
7	0.333	0.111
8	1.333	1.777
11	4.333	18.775
10	3.333	11.109
7	0.333	0.111
4	−2.667	7.113
6	−0.667	0.445
8	1.333	1.777

Total sum of squared deviations   73.335

$$s^2 = \frac{73.335}{14}$$

$$= 5.238$$

Calculating the standard deviation (*s*)

$$s = \sqrt{s^2}$$

In words, take the square root of the variance.

$$s = \sqrt{5.238} = 2.289$$

Calculating the mean and median from frequency distributions

Means

If we have asked a sample of 120 people what their age group is, we can represent it as a simple table:

Table A1.2 The frequency distribution of participants' ages

Age (in years)	20–29	30–39	40–49	50–59	60–69
Number of people	15	45	30	20	10

As we cannot know the exact ages of the people in the groups, it is usual to take the mid-value for the range in each group. Thus, in the youngest group there are fifteen people who will be treated as being aged $\frac{20 + 29}{2} = 24.5$.

The total of the ages for the group is found by multiplying the midpoint for the group by the group size. Accordingly, the total age for the first group is $24.5 \times 15 = 367.5$. It is then necessary to find the total age for all the groups and divide that total by the sample size.

$$\text{mean} = \frac{\text{total age}}{\text{sample size}}$$

$$= \frac{3790}{120}$$

$$= 31.583 \text{ years}$$

Table A1.3 Obtaining the total ages within a group

Group	midpoint	group size	Total age
1	24.5	15	367.5
2	34.5	45	1552.5
3	44.5	30	135.0
4	54.5	20	1090.0
5	64.5	10	645.0
Grand Total		120	3790.0

Medians

First find which group contains the median. As there are 120 people, the median point is between the 60th and 61st person. To find which group this is in, create what is called a *cumulative frequency*.

Table A1.4 Creating cumulative frequencies from grouped data

Group	Age range (in years)	Group size	Cumulative frequency
1	20–29	15	15
2	30–39	45	60
3	40–49	30	90
4	50–59	20	110
5	60–69	10	120

In this case, the median lies between the second group and the third group. It can be calculated by taking the mean of the highest possible age in the second group and the lowest age in the third group:

$$\text{median} = \frac{39 + 40}{2}$$

$$= 39.5 \text{ years}$$

However, when the median point lies within a group the calculation is different. Table A1.5 contains data for which the median does lie within a group: the 40–49-year-olds.

Table A1.5 Creating cumulative frequencies from grouped data

Group	Age range (in years)	Group size	Cumulative frequency
1	20–29	14	14
2	30–39	44	58
3	40–49	32	90
4	50–59	20	110
5	60–69	10	120

In this case, we find the median from the following equation:

$$\text{median} = L_m + \left[C_m \times \left(\frac{\left(\frac{1}{2} \times N \right) - F_{m-1}}{f_m} \right) \right]$$

where L_m is the lowest value in the group that contains the median
C_m is the width of the group that contains the median
F_{m-1} is the cumulative frequency of the group below the one that contains the median
f_m is the frequency within the group that contains the median
N is the total sample size

Therefore in the present case:

$$\text{median} = 40 + \left[10 \times \left(\frac{\left(\frac{1}{2} \times 120 \right) - 58}{32} \right) \right]$$

$$= 40 + \left[10 \times \left(\frac{60 - 58}{32} \right) \right]$$

$$= 40 + [10 \times 0.0625]$$

$$= 40.625$$

Winsorised mean

I mentioned in Chapter 9 that there exist versions of the mean that have been designed to lessen the effects of outliers, for example, the trimmed mean. Another method is described as *Winsorising*. This starts with the same idea as the trimmed mean in that the data are put in numerical order and then a certain number (or proportion) of the first and last scores are removed. However, in Winsorising they are replaced by the new lowest and highest scores and the mean is taken of the new set of values. As an example return to the recall data and place it in numerical order:

$$3, 4, 4, 5, 5, 6, 6, 7, 7, 7, 8, 8, 9, 10, 11$$

Now if we are Winsorising the data by just the two outer values, we need to replace 3 by 4 and 11 by 10. The new mean becomes 6.667. In other words the process has not changed the mean from what it was when it was calculated on the original data. This is no surprise as the data are relatively symmetrical. However, if the 15th person had remembered 25 words rather than 11 the normal way of calculating the mean would have produced a value of 7.6, while the Winsorised mean of the new data would have been 6.667 again. Thus, we can see that the effect of the possible outlier has been neutralised by the use of Winsorising.

Creating a pie chart

An example given in Chapter 9 was of a group of 50 males being asked whether they smoked. Twenty were found to be smokers. We can express the figures in terms of proportions. Therefore, $\frac{20}{50} = 0.4$ of the sample were smokers and the remaining 0.6 of the sample were non-smokers.

As a circle has 360 degrees, we can find the number of degrees for smokers by multiplying 360 by the proportion of smokers:

$$360 \times 0.4 = 144 \text{ degrees}$$

and for non-smokers

$$360 \times 0.6 = 216 \text{ degrees}$$

This gives us the following chart:

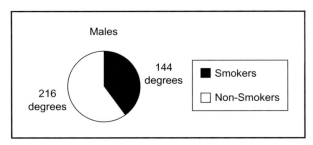

FIGURE A1.1 The degrees of a pie chart necessary to represent a given proportion of a sample

Representing relative sample size in a second pie chart

When pie charts are being created for two samples which have different sizes, Figure 9.8 (in Chapter 9) showed that the relative sample sizes can be represented through the area of the pie charts. Once the radius of one pie chart has been decided the radius of the other one can be found from the following equation:

$$r_2 = r_1 \times \sqrt{\frac{n_2}{n_1}}$$

where n_2 is the sample size of the second group
n_1 and r_1 are the sample size and radius of the group for which the radius of the pie chart has already been decided

Therefore, if the first sample was 30 and the second was 50 and we had decided to use a radius of 1 cm for the first pie chart, then the radius of the second pie chart would be:

$$1 \times \sqrt{\frac{50}{30}} = 1.291 \text{ cm}$$

Creating a box plot

Figure 9.25 (in Chapter 9) shows a labelled version of a box plot that was created in SPSS. Remember that SPSS uses slightly different conventions for the drawing of a box plot from those given here. Box plots are based on percentile points, including the median (50th percentile) and the 25th and 75th percentiles. Therefore the first stage is to put the scores in size order.

Table A1.6 The recall of fifteen participants in size order

order	recall
1	3
2	4
3	4
4	5
5	5
6	6
7	6
8	7
9	7
10	7
11	8
12	8
13	9
14	10
15	11

The median

The median is located at the $[(n + 1)/2]$th score, where n is the number of scores. In this case it is at the 8th score. Therefore, the median is 7.

Hinge location

The hinges are located at the 25th and 75th percentiles. Their location can be found using the equation:

$$\text{hinge location} = \frac{\text{median location} + 1}{2}$$

If the median location is not a whole number then ignore the decimal part of the number. For example, if the median location had been 8.5 just put 8 in the above equation.

$$\text{hinge location} = \frac{9}{2} = 4.5$$

Thus, the lower hinge is between the 4th and 5th scores from the bottom and is therefore 5. The upper hinge is between the 4th and 5th score from the top and is therefore 8.

The H-range

The H-range is the difference between the upper and lower hinge and is therefore $8 - 5 = 3$.

The inner fences

The inner fences are found from the equations:

$$\text{lower inner fence} = \text{lower hinge} - (1.5 \times \text{H-range})$$
$$\text{upper inner fence} = \text{upper hinge} + (1.5 \times \text{H-range})$$

Therefore:

$$\text{lower inner fence} = 5 - (1.5 \times 3)$$
$$= 0.5$$

and

$$\text{upper inner fence} = 8 + (1.5 \times 3)$$
$$= 12.5$$

Thus, we can see that all the scores are contained within the inner fences and we have no scores that could be considered outliers.

If the 15th score in Table A1.6 had been 25 it would have been worth calculating the outer fences. Note that because the number of scores remains the same, all the values calculated above for the box plot remain the same.

The outer fences

The outer fences are found from the equations:

lower outer fence = lower hinge − (3 × H-range)

upper outer fence = upper hinge + (3 × H-range)

Therefore:

lower outer fence = 5 − (3 × 3)

= −4.5 (which cannot exist in this example)

and

upper outer fence = 8 + (3 × 3) = 17

Therefore a score of 25 (the 15th score) would lie outside the outer fence and could be treated as a possible outlier.

Indexes of skew and kurtosis

There exist indices of both measures of the shape of a distribution curve: skew—lack of symmetry—and kurtosis—sharpness or flatness in the peak of the distribution. For each there exists a z-test that can be used, for samples below about 100, to decide whether the distribution is sufficiently non-normal that it needs transforming or that a non-parametric test would have to be used. With larger samples you would be better relying on viewing a graph of the distribution, as the tests can be over-sensitive to minor variations from a normal distribution. For both indices there are more complex variants of the index that are more suited for samples. However, I have decided to offer the simpler ones that are offered by computers as I think they are adequate for the criteria that will be recommended for deciding about non-normality, even though they are, strictly speaking, for use with the distribution in a population.

Skew

There are a number of measures of skew but the one that seems to be most commonly quoted by computers is the following:

$$\text{index of skew (IS)} = \frac{\Sigma(x - \bar{x})^3}{n \times s^3}$$

where n is the sample size
s is the standard deviation

In words, add together the cube of the deviation of each score from the mean. Divide the result by the sample size multiplied by the standard deviation cubed.

When the distribution is symmetrical then the index of skew = 0, when it is negatively skewed, IS is negative, and when the distribution is positive, so is the IS.

A z-score can be obtained from the above result, which can indicate whether the distribution is significantly skewed:

$$z = \frac{\text{IS}}{\sqrt{\dfrac{6}{n}}}$$

It is recommended that you treat $p = 0.01$ as the α-level, in other words z would have to be at least 2.58 or −2.58 for you to treat the distribution as significantly skewed.

Kurtosis

The most common measure of kurtosis has two versions: a basic one and an adjusted one. The basic version is:

$$\text{index of kurtosis (IK)} = \frac{\Sigma(x - \bar{x})^4}{n \times s^4}$$

Notice that it is almost the same as the index of skew except that instead of cubing you now raise to the fourth power. The second version involves subtracting 3 from the first index of kurtosis (this is the version given by many statistical packages, including SPSS). This is because the original version is equal to 3 when the distribution is mesokurtic (i.e. like the normal distribution, it is neither markedly tall and thin nor flat and wide). When the adjusted index produces a negative value this suggests a platykurtic distribution, while a positive value suggests a leptokurtic distribution.

The z-test for kurtosis is:

$$z = \frac{\text{IK}}{\sqrt{\dfrac{24}{n}}}$$

where IK is the adjusted version of the index of kurtosis.

APPENDIX II: SAMPLING AND CONFIDENCE INTERVALS FOR PROPORTIONS

The illustrations in this appendix are linked to examples given in Chapter 11.

Finding the confidence interval of a proportion	397
Margin of error	399
The relative size of the sample and the population	399
Estimating the required sample size	400
When no previous data are available as a guide	400
When previous data are available as a guide	400
When subsamples are of interest	401
The effect of increasing the degree of confidence on the margin of error	401

All the following statements and calculations are based on a survey that utilised a simple random (or probability) sample.

Finding the confidence interval of a proportion

The following account assumes that the sample that has been taken is smaller than 5% of the population. Refinements are given later in the appendix for situations where this is not the case. Imagine that a survey of voting patterns has been conducted. It uses a random sample of 2500 voters and finds that 900 (or 36%) of the sample say that they will vote for a right-wing party— The Right Way—while 1050 (or 42%) say that they will vote for a left-wing party—The Workers' Party. You wish to estimate what proportion of people, in the population from which the sample was taken, are likely to vote for each of the two parties. Note that the proportion in a sample is usually represented as p, while its equivalent parameter, the proportion in the population, is represented as π (the Greek letter pi). You can be confident at the 95% level that the proportion in the population (π) who will vote for The Right Way lies in the range:

$$p - 1.96 \times \sqrt{\frac{p \times (1 - p)}{n}} \text{ to } p + 1.96 \times \sqrt{\frac{p \times (1 - p)}{n}}$$

where p is the proportion of the sample who said they would vote for The Right Way

$1 - p$ is the proportion of the sample who did not say they would vote for The Right Way

n is the sample size

$\sqrt{\dfrac{p \times (1 - p)}{n}}$ is the standard error of the distribution of proportions

The figure of 1.96 is found from z-tables (see Appendix XIV). These show that 2.5% of a population will have 1.96 standard deviations or more above the mean for the population and 2.5% will have 1.96 or more standard deviations below the mean for the population. Therefore, the remaining 95% of the population will lie within 1.96 standard deviations from the mean. Accordingly, we can be confident at the 95% level that the confidence interval (CI) will contain the proportion in the population (π).[1]

Thus if 900 people in a sample of 2500 say they will vote for The Right Way,

$$p = \frac{900}{2500}$$

$$= 0.36$$

$$1 - p = 0.64$$

$$n = 2500$$

and the confidence interval for the number of supporters for The Right Way in the population is:

$$CI = 0.36 - 1.96 \times \sqrt{\frac{0.36 \times 0.64}{2500}} \text{ to } 0.36 + 1.96 \times \sqrt{\frac{0.36 \times 0.64}{2500}}$$

$$= 0.36 \pm 1.96 \times \sqrt{\frac{0.23}{2500}} = 0.36 \pm 1.96 \times \sqrt{0.000092}$$

$$= 0.36 \pm 1.96 \times 0.0096 = 0.36 \pm 0.019 = 0.341 \text{ to } 0.379$$

Therefore, if the sample was taken from a population of 100000, the number of supporters of The Right Way in the population is likely to lie between

$$0.341 \times 100000 \text{ and } 0.379 \times 100000$$

i.e. 34100 and 37900.

Margin of error

We can express the standard error used in a confidence interval as a percentage error or margin of error.

[1] Formally, the 95% confidence interval means that if we took samples of the same size and calculated a confidence interval then on 95% of occasions the confidence interval would contain the parameter in the population—in this case the proportion who vote a particular way.

$$\text{percentage error} = 0.019 \times 100$$

$$= 1.9\%$$

Note that the error is expressed as a percentage of the total sample and not of the subsample that supports a given political party.

The relative size of the sample and the population

If the sample size is less than 5% of the population then the above calculations produce a reasonable estimate of the percentage error. However, if the sample size represents a larger proportion of the population then the following adjustment needs to be made:

$$\text{adjusted percentage error} = \text{original percentage error} \times \sqrt{1 - \frac{n}{N}}$$

where n is the number in the sample
       N is the number in the population

For example, if in the above situation, the population were 25000, then the sample would represent 10% of the population. Therefore:

$$\text{adjusted percentage error} = 1.9 \times \sqrt{1 - \frac{2500}{25000}}$$

$$= 1.9 \times \sqrt{1 - 0.1}$$

$$= 1.9 \times \sqrt{0.9}$$

$$= 1.9 \times 0.949$$

$$= 1.803\%$$

This demonstrates that the larger the sample relative to the population, the smaller the percentage error. This is not surprising as the larger the sample the better the estimate of the population parameters you would expect. The logical endpoint of this trend is that there is no error if you conduct a census; that is, if you sample the entire population.

Estimating the required sample size

When no previous data are available as a guide

The nearer the proportion you are attempting to estimate is to 0.5, the larger the percentage error. If we want to work out the sample size (n) that we will

2 Those of you who know algebra will be able to see that the equations in this and the next section have been found from the original definition of a confidence interval given at the beginning of this appendix:

error (for a 95% CI)

$$= 1.96 \times \sqrt{\frac{p \times (1 - p)}{n}}$$

need in order to guarantee a particular margin of error for a proportion of 0.5, we can use the following equation:[2]

$$n = \frac{9604}{(\text{error})^2}$$

where error is the percentage margin of error we are willing to accept.

For example, if we want a 2% margin of error,

$$n = \frac{9604}{4} = 2401$$

The larger the margin of error that you are willing to have, the smaller the sample size you need.

If the proportion in the sample is smaller or larger than 0.5 then the margin of error will be smaller, for the same sample size. Therefore, the above equation will guarantee that the margin of error is no bigger than the one you require for the given sample size.

When previous data are available as a guide

Find the confidence interval, from the previous data, for the proportion in which you are interested. If this confidence interval includes 0.5, use the equation provided above for estimating the sample size. If the confidence interval does not include 0.5, take the value within the confidence interval that is nearest to 0.5 and put it into the following equation.

$$n = \frac{38416 \times p \times (1 - p)}{(\text{error})^2}$$

Accordingly, if you were using the data that was collected on voting for The Right Way, the confidence interval ranged from 0.341 to 0.379. Therefore the proportion (p) nearest to 0.5 would be 0.379 and the sample required for a 2% margin of error would be:

$$n = \frac{38416 \times 0.379 \times (1 - 0.379)}{4}$$

$$= \frac{38416 \times 0.379 \times 0.621}{4} = \frac{9041.55}{4}$$

$$= 2261 \text{ (rounded up to the nearest whole number of people)}$$

When subsamples are of interest

The above calculations have all been based on situations where the proportions of the total sample are of interest. If you are interested in proportions within subsamples then you need to calculate the size of the subsamples using the above equations. Thus, if you were interested in the proportion of males and the proportion of females in your sample who would vote for The Right Way and you were willing to accept a 2% margin of error, then you would need to include 2500 males and 2500 females in your sample. Alternatively, if you were using information from previous research to guide you, you could use the appropriate equation provided to find the number of participants required in each subsample.

The effect of increasing the degree of confidence on the margin of error

If we wish to have 99% confidence that our confidence interval will contain the parameter for the population then we need to look up the z-tables again to find how many standard deviations above and below the mean will contain 99% of the population. The z-table in Appendix XIV tells us that the figure is 2.575 because 0.005 or 0.5% of a population will have a score which is 2.575 standard deviations or more above the population mean and 0.5% of a population will have a score that is 2.575 standard deviations or more below the population mean. The confidence interval will therefore be:

$$p - 2.575 \times \sqrt{\frac{p \times (1 - p)}{n}} \text{ to } p + 2.575 \times \sqrt{\frac{p \times (1 - p)}{n}}$$

$$\text{CI} = 0.36 - 2.575 \times \sqrt{\frac{0.36 \times 0.64}{2500}} \text{ to } 0.36 + 2.575 \times \sqrt{\frac{0.36 \times 0.64}{2500}}$$

$$= 0.36 \pm 2.575 \times \sqrt{\frac{0.23}{2500}}$$

$$= 0.36 \pm 2.575 \times \sqrt{0.000092}$$

$$= 0.36 \pm 2.575 \times 0.0096$$

$$= 0.36 \pm 0.025$$

$$= 0.335 \text{ to } 0.385$$

or 33.5% to 38.5%.

Appendix III: Comparing a Sample with a Population

This appendix illustrates the techniques introduced in Chapter 12.

A single score compared with a population mean (population SD known)   402
A sample mean compared with a population mean   403
  When the standard deviation for the population is known   403
  When the standard deviation for the population is not known 403
Confidence intervals for means   404
  Sample size is at least 30   404
  Sample size is fewer than 30   405
Confidence intervals for medians   406
Quantiles and normal quantile–quantile plots   406

A single score compared with a population mean (population SD known)

A z-test is used in this situation. The equation for a z-test that compares a single participant's score with that for a population is of the form:

$$z = \frac{\text{single score} - \text{population mean for the measure}}{\text{population standard deviation for the measure}}$$

In standard notation, this is usually shown as:

$$z = \frac{x - \mu}{\sigma}$$

For example, if we know that a person has scored 70 on an IQ test that has a mean of 100 and a standard deviation of 15, then, using the equation for z, we can see how many standard deviations this is below the mean:

$$z = \frac{70 - 100}{15}$$

$$= -2$$

A sample mean compared with a population mean

When the standard deviation for the population is known

We can use a z-test to calculate the significance of the difference between a mean of a sample and the mean of a population, using the following equation:

$$z = \frac{\text{mean of sample} - \text{population mean}}{\left(\dfrac{\text{population standard deviation}}{\sqrt{\text{sample size}}}\right)}$$

In standard notation, this is usually shown as:

$$z = \frac{\bar{x} - \mu}{\left(\dfrac{\sigma}{\sqrt{n}}\right)}$$

In this way we can calculate how likely a mean from a sample is to have come from a population with a given mean and SD.

Let us assume that the IQs of twenty children are tested and that their mean IQ is 90, using a test that has a population mean of 100 and a standard deviation of 15.

$$z = \frac{90 - 100}{\left(\dfrac{15}{\sqrt{20}}\right)}$$

$$= \frac{-10}{3.354} = -2.98$$

When the standard deviation for the population is not known

We need to move from the z-test to a t-test for this situation. The equation to calculate this version of t is similar to the equation for the z when we are comparing a sample mean with a population mean: in this case the sample standard deviation is used instead of the population standard deviation:

$$t = \frac{\text{mean of sample} - \text{population mean}}{\left(\dfrac{\text{sample standard deviation}}{\sqrt{\text{sample size}}}\right)}$$

In standard notation, this is usually shown as:

$$t = \frac{\bar{x} - \mu}{\left(\dfrac{s}{\sqrt{n}}\right)}$$

Imagine that ten 6-year-olds are given a maths test that provides an arithmetic age (AA) for the sample. We can treat the children's chronological age (6 years) as the expected mean for the t-test. The SD for the population is unknown. The mean for the sample was 7 and the SD was 1.247.

$$t = \frac{7 - 6}{\left(\dfrac{1.247}{\sqrt{10}}\right)}$$

$$= \frac{1}{0.3943}$$

$$= 2.536$$

Confidence intervals for means

The usual confidence level is 95%. There are two equations for finding the confidence interval for a mean: one when the sample size is at least 30 and the other when the sample is smaller than this.

Sample size is at least 30

This version is based on the z-test.

The general equation for this version of the confidence interval (CI) for the mean is:

$$CI = \text{sample mean} \pm z \times \left(\frac{\text{sample SD}}{\sqrt{n}}\right)$$

where the z-value depends on the confidence level we require and n is the sample size.

If we required the 95% confidence interval we would consult the z-tables to see what z-value has a two-tailed probability (p) of 0.05 or 5%. Then our confidence interval will be based on $1 - p = 0.95$ or 95%. Looking in the tables we find that $z = 1.96$; remember that the z-tables show the one-tailed probabilities and so to find z for a two-tailed probability of 0.05 we need to look up the z for a one-tailed probability of $\frac{0.05}{2} = 0.025$.

If we had data from a sample of 300 for word recall with a mean of 7 words and a standard deviation of 2 then:

$$CI\ (95\%) = 7 \pm 1.96 \times \frac{2}{\sqrt{300}}$$

$$= 7 \pm 1.96 \times 0.115$$

$$= 7 \pm 0.226$$

In other words we are 95% confident that the mean word recall for the population from which this sample came lies between:

$$7 - 0.226 \text{ and } 7 + 0.226$$

or 6.774 and 7.226.

Sample size is fewer than 30

The general equation for this version of the confidence interval (CI) for the mean is very similar to the previous one:

$$CI = \text{sample mean} \pm t \times \left(\frac{\text{sample SD}}{\sqrt{n}} \right)$$

where the *t*-value depends on the confidence level we require and *n* is the sample size. However, the *t*-value will vary depending on degrees of freedom, which are linked to the sample size (df = *n* − 1).

If we required the 95% confidence interval we would consult the *t*-tables to see what *t*-value has a two-tailed probability (*p*) of 0.05 or 5% for the df in question.

If ten participants are given a maths test then the df = 9. In this case, the *t*-tables show that the *t*-value required for a 95% confidence level is 2.262. If the mean for the sample is 7 and the SD is 1.247, then:

$$CI\ (95\%) = 7 \pm 2.262 \times \frac{1.247}{\sqrt{10}}$$

$$= 7 \pm 2.262 \times 0.3943$$

$$= 7 \pm 0.892$$

In other words we are 95% confident that the mean mathematics score for the population from which this sample came lies between:

$$7 - 0.892 \text{ and } 7 + 0.892$$

or 6.108 and 7.892.

Confidence intervals for medians

The 95% confidence interval for the median, which can be used to create the notch in a notched boxplot (see Figure 12.7 in Chapter 12), can be found from the following equation:

$$CI \text{ (median)} = \text{median} \pm \frac{1.58 \times \text{H-range}}{\sqrt{n}}$$

where   H-range is the range of the mid-50% of values in the sample
n is the sample size

Thus, in the example given in Chapter 9 and Appendix I in which a sample of 15 people had a median recall of 7 words and an H-range of 3,

$$CI \text{ (median)} = 7 \pm \frac{1.58 \times 3}{\sqrt{15}}$$

$$= 7 \pm \frac{4.74}{3.873} = 7 \pm 1.224$$

Therefore the CI for the median lies between 5.776 and 8.224 words.

Quantiles and normal quantile–quantile plots

If a sample of data is put in ascending order a quantile is a point that divides the distribution such that a particular proportion is below that point. Thus, the .10 quantile—sometimes shown as Q(.10)—has 10% of the distribution below it (and therefore 90% above it). A quantile–quantile plot (a Q–Q plot) is a graph of a sample of data placed in ascending order plotted against what values the data points would have had if they conformed to a particular distribution. In Chapter 12 I gave the example of a normal Q–Q plot, in which the data was plotted against what the data points would have been had the distribution been normal. As an example of the process I have taken the data from Table 9.1 which showed the number of words recalled by a sample of 15 people.

Initially the data are placed in ascending order. Each score is then given a rank. The proportion of the data that lies at that rank or below it (the cumulative proportion) is calculated from the following equation:

$$\text{cumulative proportion} = \frac{(\text{rank} - 0.5)}{n}$$

where n is the sample size.

We can then calculate what z-score such a proportion would have if the distribution were normal. Looking at Table A14.1 we can see that if we wanted to find out the z-score for the proportion 0.0333 (the first cumulative proportion in Table A3.1) of a sample would be somewhere between 1.83 and 1.84. However, as the proportion is in the bottom 50% of the distribution, the z-value will be negative and so it would be between −1.83 and −1.84 (see Chapter 12 and in particular Figure 12.2 if this seems puzzling). Table A3.1 shows that it is −1.8339. Once we have a z-score for each cumulative proportion we can then work out what expected normal value would have that z-score by putting the mean and standard deviation from the original data into the following equation:

$$\text{expected normal value} = (z\text{-score} \times SD) + \text{mean}$$

The mean for the recall data was 6.67 and the SD was 2.29. Table A3.1 shows each of these stages leading to the normalised values and Figure A3.1 shows the plot of the original data against the expected normal values.

Table A3.1 The calculation of expected normal values for a normal quantile–quantile plot

order	recall	rank	cumulative proportion	z	expected normal value
1	3	1	0.0333	−1.8339	2.4694
2	4	2.5	0.1333	−1.1108	4.1245
3	4	2.5	0.1333	−1.1108	4.1245
4	5	4.5	0.2667	−0.6229	5.2410
5	5	4.5	0.2667	−0.6229	5.2410
6	6	6.5	0.4000	−0.2533	6.0868
7	6	6.5	0.4000	−0.2533	6.0868
8	7	9	0.5667	0.1679	7.0509
9	7	9	0.5667	0.1679	7.0509
10	7	9	0.5667	0.1679	7.0509
11	8	11.5	0.7333	0.6229	8.0923
12	8	11.5	0.7333	0.6229	8.0923
13	9	13	0.8333	0.9674	8.8808
14	10	14	0.9000	1.2816	9.5997
15	11	15	0.9667	1.8339	10.8639

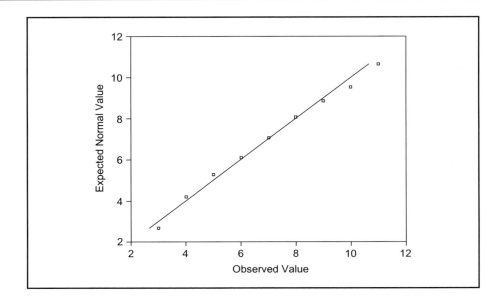

FIGURE A3.1 A normal Q–Q plot of the recall data from Table A3.1

APPENDIX IV: THE POWER OF A ONE-GROUP Z-TEST

The illustrations in this appendix are related to the material which was covered in Chapter 13.

Power analysis for a one-group z-test | 409
Choosing the sample size | 411

Power analysis for a one-group *z*-test

Once a study has been conducted it is possible to work out the power of the statistical test that was conducted on the data: that is, the probability of rejecting a false Null Hypothesis and thus avoiding a Type II error.

As an example, a sample of twenty children who have been brought up in an institution are given an enriched environment to try to enhance their IQs. The population mean IQ in the institution is 90 with a SD of 15. After a period in the enriched environment the IQs of the 20 children were tested and found to have a mean of 95.

To calculate the power of this test, we need to know whether the research hypothesis was directional and the α-level that was set.

The research hypothesis was:

H_A: Children brought up in the enriched environment will have higher IQs than the mean for those in the institution.

As this is a directional hypothesis we will be employing a one-tailed test. The α-level is set at 0.05.

Stage 1: find the critical level of the mean IQ that would just have given us a significant result

To do this we need to know what z-value would have given us a one-tailed significance level of 0.05. Looking in z-tables in Appendix XIV we find that z is 1.645. The appropriate version of the z-test is:

$$z = \frac{\bar{x}_c - \text{population mean}}{\left(\dfrac{\text{population SD}}{\sqrt{n}}\right)}$$

where $\bar{x}_c$ (calculated below) is the critical mean for the sample that would give a z of 1.645 and n is the sample size.

Therefore:

$$1.645 = \frac{\bar{x}_c - 90}{\left(\dfrac{15}{\sqrt{20}}\right)}$$

Using algebra we can find out what $\bar{x}_c$ is:

$$1.645 \times \frac{15}{\sqrt{20}} = \bar{x}_c - 90$$

$$1.645 \times \frac{15}{\sqrt{20}} + 90 = \bar{x}_c$$

$$1.645 \times 3.354 + 90 = \bar{x}_c$$

$$95.517 \qquad\qquad = \bar{x}_c$$

Therefore, we would have got a statistically significant result if the mean IQ for the sample had been as high as 95.517.

Stage 2: find ß-level (the probability of making a Type II error)
To do this we have to find the z-value that will give us the β-level; we treat the sample mean as an estimate of the mean that would be found in a population of children given the enrichment programme:

$$z = \frac{\bar{x}_c - \text{actual sample mean}}{\left(\dfrac{\text{population SD}}{\sqrt{n}}\right)}$$

$$= \frac{95.517 - 95}{\left(\dfrac{15}{\sqrt{20}}\right)}$$

$$= -0.1541$$

Looking up the one-tailed probability for this z-value we find that p is approximately 0.44. In other words, β = 0.44 and therefore the power of the test $(1 - β)$ was approximately 0.56. As this is below the 0.8 recommended by Cohen (1988) we had a low probability of avoiding a Type II error.

Choosing the sample size

It is also possible to choose the sample size that we would require in order to achieve a particular level of power. To do this we would need to know

the statistical test to be used, the α-level, whether the hypothesis was directional and the effect size.

   Imagine that we wish to replicate the above study but we want a reasonable level of statistical power. Therefore, we want to know how many
participants to use in order to get power of 0.8. We are testing the same
hypothesis and so will be using a one-tailed hypothesis and the α-level will
again be 0.05. We need to calculate the effect size (d):

$$d = \frac{\text{sample mean} - \text{population mean}}{\text{population SD}}$$

$$= \frac{95 - 90}{15}$$

$$= 0.333$$

We can use the following equation:

$$n = \left(\frac{z_\beta + z_\alpha}{d}\right)^2$$

where z_β is the z-value that will give the probability of a Type II error (in
this case, β = 0.2, so giving us power of 0.8, in which case z_β is
approximately 0.84)
z_α is the z-value that gives the α-level (in this case, a one-tailed
probability of 0.05), which, as before, is 1.645
d is the effect size we wish to detect.

   Therefore,

$$n = \left(\frac{0.84 - 1.645}{0.333}\right)^2$$

$$= 55.69$$

which means that, to the nearest person, we need a sample of 56 people to
give us power of 0.8, if the effect size is the same as that found in the
previous study.

APPENDIX V:
DATA TRANSFORMATION AND
GOODNESS-OF-FIT TESTS

This appendix illustrates the techniques introduced in Chapter 14.

Transforming data	412
Univariate data	413
Bivariate data	415
Goodness-of-fit tests	416
The Kolmogorov–Smirnov one-sample test	416
The χ^2 goodness-of-fit test	417

Transforming data

When data are not normally distributed or when levels of an IV do not have homogeneous variance, then it is often inappropriate to use a parametric statistical test. However, it is sometimes possible to transform the data so that it is more normal or so that variances are closer to each other. In addition, when looking at the relationship between two variables (bivariate data), if there appears to be a relationship between them but one that is non-linear then one of the variables can be transformed to produce a more linear relationship. To transform data is to apply the same mathematical formula to each of the values in a set of data. You may think that this appears like fiddling with the data to get the answer which you want. However, as long as you make the transformation in order to put the data into a form which would allow a parametric test or a linear test to be conducted, then it is perfectly legitimate. What is not legitimate is to try one transformation, run a statistical test on the data and then go on to try another transformation if you do not achieve statistical significance.

To demonstrate that we do use transformations, often without realising it, think of the measures we could take when we are interested in runners' performances. We could measure the time it takes them to complete a route, the distance they travelled in a given time or even their speed, which is the distance divided by the time taken. If we convert data from time to speed we have performed a transformation on the data.

Using a scientific calculator or a computer it should be possible to make all the suggested transformations.

Univariate data

Negatively skewed

If the distribution takes the following form, one possibility is to raise the data points by a value (x^a) as long as a is greater than 1; for example, we could square all the data points. Alternatively, we could raise a number to the power of each data point; for example, 10^x, that is raise 10 to the power of each data point, or e^x, which is raise the number e (approximately 2.718) to the power of each data point.

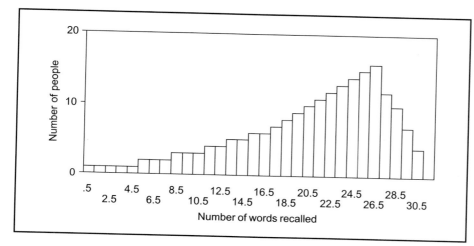

FIGURE A5.1 A negatively skewed distribution

I squared each number of words recalled to produce the more symmetrical distribution:

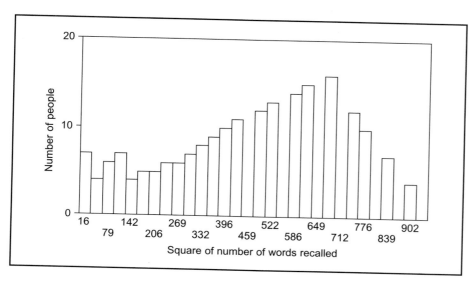

FIGURE A5.2 A negatively skewed distribution after transformation

Positively skewed

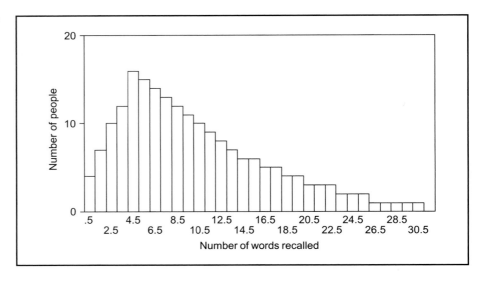

FIGURE A5.3 A positively skewed distribution

When the distribution is positively skewed there is a wide range of possible transformations that can be tried: reciprocals, logarithms, square roots or other fractional powers.

Reciprocals

Try $\dfrac{-1}{x^2}, \dfrac{-1}{x}$, or $\dfrac{-1}{\sqrt{x}}$. However, you cannot divide by zero, so you would need to use an initial transformation that made all the data points non-zero before you took a reciprocal; for example, adding 1 to each person's score.

Logarithms

Try $\log_{10}(x)$ (log to the base 10) or $\ln(x)$ (natural or Naperian logs). If any of the data points are negative or zero then add a fixed number to each data point to make them all greater than zero. Thus, if the biggest negative score in a set of data was -4, add 5 to all the scores and take the logarithm of the result.

Roots (fractional powers)

Try $\sqrt{x}$, or, particularly if the values are less than 10, $\sqrt{x + \dfrac{1}{2}}$ or $(\sqrt{x} + \sqrt{x+1})$.

Square roots can also improve homogeneity of variance. If the square root does not do the trick then try the cube root (i.e. $\sqrt[3]{x}$ or $x^{\frac{1}{3}}$). After trying a number of transformations, I found that $\sqrt{\text{recall} + 0.5}$ produced a more symmetrical distribution.

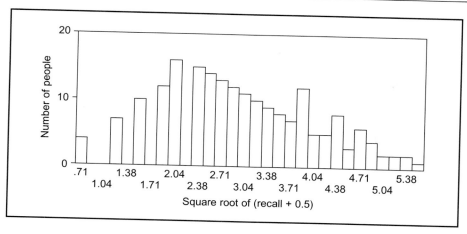

FIGURE A5.4 A positively skewed distribution after transformation

Kurtosis

When the data are proportions or percentages there may be a leptokurtic distribution (one with a tall, thin middle and long tails). In this case, try $2 \times \arcsin(\sqrt{x})$ (arcsine is sometimes shown as $\sin^{-1}$ on a calculator).

Bivariate data

When looking at the correlation between two variables, Pearson's Product Moment Correlation assumes that the relationship is linear (that is, it forms a straight line). Thus, you may need to transform data if they have a pattern but one that is non-linear.

Curving upwards

When the curve of the line is upwards, as in Figure A5.5, then transform the values that are plotted on the vertical (y) axis. Try $\sqrt{y}$, $\ln(y)$, $\log_{10}(y)$ or $\dfrac{-1}{y}$.

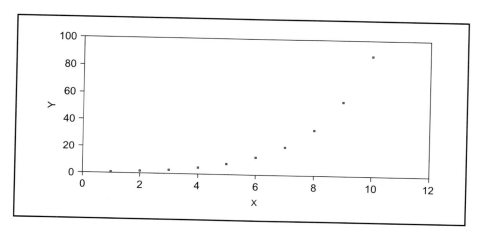

FIGURE A5.5 An upwardly curving scattergram

I took the log of the *y*-values and produced the following line:

FIGURE A5.6 The effect on an upwardly curving scattergram of transformation

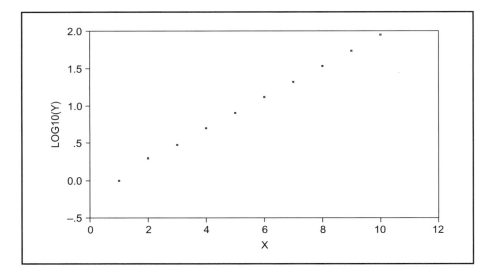

The correlation has changed from $r = 0.868$, for the non-linear relationship, to $r = 0.999$.

Curving downwards

When the curve is downwards, transform the values on the horizontal (*x*) axis. Try $\sqrt{x}$, $\ln(x)$, $\log_{10}(x)$ or $\dfrac{-1}{x}$.

Goodness-of-fit tests

Goodness-of-fit tests are used to compare the distribution in a set of data with a theoretical distribution. The theoretical distribution could either be one derived from a Null Hypothesis that the data are evenly distributed throughout the range of scores or that the data conform to a distribution such as the normal distribution. The Kolmogorov–Smirnov one-sample test can be used when the data are at least ordinal, while the χ^2 goodness-of-fit test is for nominal data. However, the χ^2 goodness-of-fit test is often used when the data are ordinal or even interval/ratio.

The Kolmogorov–Smirnov one-sample test

This test compares the cumulative frequency from the data with the cumulative frequency that would occur if the data conformed to a specified distribution. Taking the example where a sample of 120 people gave their age group, which was first presented in Chapter 9, we can see whether the distribution of ages is evenly spread across the age ranges (a *uniform* distribution).

Table A5.1 Obtaining the D_n statistic for the Kolmogorov–Smirnov one-sample test

age group	frequency	frequency as a proportion	observed cumulative frequency (F_o)	theoretical cumulative proportion (F_t)	$F_o - F_t$
20–29	15	0.125	0.125	0.2	0.075
30–39	45	0.375	0.5	0.4	0.1
40–49	30	0.25	0.75	0.6	0.15
50–59	20	0.167	0.917	0.8	0.117
60–69	10	0.083	1	1	0

As there are 5 age groups, we would expect $\frac{1}{5} = 0.2$ of the people to be in each category, if they were evenly spread across the categories.

For each category you compare the observed cumulative frequency with the theoretical cumulative frequency ($F_o - F_t$), ignoring the sign if it is negative. The statistic from this test is D_n, which is the largest value that $F_o - F_t$ reaches for the sample size n. In this case,

$$D_{120} = 0.15$$

Finding the statistical significance of D_n

Table A14.19 in Appendix XIV gives critical values that D_n has to achieve or exceed to be statistically significant. Above a sample of 35 the critical level of D_n for $p = 0.05$ is $\dfrac{1.36}{\sqrt{n}}$. In this case,

$$\frac{1.36}{\sqrt{120}} = 0.124$$

Therefore, as 0.15 is greater than 0.124, we can say that the data differ significantly from a uniform distribution.

The χ^2 goodness-of-fit test

This test is appropriate, with nominal data, when comparing the frequencies found in a set of data with those that would occur under the Null Hypothesis. Alternatively, it could be used to compare the distribution in data with what would be predicted if the data had a particular theoretical distribution, such as the normal distribution. A statistically significant result in this test suggests that the data did not conform to the Null Hypothesis or to the theoretical distribution.

An example of the use of the test was given in Chapter 14 in which children's initial preferences for particular paintings in an art gallery were being studied. Twenty children were observed as they entered a room which had five paintings in it and, in each child's case, which painting he or she approached first was noted. The research hypothesis was that the children would approach one painting first more than they would the other paintings. The Null Hypothesis was that the number of children approaching each painting first would be the same for all the paintings. Thus, according to the Null Hypothesis we would expect each painting to be approached by $\frac{25}{5} = 5$ children first.

Table A5.2 The number of children approaching a particular painting first and the expected number according to the Null Hypothesis

Painter	Approached first	Expected by H_0
Klee	11	5
Picasso	5	5
Modigliani	3	5
Cézanne	4	5
Rubens	2	5

The χ^2 test compares the actual, or observed, frequencies (f_o) with the expected frequencies (f_e) (according to the Null Hypothesis) to see whether they differ statistically significantly. It uses the following equation:

$$\chi^2 = \sum \frac{(f_o - f_e)^2}{f_e} \tag{A5.1}$$

In words, subtract each expected frequency from its observed frequency, square the result and divide that by the expected frequency. Repeat this for each category and add all the results. Therefore:

$$\chi^2 = \frac{(11 - 5)^2}{5} + \frac{(5 - 5)^2}{5} + \frac{(3 - 5)^2}{5} + \frac{(4 - 5)^2}{5} + \frac{(2 - 5)^2}{5}$$

$$= 7.2 + 0.0 + 0.8 + 0.2 + 1.8$$

$$= 10.0$$

This version of the χ^2 test has degrees of freedom that are one fewer than the number of categories. Therefore in this case df = 5 − 1 = 4. The result can now be looked up in the table of the chi-squared distribution in Appendix XIV. With df = 4, the critical level of χ^2 for $p = 0.05$ is 9.49. As the calculated value of χ^2 exceeds this critical value, we can conclude that the different pictures were approached first by the children with significantly different frequencies.

APPENDIX VI: SEEKING DIFFERENCES BETWEEN TWO LEVELS OF AN INDEPENDENT VARIABLE

This appendix illustrates the techniques introduced in Chapter 15.

Parametric tests	
The t-test	419
Between-subjects t-test	419
Between-subjects t-test with heterogeneity of variance (independent variances—Welch's t-test)	420
Within-subjects t-test	421
Calculating the effect size when two experimental groups are compared	423
Non-parametric tests	424
The Mann–Whitney U-test	425
The statistical significance of Mann–Whitney U	425
Correction for ties	427
The Wilcoxon signed-rank test for matched pairs	427
Finding the probability of Wilcoxon's signed-ranks test	428
Tied scores	429
Calculating an effect size from a z-score for Mann–Whitney U or Wilcoxon tests	430
χ^2 test for analysis of a two-way contingency table	431
Correction for continuity	431
Odds ratios	433
Confidence intervals for odds ratios	434
Risk	434
Fisher's exact probability test	435
The binomial and sign tests	436
The binomial test	437
The sign test	437
	439

Parametric tests

The t-test

There are different versions of the *t*-test, depending on whether the design is between- or within-subjects.

Between-subjects t-test

For this example researchers wish to evaluate the effectiveness of a therapeutic technique designed to rid people of arachnophobia. They have two groups of arachnophobics. One group acts as the experimental group and receives therapy; the other is the control group which does not receive therapy. The researchers measure anxiety using a self-report checklist.

Table A6.1 The anxiety scores of participants given therapy or acting as controls

Therapy	Control
85	80
65	88
70	86
70	85
65	64
75	82
83	89
60	81
62	83
70	67
65	65
79	70
76	84
72	88
74	85
69	82
76	79
71	75
68	77
75	80

Table A6.2 The means, variances and SDs of anxiety level in the therapy and control groups

	Therapy	Control
Mean	71.500	79.500
Variance	58.368	43.000
SD	7.640	6.557

The equation for the between-subjects t-test is:

$$t = \frac{\bar{x}_1 - \bar{x}_2}{\sqrt{\left(\frac{((n_1 - 1) \times s_1^2) + ((n_2 - 1) \times s_2^2)}{(n_1 + n_2 - 2)} \times \left(\frac{1}{n_1} + \frac{1}{n_2} \right) \right)}} \qquad \text{(A6.1)}$$

where $\bar{x}_1$ and $\bar{x}_2$ are the means for the two groups
n_1 and n_2 are the sample sizes for the two groups
s_1^2 and s_2^2 are the variances for the two groups

$\left(\frac{((n_1 - 1) \times s_1^2) + ((n_2 - 1) \times s_2^2)}{(n_1 + n_2 - 2)} \right)$ is the *pooled variance*; that is, the

mean (weighted by sample size) of the variances for the two groups

When the sample sizes are the same this equation becomes simpler:

$$t = \frac{\bar{x}_1 - \bar{x}_2}{\sqrt{\left(\frac{s_1^2 + s_2^2}{n} \right)}} \qquad \text{(A6.2)}$$

where n is the size of one sample.
Therefore, in the present case:

$$t = \frac{71.5 - 79.5}{\sqrt{\left(\frac{58.368 + 43.000}{20} \right)}} = -3.553$$

The degrees of freedom for this version of the t-test are $(n_1 + n_2) - 2$. Thus, in this case they would be $(20 + 20) - 2 = 38$.
The above version of the t-test assumes that the variances of the two groups are the same (homogeneous). If this is not the case then an alternative version of the t-test should be applied.

Between-subjects t-test with heterogeneity of variance (independent variances—Welch's t-test)

When the sample variances for the two groups differ by more than four times, in the case where the sample sizes are the same (or when the sample variances differ by more than two times when the samples sizes are unequal) then a version of the t-test should be used that treats the variances as separate rather than producing a pooled variance estimate:

$$t = \frac{\bar{x}_1 - \bar{x}_2}{\sqrt{\left(\frac{s_1^2}{n_1} + \frac{s_2^2}{n_2} \right)}} \qquad \text{(A6.3)}$$

When the sample sizes are the same for the two groups, this equation produces the same result as Equation A6.2 above. However, it has its own method for calculating the degrees of freedom, which it may be necessary to know in order to test whether this result is statistically significant. Although, to save time, if you have not been given the degrees of freedom by a computer then it is useful to check whether the result is likely to be statistically significant before working out the df. As the new version of the degrees of freedom will never be larger than the usual degrees of freedom for a between-subjects t-test, if the t-value is not statistically significant with the usual df, it will also not be with the modified version. Accordingly, if the t-value is not statistically significant at df = $n_1 + n_2 - 2$, then there is no need to calculate the modified df unless you want a more exact probability.

At the other end of the scale, the modified df will never be smaller than one fewer than the smaller of the two sample sizes. Accordingly, if the t-value is statistically significant when df = $n_{\text{(smaller sample)}} - 1$, then it will certainly be statistically significant for the modified version of the df. Again, there will then be no need to calculate the modified df unless you want a more exact probability.

If the t-value is not statistically significant with df of $n_{\text{(smaller sample)}} - 1$ but is statistically significant with df = $n_1 + n_2 - 2$, then you will need to calculate the modified (or *adjusted*) df.

The equation for adjusted df for a between-subjects t-test with separate variances is:

$$\text{adjusted df} = \left(\frac{\left(\dfrac{s_1^2}{n_1} + \dfrac{s_2^2}{n_2} \right)^2}{\dfrac{\left(\dfrac{s_1^2}{n_1} \right)^2}{n_1 - 1} + \dfrac{\left(\dfrac{s_2^2}{n_2} \right)^2}{n_2 - 1}} \right) - 2 \tag{A6.4}$$

For an example, imagine that the previous study had produced the following results:

Table A6.3 The means, variances and SDs of anxiety level for therapeutic and control groups (heterogeneous variance)

	Therapy	Control
Mean	71.5	79.5
Variance	112.053	24.053
SD	10.586	4.904

Notice that the variance for the group given therapy is more than four times the variance of the control group. Therefore, the t-test for groups with heterogeneous variances should be used.

$$t = \frac{71.5 - 79.5}{\sqrt{\left(\dfrac{112.053}{20} + \dfrac{24.053}{20}\right)}} = -3.0667$$

The minimum degrees of freedom that this t-value could have are $n - 1 = 19$ (as both samples are the same size) and the maximum it could have are $n_1 + n_2 - 2 = 38$. As this value of t would be statistically significant at $p \le 0.05$ with df $= 19$, it clearly will be statistically significant for whatever the adjusted df. However, as an illustration, the adjusted df are calculated:

$$\text{adjusted df} = \left(\frac{\left(\dfrac{112.053}{20} + \dfrac{24.053}{20}\right)^2}{\dfrac{\left(\dfrac{112.053}{20}\right)^2}{20 - 1} + \dfrac{\left(\dfrac{24.053}{20}\right)^2}{20 - 1}}\right) - 2$$

$$= \left(\frac{(6.8053)^2}{\dfrac{31.389}{19} + \dfrac{1.446}{19}}\right) - 2$$

$$= \left(\frac{46.312}{1.728}\right) - 2$$

$$= 26.798 - 2$$

$$= 24.798$$

Within-subjects t-test

This version of the test is based on the difference, for each participant, in the score for the two conditions. In this example, a sports psychologist has devised a technique that he hopes will enhance the performance of racing cyclists. He decides to compare performance, in terms of time taken to complete a route, before training with time taken after training. The equation for this version of the t-test is:

$$\text{within-subjects } t = \frac{\text{mean of the differences}}{\left(\dfrac{\text{SD of the differeces}}{\sqrt{\text{sample size}}}\right)} \tag{A6.5}$$

Table A6.4 The time taken (in minutes) by cyclists to complete a route before and after training, with the differences between the two times

Participant	Pre-training	Post-training	Difference
1	195	195	0
2	200	190	10
3	180	182	−2
4	170	169	1
5	210	205	5
6	220	219	1
7	190	191	−1
8	185	183	2
9	150	148	2
10	160	160	0
11	165	166	−1
		Total	17
		Mean	1.545
		SD	3.387

Therefore, in this case:

$$t = \frac{1.545}{\left(\dfrac{3.387}{\sqrt{11}}\right)} = 1.513$$

Calculating the effect size when two experimental groups are compared
The effect size for designs in which two sample means are compared is *d* and is found from:

$$d = \frac{\text{mean}_1 - \text{mean}_2}{\text{SD}}$$

If one of the groups is a control group then the SD for that group can be used in the above equation. However, if the research had involved comparing the means of two experimental groups, it would be more legitimate to use an SD that combines the information from both groups (the pooled SD). Remember that the *t*-test for a between-subjects design includes a calculation for the pooled variance (see earlier in this appendix). Remember also that the SD is the square root of the variance. Therefore:

$$\text{pooled SD} = \sqrt{\left[\frac{((n_1 - 1) \times s_1^2) + ((n_2 - 1) \times s_2^2)}{(n_1 + n_2 - 2)}\right]} \qquad \text{(A6.6)}$$

However, when the sample sizes are equal this simplifies to:

$$\text{pooled SD} = \sqrt{\frac{s_1^2 + s_2^2}{2}} \qquad \text{(A6.7)}$$

Non-parametric tests

The Mann–Whitney U-test

When the design is between-subjects, has one IV with two levels and requirements of a *t*-test are not fulfilled but the measurement is at least ordinal, then the Mann–Whitney *U*-test can be used.

Researchers wished to compare the attitudes of two groups of students —those studying physics and those studying sociology—about the hunting of animals. Each student was asked to rate his or her agreement with the statement *hunting wild animals is cruel*. The ratings were made on a five-point scale, ranging from *disagree strongly* to *agree strongly*, with a high score denoting an anti-hunting attitude.

Table A6.5 The responses of students to a statement regarding hunting

Sociology	Physics
5	1
4	2
3	3
3	4
5	5
4	2
2	1
5	3
5	4
4	2
4	1
3	3
3	2
5	3
4	3
4	5
4	4
5	3
5	2
5	1
5	2

All the scores are put in order of magnitude on a single scale, rather than separately for each level of the IV.

1	1	1	1	2	2	2	2	2	2	2	3	3	3	3	3	3	3	3	3	3
P	P	P	P	P	P	P	P	P	P	S	P	P	P	P	P	P	S	S	S	S

4	4	4	4	4	4	4	4	4	4	5	5	5	5	5	5	5	5	5	5	5
P	P	P	S	S	S	S	S	S	S	P	P	S	S	S	S	S	S	S	S	S

The statistic U is calculated by noting how many of one group are to the left of each member of the other group. As our prediction is that physicists will give low ratings, we count the number of sociologists who are to the left of each physicist; that is, counter to our prediction.

The four lowest ratings (of 1) were all made by physicists, so there are no sociologists to the left of them. Therefore, so far $U = 0$. The next lowest rating (2) was made by seven students—six physicists and one sociologist. As the sociologist has the same rating as the six physicists, each physicist is counted as having 0.5 of a sociologist to his or her left (because they have the same rank as the sociologist). Therefore we now add $(6 \times 0.5) = 3$ to U. The next rating (3) has six physicists and four sociologists. Therefore, there is one sociologist (with the rating 2) to the left of each of the six physicists, so we add $(6 \times 1) = 6$ to U. In addition, the four sociologists with the rating 3 each count as 0.5; therefore each of the six physicists has $(4 \times 0.5) = 2$ sociologists to his or her left, and so we add a further $(6 \times 2) = 12$ to U. This process continues until the relative position of each of the participants has been noted.

rating	contribution to U	U
1	0	0
2	(6×0.5)	3
3	$(6 \times 2) + (6 \times 1)$	18
4	$(3 \times 3.5) + (3 \times 4) + (3 \times 1)$	25.5
5	$(2 \times 4.5) + (2 \times 7) + (2 \times 4) + (2 \times 1)$	33
	Total U	79.5

If our prediction was a directional one that sociologists would give higher ratings than physicists, then we would seek the probability of this U-value. However, if we predicted that the physicists would give the higher ratings then we would find the U for physicists.

Once U for one group has been calculated, the other U can be found by the following equation:

$$U_2 = (n_1 \times n_2) - U_1$$

Therefore, U for physicists is:

$$U_2 = (21 \times 21) - 79.5$$

$$= 361.5$$

If the hypothesis is non-directional then you find U_1 and U_2 and the statistic used will be the smaller of the two; in this case U_1 would be the statistic.

The statistical significance of Mann–Whitney U

If you are not using a statistical package, such as later versions of SPSS, which provides exact probabilities, then if the sample size for both groups is twenty or fewer the probability of the result having occurred if the Null Hypothesis were true is given in Appendix XIV. However, if either group has more than twenty participants then you will need to use a version of a z-test to calculate the probability

$$z = \frac{U - \left(\dfrac{n_1 \times n_2}{2}\right)}{\sqrt{\dfrac{n_1 \times n_2 \times (n_1 + n_2 + 1)}{12}}} \tag{A6.8}$$

$$= \frac{79.5 - \left(\dfrac{21 \times 21}{2}\right)}{\sqrt{\dfrac{21 \times 21 \times (21 + 21 + 1)}{12}}}$$

$$= -3.5469$$

Correction for ties

It is likely that your computer program will also offer you an alternative value of z that has taken into account the number of scores that had the same value (tied scores). When the sample size is large enough to warrant using the z-test then it is worth correcting for ties as this gives a more accurate value for z and therefore for p.

To correct for ties we need to know how many scores tied and how many were in each of the ties. There were four ties for the rating 1, seven with the rating 2, and so on. Form the following table:

score	number of ties (t)	correction $= \dfrac{t^3 - t}{12}$
1	4	5
2	7	28
3	10	82.5
4	10	82.5
5	11	110
Total correction		308

We can now use the equation for z that is corrected for ties, but to simplify the equation let $N = n_1 + n_2$:

$$z \text{ (corrected for ties)} = \frac{U - \left(\dfrac{n_1 \times n_2}{2} \right)}{\sqrt{\dfrac{n_1 \times n_2}{[N \times (N - 1)]} \times \left(\dfrac{N^3 - N}{12} - \text{total correction} \right)}}$$

(A6.9)

Therefore, in this case:

$$z \text{ (corrected for ties)} = \frac{79.5 - \left(\dfrac{21 \times 21}{2} \right)}{\sqrt{\dfrac{21 \times 21}{[42 \times (42 - 1)]} \times \left(\dfrac{(42)^3 - 42}{12} - 308 \right)}}$$

$$= -3.6389$$

The Wilcoxon signed-rank test for matched pairs

When the design is within-subjects, with one IV that has two levels and the requirements of a within-subjects t-test are not fulfilled but the measurement is at least ordinal then the Wilcoxon signed-rank test for matched pairs can be used. It looks at the size of differences between the two levels of the IV. It ranks the differences according to their size and gives each difference either a positive or a negative sign, depending on whether the score in the second level is bigger or smaller than that in the first level. The ranks of the sign that occurs least often are then added together and the result forms the statistic T.

Researchers were comparing people's views of psychology as science before and after hearing a talk on the nature of psychology. Their views were found from their responses to the statement: *Psychology is a science.* They used a 5-point rating scale ranging from *agree strongly* to *disagree strongly*, with a higher score denoting a belief that psychology is a science.

When more than one score is the same (tied) the ranks are found by counting how many have the same rank, giving each the rank it would have had had they not been tied, and then finding the mean rank for them. For example, there are 3 people who had a difference of −1 in rating between the two occasions. Therefore, had they not been tied they would have had the ranks: 1, 2, and 3. Their mean rank is:

$$\text{mean rank} = \frac{1 + 2 + 3}{3}$$

$$= 2$$

The next difference would be treated as though it had a rank of 4, if it was not tied. We use the smaller of the two Ts, which in this case is the one for positive differences, $T = 0$.

Table A6.6 The ratings of participants of psychology before and after a talk on the subject

before	after	difference	rank of difference	positive	negative
1	3	−3	7.5		7.5
1	4	−3	7.5		7.5
2	2	0			
2	4	−2	5		5
3	5	−2	5		5
2	4	−2	5		5
3	4	−1	2		2
4	4	0			
5	5	0			
4	5	−1	2		2
2	3	−1	2		2
3	3	0			
			Total (*T*)	0	36

Finding the probability of Wilcoxon's signed-ranks test
This test rejects those cases where there is no difference between the two levels of the IV and the sample size is only those who did show a difference. Thus, in the present example, as four people did not change their ratings between the two occasions, the sample size is considered to be 12 − 4 = 8. If you are not using a statistical package that provides exact probabilities, then when the sample size is 25 or fewer, use Table A14.6 in Appendix XIV. Therefore, in the present case, with a sample size of 8, this is what we should do. When the sample is larger than 25 there is a *z*-test that you would have to use.

$$z = \frac{T - \dfrac{N \times (N + 1)}{4}}{\sqrt{\dfrac{N \times (N + 1) \times [(2 \times N) + 1]}{24}}} \qquad (A6.10)$$

Although it is not appropriate to use the z-test in this example, I will use the result in order to illustrate the use of the z-test.

$$z = \frac{0 - \dfrac{8 \times (8 + 1)}{4}}{\sqrt{\dfrac{8 \times (8 + 1) \times [(2 \times 8) + 1]}{24}}}$$

$$= \frac{-\dfrac{8 \times 9}{4}}{\sqrt{\dfrac{8 \times 9 \times 17}{24}}} = \frac{-18}{\sqrt{51}}$$

$$= -2.521$$

Tied scores

To correct for ties we need to know how many scores tied and how many were in each of the ties. There were three ties for the rating 1, three with the rating 2, and so on. Form the following table:

difference (regardless of sign)	number of ties (t)	correction $= \dfrac{t^3 - t}{2}$
1	3	12
2	3	12
3	2	3
Total correction		27

We can now use the equation for z that is corrected for ties:

$$z \text{ (corrected for ties)} = \frac{T - \dfrac{N \times (N + 1)}{4}}{\sqrt{\dfrac{N \times (N + 1) \times [(2 \times N) + 1]}{24} - \text{total correction}}}$$

$$(A6.11)$$

Therefore, in the present case:

$$z \text{ (corrected for ties)} = \frac{0 - \dfrac{8 \times (8 + 1)}{4}}{\sqrt{\dfrac{8 \times (8 + 1) \times [(2 \times 8) + 1]}{24} - 27}}$$

$$= \frac{-18}{\sqrt{51 - 27}}$$

$$= \frac{-18}{4.8989}$$

$$= -3.674$$

Calculating an effect size from a z-score for Mann–Whitney U or Wilcoxon tests

Now that we have a z-score for the result we can convert this into an effect size (r) using the following equation:

$$r = \frac{z}{\sqrt{N}}$$

where N is the total number of participants in the study.
Therefore, in the example above for the Mann–Whitney U-test:

$$r = \frac{-3.6389}{\sqrt{42}} = -0.56$$

which, in Cohen's (1988) terms, would be considered a large effect size.

χ^2 test for analysis of a two-way contingency table

When the design is between-subjects and there are two variables (two-way) and the data are nominal, then the χ^2 test for contingencies can be used.

Researchers wanted to see whether there were different proportions of males and females who smoked. The expected frequency (f_e) for a given cell is calculated by multiplying the total for the row in which the cell occurs by the total for the column in which that cell occurs and then dividing the result by the overall total. Therefore, for the top left-hand cell the expected frequency is:

$$f_e = \frac{38 \times 44}{88} = 19$$

Table A6.7 The numbers of male and female smokers and non-smokers

Observed Frequency Table

	male	female	Totals:
smoker	17	21	38
non-smoker	27	23	50
Totals:	44	44	88

This is a simplified version of the full equation which finds the marginal probabilities: the probability in the sample of being male is 44 out of 88; the probability of being a smoker is 38 out of 88. Therefore, if gender and smoking status are independent of each other:

$$\text{expected frequency of being a male smoker} = \frac{38}{88} \times \frac{44}{88} \times 88$$

As this involves multiplying by 88 and dividing by 88, these two operations cancel each other out and we get the simplified equation for expected frequency, shown above. The next table shows the expected frequency for each cell.

Table A6.8 The frequencies that would be expected if smoking and gender were not linked

Expected Values

	male	female	Totals:
smoker	19	19	38
non-smoker	25	25	50
Totals:	44	44	88

The χ^2 test compares the expected frequencies with those that actually occurred (the observed frequencies, f_o), using the same equation (A5.1) as for a one-group χ^2 test:

$$\chi^2 = \sum \frac{(f_o - f_e)^2}{f_e}$$

In words, subtract each expected frequency from its observed frequency, square the result and divide that by the expected frequency. Repeat this for each cell and add all the results.

$$\chi^2 = \frac{(17 - 19)^2}{19} + \frac{(21 - 19)^2}{19} + \frac{(27 - 25)^2}{25} + \frac{(23 - 25)^2}{25}$$

$$= 0.2105 + 0.2105 + 0.16 + 0.16 = 0.741$$

Correction for continuity

Yates (1934) devised a correction for the χ^2 test when it is being used for a 2×2 contingency table. As pointed out in Chapter 15, the rationale for this correction is that the probabilities given by the chi-squared distribution are calculated on the basis that the variables involved are continuous. It was felt that, as in a 2×2 table the measures are dichotomous, it was necessary to make the correction under these circumstances. However, the assumption is that the marginal totals are fixed.

This rarely happens in real research but an example would be of asking a participant to sort 32 photographs of people into two equal piles on the basis of whether he or she thought that the photograph represented someone from the north or south of England. Thus the marginal totals for the sorting would be fixed at 16 each. The photographs would be of 16 people from the south and 16 from the north of England, thus fixing the other marginal totals:

Table A6.9 The way in which a participant sorted photographs of people from the north and south of England

Sorting	Part of England person in photo comes from		
	North	South	
North	10	6	16
South	6	10	16
	16	16	32

If, in a 2×2 contingency table, the assumption of fixed marginal totals is correct then Yates's correction for χ^2 could be applied. Nonetheless, as computer programs often report the corrected version of χ^2, regardless of whether this restriction is fulfilled, it is worth being aware of the equation:

$$\text{corrected-}\chi^2 = \sum \frac{(|f_o - f_e| - 0.5)^2}{f_e} \qquad (A6.12)$$

where the vertical lines in $|f_o - f_e|$ mean ignore the sign if the result is negative.

Therefore, in the photograph sorting case:

$$\text{corrected-}\chi^2$$

$$= \frac{(|10 - 8| - 0.5)^2}{8} + \frac{(|6 - 8| - 0.5)^2}{8} + \frac{(|6 - 8| - 0.5)^2}{8} + \frac{(|10 - 8| - 0.5)^2}{8}$$

$$= \frac{(1.5)^2}{8} + \frac{(1.5)^2}{8} + \frac{(1.5)^2}{8} + \frac{(1.5)^2}{8} = 1.125$$

(For the same table, the uncorrected-$\chi^2 = 2$.)

As usual with a χ^2 for a 2×2 contingency table, df = 1.

Odds ratios

Odds ratios are also called 'cross-product ratios' because in a 2 × 2 table they can be found from the following equation:

$$\text{odds ratio} = \frac{n_{11} \times n_{22}}{n_{12} \times n_{21}} \tag{A6.13}$$

where the first subscript tells you what row the number came from and the second tells you what column it came from. Therefore n_{11} is the number from row 1 and column 1. Thus, in Table A6.7 n_{11} is 17. The odds ratio from Table A6.7 can be found from:

$$\text{odds ratio of males smokers to female smokers} = \frac{17 \times 23}{21 \times 27} = \frac{391}{567} = 0.6896$$

Confidence intervals for odds ratios

The confidence intervals (CI) for odds ratios are calculated in the following way. Because the distribution of odds ratios is skewed it is necessary to find the confidence interval for the natural log of the odds ratio and then convert back for an interval around the original ratio.

The data for Table A6.7 produced the following odds ratio:

$$\text{odds ratio of males and females being smokers} = 0.6896$$

Find the natural log of the odds ratio

$$\text{Ln}(0.6896) = -0.37164$$

Find the standard error (s.e.) for the natural log of the odds ratio (called the *asymptotic standard error*)

$$\text{s.e.} = \sqrt{\frac{1}{n_{11}} + \frac{1}{n_{12}} + \frac{1}{n_{21}} + \frac{1}{n_{22}}} \tag{A6.14}$$

where n_{11} to n_{22} are the samples in each of the cells of the 2 × 2 table. Therefore,

$$\text{s.e.} = \sqrt{\frac{1}{17} + \frac{1}{21} + \frac{1}{27} + \frac{1}{23}} = 0.43239$$

The 95% CI of the natural log

$$= \text{Ln}(\text{odds ratio}) - (1.96 \times \text{s.e.}) \text{ to Ln}(\text{odds ratio}) + (1.96 \times \text{s.e.})$$

Which, in this case

$$= -0.37164 - (1.96 \times 0.43239) \text{ to } -0.37164 + (1.96 \times 0.43239)$$

$$= -0.37164 - 0.84748 \text{ to } -0.371644 + 0.84748$$

$$= -1.21912 \text{ to } 0.47583$$

Convert these back to odds ratios by raising e by each of them, where e = 2.71828 approximately.

$$e^{-1.21912} = 0.295$$

$$e^{0.47583} = 1.609$$

Risk

In order to get SPSS to calculate an odds ratio and its confidence interval you select *Risk*. Part of the output that is provided includes the risk values, as shown in Table A6.10.

Table A6.10 The risks, odds ratio and confidence intervals for the data in Table A6.8

Risk Estimate

	Value	95% Confidence Interval	
		Lower	Upper
Odds Ratio for smoking status (smoker/non-smoker)	.690	.295	1.609
For cohort GENDER = male	.828	.536	1.282
For cohort GENDER = female	1.201	.794	1.819
N of Valid Cases	88		

$$\text{risk of being a smoker for males} = \frac{\text{probability of being male if a smoker}}{\text{probability of being male if not a smoker}}$$

where

$$\text{probability of being a male if a smoker} = \frac{17}{38} = 0.447$$

and

$$\text{probability of being a male if not a smoker} = \frac{27}{50} = 0.54$$

Therefore the risk of being a smoker for males is $\dfrac{0.447}{0.54} = 0.828$.

Incidentally, odds ratios can be found from risks, using the equation:

$$\text{odds ratio} = \text{risk } 1 / \text{risk } 2$$

Fisher's exact probability test

When there is a 2×2 contingency table and the *expected frequencies* of any of the cells are below 5 then the χ^2 test is not considered reliable. Fisher's exact probability test can be used but it is only appropriate when the levels of both variables have fixed marginal totals. (In Chapter 15 it was pointed out that when the marginal totals are not fixed, but the expected frequencies are small, then an alternative test exists, the workings for which were given in the chapter.) Imagine that we repeated the example of giving a participant photographs of people to sort as to which region they came from but only used 10 photographs and told the participant that 5 were of people from the north and 5 of people from the south:

Table A6.11 The way in which a participant sorted ten photographs of people from the north and south of England

Sorting	Part of England person in photo comes from		
	North	South	
North	4 (A)	1 (B)	5
South	1 (C)	4 (D)	5
	5	5	

As the marginal totals are fixed Fisher's exact probability test would be usable to analyse the data. The Null Hypothesis is that there is no link between participant's sorting and the place that the people photographed really came from, and so the expected frequencies for each of the cells is 2.5.

The equation for Fisher's test gives the exact probability of the outcome. Remember that usually we want the probability of that outcome plus the probabilities of more extreme probabilities that are in line with the hypothesis (see Chapter 10 for an explanation of this point). Therefore, we will want the probability of the outcome given in Table A6.11 and the probability of the more extreme outcome shown in Table A6.12:

Table A6.12 A more extreme outcome from the data shown in Table A6.11

Sorting	Part of England person in photo comes from		
	North	South	
North	5 (A)	0 (B)	5
South	0 (C)	5 (D)	5
	5	5	

Note that the marginal totals remain the same as in the previous table.

The probability from Fisher's exact probability test is found from:

$$p = \frac{(A + B)! \times (C + D)! \times (A + C)! \times (B + D)!}{N! \times A! \times B! \times C! \times D!} \qquad (A6.15)$$

Where 4! means the factorial of 4, which is $4 \times 3 \times 2 \times 1 = 24$. (Incidentally, $0! = 1$.)

Therefore, in the present case, the probability of the outcome of Table A6.11 is:

$$p = \frac{(4 + 1)! \times (1 + 4)! \times (4 + 1)! \times (1 + 4)!}{10! \times 4! \times 1! \times 4! \times 1!}$$

$$= \frac{24 \times 24 \times 24 \times 24}{3628800 \times 24 \times 1 \times 24 \times 1}$$

$$= 0.00015873$$

The probability for the more extreme outcome of Table A6.12 is:

$$p = 0.000031746$$

Therefore the probability that the results in this contingency table would have occurred if the Null Hypothesis were true is:

$$p = 0.00015873 + 0.000031746 = 0.000190476$$

To save calculating the probabilities in this way, tables of probabilities for this test are provided in Appendix XIV.

The binomial and sign tests

Two relatively simple tests that you may see referred to are the binomial test and a test that is based on it, the sign test.

The binomial test

The binomial test can be used when there are two possible types of event and we wish to calculate the likelihood of the outcomes we have found if the events had particular probabilities under the Null Hypothesis. We could use it in the case mentioned in Chapter 10 where we were interested in whether a friend could cause coins to fall as heads. Here there are two possible events for each toss of the coin—a head or a tail—and each is equally likely to occur, if the Null Hypothesis is true, so for heads $p = 0.5$ and for tails $p = 1 - 0.5$ which is also 0.5.

The basic formula for a given outcome (or set of events), say of getting all heads from 5 coins is:

$$p = {}_nC_r \times p^r \times (1 - p)^{(n-r)} \qquad (A6.16)$$

where n is the number of trials (tosses of coins)

r is the number of hits (occasions when the event we are looking for occurs)

$_nC_r$ is the number of ways in which the outcome we have achieved (e.g. 5 heads) could have occurred

$_nC_r$ is calculated from Eqn A6.17:

$$\frac{n!}{(n-r)! \times r!}$$ (A6.17)

where $n!$ means the *factorial* of n (as defined earlier).

We need one more mathematical convention to be able to work out the equation:

any number raised to the power of $0 = 1$, e.g. $5^0 = 1$

Now we can work out the probability of 5 heads:

$$p = {_5C_5} \times 0.5^5 \times (1 - 0.5)^{(5-5)} = \frac{5!}{0! \times 5!} \times 0.5^5 \times (0.5)^{(0)}$$

$$= 1 \times 0.03125 \times 1 = 0.03125$$

Unfortunately that calculation has told us the probability of one particular outcome. Remember that the probability we are told by the computer is that of the outcome that occurred plus any other possible outcome that is more extreme and in line with the hypothesis. In this example the outcome was the most extreme and so this is the probability we would be interested in. If the outcome had been 4 heads and 1 tail then we would need the probability of that outcome and we would have to add it to the probability for 5 heads to find the significance of the outcome.

The probability of exactly 4 heads out of 5 tosses is:

$$p = \frac{5!}{(5-4)! \times 4!} \times 0.5^4 \times (0.5)^{(5-4)}$$

We need yet another mathematical convention to be able to work out this equation:

any number raised to the power of 1 remains unchanged, e.g. $5^1 = 5$

$$p = \frac{5!}{(1)! \times 4!} \times 0.5^4 \times (0.5)^{(1)} = 5 \times 0.0625 \times 0.5 = 5 \times 0.03125 = 0.15625$$

Therefore the probability we need is:

the probability of 5 heads + the probability of 4 heads $= 0.03125 + 0.15625$

$$= 0.1875.$$

Rather than calculate the probability of each possible outcome, it is useful to have tables that give the probabilities. Table A14.4 allows you to find the probability of an outcome when there are up to 25 trials, as long as the probabilities of the two events you are interested in are equal. If the probabilities are unequal then you will need to use a computer or the equations above.

The sign test

The sign test can be used when we can convert our data into a format where, under the Null Hypothesis, there are two equally likely outcomes. As an example, we can re-analyse some data that were given in Chapter 15 (see Table 15.10). People were asked whether they agreed that psychology was a science, on two occasions: before they heard a talk on the subject and after the talk. We were interested in whether more people changed to have the view that psychology is a science than changed the other way. We can code those who changed from disagreeing with the statement to agreeing with it as '+' and those who changed in the opposite direction as '−'; see Table A6.13:

Table A6.13 The opinions of participants, before and after a talk, on whether psychology is a science

Person	Opinion before	Opinion afterwards	Direction of change
1	disagree	agree	+
2	disagree	agree	+
3	disagree	agree	+
4	disagree	agree	+
5	disagree	agree	+
6	disagree	agree	+
7	disagree	agree	+
8	disagree	agree	+
9	disagree	agree	+
10	disagree	disagree	0
11	disagree	disagree	0
12	disagree	disagree	0
13	agree	agree	0
14	agree	agree	0
15	agree	agree	0
16	agree	agree	0
17	agree	agree	0
18	agree	agree	0

In the example no one changed from agreeing to disagreeing, while 9 people changed from disagreeing to agreeing. Thus, we can ask of those who changed, *did a significant number change from disagreeing to agreeing?* This can be calculated using the binomial test:

$$p = \frac{9!}{(9-9)! \times 0!} \times 0.5^9 \times (0.5)^{(9-9)} = 1 \times 0.00195 \times 1 = 0.00195$$

which, when rounded to 3 decimal places, is 0.002, i.e. the one-tailed probability that was reported in Chapter 15 for these data.

This appendix illustrates the techniques introduced in Chapter 16.

Parametric tests   441
    One-way between-subjects ANOVA   441
    One-way within-subjects ANOVA   446
    Partial eta-squared   453
Non-parametric tests   454
    At least ordinal measurement   454
    Nominal data   460

The information provided in this appendix will allow you to calculate the statistics by hand or with a calculator but the techniques shown are not always the conventional ones that you would find in most text books. They are provided more to enhance understanding and to allow the checking of computer printout. The workings will be given to five decimal places so that the results are consistent with the summary tables from the computer print-out, once they have been rounded up or down; you do not normally need this level of precision.

Parametric tests

One-way between-subjects ANOVA

Researchers compared the effectiveness of two different mnemonic techniques—pegwords and method of loci—and a control condition.

Table A7.1 The number of words recalled under three memory conditions with mean and standard deviations

| | Mnemonic strategy | | |
	Control	Pegword	Loci
	10	11	10
	7	7	8
	7	9	11
	9	10	9
	5	8	12
	6	6	10
	8	12	7
	5	9	11
	7	10	8
	8	7	10
Mean	7.2	8.9	9.6
SD	1.61933	1.91195	1.57762

There are three sources of variation that we need to quantify: the overall variation in scores (Total), which can be divided into the variation between the treatments (Between-groups) and the variation in scores within the groups (Within-groups).

The Sum of Squares is the sum of squared deviations from the mean, usually shown as:

$$\text{Sum of Squares} = \Sigma(x - \bar{x})^2$$

Total Sum of Squares

To obtain this it is necessary to find the overall mean for the scores. Then take the mean from each score to find each deviation. Then square each deviation and add all the squared deviations.

In this case the overall mean is 8.56667 and the Total Sum of Squares is 109.36654 (or 109.367 to 3 decimal places).

Between-groups Sum of Squares

The Treatment or Between-groups Sum of Squares is a comparison of the results for the three treatments; it takes into account the number of scores that were in each treatment. This can be obtained by finding the deviation of each treatment mean from the overall mean. Square each deviation and multiply it by the number of scores that provided that treatment mean, then add all the results.

Table A7.2 Creating the treatments Sum of Squares for a one-way between-subjects ANOVA

treatment	mean	deviation from overall mean (8.56667)	(deviation)²	n × (deviation)²
control	7.2	−1.36667	1.86779	18.6779
pegwords	8.9	0.33333	0.11111	1.1111
loci	9.6	1.03333	1.06777	10.6777

Between-groups Sum of Squares   30.4667

Within-groups Sum of Squares

This can be obtained by finding the Sum of Squares within each group and adding them together. If we know the variance for a set of scores then we can find out their sum of squares, because:

$$\text{variance} = \frac{\text{Sum of Squares}}{n - 1}$$

Remember that:

$$\text{variance} = (SD)^2$$

Table A7.3 Creating the Within-groups Sum of Squares for a one-way between-subjects ANOVA

treatment	SD	variance	variance × (n − 1)
control	1.61933	2.62223	23.60007
pegwords	1.91195	3.65555	32.89995
loci	1.57762	2.48888	22.39992

Within-groups Sum of Squares   78.89994

The Within-groups Sum of Squares (S of S) could also have been found from:

Total S of S = Between-groups S of S + Within-groups S of S

which means that:

Within-groups S of S = Total S of S − Between-groups S of S

$$= 109.36654 - 30.4667$$

$$= 78.89984 \text{ (which is the same,}$$
to 3 decimal places, as before)

We now have the necessary sums of squares to create the summary table for the ANOVA:

Table A7.4 A summary table for a one-way between-subjects ANOVA

Source	Sum of Squares	df	Mean Square	F-test	p
Between Groups	30.467	2	15.233	5.213	0.0122
Within Groups	78.900	27	2.922		
Total	109.367	29			

See Chapter 16 for an explanation of how the degrees of freedom, Mean Squares and F-ratios are found.

Unequal sample sizes (unbalanced designs)
When the sample size is not the same for all the groups then there are two possible ways to calculate the Treatment Sum of Squares; the other sum of squares would be found as shown above.

Weighted means
The method shown above gives what is described as the *weighted means solution*, which multiplies the sum of squared deviations of each mean by the sample size of the group providing that mean. In this way, larger samples are being given more weight. This is the method used by most computer programs.

Unweighted means
An alternative method is to multiply each sum of squared deviations by the harmonic mean of the sample size. The harmonic mean is found by:

$$n_h = \frac{k}{\dfrac{1}{n_1} + \dfrac{1}{n_2} \text{ up to } \dfrac{1}{n_k}}$$

where k is the number of levels
   n_1 is the sample size in the first group
   n_k is the sample size for the last group

Therefore, if in the example given above, with three levels the sample sizes had been 8, 10 and 7, the harmonic mean of the sample size would be:

$$n_h = \frac{3}{\left(\dfrac{1}{8} + \dfrac{1}{10} + \dfrac{1}{7}\right)} = \frac{3}{(0.125 + 0.1 + 0.14286)}$$

$$= \frac{3}{0.36786} = 8.155$$

Heterogeneity of variance (Welch's F')

There is a version of between-subjects ANOVA (the Welch formula, F') which allows for lack of homogeneity of variance between the levels of the independent variable.

$$F' = \frac{\left[\dfrac{\sum\{w_j \times (\bar{x}_j - \bar{x})^2\}}{k - 1}\right]}{1 + \left[\dfrac{2 \times (k - 2)}{k^2 - 1}\right] \times \sum\left[\left(\dfrac{1}{n_j - 1}\right) \times \left(1 - \dfrac{w_j}{\sum w_j}\right)^2\right]}$$

where $w_j = \dfrac{n_j}{s_j^2}$

n_j is the sample in level j

s_j^2 is the variance in level j

$\bar{x}_j$ is the mean of level j

$\bar{x} = \dfrac{\sum(w_j \times \bar{x}_j)}{\sum w_j}$

k is the number of levels in the independent variable.

F' has the same df for treatment as a standard F-ratio $(k - 1)$ but a modified error df compared with the standard F-ratio:

$$df_2' = \frac{k^2 - 1}{3 \times \sum\left[\left(\dfrac{1}{n_j - 1}\right) \times \left(1 - \dfrac{w_j}{\sum w_j}\right)^2\right]}$$

Although the data in Table A7.1 have homogeneity of variance, the following is a re-analysis according to the Welch formula.

	Mnemonic Strategy		
	Control	Pegword	Loci
$\bar{x}_j$	7.2	8.9	9.6
SD_j	1.61933	1.91195	1.57762
Variance (s_j^2)	2.6222	3.6556	2.4889
w_j	3.8135	2.7356	4.0179
$w_j \times \bar{x}_j$	27.4572	24.3468	38.5718

$$\Sigma w_j = 10.567$$

$$\bar{x} = 8.5526$$

	Mnemonic Strategy		
	Control	Pegword	Loci
$\bar{x}_j - \bar{x}$	−1.3526	0.3474	1.0474
$(\bar{x}_j - \bar{x})^2$	1.8295	0.1207	1.0970
$w_j \times (\bar{x}_j - \bar{x})^2$	6.9768	0.3302	4.4076

$n = 10$ for each group
$k = 3$

$$F' = \cfrac{5.8573}{1 + \left(\dfrac{2}{8} \times 0.1491\right)}$$

$$= 5.6468$$

$$\mathrm{df}'_2 = \cfrac{8}{3 \times 0.1491}$$

$$= 17.8851$$

Referring to the tables for the F-distribution, we are told that with 2 and 18 degrees of freedom, the probability of F' is $0.01 < p < 0.05$. (The more exact probability is 0.013, which is very close to the probability given for the original F-ratio in Table A7.4.)

One-way within-subjects ANOVA

Researchers investigated the effects of the presence of others on judgements about the treatment of offenders. Participants were given a description of a crime and had to decide how long the criminal should spend in prison. The experiment involved three conditions: in one, each participant was alone and unaware of anyone else's judgement; in a second condition, each participant was alone but could see on a computer screen what others had 'decided'; in the third condition, each participant was in a group and aware of what the others had 'decided'. The decisions that the participants learned that others had made were, in fact, pre-set by the experimenters but the participants were unaware of this.

Table A7.5 The sentences given to criminals when participants were in one of three situations

Participant	Alone	Computer	Group	Mean for participant
1	24	24	24	24
2	18	24	24	22
3	12	15	15	14
4	3	12	12	9
5	24	24	30	26
6	18	18	24	20
7	12	15	18	15
8	15	20	20	18.33333
9	12	15	18	15
10	9	15	15	13
Mean	14.7	18.2	20	17.63333
SD	6.55	4.52	5.48	

The sources of variation in scores are the total variation, which can be split into the variation due to participants—between-subjects—and that due to a combination of the participants and the treatments—within-subjects. The within-subjects variation can be further divided into between-groups (or treatment) variation—that is, the effect of the IV—and the residual (or error) variation—that is, what cannot be accounted for by differences between the treatments.

Thus, the total sum of squared deviations can be split into:

between subjects   within subjects

Total S of S = $\boxed{\text{subjects S of S}}$ + $\boxed{\text{treatment S of S + residual S of S}}$

Total Sum of Squares

The Total Sum of Squares is obtained in the same way as for a one-way between-subjects ANOVA by finding the overall mean for the scores, then taking the mean from each score to find each deviation, then squaring each deviation and adding all the squared deviations. In this case the overall mean is 17.63333 and the Total Sum of Squares is 984.96673 (or 984.967 to 3 decimal places).

Between-subjects Sum of Squares
This is the sum of squared deviations of each participant's mean from the overall mean, multiplied by the number of treatments (k).

Table A7.6 Obtaining the Between-subjects Sum of Squares for a one-way within-subjects ANOVA

participant	mean	deviation from overall mean (17.63333)	(deviation)^2	$k \times$ (deviation)^2 (k is number of treatments)
1	24	6.36667	40.53449	121.60347
2	22	4.36667	19.06781	57.20343
3	14	−3.63333	13.20109	39.60327
4	9	−8.63333	74.53439	223.60317
5	26	8.36667	70.00117	210.00351
6	20	2.36667	5.60113	16.80339
7	15	−2.63333	6.93443	20.80329
8	18.33333	0.7	0.49	1.47
9	15	−2.63333	6.93443	20.80329
10	13	−4.63333	21.46775	64.40325

Between-subjects Sum of Squares   776.30007

Within-subjects Sum of Squares
This is the sum of the squared deviations of each participant's score from the mean for that participant. Thus the second participant's sum of squared deviation (S of S) is:

$$S \text{ of } S_{(\text{participant 2})} = (18 - 22)^2 + (24 - 22)^2 + (24 - 22)^2$$

$$= (-4)^2 + 2^2 + 2^2$$

$$= 16 + 4 + 4$$

$$= 24$$

Table A7.7 Obtaining the Within-subjects Sum of Squares for a one-way within-subjects ANOVA

participant	Alone	Computer	Group	Mean	Sum of squared deviations from own mean
1	24	24	24	24	0
2	18	24	24	22	24
3	12	15	15	14	6
4	3	12	12	9	54
5	24	24	30	26	24
6	18	18	24	20	24
7	12	15	18	15	18
8	15	20	20	18.33333	16.66667
9	12	15	18	15	18
10	9	15	15	13	24

Within-subjects S of S   208.66667

Between-groups (treatment) Sum of Squares

As with the between-subjects ANOVA, this is the sum of squares of the three treatment means multiplied by the sample size.

Table A7.8 Obtaining the between-groups Sum of Squares for a one-way within-subjects ANOVA

treatment	mean for treatment	deviation from overall mean (17.63333)	(deviation)^2	$n \times$ (deviation)^2
alone	14.7	−2.93333	8.60442	86.0442
computer	18.2	0.56667	0.32111	3.2111
group	20	2.36667	5.60113	56.0113

Between-groups Sum of Squares   145.2666

Residual Sum of Squares

The residual Sum of Squares is the sum of squares within the groups, once the between-subjects effect has been removed. The residuals can be found by subtracting each person's overall mean from his or her score in each condition.

Thus the second participant's residual for the alone treatment is $18 - 22 = -4$. Once the residuals have been found, calculate the within-group Sum of Squares for those residuals by finding how each residual differs from the mean residual for that treatment.

Table A7.9 The residuals for each participant under each condition, used to find the residual Sum of Squares for a one-way within-subjects ANOVA

Participant	Alone	Computer	Group
1	0	0	0
2	−4	2	2
3	−2	1	1
4	−6	3	3
5	−2	−2	4
6	−2	−2	4
7	−3	0	3
8	−3.33333	1.66667	1.66667
9	−3	0	3
10	−4	2	2

	Alone	Computer	Group	
Mean residual	−2.93333	0.566667	2.36667	
SD	1.60093	1.68545	1.28091	
variance	2.56296	2.84074	1.64074	residual S of S
column S of S	23.06664	25.56667	14.76667	63.39997

Once the Total and Between-subjects Sums of Squares have been found, the Within-subjects Sum of Squares can be found from:

Within-subjects S of S = Total S of S − Between-subjects S of S

Once the Treatments Sum of Squares has been found, the residual Sum of Squares can be found from:

residual S of S = Within-subjects S of S − Treatments S of S.

Now that we have obtained all the necessary sums of squares, the summary table for the ANOVA can be created. See Chapter 16 for details of how the degrees of freedom, Mean Squares and F-ratios are calculated.

Table A7.10 A summary table for a one-way within-subjects ANOVA

Source	Sum of Squares	df	Mean Square	F-ratio	p
Between subjects	776.3	9			
Within subjects	208.667	20	10.433		
treatments	145.267	2	72.633	20.621	0.0001
residual	63.399	18	3.522		
Total	984.967	29			

Sphericity

Within-subjects ANOVAs have a particular assumption that the data should fulfil. The variances of the differences between different pairs of levels of the IV will be the same (known as sphericity or circularity). That is, that the variance of the difference between the scores for the alone and the computer condition will be the same as the variance of the difference scores between computer and face-to-face and the variance of the difference scores between alone and face-to-face conditions.

When sphericity is not present, one approach to compensate for this and produce a more accurate probability for the test is to adjust the degrees of freedom for the F-ratios.

The two adjustments are the Greenhouse–Geisser epsilon (G–G) and the Huynh–Feldt epsilon (H–F). The first is conservative, in other words it is more likely to avoid a Type I error but increases the likelihood of a Type II error, and the second is more liberal.

Table A7.11 Calculating the variances of the difference scores between conditions

Participant	Alone – Computer	Differences Alone – Group	Computer – Group
1	0.00	0.00	0.00
2	−6.00	−6.00	0.00
3	−3.00	−3.00	0.00
4	−9.00	−9.00	0.00
5	0.00	−6.00	−6.00
6	0.00	−6.00	−6.00
7	−3.00	−6.00	−3.00
8	−5.00	−5.00	0.00
9	−3.00	−6.00	−3.00
10	−6.00	−6.00	0.00
Variance	9.17	5.57	6.40

A concept that is often linked to sphericity, in discussions of the issue, is *compound symmetry*. Compound symmetry exists when the variances in the original scores are homogeneous and the covariances are homogeneous. (Covariance is a measure of how closely two measures are related and is defined in Chapter 19.) Thus, for compound symmetry to be present, the variances of alone, computer and group should be the same as each other, while the covariances of alone and computer, alone and group and computer and group should be the same as each other. When compound symmetry exists, sphericity will be present. However, it is possible to have sphericity without compound symmetry.

Table A7.12 The variance–covariance matrix for the conditions under which participants sentenced criminals, including column means

	alone	computer	group
alone	42.9	27.06667	33.66667
computer	27.06667	20.2	22
group	33.66667	22	30
Mean	34.54456	23.15556	28.55556

A variance–covariance matrix contains the covariances between each of the levels of the IV and, in the diagonal of the matrix, the variances for each of the levels. In Table A7.12, 42.9 is the variance for the alone condition, while 20.2 is the variance for the computer condition.

To calculate the epsilons we need the following information, which can be derived from Table A7.12.

overall mean = 28.75189 (the mean of all the nine values)

mean variance = 31.1 (the mean of the three variances)

sum of squared column means (SS_{means}) = 2554.92659 (the sum of the square of each of the column means)

sum of squared variances and covariances (SS_{all}) = 7856.68645 (the sum of the square of each of the nine values)

(Note that SS_{means} and SS_{all} are literally sums of squares and not sums of squared deviations as in previous calculations.)

The Greenhouse–Geisser epsilon ($\hat{\varepsilon}$) is found from the following equation:

$$\hat{\varepsilon} = \frac{k^2 \times (\text{mean var} - \text{overall mean})^2}{(k-1) \times [SS_{all} - (2 \times k \times SS_{means}) + (k \times \text{overall mean})^2]}$$

$$= \frac{3^2 \times (31.1 - 28.75189)^2}{(3-1) \times [7856.68645 - (2 \times 3 \times 2554.92659) + (3 \times 28.75189)^2]}$$

$$= \frac{9 \times 5.51362}{2 \times (7856.68645 - 15269.55955 + 7440.04061)}$$

$$= \frac{49.62258}{54.33502}$$

$$= 0.91327$$

The Huynh–Feldt epsilon ($\tilde{\varepsilon}$) is based on the Greenhouse–Geisser $\hat{\varepsilon}$:

$$\tilde{\varepsilon} = \frac{[n \times (k - 1) \times \hat{\varepsilon}] - 2}{(k - 1) \times \{n - 1 - [(k - 1) \times \hat{\varepsilon}]\}}$$

$$= \frac{[10 \times (3 - 1) \times 0.91327] - 2}{(3 - 1) \times \{10 - 1 - [(3 - 1) \times 0.91327]\}}$$

$$= \frac{(10 \times 2 \times 0.91327) - 2}{2 \times [9 - (2 \times 0.91327)]}$$

$$= \frac{18.2654 - 2}{2 \times (9 - 1.82654)}$$

$$= \frac{16.2654}{14.34692}$$

$$= 1.13372$$

These epsilons can be used to adjust the degrees of freedom for a within-subjects ANOVA, using the equation:

$$\text{adjusted df} = (\text{old df}) \times \text{epsilon}$$

However, when an epsilon is greater than 1, no adjustment is made. Therefore the Greenhouse–Geisser $\hat{\varepsilon}$ is the only one that needs to be used. In the within-subjects one-way ANOVA, the degrees of freedom were 2 and 18, which means that, using the Greenhouse–Geisser $\hat{\varepsilon}$, they would become:

$$\text{adjusted df} = 2 \times 0.913 \text{ and } 18 \times 0.913$$

$$= 1.826 \text{ and } 16.434$$

Partial eta-squared

In Chapter 16 the point was made that some computer packages, including SPSS, report partial eta-squared rather than eta-squared. Partial eta-squared is calculated from the following equation:

partial eta-squared

$$= \frac{\text{Sum of Squares for treatment}}{\text{Sum of Squares for treatment} + \text{Sum of Squares for error}}$$

Thus, eta-squared and partial eta-sqaured will be the same for a one-way, between-subjects ANOVA as the elements in the equation for partial eta-squared are the only ones in the analysis and so total Sum of Squares is the same as Sum of Squares for the treatment plus Sum of Squares for error. However, in all other analyses the two versions of eta-squared will usually differ, with partial eta-squared being larger and sometimes much larger. As an illustration, in the case of the within-subjects ANOVA partial eta-squared is 0.696, while eta-squared is 0.147. The difference is due to the fact that partial eta-squared does not include the between-subjects Sum of Squares in the calculation.

Non-parametric tests

At least ordinal measurement

Between-subjects designs – Kruskal–Wallis ANOVA by ranks

When the research design is between-subjects with more than two levels of the independent variable and the requirements of a parametric ANOVA are not fulfilled then the analysis can be conducted using the Kruskal–Wallis one-way Analysis of Variance, as long as the data are at least ordinal.

Researchers wished to compare the grades given by lecturers to essays that were shown to be by a male or by a female or the gender was not specified. Twenty-four college lecturers were each given an essay to mark and they were told that the writer of the essay was a male student, or was a female student or they were not given any indication of the student's gender. In fact, the same essay was given to all the lecturers. Each essay was given a grade between A+ and C–, which was converted to a numerical grade ranging from 1 to 9.

A rank is given to each grade, with tied ranks being treated in the same way as for the Wilcoxon signed-rank test for matched pairs, in that the mean rank is given to all scores that are the same.

Table A7.13 The grades given by participants for an essay depending on the presumed gender of its author, with the grades given ranks

female		'gender' of author neutral		male	
grade	rank	grade	rank	grade	rank
2	2	3	7.5	3	7.5
3	7.5	3	7.5	4	15
2	2	4	15	5	20
3	7.5	4	15	6	22.5
4	15	5	20	7	24
4	15	6	22.5	2	2
3	7.5	4	15	3	7.5
5	20	3	7.5	4	15
Total (R)	76.5		110		113.5

The statistic used for this test is H, where:

$$H = \left[\left\{ \frac{12}{N \times (N+1)} \right\} \times \sum \left(\frac{R^2}{n_i} \right) \right] - [3 \times (N+1)]$$

where N is the overall number of participants, which in this case is $8 + 8 + 8 = 24$, and $\sum \left(\frac{R^2}{n_i} \right)$ is the sum of each the total ranks squared, divided by the number of participants in the group. Therefore:

$$\sum \left(\frac{R^2}{n_i} \right) = \frac{(76.5)^2}{8} + \frac{(110)^2}{8} + \frac{(113.5)^2}{8}$$

$$= 3854.3125$$

Therefore,

$$H = \left[\left\{ \frac{12}{24 \times (24+1)} \right\} \times (3854.3125) \right] - [3 \times (24+1)]$$

$$= \left[\left(\frac{12}{600} \right) \times 3854.3125 \right] - 75$$

$$= 77.08625 - 75 = 2.08625$$

Correction for ties

When some scores are the same, there is a version of the test which adjusts for ties. In the present example, there were five places where the grades tied.

Table A7.14 Calculating the correction for tied scores for the Kruskal–Wallis ANOVA

Grade	number of ties (t)	correction = ($t^3 - t$)
2	3	24
3	8	504
4	7	336
5	3	24
6	2	6
Total correction		894

$$\text{the corrected } H = \frac{\text{original } H}{\left[1 - \left(\dfrac{\text{total correction}}{N^3 - N}\right)\right]}$$

$$= \frac{2.08625}{\left\{1 - \left[\dfrac{894}{(24)^3 - 24}\right]\right\}}$$

$$= \frac{2.08625}{\left[1 - \left(\dfrac{894}{13824 - 24}\right)\right]}$$

$$= \frac{2.08625}{1 - 0.06478}$$

$$= 2.23076$$

Within-subjects designs: Friedman two-way ANOVA

When the design is within-subjects and the independent variable has more than two levels but the assumptions of the parametric ANOVA are not met, if the level of measurement is at least ordinal, then the Friedman two-way ANOVA is the appropriate test.

Researchers wished to see whether a group of seven students rated a particular course differently as they spent more time on it. Each student was asked to rate the course on a 7-point scale ranging from *not enjoyable at all* to *very enjoyable*, on three occasions: after one week, after five weeks and after ten weeks.

Table A7.15 The ratings given by students on three occasions of a course

Participant	week of course one	five	ten
1	3	4	5
2	4	4	4
3	5	6	6
4	2	3	4
5	6	5	5
6	1	3	5
7	5	6	6

Table A7.16 The ranks for each participant for the ratings given to the course for a Friedman two-way ANOVA

Participant	one	week of course five	ten
1	1	2	3
2	2	2	2
3	1	2.5	2.5
4	1	2	3
5	3	1.5	1.5
6	1	2	3
7	1	2.5	2.5
Total (R)	10	14.5	17.5

To calculate Friedman's ANOVA it is first necessary to give ranks to the scores for each person. Notice that the ranking is only for each person. Nonetheless, ties are treated in the usual way, as described for the Wilcoxon signed-rank test for matched pairs. However, unlike a Wilcoxon signed-rank test, a participant who scores the same in all levels of the IV is not dropped from the analysis.

The test produces a statistic called χ_F^2 (sometimes given as χ_r^2), where

$$\chi_F^2 = \left[\left\{\frac{12}{N \times k \times (k+1)}\right\} \times \left(\sum R^2\right)\right] - [3 \times N \times (k+1)]$$

where N is the sample size, in this case 7
 k is the number of levels of the IV, in this case 3
 $\sum R^2$ is the sum of the ranks squared.

Therefore:

$$\sum R^2 = (10)^2 + (14.5)^2 + (17.5)^2 = 100 + 210.25 + 306.25 = 616.5$$

Therefore:

$$\chi_F^2 = \left[\left\{\frac{12}{7 \times 3 \times (3+1)}\right\} \times 616.5\right] - [3 \times 7 \times (3+1)]$$

$$= \left[\left(\frac{12}{84}\right) \times 616.5\right] - 84 = 88.07143 - 84 = 4.07143$$

Correction for ties

Unlike previous corrections for ties, the one used with Friedman's test counts occasions when there is no tie, but counts it as a tie of 1. The ties are counted for each person.

Table A7.17 Calculating the number of tied ranks of each size for a Friedman two-way ANOVA

Participant	one	week of course five	ten	size of ties 1	2	3
1	1	2	3	3	0	0
2	2	2	2	0	0	1
3	1	2.5	2.5	1	1	0
4	1	2	3	3	0	0
5	3	1.5	1.5	1	1	0
6	1	2	3	3	0	0
7	1	2.5	2.5	1	1	0
			Total	12	3	1

Now we cube each instance of each size of tie and add the results, so for the 12 ties that had one in each tie, the sum is:

$$(1)^3 + (1)^3 + (1)^3 + (1)^3 + (1)^3 + (1)^3 + (1)^3 + (1)^3 + (1)^3 + (1)^3 + (1)^3 + (1)^3 = 12$$

For the three ties that had two in each tie, the sum is:

$$(2)^3 + (2)^3 + (2)^3 = 8 + 8 + 8 = 24$$

and for the one tie that had three in it, the sum is

$$(3)^3 = 27.$$

Therefore the sum of the ties cubed is $12 + 24 + 27 = 63$

The equation for corrected χ^2_F is:

$$\text{corrected } \chi^2_F = \frac{(12 \times \Sigma R^2) - [3 \times N^2 \times k \times (k + 1)^2]}{[N \times k \times (k + 1)] + \left[\dfrac{N \times k - \text{sum of cubed ties}}{(k - 1)} \right]}$$

Therefore:

$$\text{corrected } \chi_F^2 = \frac{(12 \times 616.5) - [3 \times (7)^2 \times 3 \times (3+1)^2]}{[7 \times 3 \times (3+1)] + \left[\dfrac{7 \times 3 - 63}{(3-1)}\right]}$$

$$= \frac{7398 - [3 \times 49 \times 3 \times (4)^2]}{(7 \times 3 \times 4) + \left(\dfrac{7 \times 3 - 63}{2}\right)}$$

$$= \frac{7398 - (3 \times 49 \times 3 \times 16)}{84 + \left(\dfrac{21 - 63}{2}\right)} = \frac{7398 - 7056}{84 - \left(\dfrac{42}{2}\right)}$$

$$= \frac{342}{63} = 5.42857$$

The power of the Friedman test

The power of the Friedman test is found in terms of its power efficiency relative to the parametric within-subjects one-way ANOVA and depends on the number of levels of the IV: the smaller the number of levels the poorer the power efficiency. To find the sample size for the Friedman test, find the sample size necessary for the parametric within-subjects one-way ANOVA, for the number of levels of the IV, the α-level and the power required, then multiply the sample size by the appropriate figure from the following table.

Table A7.18 The amount by which it is necessary to multiply the sample size suggested for a parametric ANOVA in order to achieve the same power for the Friedman test

number of levels in IV	multiply sample size by
3	1.40
4	1.31
5	1.26
6	1.22
7	1.20
8	1.18
9	1.16
10	1.15

The general rule is: multiply the sample size by $\left(1.047 \times \dfrac{k+1}{k}\right)$, where k is the number of levels.

Nominal data

Within-subjects designs: Cochran's Q

If the measure taken is dichotomous, for example, yes or no, then Cochran's Q can be used. However, it is possible to recode data to be dichotomous, as shown below. Researchers wanted to compare students' choices of modules on Social Psychology, Research Methods and Historical Issues to see whether some modules were more popular than others. It is recommended that the test be conducted with at least sixteen participants. The researchers asked this number of students what their module choices were. Twelve had chosen Social Psychology, eight Methods and six Historical Issues. As Cochran's Q requires dichotomous variables, the data had to be recoded, with 1 denoting that a student took the course and 0 that he or she did not, see Table A7.19.

Table A7.19 The modules chosen by sixteen students, coded as dummy variables, with column and row totals

Participant	Social Psychology	Research Methods	Historical Issues	Row total	Row total squared
1	1	0	0	1	1
2	1	1	0	2	4
3	0	1	0	1	1
4	1	1	1	3	9
5	0	1	1	2	4
6	1	0	0	1	1
7	1	1	1	3	9
8	0	1	1	2	4
9	1	0	0	1	1
10	1	0	0	1	1
11	0	0	0	0	0
12	1	0	0	1	1
13	1	1	0	2	4
14	1	0	0	1	1
15	1	0	1	2	4
16	1	1	1	3	9
Column total	12	8	6	26	54

Cochran's Q can be found from the following equation:

$$Q = \frac{k \times (k-1) \times \Sigma(B_i - \bar{B})^2}{k \times \Sigma L_j - \Sigma L_j^2}$$

where k is the number of levels of the IV
B_i is the sum of scores in level i of the IV
L_j is the sum of the scores for participant j
$\bar{B}$ is the mean B

Therefore, in the current case where the mean B is 8.667:

$$Q = \frac{3 \times (3-1) \times 18.667}{3 \times 26 - 54}$$

$$= \frac{112.002}{24}$$

$$= 4.667$$

Cochran's Q can also be found by running a one-way within-subjects ANOVA on the data, as per the method shown earlier in this appendix. This provides the necessary detail to form Q from:

$$Q = \frac{\text{treatments Sum of Squares}}{\text{Within-subjects Mean Square}}$$

$$= \frac{1.167}{0.25}$$

$$= 4.668$$

Table A7.20 The summary table from a one-way within-subjects ANOVA for calculating Cochran's Q

Source	Sum of Squares	df	Mean Square	F-test	p
Between subjects	3.917	15			
Within subjects	8	32	0.25		
treatments	1.167	2	0.583	2.561	0.094
residual	6.833	30	0.228		
Total	11.917	47			

Appendix VIII: Analysis of Designs with More Than One Independent Variable

This appendix illustrates the techniques introduced in Chapter 17.

Two-way between-subjects ANOVA   462
Two-way within-subjects ANOVA   466
Two-way mixed ANOVA   472

Two-way between-subjects ANOVA

Researchers looked at the effect of mnemonic strategy and the nature of the list of words to be recalled upon recall.

Table A8.1 The number of words recalled by participants when given a mnemonic strategy and a list type

	List type					
		Linked			Unlinked	
Mnemonic	Control	Pegword	Loci	Control	Pegword	Loci
	10	9	9	4	10	8
	10	10	11	6	7	8
	11	10	11	7	8	8
	11	12	10	7	8	9
	13	12	12	8	9	11
Total	55	53	53	32	42	44
Mean	11	10.6	10.6	6.4	8.4	8.8
Variance	1.5	1.8	1.3	2.3	1.3	1.7
SD	1.22474	1.34164	1.14018	1.51658	1.14018	1.30384

the overall mean = 9.3

the overall variance = 4.07931

the overall SD = 2.01973

Total Sum of Squares

The Total Sum of Squares is the sum of the squared deviations of each score from the overall mean. It can also be found from:

$$\text{Total Sum of Squares} = \text{overall variance} \times (N - 1)$$

where N is the total sample size. Therefore,

$$\text{Total Sum of Squares} = 4.07931 \times (30 - 1)$$
$$= 118.29999$$

The Total Sum of Squares can be split into:

The Sum of Squares for the first IV (SS_A)
The Sum of Squares for the second IV (SS_B)
The Sum of Squares for the interaction between the two IVs (SS_{AB})
The Sum of Squares within groups (residual or error, which is the error term for the other three Sums of Squares) (SS_{error}).

Between-groups Sum of Squares for IV₁

Find the mean for each of the levels of IV_1 (list), regardless of the levels of IV_2 (mnemonic). Thus:

$$\text{mean for linked lists} = \frac{55 + 53 + 53}{15}$$

$$= \frac{161}{15}$$

$$= 10.73333$$

Table A8.2 Obtaining the between-groups sum of squared deviations for the first independent variable in a 2 × 3 two-way between-subjects ANOVA

List	Mean	deviation from overall mean (9.3)	(deviation)²	(deviation)² × number of scores contributing to each mean (15)
Linked	10.73333	1.43333	2.05444	30.81667
Unlinked	7.86667	−1.43333	2.05444	30.81667
			Between-groups S of S for IV₁	61.63334

Notice that, not surprisingly, when you have only two values they each deviate by the same amount from their mean—one positively and one negatively.

Between-groups Sum of Squares IV₂

This is found using the same technique as for the Sum of Squares for IV₁.

Table A8.3 Obtaining the sum of squared deviations for the second independent variable in a 2 × 3 two-way between-subjects ANOVA

Mnemonic	Mean	deviation from overall mean (9.3)	(deviation)²	(deviation)² × the number of scores contributing to each mean (10)
Control	8.7	−0.6	0.36	3.6
Pegwords	9.5	0.2	0.04	0.4
Loci	9.7	0.4	0.16	1.6

Between-groups S of S for IV₂   5.6

Interaction Sum of Squares (SS_{AB})

This is obtained, initially, by finding the sum of squared deviations for the means that relate to the interaction (the between-cells Sum of Squares). In this case, the interaction involves the six means for the different groups. The interaction Sum of Squares is then found by subtracting the Sums of Squares for the main effects, involved in the interaction from the between-cells Sum of Squares:

$$SS_{AB} = IV_1 \text{ by } IV_2 \text{ cells S of S} - (SS_A + SS_B)$$

Table A8.4 Obtaining the IV₁ by IV₂ cells Sum of Squares in a 2 × 3 two-way between-subjects ANOVA

List type	Mnemonic	Mean	deviation from overall mean (9.3)	(deviation)²	(deviation)² × the number of scores contributing to each mean (5)
Linked	control	11	1.7	2.89	14.45
	pegword	10.6	1.3	1.69	8.45
	loci	10.6	1.3	1.69	8.45
Unlinked	control	6.4	−2.9	8.41	42.05
	pegword	8.4	−0.9	0.81	4.05
	loci	8.8	−0.5	0.25	1.25

IV₁ by IV₂ cells S of S   78.70

$$SS_{AB} = 78.7 - (61.63334 + 5.6)$$

$$= 78.7 - 67.23334$$

$$= 11.46667$$

Within-groups (residual) Sum of Squares

This is, as usual, obtained by finding the sum of the squared deviations for each group and adding them together. Remembering that,

$$\text{Sum of Squares (SS)} = \text{variance} \times (n - 1)$$

$$SS_{residual} = (1.5 \times 4) + (1.8 \times 4) + (1.3 \times 4) + (2.3 \times 4) + (1.3 \times 4) + (1.7 \times 4)$$

$$= 6 + 7.2 + 5.2 + 9.2 + 5.2 + 6.8$$

$$= 39.6$$

As usual, also, the residual Sum of Squares could have been found by subtracting all the other sums of squares from the Total Sum of Squares (SS_{total}):

$$SS_{residual} = SS_{total} - (SS_{interaction} + SS_A + SS_B)$$

$$= 118.29999 - (11.46667 + 61.63334 + 5.6)$$

$$= 118.29999 - 78.70001$$

$$= 39.59998 \text{ (or 39.6 to one decimal place)}.$$

Now that we have found the Sums of Squares for all the aspects of the design we can create the summary table for the ANOVA; see Chapter 17 for the ways in which the degrees of freedom, Mean Squares and F-values (F-ratios) are calculated.

Table A8.5 The summary table for a 2 × 3 two-way between-subjects ANOVA

Source	Sum of Squares	df	Mean Square	F	p
List	61.633	1	61.633	37.354	0.0001
Mnemonic	5.600	2	2.800	1.697	0.2045
List * Mnemonic	11.467	2	5.733	3.475	0.0473
Error	39.600	24	1.650		
Total	118.300	29			

Two-way within-subjects ANOVA

Participants recommended the length of sentence a criminal should serve, in one of three situations: alone, communicating with others via computer and in the presence of others. In addition, they had to sentence defendants of two types: those with no previous record (novices) and habitual criminals (experienced).

The Total Sum of Squares can be divided into the between-subjects Sum of Squares and the within-subjects Sum of Squares. The within-subjects Sum of Squares itself can be divided into:

Sum of Squares for IV_1 (defendant) (SS_A)
Sum of Squares for IV_1 by subjects (the error term for SS_A) (SS_{AS})

Sum of Squares for IV_2 (situation) (SS_B)
Sum of Squares for IV_2 by subjects (the error term for SS_B) (SS_{BS})

Sum of Squares for interaction between IV_1 and IV_2 (SS_{AB})
Sum of Squares for IV_1 by IV_2 by subjects (the error term for SS_{AB}) (SS_{ABS})

Table A8.6 The sentences (in months) given to criminals, depending on their record and the conditions under which the decision was made

	Defendant						
		Novice			Experienced		Mean for
Participant	Alone	Computer	Face-to-face	Alone	Computer	Face-to-face	participant
1	12	14	16	16	18	20	16
2	14	14	15	14	18	22	16.16667
3	13	13	17	17	17	21	16.33333
4	14	13	17	16	16	19	15.83333
5	13	14	16	17	19	21	16.66667
Mean	13.2	13.6	16.2	16.0	17.6	20.6	16.2
Variance	0.7	0.3	0.7	1.5	1.3	1.3	
SD	0.83667	0.54772	0.83667	1.22474	1.14018	1.14018	

Total Sum of Squares

As usual, this is the sum of squared deviations of each score from the overall mean (16.2). In this case it is 208.8.

The between-subjects Sum of Squares

As usual, this is the sum of squared deviations of each participant's mean score from the overall mean, multiplied by the number of conditions contributing to the means, which, in this case, is 6.

Table A8.7 Obtaining the between-subjects Sum of Squares for a 2 × 3 two-way within-subjects ANOVA

Participant	Mean	deviation from overall mean (16.2)	(deviation)²	(deviation)² × number of scores contributing to each mean (6)
1	16	−0.2	0.04	0.24
2	16.16667	−0.03333	0.00111	0.00665
3	16.33333	0.13333	0.01778	0.10668
4	15.83333	−0.36667	0.13445	0.8067
5	16.66667	0.46667	0.21778	1.30668

Between-subjects S of S   2.46671

IV_1 Sum of Squares (SS_A)

This is obtained by finding the mean (across participants and all levels of IV_2) for each level of IV_1 (defendant) and finding the sum of squared deviations of the means for the levels.

As we know the means for each condition and we know that each condition has the same number of scores, we can find the mean for each level of IV_1 in the following way:

$$\text{novice mean} = \frac{13.2 + 13.6 + 16.2}{3}$$

$$= \frac{43}{3}$$

$$= 14.33333$$

$$\text{experienced mean} = \frac{16 + 17.6 + 20.6}{3}$$

$$= \frac{54.2}{3}$$

$$= 18.06667$$

Table A8.8 Obtaining the Sum of Squares for the first independent variable of a 2 × 3 within-subjects ANOVA

Defendant	Mean	deviation from overall mean (16.2)	(deviation)^2	(deviation)^2 × number of scores contributing to each mean (15)
Novice	14.33333	−1.86667	3.48446	52.26685
Experienced	18.06667	1.86667	3.48446	52.26685

S of S for IV$_1$ 104.5337

IV$_1$ by subjects Sum of Squares (SS$_{AS}$)

The initial stage to obtain this is to find the subjects by IV$_1$ cell means. Thus, the first participant's cell mean for novice defendants is:

$$\frac{12 + 14 + 16}{3} = 14$$

We can then find the Sum of Squares for the subjects by IV$_1$ cells:

Table A8.9 Obtaining the IV$_1$ by subjects cell Sum of Squares for a 2 × 3 two-way within-subjects ANOVA

Defendant	Participant	Cell mean	deviation from overall mean (16.2)	(deviation)^2	(deviation)^2 × number of scores contributing to each mean (3)
novice	1	14	−2.2	4.84	14.52
	2	14.33333	−1.86667	3.48444	10.45333
	3	14.33333	−1.86667	3.48444	10.45333
	4	14.66667	−1.53333	2.35111	7.05333
	5	14.33333	−1.86667	3.48444	10.45333
experienced	1	18	1.8	3.24	9.72
	2	18	1.8	3.24	9.72
	3	18.33333	2.13333	4.55111	13.65333
	4	17	0.8	0.64	1.92
	5	19	2.8	7.84	23.52

Cells S of S   111.46665

We can then find the IV_1 by subjects Sum of Squares (SS_{AS}) from:

$$SS_{AS} = IV_1 \text{ by subjects cell S of S} - (SS_A + \text{between-subjects S of S})$$

Therefore,

$$\text{defendant by subjects S of S} = 111.46665 - (104.5337 + 2.46671)$$

$$= 111.46665 - 107.00041$$

$$= 4.46624$$

IV_2 Sum of Squares (SS_B)

This is obtained from the sum of the squared deviations of the means for the levels of the second independent variable, across participants and levels of the first independent variable.

The mean for the first level of IV_2 can be found from:

$$\frac{13.2 + 16}{2} = \frac{29.2}{2} = 14.6$$

Table A8.10 Obtaining the Sum of Squares for the second independent in a 2 × 3 two-way within-subjects ANOVA

condition	mean	deviation from overall mean (16.2)	(deviation)²	(deviation)² × number of scores which contributed to each mean (10)
alone	14.6	−1.6	2.56	25.6
computer	15.6	−0.6	0.36	3.6
group	18.4	2.2	4.84	48.4

IV_2 S of S   77.6

IV_2 by subjects Sum of Squares (SS_{BS})

Again we find the means for the IV_2 by subjects cells, and then the sum of squared deviations for the cells:

Table A8.11 Obtaining the IV_2 by subjects cells Sum of Squares for a 2 × 3 two-way within-subjects ANOVA

Condition	Participant	Cell mean	deviation from overall mean (16.2)	(deviation)^2	(deviation)^2 × number of scores contributing to each cell mean (2)
alone	1	14	−2.2	4.84	9.68
	2	14	−2.2	4.84	9.68
	3	15	−1.2	1.44	2.88
	4	15	−1.2	1.44	2.88
	5	15	−1.2	1.44	2.88
computer	1	16	−0.2	0.04	0.08
	2	16	−0.2	0.04	0.08
	3	15	−1.2	1.44	2.88
	4	14.5	−1.7	2.89	5.78
	5	16.5	0.3	0.09	0.18
group	1	18	1.8	3.24	6.48
	2	18.5	2.3	5.29	10.58
	3	19	2.8	7.84	15.68
	4	18	1.8	3.24	6.48
	5	18.5	2.3	5.29	10.58

Cell S of S   86.8

We can then find the IV_2 by subjects Sum of Squares (SS_{BS}) from:

$$SS_{BS} = IV_2 \text{ by subjects cell S of S} - (IV_2 \text{ S of S} + \text{between-subjects S of S})$$

Therefore,

$$\text{condition by subjects S of S} = 86.8 - (77.6 + 2.46671)$$
$$= 86.8 - 80.06671$$
$$= 6.73329$$

IV_1 by IV_2 interaction Sum of Squares (SS_{AB})

This can be obtained by firstly finding the cell means for each of the conditions; they are already given in Table A8.6. Then the sum of squared deviations for those means is found:

Table A8.12 Obtaining the IV_1 by IV_2 *cell* Sum of Squares for a 2 × 3 two-way within-subjects ANOVA

Defendant	Condition	Cell mean	deviation from overall mean (16.2)	(deviation)^2	(deviation)^2 × number of scores contributing to each cell mean (6)
novice	alone	13.2	−3	9	45
	computer	13.6	−2.6	6.76	33.8
	group	16.2	0	0	0
experienced	alone	16.0	−0.2	0.04	0.2
	computer	17.6	1.4	1.96	9.8
	group	20.6	4.4	19.36	96.8

IV_1 by IV_2 cell S of S   185.6

The IV_1 by IV_2 Sum of Squares (SS_{AB}) can be obtained from:

$$SS_{AB} = IV_1 \text{ by } IV_2 \text{ Cell S of S} - (SS_A + SS_B)$$

$$= 185.6 - (104.5337 + 77.6)$$

$$= 185.6 - 182.1337$$

$$= 3.4663$$

IV_1 by IV_2 by subjects Sum of Squares (SS_{ABS})

This can be obtained by firstly finding the Total Sum of Squares, which is the same as the IV_1 by IV_2 by subjects *cells* Sum of Squares.

The IV_1 by IV_2 by subjects Sum of Squares (SS_{ABS}) can then be found from:

$$SS_{ABS} = SS_{total} - (SS_A + SS_B + SS_{AB} + SS_{AS} + SS_{BS} + SS_S)$$

where   A is IV_1
B is IV_2
AB is the interaction between IV_1 and IV_2
AS is the interaction between IV_1 and subjects
BS is the interaction between IV_2 and subjects
S is subjects

Therefore,

$$SS_{ABS} = 208.8 - (104.5337 + 77.6 + 3.4663 + 4.46624 + 6.73329 + 2.46671)$$

$$= 9.53376$$

Table A8.13 Summary table of 2 × 3, two-way within-subjects ANOVA

Source	S of S	df	MS	F	p	G–G	H–F
subject	2.467	4	.617				
defendant	104.533	1	104.533	93.612	.0006	.0006	.0006
defendant by subject	4.467	4	1.117				
context	77.600	2	38.800	46.099	.0001	.0007	.0001
context by subject	6.733	8	.842				
defendant by context	3.467	2	1.733	1.455	.2892	.2946	.2948
defendant by context by subject	9.533	8	1.192				
Total	208.8	29					

We are now in a position to create the summary table for the ANOVA; see Chapter 17 for an explanation of how the degrees of freedom, Mean Squares and *F*-ratios are calculated and Appendix VII for an explanation of how Greenhouse–Geisser (G–G) and Huynh–Feldt (H–F) adjustments are made.

Two-way mixed ANOVA

Experimenters compared the way that males and females rate their parents' IQs. The independent variable *gender*, which has two levels—male and female—is a between-subjects variable. The independent variable *parent*, which has two levels—mother and father—is a within-subjects variable because each participant supplies data for each level of that variable.

The Total Sum of Squares can be divided into the between-subjects Sum of Squares and the within-subjects Sum of Squares. The between-subjects Sum of Squares can be further divided into:

The IV_1 (gender) Sum of Squares (SS_A)
The subjects-within-groups Sum of Squares (the error term for the IV_1 Sum of Squares) ($SS_{S(Groups)}$)

The within-subjects Sum of Squares can be subdivided into:

The IV_2 (parent) Sum of Squares, (SS_B)
The IV_1 by IV_2 Sum of Squares (the interaction between the two IVs—gender by parent) (SS_{AB})
The IV_2 by subjects within groups Sum of Squares (the error term for both SS_B and SS_{AB}) ($SS_{B \, by \, S(Groups)}$)

Table A8.14 The estimates made by males and females of their parents' IQs

Participant	Gender of participant	Parent		Mean for gender	Participant's Mean
		Father	Mother		
1	male	120	100		110
2	male	110	90		100
3	male	100	105		102.5
4	male	105	100		102.5
5	male	140	120		130
mean		115	103	109	
6	female	110	110		110
7	female	110	105		107.5
8	female	105	110		107.5
9	female	120	115		117.5
10	female	100	100		100
mean		109	108	108.5	
Mean for parent		112	105.5		

$$\text{the overall mean} = 108.75$$

$$\text{the overall SD} = 10.74526$$

$$\text{the overall variance} = 115.46053$$

Total Sum of Squares (SS_total)

As usual, this can be found from the overall variance:

SS_{total} = overall variance × $(N - 1)$ (where N is the number of scores)

= 115.46053 × 19

= 2193.75007

Between-subjects Sum of Squares

As usual, this is obtained by forming the mean score for each participant and then finding the sum of squared deviations for these means:

Table A8.15 Obtaining the between-subjects Sum of Squares for a 2 × 2 two-way mixed ANOVA

Participant	Mean rating of IQ for own parents	deviation from overall mean (108.75)	(deviation)^2	(deviation)^2 × number of scores contributing to each mean (2)
1	110	1.25	1.5625	3.125
2	100	−8.75	76.5625	153.125
3	102.5	−6.25	39.0625	78.125
4	102.5	−6.25	39.0625	78.125
5	130	21.25	451.5625	903.125
6	110	1.25	1.5625	3.125
7	107.5	−1.25	1.5625	3.125
8	107.5	−1.25	1.5625	3.125
9	117.5	8.75	76.5625	153.125
10	100	−8.75	76.5625	153.125

Between-subjects S of S   1531.25

IV_1 Sum of Squares (SS_A)

The Sum of Squares for the between-subjects IV (gender) is obtained by finding the mean IQ given by each gender of participant, regardless of the parent being rated. The sum of squared deviations of these means is then found:

Table A8.16 Obtaining the Sum of Squares for the between-subjects IV for a 2 × 2 two-way mixed ANOVA

Gender of participant	Mean estimated IQ	deviation from overall mean (108.75)	(deviation)^2	(deviation)^2 × number of scores contributing to each mean (10)
Male	109	0.25	0.0625	0.625
Female	108.5	−0.25	0.0625	0.625

SS_A 1.25

Subjects-within-Groups Sum of Squares ($SS_{S(Groups)}$)

This can be obtained from:

$$SS_{S(Groups)} = \text{between-subjects S of S} - SS_A$$

$$= 15321.25 - 1.25 = 1530$$

IV₂ Sum of Squares (SS₂)

This is obtained in the usual way for a within-subjects IV, by first finding the mean IQs for the levels of the IV (parent), regardless of the gender of the participant who supplied them.

Table A8.17 Obtaining the Sum of Squares for the within-subjects IV for a 2 × 2 two-way mixed ANOVA

Parent	Mean rating of IQ made by participants	deviation from overall mean (108.75)	(deviation)²	(deviation)² × number of scores contributing to each mean (10)
Father	112	3.25	10.5625	105.625
Mother	105.5	−3.25	10.5625	105.625

$$SS_B \quad 211.25$$

IV₁ by IV₂ Sum of Squares (SS₍AB₎)

The first stage in obtaining this, interaction Sum of Squares, is to find the means for the gender-by-parent cells. The Sum of Squares of these cell means are then found:

Table A8.18 Obtaining the Sum of Squares for the IV₁ by IV₂ cells for a 2 × 2 two-way mixed ANOVA

Gender of participants	Parent	Mean rating of IQ	deviation from overall mean (108.75)	(deviation)²	(deviation)² × number of scores contributing to each mean (5)
Male	Father	115	6.25	39.0625	195.3125
	Mother	103	−5.75	33.0625	165.3125
Female	Father	109	0.25	0.0625	0.3125
	Mother	108	−0.75	0.5625	2.8125

$$V_1 \text{ by } IV_2 \text{ cell S of S} \quad 363.75$$

Now the interaction Sum of Squares (SS₍AB₎) can be obtained from:

$$SS_{AB} = IV_1 \text{ by } IV_2 \text{ cells S of S} - (SS_A + SS_B)$$

$$= 363.75 - (1.25 + 211.25)$$

$$= 151.25$$

IV_2 by subjects within groups Sum of Squares $(SS_{\text{B by S(Groups)}})$

This can be obtained from:

$$SS_{\text{B by S(Groups)}} = SS_{\text{total}} - (SS_A + SS_{\text{S(Groups)}} + SS_B + SS_{AB})$$

where   SS is the Sum of Squares
B is IV_2 (parent)
S is subjects
S(Groups) is subjects within groups
B by S(Groups) is IV_2 by subjects within groups
AB is the interaction between IV_1 and IV_2 (gender by parent)

or, because $SS_S = SS_A + SS_{\text{S(Groups)}}$

$$SS_{\text{B by S(Groups)}} = SS_{\text{total}} - (SS_S + SS_B + SS_{AB})$$

Therefore,

$$SS_{\text{B by S(Groups)}} = 2193.75007 - (1531.25 + 211.25 + 151.25)$$
$$= 300.00007$$

The Total Sum of Squares has now been divided into its constituent parts and the summary table for the ANOVA can be formed. See Chapter 17 for an explanation of how the degrees of freedom, Mean Squares and the F-values (F-ratios) are calculated and Appendix IX for the interpretation of G–G and H–F adjustments.

Table A8.19 The summary table for a 2 × 2 two-way mixed ANOVA

Source	S of S	df	MS	F	p	G–G	H–F
gender	1.250	1	1.250	.007	.9376		
subject(group)	1530.000	8	191.250				
parent	211.250	1	211.250	5.633	.0450	.0450	.0450
parent by gender	151.250	1	151.250	4.033	.0795	.0795	.0795
parent by subject (Group)	300.000	8	37.500				
Total	2193.75	19					

APPENDIX IX: SUBSEQUENT ANALYSIS AFTER ANOVA OR χ^2

This appendix illustrates the techniques introduced in Chapter 18.

Bonferroni adjustment	477
Contrasts	478
Parametric tests	478
Pairwise contrast tests	483
Newman–Keuls test	483
Tukey's wholly significant difference (WSD)	485
Fisher's protected least significant difference (PLSD)	485
Orthogonality	485
Non-parametric tests	486
Categorical data	490
Trend tests	492
The general equation for a trend analysis	493
Adjustment for unequal intervals	495

Whenever a statistical test is used more than once, the likelihood of achieving a statistically significant result is increased, even though the Null Hypothesis of no effect is correct. That is, there is an increased danger of making a Type I error. It is possible to adjust the α-level that a given test would have to achieve before statistical significance was considered to have been reached, to allow for the number of times the same test was being conducted. A general method is described as the *Bonferroni adjustment*.

Bonferroni adjustment

A simplified version of the Bonferroni adjustment is to divide the original α-level by the number of times the test is to be repeated. Thus, if three t-tests were to be conducted and the original α-level was 0.05, then the new α-level, which each t-test would be evaluated against, would be:

$$\frac{0.05}{3} = 0.0167.$$

This approximation is adequate for α-levels of 0.05 or smaller and is the one used to find the t-values, which are contained in Bonferroni t-tables such as those in Appendix XIV.

The full equation is:

$$\text{adjusted } \alpha\text{-level} = 1 - (1 - \alpha)^{\frac{1}{k}}$$

which can be written as $1 - \sqrt[k]{1 - \alpha}$ where k is the number of times that the test is being conducted.

Therefore, if the test were being conducted three times:

$$\text{adjusted } \alpha\text{-level} = 1 - (1 - 0.05)^{\frac{1}{3}}$$

$$= 1 - (0.95)^{\frac{1}{3}}$$

$$= 1 - (0.95)^{0.333}$$

$$= 1 - 0.98306$$

$$= 0.0169$$

which is very close to the approximation given above (0.0167).

Contrasts

When an ANOVA has been conducted, it is frequently the case that researchers want to compare particular treatments to see whether they are statistically different.

Parametric tests

There is a standard equation that can be used for between-subjects designs to find a t-value, the probability of which can be tested. However, as was pointed out in Chapter 18, such contrasts can be conducted even without conducting an initial ANOVA.

General contrast equation
The most general version of the equation is:

$$t = \frac{\sum (w_j \times \bar{x}_j)}{\sqrt{MS_{error} \times \sum \dfrac{w_j^2}{n_j}}} \tag{A9.1}$$

where $\bar{x}_j$ is a mean for one of the treatments

w_j is the weighting for $\bar{x}_j$ and will depend on the nature of the contrast

MS_{error} is the appropriate Mean Square of the error term from the ANOVA

n_j is the number of scores that contributed to $\bar{x}_j$

In words, $\Sigma(w_j \times \bar{x}_j)$ tells you to multiply each mean in the contrast by an appropriate weighting and add the results; $\Sigma(w_j^2/n_j)$ tells you to square each weighting and divide it by the number of participants in the group then add the results.

Pairwise contrasts

When comparing only two treatments (a pairwise contrast) the equation simplifies to:

$$t = \frac{\text{mean}_1 - \text{mean}_2}{\sqrt{\left(\dfrac{1}{n_1} + \dfrac{1}{n_2}\right) \times \text{MS}_{\text{error}}}} \qquad (18.1)$$

where mean$_1$ is the mean for one of the conditions (condition 1)
mean$_2$ is the mean for the other condition (condition 2)
n_1 is the sample size of the group producing mean$_1$
n_2 is the sample size of the group producing mean$_2$
MS$_{\text{error}}$ is the mean square for the appropriate error term in the original F-ratio

The simplification occurs because the contrast requires the weighting for mean$_1$ to be 1 and the weighting for mean$_2$ to be −1; try putting these weightings into the original equation and see the effect.

When a pairwise contrast is being made and there are equal numbers of participants in the two groups, the equation simplifies further to:

$$t = \frac{\text{mean}_1 - \text{mean}_2}{\sqrt{\left(\dfrac{2}{n}\right) \times \text{MS}_{\text{error}}}} \qquad (18.2)$$

where n is the sample size of the group producing one of the means.

An illustration of a pairwise contrast is given in Chapter 18. I will illustrate a non-pairwise contrast, here. As an example I am using the memory experiment (introduced in Chapters 9 and 16) in which participants were given one of three conditions: a control condition under which they were given no training, a group in which they were trained to use pegwords as a mnemonic strategy and a group in which they were trained to use the method of loci. There were ten participants in each group.

Table A9.1 Means and SDs of word recall for the three memory conditions

	Control	Pegword	Loci
Mean	7.2	8.9	9.6
SD	1.62	1.91	1.58

Table A9.2 The summary table for the one-way between-subjects ANOVA on the recall data

Source	Sum of Squares	df	Mean Square	F-test	p
Between Groups	30.467	2	15.233	5.213	0.0122
Within Groups	78.9	27	2.922		
Total	109.367	29			

If we wished to compare the two mnemonic techniques with the control condition, we would have the following figures:

$$\text{mean}_1 \text{ (control)} = 7.2$$

$$\text{mean}_2 \text{ (pegwords)} = 8.9$$

$$\text{mean}_3 \text{ (loci)} = 9.6$$

$$n_1 = n_2 = n_3 = 10$$

$$\text{MS}_{\text{error}} = 2.922$$

Next we have to find the weightings, with the restriction that they must add up to zero. Thus, we could multiply mean_1 by 2, mean_2 by -1 and mean_3 by -1. This is the equivalent of contrasting the control group with the mean of the other two groups; the same result would have been found if we had use weightings of 1, $-\frac{1}{2}$ and $-\frac{1}{2}$.

Therefore:

$$\text{weight}_1 + \text{weight}_2 + \text{weight}_3 = 2 + (-1) + (-1) = 0$$

The restriction that the sum of the weights equals zero (i.e. $\Sigma w_j = 0$, where w_j is the weighting for a particular mean) is only true when the sample sizes are the same for the different groups. When the sample sizes are not the same the restriction is that $\Sigma(n_j \times w_j) = 0$, where n_j is the size of each sample. See Appendix XVI for a description of how to calculate the coefficients when the sample sizes are unequal.

Using the first equation (A9.1),

$$t = \frac{\sum(w_j \times \bar{x}_j)}{\sqrt{\text{MS}_{\text{error}} \times \sum \dfrac{w_j^2}{n_j}}}$$

$$= \frac{(w_1 \times \bar{x}_1) + (w_2 \times \bar{x}_2) + (w_3 \times \bar{x}_3)}{\sqrt{\text{MS}_{\text{error}} \times \left(\dfrac{w_1^2}{n_1} + \dfrac{w_2^2}{n_2} + \dfrac{w_3^2}{n_3} \right)}}$$

$$= \frac{(2 \times 7.2) + (-1 \times 8.9) + (-1 \times 9.6)}{\sqrt{2.922 \times \left(\frac{2^2}{10} + \frac{(-1)^2}{10} + \frac{(-1)^2}{10} \right)}}$$

$$= \frac{14.4 - 8.9 - 9.6}{\sqrt{2.922 \times \left(\frac{4}{10} + \frac{1}{10} + \frac{1}{10} \right)}}$$

$$= \frac{-4.1}{\sqrt{2.922 \times 0.6}}$$

$$= \frac{-4.1}{\sqrt{1.7532}}$$

$$= \frac{-4.1}{1.32408}$$

$$= -3.096$$

How we test the significance of this result depends on whether the contrast was planned or not and whether it was the only contrast, one of only a few contrasts or one of many. If there was a planned contrast or only a few unplanned contrasts then we can use Bonferroni's test (based on Bonferroni's adjustment). However, if it is one unplanned contrast of many we are conducting, we will need to use Scheffé's test. The latter is dealt with in the next section.

Alternative versions of Scheffé's test

Method One
Scheffé's test is sometimes given as a t-value and sometimes as an F-ratio. However, all versions will give the same protection against a Type I error. I gave one version in Chapter 18. This entailed finding the critical F-ratio which would have made the original treatment F-ratio statistically significant. In the mnemonic example, the appropriate degrees of freedom, necessary to read the F-table in Appendix XIV, are 2 and 27. For statistical significance at $\alpha = 0.05$, F would need to be at least 3.35. To find the critical level that t would need to achieve, we use the following equation:

$$\text{critical } t = \sqrt{df_{\text{treatment}} \times F(df_{\text{treatment}}, df_{\text{error}})}$$

$$= \sqrt{2 \times 3.35}$$

$$= \sqrt{6.7}$$

$$= 2.588$$

As F-tables do not give negative values we can say that t has to be equal to or greater than 2.588 or equal to or less than −2.588.

As the t-value we obtained is larger, at −3.096, than the critical value, we can conclude that the control condition produced significantly poorer recall than the two mnemonic conditions.

Method Two
This method is based very closely on the previous one. We can square the t-value that we calculated from the contrast and this is an F-ratio (remember that $(t_{27})^2 = F_{1,27}$) and we can find a critical F-ratio from:

$$\text{critical } F = \text{df}_{\text{treatment}} \times F(\text{df}_{\text{treatment}}, \text{df}_{\text{error}})$$

which, in this case, means that the F-ratio for the contrast is $(3.096)^2 = 9.585$ and the critical F-ratio is 6.7. Once again the contrast produces a larger value for the statistic than the critical value.

Method Three
In this method the critical F-ratio is simply the critical F-ratio given for the original treatment F-ratio, which, with 2 and 27 degrees of freedom, for $\alpha = 0.05$ we have already found to be 3.35. However, because we have arrived at the critical F-ratio in a different way, we need to adjust the F-ratio that we calculated for the contrast. Those of you familiar with algebra will see why the adjustment is made:

$$\text{calculated } F = \frac{(t \text{ for contrast})^2}{\text{df for treatment}}$$

$$= \frac{(3.096)^2}{2}$$

$$= \frac{9.585}{2}$$

$$= 4.793$$

Once again the calculated value is larger than the critical one.

Method Four
Following the same reasoning that took us from Method One to Method Two (or rather the reverse of it), we can say that Method Three can have a version that involves a t-value rather than an F-value. Therefore the critical t would be the square root of the critical F for the treatment:

$$\text{critical } t = \sqrt{3.35}$$

$$= 1.83$$

We now need to take the square root of the calculated F-ratio from Method Three. Therefore the calculated t is:

$$t = \sqrt{\frac{(\text{original } t \text{ for contrast})^2}{\text{df for treatment}}}$$

which is the equivalent of:

$$t = \frac{\text{original } t \text{ for contrast}}{\sqrt{\text{df for treatment}}}$$

$$= \frac{3.096}{\sqrt{2}}$$

$$= 2.189$$

which is, once again, larger than the critical value. Of the four methods, One and Two seem the most straightforward and, as so many of the contrast tests are based on the same equation for the t-test, Method One is the most consistent with other tests.

Pairwise contrast tests

As stated in Chapter 18, the equations for t for contrasts are only appropriate in between-subjects designs when the variances in the subgroups are homogeneous. If the largest variance is less than four times the smallest variance (and the subsamples are the same size) then we can treat the variances as sufficiently homogeneous. However, if the variances are more disparate than this then the t-test for independent variances (Welch's t), given in Appendix VI, should be used. Within-subjects designs have a different problem, in that they should have sphericity (see Chapter 16 and Appendix VII). Therefore, to be on the safe side, and consistent with most computer programs, you are advised to use the equation for the standard within-subjects t-test as the equation for the contrast.

In both the heterogeneous variance case and the within-subjects case, when looking up the critical value of t for a contrast, use the degrees of freedom that is used for the version of t-test you have computed. In the case of the within-subjects design this will be one fewer than the number of participants. In the independent variances case it will necessitate using the equation for df given in Appendix VI.

Newman–Keuls test
This test follows a similar principle to Tukey's HSD test, which was introduced in Chapter 18. In Tukey's HSD test the calculated t had to reach a critical value which was based on the number of means that were to be involved in the set (or family) of contrasts.

To calculate Tukey's HSD, look up the critical q-value from the tables of the Studentised range statistic, given in Appendix XIV, for the number of means involved in the contrasts and the error df (or df for the t-test, in within-subjects designs and independent variance cases). Place the value found for q in the following equation:

$$\text{critical } t = \frac{q}{\sqrt{2}}$$

In Tukey's HSD this critical value is used to assess all the calculated t values in the family of contrasts.

In the Newman–Keuls test, the means are set out in order of size and the q-value depends on the number of means apart that are involved in the particular contrast—their range. For example, we would place the three means from the mnemonic experiment in the order:

Control	Pegword	Loci
7.2	8.9	9.6

The comparison between loci and control means ranges across three means (including the two means in the contrast) and so we would look for q with three means in the table of the Studentised range statistic in Appendix XIV. This tells us that for df = 24, $q = 3.53$ and for df = 30, $q = 3.49$. Here, because the df we actually want is halfway between these values ($(24 + 30)/2 = 27$), we can use a simple form of interpolation to find the q-value for df = 27; take the mean of the two qs:

$$q = \frac{3.53 + 3.49}{2} = 3.51$$

Therefore,

$$\text{critical } t = \frac{3.51}{\sqrt{2}}$$

$$= \frac{3.51}{1.4142}$$

$$= 2.482$$

which is the same as would be found using Tukey's HSD.

To use the Newman–Keuls test for the comparison of control mean with pegword mean, and pegword mean with loci mean then, in both cases the means range across two means. Therefore, we do not need to use q to find the critical value of t: we can use the standard t-tables, with df = 27. Here the critical value of t is 2.052.

Tukey's HSD can be seen as rather conservative and therefore lacking power in comparison with the Newman–Keuls test. On the other hand, the Newman–Keuls test can be too liberal and therefore liable to commit a Type I error, if used to test contrasts among more than three means.

Tukey's wholly significant difference (WSD)

This test can be seen as a compromise between Tukey's HSD and Newman–Keuls. To find the critical value for Tukey's WSD take the mean of the critical t for Tukey's HSD and the critical t for Newman–Keuls. Thus, for the contrasts involving two means (control v. pegword and pegword v. loci), the critical t using Tukey's WSD is:

$$\text{critical } t = \frac{2.482 + 2.052}{2}$$

$$= 2.267$$

Fisher's protected least significant difference (PLSD)

This is probably the most liberal test of all and, for that reason, it is often not recommended. However, there is a restriction on this test that it should not be conducted unless the relevant F-ratio from the ANOVA is statistically significant. Once this criterion has been passed, look up the critical t in standard t-tables, with the degrees of freedom for the error term and compare each calculated t using the usual equation that is used for pairwise contrasts. Therefore, in the present case, the critical t is 2.052. Thus, this test does not take into account the number of contrasts and so, despite its initial restriction, it is not advisable to use it with more than three contrasts.

Orthogonality

As stated above, in each contrast when the sample sizes are equal, the sum of the weightings must equal zero, i.e.:

$$\Sigma w_j = 0$$

It has been suggested in the past by statisticians that the comparisons that are made should be independent of each other because we are trying to find out how much of the overall Sum of Squares for the treatment is accounted for by the contrasts. Each treatment Sum of Squares can be broken down into the same number of independent contrasts as there are degrees of freedom for the treatment. In the memory example there are two degrees of freedom for the treatment and therefore there are two independent contrasts that can be made. If the contrasts are independent then they are described as being *orthogonal*.

If they are orthogonal (and the sample sizes are equal) then:

$$\Sigma(w_{ja} \times w_{jb}) = 0$$

where j refers to the mean for which the weighting is appropriate and a and b are two different contrasts. If the sample sizes are not equal, then:

$$\Sigma(n_j \times w_{ja} \times w_{jb}) = 0$$

where n_j is the sample size that produced mean j.

To explain the equation, when the sample sizes are the same, I will use an example. The mnemonic treatment will only allow two orthogonal (independent) contrasts (there are three levels of the IV and therefore two degrees of freedom in the original F-ratio; accordingly, for the set of contrasts to be orthogonal, there can only be two of them in the set). The first contrast in the table would be comparing the mean for pegwords with the mean for loci. Notice that we could not do simple pairwise comparisons between all the means and maintain orthogonal weightings.

Table A9.3 The weightings for a set of orthogonal contrasts, when sample sizes are the same

weighting	control	Treatment pegword	loci	sum
w_{j1}	$w_{11} = 0$	$w_{21} = 1$	$w_{31} = -1$	0
w_{j2}	$w_{12} = 2$	$w_{22} = -1$	$w_{32} = -1$	0
	$w_{11} \times w_{12} = 0$	$w_{21} \times w_{22} = -1$	$w_{31} \times w_{32} = 1$	0

Non-parametric tests

At least ordinal data

Between-subjects designs: following a Kruskal–Wallis ANOVA
An example was given in Chapter 16 and Appendix VII, in which 24 college lecturers were each given an essay to mark and they were told that the writer of the essay was a male student, or was a female student or they were not given any indication of the student's gender. In fact, the same essay was given to all the lecturers. Each lecturer gave the essay a grade between C– and A+, which was converted to a numerical grade ranging from 1 to 9. The test I am going to explain should only be used if the initial Kruskal–Wallis is statistically significant and if at least five people were used in each group. However, although the result was not statistically significant I am going to use that example to illustrate the technique.

In calculating the Kruskal–Wallis test a rank is given to each grade. In Appendix VII it was shown that the three conditions had the following total ranks, from which the mean ranks (out of 8 participants) have been derived.

Table A9.4 The total and mean ranks of the grades given by participants for an essay depending on the presumed gender of its author

| | 'gender' of author | | |
	female	neutral	male
Total rank (R)	76.5	110	113.5
Mean rank ($\bar{R}$)	9.5625	13.75	14.1875

The difference between two of the mean ranks can be tested using a z-test, where:

$$z = \frac{\bar{R}_1 - \bar{R}_2}{\sqrt{\left[\frac{N \times (N + 1)}{12}\right] \times \left(\frac{1}{n_1} + \frac{1}{n_2}\right)}}$$

where N is the total sample size and n_1 and n_2 are the sizes of the two subsamples in the contrast.

Therefore, if we compare the male and female essay conditions,

$$z = \frac{14.1875 - 9.5625}{\sqrt{\left(\frac{24 \times 25}{12}\right) \times \left(\frac{1}{8} + \frac{1}{8}\right)}}$$

$$= \frac{4.625}{\sqrt{50 \times \frac{1}{4}}}$$

$$= \frac{4.625}{\sqrt{12.5}}$$

$$= \frac{4.625}{3.53553}$$

$$= 1.308$$

However, we need to adjust the α-level to take account of the number of conditions which are to be contrasted. The adjustment is:

$$\text{adjusted } \alpha = \frac{\alpha}{k \times (k - 1)}$$

where k is the number of levels of the IV.

Thus, if we set α for the family of three contrasts at 0.05, then, to be statistically significant, each contrast will have to have a probability of:

$$\text{adjusted } \alpha = \frac{0.05}{3 \times 2} = 0.0083$$

The probabilities shown in z-tables are for one-tailed tests. Therefore if we were looking for a z that produced a two-tailed probability of 0.05, we would usually look for the z that produced a one-tailed probability of 0.025 or $\alpha/2$. In the present case, we are making an adjustment that takes into account the number of pairwise contrasts that will be made. The number of pairwise contrasts that can be made from k levels of an IV will always be $[k \times (k - 1)]/2$. To make the adjustment we will divide the probability we desire for the family of contrasts by the number of possible contrasts. In other words, we divide $\alpha/2$ by $[k \times (k - 1)]/2$. Via algebra this becomes $\alpha/[k \times (k - 1)]$. Therefore, we can find the appropriate critical z-value that would produce this two-tailed probability by looking up a *one-tailed* z-value in the z-tables in Appendix XIV. This tells us that the critical z is 2.395, which is more than the calculated z.

Correction for ties
As with the Kruskal–Wallis test, when some scores are the same, there is a more accurate version of the test which adjusts for ties. In the present example, there were five places where the grades tied, and the working in Appendix VII showed that the total correction was 894.

$$z \text{ (corrected for ties)} = \frac{\bar{R}_1 - \bar{R}_2}{\sqrt{\left\{\left[\frac{N \times (N + 1)}{12}\right] - \left[\frac{\text{total correction}}{12 \times (N - 1)}\right]\right\} \times \left(\frac{1}{n_1} + \frac{1}{n_2}\right)}}$$

$$= \frac{14.1875 - 9.5625}{\sqrt{\left[\left(\frac{24 \times 25}{12}\right) - \left(\frac{894}{12 \times 23}\right)\right] \times \left(\frac{1}{8} + \frac{1}{8}\right)}}$$

$$= \frac{4.625}{\sqrt{(50 - 3.23913) \times \frac{1}{4}}}$$

$$= \frac{4.625}{\sqrt{11.69022}}$$

$$= \frac{4.625}{3.41909}$$

$$= 1.353$$

This value is still less than the critical value for z and so we cannot conclude that there is a difference in the way the lecturers rated the essay when they thought it was written by a male than when they thought it was written by a female.

Within-subjects designs: following a Friedman two-way ANOVA
An example was given in Chapter 16 and Appendix VII, in which researchers wished to see whether a group of seven students rated a particular course differently as they spent more time on it. Each student was asked to rate the course on a 7-point scale ranging from *not enjoyable at all* to *very enjoyable*, on three occasions: after one week, after five weeks and after ten weeks.

Table A9.5 The total and mean ranks for the ratings given to the course

	week of the course		
	one	five	ten
Total rank (R)	10	14.5	17.5
Mean rank (R̄)	1.42857	2.07143	2.5

The test for the pairwise comparison of levels of the independent variable follows the same principles as for the between-subjects design, in that it should only be conducted if the initial ANOVA was statistically significant, and, as long as the sample size is at least 15, there is a z-test, the value of which can be compared with a critical z-value which adjusts the α-level to take account of the number of comparisons being conducted. The z-test is derived from:

$$z = \frac{\bar{R}_1 - \bar{R}_2}{\sqrt{\dfrac{k \times (k + 1)}{n \times 6}}}$$

where k is the number of levels of the IV, in this case 3
$\bar{R}_1$ and $\bar{R}_2$ are the mean ranks for the two levels of the IV that are being compared.

(There is a version of the test that is based on the total ranks rather than the mean ranks but I am using the present version so as to be consistent with the between-subjects analysis given above.)
    In the present case:

$$z = \frac{2.5 - 1.42857}{\sqrt{\dfrac{3 \times 4}{7 \times 6}}} = \frac{1.07143}{\sqrt{0.2857}} = 2.005$$

Following the same principles for finding the critical z-value as given above for between-subjects design, with 3 levels of the IV, the critical z is 2.395, which is more than the calculated z. Accordingly, we cannot conclude that the students' opinions of the course changed between its first and tenth week.

There does not appear to be a correction for ties with this test.

Categorical data

When analysing a contingency table that is more than a 2×2 table, it is possible to conduct further analysis by *partitioning* the contingency table into a number of 2×2 sub-tables. The example I am giving is of a 3×2 table. Those wishing to partition a larger table can find details of how to do this in Agresti (2002).

As an example, imagine that researchers have looked at the occupations of 100 school-leavers, 50 from school A and 50 from school B. They find the following pattern:

Table A9.6 The occupations of school-leavers from two schools

	full time	part-time	unemployed	Total
School A	10	26	14	50
School B	22	18	10	50
Total	32	44	24	100

The appropriate initial test is a χ^2 contingency test as described in Chapter 15. The researchers conducted the test and found that $\chi^2_{(2)} = 6.621$, $p = 0.0365$. As this showed that the frequencies for the two schools differed significantly, they decided to find the source of the significance by partitioning the contingency table.

Partitioning of a $2 \times k$ table (where k is the number of columns) involves forming 2×2 sub-tables. As each sub-table has one degree of freedom, there are as many sub-tables that can be made as there were degrees of freedom in the original contingency table. Thus, as in the present case, a 2×3 table has df $= 2$ and so there are two partitions that can be made of this table. A χ^2 can be conducted on each partition. Further details of the version I am going to give are contained in Agresti (2002) which also shows how to partition a table which has more than 2 rows. (An alternative approach is given by Siegel & Castellan, 1988.)

Table A9.7 A coding of the cells from Table A9.6

	full time	part-time	unemployed
School A	a	b	c
School B	d	e	f

The first partition involves the data in the first two columns:

Table A9.8 The cells involved in the first partition of the data in Table A9.6

	full time	part-time
School A	a	b
School B	d	e

Table A9.9 The first partition of the original contingency table

	full time	part-time
School A	10	26
School B	22	18

From this we can calculate a χ^2 value using the usual equation (A5.1). From this we find $\chi^2_{(1)} = 5.760$, $p = 0.016$.

The second partition entails combining parts of the first partition and re-introducing the missing column from the original contingency table:

Table A9.10 The elements in the second partition of the data in Table A9.6

	full-time or part-time	unemployed
School A	a + b	c
School B	d + e	f

Table A9.11 The data for the second partition of Table A9.6

	full-time or part-time	unemployed
School A	36	14
School B	40	10

Applying equation A5.1 to these data we find $\chi^2_{(1)} = 0.877$, $p = 0.349$.

From these two partitions we can see that schools A and B differed significantly in the proportions who were in full- and part-time employment, while the schools did not differ significantly in the proportions who were in some form of employment.

We can check that the different partitions are independent of each other and therefore form an appropriate set of partitions. However, this involves introducing a new version of χ^2: the likelihood-ratio χ^2 (sometimes shown as G^2).

Likelihood-ratio χ^2

$$\text{Likelihood-ratio } \chi^2 = 2 \times \sum \left[\text{obs} \times \ln\left(\frac{\text{obs}}{\text{exp}}\right) \right]$$

where, as usual in such tests,

obs is the observed frequency

exp is the expected frequency if the variables are unrelated

ln refers to the natural (or Napierian) log.

Table A9.12 shows the expected frequencies for the data in Table A9.11 if school and nature of employment are not related.

Table A9.12 The expected frequencies for the second partition of Table A9.6

	full-time or part-time	unemployed
School A	38	12
School B	38	12

Using the information in Tables A9.11 and A9.12 the likelihood-ratio χ^2 is:

$$2 \times \left[\left(36 \times \ln\left(\frac{36}{38}\right) \right) + \left(14 \times \ln\left(\frac{14}{12}\right) \right) + \left(40 \times \ln\left(\frac{40}{38}\right) \right) + \left(10 \times \ln\left(\frac{10}{12}\right) \right) \right]$$

$$= 2 \times [(-1.9464) + (2.1581) + (2.0517) + (-1.8232)]$$

$$= 0.8804$$

The advantage of referring to the likelihood-ratio χ^2 is that if it is calculated for each of the partitions of the original contingency table then the sum of those values should equal the value for the original contingency table. Fortunately, you probably won't have to calculate the likelihood-ratio χ^2 by hand as it should be available in the statistical package you use; SPSS reports it automatically when you run the more usual χ^2.

The likelihood-ratio χ^2 for the data in Table A9.6 is 6.7443, for the first partition it is 5.8639. 5.8639 + 0.8804 = 6.7443. Therefore the partitions are independent of each other.

Trend tests

In Chapter 18 an example was given of participants drinking either one, two or three units of alcohol and then having their reaction times recorded; there were eight participants in each group.

Table A9.13 The means and SDs of reaction times by number of units of alcohol consumed

| | Units of alcohol consumed | | |
	one	two	three
Mean	151.25	163.38	168.75
SD	14.12	10.53	12.94

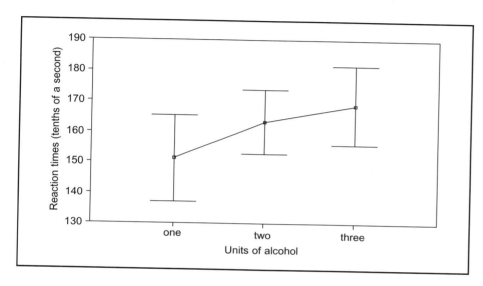

FIGURE A9.1 Mean reaction times (in tenths of seconds), with SDs, by number of units of alcohol consumed

The means form a pattern such that the more alcohol consumed the longer the reaction time. However, they do not form a completely straight line. The summary table from the preliminary ANOVA for the data was:

Table A9.14 Summary table of the between-subjects ANOVA on the effects of alcohol on reaction times

Source	Sum of Squares	df	Mean Square	F	p
Between Groups	1285.750	2	642.875	4.039	.0328
Within Groups	3342.875	21	159.185		
Total	4628.625	23			

The general equation for a trend analysis

For trend analysis you create a sum of squares for the given trend you are testing according to the following equation:

$$SS_{trend} = \frac{\left[\sum(c_j \times \bar{x}_j)\right]^2}{\sum\left(\dfrac{c_j^2}{n_j}\right)} \qquad (A9.2)$$

where $\bar{x}_j$ is a mean for one of the treatments

c_j is the coefficient for $\bar{x}_j$ and will depend on the nature of the contrast

n_j is the number of scores that contributed to $\bar{x}_j$

When the subsamples are the same size, the equation simplifies to:

$$SS_{trend} = \frac{n \times [\sum(c_j \times \bar{x}_j)]^2}{\sum(c_j^2)} \qquad (A9.3)$$

where n is the number of participants in one group.

Each trend has its own set of coefficients and, because the idea is to split up the Treatment Sum of Squares into its component parts, they should be orthogonal. Appendix XVI provides the coefficients for some trend tests.

Each trend test has 1 degree of freedom. Therefore, as the Mean Square for the trend (MS_{trend}) is found from:

$$MS_{trend} = \frac{SS_{trend}}{df_{trend}} = \frac{SS_{trend}}{1}$$

it is the same as the SS_{trend}.

An F-ratio for the trend is found from:

$$trend\ F\text{-ratio} = \frac{MS_{trend}}{MS_{error}}$$

and the F-ratio has df = 1 for MS_{trend} and the df from the original error term in the ANOVA for the error. Thus, in the present example the degrees of freedom are 1 and 21. The probability of the F-ratio for the trend can then be found from standard F-tables.

A trend analysis is, in fact, an example of a contrast test. In keeping with convention, I have referred to *coefficients* when talking about trend analysis. They are performing the same role as the weightings which are referred to in the description of contrast testing. In this particular example, the test for the linear trend across the alcohol levels would be the same as a pairwise contrast between the one unit and three unit conditions, because the coefficient for two units is 0 in the trend test. However, the trend test will produce an F-ratio, while the contrast produces a t-value. Remember, though, that when, in an F-ratio, the treatment df = 1 then $t = \sqrt{F}$. In the present example, the F-ratio for the linear trend was 7.695, in which case $t = 2.774$. Try using

Equation 18.1 to check that the pairwise contrast between one unit and three units produces the same result.

Adjustment for unequal intervals

In the above example the levels of the independent variable (units of alcohol) went up by a regular amount (1 unit at a time). If the units do not go up by a regular amount, for example if they were 1, 3, 7 and 15 units, then the coefficients need to be adjusted accordingly. Appendix XVI shows how to calculate coefficients when the intervals between the levels are unequal.

This appendix illustrates the techniques introduced in Chapter 19.

Non-parametric correlation—at least ordinal data	496
Spearman's rho	497
Kendall's tau	498
Partial correlation	501
Higher-order partial correlation	502
Method for calculating the probability of partial r	502
The difference between two correlation coefficients	502
Non-independent groups	503
Confidence Intervals for r	505
Kendall's coefficient of concordance	506
Correction for ties	507
Reliability	508
The Spearman–Brown equation for split-half reliability	508
Cronbach's coefficient alpha	509
Kuder–Richardson 20 reliability coefficient	509
Standard error of measurement	509
Inter-rater reliability—Cohen's kappa	510
Standard error of estimate	516

Non-parametric correlation—at least ordinal data

The example was given in Chapter 19 that researchers wished to investigate the relationship between the length of time students had studied psychology and the degree to which they believed that psychology is a science. Eleven psychology students were asked how long they had studied psychology and were asked to rate, on a five-point scale, ranging from 1 = *not at all* to 5 = *definitely a science*, their beliefs about whether psychology is a science.

Table A10.1 The length of time students have studied psychology and their opinion of whether it is a science

Participant	Years studied psychology	Rating of psychology as a science
1	1	1
2	2	1
3	3	2
4	4	3
5	5	4
6	1	3
7	2	3
8	3	2
9	4	5
10	5	5
11	6	5

Both Spearman's rho and Kendall's tau can be calculated by converting the scores, within a variable, to ranks. As usual in such tests, scores that have the same value (ties) are given a mean rank; see the explanation for the Wilcoxon signed-rank test for matched pairs in Appendix VI.

Table A10.2 The years spent studying psychology and the opinion over whether psychology is a science, plus rankings

year	rating	rank of year	rank of rating	difference between rankings (d)	d²
1	1	1.5	1.5	0	0
2	1	3.5	1.5	2	4
3	2	5.5	3.5	2	4
4	3	7.5	6	1.5	2.25
5	4	9.5	8	1.5	2.25
1	3	1.5	6	−4.5	20.25
2	3	3.5	6	−2.5	6.25
3	2	5.5	3.5	2	4
4	5	7.5	10	−2.5	6.25
5	5	9.5	10	−0.5	0.25
6	5	11	10	1	1

Total   50.50

Spearman's rho

There are two versions of Spearman's rho. One is very straightforward but does not correct for tied ranks. The other corrects for tied ranks and is therefore more accurate when ties are present. The method for calculating the uncorrected version is shown here. The version that corrects for ties can be found by calculating a Pearson's Product Moment Correlation on the ranks of the data. It can also be found by a laborious modification of the uncorrected version. Therefore, in the absence of a computer I would only use the following technique when there are no ties. However, to illustrate its use I have calculated the uncorrected rho for the data in Table A10.1. The equation to use for rho when there are no ties is:

$$\text{rho} = 1 - \frac{6 \times (\text{sum of } d^2)}{n^3 - n}$$

where n is the sample size. Therefore:

$$\text{rho} = 1 - \frac{6 \times 50.5}{(11)^3 - 11}$$

$$= 1 - \frac{303}{1331 - 11}$$

$$= 1 - 0.22955 = 0.77$$

Testing the statistical significance of Spearman's rho

In Chapter 19 the value of rho, corrected for ties of 0.762 was given for the correlation between the years students had spent studying psychology and their attitudes to psychology as a science.

When the sample is not more than 100 then the table for probabilities of rho given in Appendix XIV can be used. When the sample is above 100 there is an equation that converts rho to a t-value.

$$t = \text{rho} \times \sqrt{\frac{n - 2}{1 - (\text{rho})^2}} \qquad \text{(A10.1)}$$

The statistical significance of the result can be checked using standard t-tables with $n - 2$ degrees of freedom, where n is the sample size.

Alternatively, although less accurate, if you have access to more exact values for the probability of z, you should use the z-approximation:

$$z = \text{rho} \times \sqrt{(n - 1)} \qquad \text{(A10.2)}$$

and look up the probability in standard z-tables.

Kendall's tau

To re-analyse the data from the previous example using Kendall's tau, we do not, in fact, need to convert the scores to ranks; however, the same result is achieved whether ranks or the original scores are used.

Kendall's tau can be calculated in a number of ways and some of them are quicker than the one I am going to show but they become complicated when there are ties on both variables. The method I am using is applicable to all situations.

To calculate tau we first need to draw up a table that has the values from one variable, in numerical order, along the width of the table and the values of the other variable, also in numerical order, along the height of the table. The value of each pair of scores is then shown in the table by being placed in the appropriate cell, with the number of pairs that have the same value shown; e.g. the two students who had studied for three years and given the course a rating of two:

Table A10.3 The data from Table A10.1 recast into a table for initial analysis of Kendall's tau

	Rating given to course				
Years on course	1	2	3	4	5
1	1		1		
2	1		1		
3		2			
4			1		1
5				1	1
6					1

We now take each entry in the table, starting in the top left-hand corner, and note how many entries are below and to the right of that target cell; i.e. how many entries are in a position that is consistent with a positive correlation:

Table A10.4 The data from Table A10.1 recast into a table for initial analysis of Kendall's tau, showing the area to the right and below the first cell in the table

	Rating given to course				
Years on course	1	2	3	4	5
1	1		1		
2	1		1		
3		2			
4			1		1
5				1	1
6					1

Add the numbers that are in the cells below and to the right of the cell; in the first case they are, taken row by row:

$$1, 2, 1, 1, 1, 1, 1 = 8$$

Then multiply this sum by the number in the target cell, which in this case is 1. We do this for each entry in the table and add the results together to find the number of entries in the correct order (S_+). Thus,

$$S_+ = (1 \times 8) + (1 \times 4) + (1 \times 7) + (1 \times 4) + (2 \times 5) + (1 \times 3) + (1 \times 1) = 37$$

Now we need to find the number of entries that are not in the correct order (S_-). To do this we take each entry in the table and count how many are below and to the left of that target entry and multiply the result by the number in the target entry. Thus,

$$S_- = (1 \times 3) + (1 \times 2) + (1 \times 1) = 6$$

We can now find tau from the following equation:

$$\text{tau} = \frac{2 \times [(S_+) - (S_-)]}{n \times (n - 1)}$$

where n is the sample size.
    Therefore:

$$\text{tau} = \frac{2 \times (37 - 6)}{11 \times 10}$$

$$= \frac{62}{110}$$

$$= 0.564$$

Tied observations
As with Spearman's rho there is an adjustment for ties. To calculate this it is necessary to find a correction factor to allow for the ties in each of the variables.

Table A10.5 Obtaining the correction factors for Kendall's tau

rank	Years on course number in tie (t)	$t \times (t - 1)$	rank	Rating of course number in tie (t)	$t \times (t - 1)$
1.5	2	2	1.5	2	2
3.5	2	2	3.5	2	2
5.5	2	2	6	3	6
7.5	2	2	10	3	6
9.5	2	2			
	Total (correction for Var$_a$)	10		Total (correction for Var$_b$)	16

The equation for tau corrected for ties is:

$$tau = \frac{2 \times [(S_+) - (S_-)]}{\sqrt{[n \times (n-1)] - \text{correction for Var}_a} \times \sqrt{[n \times (n-1)] - \text{correction for Var}_b}}$$

$$= \frac{2 \times (37 - 6)}{\sqrt{(11 \times 10) - 10} \times \sqrt{(11 \times 10) - 16}} = \frac{62}{\sqrt{100} \times \sqrt{94}}$$

$$= \frac{62}{10 \times 9.69536} = 0.639$$

The probability of tau

As with Spearman's rho there exists an approximation to the normal distribution for Kendall's tau. However, Kendall's tau has the advantage that this approximation is accurate for smaller sample sizes. Thus, if the sample is ten or fewer you should use the appropriate table in Appendix XIV. Above this sample size use the z-approximation:

$$z = \frac{3 \times tau \times \sqrt{n \times (n-1)}}{\sqrt{2 \times [(2 \times n) + 5]}} \tag{A10.3}$$

where n is the size of the sample. The probability of this z-value can be found in standard z-tables.

Therefore,

$$z = \frac{3 \times 0.639 \times \sqrt{110}}{\sqrt{2 \times (22 + 5)}}$$

$$= \frac{1.917 \times 10.48809}{\sqrt{54}}$$

$$= \frac{20.10567}{7.34847} = 2.74$$

Partial correlation

As was pointed out in Chapter 19, partial correlation is the correlation between two variables with the possible influence of a third variable (or more variables) on the two original variables, taken out of the relationship. An example was given of the relationship between mathematical ability and ability at English with age taken out. This gave the partial correlation:

$$r_{me.a} = 0.723$$

Higher-order partial correlation

We can remove the possible influences of more than one variable on the relationship between two variables; for example, if we wished to remove the possible influences of age and socio-economic status (SES) from the relationship between mathematical ability and English ability.

$$r_{me.as} = \frac{r_{me.a} - (r_{ms.a} \times r_{es.a})}{\sqrt{(1 - r_{ms.a}^2) \times (1 - r_{es.a}^2)}}$$

where $r_{me.a}$ is the partial correlation between maths and English with age partialled out
        $r_{ms.a}$ is the partial correlation of maths and SES with age partialled out
        $r_{es.a}$ is the partial correlation between English and SES with age partialled out

Method for calculating the probability of partial r

Appendix XIV gives the equation for calculating a *t*-value in order to find the probability of a Pearson's Product Moment Correlation Coefficient *r* (when the Null Hypothesis is that $\rho = 0$). The equation can be extended to encompass partial correlations, with the same Null Hypothesis:

$$t = \frac{r \times \sqrt{n - 2 - \text{order}}}{\sqrt{1 - r^2}}$$

where *r* is the correlation coefficient or partial correlation coefficient, *n* is the sample size and order is the order of the partial correlation; if we partial one variable out then the order = 1; if we partial out two variables, as in the above example where age and SES are partialled out, then the order = 2; when it is a normal correlation, rather than a partial correlation, then order = 0. (You will sometimes see reference made to a *zero-order* correlation. This means a bivariate correlation with no variables partialled out.) In each case, the degrees of freedom of the *t*-test are df = $(n - 2 - \text{order})$.

The difference between two correlation coefficients

Chapter 19 contained an explanation of how to compare two correlation coefficients to see whether they differ significantly from each other. However, the example given there was restricted to the situation where the two coefficients are from data from separate samples of people—independent groups. A more complex calculation is involved when the two correlation coefficients are from the same sample—non-independent samples. These procedures come from a paper by Steiger (1980) in which the merits of alternative procedures are discussed.

Non-independent groups

There are two different situations in which we might want to compare two correlations that come from the same people. One is where we have correlated one measure with a second measure and we have also correlated the first measure with a third measure. For example, we might relate IQ to mathematical ability and IQ to musical ability and then compare the two correlations to see whether one of the abilities is more closely related to IQ than the other.

The second situation is where we have four measures and we wish to compare the correlations of pairs of them. Imagine that we select a group of children and we ask each child to estimate how many words he or she will be able to remember from a list of twenty words. We then give each child a list of words to remember and then test his or her recall. We can correlate the two measures to find out whether there is a relationship between the estimate and the actual scores. We then train each child in a number of mnemonic techniques, such as grouping related words together. We then test the estimates and actual memories again, and correlate them. We could compare the two correlations to see whether there has been a change in the relationship between estimated and actual memory.

In both situations, as long as the sample size is greater than 20 then we can compare the correlations.

In both of the above cases, because we are using the same participants we need to take account of the other intercorrelations between the variables. This makes the calculations appear daunting. In fact they are long-winded and require you to be very careful but they are not particularly complicated.

The first situation

Table A10.6 The correlation matrix for three variables

variable	variable 1	variable 2	variable 3
1	1		
2	r_{21}	1	
3	r_{31}	r_{32}	1

If we wished to compare the correlation between variables 1 and 2 (r_{21}) with that of variables 1 and 3 (r_{31}) then firstly we need to find what is called the *determinant* of this matrix; this is shown as: $|R|$, where:

$$|R| = [1 - (r_{21})^2 - (r_{31})^2 - (r_{32})^2] + (2 \times r_{21} \times r_{31} \times r_{32})$$

Next we need to find the mean of the two correlations we are comparing:

$$\bar{r} = \frac{r_{21} + r_{31}}{2}$$

We can now find a *t*-value that has $n - 3$ degrees of freedom, where n is the sample size.

$$t_{(n-3)} = (r_{21} - r_{31}) \times \sqrt{\frac{(n-1) \times (1 + r_{32})}{\left[2 \times \left(\frac{n-1}{n-3}\right) \times |R|\right] + [\bar{r}^2 \times (1 - r_{32})^3]}}$$

The probability of this *t*-value can looked up in the *t*-table in Appendix XIV.

The second situation

Table A10.7 The correlation matrix for four variables

		variable		
variable	1	2	3	4
1	1			
2	r_{21}	1		
3	r_{31}	r_{32}	1	
4	r_{41}	r_{42}	r_{43}	1

If we wished to compare the correlation between variables 1 and 2 (r_{21}) with the correlation between variables 3 and 4 (r_{43}), we first need to find the mean of the two correlations we are comparing ($\bar{r}$), where:

$$\bar{r} = \frac{r_{21} + r_{43}}{2}$$

We then need to find the covariance of r_{21} and r_{43}, which is denoted as $\psi_{12.34}$, where:

$$\begin{aligned}
\psi_{12.34} = 0.5 \times \{ & ([(r_{31} - (\bar{r} \times r_{32})) \times (r_{42} - (r_{32} \times \bar{r}))] \\
& + [(r_{41} - (r_{31} \times \bar{r})) \times (r_{32} - (\bar{r} \times r_{31}))] \\
& + [(r_{31} - (r_{41} \times \bar{r})) \times (r_{42} - (\bar{r} \times r_{41}))] \\
& + [(r_{41} - (\bar{r} \times r_{42})) \times (r_{32} - (r_{42} \times \bar{r}))] \}
\end{aligned}$$

We also need to find Fisher's transformation (r') for both of the correlation coefficients we wish to compare. I will denote them as r'_{21} and r'_{43} (see Appendix XVI for the transformation).

Using these results we find $\bar{s}_{12.34}$, from:

$$\bar{s}_{12.34} = \frac{\Psi_{12.34}}{(1 - \bar{r}^2)^2}$$

From these calculations we can find a z-score from:

$$z = (r'_{21} - r'_{43}) \times \left(\frac{\sqrt{n-3}}{\sqrt{2 - (2 \times \bar{s}_{12.34})}} \right)$$

The probability of this z-value can be looked up in the standard z-table in Appendix XIV.

Now you know why computers were invented.

Confidence Intervals for r

Sometimes, having found a correlation coefficient for a sample we may wish to estimate the correlation in the population. One way to do this is to find the confidence interval for the coefficient, that is, the range of values within which the population parameter (ρ) is likely to lie. Chapter 19 provided an example in which the correlation, in a sample of 30 participants, between actual and estimated memory was $r = 0.8$.

To find the confidence interval (CI) it is necessary to convert r to an r', work out the confidence interval for r' and then convert the limits shown back to r-values. The equation is:

$$CI = r' \pm z_{(prob)} \times \frac{1}{\sqrt{n-3}}$$

where r' is the Fisher's transformation for r, in this case 1.099

$z_{(prob)}$ is the z-value needed to give a particular confidence interval. In the case of 95% confidence level we need to find the z that has one-tailed probability of $p = 0.025$, i.e. 1.96 (giving a two-tailed probability of $p = 0.05$).

$\dfrac{1}{\sqrt{n-3}}$ is the standard deviation for r'

n is the sample size

Therefore,

$$CI = 1.099 \pm 1.96 \times \frac{1}{\sqrt{27}} = 1.099 \pm 0.377$$

That is, ρ' (fisher's transformation of ρ) lies between 0.722 and 1.476.

These limits have to be converted back to r values by reading the r to r' conversion tables, or using the equation to convert r' to r given in Appendix XVI. An r' of 0.722 gives $r = 0.62$ and an r' of 1.476 gives $r = 0.90$. Therefore, the 95% confidence interval for ρ is between 0.62 and 0.90.

Kendall's coefficient of concordance

This test yields a statistic W which is a measure of how much a group of judges agree when asked to put a set of objects in rank order. In Chapter 19 the example was given where four judges were asked to rank a set of five photographs on the attractiveness of the person portrayed.

Table A10.8 The attractiveness rankings given by judges for five photographs

Judge	A	B	Photograph C	D	E
one	1	2	3	4	5
two	2	1	4	3	5
three	3	2	1	5	4
four	1	3	2	4	5
Total ranking (R)	7	8	10	16	19
Mean R	1.75	2	2.5	4	4.75

$$\text{overall Mean Ranking} = \frac{\text{sum of Mean Rankings}}{k}$$

where k is the number of entities to be ranked. In the present example,

$$\text{overall Mean Ranking} = \frac{1.75 + 2 + 2.5 + 4 + 4.75}{5}$$

$$= 3$$

To find W, we can use the equation:

$$W = \frac{12 \times \Sigma(\text{Mean R} - \text{overall Mean R})^2}{k \times (k^2 - 1)}$$

where $\Sigma(\text{Mean R} - \text{overall Mean R})^2$ is the sum of squared deviations of each mean R from the overall Mean R
k is the number of photographs being judged
(the equation always has the multiplier 12)

$$W = \frac{12 \times [(1.75 - 3)^2 + (2 - 3)^2 + (2.5 - 3)^2 + (4 - 3)^2 + (4.75 - 3)^2]}{5 \times (5^2 - 1)}$$

$$= \frac{12 \times (1.5625 + 1 + 0.25 + 1 + 3.0625)}{5 \times 24} = \frac{82.5}{120} = 0.6875$$

Once W has been found the link between it and bivariate correlation can be seen as it is possible to find the mean Spearman's rho for the correlations between each of the pairs of judges (in this case $4 \times 3/2 = 6$ pairs) from:

$$\text{mean rho} = \frac{(n \times W) - 1}{n - 1}$$

where n is the number of judges.

The above technique is for situations that contain no tied scores. As with other non-parametric correlation coefficients, there is a correction that should be used when ties exist. Below is how to calculate W when ties are present. The data in Table A10.9 have been modified from those in Table A10.8 in order to include tied scores.

Table A10.9 The attractiveness rankings given by judges of five photographs

Judge	A	B	Photograph C	D	E
one	1	2	3.5	3.5	5
two	2	1	4	3	5
three	2.5	2.5	1	5	4
four	1	3	2	4	5
Total ranking (R)	6.5	8.5	10.5	15.5	19
Mean R	1.625	2.125	2.625	3.875	4.75

Correction for ties

This can be achieved by drawing up a table of the following form, such that the ties for each participant are noted:

Table A10.10 Obtaining the correction for ties for a Kendall's coefficient of concordance W

Participant (judge)	value of tied rank	number in tied rank (t)	correction ($t^3 - t$)
one	3.5	2	6
three	2.5	2	6

Total correction   12

W corrected for ties can be found from the equation:

$$W = \frac{12 \times \Sigma(\text{mean R} - \text{overall Mean R})^2}{[k \times (k^2 - 1)] - \left(\dfrac{\text{total correction}}{n}\right)}$$

where   the overall Mean R is the mean of the Mean Rs for each entity being judged, which in this case is $\dfrac{1.625 + 2.125 + 2.625 + 3.875 + 4.75}{5} = 3$

$\Sigma(\text{Mean R} - \text{overall Mean R})^2$ is the sum of squared deviations of each Mean R from the overall Mean R, which in this case is:
$(1.625 - 3)^2 + (2.125 - 3)^2 + (2.625 - 3)^2 + (3.875 - 3)^2 + (4.75 - 3)^2 = 6.625$
k is the number of photographs being judged
n is the number of judges

Therefore,

$$W = \frac{12 \times 6.625}{[5 \times (5^2 - 1)] - \left(\dfrac{12}{4}\right)}$$

$$= \frac{79.5}{(5 \times 24) - 3} = \frac{79.5}{117}$$

$$= 0.6794$$

(whereas the version uncorrected for ties would be $W = 0.6625$.) As noted in Chapter 19, SPSS reports the version corrected for ties.

Reliability

The following are the reliability coefficients, the appropriate uses of which were discussed in Chapter 19.

The Spearman–Brown equation for split-half reliability

This can be found from:

$$r_{kk} = \frac{2 \times r_{12}}{1 + r_{12}}$$

where r_{kk} is the reliability coefficient
r_{12} is the correlation between the participants' scores on the two halves of the test.

This equation can be extended to allow for the intercorrelation between all the items in the test, whence it becomes:

$$r_{kk} = \frac{k \times \text{mean}(r)}{1 + [(k-1) \times \text{mean}(r)]}$$

where k is the number of items in the test
mean(r) is the mean of the correlations between the items.

Cronbach's coefficient alpha

This is simpler to compute and produces the same result as would be found from the previous equation:

$$r_{kk} = \frac{k}{k-1} \times \left[1 - \frac{\Sigma(s_i^2)}{s_t^2}\right]$$

where s_i^2 is the variance of item i
s_t^2 is the variance of the total scores
$\Sigma(s_i^2)$ means add the variances of each of the items together.

Kuder–Richardson 20 reliability coefficient

When each item has dichotomous (binary) responses, such as pass/fail or yes/no or agree/disagree then Cronbach's alpha simplifies further to become the Kuder–Richardson 20 reliability coefficient:

$$\text{KR 20 } r_{kk} = \frac{k}{k-1} \times \left[1 - \frac{\Sigma(p \times q)}{s_t^2}\right]$$

where p is the proportion of people giving one type of response and $q = 1 - p$ (that is, the proportion of people giving the other type of response); $\Sigma(p \times q)$ means for each item in the test find the product $p \times q$ and then add each product.

Standard error of measurement

The reliability of a measure can be used to produce a confidence interval for a person's score on the measure. The confidence interval is based on the standard error of measurement for the measure:

$$\text{SEM} = \text{SD}_t \times \sqrt{(1 - r)}$$

where SD_t is standard deviation of the test
r is the reliability coefficient

The confidence interval for a person's score can be found from:

$$CI = \text{score} \pm z_{\text{prob}} \times SEM$$

where z_{prob} is the z-value that gives the required level of confidence (e.g. $z = 1.96$ for 95% confidence).

For example, if an IQ test had a SD of 15 with a reliability coefficient of 0.9, then the SEM for the test would be:

$$SEM = 15 \times \sqrt{(1 - 0.9)}$$
$$= 15 \times \sqrt{0.1}$$
$$= 15 \times 0.316$$
$$= 4.74$$

If a boy scored 90 on the test then the 95% confidence interval for his IQ can then be found from:

$$CI = 90 \pm 1.96 \times 4.74$$
$$= 90 \pm 9.2904$$

In other words, the boy's IQ is likely to lie between 80.71 and 99.29.

Inter-rater reliability—Cohen's kappa

In order to check that a measure can be used consistently by different observers we need a measure of the degree of agreement between two observers. As was noted in Chapter 19, percentage agreement fails to take into account the amount of agreement that could have been expected by chance. On the other hand, a large positive correlation coefficient does not necessarily show that two observers are agreeing, as correlation merely tells you about the direction in which the two measures move relative to each other. A measure that solves both these problems is Cohen's kappa (k).

Although the following example involves an ordinal scale, Cohen's kappa would normally be calculated on nominal data.

Two lecturers read a set of essays and each gave a grade (on a 5-point scale) to each essay, without knowing what grades the other has awarded. These grades were then summarised in a table:

Table A10.11 The grades given to 75 essays by two lecturers, working independently

Lecturer Two's grades	Lecturer One's grades 1	2	3	4	5	Total
1	5	1				6
2	2	13	2			17
3		4	20	2		26
4			1	16	2	19
5				3	4	7
Total	7	18	23	21	6	75

The 5 in the top left-hand corner of the table tells us that there were 5 essays that both lecturer one and lecturer two graded as 1's. The 2 below that tells us that there were 2 essays that lecturer one graded as 1's but lecturer 2 graded as 2's. To check that you have entered the numbers in the table correctly, the numbers in the Total row at the bottom of the table should show that lecturer one graded 7 essays as 1's, 18 as 2's etc. up to 6 as 5's. The Total column at the far right of the table should show that lecturer two graded 6 essays as 1's, 17 as 2's etc. up to 7 as 5's.

We can see along the diagonal of the matrix those essays over which the two lecturers agreed: $\frac{58}{75}$ or 77.33%.

First we need to work out the expected frequencies by chance for each cell in the matrix, where the lecturers agree. This is done in a similar way as for χ^2, in that:

$$\text{expected frequency } (f_e) = \frac{\text{row total} \times \text{column total}}{\text{overall total}}$$

Therefore the expected frequency for essays that they both gave a grade of 1 is:

$$f_e = \frac{6 \times 7}{75} = 0.56$$

and the other expected frequencies for the diagonal cells are: 4.08, 7.973, 5.32 and 0.56, which means that:

the sum of the expected diagonal values (Sum f_e) = 18.493

Cohen's kappa is calculated from:

$$K = \frac{\text{Sum } f_o - \text{Sum } f_e}{N - \text{Sum } f_e}$$

where Sum f_o is the sum of the observed frequencies of the diagonal cells, which in this case is 58, and N is the total number of entities being classified by the raters—in this case 75 essays. Therefore:

$$K = \frac{58 - 18.493}{75 - 18.493}$$

$$= 0.699$$

or just under 70% agreement, once chance has been accounted for.

Robson (2002) reports that kappa in the range 0.4 to 0.6 is considered *fair*, between 0.6 and 0.75 is *good* and above 0.75 is *excellent*.

Kappa can be calculated when there are more than two raters. To demonstrate the principle and show that when there are only two raters the result is the same as that shown above I will use the data from Table A10.11. Initially, create a table that shows, for each entity being rated (in this case essays), how many raters gave that entity a particular rating. Find p_i for each rating. To find each p_i, use the following formula:

$$p_i = \frac{1}{n \times (n - 1)} \times \sum [n_{ij} \times (n_{ij} - 1)]$$

where n is the number of raters

n_{ij} is the number of raters who rated participant i as being in category j

Thus, for the first participant $n = 2$ as there were 2 raters, $n_{11} = 2$, as both people rated the person as having a score of 1, and n_{12} to n_{15} all equal 0

So p_i for that person is

$$p_i = \frac{1}{2 \times (2 - 1)} \times \{[2 \times (2 - 1)] + [0 \times (0 - 1)]$$

$$+ [0 \times (0 - 1)] + [0 \times (0 - 1)] + [0 \times (0 - 1)]\}$$

$$= \frac{1}{2} \times (2 + 0 + 0 + 0 + 0) = 1$$

p_j is found by summing all the ratings that were given to participants in the jth category and then dividing that sum by $N \times n$, where N is the number of entities being rated and n is the number of raters.

$$\text{kappa} = \frac{\text{mean } p_i - \text{sum of } p_j^2}{1 - \text{sum of } p_j^2}$$

$$= \frac{0.77333 - 0.24728}{1 - 0.24728}$$

$$= 0.69887, \text{ or } 0.699 \text{ to 3 decimal places}$$

Table A10.12 The data from Table A10.11 reconfigured into the layout necessary to produce Cohen's kappa for any number of raters

essay	rating 1	2	3	4	5	p_i
1	2					1
2	2					1
3	2					1
4	2					1
5	2					1
6	1	1				0
7	1	1				0
8	1	1				0
9		2				1
10		2				1
11		2				1
12		2				1
13		2				1
14		2				1
15		2				1
16		2				1
17		2				1
18		2				1
19		2				1
20		2				1
21		2				1
22		1	1			0
23		1	1			0
24		1	1			0
25		1	1			0
26		1	1			0
27		1	1			0

Table A10.12 (*cont'd*)

essay	1	2	3	4	5	p_i
			rating			
28			2			1
29			2			1
30			2			1
31			2			1
32			2			1
33			2			1
34			2			1
35			2			1
36			2			1
37			2			1
38			2			1
39			2			1
40			2			1
41			2			1
42			2			1
43			2			1
44			2			1
45			2			1
46			2			1
47			2			1
48			1	1		0
49			1	1		0
50			1	1		0
51				2		1
52				2		1
53				2		1
54				2		1
55				2		1

Table A10.12 (*cont'd*)

essay	1	2	rating 3	4	5	p_i
56				2		1
57				2		1
58				2		1
59				2		1
60				2		1
61				2		1
62				2		1
63				2		1
64				2		1
65				2		1
66				2		1
67				1	1	0
68				1	1	0
69				1	1	0
70				1	1	0
71				1	1	0
72					2	1
73					2	1
74					2	1
75					2	1
Total	13	35	49	40	13	58
p_j	0.08667	0.23333	0.32667	0.26667	0.08667	
p_j^2	0.00751	0.05444	0.10671	0.07111	0.00751	

Standard error of estimate

When the validity of a measure is expressed in terms of its correlation with another measure, then a confidence interval for a person's score can be found using the standard error of estimate for the measure, where,

$$SE_{est} = SD_x \times \sqrt{(1 - r^2)}$$

where SD_x is the standard deviation of the criterion measure
r is the correlation between the criterion and the new measure

A confidence interval (CI) can then be formed from:

$$CI = score \pm z_{prob} \times SE_{est}$$

where z_{prob} is the z-value that gives the required level of confidence (e.g. $z = 1.96$ for 95% confidence).

If a new measure of extroversion had a standard deviation of 5 and correlated $r = 0.8$ with another measure of extroversion, then the standard error of estimate would be:

$$SE_{est} = 5 \times \sqrt{1 - (0.8)^2}$$
$$= 3$$

Therefore, if a girl scored 30 on the new measure, the 95% confidence interval for her score would be:

$$CI = 30 \pm 1.96 \times 3$$
$$= 30 \pm 5.88$$

Therefore, her 'true' score is likely to lie between 24.12 and 35.88.

APPENDIX XI: REGRESSION

This appendix illustrates the techniques introduced in Chapter 20.

Simple linear regression   517
   Finding the statistical significance of a regression analysis   520
Significance of difference between two regressions   522
Additional links between correlation and simple linear regression   522
Adjusted R^2 524
The standard error of a regression coefficient   524
   Testing the statistical significance of a regression coefficient   526
   Calculating a confidence interval for a regression coefficient   527
   Suppressor variables   527
   Centring   528
   Testing an interaction   528
Diagnostic statistics   529
   Residuals   529
   Leverage and influence   530
Coding categorical variables   531

Simple linear regression

In Chapter 20 an example was given of attempts to predict mathematical ability from ability at English. It was pointed out that the equation for linear regression is the equation for the straight line that could be drawn through the data points on a scattergram such that the distance between the line and the points was at a minimum. This line is called the *best-fit line* and for simple linear regression (where there is one IV and one DV) is always of the form:

$$DV = a + (b \times IV)$$

or rather, when the prediction is not perfect:

$$predicted\ DV = a + (b \times IV)$$

(*a* and *b* are described as *regression coefficients*. If we were drawing the best-fit line on a graph, *a* would be the point where the line crosses the vertical

Table A11.1 The scores on tests of mathematical ability and ability at English in a sample of 10 children

Participant	Mathematical Ability	English Ability
1	50	50
2	40	48
3	60	48
4	50	47
5	70	65
6	60	64
7	75	75
8	70	72
9	85	75
10	75	80
Mean	63.5	62.4
SD	13.95429	13.05713

axis. It is called the *intercept* and is the value the predicted DV would have if the IV were 0. The *slope* of the line would be b; that is, the amount by which the DV would change for every change of one unit in the IV.)

To find b, we use the following equation:

$$b = \frac{[n \times \text{total of (IV} \times \text{DV)}] - (\text{total for IV} \times \text{total for DV})}{[n \times \text{total of (IV}^2)] - (\text{total for IV})^2}$$

where n is the sample size and *total of (IV × DV)* means multiply each person's score on the IV by the same person's score on the DV and add the results for each person together.

Therefore,

$$b = \frac{(10 \times 41080) - (635 \times 624)}{(10 \times 40472) - (624)^2}$$

$$= \frac{410800 - 396240}{404720 - 389376}$$

$$= 0.94890511$$

(I have had to go to this number of decimal places so that the answers are compatible with the ones provided by the computer).

Table A11.2 Calculations leading to finding the slope of a best-fit line for a simple linear regression

Participant	Mathematical Ability (MA)	English Ability (EA)	(EA)²	MA × EA
1	50	50	2500	2500
2	40	48	2304	1920
3	60	48	2304	2880
4	50	47	2209	2350
5	70	65	4225	4550
6	60	64	4096	3840
7	75	75	5625	5625
8	70	72	5184	5040
9	85	75	5625	6375
10	75	80	6400	6000
Total	635	624	40472	41080

Having found b we can find a from the following equation:

$$a = \frac{\text{total for DV} - (b \times \text{total for IV})}{n}$$

or

$$a = \text{mean for DV} - (b \times \text{mean for IV})$$

which is often written as:

$$a = \bar{Y} - b\bar{X}$$

Therefore,

$$a = 63.5 - (0.94890511 \times 62.4) = 4.28832$$

Accordingly,

$$\text{predicted MA} = 4.28832 + (0.94891 \times \text{EA})$$

Therefore, if a person scored 50 for English ability, his or her mathematical ability would be predicted to be:

$$4.28832 + (0.94891 \times 50) = 51.734$$

Finding the statistical significance of a regression analysis

To find the statistical significance of a regression, we perform an ANOVA on the data, in which the total Sum of Squares is separated into the sum of squares for the regression (the variance in the DV that has been successfully accounted for by the variance in the IV(s)) and the sum of squares for the residual (the variance in the DV not accounted for by the variance in the IV(s)).

Total Sum of Squares

The total Sum of Squares is the sum of squares for the DV. As usual, if we know the standard deviation we can square it, to get the variance and multiply this by one fewer than the sample size ($n - 1$):

$$\text{total Sum of Squares} = (10 - 1) \times (13.95429)^2$$

$$= 9 \times 194.72221$$

$$= 1752.5$$

Regression Sum of Squares

The regression Sum of Squares is calculated by subtracting the mean for the DV from the predicted value of the DV for each person, squaring the result and adding these squared values together.

Table A11.3 Obtaining the regression Sum of Squares for a simple linear regression

Participant	Maths Ability (Y)	Predicted MA (Ŷ)	Predicted MA – mean for actual MA (deviation) (Ŷ – Ȳ)	(deviation)² (Ŷ – Ȳ)²
1	50	51.734	−11.76642	138.44872
2	40	49.836	−13.66423	186.71128
3	60	49.836	−13.66423	186.71128
4	50	48.887	−14.61314	213.54382
5	70	65.967	2.46715	6.08685
6	60	65.018	1.51825	2.30508
7	75	75.456	11.9562	142.95082
8	70	72.609	9.10949	82.98279
9	85	75.456	11.9562	142.95082
10	75	80.201	16.70073	278.91438

S of S for regression   1381.60600

The residual Sum of Squares

The residual Sum of Squares is the sum of the squared differences between the predicted value of the DV and the actual value for each person; it can also be found by subtracting the regression Sum of Squares from the total Sum of Squares.

Table A11.4 Obtaining the residual Sum of Squares for a simple linear regression

Participant	Maths Ability (Y)	Predicted MA (Ŷ)	MA – predicted MA (residual), i.e. (Y – Ŷ)	(residual)^2 i.e. (Y – Ŷ)^2
1	50	51.734	−1.73358	3.00529
2	40	49.836	−9.83577	96.74230
3	60	49.836	10.16423	103.31164
4	50	48.887	1.11314	1.23908
5	70	65.967	4.03285	16.26385
6	60	65.018	−5.01825	25.18281
7	75	75.456	−.45620	0.20812
8	70	72.609	−2.60949	6.80943
9	85	75.456	9.54380	91.08403
10	75	80.201	−5.20073	27.04759

S of S for residuals   370.89400

We now have sufficient detail to create the summary ANOVA for the regression analysis. See Chapter 20 for an explanation of how the degrees of freedom, Mean Square and *F*-ratio are obtained.

Table A11.5 Summary table of the analysis of variance in a simple regression of the relationship between mathematical ability and ability at English

ANOVA[b]

Model		Sum of Squares	df	Mean Square	F	Sig.
1	Regression	1381.606	1	1381.606	29.801	.001[a]
	Residual	370.894	8	46.362		
	Total	1752.500	9			

[a] Predictors: (Constant), ENGLISH
[b] Dependent Variable: MATHS

Significance of difference between two regressions

Two regressions can be compared to see whether they are significantly different when one is contained in the other—that is when one contains all the predictor variables of the other plus more predictor variables. Use the following equation:

$$F(p_1 - p_2, N - p_1 - 1) = \frac{(N - p_1 - 1) \times (R_1^2 - R_2^2)}{(p_1 - p_2) \times (1 - R_1^2)}$$

where p_1 is the number of predictors in the regression with more predictors
p_2 is the number of predictors in the regression with fewer predictors
N is the total sample size
R_1^2 is the squared multiple regression coefficient for the regression with more predictors
R_2^2 is the squared multiple regression coefficient for the regression with fewer predictors

When the larger regression has only one more predictor variable than the smaller regression then the result of this test will provide the same information as the t-test that is conducted on the extra predictor variable and the t-value will be the square root of the F-value from the above equation. Thus, if we compared the regression with SES and English ability as predictors against that with just English ability, then the F-value would be the same as the square of the t-value for SES in the larger regression. However, when the larger regression is larger than the smaller one by more than one predictor variable then this equation becomes more useful. It produces the same result as would be found from SPSS when the optional statistic *R squared change* has been chosen.

Additional links between correlation and simple linear regression

The covariance between two variables was defined in Chapter 19, where it was shown that the correlation coefficient (r) between two variables can be found from:

$$r = \frac{\text{covariance}}{SD_1 \times SD_2}$$

The covariance of mathematical ability and English ability is 161.77778.

As well as using the method described in a previous section for finding the regression coefficient b in a simple linear regression, it can be found from the equation:

$$b = \frac{\text{covariance}}{(\text{SD for IV})^2}$$

which is the same as

$$b = \frac{\text{covariance}}{\text{variance for IV}}$$

Therefore,

$$b = \frac{161.77778}{170.48889}$$

$$= 0.948905.$$

In Chapter 20 it was explained that we can convert the regression coefficients into standardised regression coefficients (or beta coefficients), using the following equation:

$$\beta = \frac{b \times SD_x}{SD_y}$$

where b is the regression coefficient for an IV
   SD_x is the standard deviation of the same IV
   SD_y is the standard deviation of the DV

If, in simple linear regression, we convert b to a beta coefficient, we get:

$$\beta = \frac{0.94890511 \times 13.05713}{13.95429}$$

$$= 0.888$$

This is the same as the correlation coefficient (r) for the relationship between mathematical ability and English ability. The reason for this is that the standardised regression coefficient is the regression coefficient that would be found if we converted the values of the IV into standardised scores and did the same for the DV, and then did a regression analysis of the two standardised variables. Remember that standardising converts a distribution into one that has a mean of 0 and a standard deviation (and variance) of 1. The covariance of two standardised variables is the same as their correlation coefficient. In addition, the standardised regression coefficient a (the intercept or constant) becomes:

standardised regression coefficient = mean for DV − β × mean for IV

$$= 0 - 0.888 \times 0$$

$$= 0$$

Thus, in simple regression, the regression equation for the standardised variables is:

$$\text{standardised DV} = r \times \text{standardised IV}$$

Adjusted R^2

The adjusted R^2 is an estimate of R^2 in the population and takes into account the sample size and the number of IVs; the smaller the sample and the greater the number of IVs the larger the adjustment. The equation for adjusted R^2 is:

$$\text{adjusted } R^2 = 1 - \left[\frac{(1 - R^2) \times (n - 1)}{(n - p - 1)} \right]$$

where n is the sample size
   p is the number of IVs in the model.

Thus, when in Chapter 20, R^2 was shown as 0.79, with two IVs and ten participants,

$$\text{adjusted } R^2 = 1 - \left[\frac{(1 - 0.79) \times (10 - 1)}{(10 - 2 - 1)} \right]$$

$$= 1 - \left(\frac{0.21 \times 9}{7} \right) = 0.73.$$

The standard error of a regression coefficient

The standard error of a regression coefficient is calculated from the following equation:

$$\text{Std Err of IV}_1 = \sqrt{\frac{\text{Mean Square}_{\text{residual}}}{\text{S of S of IV}_1 \times (1 - R^2_{1.2.})}}$$

where   Mean Square$_{\text{residual}}$ can be found from the ANOVA for the regression analysis.
   S of S of IV$_1$ is the sum of squared deviations (from the mean) of the IV for which the standard error is being calculated.
   $R^2_{1.2.}$ is the squared multiple correlation coefficient where IV$_1$ is being treated as a criterion variable and the other IVs are acting as predictor variables for it. When there are only two IVs it is the square of the correlation coefficient between the two IVs (i.e. r^2).

In the case of a simple regression (one with only one IV) the equation becomes:

$$\text{Std Err of IV} = \sqrt{\frac{\text{Mean Square}_{residual}}{\text{S of S of IV}}}$$

In Chapter 20 an example was given of a multiple regression with mathematical ability as the DV and ability at English, age, socio-economic status (SES) and IQ as IVs. Table A11.6 shows the original data entered into a stepwise regression and Table A11.7 shows the ANOVA for the regression, which only placed ability at English and SES in the model.

Table A11.6 The data entered into a stepwise regression in which maths was the DV and the other variables the IVs

Participant	Maths	English	Age	SES	IQ
1	50	50	150	2	85
2	40	48	150	1	100
3	60	48	144	4	95
4	50	47	144	3	105
5	70	65	162	4	100
6	60	64	162	1	110
7	75	75	156	2	100
8	70	72	156	2	120
9	85	75	168	2	115
10	75	80	168	1	120

Table A11.7 The ANOVA table for a multiple regression with mathematical ability as the DV and ability at English and SES as IVs

ANOVA[a]

	Sum of Squares	df	Mean Square	F	Sig.
Regression	1618.945	2	809.473	42.427	.0001[b]
Residual	133.555	7	19.079		
Total	1752.500	9			

[a] Dependent Variable: MATHS
[b] Predictors: (Constant), SES, ENGLISH

If ability at English is now treated as the DV and SES as the IV, $R^2 = 0.108$. The sum of squared deviations of English is 1534.4. Therefore:

$$\text{Std Err (for English)} = \sqrt{\frac{19.079}{1534.4 \times (1 - 0.108)}}$$

$$= \sqrt{\frac{19.079}{1534.4 \times 0.892}}$$

$$= \sqrt{\frac{19.079}{1368.6848}}$$

$$= \sqrt{0.01394}$$

$$= 0.118$$

Table A11.8 shows another part of the regression analysis when mathematical ability was the DV, while ability at English and SES were the IVs, including the standard errors of the regression coefficients.

Table A11.8 Statistics relating to the regression coefficients when mathematical ability was the DV and English and SES the IVs

Coefficients[a]

| | Unstandardised Coefficients | | Standardised Coefficients | | |
	B	Std. Error	Beta	t	Sig.
(Constant)	−14.7767	8.919		−1.657	.14152
ENGLISH	1.0856	0.118	1.016	9.196	.00004
SES	4.7887	1.358	0.390	3.527	.00964

[a] Dependent Variable: MATHS

Testing the statistical significance of a regression coefficient

A t-value can be formed, to test the statistical significance of a regression coefficient, using the following equation:

$$t_{(N-p-1)} = \frac{\text{regression coefficient}}{\text{standard error for regression coefficient}}$$

where N is the sample size
p is the number of IVs in the regression.

Therefore, in the case of ability at English:

$$t_{(7)} = \frac{1.0856}{0.118} = 9.2$$

The probability of this t-value can be checked against the critical values given in the t-tables in Appendix XIV. Use the two-tailed probability. In this case, the t-value is statistically significant at the $p = 0.001$ level and so we would conclude that ability at English is a significant predictor of mathematical ability even with SES already in the model.

In multiple regression, if we were to test the statistical significance of the regression coefficients, as this would involve more than one test we ought to adjust the alpha-level to take account of the number of tests performed. This could be done using Bonferroni's adjustment. In the present case, as there are two IVs, the critical alpha-level would become $\frac{0.05}{2} = 0.025$.

Calculating a confidence interval for a regression coefficient

As with other confidence intervals, we need to know what the critical value for t would be for the degrees of freedom and for the confidence level. If we wish to have 95% confidence level then the critical t will be the t-value for a two-tailed probability for $\alpha = 0.05$, which, with df = 7 is 2.365. Use the following equation to calculate the confidence interval (CI):

CI = regression coefficient $\pm$ ($t \times$ standard error of regression coefficient)

Therefore, in the case of ability at English:

$$CI = 1.086 \pm (2.365 \times 0.118)$$

$$= 1.086 \pm 0.279$$

In other words, we can be confident, at the 95% level, that the value for the regression coefficient, in the population, lies between 0.807 and 1.365.

Suppressor variables

When looking at the correlations between the dependent variable and the independent variables it might be assumed that because a given IV has no correlation or a very small correlation with the DV that when it is added to a regression no more variance in the DV will be explained than before. However, this is not always the case. If the IV correlates with one or more of the other IVs its inclusion in the regression could lead to more variance being explained. Such a variable is described as a *suppressor* variable. Thus if we are trying to choose what variables to include in a regression and our aim is to explain as much variance as possible then we shouldn't use the original correlations as our criterion for what variables to include. If you refer to Table 20.3 you will see that SES only correlated with mathematical ability at $r = 0.056$. However, in the regression it was found to be a significant predictor when English ability was also in the model (see Table 20.5) See Pedhazur (1997) for more on this topic.

Centring

One technique that is sometimes recommended to reduce multi-collinearity is *centring*. This involves subtracting the mean of a variable from each of the scores, in the same way that we do in the first stage when a variable is being standardised. Prior to the use of computers it was felt that this would remove problems of rounding errors. However, this is no longer necessary when computers are being used and it does not change the correlations among the original variables. Nonetheless, it can still be a useful technique for removing multi-collinearity when the analysis involves interaction terms or variables that are powers of other variables, for example if we included age and the square of age in the same analysis in order to try to explain as much variance as possible. See Howell (2002) for more details on centring in these contexts.

Testing an interaction

I mentioned, in Chapter 20, that an interaction between variables can be tested using multiple regression. However, I pointed out that it can be less straightforward than testing an interaction in ANOVA. This is for at least two reasons. Firstly, statistical packages may not have a direct way to enter an interaction term into a multiple regression. Secondly, as mentioned in the previous section, a problem with multi-collinearity can be created when interaction terms are entered in a regression. Fortunately, finding a variable that represents the interaction between two variables, which are themselves appropriate for entry into a multiple regression, is relatively simple: we can create a new variable by multiplying the two original variables. However, this will be highly correlated with each of the original variables and so we need to prevent this happening. One way is to centre the data as described above. We could also standardise the original scores as this is the equivalent of centring followed by dividing by the SD. As an example, I have saved the standardised scores for age and English ability. I have then created a variable by multiplying the values of standardised versions of age and English ability. Below (Table A11.9) are the results of a sequential multiple regression with mathematical ability as the variable to be predicted. Age and English were entered in the first stage and the interaction between them in the second stage. In this way I can see how much extra variance in mathematical ability is accounted for by their interaction and whether that amount

Table A11.9 Part of the SPSS output from a sequential multiple regression with an interaction term entered in the second stage

Model Summary

Model	R	R Square	Adjusted R Square	Std. Error of the Estimate
1	.889[a]	.790	.729	7.25845
2	.899[b]	.808	.711	7.49676

[a.] Predictors: (Constant), ENGLISH, AGE
[b.] Predictors: (Constant), ENGLISH, AGE, age by English

Coefficients[a]

Model		Unstandardised Coefficients		Standardised Coefficients		
		B	Std. Error	Beta	t	Sig.
1	(Constant)	16.979	64.663		.263	.800
	ENGLISH	1.012	.366	.947	2.768	.028
	AGE	−.107	.534	−.068	−.200	.847
2	(Constant)	17.931	66.799		.268	.797
	ENGLISH	1.062	.384	.994	2.770	.032
	AGE	−.146	.554	−.094	−.264	.801
	age by English	2.679	3.574	.137	.750	.482

[a.] Dependent Variable: MATHS

is significant. Table A11.9 shows that the interaction between age and English ability only adds 0.018 (0.808 − 0.790) to the R^2 value (i.e. it explains 1.8% more of the variance in mathematical ability). In addition, at $p = 0.482$, it does not add significantly to the model.

Diagnostic statistics

Residuals

In Chapter 20 residuals (unstandardised) and standardised were described. A residual is standardised by being divided by the *standard error of the estimate*:

$$\text{standard error of the estimate} = \sqrt{\frac{\text{sum of squares of residuals}}{N - k - 1}}$$

where N is the sample size
          k is the number of IVs

In addition to the above versions there are also *deleted, Studentised* and *Studentised deleted* residuals. A deleted residual is found by running a regression but with that particular person's data excluded and then predicting the value for the DV for that person from the regression equation and calculating the difference between the new predicted value and the actual value. A Studentised residual is similar to a standardised one except that instead of dividing each residual by the same standard error, the standard error is adjusted to take account of the individual's discrepancy from the rest of the scores on the IVs (using the leverage score for that person). A Studentised deleted residual is a combination of the last two in that the residual is calculated from the regression equation that doesn't involve that person and the standard error is adjusted to take account of the person's leverage. Unfortunately, these terms don't appear to be consistently used. Nonetheless, the descriptions I've given do apply to the use made by SPSS of these terms.

Leverage and influence

Leverage is a measure of whether an individual's set of scores on the IVs makes that person an outlier; i.e. it checks whether that person is a multivariate outlier. Its description in multiple regression involves matrix algebra so I'll spare you the details. However, you can get an idea of what it is doing from *simple* regression, where:

$$\text{leverage} = \frac{\text{squared deviation from mean on IV}}{\text{sum of squared deviations from mean on IV}} + \frac{1}{n}$$

where n is the sample size. Therefore leverage is a measure of the proportion of the overall sum of squared deviations which is accounted for by that individual's score on the IV. Stevens (2002) recommends that if the leverage is greater than $[3 \times (p + 1)]/n$ (where p is the number of IVs in the model and n is the number of participants) then the data for that person needs to be checked. Table 20.8 (p. 334) shows the leverage scores for each participant. As the critical level would be $[3 \times (2 + 1)]/10 = 0.9$, then none of the participants has a particular problem of multivariate outliers. Note that SPSS reports what it calls *centred* leverage values. To calculate these $1/n$ is subtracted from the leverage value. Thus if you want to apply the criteria suggested above you will need to subtract $1/n$ from the critical level (or add $1/n$ to the values which SPSS reports).

Mahalanobis distance is a simple transformation of leverage and so it is looking at the same thing as leverage. Mahalanobis distance can be found from:

$$\text{Mahalanobis distance} = (n - 1) \times \left[\text{leverage} - \frac{1}{n}\right]$$

where n is the sample size. Therefore, as the version of leverage that SPSS reports (centred leverage) can be found by subtracting $1/n$ from leverage, Mahalanobis distance is simply centred leverage multiplied by $n - 1$.

Cook's distance is a measure of how an individual's scores on the IVs *and* the DV are different from the other people's scores and it takes into account both the Studentised residual and the leverage for the individual. Stevens (2002) notes that the data of a person whose Cook's distance is greater than 1 should be investigated further.

DfBeta is a measure of how much each regression coefficient (including the constant) would change if a given participant were removed. In addition, there is a standardised version of each DfBeta. *DfFit* is a measure of the change in the predicted DV if a case were removed and there is a standardised version of DfFit. By all means look at all the versions of residuals and fit but my own preference would be to use only standardised residuals, leverage and Cook's distance in the ways described in Chapter 20.

Coding categorical variables

In Chapter 20 it was shown that the data that would normally be analysed via an ANOVA can be analysed using multiple regression. However, it was necessary to recode categorical variables as dummy variables.

Dummy coding

When the IV to be coded has more than two levels then we will have more than one dummy variable. We have to be careful about how we interpret the individual IVs that are put into a regression as they can't be interpreted in the same way as variables such as age or SES. When we use dummy coding we can treat the level of the original IV that has been coded as 0 in all the dummy variables as a comparison level for paired contrasts, in the same way as Dunnett's *t* does. Thus in Chapter 20 the control condition was coded as 0 in both dummy variables, while method of loci was coded as 1 in the first variable and 0 in the second and pegword was coded as 0 in the first and 1 in the second. Chapter 18 reported the paired contrasts that compared the control and method of loci conditions and the control and pegword conditions. The *t*-values were 3.139 and 0.916 respectively. The output from the regression analysis with mnemonic strategy coded as two dummy variables produced the following result:

Table A11.10 Output from a multiple regression with recall as the DV and mnemonic condition coded as two dummy variables as the IVs

Coefficients[a]

Model		Unstandardised Coefficients		Standardised Coefficients		
		B	Std. Error	Beta	*t*	Sig.
1	(Constant)	9.600	.541		17.759	.000
	dummy variable 1	−2.400	.764	−.593	−3.139	.004
	dummy variable 2	−.700	.764	−.173	−.916	.368

[a.] Dependent Variable: RECALL

Thus, we can see that the t-value for each dummy variable is the equivalent of one of those contrasts. Note that both are negative. This is because in the contrasts the control mean was subtracted from the other mean, whereas in the regression it is the equivalent of subtracting the other means from the control.

APPENDIX XII: ITEM AND DISCRIMINATIVE ANALYSIS ON LIKERT SCALES

This appendix illustrates the techniques introduced in Chapter 6.

Conducting an item analysis   533
Analysing discriminative power   534

Conducting an item analysis

1. Score each person's response to each statement. Remember to keep the scoring consistent, given that approximately half the questions are worded in the opposite direction to the others, so that a 1 always means a negative attitude and a 5 a positive attitude. A computer can be used to reverse the scoring of those items that need it. To reverse a score you need to subtract the score from a figure, the size of which will depend on the minimum and maximum possible scores for the item. To find the figure add the minimum and maximum. As an example, if you had a 5-point scale that ranged from 1 to 5 then the figure you need is $1 + 5 = 6$. If a person scored 1 on this item then the reversed score would be $6 - 1 = 5$, 2 would become 4 and so on.

   2. Calculate the total score for each participant.

   3. Calculate a Pearson's Product Moment Correlation between each statement and the total score and between all the statements (see Chapter 19). In fact, each question is only on an ordinal scale which has a limited number of possible values (5), in which case it would seem more appropriate to use a Spearman's rho or a Kendall's tau. However, the total score is likely to have a sufficient number of possible values to warrant using Pearson's r. The data are usually analysed using parametric tests. This is partly because there is a limit to the statistics that can be computed if we are restricted to non-parametric tests.

   4. Find the critical value for r for a one-tailed test at $\alpha = 0.05$ (see Appendix XIV). It is a one-tailed test because you have chosen the questions on the expectation that they correlate positively with each other. In Chapter 6, I recommended that you use at least 68 participants. This was to give the test power of 0.8 for a medium effect size, which in this case would be $r = 0.3$. If you had used 68 participants then the critical value of r, to be statistically significant at $p = 0.05$, would be 0.201.

If you decided to analyse the data using a Spearman's rho or a Kendall's tau then you should have at least 75 participants to have the same power. In the case of Spearman's rho the critical value would be rho = 0.191 for that number of participants. If you used a Kendall's tau, then the critical value of tau would be 0.129 for 75 participants.

5. Check the correlation between each statement and the total scores. Any statement that has a correlation coefficient with the total that is the same size as, or larger than, the critical value can be said to have passed this stage of the item analysis and can remain, for the moment, in the scale.

6. Examine the statements that did not pass the previous stage of the item analysis to see whether they correlate with each other (at the same critical level as before). Any statements that not only do not correlate with the total but do not correlate with any other statements should be rejected, unless they are addressing a specific aspect of what you are studying that is essential to your research. In this case, they would have to form a subscale on their own. Look at how they are worded to see why such statements might have failed.

A set of statements that do not correlate with the total but do correlate with each other may form a subscale of the attitude scale. Examine such statements to see what aspects, of the attitude you are measuring, they have in common. If there appears to be a coherent theme that relates them then treat them as forming a subscale.

If you used the attitude scale at this stage to measure attitudes you would produce different total scores for the different subscales.

Analysing discriminative power

If the item analysis identified subscales, then the following should be conducted separately for each subscale.

1. For each participant form a new total score.

2. Identify the participants with the top 25% of total scores (the high scorers) and the participants with the bottom 25% of total scores (the low scorers).

3. For each question, compare the high and low scorers (on the basis of their total scores) using a one-tailed, between-subjects t-test. Alternatively, you could conduct a one-tailed Mann–Whitney U-test, as it is the non-parametric equivalent of the between-subjects t-test.

4. Retain only statements that show a significant difference between high and low scorers. The others should be discarded as they are failing to discriminate sufficiently between high and low scorers and are therefore redundant.

Appendix XIII: Meta-Analysis

This appendix illustrates the techniques introduced in Chapter 22.

Computing a common effect size statistic   536
Computing a common probability statistic   538
Combining effect size   541
The confidence interval   542
Combining probability   542
Heterogeneity   543
   Heterogeneity for effect size   543
   Heterogeneity for probability   544
The file-drawer problem   545

Introduction

This appendix takes you through a meta-analysis that compares scores for depression of women who suffer from chronic pelvic pain (who will be described as the experimental group) with control groups of women who do not. These data are taken from McGowan, Clark-Carter and Pitts (1998).

The studies

In all but one case the relevant details given in the papers are in the form of means and standard deviations rather than probability statistics. The next stage is to create a single probability statistic for each of the studies. Given the nature of the summary statistics that each of the present studies has provided, the most appropriate statistic is the between-subjects *t*-test.

However, if the level of reporting in a paper is so poor that you have no descriptive statistics and are simply told whether the result was statistically significant then the best you can do is treat a non-significant result as having a z-value of 0 (which gives a probability of 0.5) and a statistically significant result as having a z-value of 1.645 (the critical one-tailed level for $p = 0.05$).

Table A13.1 Means, standard deviations and sample sizes for the papers to be included in the meta-analysis

Study	Experimental group			Control group			probability statistic
	n	mean	SD	n	mean	SD	
1	41	1.26	0.89	41	0.61	0.50	$t = 4.08$
2	30	46.44	10.52	30	38.40	7.50	–
3	50	64.50	11.30	50	51.90	10.40	–
4	37	61.44	12.24	23	50.50	9.20	–
5	162	54.30	12.65	46	45.50	12.40	–
6	64	61.61	8.83	46	59.11	8.45	–

A new summary table can be produced:

Table A13.2 The t-values for the studies in the meta-analysis

Study	Total N	t	Direction of effect
1	82	4.0771	+
2	60	3.4085	+
3	100	5.8015	+
4	60	3.6837	+
5	208	4.1818	+
6	110	1.4911	+

Computing a common effect size statistic

The following equations can be used for converting common statistics into r. In each case, if the original result showed a negative effect with respect to the hypothesis, that is, that the control group had a larger mean than the experimental group, then the r must be treated as negative.

To convert a t-value to r

$$r = \sqrt{\frac{t^2}{t^2 + df}}$$
(A13.1)

To convert an F-ratio to r

$$r = \sqrt{\frac{F_{1,v2}}{F_{1,v2} + df_{error}}} \qquad (A13.2)$$

where $F_{1,v2}$ is an F-ratio with df = 1 for the treatment. (An F-ratio can only be used if the independent variable has two levels; that is, the df for the treatment = 1.)

To convert a χ^2 to r

$$r = \sqrt{\frac{\chi^2}{N}} \qquad (A13.3)$$

where the χ^2 must have df = 1.

To convert a standard z-value to r

$$r = \frac{z}{\sqrt{N}} \qquad (A13.4)$$

where N is the total number of participants in the study.

To convert a d-value to r

$$r = \frac{d}{\sqrt{d^2 + \dfrac{1}{(p \times q)}}} \qquad (A13.5)$$

where d is the effect size, using Cohen's d (1988)
   p is the proportion of participants who were in the experimental group. Thus if the total number of participants in the study was 100 and the number in the experimental group was 40, $p = \frac{40}{100} = 0.4$
   q is the proportion of participants in the control group

Alternatively, when the samples are the same size, to convert a d-value to r:

$$r = \frac{d}{\sqrt{d^2 + 4}} \qquad (A13.6)$$

We are now in a position to calculate the effect size for each study. I will use Study 2 as an example:

$$r = \sqrt{\frac{t^2}{t^2 + df}}$$

$$= \sqrt{\frac{(3.4085)^2}{(3.4085)^2 + (60 - 2)}}$$

$$= \sqrt{\frac{11.6179}{11.6179 + 58}}$$

$$= \sqrt{0.1669}$$

$$= 0.4085$$

Using the same procedure all the t-values can now be converted into rs:

Table A13.3 The effect sizes (r) of the studies in the meta-analysis

Study	N	r	Direction of effect
1	82	0.4148	+
2	60	0.4085	+
3	100	0.5056	+
4	60	0.4354	+
5	208	0.2797	+
6	110	0.1420	+

Computing a common probability statistic

The following equations are for converting an inferential statistic or an effect size into a z-value. In each case, if the original finding showed a negative effect with respect to the hypothesis, that is, that the control group had a larger mean than the experimental group, then the z must be treated as negative.

To convert a t-value to z

$$z = \sqrt{df \times \log_e\left(1 + \frac{t^2}{df}\right)} \times \sqrt{\left(1 - \frac{1}{2 \times df}\right)} \qquad \text{(A13.7)}$$

where df $= N - 2$ for a between-subjects design and $N - 1$ for a within-subjects design

N is the total number of participants in the study

$\log_e$ is the natural log (often shown as LN on a calculator)

To convert an F-ratio to z

$$z = \sqrt{df_{error} \times \log_e\left(1 + \frac{F_{1,v2}}{df_{error}}\right)} \times \sqrt{\left(1 - \frac{1}{2 \times df_{error}}\right)} \qquad (A13.8)$$

where df_{error} are the degrees of freedom for the error term (the divisor) used to compute the F-ratio

$F_{1,v2}$ is an F-ratio with df $= 1$ for the treatment

(An F-ratio can only be used if the independent variable has two levels; that is, the df for the treatment $= 1$.)

To convert a χ^2 to z

$$z = \sqrt{\chi^2} \qquad (A13.9)$$

where the χ^2 must have df $= 1$.

To convert a d-value to z

$$z = \frac{d \times \sqrt{N}}{\sqrt{d^2 + \frac{1}{(p \times q)}}} \qquad (A13.10)$$

where d is the effect size, using Cohen's d (1988)

p is the proportion of participants who were in the experimental group. Thus, if the total number of participants in the study was 100 and the number in the experimental group was 40, $p = \frac{40}{100} = 0.4$

q is the proportion of participants in the control group

Alternatively, when the samples are the same size, to convert a d-value to z:

$$z = \frac{d \times \sqrt{N}}{\sqrt{d^2 + 4}} \qquad (A13.11)$$

To convert an r to z

$$z = r \times \sqrt{N} \qquad (A13.12)$$

We are now in a position to compute a z for each study ready for computing a combined probability level. Given that each conversion (transformation) is likely to produce an approximation to the exact figure, it is better to do the conversion from the original statistic, where possible, rather than via a previous conversion. Thus, I would convert t to r and t to z rather than t to r then r to z. Once again, I will use Study 2 as an example.

$$z = \sqrt{df \times \log_e\left(1 + \frac{t^2}{df}\right)} \times \sqrt{\left(1 - \frac{1}{2 \times df}\right)}$$

$$= \sqrt{58 \times \log_e\left(1 + \frac{11.6179}{58}\right)} \times \sqrt{\left(1 - \frac{1}{2 \times 58}\right)}$$

$$= \sqrt{58 \times \log_e(1 + 0.2003)} \times \sqrt{(1 - 0.0086)}$$

$$= \sqrt{58 \times 0.18257} \times \sqrt{0.9914}$$

$$= \sqrt{10.5896} \times \sqrt{0.9914}$$

$$= 3.2541 \times 0.9957$$

$$= 3.2401$$

Following the same procedure a table of z-values can be created for the studies which can be used to produce a combined probability level.

Table A13.4 The z-values for the studies in the meta-analysis

Study	N	z	Direction of effect
1	82	3.8741	+
2	60	3.2401	+
3	100	5.3652	+
4	60	3.4768	+
5	208	4.0919	+
6	110	1.4801	+

Combining effect size

Before the effect sizes can be combined we need to convert each r into a Fisher's transformation of r (r'); putting the effect size for Study 2, $r = 0.4085$, into the equation given in Appendix XVI (A16.6) produces $r' = 0.4338$.

Remember that if any of the studies had a negative direction of effect, the r for that study is negative when placed in the equation and the resultant r' will be negative.

Now a table of r's can be created for all the studies:

Table A13.5 The Fisher's transformed correlation coefficients (r') of the studies in the meta-analysis

Study	N	r'	Direction of effect
1	82	0.4414	+
2	60	0.4338	+
3	100	0.5568	+
4	60	0.4666	+
5	208	0.2874	+
6	110	0.1430	+

This information can be used to combine the effect sizes using the weighted mean ($\bar{r}'$):

$$\bar{r}' = \frac{\Sigma((N_j - 3) \times r_j')}{\Sigma(N_j - 3)} \qquad \text{(A13.13)}$$

where N_j is the number of participants in study j
r_j' is the r' for study j
$j = 1$ to k
k is the number of studies

$$\bar{r}' = \frac{(79 \times 0.4414 + 57 \times 0.4338 + 97 \times 0.5568 + 57 \times 0.4666 + 205 \times 0.2874 + 107 \times 0.1430)}{(79 + 57 + 97 + 57 + 205 + 107)}$$

$$= \frac{214.4161}{602}$$

$$= 0.3562$$

Remember that if any of the studies had a negative direction of effect, the r' for that study is negative when placed in the above equation.

We can use the weighted mean r' to find the combined effect size but we have to convert the weighted mean r' back to an r-value, using the equation given in Appendix XVI (A16.7) for transforming r' to r. This produces a combined effect size (r) = 0.3418, which, according to Cohen (1988), is a medium effect size.

The confidence interval

To find the confidence interval at the 95% level of confidence, we need to place the weighted mean effect size ($\bar{r}'$), prior to transforming to r, and the total number of participants in each study into the following equation; the example calculates the confidence interval for all six studies:

$$\text{confidence interval for } \bar{r}' \text{ (CI)} = \bar{r}' - \frac{1.96}{\sqrt{\Sigma(N_j - 3)}} \qquad \text{(A13.14)}$$

$$\text{to} \qquad \bar{r}' + \frac{1.96}{\sqrt{\Sigma(N_j - 3)}}$$

where N_j is the total number of participants in study j
$j = 1$ to k
k is the number of studies in the meta-analysis

$$CI \text{ for } \bar{r}' = 0.3562 - \frac{1.96}{\sqrt{79 + 57 + 97 + 57 + 205 + 107}}$$

$$\text{to} \qquad 0.3562 + \frac{1.96}{\sqrt{79 + 57 + 97 + 57 + 205 + 107}}$$

$$= 0.3562 - \frac{1.96}{\sqrt{602}} \text{ to } 0.3562 + \frac{1.96}{\sqrt{602}}$$

$$= 0.3562 - 0.0799 \text{ to } 0.3562 + 0.0799$$

$$= 0.2763 \text{ to } 0.4361$$

These then need to be converted into rs using the equation for transforming r' to r, given in Appendix XVI (A16.7). The CI for r becomes:

$$CI \text{ for } r = 0.2695 \text{ to } 0.4104$$

Combining probability

Probability can be combined using the standard z-scores shown in Table A13.4 in the following equation:

$$\text{combined } z = \frac{\Sigma z_j}{\sqrt{k}} \qquad \text{(A13.15)}$$

where z_j is the the the standard z-score for study j
$j = 1$ to k
k is the number of studies

$$\text{combined } z = \frac{3.8987 + 3.2673 + 5.3926 + 3.7204 + 4.1458 + 1.4951}{\sqrt{6}}$$

$$= \frac{21.52817}{2.44949}$$

$$= 8.7888$$

Remember that if any of the studies had a negative direction of effect, the z for that study is negative when placed in the above equation.

Referring to the z-table in Appendix XIV shows that this combined z-value is significant at below the $p = 0.00001$ level. We can conclude that those suffering from chronic pelvic pain are significantly more depressed than the control groups used in the studies.

Heterogeneity

Heterogeneity for effect size

The heterogeneity of the effect size can be calculated, using the equation:

$$\chi^2_{(k-1)} = \Sigma((N_j - 3) \times (r'_j - \bar{r}')^2) \qquad \text{(A13.16)}$$

where N_j is the number of participants in study j
r'_j is the r' for study j
$j = 1$ to k
k is the number of studies
$k - 1$ is the degrees of freedom for the χ^2
$\bar{r}'$ is the weighted mean r'

$$\chi^2_{(5)} = 79 \times (0.4414 - 0.3562)^2 + 57 \times (0.4338 - 0.3562)^2$$

$$+ 97 \times (0.5568 - 0.3562)^2 + 57 \times (0.4666 - 0.3562)^2$$

$$+ 205 \times (0.2874 - 0.3562)^2 + 107 \times (0.1430 - 0.3562)^2$$

$$= 0.5733 + 0.3437 + 3.9049 + 0.6948 + 0.96998 + 4.8626$$

$$= 11.3494$$

Remember that if any of the studies had a negative direction of effect, the r' for that study is negative when placed in the above equation.

Referring to the table of the chi-squared distribution in Appendix XIV we see that the probability of this χ^2 with 5 degrees of freedom lies between 0.05 and 0.02, in which case the effect sizes of the studies are significantly heterogeneous. Looking at the computation we can see that Study 6 contributed the most to this outcome. If we remove that study and re-do the calculations, including producing a new weighted mean r', we see that $\chi^2_{(4)} = 5.4356$. The probability of this new χ^2 lies between 0.3 and 0.2. In other words, the remaining five studies are not significantly heterogeneous with respect to effect size, in which case we do not need to remove any more studies from the meta-analysis.

Because we have found heterogeneity in the set of effect sizes and we have found the subset of studies which are homogeneous, we need to calculate a new confidence interval for the weighted mean r' and a new combined z of the homogeneous subset and convert the new weighted mean r' to a weighted mean r, all using the methods shown above.

Heterogeneity for probability

Heterogeneity for probability can be calculated using the standard z-values for each study. We need to calculate the mean z-value ($\bar{z}$) using the usual procedure for finding means; all six studies are included in this analysis:

$$\bar{z} = \frac{\Sigma z_j}{k} \tag{A13.17}$$

where z_j is the z-value for study j
        $j = 1$ to k
        k is the number of studies

$$\bar{z} = \frac{(3.8741 + 3.2401 + 5.3652 + 3.4768 + 4.0919 + 1.4801)}{6}$$

$$= 3.5880$$

Remember that if any of the studies had a negative direction of effect, the z for that study is negative when placed in the above equation.

The heterogeneity of the probability values can now be calculated, using the following equation:

$$\chi^2_{(k-1)} = \Sigma(z_j - \bar{z})^2 \tag{A13.18}$$

where $k - 1$ is the degrees of freedom for the χ^2.

$$\chi^2_{(5)} = (3.8741 - 3.558)^2 + (3.2401 - 3.558)^2$$
$$+ (5.3652 - 3.558)^2 + (3.4768 - 3.558)^2$$
$$+ (4.0919 - 3.558)^2 + (1.4801 - 3.558)^2$$
$$= 8.0709$$

Remember that if any of the studies had a negative direction of effect, the z for that study is negative when placed in the above equation.

Referring to the table of the chi-squared distribution in Appendix XIV we can see that the probability of this χ^2 with 5 degrees of freedom being a chance event lies between 0.2 and 0.1 and thus is not statistically significant.

In this case we can conclude that the six studies are not significantly hetero-geneous with respect to their probability levels.

Publication bias

Two methods for trying to identify whether the result of a meta-analysis is likely to be affected by publication bias are the funnel graph (described in Chapter 22) and checking fail-safe N against the likely number of unpub-lished studies.

The file-drawer problem

The fail-safe N

The fail-safe N is the number of unpublished, non-significant studies that would have to exist filed away in researchers' drawers in order to render the probability we have found for the meta-analysis non-significant. To find the fail-safe N, we use the following equation; the probability for the six studies is used as an example:

$$\text{fail-safe } N = \frac{k \times (k \times \bar{z}^2 - 2.706)}{2.706} \tag{A13.19}$$

where k is the number of studies in the meta-analysis
        $\bar{z}$ is the the mean z-value for the meta-analysis, calculated in the way shown under heterogeneity for probability, above

Therefore,

$$\text{fail-safe } N = \frac{6 \times (6 \times 3.5880^2 - 2.706)}{2.706}$$

$$= 165.2693$$

which, to the next highest whole number:

$$= 166$$

Therefore, there would have to exist at least 166 non-significant studies to render the meta-analysis non-significant. To interpret this figure we need to calculate the critical number of unpublished, non-significant studies that we could reasonably expect might be filed away.

The critical number of studies for the file-drawer problem

Rosenthal (1991) gives the following equation for the critical level of non-significant studies:

$$\text{critical number of studies} = (5 \times k) + 10 \qquad \text{(A13.20)}$$

where k is the number of studies used in the meta-analysis. Therefore,

$$\text{critical number of studies} = (5 \times 6) + 10$$

$$= 40$$

The file-drawer issue is only a problem if the critical number of studies is equal to or more than the fail-safe N. In this case, as the critical number of studies is 40 and the fail-safe N is 166, the file-drawer issue is not a problem and we can be more confident about the combined effect size and combined probabilities that we have calculated.

Clearly, the fail-safe N and the critical number of studies only need be calculated when the meta-analysis shows a significant result.

APPENDIX XIV: PROBABILITY TABLES

Finding the probability of a statistic for dfs that are not shown
   in the tables   548
    Linear interpolation   548
z, the standardised normal distribution   549
t-distributions   551
Chi-squared distributions   553
The binomial distribution   554
The Mann–Whitney U-test   556
Wilcoxon's signed-rank test for matched pairs   558
Fisher's exact probability test   559
F-distributions   561
The Kruskal–Wallis ANOVA   565
χ_F^2 (Friedman's non-parametric statistic for within-subjects ANOVA)   566
Bonferroni corrections for contrasts   567
Dunnett's t-test of contrasts   571
The Studentised range statistic q   572
r (Pearson's Product Moment Correlation Coefficient)   574
Spearman's rho   576
Kendall's tau   578
Kendall's tau as a partial correlation $\tau_{xy.z}$ 579
Kendall's coefficient of concordance (w)   580
The Kolmogorov–Smirnov statistic (D_n)   581

Most statistical computer packages will supply you with the necessary probability level for the results of your statistical tests, as will some spreadsheets such as Excel. However, there are occasions when you need to check the probability in a table. I have not included an exhaustive set of tables; instead, where a table is necessary for a single probability level, I have provided the critical levels of the statistic for $\alpha = 0.05$ on the grounds that this is the most frequently used alpha-level. However, where one-tailed probabilities are not available, or necessary, for a given statistic, then I have also provided values for $\alpha = 0.01$. A wider range of tables can be found in books devoted to the subject, such as Neave (1978).

Finding the probability of a statistic for dfs that are not shown in the tables

I will use the *t*-test to illustrate the points but the principle will be true for other tests, including non-parametric tests where probabilities are shown for given sample sizes rather than df.

When the tables do not have probabilities for the exact degrees of freedom for the test you have conducted then a quick initial check of the statistical significance is to note whether the *t*-value for the next lowest df is statistically significant. If it is then it will also be significant with the correct df. For example, if df = 45 then a *t*-value of 1.7 would be statistically significant at $\alpha = 0.05$ for a one-tailed test because the critical *t*-value for df = 40 is 1.684. On the other hand, if the *t*-value is not significant with the next highest df then it will not be for the exact df. Accordingly, if df = 45 and the *t*-value was 1.6, then it would not be statistically significant at $\alpha = 0.05$ for a one-tailed test because the critical *t*-value for df = 50 is 1.676. If using these approximate methods does not tell you whether the result is statistically significant, then use *linear interpolation*.

Linear interpolation

When you are dependent on *t*-tables, and the degrees of freedom for your study are not shown in the table, you can use what is called *linear interpolation* to work out a more exact critical *t*-value for a given probability. For example, *t* = 1.682 with df = 43. To find the critical *t*-value for df = 43, with $\alpha = 0.05$ and a one-tailed test, use the following equation:

$$\text{critical } t = t \text{ for upper df} + (t \text{ for lower df} - t \text{ for upper df})$$

$$\times \left(\frac{\text{upper df} - \text{calculated df}}{\text{upper df} - \text{lower df}} \right)$$

In the present case:

$$\text{critical } t_{(43)} = 1.676 + (1.684 - 1.676) \times \left(\frac{50 - 43}{50 - 40} \right)$$

$$= 1.682$$

As the calculated *t*-value is the same size as this critical value, it is statistically significant at $\alpha = 0.05$.

The probabilities of z, the standardised normal distribution

One-tailed probabilities are in the body of the table. The first column shows z-values up to one decimal place, while the first row shows the second decimal place. To read the table, if you wish to find the probability of a z-score of 1.72, look, in the first column, for the row that begins with 1.7; the probability will be in that row. Now look in the first row for the column that is headed by 2; the probability will be in that column. Thus, the one-tailed probability of $z = 1.72$ is 0.0427. If you wish to look up the probability of a z-value that does not contain two decimal places, for example, 2.1 or 2.10, then the probability is contained in the first column of probabilities, the one headed 0. Accordingly, the one-tailed probability of $z = 2.1$ is 0.0179.

Finding a z-value for a particular probability

To find the z-value that gives a one-tailed probability of 0.001, look in the body of the table until you find 0.001. Note the row and column that contain the probability; they are headed 3.0 and 8 respectively. Therefore the z-value is 3.08. Sometimes the exact probability you require is not shown in the table. This is true for $p = 0.05$. In this case, it is necessary to find out the probabilities just above and below the value you require: 0.0495 and 0.0505. The probability we require is halfway between the two and so the z-value will be halfway between the respective z-values, 1.64 and 1.65: i.e. $z = 1.645$.

Two-tailed probabilities

To find the two-tailed probability of a z-value, double the values shown in the body of the table. Thus the two-tailed probability of $z = 1.72$ is $0.0427 \times 2 = 0.0854$. In order to find the z-value that has a particular two-tailed probability, find the z-value that would give a one-tailed probability that is half the two-tailed probability. For example, if you wished to find the z-value that has a two-tailed probability of 0.05, look in the body of the table for $p = 0.05/2 = 0.025$. Proceed as before to find the z-value that gives this probability: $z = 1.96$.

Looking up negative z-values

The table only shows positive z-values. To look up a negative z-value, as the distribution of z is symmetrical, ignore the negative sign and use the table as described above. For example, the one-tailed probability of a z-value of -1.25 is 0.1056.

Table A14.1 The probabilities of z, the standard normal distribution

z	0	1	2	3	2nd decimal place 4	5	6	7	8	9
0.0	0.5000	0.4960	0.4920	0.4880	0.4840	0.4801	0.4761	0.4721	0.4681	0.4641
0.1	0.4602	0.4562	0.4522	0.4483	0.4443	0.4404	0.4364	0.4325	0.4286	0.4247
0.2	0.4207	0.4168	0.4129	0.4090	0.4052	0.4013	0.3974	0.3936	0.3897	0.3859
0.3	0.3821	0.3783	0.3745	0.3707	0.3669	0.3632	0.3594	0.3557	0.3520	0.3483
0.4	0.3446	0.3409	0.3372	0.3336	0.3300	0.3264	0.3228	0.3192	0.3156	0.3121
0.5	0.3085	0.3050	0.3015	0.2981	0.2946	0.2912	0.2877	0.2843	0.2810	0.2776
0.6	0.2743	0.2709	0.2676	0.2643	0.2611	0.2578	0.2546	0.2514	0.2483	0.2451
0.7	0.2420	0.2389	0.2358	0.2327	0.2296	0.2266	0.2236	0.2206	0.2177	0.2148
0.8	0.2119	0.2090	0.2061	0.2033	0.2005	0.1977	0.1949	0.1922	0.1894	0.1867
0.9	0.1841	0.1814	0.1788	0.1762	0.1736	0.1711	0.1685	0.1660	0.1635	0.1611
1.0	0.1587	0.1562	0.1539	0.1515	0.1492	0.1469	0.1446	0.1423	0.1401	0.1379
1.1	0.1357	0.1335	0.1314	0.1292	0.1271	0.1251	0.1230	0.1210	0.1190	0.1170
1.2	0.1151	0.1131	0.1112	0.1093	0.1075	0.1056	0.1038	0.1020	0.1003	0.0985
1.3	0.0968	0.0951	0.0934	0.0918	0.0901	0.0885	0.0869	0.0853	0.0838	0.0823
1.4	0.0808	0.0793	0.0778	0.0764	0.0749	0.0735	0.0721	0.0708	0.0694	0.0681
1.5	0.0668	0.0655	0.0643	0.0630	0.0618	0.0606	0.0594	0.0582	0.0571	0.0559
1.6	0.0548	0.0537	0.0526	0.0516	0.0505	0.0495	0.0485	0.0475	0.0465	0.0455
1.7	0.0446	0.0436	0.0427	0.0418	0.0409	0.0401	0.0392	0.0384	0.0375	0.0367
1.8	0.0359	0.0351	0.0344	0.0336	0.0329	0.0322	0.0314	0.0307	0.0301	0.0294
1.9	0.0287	0.0281	0.0274	0.0268	0.0262	0.0256	0.0250	0.0244	0.0239	0.0233
2.0	0.0228	0.0222	0.0217	0.0212	0.0207	0.0202	0.0197	0.0192	0.0188	0.0183
2.1	0.0179	0.0174	0.0170	0.0166	0.0162	0.0158	0.0154	0.0150	0.0146	0.0143
2.2	0.0139	0.0136	0.0132	0.0129	0.0125	0.0122	0.0119	0.0116	0.0113	0.0110
2.3	0.0107	0.0104	0.0102	0.0099	0.0096	0.0094	0.0091	0.0089	0.0087	0.0084
2.4	0.0082	0.0080	0.0078	0.0075	0.0073	0.0071	0.0069	0.0068	0.0066	0.0064
2.5	0.0062	0.0060	0.0059	0.0057	0.0055	0.0054	0.0052	0.0051	0.0049	0.0048
2.6	0.0047	0.0045	0.0044	0.0043	0.0041	0.0040	0.0039	0.0038	0.0037	0.0036
2.7	0.0035	0.0034	0.0033	0.0032	0.0031	0.0030	0.0029	0.0028	0.0027	0.0026
2.8	0.0026	0.0025	0.0024	0.0023	0.0023	0.0022	0.0021	0.0021	0.0020	0.0019
2.9	0.0019	0.0018	0.0018	0.0017	0.0016	0.0016	0.0015	0.0015	0.0014	0.0014
3.0	0.0013	0.0013	0.0013	0.0012	0.0012	0.0011	0.0011	0.0011	0.0010	0.0010
3.1	0.00097	0.00094	0.00090	0.00087	0.00084	0.00082	0.00079	0.00076	0.00074	0.00071
3.2	0.00069	0.00066	0.00064	0.00062	0.00060	0.00058	0.00056	0.00054	0.00052	0.00050
3.3	0.00048	0.00047	0.00045	0.00043	0.00042	0.00040	0.00039	0.00038	0.00036	0.00035
3.4	0.00034	0.00032	0.00031	0.00030	0.00029	0.00028	0.00027	0.00026	0.00025	0.00024
3.5	0.00023	0.00022	0.00022	0.00021	0.00020	0.00019	0.00019	0.00018	0.00017	0.00017
3.6	0.00016	0.00015	0.00015	0.00014	0.00014	0.00013	0.00013	0.00012	0.00012	0.00011
3.7	0.00011	0.00010	0.00010	0.00010	0.00009	0.00009	0.00008	0.00008	0.00008	0.00008
3.8	0.00007	0.00007	0.00007	0.00006	0.00006	0.00006	0.00006	0.00005	0.00005	0.00005
3.9	0.00005	0.00005	0.00004	0.00004	0.00004	0.00004	0.00004	0.00004	0.00003	0.00003
4.0	0.00003	0.00003	0.00003	0.00003	0.00003	0.00003	0.00002	0.00002	0.00002	0.00002

The probabilities of *t*-distributions

Degrees of freedom

For a between-subjects t-test df $= n_1 + n_2 - 2$, where n_1 and n_2 are the sizes of the two samples.

For a within-subjects t-test df $= n - 1$, where n is the sample size.

For a test where you are comparing a sample mean with a population mean (a one-group t-test), df $= n - 1$.

The values for df of infinity (∞) are there to demonstrate that when the sample size is sufficiently large—that is, well above 120—the t-distribution is the same as the z-distribution. Thus, the critical t-value for a one-tailed probability at $\alpha = 0.05$ is 1.645, when df equals infinity. The one-tailed probability for $z = 1.645$ is 0.05.

Table A14.2 The probabilities of t-distributions

a. Degrees of freedom from 1 to 20

	0.4	0.3	0.2	0.1	One-tailed probabilities 0.05	0.025	0.01	0.005	0.001	0.0005
df	0.8	0.6	0.4	0.2	Two-tailed probabilities 0.1	0.05	0.02	0.01	0.002	0.001
1	0.325	0.727	1.376	3.078	6.314	12.706	31.821	63.656	318.289	636.578
2	0.289	0.617	1.061	1.886	2.920	4.303	6.965	9.925	22.328	31.600
3	0.277	0.584	0.978	1.638	2.353	3.182	4.541	5.841	10.214	12.924
4	0.271	0.569	0.941	1.533	2.132	2.776	3.747	4.604	7.173	8.610
5	0.267	0.559	0.920	1.476	2.015	2.571	3.365	4.032	5.894	6.869
6	0.265	0.553	0.906	1.440	1.943	2.447	3.143	3.707	5.208	5.959
7	0.263	0.549	0.896	1.415	1.895	2.365	2.998	3.499	4.785	5.408
8	0.262	0.546	0.889	1.397	1.860	2.306	2.896	3.355	4.501	5.041
9	0.261	0.543	0.883	1.383	1.833	2.262	2.821	3.250	4.297	4.781
10	0.260	0.542	0.879	1.372	1.812	2.228	2.764	3.169	4.144	4.587
11	0.260	0.540	0.876	1.363	1.796	2.201	2.718	3.106	4.025	4.437
12	0.259	0.539	0.873	1.356	1.782	2.179	2.681	3.055	3.930	4.318
13	0.259	0.538	0.870	1.350	1.771	2.160	2.650	3.012	3.852	4.221
14	0.258	0.537	0.868	1.345	1.761	2.145	2.624	2.977	3.787	4.140
15	0.258	0.536	0.866	1.341	1.753	2.131	2.602	2.947	3.733	4.073
16	0.258	0.535	0.865	1.337	1.746	2.120	2.583	2.921	3.686	4.015
17	0.257	0.534	0.863	1.333	1.740	2.110	2.567	2.898	3.646	3.965
18	0.257	0.534	0.862	1.330	1.734	2.101	2.552	2.878	3.610	3.922
19	0.257	0.533	0.861	1.328	1.729	2.093	2.539	2.861	3.579	3.883
20	0.257	0.533	0.860	1.325	1.725	2.086	2.528	2.845	3.552	3.850

Table A14.2 The probabilities of *t*-distributions

b. Degrees of freedom from 21 to 120 and infinity

df	0.4 / 0.8	0.3 / 0.6	0.2 / 0.4	0.1 / 0.2	0.05 / 0.1	0.025 / 0.05	0.01 / 0.02	0.005 / 0.01	0.001 / 0.002	0.0005 / 0.001
21	0.257	0.532	0.859	1.323	1.721	2.080	2.518	2.831	3.527	3.819
22	0.256	0.532	0.858	1.321	1.717	2.074	2.508	2.819	3.505	3.792
23	0.256	0.532	0.858	1.319	1.714	2.069	2.500	2.807	3.485	3.768
24	0.256	0.531	0.857	1.318	1.711	2.064	2.492	2.797	3.467	3.745
25	0.256	0.531	0.856	1.316	1.708	2.060	2.485	2.787	3.450	3.725
26	0.256	0.531	0.856	1.315	1.706	2.056	2.479	2.779	3.435	3.707
27	0.256	0.531	0.855	1.314	1.703	2.052	2.473	2.771	3.421	3.689
28	0.256	0.530	0.855	1.313	1.701	2.048	2.467	2.763	3.408	3.674
29	0.256	0.530	0.854	1.311	1.699	2.045	2.462	2.756	3.396	3.660
30	0.256	0.530	0.854	1.310	1.697	2.042	2.457	2.750	3.385	3.646
31	0.256	0.530	0.853	1.309	1.696	2.040	2.453	2.744	3.375	3.633
32	0.255	0.530	0.853	1.309	1.694	2.037	2.449	2.738	3.365	3.622
33	0.255	0.530	0.853	1.308	1.692	2.035	2.445	2.733	3.356	3.611
34	0.255	0.529	0.852	1.307	1.691	2.032	2.441	2.728	3.348	3.601
35	0.255	0.529	0.852	1.306	1.690	2.030	2.438	2.724	3.340	3.591
36	0.255	0.529	0.852	1.306	1.688	2.028	2.434	2.719	3.333	3.582
37	0.255	0.529	0.851	1.305	1.687	2.026	2.431	2.715	3.326	3.574
38	0.255	0.529	0.851	1.304	1.686	2.024	2.429	2.712	3.319	3.566
39	0.255	0.529	0.851	1.304	1.685	2.023	2.426	2.708	3.313	3.558
40	0.255	0.529	0.851	1.303	1.684	2.021	2.423	2.704	3.307	3.551
50	0.255	0.528	0.849	1.299	1.676	2.009	2.403	2.678	3.261	3.496
60	0.254	0.527	0.848	1.296	1.671	2.000	2.390	2.660	3.232	3.460
70	0.254	0.527	0.847	1.294	1.667	1.994	2.381	2.648	3.211	3.435
80	0.254	0.526	0.846	1.292	1.664	1.990	2.374	2.639	3.195	3.416
90	0.254	0.526	0.846	1.291	1.662	1.987	2.368	2.632	3.183	3.402
100	0.254	0.526	0.845	1.290	1.660	1.984	2.364	2.626	3.174	3.390
110	0.254	0.526	0.845	1.289	1.659	1.982	2.361	2.621	3.166	3.381
120	0.254	0.526	0.845	1.289	1.658	1.980	2.358	2.617	3.160	3.373
∞	0.253	0.524	0.842	1.282	1.645	1.960	2.326	2.576	3.090	3.290

One-tailed probabilities: 0.4, 0.3, 0.2, 0.1, 0.05, 0.025, 0.01, 0.005, 0.001, 0.0005
Two-tailed probabilities: 0.8, 0.6, 0.4, 0.2, 0.1, 0.05, 0.02, 0.01, 0.002, 0.001

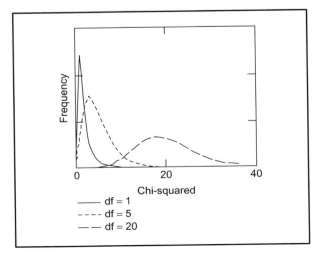

df = 1
df = 5
df = 20

The probabilities of chi-squared distributions

The shape of the chi-squared distribution becomes more symmetrical as df increases.

The probabilities are shown along the first row of Table A14.3. These are for non-directional hypotheses. See Chapters 14 and 15 for discussion of how to obtain probabilities for a directional hypothesis. The body of the table contains the minimum size that a χ^2-value would need to be, for a given df, to achieve statistical significance at a given probability level. Thus, with df = 1, χ^2 would have to be 3.84 or larger to be statistically significant at $\alpha = 0.05$.

Table A14.3 The probabilities of chi-squared distributions

df	0.99	0.95	0.90	0.80	0.70	Probability 0.50	0.30	0.20	0.10	0.05	0.02	0.01	0.001
1	0.00	0.00	0.02	0.06	0.15	0.45	1.07	1.64	2.71	3.84	5.41	6.63	10.83
2	0.02	0.10	0.21	0.45	0.71	1.39	2.41	3.22	4.61	5.99	7.82	9.21	13.82
3	0.11	0.35	0.58	1.01	1.42	2.37	3.66	4.64	6.25	7.81	9.84	11.34	16.27
4	0.30	0.71	1.06	1.65	2.19	3.36	4.88	5.99	7.78	9.49	11.67	13.28	18.47
5	0.55	1.15	1.61	2.34	3.00	4.35	6.06	7.29	9.24	11.07	13.39	15.09	20.51
6	0.87	1.64	2.20	3.07	3.83	5.35	7.23	8.56	10.64	12.59	15.03	16.81	22.46
7	1.24	2.17	2.83	3.82	4.67	6.35	8.38	9.80	12.02	14.07	16.62	18.48	24.32
8	1.65	2.73	3.49	4.59	5.53	7.34	9.52	11.03	13.36	15.51	18.17	20.09	26.12
9	2.09	3.33	4.17	5.38	6.39	8.34	10.66	12.24	14.68	16.92	19.68	21.67	27.88
10	2.56	3.94	4.87	6.18	7.27	9.34	11.78	13.44	15.99	18.31	21.16	23.21	29.59
11	3.05	4.57	5.58	6.99	8.15	10.34	12.90	14.63	17.28	19.68	22.62	24.73	31.26
12	3.57	5.23	6.30	7.81	9.03	11.34	14.01	15.81	18.55	21.03	24.05	26.22	32.91
13	4.11	5.89	7.04	8.63	9.93	12.34	15.12	16.98	19.81	22.36	25.47	27.69	34.53
14	4.66	6.57	7.79	9.47	10.82	13.34	16.22	18.15	21.06	23.68	26.87	29.14	36.12
15	5.23	7.26	8.55	10.31	11.72	14.34	17.32	19.31	22.31	25.00	28.26	30.58	37.70
16	5.81	7.96	9.31	11.15	12.62	15.34	18.42	20.47	23.54	26.30	29.63	32.00	39.25
17	6.41	8.67	10.09	12.00	13.53	16.34	19.51	21.61	24.77	27.59	31.00	33.41	40.79
18	7.01	9.39	10.86	12.86	14.44	17.34	20.60	22.76	25.99	28.87	32.35	34.81	42.31
19	7.63	10.12	11.65	13.72	15.35	18.34	21.69	23.90	27.20	30.14	33.69	36.19	43.82
20	8.26	10.85	12.44	14.58	16.27	19.34	22.77	25.04	28.41	31.41	35.02	37.57	45.31
21	8.90	11.59	13.24	15.44	17.18	20.34	23.86	26.17	29.62	32.67	36.34	38.93	46.80
22	9.54	12.34	14.04	16.31	18.10	21.34	24.94	27.30	30.81	33.92	37.66	40.29	48.27
23	10.20	13.09	14.85	17.19	19.02	22.34	26.02	28.43	32.01	35.17	38.97	41.64	49.73
24	10.86	13.85	15.66	18.06	19.94	23.34	27.10	29.55	33.20	36.42	40.27	42.98	51.18
25	11.52	14.61	16.47	18.94	20.87	24.34	28.17	30.68	34.38	37.65	41.57	44.31	52.62
26	12.20	15.38	17.29	19.82	21.79	25.34	29.25	31.79	35.56	38.89	42.86	45.64	54.05
27	12.88	16.15	18.11	20.70	22.72	26.34	30.32	32.91	36.74	40.11	44.14	46.96	55.48
28	13.56	16.93	18.94	21.59	23.65	27.34	31.39	34.03	37.92	41.34	45.42	48.28	56.89
29	14.26	17.71	19.77	22.48	24.58	28.34	32.46	35.14	39.09	42.56	46.69	49.59	58.30
30	14.95	18.49	20.60	23.36	25.51	29.34	33.53	36.25	40.26	43.77	47.96	50.89	59.70
31	15.66	19.28	21.43	24.26	26.44	30.34	34.60	37.36	41.42	44.99	49.23	52.19	61.10
32	16.36	20.07	22.27	25.15	27.37	31.34	35.66	38.47	42.58	46.19	50.49	53.49	62.49
33	17.07	20.87	23.11	26.04	28.31	32.34	36.73	39.57	43.75	47.40	51.74	54.78	63.87
34	17.79	21.66	23.95	26.94	29.24	33.34	37.80	40.68	44.90	48.60	53.00	56.06	65.25
35	18.51	22.47	24.80	27.84	30.18	34.34	38.86	41.78	46.06	49.80	54.24	57.34	66.62
36	19.23	23.27	25.64	28.73	31.12	35.34	39.92	42.88	47.21	51.00	55.49	58.62	67.98
37	19.96	24.07	26.49	29.64	32.05	36.34	40.98	43.98	48.36	52.19	56.73	59.89	69.35
38	20.69	24.88	27.34	30.54	32.99	37.34	42.05	45.08	49.51	53.38	57.97	61.16	70.70
39	21.43	25.70	28.20	31.44	33.93	38.34	43.11	46.17	50.66	54.57	59.20	62.43	72.06
40	22.16	26.51	29.05	32.34	34.87	39.34	44.16	47.27	51.81	55.76	60.44	63.69	73.40
50	29.71	34.76	37.69	41.45	44.31	49.33	54.72	58.16	63.17	67.50	72.61	76.15	86.66
60	37.48	43.19	46.46	50.64	53.81	59.33	65.23	68.97	74.40	79.08	84.58	88.38	99.61
70	45.44	51.74	55.33	59.90	63.35	69.33	75.69	79.71	85.53	90.53	96.39	100.43	112.32
80	53.54	60.39	64.28	69.21	72.92	79.33	86.12	90.41	96.58	101.88	108.07	112.33	124.84
90	61.75	69.13	73.29	78.56	82.51	89.33	96.52	101.05	107.57	113.15	119.65	124.12	137.21
100	70.06	77.93	82.36	87.95	92.13	99.33	106.91	111.67	118.50	124.34	131.14	135.81	149.45
110	78.46	86.79	91.47	97.36	101.77	109.33	117.27	122.25	129.39	135.48	142.56	147.41	161.58
120	86.92	95.70	100.62	106.81	111.42	119.33	127.62	132.81	140.23	146.57	153.92	158.95	173.62

Table A14.4: The cumulative probabilities from the binomial distribution when the probability of a success and the probability of a failure are both 0.5

The values in the table are for a one-tailed test. The result that would achieve statistical significance at $\alpha = 0.05$ for a given number of trials for a one-tailed test has had its probability printed in italics *and* bold. To find a two-tailed probability double the probabilities in the table. In some cases the number of failures/successes necessary to achieve significance with a two-tailed test will be the same as for a one-tailed test. However, where the number of successes/failures necessary to achieve significance for a two-tailed test is different from those that are bold and italic, the probability is shown in italics only. Thus, if we had no failures out of 6 trials, the one-tailed probability would be 0.016 and the two-tailed probability would be 0.032. However, if we had one failure out of 8 trials the one-tailed probability would be considered significant at 0.035 but the two-tailed probability would not at 0.07. Accordingly, the probability for no failures is shown in italics as even for a two-tailed probability this would be considered statistically significant at $2 \times 0.004 = 0.008$. Note that there is an exception to this system of signalling significance for a two-tailed test. When there are only 5 trials there is no outcome that would be significant at 0.05 for a two-tailed test, as was demonstrated in Chapter 10.

As an example of how to read the table, imagine that someone has taken a test with 20 questions in it, each of which is a simple multiple choice with only two alternatives. Under these circumstances if the person was responding purely by chance then for each question they would have an equal probability of getting the answer right or wrong. We can treat the answering of questions as the trials and so we would look down the first column until we got to 20. We can then read across to find out the probability of a given result (or one with fewer failures/successes). This tells us that if the person taking the exam got five or fewer wrong then we can assume that they have produced a result that is significantly better than chance as the probability of this result is 0.021 and thus less than 0.05. However, if they got six or more wrong we could not assume that they were significantly better than chance. Similarly if they got only five or fewer correct then we could say that they were performing significantly worse than chance.

Table A14.4 The cumulative probabilities from the binomial distribution

Number of trials	Number of failures or successes							
	0	1	2	3	4	5	6	7
5	*0.031*	0.188	0.500	0.813	0.969	1.000		
6	*0.016*	0.109	0.344	0.656	0.891	0.984	1.000	
7	*0.008*	0.063	0.227	0.500	0.773	0.938	0.992	1.000
8	*0.004*	*0.035*	0.145	0.363	0.637	0.855	0.965	0.996
9	0.002	*0.020*	0.090	0.254	0.500	0.746	0.910	0.980
10	0.001	*0.011*	0.055	0.172	0.377	0.623	0.828	0.945
11	<0.001	*0.006*	*0.033*	0.113	0.274	0.500	0.726	0.887
12	<0.001	0.003	*0.019*	0.073	0.194	0.387	0.613	0.806
13	<0.001	0.002	*0.011*	*0.046*	0.133	0.291	0.500	0.709
14	<0.001	0.001	*0.006*	*0.029*	0.090	0.212	0.395	0.605
15	<0.001	<0.001	0.004	*0.018*	0.059	0.151	0.304	0.500
16	<0.001	<0.001	0.002	*0.011*	*0.038*	0.105	0.227	0.402
17	<0.001	<0.001	0.001	0.006	*0.025*	0.072	0.166	0.315
18	<0.001	<0.001	0.001	0.004	*0.015*	*0.048*	0.119	0.240
19	<0.001	<0.001	<0.001	0.002	*0.010*	*0.032*	0.084	0.180
20	<0.001	<0.001	<0.001	0.001	0.006	*0.021*	0.058	0.132
21	<0.001	<0.001	<0.001	0.001	0.004	*0.013*	*0.039*	0.095
22	<0.001	<0.001	<0.001	<0.001	0.002	*0.008*	*0.026*	0.067
23	<0.001	<0.001	<0.001	<0.001	0.001	0.005	*0.017*	*0.047*
24	<0.001	<0.001	<0.001	<0.001	0.001	0.003	*0.011*	*0.032*
25	<0.001	<0.001	<0.001	<0.001	<0.001	0.002	0.007	*0.022*

Table A14.5: The probabilities of the Mann–Whitney U-test

If either sample has 20 or more participants it will be necessary to use the z-approximation Eqn A6.8 (or A6.9 when there are tied scores) in Appendix VI.

As an illustration, if the sample sizes were 5 and 8 then U would have to be 8 *or smaller* to be significant at $\alpha = 0.05$ for a one-tailed test.

a. The smaller sample size (n_1) = 2 to 7

		one-tailed probabilities			
		0.05	0.025	0.01	0.005
		two-tailed probabilities			
n_1	n_2	0.10	0.05	0.02	0.01
2	5	0	–	–	–
	6	0	–	–	–
	7	0	–	–	–
	8	1	0	–	–
	9	1	0	–	–
	10	1	0	–	–
	11	1	0	–	–
	12	2	1	–	–
	13	2	1	0	–
	14	3	1	0	–
	15	3	1	0	–
	16	3	1	0	–
	17	3	2	0	–
	18	4	2	0	–
	19	4	2	1	0
	20	4	2	1	0
3	3	0	–	–	–
	4	0	–	–	–
	5	1	0	–	–
	6	2	1	–	–
	7	2	1	0	–
	8	3	2	0	–
	9	4	2	1	0
	10	4	3	1	0
	11	5	3	1	0
	12	5	4	2	1
	13	6	4	2	1
	14	7	5	2	1
	15	7	5	3	2
	16	8	6	3	2
	17	9	6	4	2
	18	9	7	4	2
	19	10	7	4	3
	20	11	8	5	3

		one-tailed probabilities			
		0.05	0.025	0.01	0.005
		two-tailed probabilities			
n_1	n_2	0.10	0.05	0.02	0.01
4	4	1	0	–	–
	5	2	1	0	–
	6	3	2	1	0
	7	4	3	1	0
	8	5	4	2	1
	9	6	4	3	1
	10	7	5	3	2
	11	8	6	4	2
	12	9	7	5	3
	13	10	8	5	3
	14	11	9	6	4
	15	12	10	7	5
	16	14	11	7	5
	17	15	11	8	6
	18	16	12	9	6
	19	17	13	9	7
	20	18	14	10	8
5	5	4	2	1	0
	6	5	3	2	1
	7	6	5	3	1
	8	8	6	4	2
	9	9	7	5	3
	10	11	8	6	4
	11	12	9	7	5
	12	13	11	8	6
	13	15	12	9	7
	14	16	13	10	7
	15	18	14	11	8
	16	19	15	12	9
	17	20	17	13	10
	18	22	18	14	11
	19	23	19	15	12
	20	25	20	16	13

		one-tailed probabilities			
		0.05	0.025	0.01	0.005
		two-tailed probabilities			
n_1	n_2	0.10	0.05	0.02	0.01
6	6	7	5	3	2
	7	8	6	4	3
	8	10	8	6	4
	9	12	10	7	5
	10	14	11	8	6
	11	16	13	9	7
	12	17	14	11	9
	13	19	16	12	10
	14	21	17	13	11
	15	23	19	15	12
	16	25	21	16	13
	17	26	22	18	15
	18	28	24	19	16
	19	30	25	20	17
	20	32	27	22	18
7	7	11	8	6	4
	8	13	10	7	6
	9	15	12	9	7
	10	17	14	11	9
	11	19	16	12	10
	12	21	18	14	12
	13	24	20	16	13
	14	26	22	17	15
	15	28	24	19	16
	16	30	26	21	18
	17	33	28	23	19
	18	35	30	24	21
	19	37	32	26	22
	20	39	34	28	24

(Adapted with the kind permission of Routledge from Table G, p. 375, of Neave, H. R. and Worthington, P. L. (1988). *Distribution-free Tests*. London: Routledge.)

b. The smaller sample size (n_1) = 8 to 20

		one-tailed probabilities			
		0.05	0.025	0.01	0.005
		two-tailed probabilities			
n_1	n_2	0.10	0.05	0.02	0.01
8	8	15	13	9	7
	9	18	15	11	9
	10	20	17	13	11
	11	23	19	15	13
	12	26	22	17	15
	13	28	24	20	17
	14	31	26	22	18
	15	33	29	24	20
	16	36	31	26	22
	17	39	34	28	24
	18	41	36	30	26
	19	44	38	32	28
	20	47	41	34	30
9	9	21	17	14	11
	10	24	20	16	13
	11	27	23	18	16
	12	30	26	21	18
	13	33	28	23	20
	14	36	31	26	22
	15	39	34	28	24
	16	42	37	31	27
	17	45	39	33	29
	18	48	42	36	31
	19	51	45	38	33
	20	54	48	40	36
10	10	27	23	19	16
	11	31	26	22	18
	12	34	29	24	21
	13	37	33	27	24
	14	41	36	30	26
	15	44	39	33	29
	16	48	42	36	31
	17	51	45	38	34
	18	55	48	41	37
	19	58	52	44	39
	20	62	55	47	42

n_1	n_2	0.10	0.05	0.02	0.01
11	11	34	30	25	21
	12	38	33	28	24
	13	42	37	31	27
	14	46	40	34	30
	15	50	44	37	33
	16	54	47	41	36
	17	57	51	44	39
	18	61	55	47	42
	19	65	58	50	45
	20	69	62	53	48
12	12	42	37	31	27
	13	47	41	35	31
	14	51	45	38	34
	15	55	49	42	37
	16	60	53	46	41
	17	64	57	49	44
	18	68	61	53	47
	19	72	65	56	51
	20	77	69	60	54
13	13	51	45	39	34
	14	56	50	43	38
	15	61	54	47	42
	16	65	59	51	45
	17	70	63	55	49
	18	75	67	59	53
	19	80	72	63	57
	20	84	76	67	60

n_1	n_2	0.10	0.05	0.02	0.01
14	14	61	55	47	42
	15	66	59	51	46
	16	71	64	56	50
	17	77	69	60	54
	18	82	74	65	58
	19	87	78	60	63
	20	92	83	73	67
15	15	72	64	56	51
	16	77	70	61	55
	17	83	75	66	60
	18	88	80	70	64
	19	94	85	75	69
	20	100	90	80	73
16	16	83	75	66	60
	17	89	81	71	65
	18	95	86	76	70
	19	101	92	82	74
	20	107	98	87	79
17	17	96	87	77	70
	18	102	92	82	75
	19	109	99	88	81
	20	115	105	93	86
18	18	109	99	88	81
	19	116	106	94	87
	20	123	112	100	92
19	19	123	113	101	93
	20	130	119	107	99
20	20	138	127	114	105

(Adapted with the kind permission of Routledge from Table G, p 376, of Neave, H. R. and Worthington, P. L. (1988). *Distribution-Free Tests*. London: Routledge.)

Table A14.6: The probabilities of *T* from Wilcoxon's signed-rank test for matched pairs

If the sample has more than 25 participants then use the *z*-approximation Eqn A6.10 (or A6.11 when there are tied scores) in Appendix VI. To be statistically significant *T* has to be as small as or *smaller* than the value shown in the table.

	one-tailed probabilities			
	0.05	0.025	0.01	0.005
	two-tailed probabilities			
n	0.1	0.05	0.02	0.01
5	0			
6	2	0		
7	3	2	0	
8	5	3	1	0
9	8	5	3	1
10	10	8	5	3
11	13	10	7	5
12	17	13	9	7
13	21	17	12	9
14	25	21	15	12
15	30	25	19	15
16	35	29	23	19
17	41	34	27	23
18	47	40	32	27
19	53	46	37	32
20	60	52	43	37
21	67	58	49	42
22	75	65	55	48
23	83	73	62	54
24	91	81	69	61
25	100	89	76	68

(Adapted with the kind permission of Routledge from Table D, p. 373, of Neave, H. R. and Worthington, P. L. (1988). *Distribution-Free Tests*. London: Routledge.)

Table A14.7: The probabilities of Fisher's exact probability test

To read these tables, note which is the smallest row (or column) total; this will be S_1. Then note the next smallest or equally small column (or row) total; this will be S_2; x will then be the number in the cell with which S_1 and S_2 intersect.

		S_1	1	2	0	2
x				0	8	8
	S_2	n		2	8	10

Thus, if a result was in line with a directional hypothesis, when the sample size (n) was 10, $S_1 = 2$, $S_2 = 2$ and $x = 2$, then the probability of this outcome is $p = 0.022$.

I have only included probabilities up to 0.1. For higher probabilities see Dixon and Massey (1983) or Siegel and Castellan (1988).

a. $n = 5$ to 12

n	S_1	S_2	x	one-tailed	two-tailed
5	2	2	2	0.100	0.100
6	2	2	2	0.067	0.067
	3	3	0	0.050	0.100
			3	0.050	0.100
7	2	2	2	0.048	0.048
	3	3	3	0.029	0.029
8	2	2	2	0.036	0.036
	3	3	3	0.018	0.018
	3	4	0	0.071	0.143
			3	0.071	0.143
	4	4	0	0.014	0.029
			4	0.014	0.029
9	2	2	2	0.028	0.028
	2	3	2	0.083	0.083
	3	3	3	0.012	0.012
	3	4	3	0.048	0.048
	4	4	0	0.040	0.048
			4	0.008	0.008

n	S_1	S_2	x	one-tailed	two-tailed
10	1	1	1	0.100	0.100
	2	2	2	0.022	0.022
	2	3	2	0.067	0.067
	3	3	3	0.008	0.008
	3	4	3	0.033	0.033
	3	5	0	0.083	0.167
			3	0.083	0.167
	4	4	0	0.071	0.076
			4	0.005	0.005
	4	5	0	0.024	0.048
			4	0.024	0.048
	5	5	0	0.004	0.008
			5	0.004	0.008
11	1	1	1	0.091	0.091
	2	2	2	0.018	0.018
	2	3	2	0.055	0.055
	3	3	3	0.006	0.006
	3	4	3	0.024	0.024
	3	5	3	0.061	0.061
	4	4	3	0.088	0.088
			4	0.003	0.003
	4	5	0	0.045	0.061
			4	0.015	0.015
	5	5	0	0.013	0.015
			4	0.067	0.080
			5	0.002	0.002

n	S_1	S_2	x	one-tailed	two-tailed
12	1	1	1	0.083	0.083
	2	2	2	0.015	0.015
	2	3	2	0.045	0.045
	2	4	2	0.091	0.091
	3	3	3	0.005	0.005
	3	4	3	0.018	0.018
	3	5	3	0.045	0.045
	3	6	0	0.091	0.182
			3	0.091	0.182
	4	4	3	0.067	0.067
			4	0.002	0.002
	4	5	0	0.071	0.081
			4	0.010	0.010
	4	6	0	0.030	0.061
			4	0.030	0.061
	5	5	0	0.027	0.028
			4	0.045	0.072
			5	0.001	0.001
	5	6	0	0.008	0.015
			5	0.008	0.015
	6	6	0	0.001	0.002
			1	0.040	0.080
			5	0.040	0.080
			6	0.001	0.002

(Adapted with the kind permission of The McGraw-Hill Companies from Dixon, W. J. and Massey, F. J. Jr. (1983). *Introduction to Statistical Analysis* (4th Edn). New York: McGraw-Hill.)

Table A14.7 The probabilities of Fisher's exact probability test

b. n = 13 to 15

n	S_1	S_2	x	one-tailed	two-tailed
13	1	1	1	0.077	0.077
	2	2	2	0.013	0.013
	2	3	2	0.038	0.038
	2	4	2	0.077	0.077
	3	3	3	0.003	0.003
	3	4	3	0.014	0.014
	3	5	3	0.035	0.035
	3	6	3	0.070	0.070
	4	4	3	0.052	0.052
			4	0.001	0.001
	4	5	0	0.098	0.105
			4	0.007	0.007
	4	6	0	0.049	0.070
			4	0.021	0.021
	5	5	0	0.044	0.075
			4	0.032	0.032
			5	0.001	0.001
	5	6	0	0.016	0.021
			4	0.086	0.103
			5	0.005	0.005
	6	6	0	0.004	0.005
			1	0.078	0.103
			5	0.025	0.029
			6	0.001	0.001
14	1	1	1	0.071	0.071
	2	2	2	0.011	0.011
	2	3	2	0.033	0.033
	2	4	2	0.066	0.066
	3	3	2	0.093	0.093
			3	0.003	0.003
	3	4	3	0.011	0.011
	3	5	3	0.027	0.027
	3	6	3	0.055	0.055
	3	7	0	0.096	0.192
			3	0.096	0.192
	4	4	3	0.041	0.041
			4	0.001	0.001
	4	5	3	0.095	0.095
			4	0.005	0.005
	4	6	0	0.070	0.085
			4	0.015	0.015
	4	7	0	0.035	0.070
			4	0.035	0.070
	5	5	0	0.063	0.086
			4	0.023	0.023
			5	0.0005	0.0005
	5	6	0	0.028	0.031
			4	0.063	0.091
			5	0.003	0.003
	5	7	0	0.010	0.021
			5	0.010	0.021
	6	6	0	0.009	0.010
			5	0.016	0.026
			6	0.0003	0.0003
	6	7	0	0.002	0.005
			1	0.051	0.103
			5	0.051	0.103
			6	0.002	0.005
	7	7	0	<0.0001	<0.0001
			1	0.015	0.029
			6	0.015	0.029
			7	<0.0001	<0.0001
15	1	1	1	0.067	0.067
	2	2	2	0.010	0.010
	2	3	2	0.029	0.029
	2	4	2	0.057	0.057
	2	5	2	0.095	0.095
	3	3	2	0.081	0.081
			3	0.002	0.002
	3	4	3	0.009	0.009
	3	5	3	0.022	0.022
	3	6	3	0.044	0.044
	3	7	3	0.077	0.077
	4	4	3	0.033	0.033
			4	0.001	0.001
	4	5	3	0.077	0.077
			4	0.004	0.004
	4	6	0	0.092	0.103
			4	0.011	0.011
	4	7	0	0.051	0.077
			4	0.026	0.026
	5	5	0	0.084	0.101
			4	0.017	0.017
			5	0.0003	0.0003
	5	6	0	0.042	0.089
			4	0.047	0.089
			5	0.002	0.002
	5	7	0	0.019	0.026
			4	0.100	0.119
			5	0.007	0.007
	6	6	0	0.017	0.028
			5	0.011	0.011
			6	0.0002	0.0002
	6	7	0	0.006	0.007
			1	0.084	0.119
			5	0.035	0.041
			6	0.001	0.001
	7	7	0	0.001	0.001
			1	0.032	0.041
			5	0.100	0.132
			6	0.009	0.010
			7	0.0002	0.0002

The probabilities of *F*-distributions

The distribution of *F* depends on the degrees of freedom for the numerator (in ANOVA this is usually the treatment Mean Square) and the df for the divisor (in ANOVA this is usually the error, within-groups or residual Mean Square). The larger the df for the numerator the less positively skewed the distribution.

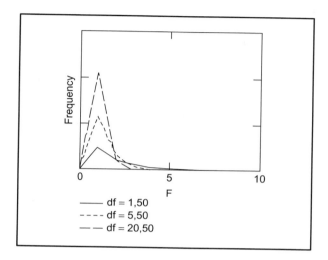

To read the tables, the numerator df is shown in the first row of the table, while the divisor df is shown in the first column. Thus, with treatment df of 2 and error df of 20, the *F*-ratio would have to be 3.49 or larger to be statistically significant at $\alpha = 0.05$.

Table A14.8 Probabilities of the *F*-distribution

a. α = 0.05, df₁ = 1 to 14

df₂	1	2	3	4	5	6	7	8	9	10	12	14
1	161.45	199.50	215.71	224.58	230.16	233.99	236.77	238.88	240.54	241.88	243.90	245.36
2	18.51	19.00	19.16	19.25	19.30	19.33	19.35	19.37	19.38	19.40	19.41	19.42
3	10.13	9.55	9.28	9.12	9.01	8.94	8.89	8.85	8.81	8.79	8.74	8.71
4	7.71	6.94	6.59	6.39	6.26	6.16	6.09	6.04	6.00	5.96	5.91	5.87
5	6.61	5.79	5.41	5.19	5.05	4.95	4.88	4.82	4.77	4.74	4.68	4.64
6	5.99	5.14	4.76	4.53	4.39	4.28	4.21	4.15	4.10	4.06	4.00	3.96
7	5.59	4.74	4.35	4.12	3.97	3.87	3.79	3.73	3.68	3.64	3.57	3.53
8	5.32	4.46	4.07	3.84	3.69	3.58	3.50	3.44	3.39	3.35	3.28	3.24
9	5.12	4.26	3.86	3.63	3.48	3.37	3.29	3.23	3.18	3.14	3.07	3.03
10	4.96	4.10	3.71	3.48	3.33	3.22	3.14	3.07	3.02	2.98	2.91	2.86
11	4.84	3.98	3.59	3.36	3.20	3.09	3.01	2.95	2.90	2.85	2.79	2.74
12	4.75	3.89	3.49	3.26	3.11	3.00	2.91	2.85	2.80	2.75	2.69	2.64
13	4.67	3.81	3.41	3.18	3.03	2.92	2.83	2.77	2.71	2.67	2.60	2.55
14	4.60	3.74	3.34	3.11	2.96	2.85	2.76	2.70	2.65	2.60	2.53	2.48
15	4.54	3.68	3.29	3.06	2.90	2.79	2.71	2.64	2.59	2.54	2.48	2.42
16	4.49	3.63	3.24	3.01	2.85	2.74	2.66	2.59	2.54	2.49	2.42	2.37
17	4.45	3.59	3.20	2.96	2.81	2.70	2.61	2.55	2.49	2.45	2.38	2.33
18	4.41	3.55	3.16	2.93	2.77	2.66	2.58	2.51	2.46	2.41	2.34	2.29
19	4.38	3.52	3.13	2.90	2.74	2.63	2.54	2.48	2.42	2.38	2.31	2.26
20	4.35	3.49	3.10	2.87	2.71	2.60	2.51	2.45	2.39	2.35	2.28	2.22
21	4.32	3.47	3.07	2.84	2.68	2.57	2.49	2.42	2.37	2.32	2.25	2.20
22	4.30	3.44	3.05	2.82	2.66	2.55	2.46	2.40	2.34	2.30	2.23	2.17
23	4.28	3.42	3.03	2.80	2.64	2.53	2.44	2.37	2.32	2.27	2.20	2.15
24	4.26	3.40	3.01	2.78	2.62	2.51	2.42	2.36	2.30	2.25	2.18	2.13
25	4.24	3.39	2.99	2.76	2.60	2.49	2.40	2.34	2.28	2.24	2.16	2.11
26	4.23	3.37	2.98	2.74	2.59	2.47	2.39	2.32	2.27	2.22	2.15	2.09
27	4.21	3.35	2.96	2.73	2.57	2.46	2.37	2.31	2.25	2.20	2.13	2.08
28	4.20	3.34	2.95	2.71	2.56	2.45	2.36	2.29	2.24	2.19	2.12	2.06
29	4.18	3.33	2.93	2.70	2.55	2.43	2.35	2.28	2.22	2.18	2.10	2.05
30	4.17	3.32	2.92	2.69	2.53	2.42	2.33	2.27	2.21	2.16	2.09	2.04
35	4.12	3.27	2.87	2.64	2.49	2.37	2.29	2.22	2.16	2.11	2.04	1.99
40	4.08	3.23	2.84	2.61	2.45	2.34	2.25	2.18	2.12	2.08	2.00	1.95
45	4.06	3.20	2.81	2.58	2.42	2.31	2.22	2.15	2.10	2.05	1.97	1.92
50	4.03	3.18	2.79	2.56	2.40	2.29	2.20	2.13	2.07	2.03	1.95	1.89
55	4.02	3.16	2.77	2.54	2.38	2.27	2.18	2.11	2.06	2.01	1.93	1.88
60	4.00	3.15	2.76	2.53	2.37	2.25	2.17	2.10	2.04	1.99	1.92	1.86
65	3.99	3.14	2.75	2.51	2.36	2.24	2.15	2.08	2.03	1.98	1.90	1.85
70	3.98	3.13	2.74	2.50	2.35	2.23	2.14	2.07	2.02	1.97	1.89	1.84
75	3.97	3.12	2.73	2.49	2.34	2.22	2.13	2.06	2.01	1.96	1.88	1.83
80	3.96	3.11	2.72	2.49	2.33	2.21	2.13	2.06	2.00	1.95	1.88	1.82
85	3.95	3.10	2.71	2.48	2.32	2.21	2.12	2.05	1.99	1.94	1.87	1.81
90	3.95	3.10	2.71	2.47	2.32	2.20	2.11	2.04	1.99	1.94	1.86	1.80
95	3.94	3.09	2.70	2.47	2.31	2.20	2.11	2.04	1.98	1.93	1.86	1.80
100	3.94	3.09	2.70	2.46	2.31	2.19	2.10	2.03	1.97	1.93	1.85	1.79
110	3.93	3.08	2.69	2.45	2.30	2.18	2.09	2.02	1.97	1.92	1.84	1.78
120	3.92	3.07	2.68	2.45	2.29	2.18	2.09	2.02	1.96	1.91	1.83	1.78

b. $\alpha = 0.05$, $df_1 = 16$ to 100

df_2	16	18	20	22	24	30	35	40	50	60	80	100
1	246.47	247.32	248.02	248.58	249.05	250.10	250.69	251.14	251.77	252.20	252.72	253.04
2	19.43	19.44	19.45	19.45	19.45	19.46	19.47	19.47	19.48	19.48	19.48	19.49
3	8.69	8.67	8.66	8.65	8.64	8.62	8.60	8.59	8.58	8.57	8.56	8.55
4	5.84	5.82	5.80	5.79	5.77	5.75	5.73	5.72	5.70	5.69	5.67	5.66
5	4.60	4.58	4.56	4.54	4.53	4.50	4.48	4.46	4.44	4.43	4.41	4.41
6	3.92	3.90	3.87	3.86	3.84	3.81	3.79	3.77	3.75	3.74	3.72	3.71
7	3.49	3.47	3.44	3.43	3.41	3.38	3.36	3.34	3.32	3.30	3.29	3.27
8	3.20	3.17	3.15	3.13	3.12	3.08	3.06	3.04	3.02	3.01	2.99	2.97
9	2.99	2.96	2.94	2.92	2.90	2.86	2.84	2.83	2.80	2.79	2.77	2.76
10	2.83	2.80	2.77	2.75	2.74	2.70	2.68	2.66	2.64	2.62	2.60	2.59
11	2.70	2.67	2.65	2.63	2.61	2.57	2.55	2.53	2.51	2.49	2.47	2.46
12	2.60	2.57	2.54	2.52	2.51	2.47	2.44	2.43	2.40	2.38	2.36	2.35
13	2.51	2.48	2.46	2.44	2.42	2.38	2.36	2.34	2.31	2.30	2.27	2.26
14	2.44	2.41	2.39	2.37	2.35	2.31	2.28	2.27	2.24	2.22	2.20	2.19
15	2.38	2.35	2.33	2.31	2.29	2.25	2.22	2.20	2.18	2.16	2.14	2.12
16	2.33	2.30	2.28	2.25	2.24	2.19	2.17	2.15	2.12	2.11	2.08	2.07
17	2.29	2.26	2.23	2.21	2.19	2.15	2.12	2.10	2.08	2.06	2.03	2.02
18	2.25	2.22	2.19	2.17	2.15	2.11	2.08	2.06	2.04	2.02	1.99	1.98
19	2.21	2.18	2.16	2.13	2.11	2.07	2.05	2.03	2.00	1.98	1.96	1.94
20	2.18	2.15	2.12	2.10	2.08	2.04	2.01	1.99	1.97	1.95	1.92	1.91
21	2.16	2.12	2.10	2.07	2.05	2.01	1.98	1.96	1.94	1.92	1.89	1.88
22	2.13	2.10	2.07	2.05	2.03	1.98	1.96	1.94	1.91	1.89	1.86	1.85
23	2.11	2.08	2.05	2.02	2.01	1.96	1.93	1.91	1.88	1.86	1.84	1.82
24	2.09	2.05	2.03	2.00	1.98	1.94	1.91	1.89	1.86	1.84	1.82	1.80
25	2.07	2.04	2.01	1.98	1.96	1.92	1.89	1.87	1.84	1.82	1.80	1.78
26	2.05	2.02	1.99	1.97	1.95	1.90	1.87	1.85	1.82	1.80	1.78	1.76
27	2.04	2.00	1.97	1.95	1.93	1.88	1.86	1.84	1.81	1.79	1.76	1.74
28	2.02	1.99	1.96	1.93	1.91	1.87	1.84	1.82	1.79	1.77	1.74	1.73
29	2.01	1.97	1.94	1.92	1.90	1.85	1.83	1.81	1.77	1.75	1.73	1.71
30	1.99	1.96	1.93	1.91	1.89	1.84	1.81	1.79	1.76	1.74	1.71	1.70
35	1.94	1.91	1.88	1.85	1.83	1.79	1.76	1.74	1.70	1.68	1.65	1.63
40	1.90	1.87	1.84	1.81	1.79	1.74	1.72	1.69	1.66	1.64	1.61	1.59
45	1.87	1.84	1.81	1.78	1.76	1.71	1.68	1.66	1.63	1.60	1.57	1.55
50	1.85	1.81	1.78	1.76	1.74	1.69	1.66	1.63	1.60	1.58	1.54	1.52
55	1.83	1.79	1.76	1.74	1.72	1.67	1.64	1.61	1.58	1.55	1.52	1.50
60	1.82	1.78	1.75	1.72	1.70	1.65	1.62	1.59	1.56	1.53	1.50	1.48
65	1.80	1.76	1.73	1.71	1.69	1.63	1.60	1.58	1.54	1.52	1.49	1.46
70	1.79	1.75	1.72	1.70	1.67	1.62	1.59	1.57	1.53	1.50	1.47	1.45
75	1.78	1.74	1.71	1.69	1.66	1.61	1.58	1.55	1.52	1.49	1.46	1.44
80	1.77	1.73	1.70	1.68	1.65	1.60	1.57	1.54	1.51	1.48	1.45	1.43
85	1.76	1.73	1.70	1.67	1.65	1.59	1.56	1.54	1.50	1.47	1.44	1.42
90	1.76	1.72	1.69	1.66	1.64	1.59	1.55	1.53	1.49	1.46	1.43	1.41
95	1.75	1.71	1.68	1.66	1.63	1.58	1.55	1.52	1.48	1.46	1.42	1.40
100	1.75	1.71	1.68	1.65	1.63	1.57	1.54	1.52	1.48	1.45	1.41	1.40
110	1.74	1.70	1.67	1.64	1.62	1.56	1.53	1.50	1.47	1.44	1.41	1.39
120	1.73	1.69	1.66	1.63	1.61	1.55	1.52	1.50	1.46	1.43	1.39	1.37

Table A14.8 Probabilities of *F*-distribution

c. α = 0.01, df$_1$ = 1 to 24

df$_2$	1	2	3	4	5	6	7	8	9	10	12	24
1	4052.18	4999.34	5403.53	5624.26	5763.96	5858.95	5928.33	5980.95	6022.40	6055.93	6106.68	6234.27
2	98.50	99.00	99.16	99.25	99.30	99.33	99.36	99.38	99.39	99.40	99.42	99.46
3	34.12	30.82	29.46	28.71	28.24	27.91	27.67	27.49	27.34	27.23	27.05	26.60
4	21.20	18.00	16.69	15.98	15.52	15.21	14.98	14.80	14.66	14.55	14.37	13.93
5	16.26	13.27	12.06	11.39	10.97	10.67	10.46	10.29	10.16	10.05	9.89	9.47
6	13.75	10.92	9.78	9.15	8.75	8.47	8.26	8.10	7.98	7.87	7.72	7.31
7	12.25	9.55	8.45	7.85	7.46	7.19	6.99	6.84	6.72	6.62	6.47	6.07
8	11.26	8.65	7.59	7.01	6.63	6.37	6.18	6.03	5.91	5.81	5.67	5.28
9	10.56	8.02	6.99	6.42	6.06	5.80	5.61	5.47	5.35	5.26	5.11	4.73
10	10.04	7.56	6.55	5.99	5.64	5.39	5.20	5.06	4.94	4.85	4.71	4.33
11	9.65	7.21	6.22	5.67	5.32	5.07	4.89	4.74	4.63	4.54	4.40	4.02
12	9.33	6.93	5.95	5.41	5.06	4.82	4.64	4.50	4.39	4.30	4.16	3.78
13	9.07	6.70	5.74	5.21	4.86	4.62	4.44	4.30	4.19	4.10	3.96	3.59
14	8.86	6.51	5.56	5.04	4.69	4.46	4.28	4.14	4.03	3.94	3.80	3.43
15	8.68	6.36	5.42	4.89	4.56	4.32	4.14	4.00	3.89	3.80	3.67	3.29
16	8.53	6.23	5.29	4.77	4.44	4.20	4.03	3.89	3.78	3.69	3.55	3.18
17	8.40	6.11	5.19	4.67	4.34	4.10	3.93	3.79	3.68	3.59	3.46	3.08
18	8.29	6.01	5.09	4.58	4.25	4.01	3.84	3.71	3.60	3.51	3.37	3.00
19	8.18	5.93	5.01	4.50	4.17	3.94	3.77	3.63	3.52	3.43	3.30	2.92
20	8.10	5.85	4.94	4.43	4.10	3.87	3.70	3.56	3.46	3.37	3.23	2.86
21	8.02	5.78	4.87	4.37	4.04	3.81	3.64	3.51	3.40	3.31	3.17	2.80
22	7.95	5.72	4.82	4.31	3.99	3.76	3.59	3.45	3.35	3.26	3.12	2.75
23	7.88	5.66	4.76	4.26	3.94	3.71	3.54	3.41	3.30	3.21	3.07	2.70
24	7.82	5.61	4.72	4.22	3.90	3.67	3.50	3.36	3.26	3.17	3.03	2.66
25	7.77	5.57	4.68	4.18	3.85	3.63	3.46	3.32	3.22	3.13	2.99	2.62
26	7.72	5.53	4.64	4.14	3.82	3.59	3.42	3.29	3.18	3.09	2.96	2.58
27	7.68	5.49	4.60	4.11	3.78	3.56	3.39	3.26	3.15	3.06	2.93	2.55
28	7.64	5.45	4.57	4.07	3.75	3.53	3.36	3.23	3.12	3.03	2.90	2.52
29	7.60	5.42	4.54	4.04	3.73	3.50	3.33	3.20	3.09	3.00	2.87	2.49
30	7.56	5.39	4.51	4.02	3.70	3.47	3.30	3.17	3.07	2.98	2.84	2.47
35	7.42	5.27	4.40	3.91	3.59	3.37	3.20	3.07	2.96	2.88	2.74	2.36
40	7.31	5.18	4.31	3.83	3.51	3.29	3.12	2.99	2.89	2.80	2.66	2.29
45	7.23	5.11	4.25	3.77	3.45	3.23	3.07	2.94	2.83	2.74	2.61	2.23
50	7.17	5.06	4.20	3.72	3.41	3.19	3.02	2.89	2.78	2.70	2.56	2.18
55	7.12	5.01	4.16	3.68	3.37	3.15	2.98	2.85	2.75	2.66	2.53	2.15
60	7.08	4.98	4.13	3.65	3.34	3.12	2.95	2.82	2.72	2.63	2.50	2.12
65	7.04	4.95	4.10	3.62	3.31	3.09	2.93	2.80	2.69	2.61	2.47	2.09
70	7.01	4.92	4.07	3.60	3.29	3.07	2.91	2.78	2.67	2.59	2.45	2.07
75	6.99	4.90	4.05	3.58	3.27	3.05	2.89	2.76	2.65	2.57	2.43	2.05
80	6.96	4.88	4.04	3.56	3.26	3.04	2.87	2.74	2.64	2.55	2.42	2.03
85	6.94	4.86	4.02	3.55	3.24	3.02	2.86	2.73	2.62	2.54	2.40	2.02
90	6.93	4.85	4.01	3.53	3.23	3.01	2.84	2.72	2.61	2.52	2.39	2.00
95	6.91	4.84	3.99	3.52	3.22	3.00	2.83	2.70	2.60	2.51	2.38	1.99
100	6.90	4.82	3.98	3.51	3.21	2.99	2.82	2.69	2.59	2.50	2.37	1.98
110	6.87	4.80	3.96	3.49	3.19	2.97	2.81	2.68	2.57	2.49	2.35	1.96
120	6.85	4.79	3.95	3.48	3.17	2.96	2.79	2.66	2.56	2.47	2.34	1.95

Table A14.9: The probabilities of H for the Kruskal–Wallis ANOVA

For samples not shown in this table use the probability values from the chi-squared distribution with df $= k - 1$.

k (number of levels) $= 3$ to 5

$k = 3$

sample sizes			probability 0.05	probability 0.01
2	2	2	–	–
3	2	1	–	–
3	2	2	4.714	–
3	3	1	5.143	–
3	3	2	5.361	–
3	3	3	5.600	7.200
4	2	1	–	–
4	2	2	5.333	–
4	3	1	5.208	–
4	3	2	5.444	6.444
4	3	3	5.791	6.745
4	4	1	4.967	6.667
4	4	2	5.455	7.036
4	4	3	5.598	7.144
4	4	4	5.692	7.654
5	2	1	5.000	–
5	2	2	5.160	6.533
5	3	1	4.960	–
5	3	2	5.251	6.909
5	3	3	5.648	7.079
5	4	1	4.985	6.955
5	4	2	5.273	7.205
5	4	3	5.656	7.445
5	4	4	5.657	7.760
5	5	1	5.127	7.309
5	5	2	5.338	7.338
5	5	3	5.705	7.578
5	5	4	5.666	7.823
5	5	5	5.780	8.000

$k = 3$

sample sizes			probability 0.05	probability 0.01
6	1	1	–	–
6	2	1	4.822	–
6	2	2	5.345	6.655
6	3	1	4.855	6.873
6	3	2	5.348	6.970
6	3	3	5.615	7.410
6	4	1	4.947	7.106
6	4	2	5.340	7.340
6	4	3	5.610	7.500
6	4	4	5.681	7.795
6	5	1	4.990	7.182
6	5	2	5.338	7.376
6	5	3	5.602	7.590
6	5	4	5.661	7.936
6	5	5	5.729	8.028
6	6	1	4.945	7.121
6	6	2	5.410	7.467
6	6	3	5.625	7.725
6	6	4	5.724	8.000
6	6	5	5.765	8.124
6	6	6	5.801	8.222
7	7	7	5.819	8.378
8	8	8	5.805	8.465

$k = 4$

sample sizes				probability 0.05	probability 0.01
2	2	1	1	–	–
2	2	2	1	5.679	–
2	2	2	2	6.167	6.667
3	1	1	1	–	–
3	2	1	1	–	–
3	2	2	1	5.833	–
3	2	2	2	6.333	7.133
3	3	1	1	6.333	–
3	3	2	1	6.244	7.200
3	3	2	2	6.527	7.636
3	3	3	1	6.600	7.400
3	3	3	2	6.727	8.015
3	3	3	3	7.000	8.538
4	1	1	1	–	–
4	2	1	1	5.833	–
4	2	2	1	6.133	7.000
4	2	2	2	6.545	7.391
4	3	1	1	6.178	7.067
4	3	2	1	6.309	7.455
4	3	2	2	6.621	7.871
4	3	3	1	6.545	7.758
4	3	3	2	6.795	8.333
4	3	3	3	6.984	8.659
4	4	1	1	5.945	7.909
4	4	2	1	6.386	7.909
4	4	2	2	6.731	8.346
4	4	3	1	6.635	8.231
4	4	3	2	6.874	8.621
4	4	3	3	7.038	8.876
4	4	4	1	6.725	8.588
4	4	4	2	6.957	8.871
4	4	4	3	7.142	9.075
4	4	4	4	7.235	9.287

$k = 5$

sample sizes					probability 0.05	probability 0.01
2	2	1	1	1	–	–
2	2	2	1	1	6.750	–
2	2	2	2	1	7.133	7.533
2	2	2	2	2	7.418	8.291
3	1	1	1	1	–	–
3	2	1	1	1	6.583	–
3	2	2	1	1	6.800	7.600
3	2	2	2	1	7.309	8.127
3	2	2	2	2	7.682	8.682
3	3	1	1	1	7.111	–
3	3	2	1	1	7.200	8.073
3	3	2	2	1	7.591	8.576
3	3	2	2	2	7.910	9.115
3	3	3	1	1	7.576	8.424
3	3	3	2	1	7.769	9.051
3	3	3	2	2	8.044	9.505
3	3	3	3	1	8.000	9.451
3	3	3	3	2	8.200	9.876
3	3	3	3	3	8.333	10.200

(Adapted with the kind permission of Routledge from Table 4.2, p. 49, of Neave, H. R. (1978). *Statistics Tables for Mathematicians, Engineers, Economists and the Behavioural and Management Sciences*. London: Routledge.)

Table A14.10: The probabilities of χ_F^2 (Friedman's non-parametric statistic for within-subjects ANOVA)

This table provides the critical values of χ_F^2 with k as the number of levels of the variable and n as the sample size.

As an example, if, in a study that involved 4 participants ($n = 4$) and had 3 levels ($k = 3$), $\chi_F^2 = 6.5$, then χ_F^2 would be statistically significant with $\alpha = 0.05$. For larger samples or where variables have more levels use the table of chi-squared distribution with df $= k - 1$.

k (number of levels of variable)

significant at	3 0.05	3 0.01	4 0.05	4 0.01	5 0.05	5 0.01	6 0.05	6 0.01
n = 2	–	–	6.00	–	7.60	8.00	9.14	9.71
3	6.00	–	7.40	9.00	8.53	10.13	9.86	11.76
4	6.50	8.00	7.80	9.60	8.80	11.20	10.29	12.71
5	6.40	8.40	7.80	9.96	8.96	11.68	10.49	13.23
6	7.00	9.00	7.60	10.20	9.07	11.87	10.57	13.62
7	7.14	8.86	7.80	10.54	9.14	12.11	10.67	13.86
8	6.25	9.00	7.65	10.50	9.20	13.20	10.71	14.00
9	6.22	9.56	7.67	10.73	9.24	12.44	10.78	14.14
10	6.20	9.60	7.68	10.68	9.28	12.48	10.80	14.23
11	6.55	9.46	7.69	10.75	9.31	12.58	10.84	14.32
12	6.50	9.50	7.70	10.80	9.33	12.60	10.86	14.38
13	6.62	9.39	7.80	10.85	9.35	12.68	10.89	14.45
14	6.14	9.14	7.71	10.89	9.37	12.74	10.90	14.49
15	6.40	8.93	7.72	10.92	9.34	12.80	10.92	14.54
16	6.50	9.38	7.80	10.95	9.40	12.80	10.96	14.57
17	6.12	9.29	7.80	10.05	9.41	12.85	10.95	14.61
18	6.33	9.00	7.73	10.93	9.42	12.89	10.95	14.63
19	6.42	9.58	7.86	11.02	9.43	12.88	11.00	14.67
20	6.30	9.30	7.80	11.10	9.40	12.92	11.00	14.66
25	6.08	8.96						
30	6.20	9.27						
35	6.17	9.31						
40	6.05	9.15						
45	6.18	9.24						
50	6.04	9.16						

(Adapted with the kind permission of Routledge from Table O, p. 395, of Neave, H. R. and Worthington, P. L. (1988). *Distribution-Free Tests*. London: Routledge and Table 4.3, p. 49, from Neave, H. R. (1978). *Statistics Tables for Mathematicians, Engineers, Economists and the Behavioural and Management Sciences*. London: Routledge.)

Table A14.11: Bonferroni corrections for contrasts

a. Error rate per family, $\alpha = 0.05$, two-tailed probabilities (or $\alpha = 0.025$, one-tailed probabilities), df for error = 1 to 20

df error	Number of contrasts											
	2	3	4	5	6	7	8	9	10	12	15
1	25.452	38.189	50.922	63.656	76.392	89.123	101.859	114.590	127.321	152.793	190.996
2	6.205	7.649	8.860	9.925	10.886	11.769	12.590	13.360	14.089	15.444	17.277
3	4.177	4.857	5.392	5.841	6.232	6.580	6.895	7.185	7.453	7.940	8.575
4	3.495	3.961	4.315	4.604	4.851	5.068	5.261	5.437	5.598	5.885	6.254
5	3.163	3.534	3.810	4.032	4.219	4.382	4.526	4.655	4.773	4.983	5.247
6	2.969	3.287	3.521	3.707	3.863	3.997	4.115	4.221	4.317	4.486	4.698
7	2.841	3.128	3.335	3.499	3.636	3.753	3.855	3.947	4.029	4.174	4.355
8	2.752	3.016	3.206	3.355	3.479	3.584	3.677	3.759	3.833	3.962	4.122
9	2.685	2.933	3.111	3.250	3.364	3.462	3.547	3.622	3.690	3.808	3.954
10	2.634	2.870	3.038	3.169	3.277	3.368	3.448	3.518	3.581	3.691	3.827
11	2.593	2.820	2.981	3.106	3.208	3.295	3.370	3.437	3.497	3.600	3.728
12	2.560	2.779	2.934	3.055	3.153	3.236	3.308	3.371	3.428	3.527	3.649
13	2.533	2.746	2.896	3.012	3.107	3.187	3.256	3.318	3.372	3.467	3.584
14	2.510	2.718	2.864	2.977	3.069	3.146	3.214	3.273	3.326	3.417	3.530
15	2.490	2.694	2.837	2.947	3.036	3.112	3.177	3.235	3.286	3.375	3.484
16	2.473	2.673	2.813	2.921	3.008	3.082	3.146	3.202	3.252	3.339	3.444
17	2.458	2.655	2.793	2.898	2.984	3.056	3.119	3.173	3.222	3.307	3.410
18	2.445	2.639	2.775	2.878	2.963	3.034	3.095	3.149	3.197	3.279	3.380
19	2.433	2.625	2.759	2.861	2.944	3.014	3.074	3.127	3.174	3.255	3.354
20	2.423	2.613	2.744	2.845	2.927	2.996	3.055	3.107	3.153	3.233	3.331

Table A14.11 Bonferroni corrections for contrasts

b. Error rate per family, α = 0.05, two-tailed tests (or α = 0.025, one-tailed tests), df for error = 21 to 120

df error	2	3	4	5	6	7	8	9	10	12	15
					Number of contrasts						
21	2.414	2.601	2.732	2.831	2.912	2.980	3.038	3.090	3.135	3.214	3.310
22	2.405	2.591	2.720	2.819	2.899	2.965	3.023	3.074	3.119	3.196	3.291
23	2.398	2.582	2.710	2.807	2.886	2.952	3.009	3.059	3.104	3.181	3.274
24	2.391	2.574	2.700	2.797	2.875	2.941	2.997	3.046	3.091	3.166	3.258
25	2.385	2.566	2.692	2.787	2.865	2.930	2.986	3.035	3.078	3.153	3.244
26	2.379	2.559	2.684	2.779	2.856	2.920	2.975	3.024	3.067	3.141	3.231
27	2.373	2.552	2.676	2.771	2.847	2.911	2.966	3.014	3.057	3.130	3.219
28	2.368	2.546	2.669	2.763	2.839	2.902	2.957	3.004	3.047	3.120	3.208
29	2.364	2.541	2.663	2.756	2.832	2.894	2.949	2.996	3.038	3.110	3.198
30	2.360	2.536	2.657	2.750	2.825	2.887	2.941	2.988	3.030	3.102	3.189
31	2.356	2.531	2.652	2.744	2.818	2.880	2.934	2.981	3.022	3.094	3.180
32	2.352	2.526	2.647	2.738	2.812	2.874	2.927	2.974	3.015	3.086	3.172
33	2.348	2.522	2.642	2.733	2.807	2.868	2.921	2.967	3.008	3.079	3.164
34	2.345	2.518	2.638	2.728	2.802	2.863	2.915	2.961	3.002	3.072	3.157
35	2.342	2.515	2.633	2.724	2.797	2.857	2.910	2.955	2.996	3.066	3.150
36	2.339	2.511	2.629	2.719	2.792	2.853	2.905	2.950	2.990	3.060	3.144
37	2.336	2.508	2.626	2.715	2.788	2.848	2.900	2.945	2.985	3.054	3.138
38	2.334	2.505	2.622	2.712	2.783	2.844	2.895	2.940	2.980	3.049	3.132
39	2.331	2.502	2.619	2.708	2.780	2.839	2.891	2.936	2.976	3.044	3.127
40	2.329	2.499	2.616	2.704	2.776	2.836	2.887	2.931	2.971	3.039	3.122
45	2.319	2.487	2.602	2.690	2.760	2.819	2.869	2.913	2.952	3.019	3.100
50	2.311	2.477	2.591	2.678	2.747	2.805	2.855	2.898	2.937	3.003	3.083
55	2.304	2.469	2.583	2.668	2.737	2.794	2.844	2.887	2.925	2.990	3.069
60	2.299	2.463	2.575	2.660	2.729	2.785	2.834	2.877	2.915	2.979	3.057
65	2.295	2.458	2.569	2.654	2.721	2.778	2.826	2.869	2.906	2.970	3.048
70	2.291	2.453	2.564	2.648	2.715	2.771	2.820	2.862	2.899	2.962	3.039
75	2.287	2.449	2.559	2.643	2.710	2.766	2.814	2.855	2.892	2.956	3.032
80	2.284	2.445	2.555	2.639	2.705	2.761	2.809	2.850	2.887	2.950	3.026
85	2.282	2.442	2.552	2.635	2.701	2.757	2.804	2.846	2.882	2.945	3.020
90	2.280	2.440	2.549	2.632	2.698	2.753	2.800	2.841	2.878	2.940	3.016
95	2.277	2.437	2.546	2.629	2.695	2.750	2.797	2.838	2.874	2.936	3.011
100	2.276	2.435	2.544	2.626	2.692	2.747	2.793	2.834	2.871	2.933	3.007
105	2.274	2.433	2.541	2.623	2.689	2.744	2.791	2.831	2.868	2.929	3.004
110	2.272	2.431	2.539	2.621	2.687	2.741	2.788	2.829	2.865	2.926	3.001
115	2.271	2.430	2.538	2.619	2.685	2.739	2.786	2.826	2.862	2.924	2.998
120	2.270	2.428	2.536	2.617	2.683	2.737	2.783	2.824	2.860	2.921	2.995

c. Error rate per family, $\alpha = 0.1$, two-tailed tests (or $\alpha = 0.05$, one-tailed tests), df for error = 1 to 30

df error	Number of contrasts											
	2	3	4	5	6	7	8	9	10	12	15
1	12.706	19.081	25.452	31.821	38.189	44.557	50.922	57.290	63.656	76.392	95.489
2	4.303	5.339	6.205	6.965	7.649	8.277	8.860	9.408	9.925	10.886	12.186
3	3.182	3.740	4.177	4.541	4.857	5.138	5.392	5.625	5.841	6.232	6.741
4	2.776	3.186	3.495	3.747	3.961	4.148	4.315	4.466	4.604	4.851	5.167
5	2.571	2.912	3.163	3.365	3.534	3.681	3.810	3.926	4.032	4.219	4.456
6	2.447	2.749	2.969	3.143	3.287	3.412	3.521	3.619	3.707	3.863	4.058
7	2.365	2.642	2.841	2.998	3.128	3.238	3.335	3.422	3.499	3.636	3.806
8	2.306	2.566	2.752	2.896	3.016	3.117	3.206	3.285	3.355	3.479	3.632
9	2.262	2.510	2.685	2.821	2.933	3.028	3.111	3.184	3.250	3.364	3.505
10	2.228	2.466	2.634	2.764	2.870	2.960	3.038	3.107	3.169	3.277	3.409
11	2.201	2.431	2.593	2.718	2.820	2.906	2.981	3.047	3.106	3.208	3.334
12	2.179	2.403	2.560	2.681	2.779	2.863	2.934	2.998	3.055	3.153	3.273
13	2.160	2.380	2.533	2.650	2.746	2.827	2.896	2.957	3.012	3.107	3.223
14	2.145	2.360	2.510	2.624	2.718	2.796	2.864	2.924	2.977	3.069	3.181
15	2.131	2.343	2.490	2.602	2.694	2.770	2.837	2.895	2.947	3.036	3.146
16	2.120	2.328	2.473	2.583	2.673	2.748	2.813	2.870	2.921	3.008	3.115
17	2.110	2.316	2.458	2.567	2.655	2.729	2.793	2.848	2.898	2.984	3.088
18	2.101	2.304	2.445	2.552	2.639	2.712	2.775	2.829	2.878	2.963	3.065
19	2.093	2.294	2.433	2.539	2.625	2.697	2.759	2.813	2.861	2.944	3.045
20	2.086	2.285	2.423	2.528	2.613	2.683	2.744	2.798	2.845	2.927	3.026
21	2.080	2.278	2.414	2.518	2.601	2.671	2.732	2.784	2.831	2.912	3.010
22	2.074	2.270	2.405	2.508	2.591	2.661	2.720	2.772	2.819	2.899	2.995
23	2.069	2.264	2.398	2.500	2.582	2.651	2.710	2.761	2.807	2.886	2.982
24	2.064	2.258	2.391	2.492	2.574	2.642	2.700	2.751	2.797	2.875	2.970
25	2.060	2.252	2.385	2.485	2.566	2.634	2.692	2.742	2.787	2.865	2.959
26	2.056	2.247	2.379	2.479	2.559	2.626	2.684	2.734	2.779	2.856	2.949
27	2.052	2.243	2.373	2.473	2.552	2.619	2.676	2.726	2.771	2.847	2.939
28	2.048	2.238	2.368	2.467	2.546	2.613	2.669	2.719	2.763	2.839	2.930
29	2.045	2.234	2.364	2.462	2.541	2.607	2.663	2.713	2.756	2.832	2.922
30	2.042	2.231	2.360	2.457	2.536	2.601	2.657	2.706	2.750	2.825	2.915

Table A14.11 Bonferroni corrections for contrasts

d. Error rate per family, $\alpha = 0.1$, two-tailed tests (or $\alpha = 0.05$, one-tailed tests), df for error = 31 to 120

df error	2	3	4	5	Number of contrasts 6	7	8	9	10	12	15
31	2.040	2.227	2.356	2.453	2.531	2.596	2.652	2.701	2.744	2.818	2.908
32	2.037	2.224	2.352	2.449	2.526	2.591	2.647	2.695	2.738	2.812	2.902
33	2.035	2.221	2.348	2.445	2.522	2.587	2.642	2.690	2.733	2.807	2.896
34	2.032	2.218	2.345	2.441	2.518	2.583	2.638	2.686	2.728	2.802	2.890
35	2.030	2.215	2.342	2.438	2.515	2.579	2.633	2.681	2.724	2.797	2.885
36	2.028	2.213	2.339	2.434	2.511	2.575	2.629	2.677	2.719	2.792	2.879
37	2.026	2.210	2.336	2.431	2.508	2.571	2.626	2.673	2.715	2.788	2.875
38	2.024	2.208	2.334	2.429	2.505	2.568	2.622	2.670	2.712	2.783	2.870
39	2.023	2.206	2.331	2.426	2.502	2.565	2.619	2.666	2.708	2.780	2.866
40	2.021	2.204	2.329	2.423	2.499	2.562	2.616	2.663	2.704	2.776	2.862
45	2.014	2.195	2.319	2.412	2.487	2.549	2.602	2.648	2.690	2.760	2.845
50	2.009	2.188	2.311	2.403	2.477	2.539	2.591	2.637	2.678	2.747	2.831
55	2.004	2.183	2.304	2.396	2.469	2.530	2.583	2.628	2.668	2.737	2.820
60	2.000	2.178	2.299	2.390	2.463	2.524	2.575	2.620	2.660	2.729	2.811
65	1.997	2.174	2.295	2.385	2.458	2.518	2.569	2.614	2.654	2.721	2.803
70	1.994	2.171	2.291	2.381	2.453	2.513	2.564	2.608	2.648	2.715	2.796
75	1.992	2.168	2.287	2.377	2.449	2.508	2.559	2.604	2.643	2.710	2.791
80	1.990	2.165	2.284	2.374	2.445	2.505	2.555	2.600	2.639	2.705	2.786
85	1.988	2.163	2.282	2.371	2.442	2.501	2.552	2.596	2.635	2.701	2.781
90	1.987	2.161	2.280	2.368	2.440	2.499	2.549	2.593	2.632	2.698	2.777
95	1.985	2.159	2.277	2.366	2.437	2.496	2.546	2.590	2.629	2.695	2.774
100	1.984	2.158	2.276	2.364	2.435	2.494	2.544	2.587	2.626	2.692	2.771
105	1.983	2.156	2.274	2.362	2.433	2.492	2.541	2.585	2.623	2.689	2.768
110	1.982	2.155	2.272	2.361	2.431	2.490	2.539	2.583	2.621	2.687	2.766
115	1.981	2.154	2.271	2.359	2.430	2.488	2.538	2.581	2.619	2.685	2.763
120	1.980	2.153	2.270	2.358	2.428	2.486	2.536	2.579	2.617	2.683	2.761

Table A14.12: Dunnett's *t*-test of contrasts

a. α = 0.05, two-tailed tests

df error	\multicolumn{13}{c}{number of means (including the control)}

df error	3	4	5	6	7	8	9	10	11	12	13	16	21
5	3.03	3.29	3.48	3.62	3.73	3.82	3.90	3.97	4.03	4.09	4.14	4.26	4.42
6	2.86	3.10	3.26	3.39	3.49	3.57	3.64	3.71	3.76	3.81	3.86	3.97	4.11
7	2.75	2.97	3.12	3.24	3.33	3.41	3.47	3.53	3.58	3.63	3.67	3.78	3.91
8	2.67	2.88	3.02	3.13	3.22	3.29	3.35	3.41	3.46	3.50	3.54	3.64	3.76
9	2.61	2.81	2.95	3.05	3.14	3.20	3.26	3.32	3.36	3.40	3.44	3.53	3.65
10	2.57	2.76	2.89	2.99	3.07	3.14	3.19	3.24	3.29	3.33	3.36	3.45	3.57
11	2.53	2.72	2.84	2.94	3.02	3.08	3.14	3.19	3.23	3.27	3.30	3.39	3.50
12	2.50	2.68	2.81	2.90	2.98	3.04	3.09	3.14	3.18	3.22	3.25	3.34	3.45
13	2.48	2.65	2.78	2.87	2.94	3.00	3.06	3.10	3.14	3.18	3.21	3.29	3.40
14	2.46	2.63	2.75	2.84	2.91	2.97	3.02	3.07	3.11	3.14	3.18	3.26	3.36
15	2.44	2.61	2.73	2.82	2.89	2.95	3.00	3.04	3.08	3.12	3.15	3.23	3.33
16	2.42	2.59	2.71	2.80	2.87	2.92	2.97	3.02	3.06	3.09	3.12	3.20	3.30
17	2.41	2.58	2.69	2.78	2.85	2.90	2.95	3.00	3.03	3.07	3.10	3.18	3.27
18	2.40	2.56	2.68	2.76	2.83	2.89	2.94	2.98	3.01	3.05	3.08	3.16	3.25
19	2.39	2.55	2.66	2.75	2.81	2.87	2.92	2.96	3.00	3.03	3.06	3.14	3.23
20	2.38	2.54	2.65	2.73	2.80	2.86	2.90	2.95	2.98	3.02	3.05	3.12	3.22
24	2.35	2.51	2.61	2.70	2.76	2.81	2.86	2.90	2.94	2.97	3.00	3.07	3.16
30	2.32	2.47	2.58	2.66	2.72	2.77	2.82	2.86	2.89	2.92	2.95	3.02	3.11
40	2.29	2.44	2.54	2.62	2.68	2.73	2.77	2.81	2.85	2.87	2.90	2.97	3.06
60	2.27	2.41	2.51	2.58	2.64	2.69	2.73	2.77	2.80	2.83	2.86	2.92	3.00
120	2.24	2.38	2.47	2.55	2.60	2.65	2.69	2.73	2.76	2.79	2.81	2.87	2.95

b. α = 0.05, one-tailed tests

df error	\multicolumn{8}{c}{number of means (including the control)}

df error	3	4	5	6	7	8	9	10
5	2.44	2.68	2.85	2.98	3.08	3.16	3.24	3.30
6	2.34	2.56	2.71	2.83	2.92	3.00	3.07	3.12
7	2.27	2.48	2.62	2.73	2.82	2.89	2.95	3.01
8	2.22	2.42	2.55	2.66	2.74	2.81	2.87	2.92
9	2.18	2.37	2.50	2.60	2.68	2.75	2.81	2.86
10	2.15	2.34	2.47	2.56	2.64	2.70	2.76	2.81
11	2.13	2.31	2.44	2.53	2.60	2.67	2.72	2.77
12	2.11	2.29	2.41	2.50	2.58	2.64	2.69	2.74
13	2.09	2.27	2.39	2.48	2.55	2.61	2.66	2.71
14	2.08	2.25	2.37	2.46	2.53	2.59	2.64	2.69
15	2.07	2.24	2.36	2.44	2.51	2.57	2.62	2.67
16	2.06	2.23	2.34	2.43	2.50	2.56	2.61	2.65
17	2.05	2.22	2.33	2.42	2.49	2.54	2.59	2.64
18	2.04	2.21	2.32	2.41	2.48	2.53	2.58	2.62
19	2.03	2.20	2.31	2.40	2.47	2.52	2.57	2.61
20	2.03	2.19	2.30	2.39	2.46	2.51	2.56	2.60
24	2.01	2.17	2.28	2.36	2.43	2.48	2.53	2.57
30	1.99	2.15	2.25	2.33	2.40	2.45	2.50	2.54
40	1.97	2.13	2.23	2.31	2.37	2.42	2.47	2.51
60	1.95	2.10	2.21	2.28	2.35	2.39	2.44	2.48
120	1.93	2.08	2.18	2.26	2.32	2.37	2.41	2.45

(Adapted with the kind permission of the Biometrics Society from Table II of Dunnett, C. W. (1964). New Tables for multiple comparisons with a control. *Biometrics*, 20, 482–491.)

Table A14.13: The distribution of the Studentised range statistic q

a. Error rate per family $\alpha = 0.05$, two-tailed tests

df error	\multicolumn{11}{c}{Number of means to be contrasted}
	3	4	5	6	7	8	9	10	11	12	15
1	26.98	32.82	37.08	40.41	43.12	45.40	47.36	49.07	50.59	51.96	55.36
2	8.33	9.80	10.88	11.74	12.44	13.03	13.54	13.99	14.39	14.75	15.65
3	5.91	6.82	7.50	8.04	8.48	8.85	9.18	9.46	9.72	9.95	10.52
4	5.04	5.76	6.29	6.71	7.05	7.35	7.60	7.83	8.03	8.21	8.66
5	4.60	5.22	5.67	6.03	6.33	6.58	6.80	6.99	7.17	7.32	7.72
6	4.34	4.90	5.30	5.63	5.90	6.12	6.32	6.49	6.65	6.79	7.14
7	4.16	4.68	5.06	5.36	5.61	5.82	6.00	6.16	6.30	6.43	6.76
8	4.04	4.53	4.89	5.17	5.40	5.60	5.77	5.92	6.05	6.18	6.48
9	3.95	4.41	4.76	5.02	5.24	5.43	5.59	5.74	5.87	5.98	6.28
10	3.88	4.33	4.65	4.91	5.12	5.30	5.46	5.60	5.72	5.83	6.11
11	3.82	4.26	4.57	4.82	5.03	5.20	5.35	5.49	5.61	5.71	5.98
12	3.77	4.20	4.51	4.75	4.95	5.12	5.27	5.39	5.51	5.61	5.88
13	3.73	4.15	4.45	4.69	4.88	5.05	5.19	5.32	5.43	5.53	5.79
14	3.70	4.11	4.41	4.64	4.83	4.99	5.13	5.25	5.36	5.46	5.71
15	3.67	4.08	4.37	4.59	4.78	4.94	5.08	5.20	5.31	5.40	5.65
16	3.65	4.05	4.33	4.56	4.74	4.90	5.03	5.15	5.26	5.35	5.59
17	3.63	4.02	4.30	4.52	4.70	4.86	4.99	5.11	5.21	5.31	5.54
18	3.61	4.00	4.28	4.49	4.67	4.82	4.96	5.07	5.17	5.27	5.50
19	3.59	3.98	4.25	4.47	4.65	4.79	4.92	5.04	5.14	5.23	5.46
20	3.58	3.96	4.23	4.45	4.62	4.77	4.90	5.01	5.11	5.20	5.43
24	3.53	3.90	4.17	4.37	4.54	4.68	4.81	4.92	5.01	5.10	5.32
30	3.49	3.85	4.10	4.30	4.46	4.60	4.72	4.82	4.92	5.00	5.21
40	3.44	3.79	4.04	4.23	4.39	4.52	4.63	4.73	4.82	4.90	5.11
60	3.40	3.74	3.98	4.16	4.31	4.44	4.55	4.65	4.73	4.81	5.00
120	3.36	3.68	3.92	4.10	4.24	4.36	4.47	4.56	4.64	4.71	4.90

(Adapted with the kind permission of the authors and Edward Arnold (Publishers) Ltd from Pearson, E. S. and Hartley, H. O. (1970). *Biometrika Tables for Statisticians* (3rd Edn) London: Charles Griffin & Co Ltd.)

b. Error rate per family $\alpha = 0.01$, two-tailed tests

df error	Number of means to be contrasted											
	3	4	5	6	7	8	9	10	11	12	15
1	135.00	164.30	185.60	202.20	215.80	227.20	237.00	245.60	253.20	260.00	277.00
2	19.02	22.29	24.72	26.63	28.20	29.53	30.68	31.69	32.59	33.40	35.43
3	10.62	12.17	13.33	14.24	15.00	15.64	16.20	16.69	17.13	17.53	18.52
4	8.12	9.17	9.96	10.58	11.10	11.55	11.93	12.27	12.57	12.84	13.53
5	6.98	7.80	8.42	8.91	9.32	9.67	9.97	10.24	10.48	10.70	11.24
6	6.33	7.03	7.56	7.97	8.32	8.61	8.87	9.10	9.30	9.48	9.95
7	5.92	6.54	7.01	7.37	7.68	7.94	8.17	8.37	8.55	8.71	9.12
8	5.64	6.20	6.62	6.96	7.24	7.47	7.68	7.86	8.03	8.18	8.55
9	5.43	5.96	6.35	6.66	6.91	7.13	7.33	7.49	7.65	7.78	8.13
10	5.27	5.77	6.14	6.43	6.67	6.87	7.05	7.21	7.36	7.49	7.81
11	5.15	5.62	5.97	6.25	6.48	6.67	6.84	6.99	7.13	7.25	7.56
12	5.05	5.50	5.84	6.10	6.32	6.51	6.67	6.81	6.94	7.06	7.36
13	4.96	5.40	5.73	5.98	6.19	6.37	6.53	6.67	6.79	6.90	7.19
14	4.89	5.32	5.63	5.88	6.08	6.26	6.41	6.54	6.66	6.77	7.05
15	4.84	5.25	5.56	5.80	5.99	6.16	6.31	6.44	6.55	6.66	6.93
16	4.79	5.19	5.49	5.72	5.92	6.08	6.22	6.35	6.46	6.56	6.82
17	4.74	5.14	5.43	5.66	5.85	6.01	6.15	6.27	6.38	6.48	6.73
18	4.70	5.09	5.38	5.60	5.79	5.94	6.08	6.20	6.31	6.41	6.65
19	4.67	5.05	5.33	5.55	5.73	5.89	6.02	6.14	6.25	6.34	6.58
20	4.64	5.02	5.29	5.51	5.69	5.84	5.97	6.09	6.19	6.28	6.52
24	4.55	4.91	5.17	5.37	5.54	5.69	5.81	5.92	6.02	6.11	6.33
30	4.45	4.80	5.05	5.24	5.40	5.54	5.65	5.76	5.85	5.93	6.14
40	4.37	4.70	4.93	5.11	5.26	5.39	5.50	5.60	5.69	5.76	5.96
60	4.28	4.59	4.82	4.99	5.13	5.25	5.36	5.45	5.53	5.60	5.78
120	4.20	4.50	4.71	4.87	5.01	5.12	5.21	5.30	5.37	5.44	5.61

(Adapted with the kind permission of the authors and Edward Arnold (Publishers) Ltd from Pearson, E. S. and Hartley, H. O. (1970). *Biometrika Tables for Statisticians* (3rd Edn) London: Charles Griffin & Co Ltd.)

Table A14.14: The probabilities of the distribution of *r* (Pearson's Product Moment Correlation Coefficient)

The probability of an *r*-value can also be found by converting *r* to a *t*-value and using the *t*-tables (Table A14.2).
To convert *r* to *t* use:

$$t = \frac{r \times \sqrt{n-2}}{\sqrt{1-r^2}}$$

where *n* is the number of pairs of scores in the correlation.

a. df = 1 to 20

					One-tailed probabilities					
	0.4	0.3	0.2	0.1	0.05	0.025	0.01	0.005	0.001	0.0005
					Two-tailed probabilities					
df = *n*−2	0.8	0.6	0.4	0.2	0.1	0.05	0.02	0.01	0.002	0.001
1	0.3090	0.5878	0.8090	0.9511	0.9877	0.9969	0.9995	0.9999	1.0000	1.0000
2	0.2000	0.4000	0.6000	0.8000	0.9000	0.9500	0.9800	0.9900	0.9980	0.9990
3	0.1577	0.3197	0.4919	0.6870	0.8054	0.8783	0.9343	0.9587	0.9859	0.9911
4	0.1341	0.2735	0.4257	0.6084	0.7293	0.8114	0.8822	0.9172	0.9633	0.9741
5	0.1186	0.2427	0.3803	0.5509	0.6694	0.7545	0.8329	0.8745	0.9350	0.9509
6	0.1075	0.2204	0.3468	0.5067	0.6215	0.7067	0.7887	0.8343	0.9049	0.9249
7	0.0990	0.2032	0.3208	0.4716	0.5822	0.6664	0.7498	0.7977	0.8751	0.8983
8	0.0922	0.1895	0.2998	0.4428	0.5494	0.6319	0.7155	0.7646	0.8467	0.8721
9	0.0867	0.1783	0.2825	0.4187	0.5214	0.6021	0.6851	0.7348	0.8199	0.8470
10	0.0820	0.1688	0.2678	0.3981	0.4973	0.5760	0.6581	0.7079	0.7950	0.8233
11	0.0780	0.1607	0.2552	0.3802	0.4762	0.5529	0.6339	0.6835	0.7717	0.8010
12	0.0746	0.1536	0.2443	0.3646	0.4575	0.5324	0.6120	0.6614	0.7501	0.7800
13	0.0715	0.1474	0.2346	0.3507	0.4409	0.5140	0.5923	0.6411	0.7301	0.7604
14	0.0688	0.1419	0.2260	0.3383	0.4259	0.4973	0.5742	0.6226	0.7114	0.7419
15	0.0664	0.1370	0.2183	0.3271	0.4124	0.4821	0.5577	0.6055	0.6940	0.7247
16	0.0643	0.1326	0.2113	0.3170	0.4000	0.4683	0.5425	0.5897	0.6777	0.7084
17	0.0623	0.1285	0.2049	0.3077	0.3887	0.4555	0.5285	0.5751	0.6624	0.6932
18	0.0605	0.1248	0.1991	0.2992	0.3783	0.4438	0.5155	0.5614	0.6481	0.6788
19	0.0588	0.1214	0.1938	0.2914	0.3687	0.4329	0.5034	0.5487	0.6346	0.6652
20	0.0573	0.1183	0.1888	0.2841	0.3598	0.4227	0.4921	0.5368	0.6219	0.6524

b. df = 21 to 120

df = $n-2$	One-tailed probabilities									
	0.4	0.3	0.2	0.1	0.05	0.025	0.01	0.005	0.001	0.0005
	Two-tailed probabilities									
	0.8	0.6	0.4	0.2	0.1	0.05	0.02	0.01	0.002	0.001
21	0.0559	0.1154	0.1843	0.2774	0.3515	0.4132	0.4815	0.5256	0.6099	0.6402
22	0.0546	0.1127	0.1800	0.2711	0.3438	0.4044	0.4716	0.5151	0.5986	0.6287
23	0.0534	0.1102	0.1760	0.2653	0.3365	0.3961	0.4622	0.5052	0.5879	0.6178
24	0.0522	0.1078	0.1723	0.2598	0.3297	0.3882	0.4534	0.4958	0.5776	0.6074
25	0.0511	0.1056	0.1688	0.2546	0.3233	0.3809	0.4451	0.4869	0.5679	0.5974
26	0.0501	0.1036	0.1655	0.2497	0.3172	0.3739	0.4372	0.4785	0.5587	0.5880
27	0.0492	0.1016	0.1624	0.2451	0.3115	0.3673	0.4297	0.4705	0.5499	0.5789
28	0.0483	0.0997	0.1594	0.2407	0.3061	0.3610	0.4226	0.4629	0.5415	0.5703
29	0.0474	0.0980	0.1567	0.2366	0.3009	0.3550	0.4158	0.4556	0.5334	0.5621
30	0.0466	0.0963	0.1540	0.2327	0.2960	0.3494	0.4093	0.4487	0.5257	0.5541
31	0.0458	0.0947	0.1515	0.2289	0.2913	0.3440	0.4032	0.4421	0.5184	0.5465
32	0.0451	0.0932	0.1491	0.2254	0.2869	0.3388	0.3972	0.4357	0.5113	0.5392
33	0.0444	0.0918	0.1468	0.2220	0.2826	0.3338	0.3916	0.4296	0.5045	0.5322
34	0.0437	0.0904	0.1446	0.2187	0.2785	0.3291	0.3862	0.4238	0.4979	0.5254
35	0.0431	0.0891	0.1425	0.2156	0.2746	0.3246	0.3810	0.4182	0.4916	0.5189
36	0.0425	0.0878	0.1405	0.2126	0.2709	0.3202	0.3760	0.4128	0.4856	0.5126
37	0.0419	0.0866	0.1386	0.2097	0.2673	0.3160	0.3712	0.4076	0.4797	0.5066
38	0.0414	0.0855	0.1368	0.2070	0.2638	0.3120	0.3665	0.4026	0.4741	0.5007
39	0.0408	0.0844	0.1350	0.2043	0.2605	0.3081	0.3621	0.3978	0.4686	0.4950
40	0.0403	0.0833	0.1333	0.2018	0.2573	0.3044	0.3578	0.3932	0.4634	0.4896
50	0.0360	0.0744	0.1192	0.1806	0.2306	0.2732	0.3218	0.3542	0.4188	0.4432
60	0.0328	0.0679	0.1088	0.1650	0.2108	0.2500	0.2948	0.3248	0.3850	0.4079
70	0.0304	0.0628	0.1007	0.1528	0.1954	0.2319	0.2737	0.3017	0.3583	0.3798
80	0.0284	0.0588	0.0942	0.1430	0.1829	0.2172	0.2565	0.2830	0.3364	0.3568
90	0.0268	0.0554	0.0888	0.1348	0.1726	0.2050	0.2422	0.2673	0.3181	0.3375
100	0.0254	0.0525	0.0842	0.1279	0.1638	0.1946	0.2301	0.2540	0.3025	0.3211
110	0.0242	0.0501	0.0803	0.1220	0.1562	0.1857	0.2196	0.2425	0.2890	0.3068
120	0.0232	0.0479	0.0769	0.1168	0.1496	0.1779	0.2104	0.2324	0.2771	0.2943

Table A14.15: The critical values of Spearman's rho

When the sample size is greater than 100 use either the t-approximation Eqn A10.1 or the z-approximation Eqn A10.2 in Appendix X.

a. n = 4 to 40

	one-tailed probabilities								
	0.25	0.10	0.05	0.025	0.01	0.005	0.0025	0.001	0.0005
	two-tailed probabilities								
n	0.50	0.20	0.10	0.05	0.02	0.01	0.005	0.002	0.001
4	0.600	1.000	1.000						
5	0.500	0.800	0.900	1.000	1.000				
6	0.371	0.657	0.829	0.886	0.943	1.000	1.000		
7	0.321	0.571	0.714	0.786	0.893	0.929	0.964	1.000	1.000
8	0.310	0.524	0.643	0.738	0.833	0.881	0.905	0.952	0.976
9	0.267	0.483	0.600	0.700	0.783	0.833	0.867	0.917	0.933
10	0.248	0.455	0.564	0.648	0.745	0.794	0.830	0.879	0.903
11	0.236	0.427	0.536	0.618	0.709	0.755	0.800	0.845	0.873
12	0.224	0.406	0.503	0.587	0.671	0.727	0.776	0.825	0.860
13	0.209	0.385	0.484	0.560	0.648	0.703	0.747	0.802	0.835
14	0.200	0.367	0.464	0.538	0.622	0.675	0.723	0.776	0.811
15	0.189	0.354	0.443	0.521	0.604	0.654	0.700	0.754	0.786
16	0.182	0.341	0.429	0.503	0.582	0.635	0.679	0.732	0.765
17	0.176	0.328	0.414	0.485	0.566	0.615	0.662	0.713	0.748
18	0.170	0.317	0.401	0.472	0.550	0.600	0.643	0.695	0.728
19	0.165	0.309	0.391	0.460	0.535	0.584	0.628	0.677	0.712
20	0.161	0.299	0.380	0.447	0.520	0.570	0.612	0.662	0.696
21	0.156	0.292	0.370	0.435	0.508	0.556	0.599	0.648	0.681
22	0.152	0.284	0.361	0.425	0.496	0.544	0.586	0.634	0.667
23	0.148	0.278	0.353	0.415	0.486	0.532	0.573	0.622	0.654
24	0.144	0.271	0.344	0.406	0.476	0.521	0.562	0.610	0.642
25	0.142	0.265	0.337	0.398	0.466	0.511	0.551	0.598	0.630
26	0.138	0.259	0.331	0.390	0.457	0.501	0.541	0.587	0.619
27	0.136	0.255	0.324	0.382	0.448	0.491	0.531	0.577	0.608
28	0.133	0.250	0.317	0.375	0.440	0.483	0.522	0.567	0.598
29	0.130	0.245	0.312	0.368	0.433	0.475	0.513	0.558	0.589
30	0.128	0.240	0.306	0.362	0.425	0.467	0.504	0.549	0.580
31	0.126	0.236	0.301	0.356	0.418	0.459	0.496	0.541	0.571
32	0.124	0.232	0.296	0.350	0.412	0.452	0.489	0.533	0.563
33	0.121	0.229	0.291	0.345	0.405	0.446	0.482	0.525	0.554
34	0.120	0.225	0.287	0.340	0.399	0.439	0.475	0.517	0.547
35	0.118	0.222	0.283	0.335	0.394	0.433	0.468	0.510	0.539
36	0.116	0.219	0.279	0.330	0.388	0.427	0.462	0.504	0.533
37	0.114	0.216	0.275	0.325	0.383	0.421	0.456	0.497	0.526
38	0.113	0.212	0.271	0.321	0.378	0.415	0.450	0.491	0.519
39	0.111	0.210	0.267	0.317	0.373	0.410	0.444	0.485	0.513
40	0.110	0.207	0.264	0.313	0.368	0.405	0.439	0.479	0.507

(Adapted from Table I of Zar, J. H. (1972) Significance testing of the Spearman rank correlation coefficient. *Journal of the American Statistical Association*. 76, 578–580. Reprinted with permission from the Journal of the American Statistical Association. Copyright 1972 by the American Statistical Association. All rights reserved.)

b. $n = 41$ to 100

	0.25	0.10	0.05	one-tailed probabilities 0.025	0.01	0.005	0.0025	0.001	0.0005
n	0.50	0.20	0.10	two-tailed probabilities 0.05	0.02	0.01	0.005	0.002	0.001
41	0.108	0.204	0.261	0.309	0.364	0.400	0.433	0.473	0.501
42	0.107	0.202	0.257	0.305	0.359	0.395	0.428	0.468	0.495
43	0.105	0.199	0.254	0.301	0.355	0.391	0.423	0.463	0.490
44	0.104	0.197	0.251	0.298	0.351	0.386	0.419	0.458	0.484
45	0.103	0.194	0.248	0.294	0.347	0.382	0.414	0.453	0.479
46	0.102	0.192	0.246	0.291	0.343	0.378	0.410	0.448	0.474
47	0.101	0.190	0.243	0.288	0.340	0.374	0.405	0.443	0.469
48	0.100	0.188	0.240	0.285	0.336	0.370	0.401	0.439	0.465
49	0.098	0.186	0.238	0.282	0.333	0.366	0.397	0.434	0.460
50	0.097	0.184	0.235	0.279	0.329	0.363	0.393	0.430	0.456
52	0.095	0.180	0.231	0.274	0.323	0.356	0.386	0.422	0.447
54	0.094	0.177	0.226	0.268	0.317	0.349	0.379	0.414	0.439
56	0.092	0.174	0.222	0.264	0.311	0.343	0.372	0.407	0.432
58	0.090	0.171	0.218	0.259	0.306	0.337	0.366	0.400	0.424
60	0.089	0.168	0.214	0.255	0.300	0.331	0.360	0.394	0.418
62	0.087	0.165	0.211	0.250	0.296	0.326	0.354	0.388	0.411
64	0.086	0.162	0.207	0.246	0.291	0.321	0.348	0.382	0.405
66	0.084	0.160	0.204	0.243	0.287	0.316	0.343	0.376	0.399
68	0.083	0.157	0.201	0.239	0.282	0.311	0.338	0.370	0.393
70	0.082	0.155	0.198	0.235	0.278	0.307	0.333	0.365	0.388
72	0.081	0.153	0.195	0.232	0.274	0.303	0.329	0.360	0.382
74	0.080	0.151	0.193	0.229	0.271	0.299	0.324	0.355	0.377
76	0.078	0.149	0.190	0.226	0.267	0.295	0.320	0.351	0.372
78	0.077	0.147	0.188	0.223	0.264	0.291	0.316	0.346	0.368
80	0.076	0.145	0.185	0.220	0.260	0.287	0.312	0.342	0.363
82	0.075	0.143	0.183	0.217	0.257	0.284	0.308	0.338	0.359
84	0.074	0.141	0.181	0.215	0.254	0.280	0.305	0.334	0.355
86	0.074	0.139	0.179	0.212	0.251	0.277	0.301	0.330	0.351
88	0.073	0.138	0.176	0.210	0.248	0.274	0.298	0.327	0.347
90	0.072	0.136	0.174	0.207	0.245	0.271	0.294	0.323	0.343
92	0.071	0.135	0.173	0.205	0.243	0.268	0.291	0.319	0.339
94	0.070	0.133	0.171	0.203	0.240	0.265	0.288	0.316	0.336
96	0.070	0.132	0.169	0.201	0.238	0.262	0.285	0.313	0.332
98	0.069	0.130	0.167	0.199	0.235	0.260	0.282	0.310	0.329
100	0.068	0.129	0.165	0.197	0.233	0.257	0.279	0.307	0.326

Table A14.16: The critical values of Kendall's tau

If the sample is greater than 10 use the z-approximation Eqn A10.3 in Appendix X.

Critical values of α: one-tailed probabilities

n	0.1	0.05	0.025	0.01	0.005	0.001
4	1.0000	1.0000				
5	0.8000	0.8000	1.0000	1.0000		
6	0.6000	0.7333	0.8667	0.8667	1.0000	
7	0.5238	0.6190	0.7143	0.8095	0.9048	1.0000
8	0.4286	0.5714	0.6429	0.7143	0.7857	0.8571
9	0.3889	0.5000	0.5556	0.6667	0.7222	0.8333
10	0.3778	0.4667	0.5111	0.6000	0.6444	0.7778

Critical values of α: two-tailed probabilities

n	0.1	0.05	0.025	0.01	0.005	0.001
4	1.0000					
5	0.8000	1.0000	1.0000			
6	0.7333	0.8667	0.8667	1.0000	1.0000	
7	0.6190	0.7143	0.8095	0.9048	0.9048	1.0000
8	0.5714	0.6429	0.7143	0.7857	0.8571	0.9286
9	0.5000	0.5556	0.6111	0.7222	0.7778	0.8333
10	0.4667	0.5111	0.6000	0.6444	0.6889	0.7778

(Adapted with the kind permission of the author and Edward Arnold (Publishers) Ltd from Kendall, M. G. (1970). *Rank Correlation Methods* (4th Edn.). London: Charles Griffin & Co. Ltd.)

Table A14.17: The probabilities of Kendall's tau as a partial correlation $\tau_{xy.z}$

The table shows the probabilities of tau for sample sizes up to 50. Maghsoodloo and Pallos (1981) note that beyond this sample size there is a normal approximation which can be used to find out the probability of Kendall's partial correlation coefficient:

$$z = \frac{\tau_{xy.z}}{\sqrt{\left(-0.0008855 + \dfrac{0.5179}{n} + \dfrac{10.344}{n^3}\right)}}$$

where n is the sample size.

	two-tailed test					
	0.2	0.1	0.05	0.02	0.01	0.002
	one-tailed test					
n	0.1	0.05	0.025	0.01	0.005	0.001
4	0.707	0.707	1.000			
5	0.535	0.667	0.802	0.817	1.000	
6	0.473	0.600	0.667	0.764	0.866	1.000
7	0.421	0.527	0.617	0.712	0.761	0.901
8	0.382	0.484	0.565	0.648	0.713	0.807
9	0.347	0.443	0.515	0.602	0.660	0.757
10	0.325	0.413	0.480	0.562	0.614	0.718
11	0.305	0.387	0.453	0.530	0.581	0.677
12	0.288	0.465	0.430	0.505	0.548	0.643
13	0.273	0.347	0.410	0.481	0.527	0.616
14	0.260	0.331	0.391	0.458	0.503	0.590
15	0.251	0.319	0.377	0.442	0.485	0.570
16	0.240	0.305	0.361	0.423	0.466	0.549
17	0.231	0.294	0.348	0.410	0.450	0.532
18	0.222	0.284	0.336	0.395	0.434	0.514
19	0.215	0.275	0.326	0.382	0.421	0.498
20	0.210	0.268	0.318	0.374	0.412	0.488
25	0.185	0.236	0.279	0.329	0.363	0.430
30	0.167	0.213	0.253	0.298	0.329	0.390
35	0.153	0.196	0.232	0.274	0.303	0.361
40	0.142	0.182	0.216	0.255	0.282	0.335
45	0.133	0.171	0.203	0.240	0.265	0.316
50	0.126	0.161	0.192	0.225	0.250	0.298

(Adapted with the kind permission of Gordon and Breach Publishers from Tables II and V of Maghsoodloo, S. (1975). Estimates of the quantiles of Kendall's partial rank correlation coefficient. *Journal of Statistical Computing and Simulation 4*, 155–164, and Tables I and II of Maghsoodloo, S. and Pallos, L. L. (1981). Asymptotic behavior of Kendall's partial rank correlation coefficient and additional quantile estimates. *Journal of Statistical Computing and Simulation.* 13, 41–48.)

Table A14.18: Kendall's coefficient of concordance (W)

k (number of items to be ranked) = 3 to 7, n (number of judges) = 3 to 20.

When k is more than 7 find the probability from the chi-squared distribution for:

$$\chi^2_{(k-1)} = n \times (k-1) \times W$$

	$k = 3$ probability	
n	0.05	0.01
8	0.3758	0.5219
9	0.3333	0.4685
10	0.3000	0.4255
12	0.2497	0.3594
14	0.2138	0.3110
15	0.1996	0.2911
16	0.1871	0.2738
18	0.1662	0.2448
20	0.1496	0.2213

	$k = 4$ probability		$k = 5$ probability		$k = 6$ probability		$k = 7$ probability	
n	0.05	0.01	0.05	0.01	0.05	0.01	0.05	0.01
3	–	–	0.7156	0.8400	0.6597	0.7797	0.6242	0.7365
4	0.6188	0.7675	0.5525	0.6831	0.5118	0.6293	0.4844	0.5915
5	0.5008	0.6440	0.4492	0.5712	0.4169	0.5243	0.3946	0.4911
6	0.4206	0.5528	0.3781	0.4892	0.3514	0.4483	0.3325	0.4192
8	0.3178	0.4294	0.2870	0.3792	0.2670	0.3467	0.2528	0.3236
10	0.2556	0.3506	0.2312	0.3091	0.2153	0.2823	0.2039	0.2632
15	0.1715	0.2398	0.1555	0.2112	0.1449	0.1926	0.1373	0.1793
20	0.1290	0.1821	0.1171	0.1603	0.1092	0.1460	0.1035	0.1359

(Adapted with the kind permission of the author and Edward Arnold (Publishers) from Kendall, M. G. (1970). *Rank Correlation Methods* (4th Edn.). London: Charles Griffin & Co. Ltd.)

Table A14.19: The critical values of the Kolmogorov–Smirnov statistic (D_n)

To be statistically significant, D_n has to be as large as or larger than the critical value shown in the table. For example, with a sample size of 20, to be significant at $\alpha = 0.05$, D_n has to be at least 0.294.

n	0.20	0.15	0.10	0.05
1	0.900	0.925	0.950	0.975
2	0.684	0.726	0.776	0.842
3	0.565	0.597	0.642	0.708
4	0.494	0.525	0.564	0.624
5	0.446	0.474	0.510	0.565
6	0.410	0.436	0.470	0.521
7	0.381	0.405	0.438	0.486
8	0.358	0.381	0.411	0.457
9	0.339	0.360	0.388	0.432
10	0.322	0.342	0.368	0.410
11	0.307	0.326	0.352	0.391
12	0.295	0.313	0.338	0.375
13	0.284	0.302	0.325	0.361
14	0.274	0.292	0.314	0.349
15	0.266	0.283	0.304	0.338
16	0.258	0.274	0.295	0.328
17	0.250	0.266	0.286	0.318
18	0.244	0.259	0.278	0.309
19	0.237	0.252	0.272	0.301
20	0.231	0.246	0.264	0.294
25	0.210	0.220	0.240	0.270
30	0.190	0.200	0.220	0.240
35	0.180	0.190	0.210	0.230
over 35	$\dfrac{1.07}{\sqrt{n}}$	$\dfrac{1.14}{\sqrt{n}}$	$\dfrac{1.22}{\sqrt{n}}$	$\dfrac{1.36}{\sqrt{n}}$

(Adapted from Table 1 of Massey, F. J. (1951) The Kolmogorov–Smirnov test for goodness of fit. *Journal of the American Statistical Association.* 46, 68–78.)

APPENDIX XV: POWER TABLES

Adjusted sample size for power tables when using unequal samples   582
Interpolation   583
The effect size of a within-subjects t-test   584
Explanation of the tables for ANOVA and multiple regression   585
Multifactorial between-subjects ANOVA   585
The power of within-subjects ANOVA   587
The power of mixed ANOVA   587
One-group z-test   588
Between-subjects t-test   590
Within-subjects t-test or one-group t-test   592
χ^2 594
F-ratio in Analysis of Variance   603
Pearson's Product Moment Correlation Coefficient r   612
Multiple regression   614

Introduction

I have attempted to simplify the process of calculating power, while at the same time not overbalancing the book with power tables. This has involved a number of compromises. Firstly, I have only given tables for $\alpha = 0.05$. Secondly, for tests such as χ^2, ANOVA and multiple regression I have given tables for a restricted set of degrees of freedom. Thirdly, in the case of ANOVA I have used η^2 as the measure of effect size. In addition to these points, some explanation is necessary on how to use the tables for within-subjects designs, for between-subjects designs with unequal sample sizes, for between-subjects ANOVA with more than one IV, for mixed designs and for working out power for sample sizes and df that are not in the tables. Throughout the tables * denotes that the power of the test is over 0.995.

Adjusted sample size for power tables when using unequal samples

Between-subjects t-tests

When unequal-sized samples are used in a between-subjects *t*-test, power is reduced relative to what it would be for a design with equal-sized samples. To read the standard power tables it is necessary to calculate an adjusted sample size n_h, which is the *harmonic mean* of the two samples' sizes.

$$n_h = \frac{2 \times n_1 \times n_2}{n_1 + n_2}$$

where n_1 is the size of one sample
n_2 is the size of the other sample

Thus, if $n_1 = 10$ and $n_2 = 30$:

$$n_h = \frac{2 \times 10 \times 30}{10 + 30}$$

$$= 15$$

In this case, the power of the test will be the same as that for a design with 15 people in each group, despite having 40 participants altogether.

Between-subjects ANOVA

In this case, use the arithmetic mean. Thus if there were three groups with 15, 20 and 30 in each, then the sample size per group should be treated as:

$$n = \frac{15 + 20 + 30}{3} = 21.67, \text{ or } 21 \text{ to the next lowest person}$$

Interpolation

Using the technique of linear interpolation, described in Appendix XIV for probability tables, approximate power values and sample sizes can be found where these are not contained in the tables given in the present appendix. Cohen (1988) gives a much wider range of tabled values.

Finding power for an intermediate sample size
Use the following equation:

$$\text{power} = \text{lower power} + (\text{upper power} - \text{lower power}) \times \left(\frac{\text{actual } n - \text{lower } n}{\text{upper } n - \text{lower } n} \right)$$

where upper and lower powers and sample sizes are those shown in the tables.

Imagine we were conducting a one-tailed, between-subjects t-test with $\alpha = 0.05$, we had a sample of 22 people in each group and we found an effect size (d) of 0.5.

$$\text{power} = 0.46 + (0.54 - 0.46) \times \left(\frac{22 - 20}{25 - 20}\right)$$

$$= 0.492$$

Finding power for an intermediate effect size
Use the following equation:

$$\text{power} = \text{lower power} + (\text{upper power} - \text{lower power})$$

$$\times \left(\frac{\text{actual ES} - \text{lower ES}}{\text{upper ES} - \text{lower ES}}\right)$$

If we conducted a one-tailed, between-subjects t-test on data that we had found had an effect size of 0.56, with a sample of 20 participants in each group, using $\alpha = 0.05$, then:

$$\text{power} = 0.46 + (0.58 - 0.46) \times \left(\frac{0.56 - 0.5}{0.6 - 0.5}\right)$$

$$= 0.532$$

Finding a sample size for an intermediate level of power
Use the following equation:

$$n = \text{lower } n + (\text{upper } n - \text{lower } n) \times \left(\frac{\text{actual power} - \text{lower power}}{\text{upper power} - \text{lower power}}\right)$$

If we wished to have power of 0.8 for a one-tailed, between-subjects t-test with an effect size of 0.4 then the number of people we would need in each group would be:

$$n = 70 + (80 - 70) \times \left(\frac{0.80 - 0.76}{0.81 - 0.76}\right)$$

$$= 78$$

If this had not been a whole number, then I would have rounded up to the next whole number.

The effect size of a within-subjects t-test

In Chapter 15 it was pointed out that the effect size for a within-subjects design with two levels of the IV can be calculated in two ways: one way produces d and allows comparison with between-subjects designs while the other way produces d' and allows calculation of statistical power. The example given showed $d = 0.07$ and $d' = 0.456$. The reason for the discrepancy is that d' is affected by the degree to which the participants' scores on the two levels of the IV are correlated. In the example given, the correlation was very high at $r = 0.9883$. The following equation can be used to convert d to d':

$$d' = \frac{d}{\sqrt{2 \times (1 - r)}}$$

Thus,

$$d' = \frac{0.07}{\sqrt{2 \times (1 - 0.9883)}}$$

$$= 0.458 \text{ (which, to two decimal places, agrees with the figure given above)}$$

Explanation of the tables for ANOVA and multiple regression

I have based the power tables for ANOVA on η^2 as the effect size and for multiple regression I have used R^2. In both cases this means that the tables are different from those provided by Cohen (1988). Nonetheless, I have provided tabled values for what he considers constitute small, medium and large effect sizes.

Effect size	η^2	R^2
small	0.01	0.0196
medium	0.059	0.13
large	0.138	0.2

Multifactorial between-subjects ANOVA

Calculating power

When a between-subjects ANOVA has more than one IV it is necessary to adjust the sample size that is used to read the power tables. The adjusted sample size (n') is found using the following equation:

$$n' = \frac{\text{error df}}{\text{treatment df} + 1} + 1$$

The example given in Chapter 17 had the IVs mnemonic strategy (with three levels) and type of list (with two levels). Therefore, there were three possible effects: two main effects and the interaction between them. The main effect of mnemonic strategy had df = 2, the main effect of type of list had df = 1 and the interaction had df = 2. The error term is the same for each of the F-ratios and had df = 24. Therefore, in the case of mnemonic strategy (and the interaction),

$$n' = \frac{24}{2 + 1} + 1 = 9$$

For type of list n' is 13.

The effect sizes (η^2) for the three effects were 0.57 for type of list, 0.05 for mnemonic strategy and 0.11 for the interaction. Table A15.5a shows that the power for the test with $\eta^2 = 0.57$, treatment df = 1 and $n' = 13$ was over 0.95. Table A15.5b shows that the power for the test with $\eta^2 = 0.05$, treatment df = 2 and $n' = 9$ was 0.16 and for $\eta^2 = 0.11$, treatment df = 2 and $n' = 9$ it was just over 0.29.

As the main effect of mnemonic strategy was not statistically significant it is worth finding what sample size would be necessary in order to achieve power of 0.8. The next section shows how to do this.

Choosing the sample size

I will use the example from the previous section in which the effect size (η^2) being sought is 0.05, treatment df = 2 and the design is a 2 by 3 ANOVA. Table A15.5b shows that n' would be between 60 and 70 to achieve power of 0.8. Using linear interpolation the figure is 62. The total sample size required can be found from:

total sample size = (treatment df + 1) × ($n' - 1$) + number of conditions

In the present case there are 3 × 2 conditions, therefore:

total sample size = 3 × (62 − 1) + 6

= 189

In order to have a balanced design the number of participants in each condition will be:

$$\frac{\text{total sample size}}{\text{number of conditions}}$$

which, in the present case will be:

$$\frac{189}{6} = 31.5$$

In other words, 32 people will be needed in each condition to give power of at least 0.8 for the test of the main effect of mnemonic strategy.

If the effect sizes that are being sought for the different treatments differ then the above analysis would be conducted using the treatment with the smallest expected effect size.

The power of within-subjects ANOVA

The power of a within-subjects ANOVA is affected by a number of factors. It is enhanced by the degree to which participants' scores correlate between the pairs of levels of the IV. However, it is lowered by lack of sphericity. In order to simplify the process, I recommend reading the tables in the same way as for a between-subjects ANOVA but treating the sample size suggested as the overall sample size. To illustrate the procedure I will use the example that entails participants recommending a sentence for a criminal under three different conditions. The analysis is by a one-way ANOVA with three levels of the IV. If the researchers wished to detect a large effect size ($\eta^2 = 0.138$), as defined by Cohen (1988), using power of 0.8, then they would find from Table A15.5b that the recommended sample size was between 20 and 25, giving power between 0.78 and 0.87. Using linear interpolation, this would show that the overall sample size required was 21.1. Therefore they require a sample of 22 people.

The power of mixed ANOVA

To simplify the process again I recommend the following procedure, using the example of the two-way ANOVA described in Chapter 17. The between-subjects IV was gender of rater, the within-subjects IV was the gender of the parent being rated and the DV was the IQ that was estimated for the parent. For the between-subjects variable—gender of rater—the power and necessary sample size can be found in the way shown above for multifactorial between-subjects designs. Accordingly, as the treatment df was 1 and the error df was 8, n' is 5. The effect size for the main effect of gender of rater was $\eta^2 = 0.0006$. From Table A15.5a we can see that even if the effect size had been $\eta^2 = 0.01$, the level of power with n of 5 would be as low as 0.06. For the within-subjects IV—parent being rated—ignore the fact that it is a mixed design, read the tables as though for a one-way between-subjects ANOVA and treat the n as the total sample required. Thus, if during the design stage a medium effect size was being considered, as the treatment df would be 1, the necessary sample size would be between 60 and 70, or 62 after interpolation.

Table A15.1 Power tables for a one-group z-test

a. One-tailed tests

n	\multicolumn{14}{c}{Effect size (d)}
	0.1	0.2	0.3	0.4	0.5	0.6	0.7	0.8	0.9	1.0	1.1	1.2	1.3	1.4
4	0.07	0.11	0.15	0.20	0.26	0.33	0.40	0.48	0.56	0.64	0.71	0.77	0.83	0.88
5	0.08	0.12	0.17	0.23	0.30	0.38	0.47	0.56	0.64	0.72	0.79	0.85	0.90	0.93
6	0.08	0.12	0.18	0.25	0.34	0.43	0.53	0.62	0.71	0.79	0.85	0.90	0.94	0.96
7	0.08	0.13	0.20	0.28	0.37	0.48	0.58	0.68	0.77	0.84	0.90	0.94	0.96	0.98
8	0.09	0.14	0.21	0.30	0.41	0.52	0.63	0.73	0.82	0.88	0.93	0.96	0.98	0.99
9	0.09	0.15	0.23	0.33	0.44	0.56	0.68	0.77	0.85	0.91	0.95	0.97	0.99	0.99
10	0.09	0.16	0.24	0.35	0.47	0.60	0.72	0.81	0.89	0.94	0.97	0.98	0.99	*
11	0.09	0.16	0.26	0.38	0.51	0.63	0.75	0.84	0.91	0.95	0.98	0.99	*	*
12	0.10	0.17	0.27	0.40	0.53	0.67	0.78	0.87	0.93	0.97	0.98	0.99	*	*
13	0.10	0.18	0.29	0.42	0.56	0.70	0.81	0.89	0.95	0.98	0.99	*	*	*
14	0.10	0.18	0.30	0.44	0.59	0.73	0.84	0.91	0.96	0.98	0.99	*	*	*
15	0.10	0.19	0.31	0.46	0.61	0.75	0.86	0.93	0.97	0.99	*	*	*	*
16	0.11	0.20	0.33	0.48	0.64	0.77	0.88	0.94	0.97	0.99	*	*	*	*
17	0.11	0.21	0.34	0.50	0.66	0.80	0.89	0.95	0.98	0.99	*	*	*	*
18	0.11	0.21	0.35	0.52	0.68	0.82	0.91	0.96	0.99	*	*	*	*	*
19	0.11	0.22	0.37	0.54	0.70	0.83	0.92	0.97	0.99	*	*	*	*	*
20	0.12	0.23	0.38	0.56	0.72	0.85	0.93	0.97	0.99	*	*	*	*	*
25	0.13	0.26	0.44	0.64	0.80	0.91	0.97	0.99	*	*	*	*	*	*
30	0.14	0.29	0.50	0.71	0.86	0.95	0.99	*	*	*	*	*	*	*
35	0.15	0.32	0.55	0.76	0.91	0.97	0.99	*	*	*	*	*	*	*
40	0.16	0.35	0.60	0.81	0.94	0.98	*	*	*	*	*	*	*	*
45	0.17	0.38	0.64	0.85	0.96	0.99	*	*	*	*	*	*	*	*
50	0.17	0.41	0.68	0.88	0.97	*	*	*	*	*	*	*	*	*
60	0.19	0.46	0.75	0.93	0.99	*	*	*	*	*	*	*	*	*
70	0.21	0.51	0.81	0.96	0.99	*	*	*	*	*	*	*	*	*
80	0.23	0.56	0.85	0.97	*	*	*	*	*	*	*	*	*	*
90	0.24	0.60	0.89	0.98	*	*	*	*	*	*	*	*	*	*
100	0.26	0.64	0.91	0.99	*	*	*	*	*	*	*	*	*	*
120	0.29	0.71	0.95	*	*	*	*	*	*	*	*	*	*	*
140	0.32	0.76	0.97	*	*	*	*	*	*	*	*	*	*	*
160	0.35	0.81	0.98	*	*	*	*	*	*	*	*	*	*	*
180	0.38	0.85	0.99	*	*	*	*	*	*	*	*	*	*	*
200	0.41	0.88	*	*	*	*	*	*	*	*	*	*	*	*
300	0.53	0.97	*	*	*	*	*	*	*	*	*	*	*	*
400	0.64	0.99	*	*	*	*	*	*	*	*	*	*	*	*
500	0.72	*	*	*	*	*	*	*	*	*	*	*	*	*
600	0.79	*	*	*	*	*	*	*	*	*	*	*	*	*
700	0.84	*	*	*	*	*	*	*	*	*	*	*	*	*
800	0.88	*	*	*	*	*	*	*	*	*	*	*	*	*
900	0.91	*	*	*	*	*	*	*	*	*	*	*	*	*
1000	0.94	*	*	*	*	*	*	*	*	*	*	*	*	*

b. Two-tailed tests

n	\multicolumn{15}{c}{Effect size (d)}
	0.1	0.2	0.3	0.4	0.5	0.6	0.7	0.8	0.9	1.0	1.1	1.2	1.3	1.4
4	0.04	0.06	0.09	0.12	0.17	0.22	0.29	0.36	0.44	0.52	0.59	0.67	0.74	0.80
5	0.04	0.07	0.10	0.14	0.20	0.27	0.35	0.43	0.52	0.61	0.69	0.77	0.83	0.88
6	0.04	0.07	0.11	0.16	0.23	0.31	0.40	0.50	0.60	0.69	0.77	0.84	0.89	0.93
7	0.05	0.08	0.12	0.18	0.26	0.35	0.46	0.56	0.66	0.75	0.83	0.89	0.93	0.96
8	0.05	0.08	0.13	0.20	0.29	0.40	0.51	0.62	0.72	0.81	0.88	0.92	0.96	0.98
9	0.05	0.09	0.14	0.22	0.32	0.44	0.56	0.67	0.77	0.85	0.91	0.95	0.97	0.99
10	0.05	0.09	0.16	0.24	0.35	0.48	0.60	0.72	0.81	0.89	0.94	0.97	0.98	0.99
11	0.05	0.10	0.17	0.26	0.38	0.51	0.64	0.76	0.85	0.91	0.95	0.98	0.99	*
12	0.05	0.10	0.18	0.28	0.41	0.55	0.68	0.79	0.88	0.93	0.97	0.99	0.99	*
13	0.05	0.11	0.19	0.30	0.44	0.58	0.71	0.82	0.90	0.95	0.98	0.99	*	*
14	0.06	0.11	0.20	0.32	0.46	0.61	0.75	0.85	0.92	0.96	0.98	0.99	*	*
15	0.06	0.12	0.21	0.34	0.49	0.64	0.77	0.87	0.94	0.97	0.99	*	*	*
16	0.06	0.12	0.22	0.36	0.52	0.67	0.80	0.89	0.95	0.98	0.99	*	*	*
17	0.06	0.13	0.23	0.38	0.54	0.70	0.82	0.91	0.96	0.98	0.99	*	*	*
18	0.06	0.13	0.25	0.40	0.56	0.72	0.84	0.92	0.97	0.99	*	*	*	*
19	0.06	0.14	0.26	0.41	0.59	0.74	0.86	0.94	0.98	0.99	*	*	*	*
20	0.07	0.14	0.27	0.43	0.61	0.77	0.88	0.95	0.98	0.99	*	*	*	*
25	0.07	0.17	0.32	0.52	0.71	0.85	0.94	0.98	0.99	*	*	*	*	*
30	0.08	0.19	0.38	0.59	0.78	0.91	0.97	0.99	*	*	*	*	*	*
35	0.09	0.22	0.43	0.66	0.84	0.94	0.99	*	*	*	*	*	*	*
40	0.09	0.24	0.48	0.72	0.89	0.97	0.99	*	*	*	*	*	*	*
45	0.10	0.27	0.52	0.77	0.92	0.98	*	*	*	*	*	*	*	*
50	0.11	0.29	0.56	0.81	0.94	0.99	*	*	*	*	*	*	*	*
60	0.12	0.34	0.64	0.87	0.97	*	*	*	*	*	*	*	*	*
70	0.13	0.39	0.71	0.92	0.99	*	*	*	*	*	*	*	*	*
80	0.14	0.43	0.77	0.95	0.99	*	*	*	*	*	*	*	*	*
90	0.16	0.48	0.81	0.97	*	*	*	*	*	*	*	*	*	*
100	0.17	0.52	0.85	0.98	*	*	*	*	*	*	*	*	*	*
120	0.19	0.59	0.91	0.99	*	*	*	*	*	*	*	*	*	*
140	0.22	0.66	0.94	*	*	*	*	*	*	*	*	*	*	*
160	0.24	0.72	0.97	*	*	*	*	*	*	*	*	*	*	*
180	0.27	0.77	0.98	*	*	*	*	*	*	*	*	*	*	*
200	0.29	0.81	0.99	*	*	*	*	*	*	*	*	*	*	*
300	0.41	0.93	*	*	*	*	*	*	*	*	*	*	*	*
400	0.52	0.98	*	*	*	*	*	*	*	*	*	*	*	*
500	0.61	0.99	*	*	*	*	*	*	*	*	*	*	*	*
600	0.69	*	*	*	*	*	*	*	*	*	*	*	*	*
700	0.75	*	*	*	*	*	*	*	*	*	*	*	*	*
800	0.81	*	*	*	*	*	*	*	*	*	*	*	*	*
900	0.85	*	*	*	*	*	*	*	*	*	*	*	*	*
1000	0.89	*	*	*	*	*	*	*	*	*	*	*	*	*

Table A15.2 Power of a between-subjects *t*-test

a. One-tailed tests (*n* is the number of people in each group)

n	Effect size (*d*)													
	0.1	0.2	0.3	0.4	0.5	0.6	0.7	0.8	0.9	1.0	1.1	1.2	1.3	1.4
8	0.07	0.10	0.13	0.18	0.23	0.29	0.36	0.44	0.52	0.59	0.67	0.73	0.79	0.84
9	0.07	0.10	0.14	0.19	0.25	0.32	0.40	0.48	0.56	0.64	0.72	0.78	0.84	0.88
10	0.07	0.11	0.15	0.21	0.27	0.35	0.43	0.52	0.61	0.69	0.76	0.82	0.87	0.91
11	0.08	0.11	0.16	0.22	0.29	0.38	0.47	0.56	0.65	0.73	0.80	0.86	0.90	0.93
12	0.08	0.12	0.17	0.23	0.31	0.40	0.50	0.59	0.68	0.76	0.83	0.88	0.92	0.95
13	0.08	0.12	0.18	0.25	0.33	0.43	0.53	0.63	0.72	0.80	0.86	0.90	0.94	0.96
14	0.08	0.13	0.19	0.26	0.35	0.45	0.56	0.66	0.75	0.82	0.88	0.92	0.95	0.97
15	0.08	0.13	0.19	0.27	0.37	0.48	0.58	0.69	0.77	0.85	0.90	0.94	0.96	0.98
16	0.08	0.13	0.20	0.29	0.39	0.50	0.61	0.71	0.80	0.87	0.92	0.95	0.97	0.98
17	0.09	0.14	0.21	0.30	0.41	0.52	0.63	0.74	0.82	0.88	0.93	0.96	0.98	0.99
18	0.09	0.14	0.22	0.31	0.42	0.54	0.66	0.76	0.84	0.90	0.94	0.97	0.98	0.99
19	0.09	0.15	0.23	0.33	0.44	0.56	0.68	0.78	0.86	0.91	0.95	0.97	0.99	0.99
20	0.09	0.15	0.23	0.34	0.46	0.58	0.70	0.80	0.87	0.93	0.96	0.98	0.99	*
25	0.10	0.17	0.27	0.40	0.54	0.67	0.79	0.87	0.93	0.97	0.98	0.99	*	*
30	0.10	0.19	0.31	0.45	0.60	0.74	0.85	0.92	0.96	0.98	0.99	*	*	*
35	0.11	0.20	0.34	0.50	0.66	0.80	0.89	0.95	0.98	0.99	*	*	*	*
40	0.11	0.22	0.37	0.55	0.72	0.84	0.93	0.97	0.99	*	*	*	*	*
45	0.12	0.24	0.41	0.59	0.76	0.88	0.95	0.98	0.99	*	*	*	*	*
50	0.12	0.26	0.44	0.63	0.80	0.91	0.97	0.99	*	*	*	*	*	*
60	0.13	0.29	0.49	0.70	0.86	0.95	0.98	*	*	*	*	*	*	*
70	0.14	0.32	0.55	0.76	0.90	0.97	0.99	*	*	*	*	*	*	*
80	0.15	0.35	0.60	0.81	0.93	0.98	*	*	*	*	*	*	*	*
90	0.16	0.38	0.64	0.85	0.95	0.99	*	*	*	*	*	*	*	*
100	0.17	0.41	0.68	0.88	0.97	0.99	*	*	*	*	*	*	*	*
110	0.18	0.43	0.72	0.90	0.98	*	*	*	*	*	*	*	*	*
120	0.19	0.46	0.75	0.93	0.99	*	*	*	*	*	*	*	*	*
130	0.20	0.48	0.78	0.94	0.99	*	*	*	*	*	*	*	*	*
140	0.21	0.51	0.80	0.95	0.99	*	*	*	*	*	*	*	*	*
150	0.22	0.53	0.83	0.96	*	*	*	*	*	*	*	*	*	*
160	0.23	0.56	0.85	0.97	*	*	*	*	*	*	*	*	*	*
170	0.23	0.58	0.87	0.98	*	*	*	*	*	*	*	*	*	*
180	0.24	0.60	0.88	0.98	*	*	*	*	*	*	*	*	*	*
190	0.25	0.62	0.90	0.99	*	*	*	*	*	*	*	*	*	*
200	0.26	0.64	0.91	0.99	*	*	*	*	*	*	*	*	*	*
300	0.34	0.79	0.98	*	*	*	*	*	*	*	*	*	*	*
400	0.41	0.88	*	*	*	*	*	*	*	*	*	*	*	*
500	0.47	0.94	*	*	*	*	*	*	*	*	*	*	*	*
600	0.53	0.97	*	*	*	*	*	*	*	*	*	*	*	*
700	0.59	0.98	*	*	*	*	*	*	*	*	*	*	*	*
800	0.64	0.99	*	*	*	*	*	*	*	*	*	*	*	*
900	0.68	*	*	*	*	*	*	*	*	*	*	*	*	*
1000	0.72	*	*	*	*	*	*	*	*	*	*	*	*	*

b. Two-tailed tests (*n* is the number of people in each group)

n	0.1	0.2	0.3	0.4	0.5	0.6	Effect size (*d*) 0.7	0.8	0.9	1.0	1.1	1.2	1.3	1.4
8	0.04	0.05	0.07	0.10	0.14	0.18	0.23	0.30	0.37	0.44	0.52	0.60	0.67	0.74
9	0.04	0.05	0.08	0.11	0.15	0.20	0.27	0.34	0.42	0.50	0.58	0.66	0.73	0.80
10	0.04	0.06	0.08	0.12	0.17	0.23	0.30	0.38	0.47	0.55	0.64	0.72	0.78	0.84
11	0.04	0.06	0.09	0.13	0.19	0.25	0.33	0.42	0.51	0.60	0.69	0.76	0.83	0.88
12	0.04	0.06	0.10	0.14	0.20	0.28	0.36	0.46	0.55	0.64	0.73	0.80	0.86	0.91
13	0.04	0.07	0.10	0.15	0.22	0.30	0.39	0.49	0.59	0.68	0.77	0.84	0.89	0.93
14	0.04	0.07	0.11	0.16	0.24	0.32	0.42	0.52	0.63	0.72	0.80	0.86	0.91	0.94
15	0.04	0.07	0.12	0.17	0.25	0.34	0.45	0.56	0.66	0.75	0.83	0.89	0.93	0.96
16	0.04	0.08	0.12	0.18	0.27	0.37	0.48	0.59	0.69	0.78	0.85	0.91	0.94	0.97
17	0.05	0.08	0.13	0.20	0.28	0.39	0.50	0.62	0.72	0.81	0.87	0.92	0.96	0.98
18	0.05	0.08	0.13	0.21	0.30	0.41	0.53	0.64	0.75	0.83	0.89	0.94	0.96	0.98
19	0.05	0.08	0.14	0.22	0.31	0.43	0.55	0.67	0.77	0.85	0.91	0.95	0.97	0.99
20	0.05	0.09	0.14	0.23	0.33	0.45	0.57	0.69	0.79	0.87	0.92	0.96	0.98	0.99
25	0.05	0.10	0.17	0.28	0.40	0.54	0.68	0.79	0.88	0.93	0.97	0.98	0.99	*
30	0.06	0.11	0.20	0.33	0.47	0.63	0.76	0.86	0.93	0.97	0.99	0.99	*	*
35	0.06	0.13	0.23	0.37	0.54	0.70	0.82	0.91	0.96	0.98	0.99	*	*	*
40	0.06	0.14	0.26	0.42	0.60	0.75	0.87	0.94	0.98	0.99	*	*	*	*
45	0.07	0.15	0.29	0.46	0.65	0.80	0.91	0.96	0.99	*	*	*	*	*
50	0.07	0.16	0.31	0.51	0.70	0.84	0.93	0.98	0.99	*	*	*	*	*
60	0.08	0.19	0.37	0.58	0.78	0.90	0.97	0.99	*	*	*	*	*	*
70	0.08	0.21	0.42	0.65	0.84	0.94	0.98	*	*	*	*	*	*	*
80	0.09	0.24	0.47	0.71	0.88	0.96	0.99	*	*	*	*	*	*	*
90	0.10	0.26	0.52	0.76	0.92	0.98	*	*	*	*	*	*	*	*
100	0.10	0.29	0.56	0.80	0.94	0.99	*	*	*	*	*	*	*	*
110	0.11	0.31	0.60	0.84	0.96	0.99	*	*	*	*	*	*	*	*
120	0.12	0.34	0.64	0.87	0.97	*	*	*	*	*	*	*	*	*
130	0.12	0.36	0.67	0.89	0.98	*	*	*	*	*	*	*	*	*
140	0.13	0.38	0.71	0.92	0.99	*	*	*	*	*	*	*	*	*
150	0.14	0.41	0.74	0.93	0.99	*	*	*	*	*	*	*	*	*
160	0.14	0.43	0.76	0.95	0.99	*	*	*	*	*	*	*	*	*
170	0.15	0.45	0.79	0.96	*	*	*	*	*	*	*	*	*	*
180	0.15	0.47	0.81	0.97	*	*	*	*	*	*	*	*	*	*
190	0.16	0.49	0.83	0.97	*	*	*	*	*	*	*	*	*	*
200	0.17	0.51	0.85	0.98	*	*	*	*	*	*	*	*	*	*
300	0.23	0.69	0.96	*	*	*	*	*	*	*	*	*	*	*
400	0.29	0.81	0.99	*	*	*	*	*	*	*	*	*	*	*
500	0.35	0.88	*	*	*	*	*	*	*	*	*	*	*	*
600	0.41	0.93	*	*	*	*	*	*	*	*	*	*	*	*
700	0.46	0.96	*	*	*	*	*	*	*	*	*	*	*	*
800	0.52	0.98	*	*	*	*	*	*	*	*	*	*	*	*
900	0.56	0.99	*	*	*	*	*	*	*	*	*	*	*	*
1000	0.61	0.99	*	*	*	*	*	*	*	*	*	*	*	*

Table A15.3 Power of a within-subjects *t*-test or one-group *t*-test

a. One-tailed tests

						Effect size (*d*)							
n	0.1	0.2	0.3	0.4	0.5	0.6	0.7	0.8	0.9	1	1.1	1.2	1.3	1.4
5	0.06	0.08	0.11	0.14	0.18	0.24	0.30	0.37	0.46	0.54	0.62	0.69	0.76	0.81
6	0.07	0.09	0.13	0.17	0.23	0.30	0.39	0.48	0.57	0.66	0.74	0.80	0.85	0.89
7	0.07	0.10	0.15	0.21	0.28	0.37	0.47	0.57	0.66	0.75	0.81	0.87	0.91	0.94
8	0.08	0.11	0.17	0.24	0.32	0.42	0.53	0.64	0.73	0.81	0.87	0.91	0.94	0.96
9	0.08	0.12	0.18	0.26	0.36	0.48	0.59	0.70	0.79	0.86	0.91	0.94	0.96	0.98
10	0.08	0.13	0.20	0.29	0.40	0.52	0.64	0.75	0.83	0.89	0.93	0.96	0.98	0.99
11	0.08	0.14	0.22	0.32	0.44	0.57	0.69	0.79	0.87	0.92	0.95	0.97	0.98	0.99
12	0.09	0.15	0.23	0.34	0.48	0.61	0.73	0.82	0.89	0.94	0.97	0.98	0.99	0.99
13	0.09	0.15	0.25	0.37	0.49	0.65	0.76	0.85	0.92	0.95	0.98	0.99	0.99	*
14	0.09	0.16	0.26	0.39	0.54	0.68	0.79	0.88	0.93	0.96	0.98	0.99	*	*
15	0.10	0.17	0.28	0.42	0.57	0.71	0.82	0.90	0.95	0.97	0.99	0.99	*	*
16	0.10	0.18	0.29	0.44	0.60	0.74	0.84	0.92	0.96	0.98	0.99	*	*	*
17	0.10	0.19	0.31	0.46	0.62	0.76	0.86	0.93	0.97	0.98	0.99	*	*	*
18	0.10	0.19	0.32	0.48	0.65	0.78	0.88	0.94	0.97	0.99	*	*	*	*
19	0.11	0.20	0.34	0.50	0.67	0.81	0.90	0.95	0.98	0.99	*	*	*	*
20	0.11	0.21	0.35	0.52	0.69	0.82	0.91	0.96	0.98	0.99	*	*	*	*
25	0.12	0.24	0.42	0.61	0.78	0.90	0.96	0.98	0.99	*	*	*	*	*
30	0.13	0.28	0.48	0.69	0.85	0.94	0.98	0.99	*	*	*	*	*	*
35	0.14	0.31	0.53	0.75	0.89	0.96	0.99	*	*	*	*	*	*	*
40	0.15	0.34	0.58	0.80	0.93	0.98	*	*	*	*	*	*	*	*
45	0.16	0.37	0.63	0.84	0.95	0.99	*	*	*	*	*	*	*	*
50	0.17	0.40	0.67	0.87	0.97	0.99	*	*	*	*	*	*	*	*
60	0.19	0.45	0.74	0.92	0.98	*	*	*	*	*	*	*	*	*
70	0.20	0.50	0.80	0.95	0.99	*	*	*	*	*	*	*	*	*
80	0.22	0.55	0.84	0.97	*	*	*	*	*	*	*	*	*	*
90	0.24	0.59	0.88	0.98	*	*	*	*	*	*	*	*	*	*
100	0.26	0.63	0.91	0.99	*	*	*	*	*	*	*	*	*	*
110	0.27	0.67	0.93	0.99	*	*	*	*	*	*	*	*	*	*
120	0.29	0.70	0.95	*	*	*	*	*	*	*	*	*	*	*
130	0.30	0.73	0.96	*	*	*	*	*	*	*	*	*	*	*
140	0.32	0.76	0.97	*	*	*	*	*	*	*	*	*	*	*
150	0.33	0.79	0.98	*	*	*	*	*	*	*	*	*	*	*
160	0.35	0.81	0.98	*	*	*	*	*	*	*	*	*	*	*
170	0.36	0.83	0.99	*	*	*	*	*	*	*	*	*	*	*
180	0.38	0.85	0.99	*	*	*	*	*	*	*	*	*	*	*
190	0.39	0.86	0.99	*	*	*	*	*	*	*	*	*	*	*
200	0.41	0.88	0.99	*	*	*	*	*	*	*	*	*	*	*
300	0.53	0.96	*	*	*	*	*	*	*	*	*	*	*	*
400	0.64	0.99	*	*	*	*	*	*	*	*	*	*	*	*
500	0.72	*	*	*	*	*	*	*	*	*	*	*	*	*
600	0.79	*	*	*	*	*	*	*	*	*	*	*	*	*
700	0.84	*	*	*	*	*	*	*	*	*	*	*	*	*
800	0.88	*	*	*	*	*	*	*	*	*	*	*	*	*
900	0.91	*	*	*	*	*	*	*	*	*	*	*	*	*
1000	0.94	*	*	*	*	*	*	*	*	*	*	*	*	*

b. Two-tailed tests

n	Effect size (d) 0.1	0.2	0.3	0.4	0.5	0.6	0.7	0.8	0.9	1	1.1	1.2	1.3	1.4
6	0.03	0.05	0.06	0.09	0.12	0.16	0.22	0.28	0.36	0.45	0.55	0.64	0.72	0.79
7	0.04	0.05	0.07	0.11	0.15	0.21	0.29	0.38	0.47	0.58	0.67	0.75	0.82	0.87
8	0.04	0.06	0.09	0.13	0.19	0.26	0.36	0.46	0.57	0.67	0.76	0.83	0.88	0.92
9	0.04	0.06	0.10	0.15	0.22	0.31	0.42	0.54	0.65	0.75	0.83	0.88	0.93	0.95
10	0.04	0.07	0.11	0.17	0.26	0.36	0.48	0.60	0.71	0.80	0.87	0.92	0.95	0.97
11	0.04	0.07	0.12	0.19	0.29	0.41	0.54	0.66	0.77	0.85	0.91	0.94	0.97	0.98
12	0.05	0.08	0.13	0.22	0.32	0.45	0.59	0.71	0.81	0.88	0.93	0.96	0.98	0.99
13	0.05	0.09	0.15	0.24	0.36	0.49	0.63	0.75	0.85	0.91	0.95	0.97	0.99	0.99
14	0.05	0.09	0.16	0.26	0.39	0.53	0.67	0.79	0.88	0.93	0.96	0.98	0.99	*
15	0.05	0.10	0.17	0.28	0.42	0.57	0.71	0.82	0.90	0.95	0.97	0.99	0.99	*
16	0.05	0.10	0.18	0.30	0.45	0.60	0.74	0.85	0.92	0.96	0.98	0.99	*	*
17	0.05	0.11	0.20	0.32	0.48	0.64	0.77	0.87	0.93	0.97	0.99	0.99	*	*
18	0.06	0.11	0.21	0.34	0.50	0.67	0.80	0.89	0.95	0.98	0.99	*	*	*
19	0.06	0.12	0.22	0.36	0.53	0.69	0.82	0.91	0.96	0.98	0.99	*	*	*
20	0.06	0.12	0.23	0.38	0.56	0.72	0.84	0.92	0.97	0.99	0.99	*	*	*
25	0.07	0.15	0.29	0.47	0.67	0.82	0.92	0.97	0.99	*	*	*	*	*
30	0.07	0.18	0.35	0.56	0.75	0.89	0.96	0.99	*	*	*	*	*	*
35	0.08	0.20	0.40	0.63	0.82	0.93	0.98	0.99	*	*	*	*	*	*
40	0.09	0.23	0.45	0.69	0.87	0.96	0.99	*	*	*	*	*	*	*
45	0.09	0.25	0.50	0.75	0.91	0.97	0.99	*	*	*	*	*	*	*
50	0.10	0.28	0.54	0.79	0.93	0.98	*	*	*	*	*	*	*	*
60	0.11	0.33	0.63	0.86	0.97	0.99	*	*	*	*	*	*	*	*
70	0.13	0.37	0.70	0.91	0.98	*	*	*	*	*	*	*	*	*
80	0.14	0.42	0.75	0.94	0.99	*	*	*	*	*	*	*	*	*
90	0.15	0.46	0.80	0.96	*	*	*	*	*	*	*	*	*	*
100	0.16	0.51	0.84	0.98	*	*	*	*	*	*	*	*	*	*
110	0.18	0.55	0.88	0.99	*	*	*	*	*	*	*	*	*	*
120	0.19	0.58	0.90	0.99	*	*	*	*	*	*	*	*	*	*
130	0.20	0.62	0.92	0.99	*	*	*	*	*	*	*	*	*	*
140	0.21	0.65	0.94	*	*	*	*	*	*	*	*	*	*	*
150	0.23	0.68	0.95	*	*	*	*	*	*	*	*	*	*	*
160	0.24	0.71	0.96	*	*	*	*	*	*	*	*	*	*	*
170	0.25	0.74	0.97	*	*	*	*	*	*	*	*	*	*	*
180	0.26	0.76	0.98	*	*	*	*	*	*	*	*	*	*	*
190	0.28	0.78	0.98	*	*	*	*	*	*	*	*	*	*	*
200	0.29	0.80	0.99	*	*	*	*	*	*	*	*	*	*	*
300	0.41	0.93	*	*	*	*	*	*	*	*	*	*	*	*
400	0.51	0.98	*	*	*	*	*	*	*	*	*	*	*	*
500	0.61	0.99	*	*	*	*	*	*	*	*	*	*	*	*
600	0.69	*	*	*	*	*	*	*	*	*	*	*	*	*
700	0.75	*	*	*	*	*	*	*	*	*	*	*	*	*
800	0.81	*	*	*	*	*	*	*	*	*	*	*	*	*
900	0.85	*	*	*	*	*	*	*	*	*	*	*	*	*
1000	0.88	*	*	*	*	*	*	*	*	*	*	*	*	*

Table A15.4 Power of a χ^2 test

a. df = 1

n	0.1	0.2	0.3	0.4	effect size (w) 0.5	0.6	0.7	0.8	0.9
20	<0.20	<0.20	0.27	0.43	0.61	0.76	0.88	0.95	0.98
22	<0.20	<0.20	0.29	0.46	0.65	0.80	0.91	0.96	0.99
24	<0.20	<0.20	0.31	0.50	0.69	0.84	0.93	0.97	*
26	<0.20	<0.20	0.33	0.53	0.72	0.86	0.95	0.98	*
28	<0.20	<0.20	0.35	0.56	0.75	0.89	0.96	0.99	*
30	<0.20	<0.20	0.38	0.59	0.78	0.91	0.97	0.99	*
35	<0.20	0.22	0.42	0.66	0.84	0.94	0.98	*	*
40	<0.20	0.25	0.47	0.71	0.89	0.97	*	*	*
45	<0.20	0.27	0.52	0.76	0.92	0.98	*	*	*
50	<0.20	0.30	0.56	0.81	0.94	0.99	*	*	*
55	<0.20	0.32	0.60	0.84	0.96	*	*	*	*
60	<0.20	0.34	0.64	0.87	0.97	*	*	*	*
65	<0.20	0.36	0.68	0.90	0.98	*	*	*	*
70	<0.20	0.39	0.71	0.92	0.99	*	*	*	*
75	<0.20	0.41	0.74	0.93	0.99	*	*	*	*
80	<0.20	0.43	0.76	0.95	*	*	*	*	*
85	<0.20	0.45	0.79	0.96	*	*	*	*	*
90	<0.20	0.47	0.81	0.97	*	*	*	*	*
95	<0.20	0.49	0.83	0.97	*	*	*	*	*
100	<0.20	0.51	0.85	0.98	*	*	*	*	*
110	<0.20	0.55	0.88	0.99	*	*	*	*	*
120	<0.20	0.59	0.91	0.99	*	*	*	*	*
130	0.21	0.62	0.93	*	*	*	*	*	*
140	0.22	0.66	0.94	*	*	*	*	*	*
150	0.23	0.69	0.96	*	*	*	*	*	*
160	0.25	0.71	0.97	*	*	*	*	*	*
170	0.26	0.74	0.97	*	*	*	*	*	*
180	0.27	0.76	0.98	*	*	*	*	*	*
190	0.28	0.79	0.98	*	*	*	*	*	*
200	0.30	0.81	0.99	*	*	*	*	*	*
250	0.35	0.89	*	*	*	*	*	*	*
300	0.41	0.93	*	*	*	*	*	*	*
350	0.46	0.96	*	*	*	*	*	*	*
400	0.51	0.98	*	*	*	*	*	*	*
450	0.56	0.99	*	*	*	*	*	*	*
500	0.61	*	*	*	*	*	*	*	*
600	0.69	*	*	*	*	*	*	*	*
700	0.75	*	*	*	*	*	*	*	*
800	0.81	*	*	*	*	*	*	*	*
900	0.85	*	*	*	*	*	*	*	*
1000	0.89	*	*	*	*	*	*	*	*

b. df = 2

n	effect size (w)								
	0.1	0.2	0.3	0.4	0.5	0.6	0.7	0.8	0.9
20	<0.20	<0.20	0.21	0.34	0.50	0.67	0.81	0.90	0.96
22	<0.20	<0.20	0.23	0.37	0.54	0.71	0.85	0.93	0.97
24	<0.20	<0.20	0.24	0.40	0.58	0.75	0.88	0.95	0.98
26	<0.20	<0.20	0.26	0.43	0.62	0.79	0.90	0.96	0.99
28	<0.20	<0.20	0.28	0.46	0.66	0.82	0.92	0.97	0.99
30	<0.20	<0.20	0.29	0.48	0.69	0.85	0.94	0.98	*
35	<0.20	<0.20	0.34	0.55	0.76	0.90	0.97	0.99	*
40	<0.20	<0.20	0.38	0.61	0.82	0.93	0.99	*	*
45	<0.20	0.21	0.42	0.67	0.86	0.96	0.99	*	*
50	<0.20	0.23	0.46	0.72	0.90	0.98	*	*	*
55	<0.20	0.25	0.50	0.76	0.92	0.99	*	*	*
60	<0.20	0.27	0.54	0.80	0.94	0.99	*	*	*
65	<0.20	0.28	0.57	0.83	0.96	*	*	*	*
70	<0.20	0.30	0.61	0.86	0.97	*	*	*	*
75	<0.20	0.32	0.64	0.88	0.98	*	*	*	*
80	<0.20	0.34	0.67	0.90	0.99	*	*	*	*
85	<0.20	0.36	0.70	0.92	0.99	*	*	*	*
90	<0.20	0.38	0.72	0.93	0.99	*	*	*	*
95	<0.20	0.40	0.75	0.95	*	*	*	*	*
100	<0.20	0.41	0.77	0.96	*	*	*	*	*
110	<0.20	0.45	0.81	0.97	*	*	*	*	*
120	<0.20	0.48	0.85	0.98	*	*	*	*	*
130	<0.20	0.52	0.88	0.99	*	*	*	*	*
140	<0.20	0.55	0.90	0.99	*	*	*	*	*
150	<0.20	0.58	0.92	*	*	*	*	*	*
160	<0.20	0.61	0.93	*	*	*	*	*	*
170	0.20	0.64	0.95	*	*	*	*	*	*
180	0.21	0.67	0.96	*	*	*	*	*	*
190	0.22	0.69	0.97	*	*	*	*	*	*
200	0.23	0.72	0.98	*	*	*	*	*	*
250	0.28	0.82	0.99	*	*	*	*	*	*
300	0.32	0.88	*	*	*	*	*	*	*
350	0.37	0.93	*	*	*	*	*	*	*
400	0.41	0.96	*	*	*	*	*	*	*
450	0.46	0.98	*	*	*	*	*	*	*
500	0.50	0.99	*	*	*	*	*	*	*
600	0.58	*	*	*	*	*	*	*	*
700	0.66	*	*	*	*	*	*	*	*
800	0.72	*	*	*	*	*	*	*	*
900	0.77	*	*	*	*	*	*	*	*
1000	0.82	*	*	*	*	*	*	*	*

Table A15.4 Power of a χ^2 test

c. df = 3

	effect size (w)								
n	0.1	0.2	0.3	0.4	0.5	0.6	0.7	0.8	0.9
20	<0.20	<0.20	<0.20	0.29	0.44	0.60	0.75	0.87	0.94
22	<0.20	<0.20	<0.20	0.32	0.48	0.65	0.80	0.90	0.96
24	<0.20	<0.20	0.21	0.35	0.52	0.69	0.83	0.92	0.98
26	<0.20	<0.20	0.22	0.37	0.55	0.73	0.86	0.94	0.99
28	<0.20	<0.20	0.23	0.40	0.59	0.77	0.89	0.96	0.99
30	<0.20	<0.20	0.25	0.42	0.62	0.80	0.91	0.97	*
35	<0.20	<0.20	0.29	0.49	0.70	0.86	0.95	0.99	*
40	<0.20	<0.20	0.32	0.55	0.76	0.91	0.98	*	*
45	<0.20	<0.20	0.36	0.60	0.82	0.94	0.99	*	*
50	<0.20	0.20	0.40	0.65	0.86	0.96	*	*	*
55	<0.20	0.21	0.44	0.70	0.89	0.98	*	*	*
60	<0.20	0.22	0.47	0.74	0.92	0.99	*	*	*
65	<0.20	0.24	0.51	0.78	0.94	0.99	*	*	*
70	<0.20	0.26	0.54	0.81	0.95	*	*	*	*
75	<0.20	0.27	0.57	0.84	0.97	*	*	*	*
80	<0.20	0.29	0.60	0.87	0.98	*	*	*	*
85	<0.20	0.31	0.63	0.89	0.99	*	*	*	*
90	<0.20	0.32	0.66	0.91	0.99	*	*	*	*
95	<0.20	0.34	0.69	0.92	0.99	*	*	*	*
100	<0.20	0.36	0.71	0.93	*	*	*	*	*
110	<0.20	0.39	0.76	0.96	*	*	*	*	*
120	<0.20	0.42	0.80	0.97	*	*	*	*	*
130	<0.20	0.46	0.83	0.99	*	*	*	*	*
140	<0.20	0.49	0.86	0.99	*	*	*	*	*
150	<0.20	0.52	0.88	*	*	*	*	*	*
160	<0.20	0.55	0.91	*	*	*	*	*	*
170	<0.20	0.58	0.92	*	*	*	*	*	*
180	<0.20	0.60	0.94	*	*	*	*	*	*
190	<0.20	0.63	0.95	*	*	*	*	*	*
200	0.20	0.65	0.96	*	*	*	*	*	*
250	0.23	0.76	0.99	*	*	*	*	*	*
300	0.27	0.84	*	*	*	*	*	*	*
350	0.32	0.90	*	*	*	*	*	*	*
400	0.36	0.93	*	*	*	*	*	*	*
450	0.40	0.96	*	*	*	*	*	*	*
500	0.44	0.98	*	*	*	*	*	*	*
600	0.52	0.98	*	*	*	*	*	*	*
700	0.59	*	*	*	*	*	*	*	*
800	0.65	*	*	*	*	*	*	*	*
900	0.71	*	*	*	*	*	*	*	*
1000	0.76	*	*	*	*	*	*	*	*
1100	0.81	*	*	*	*	*	*	*	*

d. df = 4

n	effect size (w)								
	0.1	0.2	0.3	0.4	0.5	0.6	0.7	0.8	0.9
20	<0.20	<0.20	<0.20	0.26	0.40	0.55	0.71	0.83	0.91
22	<0.20	<0.20	<0.20	0.29	0.43	0.60	0.75	0.87	0.94
24	<0.20	<0.20	<0.20	0.31	0.47	0.64	0.80	0.90	0.96
26	<0.20	<0.20	0.20	0.33	0.50	0.69	0.83	0.92	0.97
28	<0.20	<0.20	0.21	0.36	0.54	0.72	0.86	0.94	0.99
30	<0.20	<0.20	0.23	0.38	0.57	0.76	0.88	0.96	0.99
35	<0.20	<0.20	0.26	0.44	0.65	0.82	0.93	0.98	*
40	<0.20	<0.20	0.29	0.50	0.72	0.88	0.96	0.99	*
45	<0.20	<0.20	0.33	0.55	0.77	0.91	0.98	*	*
50	<0.20	<0.20	0.36	0.61	0.82	0.94	0.99	*	*
55	<0.20	<0.20	0.39	0.65	0.86	0.96	*	*	*
60	<0.20	0.20	0.42	0.70	0.89	0.98	*	*	*
65	<0.20	0.22	0.46	0.74	0.91	0.99	*	*	*
70	<0.20	0.23	0.49	0.77	0.93	0.99	*	*	*
75	<0.20	0.25	0.52	0.80	0.95	*	*	*	*
80	<0.20	0.26	0.55	0.83	0.96	*	*	*	*
85	<0.20	0.28	0.58	0.86	0.98	*	*	*	*
90	<0.20	0.29	0.61	0.88	0.98	*	*	*	*
95	<0.20	0.31	0.64	0.89	0.99	*	*	*	*
100	<0.20	0.32	0.67	0.91	0.99	*	*	*	*
110	<0.20	0.35	0.71	0.94	*	*	*	*	*
120	<0.20	0.38	0.76	0.96	*	*	*	*	*
130	<0.20	0.41	0.79	0.97	*	*	*	*	*
140	<0.20	0.44	0.82	0.98	*	*	*	*	*
150	<0.20	0.47	0.85	0.99	*	*	*	*	*
160	<0.20	0.50	0.88	0.99	*	*	*	*	*
170	<0.20	0.53	0.90	*	*	*	*	*	*
180	<0.20	0.55	0.91	*	*	*	*	*	*
190	<0.20	0.58	0.93	*	*	*	*	*	*
200	<0.20	0.61	0.94	*	*	*	*	*	*
250	0.21	0.72	0.98	*	*	*	*	*	*
300	0.25	0.80	0.98	*	*	*	*	*	*
350	0.28	0.87	*	*	*	*	*	*	*
400	0.32	0.91	*	*	*	*	*	*	*
450	0.36	0.94	*	*	*	*	*	*	*
500	0.40	0.96	*	*	*	*	*	*	*
600	0.47	0.99	*	*	*	*	*	*	*
700	0.54	*	*	*	*	*	*	*	*
800	0.61	*	*	*	*	*	*	*	*
900	0.67	*	*	*	*	*	*	*	*
1000	0.72	*	*	*	*	*	*	*	*
1100	0.76	*	*	*	*	*	*	*	*
1200	0.80	*	*	*	*	*	*	*	*

Table A15.4 Power of a χ^2 test

e. df = 5

| n | \multicolumn{9}{c}{effect size (w)} |
	0.1	0.2	0.3	0.4	0.5	0.6	0.7	0.8	0.9
20	<0.20	<0.20	<0.20	0.24	0.36	0.51	0.67	0.80	0.89
22	<0.20	<0.20	<0.20	0.26	0.40	0.56	0.72	0.84	0.92
24	<0.20	<0.20	<0.20	0.28	0.43	0.60	0.76	0.88	0.94
26	<0.20	<0.20	<0.20	0.30	0.47	0.64	0.80	0.90	0.96
28	<0.20	<0.20	<0.20	0.33	0.50	0.68	0.83	0.93	0.97
30	<0.20	<0.20	0.20	0.35	0.53	0.72	0.86	0.94	0.98
35	<0.20	<0.20	0.23	0.40	0.61	0.79	0.91	0.97	*
40	<0.20	<0.20	0.26	0.46	0.68	0.85	0.95	0.99	*
45	<0.20	<0.20	0.29	0.51	0.74	0.89	0.97	*	*
50	<0.20	<0.20	0.33	0.56	0.79	0.93	0.98	*	*
55	<0.20	<0.20	0.36	0.61	0.83	0.95	0.99	*	*
60	<0.20	<0.20	0.39	0.66	0.87	0.96	*	*	*
65	<0.20	<0.20	0.42	0.70	0.90	0.98	*	*	*
70	<0.20	0.21	0.45	0.73	0.92	0.98	*	*	*
75	<0.20	0.22	0.48	0.77	0.94	0.99	*	*	*
80	<0.20	0.24	0.51	0.80	0.95	*	*	*	*
85	<0.20	0.25	0.54	0.83	0.96	*	*	*	*
90	<0.20	0.26	0.57	0.85	0.97	*	*	*	*
95	<0.20	0.28	0.60	0.87	0.98	*	*	*	*
100	<0.20	0.29	0.62	0.89	0.98	*	*	*	*
110	<0.20	0.32	0.67	0.92	0.99	*	*	*	*
120	<0.20	0.35	0.72	0.94	*	*	*	*	*
130	<0.20	0.38	0.76	0.96	*	*	*	*	*
140	<0.20	0.40	0.79	0.97	*	*	*	*	*
150	<0.20	0.43	0.82	0.98	*	*	*	*	*
160	<0.20	0.46	0.85	0.99	*	*	*	*	*
170	<0.20	0.49	0.87	0.99	*	*	*	*	*
180	<0.20	0.51	0.89	*	*	*	*	*	*
190	<0.20	0.54	0.91	*	*	*	*	*	*
200	<0.20	0.56	0.93	*	*	*	*	*	*
250	<0.20	0.68	0.97	*	*	*	*	*	*
300	0.22	0.77	0.99	*	*	*	*	*	*
350	0.26	0.84	*	*	*	*	*	*	*
400	0.29	0.89	*	*	*	*	*	*	*
450	0.33	0.93	*	*	*	*	*	*	*
500	0.36	0.95	*	*	*	*	*	*	*
600	0.43	0.98	*	*	*	*	*	*	*
700	0.50	0.99	*	*	*	*	*	*	*
800	0.56	*	*	*	*	*	*	*	*
900	0.62	*	*	*	*	*	*	*	*
1000	0.68	*	*	*	*	*	*	*	*
1100	0.73	*	*	*	*	*	*	*	*
1200	0.77	*	*	*	*	*	*	*	*
1300	0.84	*	*	*	*	*	*	*	*

f. df = 6

| | effect size (w) | | | | | | | | |
n	0.1	0.2	0.3	0.4	0.5	0.6	0.7	0.8	0.9
20	<0.20	<0.20	<0.20	0.22	0.34	0.48	0.63	0.77	0.87
22	<0.20	<0.20	<0.20	0.24	0.37	0.52	0.68	0.81	0.91
24	<0.20	<0.20	<0.20	0.26	0.40	0.57	0.73	0.85	0.93
26	<0.20	<0.20	<0.20	0.28	0.43	0.61	0.77	0.88	0.95
28	<0.20	<0.20	<0.20	0.30	0.47	0.65	0.80	0.91	0.96
30	<0.20	<0.20	<0.20	0.32	0.50	0.68	0.83	0.93	0.98
35	<0.20	<0.20	0.22	0.38	0.57	0.76	0.89	0.96	0.99
40	<0.20	<0.20	0.25	0.43	0.64	0.82	0.93	0.98	*
45	<0.20	<0.20	0.27	0.48	0.70	0.87	0.96	0.99	*
50	<0.20	<0.20	0.30	0.53	0.76	0.91	0.98	*	*
55	<0.20	<0.20	0.33	0.58	0.80	0.94	0.99	*	*
60	<0.20	<0.20	0.36	0.62	0.84	0.96	0.99	*	*
65	<0.20	<0.20	0.39	0.66	0.87	0.97	*	*	*
70	<0.20	0.20	0.42	0.70	0.90	0.98	*	*	*
75	<0.20	0.21	0.45	0.74	0.92	0.99	*	*	*
80	<0.20	0.22	0.48	0.77	0.94	0.99	*	*	*
85	<0.20	0.23	0.51	0.80	0.95	*	*	*	*
90	<0.20	0.25	0.53	0.82	0.96	*	*	*	*
95	<0.20	0.26	0.56	0.85	0.97	*	*	*	*
100	<0.20	0.27	0.59	0.87	0.98	*	*	*	*
110	<0.20	0.30	0.64	0.90	0.99	*	*	*	*
120	<0.20	0.32	0.68	0.93	*	*	*	*	*
130	<0.20	0.35	0.72	0.95	*	*	*	*	*
140	<0.20	0.38	0.76	0.96	*	*	*	*	*
150	<0.20	0.40	0.79	0.97	*	*	*	*	*
160	<0.20	0.43	0.82	0.98	*	*	*	*	*
170	<0.20	0.45	0.85	0.99	*	*	*	*	*
180	<0.20	0.48	0.87	0.99	*	*	*	*	*
190	<0.20	0.50	0.89	*	*	*	*	*	*
200	<0.20	0.53	0.91	*	*	*	*	*	*
250	<0.20	0.64	0.96	*	*	*	*	*	*
300	0.21	0.74	0.99	*	*	*	*	*	*
350	0.24	0.81	*	*	*	*	*	*	*
400	0.27	0.87	*	*	*	*	*	*	*
450	0.30	0.91	*	*	*	*	*	*	*
500	0.34	0.94	*	*	*	*	*	*	*
600	0.40	0.97	*	*	*	*	*	*	*
700	0.47	0.99	*	*	*	*	*	*	*
800	0.53	*	*	*	*	*	*	*	*
900	0.59	*	*	*	*	*	*	*	*
1000	0.64	*	*	*	*	*	*	*	*
1100	0.69	*	*	*	*	*	*	*	*
1200	0.74	*	*	*	*	*	*	*	*
1300	0.81	*	*	*	*	*	*	*	*

Table A15.4 Power of a χ^2 test

g. df = 7

				effect size *(w)*					
n	0.1	0.2	0.3	0.4	0.5	0.6	0.7	0.8	0.9
20	<0.20	<0.20	<0.20	0.20	0.32	0.45	0.60	0.75	0.85
22	<0.20	<0.20	<0.20	0.22	0.35	0.50	0.66	0.79	0.89
24	<0.20	<0.20	<0.20	0.24	0.38	0.54	0.70	0.83	0.92
26	<0.20	<0.20	<0.20	0.26	0.41	0.58	0.74	0.87	0.94
28	<0.20	<0.20	<0.20	0.28	0.44	0.62	0.78	0.89	0.96
30	<0.20	<0.20	<0.20	0.30	0.47	0.66	0.81	0.92	0.97
35	<0.20	<0.20	0.20	0.35	0.55	0.74	0.88	0.96	0.99
40	<0.20	<0.20	0.23	0.40	0.62	0.80	0.92	0.98	*
45	<0.20	<0.20	0.26	0.45	0.68	0.85	0.95	0.99	*
50	<0.20	<0.20	0.28	0.50	0.73	0.89	0.97	*	*
55	<0.20	<0.20	0.31	0.55	0.78	0.92	0.99	*	*
60	<0.20	<0.20	0.34	0.59	0.82	0.95	0.99	*	*
65	<0.20	<0.20	0.37	0.64	0.86	0.97	*	*	*
70	<0.20	<0.20	0.40	0.68	0.88	0.98	*	*	*
75	<0.20	<0.20	0.43	0.71	0.91	0.99	*	*	*
80	<0.20	0.20	0.45	0.75	0.93	0.99	*	*	*
85	<0.20	0.22	0.48	0.78	0.94	0.99	*	*	*
90	<0.20	0.23	0.51	0.80	0.96	*	*	*	*
95	<0.20	0.24	0.53	0.83	0.97	*	*	*	*
100	<0.20	0.25	0.56	0.85	0.98	*	*	*	*
110	<0.20	0.28	0.61	0.89	0.99	*	*	*	*
120	<0.20	0.30	0.66	0.92	0.99	*	*	*	*
130	<0.20	0.33	0.70	0.94	*	*	*	*	*
140	<0.20	0.35	0.74	0.96	*	*	*	*	*
150	<0.20	0.38	0.77	0.97	*	*	*	*	*
160	<0.20	0.40	0.80	0.98	*	*	*	*	*
170	<0.20	0.43	0.83	0.99	*	*	*	*	*
180	<0.20	0.45	0.85	0.99	*	*	*	*	*
190	<0.20	0.48	0.88	0.99	*	*	*	*	*
200	<0.20	0.50	0.89	*	*	*	*	*	*
250	<0.20	0.62	0.96	*	*	*	*	*	*
300	<0.20	0.71	0.99	*	*	*	*	*	*
350	0.22	0.79	*	*	*	*	*	*	*
400	0.25	0.85	*	*	*	*	*	*	*
450	0.28	0.89	*	*	*	*	*	*	*
500	0.32	0.93	*	*	*	*	*	*	*
600	0.38	0.97	*	*	*	*	*	*	*
700	0.44	0.99	*	*	*	*	*	*	*
800	0.50	*	*	*	*	*	*	*	*
900	0.56	*	*	*	*	*	*	*	*
1000	0.62	*	*	*	*	*	*	*	*
1100	0.67	*	*	*	*	*	*	*	*
1200	0.71	*	*	*	*	*	*	*	*
1300	0.79	*	*	*	*	*	*	*	*
1400	0.82	*	*	*	*	*	*	*	*

h. df = 8

n	effect size (w)								
	0.1	0.2	0.3	0.4	0.5	0.6	0.7	0.8	0.9
20	<0.20	<0.20	<0.20	<0.20	0.30	0.43	0.58	0.72	0.84
22	<0.20	<0.20	<0.20	0.21	0.33	0.47	0.63	0.77	0.87
24	<0.20	<0.20	<0.20	0.23	0.36	0.51	0.67	0.81	0.91
26	<0.20	<0.20	<0.20	0.25	0.39	0.55	0.72	0.85	0.93
28	<0.20	<0.20	<0.20	0.27	0.42	0.59	0.76	0.88	0.95
30	<0.20	<0.20	<0.20	0.29	0.45	0.63	0.79	0.90	0.96
35	<0.20	<0.20	<0.20	0.33	0.52	0.71	0.86	0.95	0.98
40	<0.20	<0.20	0.22	0.38	0.59	0.78	0.91	0.97	0.99
45	<0.20	<0.20	0.24	0.43	0.65	0.84	0.94	0.99	*
50	<0.20	<0.20	0.27	0.47	0.71	0.88	0.96	0.99	*
55	<0.20	<0.20	0.30	0.52	0.76	0.91	0.98	*	*
60	<0.20	<0.20	0.32	0.56	0.80	0.94	0.99	*	*
65	<0.20	<0.20	0.35	0.61	0.84	0.96	0.99	*	*
70	<0.20	<0.20	0.37	0.65	0.87	0.97	0.99	*	*
75	<0.20	<0.20	0.40	0.68	0.89	0.98	*	*	*
80	<0.20	<0.20	0.43	0.72	0.92	0.99	*	*	*
85	<0.20	0.20	0.45	0.75	0.93	0.99	*	*	*
90	<0.20	0.22	0.48	0.78	0.95	0.99	*	*	*
95	<0.20	0.23	0.51	0.81	0.96	0.99	*	*	*
100	<0.20	0.24	0.53	0.83	0.97	*	*	*	*
110	<0.20	0.26	0.58	0.87	0.98	*	*	*	*
120	<0.20	0.29	0.63	0.90	0.99	*	*	*	*
130	<0.20	0.31	0.67	0.93	0.99	*	*	*	*
140	<0.20	0.33	0.71	0.95	*	*	*	*	*
150	<0.20	0.36	0.75	0.96	*	*	*	*	*
160	<0.20	0.38	0.78	0.97	*	*	*	*	*
170	<0.20	0.40	0.81	0.98	*	*	*	*	*
180	<0.20	0.43	0.84	0.99	*	*	*	*	*
190	<0.20	0.45	0.86	0.99	*	*	*	*	*
200	<0.20	0.47	0.88	0.99	*	*	*	*	*
250	<0.20	0.59	0.95	*	*	*	*	*	*
300	<0.20	0.68	0.98	*	*	*	*	*	*
350	0.21	0.77	0.99	*	*	*	*	*	*
400	0.24	0.83	*	*	*	*	*	*	*
450	0.27	0.88	*	*	*	*	*	*	*
500	0.30	0.92	*	*	*	*	*	*	*
600	0.36	0.96	*	*	*	*	*	*	*
700	0.42	0.98	*	*	*	*	*	*	*
800	0.47	0.99	*	*	*	*	*	*	*
900	0.53	*	*	*	*	*	*	*	*
1000	0.59	*	*	*	*	*	*	*	*
1100	0.64	*	*	*	*	*	*	*	*
1200	0.68	*	*	*	*	*	*	*	*
1300	0.77	*	*	*	*	*	*	*	*
1400	0.80	*	*	*	*	*	*	*	*

Table A15.4 Power of a χ^2 test

i. df = 10

				effect size *(w)*					
n	0.1	0.2	0.3	0.4	0.5	0.6	0.7	0.8	0.9
20	<0.20	<0.20	<0.20	<0.20	0.27	0.39	0.53	0.68	0.80
22	<0.20	<0.20	<0.20	<0.20	0.30	0.43	0.58	0.73	0.84
24	<0.20	<0.20	<0.20	0.21	0.32	0.47	0.63	0.77	0.88
26	<0.20	<0.20	<0.20	0.23	0.35	0.51	0.67	0.81	0.91
28	<0.20	<0.20	<0.20	0.24	0.38	0.55	0.71	0.84	0.93
30	<0.20	<0.20	<0.20	0.26	0.41	0.58	0.75	0.87	0.95
35	<0.20	<0.20	<0.20	0.30	0.48	0.67	0.82	0.93	0.98
40	<0.20	<0.20	<0.20	0.35	0.54	0.74	0.88	0.96	0.99
45	<0.20	<0.20	0.22	0.39	0.61	0.80	0.92	0.98	*
50	<0.20	<0.20	0.24	0.44	0.66	0.85	0.95	0.99	*
55	<0.20	<0.20	0.27	0.48	0.71	0.88	0.97	*	*
60	<0.20	<0.20	0.29	0.52	0.76	0.91	0.99	*	*
65	<0.20	<0.20	0.32	0.56	0.80	0.94	0.99	*	*
70	<0.20	<0.20	0.34	0.60	0.83	0.96	*	*	*
75	<0.20	<0.20	0.37	0.64	0.86	0.97	*	*	*
80	<0.20	<0.20	0.39	0.68	0.89	0.98	*	*	*
85	<0.20	<0.20	0.42	0.71	0.91	0.99	*	*	*
90	<0.20	<0.20	0.44	0.74	0.93	0.99	*	*	*
95	<0.20	0.21	0.47	0.77	0.94	*	*	*	*
100	<0.20	0.22	0.49	0.79	0.96	*	*	*	*
110	<0.20	0.24	0.54	0.84	0.98	*	*	*	*
120	<0.20	0.26	0.58	0.87	0.99	*	*	*	*
130	<0.20	0.28	0.63	0.90	0.99	*	*	*	*
140	<0.20	0.30	0.67	0.93	*	*	*	*	*
150	<0.20	0.32	0.70	0.95	*	*	*	*	*
160	<0.20	0.35	0.74	0.96	*	*	*	*	*
170	<0.20	0.37	0.77	0.97	*	*	*	*	*
180	<0.20	0.39	0.80	0.98	*	*	*	*	*
190	<0.20	0.41	0.82	0.99	*	*	*	*	*
200	<0.20	0.44	0.85	0.99	*	*	*	*	*
250	<0.20	0.54	0.93	*	*	*	*	*	*
300	<0.20	0.64	0.97	*	*	*	*	*	*
350	<0.20	0.72	0.99	*	*	*	*	*	*
400	0.22	0.79	*	*	*	*	*	*	*
450	0.24	0.85	*	*	*	*	*	*	*
500	0.27	0.89	*	*	*	*	*	*	*
600	0.32	0.95	*	*	*	*	*	*	*
700	0.38	0.98	*	*	*	*	*	*	*
800	0.44	0.99	*	*	*	*	*	*	*
900	0.49	*	*	*	*	*	*	*	*
1000	0.54	*	*	*	*	*	*	*	*
1100	0.59	*	*	*	*	*	*	*	*
1200	0.64	*	*	*	*	*	*	*	*
1300	0.72	*	*	*	*	*	*	*	*
1400	0.76	*	*	*	*	*	*	*	*
1500	0.79	*	*	*	*	*	*	*	*
1700	0.82	*	*	*	*	*	*	*	*

Table A15.5 Power of an *F*-ratio in Analysis of Variance

a. Treatment df = 1 (*n* is the number of people in each condition for a between-subjects design)

n	0.01	0.05	0.059	0.10	effect size (η^2) 0.138	0.15	0.20	0.25	0.30	0.35
3	0.06	0.08	0.08	0.11	0.13	0.13	0.17	0.20	0.24	0.29
4	0.06	0.09	0.09	0.13	0.16	0.17	0.23	0.28	0.35	0.42
5	0.06	0.10	0.11	0.15	0.20	0.22	0.29	0.37	0.45	0.54
6	0.06	0.11	0.12	0.18	0.24	0.26	0.35	0.45	0.54	0.64
7	0.06	0.12	0.14	0.21	0.28	0.31	0.41	0.52	0.62	0.72
8	0.06	0.13	0.15	0.24	0.32	0.35	0.47	0.58	0.69	0.79
9	0.06	0.15	0.17	0.27	0.36	0.39	0.52	0.64	0.75	0.84
10	0.06	0.16	0.18	0.30	0.40	0.44	0.57	0.69	0.80	0.88
11	0.07	0.17	0.20	0.32	0.44	0.47	0.62	0.74	0.84	0.91
12	0.07	0.19	0.22	0.35	0.47	0.51	0.66	0.78	0.87	0.93
13	0.07	0.20	0.23	0.38	0.51	0.55	0.70	0.81	0.90	0.95
14	0.07	0.21	0.25	0.40	0.54	0.58	0.73	0.84	0.92	0.96
15	0.07	0.23	0.26	0.43	0.57	0.61	0.76	0.87	0.94	0.97
16	0.08	0.24	0.28	0.46	0.60	0.64	0.79	0.89	0.95	0.98
17	0.08	0.26	0.30	0.48	0.63	0.67	0.82	0.91	0.96	0.99
18	0.08	0.27	0.31	0.50	0.66	0.70	0.84	0.92	0.97	0.99
19	0.08	0.28	0.33	0.53	0.68	0.72	0.86	0.94	0.98	0.99
20	0.09	0.30	0.34	0.55	0.70	0.75	0.88	0.95	0.98	*
25	0.10	0.36	0.42	0.65	0.80	0.84	0.94	0.98	*	*
30	0.11	0.42	0.49	0.73	0.87	0.90	0.97	0.99	*	*
35	0.12	0.48	0.55	0.79	0.92	0.94	0.99	*	*	*
40	0.14	0.54	0.61	0.85	0.95	0.96	0.99	*	*	*
45	0.15	0.59	0.66	0.89	0.97	0.98	*	*	*	*
50	0.16	0.63	0.71	0.92	0.98	0.99	*	*	*	*
60	0.19	0.71	0.79	0.96	0.99	*	*	*	*	*
70	0.22	0.78	0.85	0.98	*	*	*	*	*	*
80	0.24	0.83	0.89	0.99	*	*	*	*	*	*
90	0.27	0.87	0.92	0.99	*	*	*	*	*	*
100	0.30	0.90	0.95	*	*	*	*	*	*	*
120	0.35	0.95	0.97	*	*	*	*	*	*	*
140	0.40	0.97	0.99	*	*	*	*	*	*	*
160	0.44	0.98	0.99	*	*	*	*	*	*	*
180	0.49	0.99	*	*	*	*	*	*	*	*
200	0.53	*	*	*	*	*	*	*	*	*
300	0.70	*	*	*	*	*	*	*	*	*
400	0.82	*	*	*	*	*	*	*	*	*
500	0.89	*	*	*	*	*	*	*	*	*
600	0.94	*	*	*	*	*	*	*	*	*
700	0.97	*	*	*	*	*	*	*	*	*
800	0.98	*	*	*	*	*	*	*	*	*
900	0.99	*	*	*	*	*	*	*	*	*
1000	0.99	*	*	*	*	*	*	*	*	*

Table A15.5 Power of an *F*-ratio in Analysis of Variance

b. Treatment df = 2 (*n* is the number of people in each condition for a between-subjects design)

n	0.01	0.05	0.059	0.10	0.138	0.15	0.20	0.25	0.30	0.35
3	0.06	0.08	0.08	0.11	0.13	0.14	0.17	0.21	0.26	0.32
4	0.06	0.09	0.09	0.13	0.17	0.18	0.24	0.31	0.39	0.47
5	0.06	0.10	0.11	0.16	0.22	0.23	0.32	0.41	0.51	0.61
6	0.06	0.11	0.13	0.19	0.26	0.29	0.39	0.50	0.61	0.72
7	0.06	0.13	0.14	0.23	0.31	0.34	0.46	0.58	0.70	0.80
8	0.06	0.14	0.16	0.26	0.36	0.39	0.53	0.66	0.77	0.86
9	0.06	0.16	0.18	0.29	0.40	0.44	0.59	0.72	0.83	0.91
10	0.07	0.17	0.20	0.32	0.45	0.49	0.64	0.77	0.87	0.94
11	0.07	0.19	0.22	0.36	0.49	0.53	0.69	0.82	0.91	0.96
12	0.07	0.20	0.23	0.39	0.53	0.58	0.74	0.85	0.93	0.97
13	0.07	0.22	0.25	0.42	0.57	0.62	0.77	0.89	0.95	0.98
14	0.08	0.23	0.27	0.45	0.61	0.65	0.81	0.91	0.96	0.99
15	0.08	0.25	0.29	0.48	0.64	0.69	0.84	0.93	0.97	0.99
16	0.08	0.26	0.31	0.51	0.68	0.72	0.86	0.95	0.98	*
17	0.08	0.28	0.33	0.54	0.71	0.75	0.89	0.96	0.99	*
18	0.09	0.30	0.35	0.57	0.73	0.78	0.90	0.97	0.99	*
19	0.09	0.31	0.36	0.59	0.76	0.80	0.92	0.98	0.99	*
20	0.09	0.33	0.38	0.62	0.78	0.82	0.93	0.98	*	*
25	0.10	0.40	0.47	0.72	0.87	0.90	0.98	*	*	*
30	0.12	0.48	0.55	0.81	0.93	0.95	0.99	*	*	*
35	0.13	0.54	0.62	0.87	0.96	0.98	*	*	*	*
40	0.15	0.60	0.69	0.91	0.98	0.99	*	*	*	*
45	0.16	0.66	0.74	0.94	0.99	0.99	*	*	*	*
50	0.18	0.71	0.79	0.96	0.99	*	*	*	*	*
60	0.21	0.79	0.86	0.98	*	*	*	*	*	*
70	0.24	0.85	0.91	0.99	*	*	*	*	*	*
80	0.27	0.90	0.94	*	*	*	*	*	*	*
90	0.30	0.93	0.97	*	*	*	*	*	*	*
100	0.33	0.95	0.98	*	*	*	*	*	*	*
120	0.39	0.98	0.99	*	*	*	*	*	*	*
140	0.44	0.99	*	*	*	*	*	*	*	*
160	0.50	*	*	*	*	*	*	*	*	*
180	0.55	*	*	*	*	*	*	*	*	*
200	0.60	*	*	*	*	*	*	*	*	*
300	0.78	*	*	*	*	*	*	*	*	*
400	0.89	*	*	*	*	*	*	*	*	*
500	0.95	*	*	*	*	*	*	*	*	*
600	0.98	*	*	*	*	*	*	*	*	*
700	0.99	*	*	*	*	*	*	*	*	*
800	*	*	*	*	*	*	*	*	*	*

c. Treatment df = 3 (*n* is the number of people in each condition for a between-subjects design)

n	0.01	0.05	0.059	0.10	effect size (η^2) 0.138	0.15	0.20	0.25	0.30	0.35
3	0.06	0.08	0.08	0.11	0.14	0.15	0.19	0.24	0.30	0.36
4	0.06	0.09	0.10	0.14	0.18	0.20	0.27	0.35	0.44	0.54
5	0.06	0.10	0.12	0.17	0.24	0.26	0.36	0.46	0.57	0.68
6	0.06	0.12	0.13	0.21	0.29	0.32	0.44	0.57	0.69	0.79
7	0.06	0.13	0.15	0.25	0.35	0.38	0.52	0.65	0.77	0.87
8	0.06	0.15	0.17	0.29	0.40	0.44	0.59	0.73	0.84	0.92
9	0.07	0.17	0.19	0.33	0.46	0.50	0.66	0.79	0.89	0.95
10	0.07	0.19	0.22	0.36	0.51	0.55	0.71	0.84	0.93	0.97
11	0.07	0.20	0.24	0.40	0.55	0.60	0.76	0.88	0.95	0.98
12	0.07	0.22	0.26	0.44	0.60	0.65	0.81	0.91	0.97	0.99
13	0.08	0.24	0.28	0.47	0.64	0.69	0.84	0.93	0.98	0.99
14	0.08	0.26	0.30	0.51	0.68	0.73	0.87	0.95	0.99	*
15	0.08	0.27	0.32	0.54	0.71	0.76	0.90	0.97	0.99	*
16	0.08	0.29	0.34	0.57	0.75	0.79	0.92	0.98	0.99	*
17	0.09	0.31	0.37	0.60	0.78	0.82	0.94	0.98	*	*
18	0.09	0.33	0.39	0.63	0.80	0.84	0.95	0.99	*	*
19	0.09	0.35	0.41	0.66	0.83	0.87	0.96	0.99	*	*
20	0.10	0.37	0.43	0.69	0.85	0.88	0.97	0.99	*	*
25	0.11	0.45	0.53	0.80	0.93	0.95	0.99	*	*	*
30	0.13	0.53	0.62	0.87	0.97	0.98	*	*	*	*
35	0.14	0.61	0.69	0.92	0.98	0.99	*	*	*	*
40	0.16	0.67	0.76	0.95	0.99	*	*	*	*	*
45	0.18	0.73	0.81	0.97	*	*	*	*	*	*
50	0.19	0.78	0.85	0.98	*	*	*	*	*	*
60	0.23	0.86	0.92	*	*	*	*	*	*	*
70	0.26	0.91	0.95	*	*	*	*	*	*	*
80	0.30	0.94	0.97	*	*	*	*	*	*	*
90	0.33	0.97	0.99	*	*	*	*	*	*	*
100	0.37	0.98	0.99	*	*	*	*	*	*	*
120	0.43	0.99	*	*	*	*	*	*	*	*
140	0.50	*	*	*	*	*	*	*	*	*
160	0.56	*	*	*	*	*	*	*	*	*
180	0.61	*	*	*	*	*	*	*	*	*
200	0.66	*	*	*	*	*	*	*	*	*
300	0.85	*	*	*	*	*	*	*	*	*
400	0.94	*	*	*	*	*	*	*	*	*
500	0.98	*	*	*	*	*	*	*	*	*
600	0.99	*	*	*	*	*	*	*	*	*
700	*	*	*	*	*	*	*	*	*	*

Table A15.5 Power of an *F*-ratio in Analysis of Variance

d. Treatment df = 4 (*n* is the number of people in each condition for a between-subjects design)

n	effect size (η^2)									
	0.01	0.05	0.059	0.10	0.138	0.15	0.20	0.25	0.30	0.35
3	0.06	0.08	0.09	0.11	0.14	0.16	0.20	0.26	0.33	0.41
4	0.06	0.09	0.10	0.15	0.20	0.22	0.30	0.39	0.50	0.60
5	0.06	0.11	0.12	0.19	0.26	0.29	0.40	0.52	0.64	0.75
6	0.06	0.13	0.14	0.23	0.32	0.36	0.49	0.63	0.75	0.85
7	0.06	0.14	0.16	0.27	0.39	0.42	0.58	0.72	0.83	0.91
8	0.07	0.16	0.19	0.32	0.45	0.49	0.65	0.79	0.89	0.95
9	0.07	0.18	0.21	0.36	0.51	0.55	0.72	0.85	0.93	0.97
10	0.07	0.20	0.23	0.40	0.56	0.61	0.78	0.89	0.96	0.99
11	0.07	0.22	0.26	0.45	0.61	0.66	0.82	0.92	0.97	0.99
12	0.08	0.24	0.28	0.49	0.66	0.71	0.86	0.95	0.98	*
13	0.08	0.26	0.31	0.53	0.70	0.75	0.89	0.96	0.99	*
14	0.08	0.28	0.33	0.56	0.74	0.79	0.92	0.98	0.99	*
15	0.08	0.30	0.36	0.60	0.78	0.82	0.94	0.98	*	*
16	0.09	0.32	0.38	0.63	0.81	0.85	0.95	0.99	*	*
17	0.09	0.34	0.41	0.66	0.83	0.87	0.96	0.99	*	*
18	0.09	0.36	0.43	0.69	0.86	0.89	0.97	*	*	*
19	0.10	0.38	0.45	0.72	0.88	0.91	0.98	*	*	*
20	0.10	0.40	0.48	0.75	0.90	0.93	0.99	*	*	*
25	0.12	0.50	0.58	0.85	0.96	0.97	*	*	*	*
30	0.13	0.59	0.68	0.92	0.98	0.99	*	*	*	*
35	0.15	0.67	0.75	0.95	0.99	*	*	*	*	*
40	0.17	0.73	0.81	0.98	*	*	*	*	*	*
45	0.19	0.79	0.86	0.99	*	*	*	*	*	*
50	0.21	0.84	0.90	0.99	*	*	*	*	*	*
60	0.25	0.90	0.95	*	*	*	*	*	*	*
70	0.29	0.95	0.98	*	*	*	*	*	*	*
80	0.33	0.97	0.99	*	*	*	*	*	*	*
90	0.37	0.98	0.99	*	*	*	*	*	*	*
100	0.40	0.99	*	*	*	*	*	*	*	*
120	0.48	*	*	*	*	*	*	*	*	*
140	0.55	*	*	*	*	*	*	*	*	*
160	0.61	*	*	*	*	*	*	*	*	*
180	0.67	*	*	*	*	*	*	*	*	*
200	0.72	*	*	*	*	*	*	*	*	*
300	0.90	*	*	*	*	*	*	*	*	*
400	0.97	*	*	*	*	*	*	*	*	*
500	0.99	*	*	*	*	*	*	*	*	*
600	*	*	*	*	*	*	*	*	*	*

e. Treatment df = 5 (*n* is the number of people in each condition for a between-subjects design)

n	0.01	0.05	0.059	0.10	effect size (η^2) 0.138	0.15	0.20	0.25	0.30	0.35
3	0.06	0.08	0.09	0.12	0.15	0.17	0.22	0.29	0.37	0.46
4	0.06	0.10	0.11	0.16	0.22	0.24	0.33	0.43	0.55	0.66
5	0.06	0.11	0.13	0.20	0.29	0.31	0.44	0.57	0.69	0.80
6	0.06	0.13	0.15	0.25	0.36	0.39	0.54	0.68	0.80	0.89
7	0.06	0.15	0.18	0.30	0.42	0.46	0.63	0.77	0.88	0.95
8	0.07	0.17	0.20	0.35	0.49	0.54	0.71	0.84	0.93	0.97
9	0.07	0.19	0.23	0.39	0.55	0.60	0.77	0.89	0.96	0.99
10	0.07	0.22	0.25	0.44	0.61	0.66	0.83	0.93	0.98	0.99
11	0.08	0.24	0.28	0.49	0.66	0.71	0.87	0.95	0.99	*
12	0.08	0.26	0.31	0.53	0.71	0.76	0.90	0.97	0.99	*
13	0.08	0.28	0.34	0.57	0.75	0.80	0.93	0.98	*	*
14	0.08	0.31	0.36	0.61	0.79	0.84	0.95	0.99	*	*
15	0.09	0.33	0.39	0.65	0.83	0.86	0.96	0.99	*	*
16	0.09	0.35	0.42	0.68	0.85	0.89	0.97	*	*	*
17	0.09	0.37	0.44	0.72	0.88	0.91	0.98	*	*	*
18	0.10	0.40	0.47	0.75	0.90	0.93	0.99	*	*	*
19	0.10	0.42	0.49	0.77	0.92	0.94	0.99	*	*	*
20	0.10	0.44	0.52	0.80	0.93	0.95	0.99	*	*	*
25	0.12	0.55	0.63	0.89	0.98	0.99	*	*	*	*
30	0.14	0.64	0.73	0.95	0.99	*	*	*	*	*
35	0.16	0.72	0.80	0.97	*	*	*	*	*	*
40	0.18	0.79	0.86	0.99	*	*	*	*	*	*
45	0.20	0.84	0.90	0.99	*	*	*	*	*	*
50	0.22	0.88	0.93	*	*	*	*	*	*	*
60	0.27	0.94	0.97	*	*	*	*	*	*	*
70	0.31	0.97	0.99	*	*	*	*	*	*	*
80	0.36	0.98	*	*	*	*	*	*	*	*
90	0.40	0.99	*	*	*	*	*	*	*	*
100	0.44	*	*	*	*	*	*	*	*	*
120	0.52	*	*	*	*	*	*	*	*	*
140	0.60	*	*	*	*	*	*	*	*	*
160	0.67	*	*	*	*	*	*	*	*	*
180	0.72	*	*	*	*	*	*	*	*	*
200	0.78	*	*	*	*	*	*	*	*	*
300	0.93	*	*	*	*	*	*	*	*	*
400	0.98	*	*	*	*	*	*	*	*	*
500	*	*	*	*	*	*	*	*	*	*

Table A15.5 Power of an *F*-ratio in Analysis of Variance

f. Treatment df = 6 (*n* is the number of people in each condition for a between-subjects design)

n	0.01	0.05	0.059	0.10	effect size (η^2) 0.138	0.15	0.20	0.25	0.30	0.35
3	0.06	0.08	0.09	0.13	0.16	0.18	0.24	0.32	0.40	0.50
4	0.06	0.10	0.11	0.17	0.23	0.26	0.36	0.47	0.59	0.71
5	0.06	0.12	0.13	0.22	0.31	0.34	0.48	0.62	0.74	0.85
6	0.06	0.14	0.16	0.27	0.39	0.42	0.58	0.73	0.85	0.93
7	0.06	0.16	0.19	0.32	0.46	0.50	0.68	0.82	0.91	0.97
8	0.07	0.18	0.21	0.37	0.53	0.58	0.76	0.88	0.95	0.99
9	0.07	0.21	0.24	0.43	0.60	0.65	0.82	0.92	0.98	0.99
10	0.07	0.23	0.27	0.48	0.66	0.71	0.87	0.95	0.99	*
11	0.08	0.26	0.30	0.53	0.71	0.76	0.90	0.97	0.99	*
12	0.08	0.28	0.33	0.57	0.76	0.80	0.93	0.98	*	*
13	0.08	0.31	0.36	0.62	0.80	0.84	0.95	0.99	*	*
14	0.09	0.33	0.39	0.66	0.83	0.87	0.97	0.99	*	*
15	0.09	0.36	0.42	0.70	0.86	0.90	0.98	*	*	*
16	0.09	0.38	0.45	0.73	0.89	0.92	0.98	*	*	*
17	0.10	0.41	0.48	0.76	0.91	0.94	0.99	*	*	*
18	0.10	0.43	0.51	0.79	0.93	0.95	0.99	*	*	*
19	0.11	0.45	0.53	0.82	0.94	0.96	*	*	*	*
20	0.11	0.48	0.56	0.84	0.95	0.97	*	*	*	*
25	0.13	0.59	0.68	0.92	0.99	0.99	*	*	*	*
30	0.15	0.69	0.77	0.97	*	*	*	*	*	*
35	0.17	0.76	0.84	0.99	*	*	*	*	*	*
40	0.19	0.83	0.90	0.99	*	*	*	*	*	*
45	0.22	0.88	0.93	*	*	*	*	*	*	*
50	0.24	0.91	0.96	*	*	*	*	*	*	*
60	0.29	0.96	0.98	*	*	*	*	*	*	*
70	0.34	0.98	0.99	*	*	*	*	*	*	*
80	0.38	0.99	*	*	*	*	*	*	*	*
90	0.43	*	*	*	*	*	*	*	*	*
100	0.48	*	*	*	*	*	*	*	*	*
120	0.56	*	*	*	*	*	*	*	*	*
140	0.64	*	*	*	*	*	*	*	*	*
160	0.71	*	*	*	*	*	*	*	*	*
180	0.77	*	*	*	*	*	*	*	*	*
200	0.82	*	*	*	*	*	*	*	*	*
300	0.95	*	*	*	*	*	*	*	*	*
400	0.99	*	*	*	*	*	*	*	*	*
500	*	*	*	*	*	*	*	*	*	*

g. Treatment df = 7 (*n* is the number of people in each condition for a between-subjects design)

n	0.01	0.05	0.059	0.10	0.138	0.15	0.20	0.25	0.30	0.35
3	0.06	0.09	0.09	0.13	0.17	0.19	0.26	0.34	0.44	0.54
4	0.06	0.10	0.12	0.18	0.25	0.27	0.39	0.51	0.64	0.76
5	0.06	0.12	0.14	0.23	0.33	0.37	0.51	0.66	0.79	0.88
6	0.06	0.15	0.17	0.29	0.41	0.46	0.63	0.77	0.88	0.95
7	0.07	0.17	0.20	0.35	0.49	0.54	0.72	0.85	0.94	0.98
8	0.07	0.19	0.23	0.40	0.57	0.62	0.80	0.91	0.97	0.99
9	0.07	0.22	0.26	0.46	0.64	0.69	0.85	0.95	0.99	*
10	0.08	0.25	0.29	0.51	0.70	0.75	0.90	0.97	0.99	*
11	0.08	0.27	0.32	0.56	0.75	0.80	0.93	0.98	*	*
12	0.08	0.30	0.36	0.61	0.80	0.84	0.95	0.99	*	*
13	0.09	0.33	0.39	0.66	0.84	0.88	0.97	0.99	*	*
14	0.09	0.35	0.42	0.70	0.87	0.90	0.98	*	*	*
15	0.09	0.38	0.45	0.74	0.90	0.93	0.99	*	*	*
16	0.10	0.41	0.48	0.77	0.92	0.94	0.99	*	*	*
17	0.10	0.43	0.51	0.80	0.94	0.96	0.99	*	*	*
18	0.11	0.46	0.54	0.83	0.95	0.97	*	*	*	*
19	0.11	0.49	0.57	0.85	0.96	0.98	*	*	*	*
20	0.11	0.51	0.60	0.87	0.97	0.98	*	*	*	*
25	0.13	0.63	0.72	0.95	0.99	*	*	*	*	*
30	0.16	0.73	0.81	0.98	*	*	*	*	*	*
35	0.18	0.80	0.88	0.99	*	*	*	*	*	*
40	0.20	0.86	0.92	*	*	*	*	*	*	*
45	0.23	0.91	0.95	*	*	*	*	*	*	*
50	0.26	0.94	0.97	*	*	*	*	*	*	*
60	0.31	0.97	0.99	*	*	*	*	*	*	*
70	0.36	0.99	*	*	*	*	*	*	*	*
80	0.41	*	*	*	*	*	*	*	*	*
90	0.46	*	*	*	*	*	*	*	*	*
100	0.51	*	*	*	*	*	*	*	*	*
120	0.60	*	*	*	*	*	*	*	*	*
140	0.68	*	*	*	*	*	*	*	*	*
160	0.75	*	*	*	*	*	*	*	*	*
180	0.81	*	*	*	*	*	*	*	*	*
200	0.85	*	*	*	*	*	*	*	*	*
300	0.97	*	*	*	*	*	*	*	*	*
400	0.99	*	*	*	*	*	*	*	*	*
500	*	*	*	*	*	*	*	*	*	*

Table A15.5 Power of an *F*-ratio in Analysis of Variance

h. Treatment df = 8 (*n* is the number of people in each condition for a between-subjects design)

n	0.01	0.05	0.059	0.10	0.138	0.15	0.20	0.25	0.30	0.35
3	0.06	0.09	0.10	0.14	0.18	0.20	0.28	0.37	0.47	0.58
4	0.06	0.11	0.12	0.19	0.27	0.29	0.42	0.55	0.68	0.79
5	0.06	0.13	0.15	0.25	0.35	0.39	0.55	0.70	0.82	0.91
6	0.06	0.15	0.18	0.31	0.44	0.49	0.66	0.81	0.91	0.97
7	0.07	0.18	0.21	0.37	0.53	0.58	0.76	0.88	0.96	0.99
8	0.07	0.20	0.24	0.43	0.60	0.66	0.83	0.93	0.98	*
9	0.07	0.23	0.28	0.49	0.67	0.73	0.88	0.96	0.99	*
10	0.08	0.26	0.31	0.55	0.74	0.78	0.92	0.98	*	*
11	0.08	0.29	0.34	0.60	0.79	0.83	0.95	0.99	*	*
12	0.08	0.32	0.38	0.65	0.83	0.87	0.97	0.99	*	*
13	0.09	0.35	0.41	0.69	0.87	0.90	0.98	*	*	*
14	0.09	0.38	0.45	0.74	0.90	0.93	0.99	*	*	*
15	0.10	0.41	0.48	0.77	0.92	0.95	0.99	*	*	*
16	0.10	0.43	0.51	0.81	0.94	0.96	*	*	*	*
17	0.10	0.46	0.55	0.83	0.95	0.97	*	*	*	*
18	0.11	0.49	0.58	0.86	0.97	0.98	*	*	*	*
19	0.11	0.52	0.61	0.88	0.97	0.99	*	*	*	*
20	0.12	0.54	0.63	0.90	0.98	0.99	*	*	*	*
25	0.14	0.66	0.75	0.96	*	*	*	*	*	*
30	0.16	0.76	0.84	0.99	*	*	*	*	*	*
35	0.19	0.84	0.90	*	*	*	*	*	*	*
40	0.22	0.89	0.94	*	*	*	*	*	*	*
45	0.24	0.93	0.97	*	*	*	*	*	*	*
50	0.27	0.95	0.98	*	*	*	*	*	*	*
60	0.33	0.98	0.99	*	*	*	*	*	*	*
70	0.38	0.99	*	*	*	*	*	*	*	*
80	0.44	*	*	*	*	*	*	*	*	*
90	0.49	*	*	*	*	*	*	*	*	*
100	0.54	*	*	*	*	*	*	*	*	*
120	0.64	*	*	*	*	*	*	*	*	*
140	0.72	*	*	*	*	*	*	*	*	*
160	0.78	*	*	*	*	*	*	*	*	*
180	0.84	*	*	*	*	*	*	*	*	*
200	0.88	*	*	*	*	*	*	*	*	*
300	0.98	*	*	*	*	*	*	*	*	*
400	*	*	*	*	*	*	*	*	*	*

i. Treatment df = 10 (*n* is the number of people in each condition for a between-subjects design)

n	0.01	0.05	0.059	0.10	effect size (η^2) 0.138	0.15	0.20	0.25	0.30	0.35
3	0.06	0.09	0.10	0.15	0.20	0.22	0.31	0.42	0.53	0.65
4	0.06	0.11	0.13	0.21	0.30	0.33	0.47	0.61	0.75	0.86
5	0.06	0.14	0.16	0.27	0.40	0.44	0.61	0.76	0.88	0.95
6	0.07	0.17	0.19	0.34	0.50	0.54	0.73	0.87	0.95	0.98
7	0.07	0.19	0.23	0.41	0.59	0.64	0.82	0.93	0.98	*
8	0.07	0.22	0.27	0.48	0.67	0.72	0.88	0.96	0.99	*
9	0.08	0.26	0.31	0.55	0.74	0.79	0.93	0.98	*	*
10	0.08	0.29	0.35	0.61	0.80	0.84	0.96	0.99	*	*
11	0.08	0.32	0.39	0.66	0.85	0.88	0.97	*	*	*
12	0.09	0.35	0.42	0.71	0.88	0.92	0.98	*	*	*
13	0.09	0.39	0.46	0.76	0.91	0.94	0.99	*	*	*
14	0.10	0.42	0.50	0.80	0.94	0.96	*	*	*	*
15	0.10	0.45	0.54	0.83	0.95	0.97	*	*	*	*
16	0.11	0.48	0.57	0.86	0.97	0.98	*	*	*	*
17	0.11	0.52	0.61	0.89	0.98	0.99	*	*	*	*
18	0.12	0.55	0.64	0.91	0.98	0.99	*	*	*	*
19	0.12	0.57	0.67	0.92	0.99	0.99	*	*	*	*
20	0.13	0.60	0.70	0.94	0.99	*	*	*	*	*
25	0.15	0.73	0.81	0.98	*	*	*	*	*	*
30	0.18	0.82	0.89	0.99	*	*	*	*	*	*
35	0.21	0.89	0.94	*	*	*	*	*	*	*
40	0.24	0.93	0.97	*	*	*	*	*	*	*
45	0.27	0.96	0.98	*	*	*	*	*	*	*
50	0.30	0.98	0.99	*	*	*	*	*	*	*
60	0.36	0.99	*	*	*	*	*	*	*	*
70	0.43	*	*	*	*	*	*	*	*	*
80	0.49	*	*	*	*	*	*	*	*	*
90	0.55	*	*	*	*	*	*	*	*	*
100	0.60	*	*	*	*	*	*	*	*	*
120	0.70	*	*	*	*	*	*	*	*	*
140	0.78	*	*	*	*	*	*	*	*	*
160	0.84	*	*	*	*	*	*	*	*	*
180	0.89	*	*	*	*	*	*	*	*	*
200	0.92	*	*	*	*	*	*	*	*	*
300	0.99	*	*	*	*	*	*	*	*	*
400	*	*	*	*	*	*	*	*	*	*

Table A15.6 Power of a Pearson's Product Moment Correlation Coefficient *r*

a. One-tailed tests

n	0.1	0.2	0.3	0.4	0.5	0.6	0.7	0.8	0.9	0.95	0.99
					effect size (*r*)						
4	0.07	0.08	0.10	0.13	0.16	0.20	0.26	0.35	0.50	0.64	0.88
5	0.06	0.08	0.11	0.15	0.20	0.26	0.36	0.49	0.70	0.85	0.99
6	0.06	0.09	0.13	0.18	0.24	0.33	0.46	0.62	0.83	0.95	*
7	0.07	0.10	0.14	0.21	0.29	0.40	0.55	0.73	0.91	0.98	*
8	0.07	0.11	0.16	0.24	0.34	0.47	0.63	0.80	0.96	0.99	*
9	0.07	0.12	0.18	0.27	0.38	0.53	0.70	0.86	0.98	*	*
10	0.08	0.13	0.20	0.30	0.43	0.58	0.75	0.90	0.99	*	*
11	0.08	0.13	0.21	0.32	0.47	0.63	0.80	0.93	*	*	*
12	0.08	0.14	0.23	0.35	0.50	0.68	0.84	0.96	*	*	*
13	0.09	0.15	0.25	0.38	0.54	0.72	0.87	0.97	*	*	*
14	0.09	0.16	0.26	0.40	0.57	0.75	0.90	0.98	*	*	*
15	0.09	0.17	0.28	0.43	0.61	0.78	0.92	0.99	*	*	*
16	0.09	0.17	0.29	0.45	0.64	0.81	0.94	0.99	*	*	*
17	0.10	0.18	0.31	0.48	0.66	0.84	0.95	0.99	*	*	*
18	0.10	0.19	0.33	0.50	0.69	0.86	0.96	*	*	*	*
19	0.10	0.20	0.34	0.52	0.72	0.88	0.97	*	*	*	*
20	0.10	0.20	0.35	0.54	0.74	0.89	0.98	*	*	*	*
25	0.12	0.24	0.42	0.64	0.83	0.95	0.99	*	*	*	*
30	0.13	0.27	0.49	0.71	0.89	0.98	*	*	*	*	*
35	0.14	0.31	0.54	0.78	0.93	0.99	*	*	*	*	*
40	0.15	0.34	0.60	0.83	0.96	*	*	*	*	*	*
45	0.16	0.37	0.64	0.87	0.97	*	*	*	*	*	*
50	0.17	0.40	0.69	0.90	0.98	*	*	*	*	*	*
60	0.19	0.45	0.76	0.94	0.99	*	*	*	*	*	*
70	0.20	0.51	0.81	0.97	*	*	*	*	*	*	*
80	0.22	0.55	0.86	0.98	*	*	*	*	*	*	*
90	0.24	0.60	0.89	0.99	*	*	*	*	*	*	*
100	0.25	0.64	0.92	0.99	*	*	*	*	*	*	*
110	0.27	0.68	0.94	*	*	*	*	*	*	*	*
120	0.29	0.71	0.96	*	*	*	*	*	*	*	*
130	0.30	0.74	0.97	*	*	*	*	*	*	*	*
140	0.32	0.77	0.98	*	*	*	*	*	*	*	*
150	0.33	0.79	0.98	*	*	*	*	*	*	*	*
160	0.35	0.82	0.99	*	*	*	*	*	*	*	*
170	0.36	0.84	0.99	*	*	*	*	*	*	*	*
180	0.38	0.85	0.99	*	*	*	*	*	*	*	*
190	0.39	0.87	*	*	*	*	*	*	*	*	*
200	0.41	0.89	*	*	*	*	*	*	*	*	*
300	0.53	0.97	*	*	*	*	*	*	*	*	*
400	0.64	0.99	*	*	*	*	*	*	*	*	*
500	0.72	*	*	*	*	*	*	*	*	*	*
600	0.79	*	*	*	*	*	*	*	*	*	*
700	0.84	*	*	*	*	*	*	*	*	*	*
800	0.88	*	*	*	*	*	*	*	*	*	*
900	0.91	*	*	*	*	*	*	*	*	*	*
1000	0.94	*	*	*	*	*	*	*	*	*	*

b. Two-tailed tests

n	effect size (r)										
	0.1	0.2	0.3	0.4	0.5	0.6	0.7	0.8	0.9	0.95	0.99
4	0.03	0.04	0.05	0.07	0.09	0.12	0.16	0.22	0.36	0.50	0.79
5	0.03	0.04	0.05	0.08	0.11	0.16	0.23	0.35	0.56	0.75	0.97
6	0.03	0.04	0.07	0.10	0.14	0.21	0.32	0.48	0.73	0.89	*
7	0.03	0.05	0.08	0.12	0.18	0.27	0.40	0.59	0.84	0.96	*
8	0.03	0.06	0.09	0.14	0.22	0.33	0.49	0.69	0.91	0.98	*
9	0.04	0.06	0.10	0.17	0.26	0.39	0.56	0.77	0.95	0.99	*
10	0.04	0.07	0.12	0.19	0.30	0.44	0.63	0.83	0.98	*	*
11	0.04	0.07	0.13	0.21	0.33	0.50	0.69	0.88	0.99	*	*
12	0.04	0.08	0.14	0.24	0.37	0.55	0.74	0.91	0.99	*	*
13	0.04	0.08	0.15	0.26	0.41	0.59	0.79	0.94	*	*	*
14	0.05	0.09	0.17	0.28	0.44	0.63	0.82	0.96	*	*	*
15	0.05	0.10	0.18	0.30	0.47	0.67	0.86	0.97	*	*	*
16	0.05	0.10	0.19	0.33	0.51	0.71	0.88	0.98	*	*	*
17	0.05	0.11	0.20	0.35	0.54	0.74	0.90	0.99	*	*	*
18	0.05	0.11	0.22	0.37	0.57	0.77	0.92	0.99	*	*	*
19	0.05	0.12	0.23	0.39	0.59	0.79	0.94	0.99	*	*	*
20	0.06	0.12	0.24	0.41	0.62	0.82	0.95	*	*	*	*
25	0.06	0.15	0.30	0.51	0.73	0.90	0.98	*	*	*	*
30	0.07	0.18	0.36	0.60	0.82	0.95	0.99	*	*	*	*
35	0.08	0.20	0.41	0.67	0.88	0.98	*	*	*	*	*
40	0.09	0.23	0.47	0.73	0.92	0.99	*	*	*	*	*
45	0.09	0.26	0.52	0.79	0.95	0.99	*	*	*	*	*
50	0.10	0.28	0.56	0.83	0.97	*	*	*	*	*	*
60	0.11	0.33	0.65	0.89	0.99	*	*	*	*	*	*
70	0.13	0.38	0.72	0.94	0.99	*	*	*	*	*	*
80	0.14	0.43	0.78	0.96	*	*	*	*	*	*	*
90	0.15	0.47	0.82	0.98	*	*	*	*	*	*	*
100	0.16	0.51	0.86	0.99	*	*	*	*	*	*	*
110	0.18	0.55	0.89	0.99	*	*	*	*	*	*	*
120	0.19	0.59	0.92	*	*	*	*	*	*	*	*
130	0.20	0.63	0.94	*	*	*	*	*	*	*	*
140	0.21	0.66	0.95	*	*	*	*	*	*	*	*
150	0.23	0.69	0.96	*	*	*	*	*	*	*	*
160	0.24	0.72	0.97	*	*	*	*	*	*	*	*
170	0.25	0.75	0.98	*	*	*	*	*	*	*	*
180	0.27	0.77	0.98	*	*	*	*	*	*	*	*
190	0.28	0.79	0.99	*	*	*	*	*	*	*	*
200	0.29	0.81	0.99	*	*	*	*	*	*	*	*
300	0.41	0.94	*	*	*	*	*	*	*	*	*
400	0.52	0.98	*	*	*	*	*	*	*	*	*
500	0.61	0.99	*	*	*	*	*	*	*	*	*
600	0.69	*	*	*	*	*	*	*	*	*	*
700	0.75	*	*	*	*	*	*	*	*	*	*
800	0.81	*	*	*	*	*	*	*	*	*	*
900	0.85	*	*	*	*	*	*	*	*	*	*
1000	0.89	*	*	*	*	*	*	*	*	*	*

Table A15.7 Power tables for multiple regression

a. One or two predictor variables

one predictor variable effect size (R^2)

n	0.01	0.0196	0.05	0.10	0.13	0.15	0.20	0.25	0.26	0.30
10	0.06	0.07	0.10	0.15	0.19	0.22	0.29	0.37	0.38	0.45
15	0.06	0.07	0.13	0.22	0.29	0.33	0.44	0.55	0.57	0.66
20	0.06	0.08	0.16	0.30	0.38	0.44	0.57	0.69	0.72	0.80
30	0.07	0.11	0.23	0.43	0.54	0.61	0.76	0.87	0.89	0.94
40	0.09	0.13	0.30	0.55	0.67	0.75	0.88	0.95	0.96	0.98
50	0.10	0.16	0.36	0.65	0.77	0.84	0.94	0.98	0.99	1.00
60	0.11	0.19	0.42	0.73	0.85	0.90	0.97	0.99	*	*
80	0.14	0.24	0.54	0.85	0.93	0.96	0.99	*	*	*
100	0.16	0.29	0.63	0.92	0.97	0.99	*	*	*	*
120	0.19	0.34	0.71	0.96	0.99	*	*	*	*	*
150	0.23	0.41	0.81	0.98	*	*	*	*	*	*
200	0.30	0.52	0.90	*	*	*	*	*	*	*
250	0.36	0.62	0.95	*	*	*	*	*	*	*
500	0.62	0.89	*	*	*	*	*	*	*	*
750	0.79	0.97	*	*	*	*	*	*	*	*
1000	0.89	0.99	*	*	*	*	*	*	*	*

two predictor variables effect size (R^2)

n	0.01	0.0196	0.05	0.10	0.13	0.15	0.20	0.25	0.26	0.30
10	0.05	0.06	0.08	0.12	0.14	0.16	0.20	0.25	0.27	0.31
15	0.05	0.06	0.10	0.16	0.20	0.23	0.31	0.40	0.41	0.48
20	0.06	0.07	0.12	0.21	0.27	0.31	0.41	0.52	0.54	0.62
30	0.06	0.09	0.16	0.30	0.39	0.45	0.59	0.71	0.73	0.81
40	0.07	0.10	0.21	0.40	0.50	0.57	0.72	0.84	0.85	0.91
50	0.08	0.12	0.26	0.48	0.60	0.67	0.82	0.91	0.92	0.96
60	0.09	0.14	0.30	0.56	0.68	0.75	0.88	0.95	0.96	0.98
80	0.10	0.17	0.39	0.68	0.81	0.87	0.95	0.99	0.99	*
100	0.12	0.21	0.47	0.78	0.88	0.93	0.98	*	*	*
120	0.14	0.24	0.54	0.85	0.93	0.96	0.99	*	*	*
150	0.17	0.29	0.64	0.92	0.97	0.99	*	*	*	*
200	0.21	0.38	0.76	0.97	0.99	*	*	*	*	*
250	0.25	0.45	0.85	0.99	*	*	*	*	*	*
500	0.46	0.74	0.99	*	*	*	*	*	*	*
750	0.62	0.89	*	*	*	*	*	*	*	*
1000	0.75	0.96	*	*	*	*	*	*	*	*
1250	0.84	0.98	*	*	*	*	*	*	*	*

b. Three or four predictor variables

three predictor variables effect size (R^2)

n	0.01	0.0196	0.05	0.10	0.13	0.15	0.20	0.25	0.26	0.30
10	0.06	0.07	0.08	0.10	0.11	0.12	0.15	0.18	0.19	0.22
15	0.06	0.06	0.09	0.13	0.16	0.19	0.25	0.32	0.34	0.41
20	0.06	0.07	0.10	0.17	0.22	0.26	0.36	0.46	0.49	0.57
30	0.06	0.08	0.14	0.27	0.35	0.41	0.56	0.69	0.72	0.81
40	0.07	0.09	0.19	0.36	0.48	0.55	0.71	0.84	0.86	0.93
50	0.07	0.11	0.23	0.46	0.59	0.67	0.83	0.92	0.94	0.97
60	0.08	0.12	0.27	0.54	0.68	0.76	0.90	0.97	0.97	0.99
80	0.10	0.15	0.37	0.69	0.82	0.88	0.97	0.99	*	*
100	0.11	0.19	0.45	0.80	0.91	0.95	0.99	*	*	*
120	0.13	0.22	0.53	0.87	0.95	0.98	*	*	*	*
150	0.15	0.27	0.64	0.94	0.98	0.99	*	*	*	*
200	0.19	0.36	0.78	0.98	*	*	*	*	*	*
250	0.24	0.44	0.87	*	*	*	*	*	*	*
500	0.45	0.76	*	*	*	*	*	*	*	*
750	0.63	0.92	*	*	*	*	*	*	*	*
1000	0.77	0.97	*	*	*	*	*	*	*	*
1250	0.86	0.99	*	*	*	*	*	*	*	*

four predictor variables effect size (R^2)

n	0.01	0.0196	0.05	0.10	0.13	0.15	0.20	0.25	0.26	0.30
15	0.06	0.06	0.08	0.11	0.14	0.15	0.20	0.26	0.27	0.32
20	0.06	0.06	0.09	0.15	0.18	0.21	0.29	0.37	0.39	0.47
30	0.06	0.07	0.12	0.22	0.28	0.33	0.46	0.58	0.61	0.70
40	0.06	0.08	0.15	0.29	0.39	0.45	0.61	0.74	0.77	0.85
50	0.07	0.09	0.19	0.37	0.49	0.56	0.73	0.85	0.87	0.93
60	0.07	0.11	0.22	0.45	0.57	0.65	0.81	0.92	0.93	0.97
80	0.08	0.13	0.30	0.58	0.72	0.80	0.92	0.98	0.98	*
100	0.10	0.16	0.37	0.69	0.83	0.89	0.97	*	*	*
120	0.11	0.18	0.44	0.78	0.90	0.94	0.99	*	*	*
150	0.13	0.22	0.54	0.87	0.95	0.98	*	*	*	*
200	0.16	0.29	0.68	0.95	0.99	*	*	*	*	*
250	0.19	0.36	0.78	0.98	*	*	*	*	*	*
500	0.37	0.66	0.98	*	*	*	*	*	*	*
750	0.53	0.84	*	*	*	*	*	*	*	*
1000	0.66	0.93	*	*	*	*	*	*	*	*
1250	0.77	0.97	*	*	*	*	*	*	*	*
1500	0.85	0.99	*	*	*	*	*	*	*	*

Table A15.7 Power tables for multiple regression

c. Six or eight predictor variables

six predictor variables effect size (R^2)

n	0.01	0.0196	0.05	0.10	0.13	0.15	0.20	0.25	0.26	0.30
15	0.06	0.06	0.07	0.09	0.11	0.12	0.15	0.19	0.19	0.23
20	0.06	0.06	0.08	0.12	0.15	0.17	0.22	0.29	0.31	0.37
30	0.06	0.07	0.11	0.18	0.24	0.28	0.39	0.52	0.54	0.64
40	0.06	0.08	0.13	0.25	0.34	0.40	0.55	0.70	0.73	0.82
50	0.07	0.09	0.16	0.33	0.44	0.52	0.69	0.83	0.85	0.92
60	0.07	0.10	0.20	0.40	0.54	0.62	0.79	0.91	0.92	0.97
80	0.08	0.12	0.27	0.55	0.70	0.78	0.92	0.98	0.98	*
100	0.09	0.14	0.34	0.67	0.81	0.88	0.97	*	*	*
120	0.10	0.16	0.41	0.77	0.89	0.94	0.99	*	*	*
150	0.11	0.20	0.51	0.87	0.96	0.98	*	*	*	*
200	0.14	0.27	0.66	0.96	0.99	*	*	*	*	*
250	0.17	0.33	0.77	0.99	*	*	*	*	*	*
500	0.34	0.64	0.98	*	*	*	*	*	*	*
750	0.51	0.84	*	*	*	*	*	*	*	*
1000	0.65	0.94	*	*	*	*	*	*	*	*
1250	0.76	0.98	*	*	*	*	*	*	*	*
1500	0.85	0.99	*	*	*	*	*	*	*	*

eight predictor variables effect size (R^2)

n	0.01	0.0196	0.05	0.10	0.13	0.15	0.20	0.25	0.26	0.30
15	0.06	0.06	0.07	0.09	0.09	0.10	0.12	0.14	0.15	0.17
20	0.06	0.06	0.08	0.10	0.12	0.14	0.18	0.23	0.24	0.29
30	0.06	0.07	0.09	0.15	0.20	0.23	0.32	0.43	0.45	0.55
40	0.06	0.07	0.12	0.21	0.28	0.34	0.48	0.62	0.65	0.75
50	0.06	0.08	0.14	0.28	0.38	0.44	0.61	0.76	0.79	0.88
60	0.07	0.09	0.17	0.35	0.47	0.55	0.73	0.86	0.88	0.94
80	0.07	0.10	0.23	0.48	0.63	0.72	0.88	0.96	0.97	*
100	0.08	0.12	0.29	0.60	0.76	0.84	0.95	*	*	*
120	0.09	0.14	0.36	0.71	0.85	0.91	*	*	*	*
150	0.10	0.17	0.45	0.82	0.93	0.97	*	*	*	*
200	0.13	0.23	0.60	0.93	*	*	*	*	*	*
250	0.15	0.29	0.72	0.98	*	*	*	*	*	*
500	0.30	0.59	0.97	*	*	*	*	*	*	*
750	0.46	0.80	*	*	*	*	*	*	*	*
1000	0.60	0.91	*	*	*	*	*	*	*	*
1250	0.71	0.97	*	*	*	*	*	*	*	*
1500	0.80	0.99	*	*	*	*	*	*	*	*

d. Ten or twelve predictor variables

n	\multicolumn{10}{c}{ten predictor variables effect size (R^2)}
	0.01	0.0196	0.05	0.10	0.13	0.15	0.20	0.25	0.26	0.30
20	0.05	0.06	0.07	0.09	0.10	0.11	0.14	0.18	0.18	0.22
30	0.05	0.06	0.08	0.13	0.16	0.19	0.26	0.35	0.37	0.45
40	0.06	0.07	0.10	0.18	0.24	0.29	0.41	0.55	0.57	0.68
50	0.06	0.07	0.13	0.24	0.33	0.39	0.55	0.70	0.73	0.83
60	0.06	0.08	0.15	0.30	0.41	0.49	0.67	0.81	0.84	0.91
80	0.07	0.10	0.20	0.43	0.57	0.66	0.84	0.94	0.95	0.98
100	0.08	0.11	0.26	0.55	0.71	0.79	0.93	0.98	0.99	*
120	0.08	0.13	0.32	0.66	0.81	0.88	0.97	*	*	*
150	0.10	0.16	0.41	0.78	0.91	0.95	0.99	*	*	*
200	0.12	0.21	0.55	0.91	0.98	0.99	*	*	*	*
250	0.14	0.26	0.67	0.97	*	*	*	*	*	*
500	0.27	0.54	0.96	*	*	*	*	*	*	*
750	0.41	0.76	*	*	*	*	*	*	*	*
1000	0.55	0.89	*	*	*	*	*	*	*	*
1250	0.67	0.95	*	*	*	*	*	*	*	*
1500	0.77	0.98	*	*	*	*	*	*	*	*
1750	0.84	0.99	*	*	*	*	*	*	*	*

n	\multicolumn{10}{c}{twelve predictor variables effect size (R^2)}
	0.01	0.0196	0.05	0.10	0.13	0.15	0.20	0.25	0.26	0.30
20	0.05	0.06	0.07	0.09	0.09	0.10	0.12	0.14	0.15	0.17
30	0.05	0.06	0.08	0.11	0.14	0.16	0.22	0.29	0.30	0.37
40	0.06	0.07	0.10	0.16	0.21	0.25	0.36	0.48	0.51	0.61
50	0.06	0.07	0.12	0.21	0.29	0.34	0.49	0.64	0.67	0.78
60	0.06	0.08	0.13	0.27	0.37	0.44	0.61	0.77	0.79	0.88
80	0.07	0.09	0.18	0.39	0.53	0.61	0.80	0.92	0.93	0.97
100	0.07	0.10	0.23	0.51	0.66	0.75	0.91	0.97	0.98	*
120	0.08	0.12	0.29	0.61	0.77	0.85	0.96	0.99	*	*
150	0.09	0.14	0.37	0.74	0.88	0.94	0.99	*	*	*
200	0.11	0.19	0.51	0.89	0.97	0.99	*	*	*	*
250	0.13	0.24	0.63	0.96	0.99	*	*	*	*	*
500	0.25	0.50	0.95	*	*	*	*	*	*	*
750	0.38	0.72	*	*	*	*	*	*	*	*
1000	0.51	0.86	*	*	*	*	*	*	*	*
1250	0.63	0.94	*	*	*	*	*	*	*	*
1500	0.73	0.97	*	*	*	*	*	*	*	*
1750	0.81	0.99	*	*	*	*	*	*	*	*

APPENDIX XVI: MISCELLANEOUS TABLES

Table of random numbers   618
Coefficients for trend tests   621
  Calculating linear coefficients   621
    With equal intervals and equal sample sizes   621
    With unequal intervals and unequal sample sizes   622
    With unequal intervals but equal sample sizes   623
    With equal intervals but unequal sample sizes   623
  Finding the weightings for a paired contrast with unequal sample sizes   624
Table of coefficients for trend tests   625
Conversion of r to r' (Fisher's transformation)   626
Conversion of r' to r   626
Table of Fisher's transformation   627

Table A16.1: Random numbers

To use the tables decide on a starting point by choosing a row and column; for example, row 7 and column 10. Then read off the numbers of the appropriate size. Thus, if the numbers to be chosen were between 0 and 99, then the first three numbers would be: 66, 74 and 13. When looking for numbers in the range 0 to 9 treat 00 as 0, 01 as 1 and so on.

Table A16.1 Random numbers

```
                                                      column
row   1 2  3  4  5  6  7  8  9 10 11 12 13 14 15 16 17 18 19 20 21 22 23 24 25 26 27 28 29 30
  1   2 4  1  3  0  3  6  3  7  8  0  3  5  7  2  3  5  3  6  5  7  4  2  8  7  5  8  1  5  0
  2   4 3  1  3  8  2  7  7  6  1  4  8  2  4  4  5  7  3  5  8  6  3  5  5  2  0  7  4  5  4
  3   7 1  6  4  7  3  5  6  7  2  2  1  3  0  2  4  6  5  4  4  0  0  8  2  5  2  8  0  8  6
  4   6 2  0  5  3  0  3  0  5  4  8  6  5  8  6  1  6  7  8  3  5  0  1  8  6  4  8  1  0  4
  5   1 3  8  3  7  1  2  5  5  6  3  4  0  4  5  5  1  0  2  4  8  3  5  7  6  6  2  3  6  3
  6   8 4  5  2  4  7  2  4  7  5  4  5  0  2  3  6  6  4  4  2  7  5  3  2  0  8  1  2  5  0
  7   1 7  0  0  5  6  3  4  5  6  6  7  4  1  3  4  6  4  8  5  1  6  0  8  3  0  0  8  7  7
  8   1 8  0  3  1  2  8  6  6  0  6  1  6  4  6  1  3  8  6  1  5  3  4  1  6  2  0  4  5  5
  9   1 4  8  6  2  4  2  2  4  0  7  7  7  6  1  8  7  0  1  0  4  1  1  2  0  7  1  1  0  3
 10   6 2  0  3  5  2  2  7  0  3  8  8  7  3  8  6  5  2  7  3  1  8  3  2  7  2  1  2  2  0
 11   8 1  6  1  7  2  1  0  0  0  2  4  8  0  0  7  1  3  0  1  2  7  2  1  3  4  8  5  4  5
 12   0 1  7  0  7  5  8  2  3  0  3  7  5  1  4  6  6  8  1  3  5  4  7  5  1  5  7  5  4  8
 13   1 5  5  0  6  0  8  5  2  4  7  2  5  7  2  4  6  1  6  8  7  0  2  0  2  8  4  4  4  7
 14   2 4  2  1  1  1  2  7  8  4  1  2  2  5  7  7  2  6  1  5  5  7  6  5  2  7  1  4  5  6
 15   5 3  8  4  5  4  1  0  4  0  1  6  1  4  3  0  4  0  2  1  7  5  0  1  5  7  5  5  2  5
 16   0 7  1  7  3  5  2  0  7  3  7  2  2  6  8  7  4  7  1  2  4  2  0  2  0  4  2  4  6  1
 17   7 8  0  7  4  4  4  5  0  7  2  1  7  1  1  1  7  2  2  2  3  4  7  4  3  4  7  5  0  6
 18   2 6  6  4  7  3  6  1  6  2  2  5  3  4  0  7  3  3  0  7  5  4  2  4  4  5  4  7  0  7
 19   4 3  5  0  6  6  8  5  8  4  0  8  6  7  0  4  0  3  7  1  5  8  3  8  1  2  6  4  6  8
 20   1 2  5  3  2  0  0  2  1  0  1  5  2  8  7  7  2  5  7  6  8  3  1  5  3  0  8  8  0  3
 21   0 4  4  5  5  1  0  3  3  4  2  0  6  7  6  7  3  1  2  3  5  6  8  5  8  2  0  5  6  2
 22   2 7  8  7  0  0  5  6  1  6  8  3  8  3  6  2  8  7  5  3  2  5  5  6  6  0  4  7  4  1
 23   4 0  8  3  0  0  5  4  3  6  6  4  1  8  6  2  7  4  3  3  2  1  4  1  6  0  4  8  1  7
 24   4 2  6  1  2  4  2  0  2  5  2  6  7  7  6  3  7  3  4  4  6  2  7  8  1  2  8  0  2  6
 25   1 2  8  2  2  6  6  8  4  0  2  1  6  6  2  2  4  2  0  8  6  8  0  8  0  1  4  6  6  6
 26   4 3  3  3  2  8  6  0  0  3  2  0  0  3  8  4  4  4  0  4  6  0  0  7  7  3  8  3  7  6
 27   6 2  7  6  1  1  4  5  2  2  5  8  6  0  1  6  5  6  0  5  3  2  6  2  6  6  3  8  2  6
 28   0 4  6  3  0  2  6  2  4  4  8  8  6  5  0  6  0  6  3  0  4  4  8  0  5  4  0  8  0  0
 29   1 8  4  7  7  8  6  0  0  3  7  8  1  4  5  4  3  3  0  7  8  0  0  8  6  0  6  1  4  2
 30   7 2  8  6  0  3  4  7  4  7  8  7  6  6  5  6  4  5  7  8  4  4  6  1  2  6  3  1  6
 31   1 3  1  0  8  4  8  4  5  8  7  4  5  6  5  8  7  5  1  2  2  5  6  8  3  7  7  1  6  2
 32   0 5  4  5  6  1  0  8  4  0  3  7  2  5  3  3  5  3  0  2  7  4  7  4  0  3  7  5  2  4
 33   6 1  1  1  0  8  8  3  6  5  7  2  1  6  8  4  1  2  6  5  6  2  4  4  3  2  4  6  1  2
 34   1 4  6  5  4  6  2  3  4  7  8  2  4  6  7  4  2  6  6  8  6  4  1  1  0  8  6  0  3  5
 35   2 2  1  8  5  1  6  1  3  8  8  8  3  7  4  8  5  2  2  5  3  1  3  6  0  3  6  2  0  4
 36   0 4  4  5  7  8  7  4  0  0  6  5  2  1  7  2  0  4  0  7  8  7  3  7  4  2  6  7  3  8
 37   5 7  8  4  2  5  8  6  3  0  5  1  7  1  1  8  8  6  6  4  7  0  5  1  6  5  7  1  7  8
 38   5 0  6  7  4  0  4  6  2  3  6  5  7  3  8  0  2  4  3  4  0  4  5  1  1  5  2  0  0  2
 39   0 2  3  0  3  4  4  8  4  2  8  1  3  7  8  4  7  1  8  7  5  1  3  6  0  8  5  5  4  1
 40   5 3  0  1  4  1  7  6  4  1  8  8  4  2  3  4  8  7  2  8  0  2  1  3  8  4  2  1  0  0
 41   0 6  7  1  5  6  3  3  1  8  0  6  1  1  6  7  5  0  7  5  3  3  3  3  1  2  8  5  4  2
 42   6 1  8  6  1  5  6  7  2  5  3  6  4  3  0  2  4  4  5  8  2  3  5  8  2  1  2  3  0  3
 43   0 4  1  8  7  6  2  7  3  5  6  8  1  1  5  6  4  4  3  7  3  0  1  7  7  3  8  5  7  1
 44   0 1  1  7  6  7  5  2  1  7  3  6  8  3  0  0  5  3  4  4  6  3  2  6  5  4  3  2  6  2
 45   2 2  0  4  7  1  5  6  7  4  7  5  1  8  6  7  3  5  2  0  0  7  1  7  3  0  6  8  6  6
 46   8 2  7  5  2  5  2  6  4  1  5  4  0  0  3  4  4  4  8  5  2  4  1  2  1  8  5  3  4  2
 47   2 0  4  1  4  8  4  5  3  8  6  2  7  3  2  2  3  8  1  2  3  7  1  1  2  6  5  0  2  4
 48   2 0  7  8  3  5  0  6  8  2  4  4  5  8  0  6  5  8  8  0  7  2  8  8  1  6  2  3  0  3
 49   0 7  5  5  7  7  8  0  1  3  2  8  0  8  0  3  6  6  5  5  3  3  4  8  2  8  4  0  1  1
 50   1 7  4  7  3  6  8  3  0  5  6  2  8  6  8  1  4  3  7  0  5  2  2  6  8  1  8  2  5  5
```

Table A16.1 Random numbers

row	1	2	3	4	5	6	7	8	9	10	11	12	13	14	15	16	17	18	19	20	21	22	23	24	25	26	27	28	29	30
51	7	1	3	3	4	2	1	8	0	5	4	3	2	2	3	3	7	6	1	0	8	3	1	1	5	0	8	8	0	6
52	5	4	7	6	6	6	4	0	2	4	4	2	2	0	6	8	1	1	6	3	4	2	0	2	1	7	6	0	4	2
53	7	4	6	8	8	0	7	4	5	0	1	6	7	3	8	1	1	0	1	3	2	4	1	8	2	2	6	6	4	3
54	3	0	7	2	3	8	6	4	6	4	1	8	0	6	4	3	0	6	2	6	5	4	3	7	2	2	5	0	1	4
55	0	1	0	2	0	7	1	6	5	3	2	0	1	4	4	5	8	5	7	0	4	8	4	7	5	5	6	4	8	7
56	8	3	6	4	7	2	8	6	1	8	5	7	6	8	0	2	6	7	6	7	5	7	6	2	7	7	0	3	4	7
57	2	8	7	0	4	6	3	8	8	3	2	5	2	5	3	6	3	2	7	7	2	8	8	3	6	1	3	2	8	8
58	6	5	0	4	6	0	7	4	8	6	6	3	2	1	7	1	0	2	0	1	0	7	6	8	7	4	2	1	3	6
59	3	7	2	3	4	3	3	6	5	5	0	8	1	2	1	5	3	5	2	2	3	3	7	3	7	4	2	8	5	2
60	8	5	6	7	3	5	3	4	3	4	6	3	0	6	2	3	1	0	8	3	1	6	2	2	0	2	0	3	0	4
61	7	1	8	4	7	6	0	8	1	1	1	5	2	6	6	7	7	8	4	1	0	1	8	3	1	5	2	1	7	0
62	0	5	4	3	3	3	4	7	1	6	7	5	2	8	7	1	8	3	1	0	2	1	6	6	5	7	7	5	5	7
63	5	2	5	0	3	1	8	5	6	5	5	7	1	3	7	6	4	5	0	8	5	8	6	8	8	8	0	0	2	8
64	4	2	2	2	0	1	3	0	3	6	1	0	0	7	5	8	2	6	1	1	4	8	1	1	1	2	4	4	4	4
65	5	5	2	3	8	3	0	1	6	6	5	8	8	0	5	4	5	7	6	1	3	3	7	2	6	6	4	6	6	8
66	6	3	1	8	3	1	7	2	2	3	7	5	8	7	1	4	6	8	3	2	6	1	1	5	3	8	4	5	2	3
67	7	2	2	7	2	4	7	2	7	5	7	8	4	5	5	0	2	6	6	6	8	6	5	8	1	7	6	5	0	4
68	3	1	1	6	3	4	7	1	1	5	0	5	6	6	0	5	3	8	0	6	5	6	5	5	4	2	2	8	6	3
69	1	2	3	5	6	0	1	6	1	3	3	8	7	6	6	6	7	5	0	2	0	5	0	4	1	7	6	4	8	8
70	7	0	2	3	6	3	4	7	4	2	4	8	1	4	0	8	7	8	5	2	1	0	7	7	7	0	4	1	7	3
71	1	3	2	1	8	1	5	6	6	2	5	5	4	3	1	0	8	3	0	7	4	2	7	5	5	2	8	0	5	2
72	5	6	1	6	2	2	7	0	0	3	8	1	3	3	1	0	0	2	4	1	2	6	7	4	8	3	4	3	7	5
73	6	0	5	1	1	3	6	1	7	0	5	7	3	3	8	6	6	1	8	6	4	3	6	1	7	8	1	2	0	2
74	8	7	6	0	0	8	5	4	0	3	2	6	7	5	1	6	4	5	8	8	1	2	4	8	4	2	4	1	8	1
75	1	3	7	2	2	0	1	3	2	7	5	1	8	5	3	6	6	1	7	3	4	6	4	2	6	4	4	8	2	1
76	8	6	7	3	8	1	3	7	0	4	8	7	3	3	8	7	3	0	5	0	8	6	3	4	6	6	2	3	0	2
77	0	4	6	8	1	2	8	6	2	8	0	1	8	3	3	8	5	8	6	4	2	1	5	2	8	5	1	4	7	3
78	6	8	8	7	4	3	5	8	4	2	8	4	4	6	2	4	7	0	2	0	5	4	4	7	2	0	0	0	1	0
79	6	3	4	5	4	4	6	3	8	8	0	0	5	6	8	7	6	0	0	7	0	3	3	5	6	5	5	7	8	1
80	3	0	1	3	2	2	8	1	0	6	1	5	7	8	8	3	1	6	0	8	7	4	5	2	1	8	5	4	4	3
81	7	1	4	6	4	1	3	2	0	0	7	4	2	0	5	2	8	6	4	2	5	6	6	3	0	2	6	4	5	7
82	8	3	8	4	8	3	6	0	5	8	1	5	5	3	8	3	8	4	8	4	0	5	1	3	0	8	5	4	4	6
83	6	3	6	7	2	5	1	3	6	7	8	7	5	8	6	6	5	6	6	2	0	8	8	7	8	7	5	5	7	5
84	6	8	5	5	2	3	4	1	5	6	5	3	3	6	8	1	0	2	6	5	3	8	5	5	3	6	8	7	0	8
85	2	7	3	4	4	0	2	6	5	4	4	4	1	5	8	3	6	2	4	6	2	2	2	5	4	8	1	1	1	0
86	1	8	7	1	3	4	1	7	5	5	0	2	8	2	8	6	8	4	0	7	2	2	6	2	1	7	2	2	5	6
87	3	0	8	1	1	5	1	1	5	8	6	7	1	1	7	5	3	3	8	4	1	6	8	7	6	8	3	4	8	7
88	2	5	5	4	4	2	1	8	0	2	1	6	4	4	2	7	7	1	2	5	2	0	3	2	5	0	4	0	1	6
89	7	3	7	4	4	5	2	1	2	1	2	1	8	2	7	0	7	5	2	6	8	4	5	4	1	3	4	6	3	6
90	0	5	0	0	1	7	3	6	7	2	8	3	7	8	7	4	3	0	2	4	5	1	5	3	0	7	5	1	5	6
91	1	6	4	2	7	2	6	1	7	8	6	3	4	0	6	6	0	4	3	8	4	2	6	5	5	0	2	5	0	4
92	7	4	6	4	5	7	3	5	4	7	0	0	3	7	1	0	1	8	1	4	0	2	5	0	1	4	0	4	2	1
93	8	6	6	1	7	1	3	8	0	7	5	1	3	4	5	1	3	8	3	6	6	4	0	6	5	8	2	6	5	1
94	3	3	7	7	2	4	8	3	1	1	2	6	7	7	7	7	1	1	5	2	4	3	3	1	7	4	3	5	1	4
95	5	8	6	8	3	3	0	5	0	6	3	8	5	5	0	8	5	3	4	8	8	4	4	2	1	6	8	2	4	1
96	1	3	3	1	8	7	8	8	3	3	0	6	8	6	5	3	4	7	2	8	6	4	1	6	3	4	2	6	1	7
97	7	7	6	2	4	4	3	1	7	5	1	1	5	4	1	6	0	3	8	0	6	3	4	5	8	3	8	0	7	4
98	3	6	4	5	1	7	6	1	6	1	5	3	8	4	7	6	3	5	3	5	5	0	8	2	1	8	6	0	3	4
99	0	8	3	5	6	1	4	1	8	7	2	6	2	3	5	2	4	0	8	3	7	5	6	6	8	8	0	4	8	3
100	4	3	6	4	4	8	1	8	0	8	2	5	2	2	3	4	4	6	8	3	4	8	4	0	5	2	2	1	1	3

Coefficients for trend tests

Table A16.2 provides the coefficients (c_j) that are appropriate for trend tests when the sample sizes in each level of the independent variable are the same and when the levels of the independent variable differ by a regular amount; an example of this would be if the independent variable was delay, in seconds, before participants were required to recall a list of words, with delays of 5, 10, 15 and 20 seconds. In addition, I have only provided coefficients for linear, quadratic and cubic trends (where applicable). See Myers and Well (1991) for the coefficients for other trends and details of how to calculate the coefficients for trends other than linear ones.

Calculating linear coefficients

With equal intervals and equal sample sizes
The two equations we need for a linear coefficient, if the intervals between levels of the IV are equal and the sample sizes are the same, are:

$$c_j = a + j \qquad \text{(A16.1)}$$

and

$$\Sigma(c_j) = 0 \qquad \text{(A16.2)}$$

where a is an algebraic value that will help us to find each c_j
j is the level of the IV
c_j is the coefficient for mean j

Therefore if we had three levels in the IV:

$$c_1 = a + 1$$
$$c_2 = a + 2$$
$$c_3 = a + 3$$

In this case, from Eqn A16.2:

$$3a + 6 = 0$$

Therefore:

$$a = -2$$

which means that:

$$c_1 = -2 + 1 \quad -1$$
$$c_2 = -2 + 2 \quad 0$$
$$c_3 = -2 + 3 \quad 1$$

With unequal intervals and unequal sample sizes
In this case, Eqn A16.1 becomes:

$$c_j = a + X_j \qquad\qquad (A16.3)$$

where X_j is the value of the jth level of the IV, and Eqn A16.2 becomes:

$$\Sigma(n_j \times c_j) = 0 \qquad\qquad (A16.4)$$

where n_j is the sample size in the jth level of the IV.

As an example, imagine that we wanted the coefficients for a linear trend when there were three levels of an IV, we had samples of 10, 15 and 25 participants and the levels of the IV (years spent learning a skill) were 5, 12 and 20. Therefore, from Eqn A16.3:

$$c_1 = a + 5$$

$$c_2 = a + 12$$

$$c_3 = a + 20$$

and from Eqn A16.4:

$$10 \times (a + 5) + 15 \times (a + 12) + 25 \times (a + 20) = 0$$

Therefore,

$$50 \times a + 730 = 0$$

which means that:

$$a = \frac{-73}{5}$$

and, from Eqn A16.3:

$$c_1 = \frac{-48}{5}$$

$$c_2 = \frac{-13}{5}$$

$$c_3 = \frac{27}{5}$$

To simplify the calculations for the linear trend test, we can multiply each of the coefficients by 5 to make them into whole numbers.

With unequal intervals but equal sample sizes

In this case, we can use Eqn A16.3 and Eqn A16.2. Therefore, if in the previous example the sample sizes had been the same, from Eqn 16.3:

$$c_1 = a + 5$$
$$c_2 = a + 12$$
$$c_3 = a + 20$$

and from Eqn A16.2:

$$3 \times a + 37 = 0$$

in which case:

$$a = \frac{-37}{3}$$

Therefore, from Eqn A16.3

$$c_1 = \frac{-22}{3}$$

$$c_2 = \frac{-1}{3}$$

$$c_3 = \frac{23}{3}$$

As with the last example we could simplify the coefficients; in this case, by multiplying each of them by 3.

With equal intervals but unequal sample sizes

In this case, we need Eqn A16.1 and A16.4. Therefore,

$$c_1 = a + 1$$
$$c_2 = a + 2$$
$$c_3 = a + 3$$

and if the samples had had 10, 15 and 25 participants in them:

$$10 \times (a + 1) + 15 \times (a + 2) + 25 \times (a + 3) = 0$$

which means that;

$$50 \times a + 115 = 0$$

Therefore,

$$a = \frac{-115}{50} \text{ or } \frac{-23}{10}$$

In which case:

$$c_1 = \frac{-13}{10}$$

$$c_2 = \frac{-3}{10}$$

$$c_3 = \frac{7}{10}$$

We can multiply each coefficient by 10 to make the calculations for the trend test simpler.

Finding the weightings for a paired contrast with unequal sample sizes

We can use the same procedure as that shown above for finding the coefficients for a linear trend when the sample sizes are unequal but the intervals are the same. However, we are only looking for two coefficients. For example, if we had an IV with three levels, with samples of 5, 10 and 25 and we wished to contrast two conditions then the equations we would use would be adaptations of Eqn A16.1 and Eqn A16.4, but with w_j substituted for c_j. Thus:

$$w_1 = a + 1$$
$$w_2 = a + 2$$

(in a pairwise contrast, always use 1 and 2 in these equations, regardless of the levels of the IV being contrasted.)
and

$$\Sigma(n_j \times w_j) = 0 \tag{A16.5}$$

Therefore, if we were contrasting the first and the third samples,

$$5 \times (a + 1) + 25 \times (a + 2) = 0$$

which means that

$$30 \times a + 55 = 0$$

and

$$a = \frac{-55}{30} \text{ or } \frac{-11}{6}$$

which means that:

$$w_1 = \frac{-5}{6}$$

$$w_2 = \frac{1}{6}$$

To simplify the calculations in the contrast, we can multiply the weightings by 6, to get −5 and 1.

Table A16.2 Coefficients for trend tests

| Number of levels of IV | Type of trend | \multicolumn{10}{c}{Level of IV} | $\Sigma(c_j)^2$ |

Number of levels of IV	Type of trend	1	2	3	4	5	6	7	8	9	10	$\Sigma(c_j)^2$
3	linear	−1	0	1								2
	quadratic	1	2	1								6
4	linear	−3	−1	1	3							20
	quadratic	1	−1	−1	1							4
	cubic	−1	3	−3	1							20
5	linear	−2	−1	0	1	2						10
	quadratic	2	−1	−2	−1	2						14
	cubic	−1	2	0	−2	1						10
6	linear	−5	−3	−1	1	3	5					70
	quadratic	5	−1	−4	−4	−1	5					84
	cubic	−5	7	4	−4	−7	5					180
7	linear	−3	−2	−1	0	1	2	3				28
	quadratic	5	0	−3	−4	−3	0	5				84
	cubic	−1	1	1	0	−1	−1	1				6
8	linear	−7	−5	−3	−1	1	3	5	7			168
	quadratic	7	1	−3	−5	−5	−3	1	7			168
	cubic	−7	5	7	3	−3	−7	−5	7			264
9	linear	−4	−3	−2	−1	0	1	2	3	4		60
	quadratic	28	7	−8	−17	−20	−17	−8	7	28		2772
	cubic	−14	7	13	9	0	−9	−13	−7	14		990
10	linear	−9	−7	−5	−3	−1	1	3	5	7	9	330
	quadratic	6	2	−1	−3	−4	−4	−3	−1	2	6	108
	cubic	−42	14	35	31	12	−12	−31	−35	−14	42	8580

Conversion of *r* to *r'* (Fisher's transformation)

Table A16.3 provides the conversion for a range of values of r. However, when you need to convert a value that is not shown in the table you can use the following equation:

$$r' = 0.5 \times \log_e \left(\frac{1 + r}{1 - r} \right) \qquad (A16.6)$$

This means find the value of $(1 + r)/(1 - r)$, look up the logarithm to the base e of the result (the natural log, often shown as LN or ln on a calculator) and multiply the answer by 0.5.

For example, if $r = 0.7$, then:

$$r' = 0.5 \times \log_e \left(\frac{1 + 0.7}{1 - 0.7} \right)$$

$$= 0.5 \times \log_e \left(\frac{1.7}{0.3} \right)$$

$$= 0.5 \times \log_e 5.6667$$

$$= 0.5 \times 1.7346 = 0.8673$$

Conversion of *r'* to *r*

$$r = \frac{e^{(2 \times r')} - 1}{e^{(2 \times r')} + 1} \qquad (A16.7)$$

where e = 2.71828 (approximately).

For example, if $r' = 0.8673$, then

$$r = \frac{e^{(2 \times 0.8673)} - 1}{e^{(2 \times 0.8673)} + 1}$$

$$= \frac{e^{(1.7346)} - 1}{e^{(1.7346)} + 1}$$

$$= \frac{5.6667 - 1}{5.6667 + 1}$$

$$= \frac{4.6667}{6.6667} = 0.7$$

Table A16.3 Fisher's transformation

r	r'	r	r'	r	r'	r	r'	r	r'
0.000	0.000	0.200	0.203	0.400	0.424	0.600	0.693	0.800	1.099
0.005	0.005	0.205	0.208	0.405	0.430	0.605	0.701	0.805	1.113
0.010	0.010	0.210	0.213	0.410	0.436	0.610	0.709	0.810	1.127
0.015	0.015	0.215	0.218	0.415	0.442	0.615	0.717	0.815	1.142
0.020	0.020	0.220	0.224	0.420	0.448	0.620	0.725	0.820	1.157
0.025	0.025	0.225	0.229	0.425	0.454	0.625	0.733	0.825	1.172
0.030	0.030	0.230	0.234	0.430	0.460	0.630	0.741	0.830	1.188
0.035	0.035	0.235	0.239	0.435	0.466	0.635	0.750	0.835	1.204
0.040	0.040	0.240	0.245	0.440	0.472	0.640	0.758	0.840	1.221
0.045	0.045	0.245	0.250	0.445	0.478	0.645	0.767	0.845	1.238
0.050	0.050	0.250	0.255	0.450	0.485	0.650	0.775	0.850	1.256
0.055	0.055	0.255	0.261	0.455	0.491	0.655	0.784	0.855	1.274
0.060	0.060	0.260	0.266	0.460	0.497	0.660	0.793	0.860	1.293
0.065	0.065	0.265	0.271	0.465	0.504	0.665	0.802	0.865	1.313
0.070	0.070	0.270	0.277	0.470	0.510	0.670	0.811	0.870	1.333
0.075	0.075	0.275	0.282	0.475	0.517	0.675	0.820	0.875	1.354
0.080	0.080	0.280	0.288	0.480	0.523	0.680	0.829	0.880	1.376
0.085	0.085	0.285	0.293	0.485	0.530	0.685	0.838	0.885	1.398
0.090	0.090	0.290	0.299	0.490	0.536	0.690	0.848	0.890	1.422
0.095	0.095	0.295	0.304	0.495	0.543	0.695	0.858	0.895	1.447
0.100	0.100	0.300	0.310	0.500	0.549	0.700	0.867	0.900	1.472
0.105	0.105	0.305	0.315	0.505	0.556	0.705	0.877	0.905	1.499
0.110	0.110	0.310	0.321	0.510	0.563	0.710	0.887	0.910	1.528
0.115	0.116	0.315	0.326	0.515	0.570	0.715	0.897	0.915	1.557
0.120	0.121	0.320	0.332	0.520	0.576	0.720	0.908	0.920	1.589
0.125	0.126	0.325	0.337	0.525	0.583	0.725	0.918	0.925	1.623
0.130	0.131	0.330	0.343	0.530	0.590	0.730	0.929	0.930	1.658
0.135	0.136	0.335	0.348	0.535	0.597	0.735	0.940	0.935	1.697
0.140	0.141	0.340	0.354	0.540	0.604	0.740	0.950	0.940	1.738
0.145	0.146	0.345	0.360	0.545	0.611	0.745	0.962	0.945	1.783
0.150	0.151	0.350	0.365	0.550	0.618	0.750	0.973	0.950	1.832
0.155	0.156	0.355	0.371	0.555	0.626	0.755	0.984	0.955	1.886
0.160	0.161	0.360	0.377	0.560	0.633	0.760	0.996	0.960	1.946
0.165	0.167	0.365	0.383	0.565	0.640	0.765	1.008	0.965	2.014
0.170	0.172	0.370	0.388	0.570	0.648	0.770	1.020	0.970	2.092
0.175	0.177	0.375	0.394	0.575	0.655	0.775	1.033	0.975	2.185
0.180	0.182	0.380	0.400	0.580	0.662	0.780	1.045	0.980	2.298
0.185	0.187	0.385	0.406	0.585	0.670	0.785	1.058	0.985	2.443
0.190	0.192	0.390	0.412	0.590	0.678	0.790	1.071	0.990	2.647
0.195	0.198	0.395	0.418	0.595	0.685	0.795	1.085	0.995	2.994
								0.999	3.800

References

Abelson, R. P. (1995). *Statistics as principled argument*. Hillsdale, New Jersey: Lawrence Erlbaum Associates, Inc.

Agresti, A. (1996). *An introduction to categorical data analysis*. New York: Wiley.

Agresti, A. (2002). *Categorical data analysis* (2nd ed.). New York: Wiley.

American Psychological Association (1992). Ethical principles of psychologists and code of conduct. *American Psychologist*, 47, 1597–1611.

American Psychological Association (2001). *Publication manual of the American Psychological Association* (5th ed.). Washington, DC: American Psychological Association.

Atkinson, R. C. & Shiffrin, R. M. (1971). The control of short-term memory. *Scientific American*, 225, 82–90.

Baddeley, A. (1990). *Human memory: Theory and practice*. Hove: Lawrence Erlbaum Associates Ltd.

Bales, R. F. (1950). A set of categories for analysis of small group interaction. *American Sociological Review*, 15, 257–263.

Banister, P., Burman, E., Parker, I., Taylor, M. & Tindall, C. (1994). *Qualitative methods in psychology: A research guide*. Buckingham: Open University Press.

Belsley, D. A. (1991). *Conditioning diagnostics: Collinearity and weak data in regression*. New York: Wiley.

Boden, M. A. (1987). *Artificial intelligence and natural man* (2nd revised ed.). London: The MIT Press.

Bogardus, E. S. (1925). Measuring social distances. *Journal of applied sociology*, 9, 299–308.

Bollen, K. & Lennox, R. (1991). Conventional wisdom on measurement: A structural equation perspective. *Psychological Bulletin*, 110, 305–314.

Bonge, D. R., Schuldt, W. J. & Harper, Y. Y. (1992). The experimenter-as-fixed-effect fallacy. *The Journal of Psychology*, 126 (5), 477–486.

Borenstein, M., Rothstein, H. & Cohen, J. (1997). *SamplePower 1.0*. Chicago: SPSS Inc.

British Psychological Society (2000). *Code of conduct, Ethical principles and guidelines*. Leicester: The British Psychological Society.

Byrne, B. M. (2001). *Structural equation modeling with AMOS: Basic concepts, applications and programming*. Mahwah, New Jersey: Lawrence Erlbaum Associates, Inc.

Chambless, D. L. & Ollendick, T. H. (2001). Empirically supported psychological interventions: Controversies and evidence. *Annual Review of Psychology*, 52, 685–716.

Chatterjee, S. & Hadi, A. S. (1988). *Sensitivity analysis in linear regression*. New York: Wiley.

Chatterjee, S., Hadi, A. S. & Price, B. (2000). *Regression analysis by example* (3rd ed.). New York: Wiley.

Clark-Carter, D. (1997). The account taken of statistical power in research published in the *British Journal of Psychology*. *British Journal of Psychology*, 88, 71–83.

Cleveland, W. S. (1985). *The elements of graphing data*. Monterey, California: Wadsworth.

Cochran, W. G. & Cox, G. M. (1957). *Experimental designs* (2nd ed.). London: Wiley.

Cohen, J. (1962). The statistical power of abnormal-social psychological research: a review. *Journal of Abnormal and Social Psychology*, 65, 145–153.

Cohen, J. (1988). *Statistical power analysis for the behavioral sciences* (2nd ed.). Hillsdale, New Jersey: Lawrence Erlbaum Associates, Inc.

Comrey, A. L. & Lee, H. B. (1992). *A first course in factor analysis* (2nd ed.). Hillsdale, New Jersey: Lawrence Erlbaum Associates, Inc.

Cook, T. D. & Campbell, D. T. (1979). *Quasi-experimentation: Design and analysis issues for field settings.* Boston: Houghton Mifflin Company.

Danziger, K. (1990). *Constructing the subject.* Cambridge: Cambridge University Press.

Dixon, W. J. & Massey, F. J. (Jr.) (1983). *Introduction to statistical analysis* (4th ed.). London: McGraw-Hill.

Dracup, C. (2000). Hypothesis testing: Further misconceptions. *Psychology Teaching Review*, 9, 103–110.

Duncan, D. (2001). Eighty years of human resource accountancy. *History and Philosophy of Psychology*, 3, 27–31.

Erdfelder, E., Faul, F. & Buchner, A. (1996). Gpower: A general power analysis program. *Behavior Research Methods, Instruments, and Computers*, 28, 1–11.

Ericsson, K. A. & Simon, H. A. (1980). Verbal reports as data. *Psychological Review*, 87, 215–251.

Estes, W. K. (1993). Mathematical models in psychology. In G. Keren and C. Lewis (Eds.), *A handbook for data analysis in the behavioral sciences: Methodological issues* (pp. 3–19). Hillsdale, New Jersey: Lawrence Erlbaum Associates, Inc.

Fisher, R. A. (1925). *Statistical methods for research workers.* Edinburgh: Oliver and Boyd.

Fisher, R. A. (1935). *The design of experiments.* Edinburgh: Oliver and Boyd.

Gregg, V. H. (1986). *Introduction to human memory.* London: Routledge.

Guttman, L. (1944). A basis for scaling qualitative data. *American Sociological Review*, 9, 139–150.

Harris, R. J. (1997). Reforming significance testing via three-valued logic. In L. L. Harlow, S. A. Mulaik & J. H. Steiger (Eds.). *What if there were no significance tests?* (pp. 145–174). Mahwah, New Jersey: Lawrence Erlbaum Associates, Inc.

Hayes, N. (1997). *Doing qualitative analysis in psychology.* Hove: Psychology Press.

Hewson, C. (2003). Conducting research on the Internet. *The Psychologist*, 16, 290–293.

Hewstone, M., Stroebe, W. & Stephenson, G. M. (Eds.) (1996). *Introduction to social psychology* (2nd ed.). Oxford: Blackwell.

Hosmer, D. W. & Lemeshow, S. (2000). *Applied logistic regression* (2nd ed.). New York: Wiley.

Howell, D. C. (1997). *Statistical methods for psychology* (4th ed.). Boston: Duxbury.

Howell, D. C. (2002). *Statistical methods for psychology* (5th ed.). Boston: Duxbury.

Huberty, C. J. (1994). *Applied discriminant analysis.* New York: Wiley

Humphreys, G. & Riddoch, J. M. (1987). *To see but not to be seen: A case study of visual agnosia.* Hove: Lawrence Erlbaum Associates Ltd.

Jones, L. V. & Tukey, J. W. (2000). A sensible formulation of the significance test. *Psychological Methods*, 5, 411–414.

Kelly, G. (1955). *The psychology of personal constructs.* New York: Norton.

Kerlinger, F. N. (1973). *Foundations of behavioral research* (2nd ed.). London: Holt, Rinehart & Winston.

Kinnear, P. R. & Gray, C. D. (2000). *SPSS for Windows made simple (Release 10).* Hove: Psychology Press.

Kline, P. (2000). *The handbook of psychological testing* (2nd ed.). London: Routledge.

Kline, R. B. (1998). *Principles and practice of structural equation modeling.* New York: The Guilford Press.

Leventhal, L. & Huynh C.-L. (1996). Directional decisions for two-tailed tests: Power, error rates and sample size. *Psychological Methods*, 1, 278–292.

Likert, R. (1932). A technique for the measurement of attitudes. *Archives of Psychology*, No. 140.

Luria, A. R. (1975a). *The mind of a mnemonist.* Harmondsworth: Penguin.

Luria, A. R. (1975b). *The man with a shattered world.* Harmondsworth: Penguin.

McCain, L. J. & McCleary, R. (1979). The statistical analysis of the simple interrupted time-series quasi-experiment. In T. D. Cook & D. T. Campbell, *Quasi-experimentation: Design and analysis issues for field settings* (pp. 233–293). Boston: Houghton Mifflin.

McDonald, R. P. (1999). *Test theory: A unified treatment.* Mahwah, New Jersey: Lawrence Erlbaum Associates, Inc.

McGowan, L., Clark-Carter, D. & Pitts, M. (1998). Chronic pelvic pain: A meta-analytic review. *Psychology and Health*, 13, 937–951.

McGowan, L., Pitts, M. K. & Clark-Carter, D. (1999). Chronic pelvic pain: The general practitioner's perspective. *Psychology, Health and Medicine*, 4, 303–317.

Maghsoodloo, S. & Pallos, L. L. (1981). Asymptotic behaviour of Kendall's partial rank correlation coefficient and additional quantile estimates. *Journal of Statistical Computing and Simulation*, 13, 41–48.

Manstead, A. S. R. & McCulloch, C. (1981). Sex-role stereotyping in British television advertisements. *British Journal of Psychology*, 20, 171–180.

Meddis, R. (1984). *Statistics using ranks: A unified approach*. Oxford: Blackwell.

Milgram, S. (1974). *Obedience to authority*. London: Tavistock Publications.

Miller, G. A. (1985). Trends and debates in cognitive psychology. In A. M Aitkenhead & J. M Slack (Eds.), *Issues in cognitive modelling*. Hove: Lawrence Erlbaum Associates Ltd.

Morgan, D. L. (1998). Planning focus groups. Vol. 2 of D. L. Morgan & R. A. Krueger. *The focus group kit*. London: Sage.

Myers, J. L. & Well, A. D. (1991). *Research design and statistical analysis*. New York: HarperCollins.

Neave, H. R. (1978). *Statistics tables: for mathematicians, engineers, economists and the behavioural and management sciences*. London: Unwin Hyman.

Neave, H. R. & Worthington, P. L. (1988). *Distribution-free tests*. London: Routledge.

Newell, A. & Simon, H. A. (1972). *Human problem solving*. Englewood Cliffs, New Jersey: Prentice-Hall.

Neyman, J. & Pearson, E. S. (1933). On the problem of the most efficient tests of statistical hypotheses. *Philosophical Transactions of the Royal Society (A)*, 231, 289–337.

Nisbett, R. E. & Wilson, T. D. (1977). Telling more than we can know: Verbal reports on mental processes. *Psychological Review*, 84, 231–259.

Orne, M. T. (1962). On the social psychology of the psychological experiment: With particular reference to demand characteristics and their implications. *American Psychologist*, 17, 776–783.

Osgood, C. E. & Luria, Z. (1954). A blind analysis of a case of multiple personality using the semantic differential. *Journal of Abnormal and Social Psychology*, 49, 579–591. Reprinted in C. H. Thigpen & H. M. Cleckley (1957) *The three faces of Eve*. London: Secker and Warburg

Osgood, C. E., Suci, G. J. & Tannenbaum, P. H. (1957). *The measurement of meaning*. Urbana, Illinois: University of Illinois Press.

Pedhazur, E. J. (1997). *Multiple regression in behavioural research: Explanation and prediction* (3rd ed.). Orlando: Holt, Rinehart & Winston.

Pedhazur, E. J. & Schmelkin, L. P. (1991). *Measurement, design, and analysis: An integrated approach*. Hillsdale, New Jersey: Lawrence Erlbaum Associates, Inc.

Pfungst, O. (1965). *Clever Hans: The horse of Mr von Osten* (C. L. Rahn, Trans.). New York: Holt, Rinehart & Winston. (Original work published in 1911)

Pitts, M. & Jackson, H. (1989). AIDS and the press: An analysis of the coverage of AIDS by Zimbabwe newspapers. *AIDS CARE*, 1, 77–83.

Popper, K. R. (1972). *The logic of scientific discovery* (5th impression (revised) ed.). London: Hutchinson.

Popper, K. R. (1974). *Conjectures and refutations: The growth of scientific knowledge* (5th ed.). London: Routledge.

Potter, J. & Wetherall, M. (1995). Discourse analysis. In J. A. Smith, R. Harré & L. Van Langenhove (Eds.), *Rethinking methods in psychology*. London: Sage.

Putnam, H. (1979). The 'corroboration' of theories. In T. Honderich & M. Burnyeat (Eds.), *Philosophy as it is*. Harmondsworth: Penguin.

Robson, C. (2002). *Real world research: A resource for social scientists and practitioner–researchers* (2nd ed.). Oxford: Blackwell.

Rogers, C. R. (1951). *Client-centred therapy*. London: Constable.

Rogers, C. R. (1961). *On becoming a person: A therapist's view of psychotherapy*. London: Constable.

Rosenthal, R. (1991). *Meta-analytic procedures for social research*. London: Sage.

Rosnow, R. L. & Rosenthal, R. (1989). Statistical procedures and the justification of knowledge in Psychological Science. *American Psychologist*, 44, 1276–1284.

Schumacker, R. E. & Lomax, R. G. (1996). *A beginner's guide to structural equation modelling*. Mahwah, New Jersey: Lawrence Erlbaum Associates, Inc.

Sears, D. O. (1986). College sophomores in the laboratory: Influences of a narrow data base on psychology's view of human nature. *Journal of Personality and Social Psychology*, 51, 513–530.

Sedlmeier, P. & Gigerenzer, G. (1989). Do studies of statistical power have an effect on the power of studies? *Psychological Bulletin*, 105, 309–316.

Shaughnessy, J. J., Zechmeister, E. B. & Zechmeister, J. S. (2003). *Research methods in psychology* (7th ed.). New York: McGraw-Hill.

Shye, S., Elizur, D. & Hoffman, M. (1994). *Introduction to facet theory: Content design and intrinsic data analysis in behavioral research.* London: Sage

Siegel, S. & Castellan, N. J. (1988). *Nonparametric statistics for the behavioral sciences* (2nd ed.). New York: McGraw-Hill.

Stainton Rogers, R. (1995). Q methodology. In J. A. Smith, R. Harré & L. Van Langenhove (Eds.), *Rethinking methods in psychology.* London: Sage.

Steiger, J. H. (1980). Tests for comparing elements of a correlation matrix. *Psychological Bulletin*, 87, 245–251.

Stenner, P. & Marshall, H. (1995). A Q methodological study of rebelliousness. *European Journal of Social Psychology*, 25, 621–636.

Stenner, P. & Marshall, H. (1999). On developmentality: Researching the varied meanings of 'independence' and 'maturity' extant amongst a sample of young people in East London. *Journal of Youth Studies*, 2, 297–315.

Stenner, P. & Stainton Rogers, R. (1998). Jealousy as a manifold of divergent understandings: A Q methodological investigation. *European Journal of Social Psychology*, 28, 71–94.

Stephenson, W. (1953). *The study of behavior: Q-technique and its methodology.* Chicago: University of Chicago Press.

Stevens, J. (2002). *Applied multivariate statistics for the social sciences* (4th ed.). Mahwah, New Jersey: Lawrence Erlbaum Associates, Inc.

Sudman, S. (1976). *Applied sampling.* London: Academic Press.

Suedfeld, P. (1980). *Restricted environmental stimulation: Research and clinical applications.* New York: Wiley.

Tabachnick, B. G. & Fidell, L. S. (2001). *Using multivariate statistics* (4th ed.). Boston: Allyn and Bacon.

Thurstone, L. L. (1931). The measurement of social attitudes. *Journal of Abnormal and Social Psychology*, 26, 249–269.

Thurstone, L. L. & Chave, E. J. (1929). *The measurement of attitude: A psychophysical method and some experiments with a scale for measuring attitude toward the Church.* Chicago: The University of Chicago Press.

Todman, J. B. & Dugard, P. (2001). *Single-case and small-n experimental designs: A practical guide to randomization tests.* Mahwah, New Jersey: Lawrence Erlbaum Associates, Inc.

Tukey, J. W. (1977). *Exploratory data analysis.* Reading Massachusetts: Addison-Wesley.

Valentine, E. R. (1992). *Conceptual issues in psychology* (2nd ed.). London: Routledge.

Wickens, T. D. (1989). *Multiway contingency table analysis for the social sciences.* Hillsdale, New Jersey: Lawrence Erlbaum Associates, Inc.

Winer, B. J., Brown, D. R. & Michels, K. M. (1991). *Statistical principles in experimental design* (3rd ed.). London: McGraw-Hill.

Winter, D. A. (1992). *Personal construct psychology in clinical practice: Theory, research and applications.* London: Routledge.

Wright, P. (1983). Writing and reading technical information. In J. Nicholson & B. Foss (Eds.), *Psychology Survey No 4* (pp. 323–354). Leicester: The British Psychological Society.

Yates, F. (1934). Contingency tables involving small numbers and the χ^2 test. *Supplement to the Journal of the Royal Statistical Society*, 1, 217–235.

Young, A. W., Hay, D. C. & Ellis, A. W. (1985). The faces that launched a thousand slips: Everyday difficulties and errors in recognizing people. *British Journal of Psychology*, 76, 495–523.

Zimmerman, D. W. & Zumbo, B. D. (1993). The relative power of parametric and non-parametric statistics. In G. Keren & C. Lewis (Eds.), *A handbook for data analysis in the behavioral Sciences: Methodological issues* (pp. 481–517). Hillsdale, New Jersey: Lawrence Erlbaum Associates, Inc.

Glossary of symbols

Using the English alphabet

d an effect size for designs measuring the difference between two levels of an IV

F a statistic used in parametric ANOVA, when comparing more than two levels of an IV or more than one IV

M the mean of a variable in a sample

n_h the harmonic mean sample size

r Pearson's Product Moment Correlation Coefficient in a sample

r^2 an effect size measure in correlation (the proportion of variance in one variable which can be explained by the variance in a second variable with which it is correlated)

R the multiple correlation coefficient from multiple regression

R^2 an effect size in regression analysis (the proportion of variance in a variable which can be explained by the variance in a set of predictor variables)

s the standard deviation of a variable in a sample

s^2 the variance of a variable in a sample

t a parametric statistic used for designs comparing two levels of an IV

w an effect size for nominal data

$\bar{x}$ the mean of a variable in a sample

Using the Greek alphabet

α	alpha	the probability of committing a Type I error
β	beta	the probability of committing a Type II error or a standardised regression coefficient
η^2	eta-squared	an effect size in ANOVA
χ^2	chi-squared	a statistic for nominal data
μ	mu	the mean of a variable in the population
π	pi	the proportion in the population (e.g. the proportion of smokers)
ρ	rho	the correlation coefficient for a relationship in the population
σ	sigma	the standard deviation of a variable in the population
σ^2	sigma-squared	the variance of a variable in the population

Author index

Abelson, R. P., 174
Agresti, A., 343, 346, 490
Atkinson, R. C., 6

Bales, R. F., 9, 102
Banister, P., 11
Belsley, D. A., 329
Boden, M. A., 6
Bogardus, E. S., 88
Bollen, K., 315
Bonge, D. R., 39
Borenstein, M., 187
Brown, D. R., 66, 259
Buchner, A., 187
Burman, E., 11
Byrne, B. M., 350

Campbell, D. T., 66
Castellan, N. J., 272, 490, 559
Chambless, D. L., 46
Chatterjee, S., 329
Chave, E. J., 86
Clark-Carter, D., 72, 180, 353, 535
Cleveland, W. S., 137
Cochran, W. G., 66
Cohen, J., 180, 181, 183, 187, 197,
    201, 205, 210, 212, 215, 237, 296,
    330, 361, 374, 410, 431, 537, 539,
    541, 583, 585, 587
Comrey, A. L., 350
Cook, T. D., 66
Cox, G. M., 66

Danziger, K., 50
Dixon, W. J., 559
Dracup, C., 175
Dugard, P., 61
Duncan, D., 43

Elizur, D., 95
Ellis, A. W., 103
Erdfelder, E., 187

Ericsson, K. A., 28
Estes, W. K., 6
Faul, F., 187
Fidell, L. S., 61, 189, 233, 330, 339,
    341, 350
Fisher, R. A., 146, 180

Gauss, C. F., 138
Gigerenzer, G., 180
Gossett, W., 170
Gregg, V. H., 6
Guttman, L., 87, 94

Hadi, A. S., 329
Harper, Y. Y., 39
Harris, R. J., 175
Hay, D. C., 103
Hayes, N., 11
Hewson, C., 72
Hewstone, M., 9
Hoffman, M., 95
Hosmer, D. W., 346
Howell, D. C., 259, 281, 299, 303,
    304, 339, 528
Huberty, C. J., 345
Humphreys, G., 10
Huynh, C.-L., 175

Jackson, H., 10
Jones, L. V., 175

Kelly, G., 94, 346
Kerlinger, F. N., 91
Kline, P., 314
Kline, R. B., 350

Lee, H. B., 350
Lemeshow, S., 346
Lennox, R., 315
Leventhal, L., 175
Likert, R., 88
Lomax, R. G., 350

Lucas, D., 103
Luria, A. R., 10
Luria, Z., 93

Maghsoodloo, S., 579
Manstead, A. S. R., 10, 103
Marshall, H., 92
Massey, F. J., 559
McCain, L. J., 61
McCleary, R., 61
McCulloch, C., 10, 103
McDonald, R. P., 313
McGowan, L., 72, 353, 535
Meddis, R., 260
Michels, K. M., 66, 259
Milgram, S., 17, 30
Miller, G. A., 6
Morgan, D. L., 76
Myers, J. L., 54, 66, 259, 265, 278,
    621

Neyman, J., 180
Neave, H. R., 216, 260, 547
Newell, A., 6
Nisbett, R. E., 28

Ollendick, T. H., 46
Orne, M. T., 30
Osgood, C. E., 92, 93

Pallos, L. L., 579
Parker, I., 11
Pearson, E. S., 180
Pedhazur, E. J., 111, 313, 314, 315,
    528
Pfungst, O., 15
Pitts, M., 10, 72, 353, 535
Plato, 6
Popper, K. R., 11, 12
Potter, J., 7
Price, B., 329
Putnam, H., 12

Reason, J., 103
Riddoch, J. M., 10
Robson, C., 512
Rogers, C. R., 92
Rosenthal, R., 182, 359, 360, 545
Rosnow, R. L., 182
Rothstein, H., 187

Schmelkin, L. P., 111, 313, 314, 315
Schumacker, R. E., 350
Schuldt, W. J., 39
Sears, D. O., 39
Sedlmeier, P., 180
Shaughnessy, J. J., 13
Shiffrin, R. M., 6
Shye, S., 95
Siegel, S., 272, 490, 559
Simon, H. A., 6, 28

Stainton Rogers, R., 92
Steiger, J. H., 503
Stenner, P., 92
Stephenson, G., 91
Stephenson, G. M., 9
Stevens, J., 330, 341, 530, 531
Stroebe, W., 9
Suci, G. J., 92
Sudman, S., 153, 156, 162
Suedfeld, P., 40

Tabachnick, B. G., 61, 189, 233, 330, 339, 341, 350
Tannenbaum, P. H., 92
Taylor, M., 11
Thurstone, L. L., 86
Tindall, C., 11
Todman, J. B., 61
Tukey, J. W., 114, 175

Valentine, E. R., 12

Well, A. D., 54, 66, 259, 265, 278, 621
Wetherall, M., 7
Wickens, T. D., 343
Wilson, T. D., 28
Winer, B. J., 66, 259
Winter, D. A., 94
Worthington, P. L., 216, 260
Wright, P., 81

Yates, F., 215, 433
Young, A. W., 103

Zechmeister, E. B., 13
Zechmeister, J. S., 13
Zimmerman, D. W., 189, 207, 234
Zumbo, B. D., 189, 207, 234

Subject index

Abstracts of research, 23, 367–368
Academic journal article, 23
  writing, 377–378
Accidental sampling, 157, *see also*
  Sampling: opportunity
Adjusted R^2, 324, *see also*
  Regression
Alpha (α), 146, 222–223, *see also*
  Hypothesis testing
  adjusted, 223, 262
Alternative form reliability, 314,
  see also Reliability
Alternative Hypothesis, 142
  defined, 46
  directional, 47, 149
  non-directional, 46, 149
American Psychological
  Association (APA),
  ethical guidelines, 13
  conferences, 22
  journals, 377
  publication manual, 371, 373,
  375, 377
AMOS, 350
Analysing discriminatory power,
  89, 90–91, 534
Analysis, choice of, 32
Analysis of Covariance, 339,
  see also ANCOVA
Analysis of Variance, 223–242,
  see also ANOVA
ANCOVA, 339, 343–344
Anonymity, 15, 73, 77
ANOVA
  Alternative hypothesis, 225, 229,
  246
  assumptions of, 232–236
  between-subjects, 224–228,
  245–251, 441–446, 462–465
  heterogeneous variance,
  233–234, 445–446
  homogeneous variance, 233

interpreting, 226, 248–250
one-way, 224–228, 441–446
partitioning variance, 224,
  247
power, 237, 260, 585–587
reporting the results, 228, 250
summary table, 226, 248
two-way, 245–251, 462–465
unequal sample size, 233, 236,
  250–251, 444, 583
weighted means, 236, 444
Cochran's Q, 241–242
contrasts, 261–271, *see also*
  Contrasts
degrees of freedom, 226,
  227–228, 231, 248–249, 254,
  258
designs with more than two IVs,
  259, 285–286
effect size, 236–237, 259, 453–454,
  585
error variance, 226, 228
Factorial, 245, *see also* ANOVA:
  between-subjects
F-distribution, 227–228, 561–564
F-ratio, 224, 227–228, 231–232,
  249, 254, 258, 561–564
Friedman's test, 240–241,
  456–460
interaction, 244–246, 248–249,
  254
Kruskal-Wallis test, 238–240,
  454–456
level of measurement, 232–234
main effect, 250, 254, 283–285
Mean Square (MS), 223, 226, 227,
  231, 248, 254, 258
mixed designs, 255–259, 472–476
  interpreting, 257–258
  missing data, 258–259
  partitioning variance, 256–257
  power, 587

reporting, 258
summary table, 257
more than 2 IVs, 259, 285–286
non-parametric, 238–242, 260
Null Hypothesis, 223, 224, 225,
  227, 229, 246
power, 237, 260, 585–587
power tables, 603–611
probability tables, 561–564
rationale for, 222–223
relationship with t-test, 238
reporting the results, 228, 232,
  250, 254, 255, 258
residual, 228
robustness, 233–234
similarity with regression,
  337–339
simple effects, 276–283, *see also*
  Simple effects
sphericity, 234–236, 255, 451–453
split-plot designs, 255–259,
  see also ANOVA: mixed
  designs
statistical significance, 227–228,
  561–564
Sum of Squares, 223, 226,
  442–444, 447–450, 463–465,
  473–476
tails of test, 226–227
treatment, 224, 227, 228
trend tests, 272–276, *see also*
  Trend tests
two-way,
  defined, 246
  interpreting main effects,
  283–285
unbalanced designs, 250–251,
  444
unequal sample sizes, 236,
  250–251
unweighted means, 250–251,
  444

637

weighted means, 236, 250–251, 444
Welch's F', 233–234, 445–446
  adjusted df, 445–446
within-group, 224, 226, 227, 443
within-subjects, 228–232, 251–255, 446–453, 466–472
  between-subjects variance, 228–229, 252–253, 447, 467
  interpreting, 232, 254–255
  one-way, 228–232, 446–453
  partitioning variance, 228, 252–253
  power, 237, 587
  reporting the results, 232, 254–255
  sphericity, 234–236, 255, 451–453
  summary table, 230, 253
  two-way, 251–255, 466–472
a posteriori contrasts, 262–263, see also Contrasts: unplanned
a priori contrasts, 262–263, see also Contrasts: planned
Artificial intelligence, 6
  contrasted with computer simulation, 6
Asking questions, 5, 7–8
  abbreviations, use of, 79
  ambiguous questions, 79
  anonymity of respondents, 73, 77
  attitude scales, 84–91
  badly worded questions, 79–80, 85
  behaviour questions, 69, 81, 82
  Bogardus Social Distance scales, 88
  census, 77, 399
  checking responses, 75
  choice of participants, 77, 72
  choice of setting, 77
  closed questions, 78–79, 82
  computerised, 75
  control over order, 76
  cost, 74, 77
  demographic questions, 69, 81
  dimensions, 85, 87, 88, 89
  double-barrelled questions, 80
  double negatives, 80
  e-mail surveys, 72, 75, 77
  establishing rapport, 73, 74
  face-to-face interviews, 71, 72, 73, 74, 75, 77
  filter questions, 79
  focus groups, 8, 76–77

format, 70
  choosing, 70–71
free interviews, 70
groups size, 76–77
Guttman scales, 85, 87–88, 94
health status questions, 70
internet surveys, 72, 75, 77
interviewer effects, 71, 73–74, 77
interviews, 69–83
jargon, use of, 79
layout of questionnaire, 81–82
leading questions, 80
length of interview, 74, 77
Likert scales, 85, 88–91
motivation of respondents, 73, 82
open-ended questions, 78, 82
order of questions, 82
pilot study, 35, 82
postal surveys, 71, 72, 73, 74, 76, 77
probe questions, 74
Q-methodology, 91–92
questionnaires, 69–83
reliability of measures, 84–85, 313–316
Repertory grids, 94
response bias, 89
response rate, 72, 77
sample, 72, 77
self-completed surveys, 71–72
Semantic differential, 92–93
semi-structured interviews, 7–8, 70
sensitive questions, 76, 80–81
settings, 71–72, 77
speed, 75, 77
split-ballot, 82
structured interviews, 8, 70
structured questionnaire, 8, 70
supervision of interviewers, 75
surveys, 63, 69–83
telephone surveys, 72, 74, 75, 76, 77, 155
Thurstone scales, 85, 86–87
topics for questions, 69–70
unstructured interviews, 7, 70
vague questions, 80
visual analogue scale (VAS), 78–79
Assumptions of tests, 188–189
  ANOVA, 232–233
  between-subjects t-test, 198–199
  χ^2, 195, 216, 241
  homogeneity of variance, 199, 233

independence of scores, 188–189, 233, 234
  Kruskal-Wallis ANOVA, 238
  Mann-Whitney U test, 207
  normal distribution, 188, 233
  sphericity, 234–236
  Wilcoxon signed rank test for matched pairs, 210
Attitude scales, 84–91
  Guttman scales, 85, 87–88, 94, see also Asking questions
  Likert scales, 85, 88–91, see also Asking questions
  reversing scores, 90, 533
  Thurstone scales, 85, 86–87, see also Asking questions
Attrition (as a threat to internal validity), 43, see also Internal validity
Audio-Visual Aids, use of, 382–384
Average, 114–116

Badly worded questions, 79–80, 85
Balanced designs, 55, see also Designs
Bar Charts, 123, 132–133, 134, 135
Behaviour, 69
  molar, 97
  molecular, 97
Best-fit line, 292–293, 299, 318, 517–519
  equation for, 318–319, 517–519
Beta (β)
  probability of Type II error, 182–183, 410
  standardised regression coefficient, 328, 523
Between-subjects ANOVA, 224–228, see also ANOVA
Between-subjects designs, 51–52, 57–58, 59–60, 62–63, 198–203, 224–228, 245–251
  defined, 51
Between-subjects t-tests, 198–203, see also t-test
Bi-directional hypothesis, 46, 149, see also Alternative Hypothesis
Bi-modal, 117
Binary data, 108, see also Measurement
Binomial distribution, 220, 554–555
Binomial test, 437–439, 554–555
Bipolar adjective pairs, 93
Bi-serial correlation, 299–300, see also Correlation

Bivariately normal, 297–298
Bivariate designs, 49, *see also*
    Designs
Blind condition, 15
Block designs, 52, 62–63
Bogardus Social Distance scales,
    88, *see also* Asking questions
Bonferroni adjustment, 266, 271,
    272, 282, 477–478, 527,
    567–570
Bonferroni corrections, 266, *see also*
    Bonferroni adjustment
Bonferroni's t, 266–267, *see also*
    Contrasts
Box-and-whisker plots, 135–137,
    see also Box plots
Box Plots, 135–137, 176–177
    creating, 393–395
    extreme score, 136–137
    hinge location, 136, 394
    H-range, 136, 394
    inner fences, 136–137, 394–395
    notched, 176–177
    outer fences, 136–137, 395
    whiskers, 136
British Psychological Society (BPS)
    ethical guidelines, 13
    conferences, 22

Canonical Correlation, 347
Carry-over effects, 54
Case study, 55–56, 61–62
Causality, identifying, 7, 291, 347
Categorical data, 108, *see also*
    Measurement
Ceiling effects, 32
Census, 77, 399
Central limit theorem, 190
Centring, 528, *see also* Regression
χ^2, 193–197, 212–216, 241, 417–418,
    431–433
    assumptions of, 195–196, 216,
        241
    chi-squared distribution,
        193–194, 418, 552–553
    contingency tables, 121–122,
        212–217, 241, 431–433
    correction for continuity,
        215–216, 433
    degrees of freedom, 194,
        213–214, 418, 552
    effect size, 194–195, 212, 215
    expected frequencies, 195–196,
        216, 241, 418, 431–432
    goodness-of-fit test, 196–197,
        417–418

likelihood-ratio χ^2 (G^2), 491–492
marginal probabilities, 432
marginal totals, 213–214
Null Hypothesis, 193, 213, 418
one-group, 193–197, 417–418
one-sample test, 193–197,
    417–418
one-tailed tests, 214
power, 195, 212
power tables, 195, 594–602
probability tables, 194, 552–553
reporting the results, 194,
    214–215
small expected frequencies, 195
statistical significance of,
    193–194, 552–553
test of contingencies, 212–216,
    241, 431–433
    degrees of freedom, 213–214
Chi-squared distributions, 193–194,
    220, 552
    probability tables, 194, 552–553
Choice of test, 32
    contrasts, 270
    correlation, 306
    multivariate techniques,
        351–352
    one IV
        more than two levels, 243
        two levels, 221
Circularity, 234, *see also* Sphericity
Clever Hans, 15
Closed questions, 78–79, *see also*
    Asking questions
Cluster Analysis, 94, 346
Cochran's Q, 241–242, 460–461
Cohen's d, 181, *see also* Effect size
Cohen's Kappa, 315, *see also*
    Correlation
Collective responsibility, 16
Comparisons, 261–272, *see also*
    Contrasts
Compensation (as a threat to
    internal validity), 44, *see also*
    Internal validity
Compensatory rivalry (as a threat
    to internal validity), 44,
    see also Internal validity
Compound symmetry, 451, *see also*
    ANOVA: sphericity
Computer simulation, 6, 12
Concurrent Validity, 31, *see also*
    Validity
Condition, 37
Conferences, as sources of
    research, 22, 23

Confidence intervals, 158–162
    correlation coefficients, 311–312,
        505–506
    defined, 158, 398
    effect of confidence level, 161, 401
    effect of proportion, 159
    effect of sample size, 160–161
    in meta-analysis, 358–359, 542
    means, 175, 404–405
    medians, 406
    odds ratios, 219, 434–435
    proportions, 159–162, 397–398,
        400
    regression coefficients, 527
Confidence level, 161–162, 401
Confidentiality, 15, 16
Confirmatory analysis, 348, 350
Confounding variables, 38, 44, 50,
    51
Content Analysis, 100–104
    defined, 10
Content validity, 31, *see also*
    Validity
Contingency coefficient, 304–306,
    see also Correlation
Contingency tables, 121–122,
    212–217, 219–220, 241,
    431–433
Continuous scales, 111, *see also*
    Measurement
Contrasts, 261–272, 478–492
    between-subjects designs, 264
    Bonferroni's t, 266–267, 271
        probability tables, 266,
        567–570
    categorical data, 272, 490–492
    choice of, 271
    computers and, 270–271
    Dunnett's t, 267, 271
        probability tables, 267, 571
    family of contrasts, 262
    Fisher's Protected Least
        Significant Difference
        (PLSD), 485
    following χ^2, 490–492
    following Friedman ANOVA,
        271–272, 489–490
    following Kruskal-Wallis
        ANOVA, 271–272, 486–489
    Games-Howell, 271
    general equation, 264, 478
    heterogeneous variance, 264
    Newman-Keuls, 483–485
    non-pairwise, 479–481
    non-parametric, 271–272,
        486–492

one-tailed tests, 270
orthogonality, 263–264, 485–486
paired, 264
   weightings with unequal
      sample sizes, 624–625
pairwise, 264, 479, 483–485
planned, 262–263, 271
Scheffé's t, 267–268
Scheffé's test, alternative
   versions, 481–483
studentised range statistic (q),
   269
   probability tables, 269,
      572–573
tail of test, 270
Tukey-Kramer test, 269, 271
Tukey's Honestly Significant
   Difference (HSD), 268–269,
   271
Tukey's Wholly Significant
   Difference (WSD), 271, 485
unplanned, 262–263, 270–271
weightings, 480, 485–486
weightings for unequal sample
   size, 480, 624–625
Welch's t-test, 264, 271
within-subjects designs, 265, 268
Control, 51
   versus ecological validity, 4–5
Control group, 45, 57, 58, 59
Convenience sampling, 157, see also
   Sampling: opportunity
Convergence, 30, see also Validity
Convergent construct validity, 30,
   see also Validity
Cook's distance, 333–334, see also
   Regression
Correlation, 287–316
   best-fit line, 292
   biserial, 299–300
   causality, 291
   choice of, 306
   coefficient, 288–289
   Cohen's Kappa, 315, 510–515
   comparing sample and
      population, 310–311
   confidence intervals, 311–312,
      505–506
   contingency coefficient, 304–306
   Cramér's phi, 300, 304–306
   Cramér's V, see Cramér's phi
   difference between two
      coefficients
      independent groups, 309–310
      non-independent groups, 310,
         503–505

directional hypothesis, 290
effect size, 296, 305
interpretation, 291
inter-rater agreement, 315
inverse, 287
Kendall's coefficient of
   concordance (W), 312–313,
   506–508, 580
   correction for ties, 507–508
   exact probability, 312
   probability tables, 312, 580
   relationship to Spearman's
      rho, 507
Kendall's tau, 300, 302–304,
   498–501
   partial correlation, 300, 303,
      309, 579
   power, 303–304
   probability tables, 578
   relative merits, 300, 303
   statistical significance, 303,
      501, 578
   tied scores, 303, 500–501
links with regression, 321
matrix, 307, 326
negative, 287, 290, 293
nominal data, 304–306
non-directional hypothesis, 291
non-linear relationships, 295
non-parametric, 300–305,
   496–501
Null Hypothesis, 290
one-tailed tests, 290
outliers, effect of, 294
parameter (ρ), 289
partial, 306–309, 326, 501–502
   degrees of freedom, 307, 502
   higher-order, 502
   Kendall's tau, 300, 303, 579
   statistical significance, 307–308
Pearson's Product Moment
   Correlation coefficient (r),
   288–289
   assumptions, 297–298
   degrees of freedom, 290
   distribution, 289–290
   effect size, 296, 305
   power, 296–297
   power tables, 297, 612–613
   probability tables, 574–575
   statistical significance,
      289–291, 574–575
phi, 304–306
point biserial, 298–299
polynomial, 295
positive, 287, 290, 292

power, 296–297, 303–304
reliability, 313–316, see also
   Reliability
reporting results, 290
restricted range, effect of,
   295–296
scattergrams, 127–130, 291–296
semi-partial, 308, 323
Spearman's rho, 300–302,
   497–498
   power, 303–304
   probability tables, 576–577
   relative merits, 300, 303
   reporting, 302
   statistical significance,
      301–302, 498
   tied scores, 301
spurious, 294–295
statistical significance, 289–291,
   574–575
   when H_0 is not $\rho = 0$, 310–311
two-tailed tests, 291
validity, 316, see also Validity
variance accounted for, 296, 308
zero-order, 502
Cost-benefit analysis, 21
Counterbalancing, 53
Covariance, 287–288, 522
Cover story, 15, 17, 34
Cramer's phi, 304–306 see also
   Correlation
Criterion contamination, 32
Criterion-related validity, 31–32,
   see also Validity
Criterion variable, 38, 317
Critical probability, 146
Cronbach's alpha reliability,
   314–315, see also Reliability
Crossed designs, 54, see also
   Designs
Cross-sectional designs, 57, see also
   Designs
Cubic trend, 274, see also Trend
   tests
Current Contents, 25, 378

Databases, of research, 24–25
Data distribution, 137–141
Data transformation, 191, 412–416
   bivariate data, 333, 415–416
   kurtosis, 415
   negatively skewed, 413
   positively skewed, 414–415
Debriefing, 17, 137
Degrees of freedom, 171–173
Demand characteristics, 30, 34

Demoralisation (as a threat to internal validity), 44, *see also* Internal validity
Dependent designs, 52, *see also* Within-subjects designs
Dependent variable, 37
Descriptive Discriminative Analysis (DDA), 345
Descriptive statistics, 114–122, 387–396
  reporting, 372–373
Designs
  balanced, 55, 236
  between-subjects, 51–52, 57–58, 59–60, 62–63, *see also* Between-subjects designs
  bi-variate, 49
  blocks, 52, 62
  choice of, 27
  classic experiment, 63
  crossed, 54
  cross-sectional, 57, 59
  efficiency, 50
  fully factorial, 62, 245
  hierarchical, 55
  interrupted time series, 61–62, 65
  Latin squares, 53–54, 64
  longitudinal, 57
  matched, 52, 58, 60
  mixed, 63–64, 255–259
  multivariate, 50
  nested, 55, 63
  non-equivalent group, 57–58, 59
  one-shot case study, 55–56
  panel, 59, 61
  post-test only, 56, 57, 58, 59, 61
  pre-test, post-test, 59, 63
  quasi-panel, 58, 60
  replicated, interrupted, time series, 65
  retrospective panel, 59
  simple panel, 59
  single-case, 61–62
  Solomon four group, 64–65
  split-plot, 63–64, 255–259
  static group, 57–58, 59
  time series, 61–62, 64, 65
  two-way, 62, 64
  types, 48–66
  unbalanced, 250–251
  uni-variate, 49
  within-subjects, 52–54, 58–59, 61–62, 66, *see also* Within-subjects designs

Diaries, 103–104
Dichotomous scales, 108, *see also* Measurement
Dimensional sampling, 157–158, *see also* Non-random sampling
Directional hypothesis, 47, 149, *see also* Alternative hypothesis
Discourse Analysis, 7
Discrete scales, 111, *see also* Measurement
Discriminant Analysis, 345, 346
Discriminative power, 89, 90–91, 534
Distribution of means, 169–170
Divergence, 30, 31, *see also* Validity
Divergent construct validity, 30, 31, *see also* Validity
Dummy coding, 338, 531
Dummy variables, 337–338, 531–532
Dunn Multiple Comparison Test, 266–267, *see also* Contrasts: Bonferroni's t
Dunnett's t, 267, *see also* Contrasts

Ecological observation, 98, *see also* Observation
Ecological validity, 99, 103
  defined, 5
  versus control, 4–5
Effect size, 180–185
  ANOVA (η^2), 236–237, 259
    small, medium, large, 237
  between-subjects t-test, 200–201, *see also* Effect size: (d)
  χ^2 tests, 194–195, *see also* Effect size: (w)
  choosing, 183–184
  correlation (r), *see also* Effect size: (r)
  (d), 181, 200–201, 205
    between-subjects t-test, 200–201
    comparing two experimental conditions, 424–425
    one-group z-test, 411
    small, medium, large, 181
    within-subjects t-test, 205, 584–585
  defined, 181–182
  difference between two means, 200–201, *see also* Effect size: (d)
  importance of, 182

Mann-Whitney U test, 431
(r), 296
  from χ^2, 537
  from d-value, 537
  from F-ratio, 537
  from t-value, 536, 538
  from z-value, 537
  small, medium, large, 296
R^2, 330–331
  small, medium, large, 330
  regression, 330–331, *see also* Effect size: R^2
  t-test, 181, *see also* Effect size: (d)
  (w), 194–195, 305
    small, medium, large, 195
  Wilcoxon signed rank test for matched pairs, 431
  within-subjects t-test, 205, *see also* Effect size: (d)
Effectiveness (of treatment), 46
Efficacy (of treatment), 46
Efficiency (of design), 50
E-mail, surveys, 72, 75, 77, *see also* Asking questions
EQS, 350
Error bar graph, 134–135, 175–177
Error rate per contrast, 262
Error rate per family, 262
Error types, 147–148
  Type I error, 147, 183, 222–223
  Type II error, 147, 182–183, 197, 409–410
Eta-squared (η^2), 236–237, *see also* Effect size
Ethics, 13–17, 103
  anonymity, 15
  collective responsibility, 16
  confidentiality, 15, 16
  cover story, 15, 17
  covert observation, 98
  debriefing, 17
  informed consent, 14
  in loco parentis, 14
  minimal risk, 13
  psychometric tests, 15
  risk/benefit ratio, 13
Ethnography, 97, 98, *see also* Observation
Ethology, 98, *see also* Observation
Exact probability, 191–192, 209, 211, 239, 240, 242, 312
Expected frequencies, 195–196
Experiment, 5, 6–7, 63, *see also* Method
  variables in, 36–37

Experimental Hypothesis, 46, 142, *see also* Alternative Hypothesis
Experts, seeking advice from, 22
Exploratory analysis, 348
Exploratory Data Analysis (EDA), 114
External validity, 27, 39–41, 52
  defined, 39
  improving, 41
  threats to, 39–41
    setting, 40
    task, 39–40
    time, 40
Extreme score, 127, 136–137

Facet theory, 94–95
Face-to-face interviews, 71, 72, 73, 74, 75, 77, *see also* Asking questions
Face validity, 29–30, *see also* Validity
Factor Analysis, 350
Factorial (of a number), 438
Factorial designs, 51, 62, *see also* Between-subjects designs
Fatigue effects, 52, *see also* Order effects
F-distributions, probability tables, 227–228, 561–564
File-drawer problem, 356, *see also* Meta-analysis
Filter questions, 79, *see also* Asking questions
Fisher's Exact probability Test, 216, 436–437
  probability tables, 559–560
Fisher's transformation, 310, 311, 357, 540
  equation, 626
  table, 627
Fixed variables, 37
Floor effects, 32
Focus groups, 8, 76–77, *see also* Asking questions
Formal observation, 98, *see also* Observation: systematic
Fractions, 120
F-ratio, 224, *see also* ANOVA
  power tables, 603–611
  probability tables, 562–564
  reading, 227–228
  relation to t, 238
Free interviews, 70, *see also* Unstructured interviews

Frequency distributions, 120–121, 126
Friedman's ANOVA, 240–241, 456–460
  correction for ties, 240, 458–459
  power, 240–241, 459–460
  probability tables, 240, 566
  reporting the results, 240
  statistical significance, 240, 566
F-test, 224, *see also* ANOVA
Funnel Plot, 359, *see also* Meta-analysis: funnel graph

G^2, 491–492, *see also* Likelihood-ratio χ^2
Gaussian curve, 138, *see also* Normal distribution
General Linear Model, 339
Generalising, 40, 41, 52
G-G, 235, *see also* Greenhouse-Geisser epsilon
Giving a talk, 379–384
  delivery, 380–384
  preparation, 380
  use of illustrations, 381–384
Goodness-of-fit tests, 196–197, 416–418
  power, 197
Graphical methods, 122–141, 175–178
  truncated range, 132
Greenhouse-Geisser epsilon, 235, 255, 451–453
Guttman scales, 85, 87–88, 94, *see also* Asking questions

Hat element, 333, *see also* Regression: leverage
Handouts, 381–382
Harmonic mean, 444, *see also* Measures of central tendency: mean
Heterogeneity of variance, 203, 233, 264
Heteroscedasticity, 333, *see also* Regression
H-F, 235, *see also* Huynh-Feldt epsilon
Hierarchical designs, 55, *see also* Designs
Histograms, 124
History (as a threat to internal validity), 42–43, *see also* Internal validity

Homogeneity of variance, 199
Homoscedasticity, 333, *see also* Regression
Hotelling's T^2, 343
Huynh-Feldt epsilon, 235, 255, 451–453
Hypothesis,
  Alternative, 46, 142
  ANOVA, 225, 227, 246
  bi-directional, 46, 149
  choice of, 11, 26, 46–47
  defined, 11
  directional, 47
  non-directional, 46, 149, 169
  Null, 46, 142, 222–223
  uni-directional, 47
  wording of, 46
Hypothesis testing, 142–151
  alpha level, 146, 222–223, 262
  critical probability, 146
  lopsided test, 174
  rejection region, 146, 150–151
  statistical significance, 146–147
  tail of test, 149–151
Hypothetico-deductive, 12

Imitation (as a threat to internal validity), 44, *see also* Internal validity
Independence of scores, 188–189, 234
Independent groups designs, 51, *see also* Between-subjects designs
Independent variables, 36–37
Indicator, 110–111, *see also* Measurement
Inferential statistics, 164
  reporting, 373–374
Influence, 333–334, *see also* Regression
Informed consent, 14
in loco parentis, 14
Instrumentation (as a threat to internal validity), 43, *see also* Internal validity
Interaction, 49, 54, 244–245, 254, 339, 464–465, 470–471, 475–476, 528–529
Interaction Process Analysis (IPA), 9, 102, *see also* Observation
Intercept, 319, *see also* Regression
Inter-Library Loans, 25
Internal consistency reliability, 314–315, *see also* Reliability

Internal validity, 27, 41–46
  defined, 41
  improving, 45–46, 64
  threats to, 42–45, 64
    attrition, 43
    compensation, 44
    compensatory rivalry, 44
    contamination, 44
    demoralisation, 44
    history, 42–43
    imitation, 44
    instrumentation, 43
    maturation, 42
    mortality, 43
    regression to the mean, 45
    selection, 42
    selection by maturation,
      43–44
    testing, 43
Internet
  journals, 23
  surveys, 72, 75, 77, see also
    Asking questions
Interpolation, 203, see also Linear
    interpolation
Interquartile range, 118, see also
    Measures of spread
Inter-rater reliability, 29, 100,
    see also Reliability
Intra-rater reliability, 29, see also
    Reliability
Interval scale, 108, see also
    Measurement
Interviews, 69–83
Interviewer effects, 71, 73–74, 77,
    see also Asking questions
Irrelevant variables, 38–39
Item Analysis, 86–87, 89–90,
    533–534

Journals, 23, 377–378

Kelly's Personal Construct Theory,
    94, 346
Kendall's coefficient of
    concordance (W), 312–313,
    see also Correlation
Kendall's tau, 302–304, see also
    Correlation
Kolmogorov-Smirnov One-Sample
    Test, 416–417
  probability tables, 581
Kruskal-Wallis ANOVA, 238–240,
    454–456
  assumptions, 238
  correction for ties, 239, 455–456

Null hypothesis, 238
  power, 239–240
  probability tables, 239, 565
  reporting the results, 239
  statistical significance, 239,
    565
Kuder-Richardson 20 reliability,
    315, see also Reliability
Kurtosis, 140–141
  defined, 140
  index of, 396
  leptokurtic, 140, 141
  mesokurtic, 140
  platykurtic, 140

Latent variables, 345, 347–351
Latin Squares, 53–54, 64
Least squares, 250, 318
Level of variable, 36–37
Leverage, 333–334, see also
    Regression
Likelihood-ratio χ^2 (G^2), 491–492
Likert scales, 85, 88–91, see also
    Asking questions
Line charts, 131–133
  with confidence intervals, 176
  with standard error of the mean,
    175–176
Linear interpolation, 203, 548,
    583–584
Linear trend, 272–273, see also
    Trend tests
LISREL (LInear Structural
    RELations), 350
Logistic Regression, 346
Logit Analysis, 346
Log-linear modelling, 342–343
Logs, and diaries, 103–104
Longitudinal design, 57, see also
    Design
Lopsided test, 174

Mahalanobis distance, 530, see also
    Regression
Main effect, in ANOVA, 250, 254
MANCOVA, 339, 345
Mann-Whitney U test, 207–210,
    425–428
  assumptions, 207
  correction for ties, 209, 427–428
  effect size, 208, 210, 431
  following Kruskal-Wallis, 272
  Null Hypothesis, 208
  power, 208
  probability tables, 556–557
  reporting the results, 209–210

statistical significance, 209,
    427–428, 556–557
  z-approximation, 427
MANOVA, 339, 343
Marginal totals, 213–214, 436
Margin of error, 159, 398–401
  relative size of sample and
    population, 399
Matched designs, 52, 58, 60
Matching, 52
  precision matching, 52
  range matching, 52
Maturation (as a threat to internal
    validity), 42, see also Internal
    validity
Maxima, 117, see also Measures of
    spread
McNemar's test of change,
    219–220
  statistical significance, 220,
    439–440
MDS, see Multidimensional scaling
Mean, 115, see also Measures of
    central tendency
Mean Square (MS), 223
Means, distribution of, 169–170
Measurement
  indicators, 110–111
    effect, 315–316
    causal, 315–316
  in psychology, 27–28
    covert behaviour, 27
    overt behaviour, 27
    verbal behaviour, 27, 28
  scales, 107–113
    binary, 108, 111
    categorical, 108
    continuous, 111, 112, 124
    dichotomous, 108, 111, 112
    discrete, 111, 112, 124
    interval, 108, 109, 110, 114
    nominal, 108, 109, 110,
      120–122
    ordinal, 108, 109, 110, 114
    ratio, 108–109, 110, 114
Measures
  choice of, 28
  reliability of, 28–29, 84–85, 100,
    313–316, see also Reliability
  true score, 313
Measures of central tendency,
    114–117, 139, 140
  average, 114–116
  mean, 115, 117
    calculating from frequencies,
      389–390

calculation, 387–388
disadvantages, 117
distribution of, 169–170
harmonic mean, 444, 583
graphs of, 131–135, 175–177
symbol for, 115
trimmed mean, 116
Winsorised, 391–392
median, 115–116, 117, 136
calculation from frequencies,
390–391
disadvantages, 117
mode, 116, 117
disadvantages, 117
trimmed mean, 116
Measures of Dispersion, 117–120,
see also Measures of spread
Measures of spread, 117–120,
134–137
interquartile range, 118, 127
maxima and minima, 117, 118
range, 117–118
semi-interquartile range,
119–120
standard deviation, 119
calculation, 389
pooled, 201, 424–425
variance, 118–119
calculation, 388–389
pooled, 421
Median, 115–116, see also Measures
of central tendency
Mediator, 291
Meta-analysis, 353–362, 535–546
choosing hypotheses to be
tested, 354–355
classifying studies, 356
coding sheets, 355
combining effect sizes, 357,
540–541
combining probabilities, 358,
542–543
computing a common effect size,
357, 536–538
computing a common
probability statistic, 357,
538–540
confidence interval for effect
size, 358–359, 542
critical number of studies for
file drawer problem, 359,
545–546
defined, 10
extracting information from
studies, 355
Fail-safe N, 359, 545

file drawer problem, 353,
359–360, 545–546
focused comparison, 360
funnel graph, 359–360
heterogeneity for probability,
358, 544–545
heterogeneity of effect size, 358,
543–544
homogeneity of studies, 358
hypotheses to be tested, 354–355
identifying the research, 353–354
inadequately reported studies,
355
inclusion criteria, 354–355
publication bias, 545–546
reliability of coding, 356
reporting, 360–361, 379
standard measure of effect size,
357
standard measure of probability,
357
weighting, 357
Method
choice of, 26
defined, 3
experimental, 5, 6–7, 26
defined, 5, 6–7
observational, 5, 8–10, 96–102,
see also Observation
defined, 5, 8
quasi-experiment, 7, 42, 55, 63,
251
defined, 7
questioning, 5, 7–8, 69–95,
see also Asking questions
defined, 5, 7
rationale for, 4
Minima, 117, see also Measures of
spread
Minimal risk, 13
Missing data, 258–259
Mixed designs, 63–64, see also
Designs
Mode, 116, see also Measures of
central tendency
Modelling, 6, 12, 317
Moderator variable, 245
Monte Carlo Method, 192
Mortality (as a threat to internal
validity), 43, see also Internal
validity
Multicollinearity, 329–330, see also
Regression
Multidimensional scaling (MDS),
93, 95, 348–349
Multi-modal, 117

Multiple correlation coefficient R,
321, 322
Multiple regression, 321–340,
see also Regression
Multivariate, 50, 341–342
Multivariate Analysis of
Covariance, 339, see also
MANCOVA
Multivariate Analysis of Variance,
339, see also MANOVA
Multivariate outlier, 333–334,
530–531
Multivariate techniques, 341–352
advantages, 341–342
choice of, 351–352
Multi-way frequency analysis, see
Log-linear modelling

Nested Designs, 55, 63, see also
Designs
Nominal scale, 108, see also
Measurement
Non-directional hypotheses, 46,
see also Alternative
hypothesis
Non-equivalent group design,
57–58, 59, see also Design
Non-parametric tests, 188–192
correlation, 300–305, 496–501
one group designs, 192–197,
416–418
one IV with 2 levels, 207–217,
219–221, 425–433, 436–440
one IV with more than 2 levels,
238–242, 454–461
power, 189, 208
statistical significance, 191–192
z-approximation, 191
Non-probability sampling, 153,
see also Non-random
sampling
Non-random sampling, 157–158
dimensional, 157–158
opportunity, 74, 157
purposive, 158
quota sample, 157–158
snowball, 158
Non-sexist language, 365–366
Non-verbal behaviour, 27
Normal Distribution, 137–138, 140
standardised, 165
Normal Quantile-Quantile plots,
176–178, 332, 406–408
Norms, 163
Notched box plots, 176–177,
see also Box plots

Null Hypothesis, 46, 142, 222–223
  ANOVA, 223, 224, 225
  as predicted hypothesis, 197
  between-subjects t-test, 199
  defined, 46
  χ^2, 193, 213
  correlation, 289–291
  Mann-Whitney U test, 208
  McNemar's test of change,
    219–220
  rejecting, 146, 148
  within-subjects t-test, 204

Observation, 5, 8–10, 96–102
  access, 98–99
  audio recording, 99–100, 101
  casual, 98
  complete observer, 97
  complete participant, 97
  covert, 98
  ecological, 98
  ethnography, 97, 98
  ethology, 98
  informal, 98
  Interaction Process Analysis
    (IPA), 9, 102
  marginal participant, 97
  methods of recording, 99–100
  observer bias, 100–101
  observer drift, 101
  observer-as-participant, 97
  participant-as-observer, 97
  sampling, 101–102
    continuous real-time, 101
    time interval, 101
    time-point, 101
  structured, 9–10, 102
  systematic, 98, 102
  transcribing, 101
  video cameras, 99–100, 101
Odds, 217–218
Odds ratio, 217–219, 434–436
  confidence intervals, 219,
    434–435
  risk, 435–436
OHPs, 382, see also Over head
    projectors
OHP tablets, use of, 384
One-group t-test, 170–174, see also
    t-test
One-group z-test, 169–170
One-tailed test, 149–151
One-way, defined, 226
Open-ended questions, 78, 82,
    see also Asking questions
Operational definition, 33

Opportunity sampling, 74, 157,
    see also Non-random
    sampling
Order effects, 52–54, 58, 64
  defined, 52
  fatigue effect, 52
  practice effect, 52
Ordinal scale, 108, see also
    Measurement
Orthogonality, 263–264, 485–486
Outliers
  defined, 116
  identifying, 136–137, 176–177,
    178–179
  multivariate, 333, 530–531
Over head projectors (OHPs),
    382–383, 384

Paired designs, 52, see also Within-
    subjects designs
Panel designs, 59, 61, see also
    Designs
Parallel form reliability, 314,
    see also Reliability:
    alternative form
Parameters, 152–153, 163
  defined, 152
  estimating, 153
Parametric tests
  assumptions of, 188–189
  defined, 188
  robustness, 189–191
Partial correlation, 306–308, see also
    Correlation
Partial eta-squared, 237, 259,
    453–454
Participant observation, 97, see also
    Observation
Participants
  allocation of, 45–46, 51–55, 61,
    64
  choice of, 33, 40, 41, 77
  treatment of, 14–15
Partitioning contingency tables,
    272, 490–492
Path Analysis, 347, 350
Path coefficients, 347
PCA, see Principal components
    analysis
Pearson's Product Moment
    Correlation Coefficient (r),
    288–289, see also Correlation
Percentages, 120, 121
Permutation tests, 191–192
Personal construct theory, 94, 346
Phi, 304–306, see also Correlation

Physiological responses, 27
Pie Charts, 124–126
  creating, 392–393
Pilot study, 34–35, 371
  in surveys, 82
Placebo, 4
Point bi-serial, 298–299, see also
    Correlation
Pooled standard deviation, 201,
    425
Pooled variance, 421
Population, 77, 153
Population elements, 153, 154–155
Positivism, 11
Postal surveys, 71, 72, 74, 76, 77,
    see also Asking questions
Poster presentation, 385
Post-hoc contrasts, 262–263, see also
    Contrasts: unplanned
Power, 180, 182–187
  α-level and, 185
  ANOVA, 237, 260, 585–587,
    603–611
  between-subjects t-test, 199–200,
    582–583, 590–591
  χ^2, 195, 212, 594–602
  correlation (r), 296–297, 612–613
  defined, 182–183
  effect size and, 185
  Friedman's ANOVA, 240–241,
    459–460
  Kendall's tau, 303–304
  Kruskal-Wallis ANOVA,
    239–240
  Mann-Whitney U, 208
  mixed ANOVA, 587
  multiway ANOVA, 260, 585–587
  one-group z-test, 184–185,
    409–411, 588–589
  one-group t-test, 185–187,
    592–593
  one-way ANOVA, 237
  Pearson's Product Moment
    Correlation coefficient (r),
    296–297, 612–613
  prospective, 183–184
  recommended level, 183
  regression, 331, 585, 614–617
  research hypothesis and, 185
  retrospective analysis, 186–187,
    206–207
  sample size and, 185, 410–411,
    582–583
  Spearman's rho, 303–304
  Wilcoxon signed rank test for
    matched pairs, 210–211

within-subjects ANOVA, 237, 587
within-subjects t-test, 204, 206–207, 592–593
Power efficiency, 208, 210, 219, 239, 240–241, 459
PowerPoint, 382, 384
Practice effects, 52, *see also* Order effects
Precision matching, 52, *see also* Matching
Predictive Discriminative Analysis (PDA), 345
Predictive Validity, 32, *see also* Validity
Predictor variable, 38, 317
Principal Component Analysis (PCA), 330, 349, 350
Probability, 142–146
  calculating, 143–146, 148–149
  exact, 191–192, 209, 211, 239, 240, 242
  Monte Carlo method, 192
  permutation tests, 191–192
Probability of r when H_0 is not $\rho = 0$, 310–311
Probability samples, 153, *see also* Random sampling
Probe questions in interviews, 74
Procedural knowledge, 28
Procedure, 33–34, 372
Proportions, 120, 121
PsycINFO, 24, 353, 367, 378
Psychological Abstracts, 24, 353
Psychology as a science, 11–12
Psychometric tests, ethical use of, 15
Purposive sampling, 158, *see also* Non-random sampling

Q-Methodology, 91–92
Q-sort, 91–92
Quadratic trend, 273, *see also* Trend tests
Qualitative methods, 10–11, 26
  contrasted with quantitative methods, 5
  defined, 3
Quantile, defined, 176–177, 406
Quantitative methods, 5–10
  classifications of, 5
  contrasted with qualitative methods, 5
  defined, 3
  examples, 5–10
Quasi-experiment, 7, 42, 55, 63, 251, *see also* Method

Questionnaires, 8, *see also* Asking questions
Quota sampling, 157–158, *see also* Non-random sampling

Random allocation, 46, 51, 52, 61, 64
Random numbers, 618–620
  table, 618–620
Random sampling, 41, 153–157
  advantages of, 158
  cluster sampling, 156–157
  non-responders, 157
  simple random sampling, 154–155
  stratified sampling, 155–156
    disproportionate, 156
    proportionate, 156
  systematic sampling, 102, 155
  telephone surveys, 155
Random variables, 37
Range, 117–118, *see also* Measures of spread
Range matching, 52, *see also* Matching
Rapport, establishing, 73, 74, *see also* Asking questions
Ratio scale, 108–109, *see also* Measurement
Reductionism, 11
Regression, 317–340
  Adjusted R^2, 324, 524
  best-fit line, 318, 517–519
  beta coefficient, 328, *see also* Regresssion: standardised regression coefficient
  centred leverage, 530
  centring, 528
  coefficients, 319, 328–329, 517–519
    confidence interval, 527
    statistical significance, 328–329, 526–527
  collinearity, 329, *see also* Regression: multicollinearity
  confidence interval for a regression coefficient, 527
  constant, 523, *see also* Regression: intercept
  Cook's distance, 333–334, 335, 531
  criterion variable, 38, 317
  curvilinearity, 333
  data splitting, 336
  degress of freedom, 320–321
  deleted residuals, 529–530

DfBeta, 531
DfFit, 531
diagnostic checks, 331–335, 529–531
difference between two regressions (significance of), 522
dummy variables, 337–338, 531–532
effect size, 330–331, 585
F-ratio, 320
hat element, 333–334, *see also* Regression: leverage
heteroscedasticity, 333
homoscedasticity, 333
influence, 333–334, 530–531
interaction, 339, 528–529
intercept, 319, 518–519, 523
least squares, 318
leverage, 333–334, 335, 530–531
linear, 317–340
links with correlation, 321, 522–524
logistic, 346
Mahalanobis distance, 530
model validation, 336
multicollinearity, 329–330, 335, 528
multiple, 317, 321–340
  Adjusted R^2, 324, 524
  all sub-set, 324–325
  backward deletion, 325
  equation for, 322
  forward selection, 325
  hierarchical, 324, 347
  interpreting, 328–329
  rationale for, 322
  sequential, 324, 325
  standard, 324
  statistical, 325–327
  stepwise, 325–327, 328
  summary table, 323
  types of, 324–325
  use of, 322
power, 331
power tables, 614–617
predictor variable, 38, 317
PRESS statistic, 336
reporting, 336–337
residual plot, 332–333
residuals, 320, 331–333, 335, 521, 529–530
R squared change, 522
sample size, 330
semi-partial correlation, 323, *see also* Correlation

similarity with ANOVA, 337–339
simple, 317, 318–321, 517–524
    equation for, 318–319, 517–519
    links with correlation, 321, 522–524
simple linear, 317–321, 517–524
slope, 319, 518–519
standard error of the estimate, 529
standard error of a regression coefficient, 327, 524–526
standardised predicted value, 332
standardised regression coefficient, 328, 523–524, 526–527
standardised residuals, 331–332
statistical significance, 320–321, 328–329, 520–521
Std. Error, 327, *see also* Regression: standard error of a regression coefficient
Studentised deleted residuals, 529–530
Studentised residuals, 529–530
summary table, 320–321
suppressor variables, 527–528
tolerance, 329–330, 335
to the mean, 45
variance inflation factor (VIF), 329–330, 335
Rejection region, defined, 146, *see also* Hypothesis testing
Related designs, 52, *see also* Within-subjects designs
Reliability, 28–29, 84–85, 100, 313–316, 508–515
    alternative form, 314
    attitude scales, 84–85
    Cohen's Kappa, 315, 510–515
        more than two raters, 512–515
    Cronbach's coefficient alpha, 314–315, 509
    defined, 28–29
    internal consistency, 314–315
    inter-rater, 29, 100, 315, 510–515
    intra-rater, 29
    Kuder-Richardson 20, 315, 509
    Spearman-Brown split-half, 314, 508–509
    split-half, 314–315, 508–509
    standard error of measurement, 315, 509–510
    subjective measures, 29

test, 28–29, 313
test-retest, 313–314
Repeated measures designs, 52, *see also* Within-subjects designs
Repertory Grids, 94
Replication of condition, 50–51
Replication of study, 41
Reports of research, 22–23
Report writing, 366–379
    Abstract, 367–368
    Appendixes, 377
    citing authors, 368–370
    Design, 370–371
    Discussion and conclusion, 375
    Introduction, 368–370
    Materials/apparatus, 371–372
    Method, 370–372
    Participants, 371
    Procedure section, 372
    quoting in, 369–370
    References, 375–377
    Results section, 372–374
    Title, 366–367
Request-a-print, 25
Research
    aims, 48–50, 70–71
    cost-benefit analysis of, 21
    focusing on an area, 25–26
    stages, 3, 21
Research design
    choice of, 27
    types, 48–66
Research Hypothesis, 46, *see also* Alternative Hypothesis
Response bias, 89
Retrospective power, 186–187, 206–207
Reversing scoring in attitude scale, 90, 533
Reviewing the literature, 22–25, 368–370
Risk (and odds ratios), 435–436
Risk/benefit ratio, 13
Robustness of parametric tests, 189–190, 233

Sample, choosing, 72, 77 153–158
Sampling
    non-random, 153, *see also* Non-random sampling
    non-responders, 157
    random, 153, *see also* Random sampling
    systematic, 102, 155
Scales of measurement, 107–113

Scattergrams, 127–130, 291–296, 318, 332–334
    sunflowers, 130
    tied scores, representing, 129–130
Scatterplots, 127, *see also* Scattergrams
Scheffé's t, 267–268, *see also* Contrasts
SCI *see* Science Citation Index
Science, definitions of, 11–12
Science Citation Index (SCI), 25
Scientific notation (of numbers), 374
Selection (as threat to internal validity), 42, *see also* Internal validity
Self-completed surveys, 71–72, *see* Asking questions
SEM, *see* Structural Equation Modelling
Semantic Differential, 92–93
Semi-interquartile range, 119–120, *see also* Measures of spread
Semi-partial correlation, 308, *see also* Correlation
Semi-structured interviews, 7–8, 70, *see also* Asking questions
Sequential multiple regression, 324, *see also* Regression
Sign test, 439–440
Simple effects, 276–283
    between-subjects designs, 277–280
    degrees of freedom, 278
    effect size, 279
    F-ratio, 278
    heterogeneity of variance, 277–278
    mixed designs, 281–282
    partitioning Sums of Squares, 279–280
    simple main effect, 277
    simple interaction effects, 286
    Type I errors, 282–283
    within-subjects designs, 280–281
Simple regression, 317, *see also* Regression
Single-case design, 61–62
Skew, 139–140, 141, 191
    index of, 395–396
    negative, 139–140
    positive, 139
Slide projectors, use of, 383–384
Slope, 319, *see also* Regression

Snowball sampling, 158, *see also* Non-random sampling
Social Science Citation Index (SSCI), 24–25, 353
Solomon four group design, 64–65, *see also* Design
Spearman's rho, 300–302, *see also* Correlation
Spearman-Brown reliability, 314, *see also* Reliability
Sphericity, 234–236, 451–453
Split-half reliability, 314–315, *see also* Reliability
Split-plot designs, 63–64, *see also* Designs: mixed
SSCI, *see* Social Science Citation Index
Standard deviation, 119, *see also* Measures of spread
Standard error of estimate, 316, *see also* Validity
Standard error of measurement, 315, *see also* Reliability
Standard error of the mean, 170
Standardised Normal Distribution, 165, *see also* Normal distribution
Standardised regression coefficient, 328, *see also* Regression
Standardised scores, 178–179
Static group design, 57–58, 59, *see also* Design
Statistical power, 182–187, *see also* Power
Statistical significance, 146–147
    ANOVA, 227–228, 561–564
    between-subjects t-test, 202–203, 551–552
    χ^2, 193–194, 213, 552–553
    correlation (r), 289–291, 574–575
    defined, 146–147
    effect of sample size, 180
    Friedman's 2-way within-subjects ANOVA, 240, 457–459, 566
    Kendall's tau, 303, 501, 578
    Kruskal-Wallis, 239, 455–456, 565
    limitations, 180
    Mann-Whitney U test, 209, 556–557
    one-group t-test, 173, 551–552
    regression, 320–321, 328–329
    Spearman's rho, 301–302, 498, 576–577

Wilcoxon signed rank test for matched pairs, 211, 429–431, 558
within-subjects t-test, 206, 551–552
Statistical Test, choice of
    contrasts, 271
    correlation, 306
    multivariate, 351–352
    one independent variable with more than two levels, 243
    one independent variable with two levels, 221
Stem-and-leaf plots, 127
Structural Equation Modelling (SEM), 350–351
Structured interviews, 8, 70, *see also* Asking questions
Structured observation, 9–10, 102, *see also* Observation
Structured questionnaire, 8, 70, *see also* Asking questions
Studentised range statistic (q), 269, *see also* Contrasts
Student's t, 170–174, *see also* t-test
Summary statistics, 114–122, 387–396
    reporting, 372–373
Sum of Squared deviations, 223, *see also* ANOVA
Sum of Squares, 223, *see also* ANOVA
Sunflowers, 130, *see also* Scattergrams
SuperANOVA, 234
Suppressor variables, 527–528, *see also* Regression
Survey, 63, 69–83, *see also* Asking questions
    reporting, 378–379
    required sample size, 399–401

Tail of test
    ANOVA, 226–227
    χ^2, 214
    contrasts, 270
    correlation, 290–291
    one-tailed, 149–151
    two-tailed, 149–151, 169
t-distribution, 171–173, 551–552
    probability tables, 551–552
Telephone surveys, 72, 74, 75, 76, 77, 155, *see also* Asking questions
Test, choice of
    contrasts, 271
    correlation, 306

multivariate, 351–352
one IV
    more than two levels, 243
    two levels, 221
Testing (as a threat to internal validity), 43, *see also* Internal validity
Test reliability, 28–29, *see also* Reliablity
Test-retest reliability, 313–314, *see also* Reliability
Thurstone scales, 85, 86–87, *see also* Asking questions
Time series, 61–62, 64, 65
Tolerance, 329–330, *see also* Regression
Topic, choice of, 21–26
Transforming data, 191, *see also* Data transformation
Trend analysis, 272–276
    general equation, 493–494
Trend tests, 272–276, 492–495
    coefficients, 275, 494, 621–624
    cubic trend, 274
    degrees of freedom, 276
    F-ratio, 276, 494
    general equation, 493–494
    linear coefficients, calculating, 621–624
    linear trend, 272–273
    partitioning variance, 276
    quadratic trend, 273
    table of coefficients, 275, 625
    unequal intervals, 495, 622–623
Triangulation, 26
Trimmed mean, 116, *see also* Measures of central tendency
True score, 313
t-tables, 551–552
    reading, 173, 551
t-test
    between-subjects, 198–203, 420–423
    assumptions, 198–199
    correlation coefficient (r), 574
    degrees of freedom, 202
    effect size (d), 200–201, 424–425
    equation for, 421
    heterogeneity of variance, 203, 421–423
    Null Hypothesis, 199
    pooled variance, 421
    pooled SD, 201, 425
    power, 199–200, 203, 590–591

power tables, 590–591
reporting the results, 202
statistical significance,
    202–203, 551–552
unequal sample size, effect on
    power, 203, 582–583
Welch's t-test, 203, 207, 264,
    421–423
degrees of freedom, 551
one-group, 170–174, 403–404
    degrees of freedom, 171–172
    power tables, 185, 592–593
    reporting results, 174
    statistical significance, 173
partial correlation, 502
probability tables, 551–552
regression coefficients, 328–329
relation to F-ratio, 238
reporting the results, 174, 202,
    206
single sample mean compared
    with population mean,
    170–174, 403–404
Spearman's rho, 302, 498
statistical significance, 173,
    202–203, 551–552
Welch's t, 203, 207, 264, 421–423
    adjusted df, 422–423
within-subjects, 203–207,
    423–424
    degrees of freedom, 204, 254
    effect size, 205, 584–585
    Null Hypothesis, 204
    power, 204, 206–207, 584–585,
        592–593
    power tables, 592–593
    reporting, 206
    statistical significance, 206,
        551–552
Tukey-Kramer contrast test, 269,
    see also Contrasts
Tukey's Honestly Significant
    Difference (HSD), 268–269,
    see also Contrasts
Two by two frequency table quick
    test, 216–217
Two-tailed test, 149–151, 169
Type I error, 147, see also Error
    types
Type II error, 147, see also Error types

Unexpected results, dealing with,
    174–175
Uni-directional hypothesis, 47,
    149, see also Alternative
    Hypothesis: directional

Uniform distribution, 416
Univariate designs, 49–50, see also
    Designs
Unpaired designs, 51, see also
    Between-subjects designs
Unrelated designs, 51, see also
    Between-subjects designs
Unstructured interviews, 7, 70,
    see also Asking questions

Validity (of measures), 29–32,
    316
    Construct validity, 30–31
        Convergent, 30
        Divergent, 31, 316
    Content validity, 31
    Criterion-related validity, 31–32
        Concurrent, 31
        Predictive, 32
    defined, 29
    Face validity, 29–30
    Standard error of estimate, 316,
        516
Validity of research designs, 27,
    39–46
Variables, 36–39
Variance, 118–119, see also
    Measures of spread
Variance-covariance matrix, 452
Variance inflation factor (VIF),
    329–330
Verbal presentation, 379–384
    delivering, 380–381
    illustrating, 381–384
    preparing, 380
Visual analogue scale (VAS),
    78–79, see also Asking
    questions

Welch's t-test, 203, see also t-test
Welch's F', 233, see also ANOVA
Wilcoxon signed rank test for
    matched pairs, 210–212,
    428–431
    assumptions, 210
    effect size, 431
    following Friedman's ANOVA,
        272
    mean rank, 429
    power, 210–211
    probability tables, 558
    reporting the results, 211–212
    statistical significance, 211,
        429–431, 558
    tied scores, 211, 429, 430–431
    z-approximation, 430–431

White space, use of, 81
Winsorising, 391–392
Within-subjects designs, 52–54,
    58–59, 61–62, 66, 203–207,
    210–212, 219–220, 228–232,
    240–242, 251–255
    defined, 52
Within-subjects t-test, 203–207,
    see also t-test

Yates' correction, 215–216, 433

z-approximation tests, 191
Zero-order correlation, 502
z-score
    from χ^2, 539
    from d-value, 539
    from F-ratio, 539
    from r, 539
    from t-value, 538, 540
    negative values, 549
    statistical significance, 168–169
z-tables, 549–550
    negative values, 549
    reading, 166–169, 549
    two-tailed test, 169, 549
z-tests, 163–170
    for difference between two
        correlation coefficients, 310,
        505
    for Kendall's tau, 303, 501
    for Kendall's tau as a partial
        correlation, 579
    for Mann-Whitney U test, 209,
        427
    for sample mean, 169–170, 403
    for single score, 164–169, 402
    for Spearman's rho, 302, 498
    for Wilcoxon signed rank test
        for matched pairs, 211,
        430–431
    one-group, 169–170, 403
        choosing sample size,
            410–411
        power, 184–185, 409–410,
            588–589
        power tables, 588–589
    probability tables, 549–550
    sample mean compared with
        population mean, 169–170,
        403
    single score compared with
        population mean, 164–169,
        402
    statistical significance, 168–169,
        549–550

DATE DUE